Java™ Network Programming

THE JAVA™ SERIES

Java™ Network Programming

Second Edition

Elliotte Rusty Harold

O'REILLY®

Beijing · Cambridge · Farnham · Köln · Paris · Sebastopol · Taipei · Tokyo

Java™ Network Programming, Second Edition
by Elliotte Rusty Harold

Copyright © 2000, 1997 O'Reilly & Associates, Inc. All rights reserved.
Printed in the United States of America.

Published by O'Reilly & Associates, Inc., 1005 Gravenstein Highway North, Sebastopol, CA 95472.

Editor: Mike Loukides

Production Editors: Claire Cloutier and Sarah Jane Shangraw

Cover Designer: Emma Colby

Printing History:

February 1997:	First Edition.
August 2000:	Second Edition.

Library of Congress Cataloging-in-Publication data is available online at:
http://www.oreilly.com/catalog/javanp2/.

ISBN: 1-56592-870-9
[M]

To Grandmama, a great grandmother

Table of Contents

Preface

Java™'s growth over the last five years has been nothing short of phenomenal. Given Java's rapid rise to prominence and the general interest in networking, it's a little surprising that network programming in Java is still so mysterious to so many. This doesn't have to be. In fact, writing network programs in Java is quite simple, as this book will show. Readers with previous experience in network programming in a Unix, Windows, or Macintosh environment should be pleasantly surprised at how much easier it is to write equivalent programs in Java. That's because the Java core API includes well-designed interfaces to most network features. Indeed, there is very little application layer network software you can write in C or C++ that you can't write more easily in Java. *Java Network Programming* endeavors to show you how to take advantage of Java's network class library to quickly and easily write programs that accomplish many common networking tasks. These include:

- Browsing pages on the Web
- Parsing and rendering HTML
- Sending email with SMTP
- Receiving email with POP and IMAP
- Writing multithreaded servers
- Installing new protocol and content handlers into browsers
- Encrypting communications for confidentiality, authentication, and guaranteed message integrity
- Designing GUI clients for network services
- Posting data to CGI programs
- Looking up hosts using DNS
- Downloading files with anonymous FTP

- Connecting sockets for low-level network communication

- Distributing applications across multiple systems with Remote Method Invocation

Java is the first language to provide such a powerful cross-platform network library that handles all these diverse tasks. *Java Network Programming* exposes the power and sophistication of this library. This book's goal is to enable you to start using Java as a platform for serious network programming. To do so, this book provides a general background in network fundamentals as well as detailed discussions of Java's facilities for writing network programs. You'll learn how to write Java applets and applications that share data across the Internet for games, collaboration, software updates, file transfer and more. You'll also get a behind-the-scenes look at HTTP, CGI, TCP/IP, and the other protocols that support the Internet and the Web. When you finish this book, you'll have the knowledge and the tools to create the next generation of software that takes full advantage of the Internet.

About the Second Edition

In the first chapter of the first edition of this book, I wrote extensively about the sort of dynamic, distributed network applications I thought Java would make possible. One of the most exciting parts of writing this second edition was seeing that virtually all of the applications I had postulated have indeed come to pass. Programmers are using Java to query database servers, monitor web pages, control telescopes, manage multiplayer games, and more, all by using Java's ability to access the Internet. Java in general, and network programming in Java in particular, has moved well beyond the hype stage and into the realm of real, working applications. Not all network software is written in Java yet, but it's not for a lack of trying. Efforts are well under way to subvert the existing infrastructure of C-based network clients and servers with pure Java replacements. It's unlikely that Java will replace C for all network programming in the near future. However, the mere fact that many people are willing to use web browsers, web servers, and more written in Java shows just how far we've come since 1996.

This book has come a long way too. The second edition has been rewritten almost from scratch. There are five completely new chapters, some of which reflect new APIs and abilities of Java introduced since the first edition was published (Chapter 8, *HTML in Swing*, Chapter 12, *Secure Sockets*, and Chapter 19, *The Java-Mail API*), and some of which reflect my greater experience in teaching this material and noticing exactly where students' trouble spots are (Chapter 4, *Java I/O*, and Chapter 5, *Threads*). In addition, one chapter on the Java Servlet API has been removed, since the topic really deserves a book of its own; and indeed Jason Hunter has written that book, *Java Servlet Programming* (O'Reilly & Associates, Inc., 1998).

However, much more important than the added and deleted chapters are the changes inside the chapters that we kept. The most obvious change to the first edition is that all of the examples have been rewritten with the Java 1.1 I/O API. The deprecation messages that tormented readers who compiled the first edition's examples using Java 1.1 or later are now a thing of the past. Less obviously, but far more importantly, all the examples have been rewritten from the ground up to use clean, object-oriented design that follows Java's naming conventions and design principles. Like almost everyone (Sun not excepted), I was still struggling to figure out a lot of the details of just what one did with Java and how one did it when I wrote the first edition in 1996. The old examples got the network code correct, but in most other respects they now look embarrassingly amateurish. I've learned a lot about both Java and object-oriented programming since then, and I think my increased experience shows in this edition. For just one example, I no longer use standalone applets where a simple frame-based application would suffice. I hope that the new examples will serve as models not just of how to write network programs, but also of how to write Java code in general.

And of course the text has been cleaned up too. In fact, I took as long to write this second, revised edition as I did to write the original edition. As previously mentioned, there are 5 completely new chapters, but the 14 revised chapters have been extensively rewritten and expanded to bring them up-to-date with new developments, as well as to make them clearer and more engaging. This edition is, to put it frankly, a much better written book than the first edition, even leaving aside all the changes to the examples. I hope you'll find this edition an even stronger, longer lived, more accurate, and more enjoyable tutorial and reference to network programming in Java than the first edition.

Organization of the Book

This book begins with three chapters that outline how networks and network programs work. Chapter 1, *Why Networked Java?*, is a gentle introduction to network programming in Java and the applications that it makes possible. All readers should find something of interest in this chapter. It explores some of the unique programs that become feasible when networking is combined with Java. Chapter 2, *Basic Network Concepts*, and Chapter 3, *Basic Web Concepts*, explain in detail what a programmer needs to know about how the Internet and the Web work. Chapter 2 describes the protocols that underlie the Internet, such as TCP/IP and UDP/IP. Chapter 3 describes the standards that underlie the Web such, as HTTP, HTML, and CGI. If you've done a lot of network programming in other languages on other platforms, you may be able to skip these two chapters.

The next two chapters throw some light on two parts of Java that are critical to almost all network programs but are often misunderstood and misused: I/O and threading. Chapter 4 explores Java's unique way of handling input and output. Understanding how Java handles I/O in the general case is a prerequisite for understanding the special case of how Java handles network I/O. Chapter 5 explores multithreading and synchronization, with a special emphasis on how they can be used for asynchronous I/O and network servers. Experienced Java programmers may be able to skim or skip these two chapters. However, Chapter 6, *Looking Up Internet Addresses*, is essential reading for everyone. It shows how Java programs interact with the Domain Name System through the InetAddress class, the one class that's needed by essentially all network programs. Once you've finished this chapter, it's possible to jump around in the book as your interests and needs dictate. There are, however, some interdependencies between specific chapters. Figure P-1 should allow you to map out possible paths through the book.

Chapter 7, *Retrieving Data with URLs*, explores Java's URL class, a powerful abstraction for downloading information and files from network servers of many kinds. The URL class enables you to connect to and download files and documents from a network server without concerning yourself with the details of the protocol that the server speaks. It lets you connect to an FTP server using the same code you use to talk to an HTTP server or to read a file on the local hard disk.

Once you've retrieved an HTML file from a server, you're going to want to do something with it. Parsing and rendering HTML is one of the most difficult challenges network programmers face. Indeed, the Mozilla project has been struggling with that exact problem for more than two years. Chapter 8, *HTML in Swing*, introduces some little-known classes for parsing and rendering HTML documents that take this burden off your shoulders and put it on Sun's.

Chapter 9, *The Network Methods of java.applet.Applet*, investigates the network methods of one the first classes every Java programmer learns about, Applet. You'll see how to load images and audio files from network servers and track their progress. Without using undocumented classes, this is the only way to handle audio in Java 1.2 and earlier.

Chapters 10 through 14 discuss Java's low-level socket classes for network access. Chapter 10, *Sockets for Clients*, introduces the Java sockets API and the Socket class in particular. It shows you how to write network clients that interact with TCP servers of all kinds, including whois, finger, and HTTP. Chapter 11, *Sockets for Servers*, shows you how to use the ServerSocket class to write servers for these and other protocols in Java. Chapter 12, shows you how to protect your client/server communications using the Secure Sockets Layer (SSL) and the Java Secure Sockets Extension (JSSE). Chapter 13, *UDP Datagrams and Sockets*, introduces the User Datagram Protocol (UDP) and the associated classes DatagramPacket and Datagram- Socket for fast, reliable communication. Finally, Chapter 14, *Multicast Sockets*, shows you how to use UDP to communicate with multiple hosts at the same time.

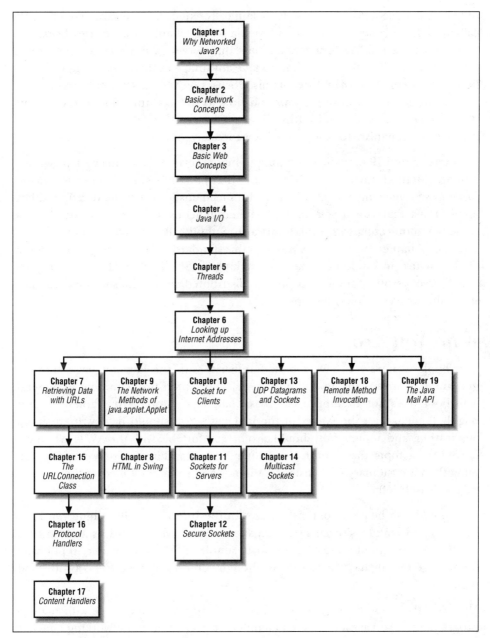

Figure P-1. Chapter prerequisites

All the other classes that access the network from Java rely on the classes described in these five chapters.

Chapters 15 through 17 look more deeply at the infrastructure supporting the URL class. These chapters introduce protocol and content handlers, concepts unique to Java that make it possible to write dynamically-extensible software that automatically understands new protocols and media types. Chapter 15, *The URLConnection Class*, describes the URLConnection class that serves as the engine for the URL class of Chapter 7. It shows you how to take advantage of this class through its public API. Chapter 16, *Protocol Handlers*, also focuses on the URLConnection class but from a different direction; it shows you how to subclass this class to create handlers for new protocols and URLs. Finally, Chapter 17 explores Java's somewhat moribund mechanism for supporting new media types.

Chapters 18 and 19 introduce two unique higher-level APIs for network programs, Remote Method Invocation (RMI) and the JavaMail API. Chapter 18, *Remote Method Invocation*, introduces this powerful mechanism for writing distributed Java applications that run across multiple heterogeneous systems at the same time while communicating with straightforward method calls just like a nondistributed program. Chapter 19, acquaints you with this standard extension to Java that offers an alternative to low-level sockets for talking to SMTP, POP, IMAP, and other email servers. Both of these APIs provide distributed applications with less cumbersome alternatives to lower-level protocols.

Who You Are

This book assumes you have a basic familiarity with the Java language and programming environment, in addition to object-oriented programming in general. This book does not attempt to be a basic language tutorial. You should be thoroughly familiar with the syntax of the language. You should have written simple applications and applets. You should also be comfortable with the AWT. When you encounter a topic that requires a deeper understanding for network programming than is customary—for instance, threads and streams—I'll cover that topic as well, at least briefly.

You should also be an accomplished user of the Internet. I will assume you know how to *ftp* files and visit web sites. You should know what a URL is and how you locate one. You should know how to write simple HTML and be able to publish a home page that includes Java applets, though you do not need to be a super web designer.

However, this book doesn't assume that you have prior experience with network programming. You should find it a complete introduction to networking concepts and network application development. I don't assume that you have a few thousand networking acronyms (TCP, UDP, SMTP . . .) at the tip of your tongue. You'll learn what you need to know about these here. It's certainly possible that you could use this book as a general introduction to network programming with a socket-like interface, then go on to learn the Windows Socket Architecture (WSA), and figure out how to write network applications in C++. But it's not clear why you would want to: Java lets you write very sophisticated applications with ease.

Java Versions

Java's network classes have changed much more slowly since Java 1.0 than other parts of the core API. In comparison to the AWT or I/O, there have been almost no changes and only a few additions. Of course, all network programs make extensive use of the I/O classes, and many make heavy use of GUIs. This book is written with the assumption that you and your customers are using at least Java 1.1 (an assumption that may finally become safe in 2001). In general, I use Java 1.1 features such as readers and writers and the new event model freely without further explanation.

Java 2 is a bit more of a stretch. Although I wrote almost all of this book using Java 2, and although Java 2 has been available on Windows and Solaris for more than a year, no Java 2 runtime or development environment is yet available for the Mac. While Java 2 has gradually made its way onto most Unix platforms, including Linux, it is almost certain that neither Apple nor Sun will ever port any version of Java 2 to MacOS 9.x or earlier, thus effectively locking out 100% of the current Mac installed base from future developments. (Java 2 will probably appear on MacOS X sometime in 2001.) This is not a good thing for a language that claims to be "write once, run anywhere". Furthermore, Microsoft's Java virtual machine supports only Java 1.1 and does not seem likely to improve in this respect the foreseeable future (the settlement of various lawsuits perhaps withstanding). Finally, almost all currently installed browsers, including Internet Explorer 5.5 and earlier and Netscape Navigator 4.7 and earlier, support only Java 1.1. Applet developers are pretty much limited to Java 1.1 by the capabilities of their customers. Consequently, Java 2 seems likely to be restricted to standalone applications on Windows and Unix for at least the near term. Thus, while I have not shied away from using Java 2-specific features where they seemed useful or convenient—for instance, the ASCII encoding for the `InputStreamReader` and the *keytool* program—I have been careful to point out my use of such features. Where 1.1-safe alternatives exist, they are noted. When a particular method or class is new in Java 1.2 or later, it is noted by a comment following its declaration like this:

```
public void setTimeToLive(int ttl) throws IOException // Java 1.2
```

To further muddy the waters, there are multiple versions of Java 2. At the time this book was completed, the current release was the Java™ 2 SDK, Standard Edition, v1.2.2. At least that's what it was called then. Sun seems to change names at the drop of a marketing consultant. In previous incarnations, this is what was simply known as the JDK. Sun also makes available the Java™ 2 Platform, Enterprise

Edition (J2EE™) and Java™ 2 Platform, Micro Edition (J2ME™). The Enterprise Edition is a superset of the Standard Edition that adds features such as the Java Naming and Directory Interface and the JavaMail API that provide high-level APIs for distributed applications. Some of these additional APIs are also available as extensions to the Standard Edition, and will be so treated here. The Micro Edition is a subset of the Standard Edition targeted at cell phones, set-top boxes and other memory, CPU, and display-challenged devices. It removes a lot of the GUI APIs that programmers have learned to associate with Java, though surprisingly it retains almost all of the basic networking and I/O classes discussed in this book. Finally, when this book was about half complete, Sun released a beta of the Java™ 2 SDK, Standard Edition, v1.3. This added a few pieces to the networking API, but left most of the existing API untouched. Over the next few months, Sun released several more betas of JDK 1.3. The finishing touches were placed in this book, and all the code was tested with the final release of JDK 1.3.

To be honest, the most annoying problem with all these different versions and editions was not the rewriting they necessitated. It was figuring out how to identify them in the text. I simply refuse to write *Java™ 2 SDK, Standard Edition, v1.3*, or even *Java 2 1.3* every time I want to point out a new feature in the latest release of Java. Consequently, I've adopted the following convention:

- *Java 1.0* refers to all versions of Java that more or less implement the Java API as defined in Sun's Java Development Kit 1.0.2.

- *Java 1.1* refers to all versions of Java that more or less implement the Java API as defined in any version of Sun's Java Development Kit 1.1.x. This includes third-party efforts such as Macintosh Runtime for Java (MRJ) 2.0, 2.1, and 2.2.

- *Java 1.2* refers to all versions of Java that more or less implement the Java API as defined in the Standard Edition of Sun's Java Development Kit 1.2.x. This does not include the Enterprise Edition additions, which will be treated as extensions to the standard. These normally come in the `javax` package rather than the `java` packages.

- *Java 1.3* refers to all versions of Java that more or less implement the Java API as defined in the Standard Edition of Sun's Java Development Kit 1.3.

In short, this book covers the state-of-the-art for network programming in Java 2, which isn't really all that different from network programming in Java 1.1. I'll post updates and corrections on my web site at *http://metalab.unc.edu/javafaq/books/ jnp2e/* as more information becomes available. However, the networking API seems fairly stable.

Security

I don't know if there was one most frequently asked question about the first edition of *Java Network Programming*, but there was definitely one most frequent answer, and it applies to this edition too. My mistake in the first edition was hiding that answer in the back of a chapter that most people didn't read. Since that very same answer should answer an equal number of questions from readers of this book, I want to get it out of the way right up front (and then repeat it several times throughout the book for readers who habitually skip prefaces): *Java's security constraints prevent almost all the examples and methods discussed in this book from working in an applet.*

This book focuses very much on applications. Untrusted Java applets are prohibited from communicating over the Internet with any host other than the one they came from. This includes the host they're running on. The problem may not always be obvious—not all web browsers properly report security exceptions—but it is there. In Java 1.2 and later, there are ways to relax the restrictions on applets so that they get less limited access to the network. However, these are exceptions, not the rule. If you can make an applet work when run as a standalone application and you cannot get it to work inside a web browser, the problem is almost certainly a conflict with the browser's security manager.

About the Examples

Most methods and classes described in this book are illustrated with at least one complete working program, simple though it may be. In my experience, a complete working program is essential to showing the proper use of a method. Without a program, it is too easy to drop into jargon or to gloss over points about which the author may be unclear in his own mind. The Java API documentation itself often suffers from excessively terse descriptions of the method calls. In this book, I have tried to err on the side of providing too much explication rather than too little. If a point is obvious to you, feel free to skip over it. You do not need to type in and run every example in this book, but if a particular method does give you trouble, you are guaranteed to have at least one working example.

Each chapter includes at least one (and often several) more complex program that demonstrates the classes and methods of that chapter in a more realistic setting. These often rely on Java features not discussed in this book. Indeed, in many of the programs, the networking components are only a small fraction of the source code and often the least difficult parts. Nonetheless, none of these programs could be written as easily in languages that didn't give networking the central position it occupies in Java. The apparent simplicity of the networked sections of the code reflects the extent to which networking has been made a core feature of Java and not any triviality of the program itself. All example programs presented in this book are available online, often with corrections and additions. You can download the source code from *http://metalab.unc.edu/javafaq/books/jnp2e* and *http://www.oreilly.com/catalog/javanp2/*.

This book assumes you are using Sun's Java Development Kit. I have tested all the examples on Windows and many on Solaris and the Macintosh. Almost all the examples given here *should* work on other platforms and with other compilers and virtual machines that support Java 1.2 (and many on Java 1.1). The few that require Java 1.3 are clearly noted. In reality, every implementation of Java that I have tested has had nontrivial bugs in networking, so actual performance is not guaranteed. I have tried to note any places where a method behaves other than as advertised by Sun.

Conventions Used in This Book

Body text is Times Roman, normal, like you're reading now.

A `Constant width` font is used for:

- Code examples and fragments

- Keywords, operators, data types, variable names, class names, and interface names that might appear in a Java program

- Program output

- Tags that might appear in an HTML document

A **`bold constant width`** is used for:

- Command lines and options that should be typed verbatim on the screen

An *`italicized constant width`* font is used for:

- Replaceable or variable code fragments

An *italicized* font is used for:

- New terms where they are defined

- Pathnames, filenames, and program names. (However, if the program name is also the name of a Java class, it is given in a monospaced font, like other class names.)

- Host and domain names (*java.oreilly.com*)

- URLs (*http://metalab.unc.edu/javafaq/*)

- Titles of other chapters and books (*Java I/O*)

Significant code fragments and complete programs are generally placed in a separate paragraph like this:

```
Socket s = new Socket("java.oreilly.com", 80);
if (!s.getTcpNoDelay()) s.setTcpNoDelay(true);
```

When code is presented as fragments rather than complete programs, the existence of the appropriate `import` statements should be inferred. For example, in the previous code fragment you may assume that `java.net.Socket` was imported.

Some examples intermix user input with program output. In these cases, the user input will be displayed in bold, as in this example from Chapter 10:

```
% telnet localhost 7
Trying 127.0.0.1...
Connected to localhost.
Escape character is '^]'.
This is a test
This is a test
This is another test
This is another test
9876543210
9876543210
^]
telnet> close
Connection closed.
```

The Java programming language is case-sensitive. `Java.net.socket` is not the same thing as `java.net.Socket`. Case-sensitive programming languages do not always allow authors to adhere to standard English grammar. Most of the time, it's possible to rewrite the sentence in such a way that the two do not conflict, and when possible, I have endeavored to do so. However, on those rare occasions when there is simply no way around the problem, I have let standard English come up the loser. In keeping with this principle, when I want to refer to a class or an instance of a class in body text, I use the capitalization that you'd see in source code, generally an initial capital with internal capitalization—for example, `ServerSocket`.

Throughout this book, I use the British convention of placing punctuation inside quotation marks only when punctuation is part of the material quoted. Although I learned grammar under the American rules, the British system has always seemed far more logical to me, even more so than usual when one must quote source code where a missing or added comma, period, or semicolon can make the difference between code that compiles and code that doesn't.

Finally, although many of the examples used here are toy examples unlikely to be reused, a few of the classes I develop have real value. Please feel free to reuse them or any parts of them in your own code. No special permission is required. As far as I am concerned, they are in the public domain (though the same is most definitely not true of the explanatory text!). Such classes are placed somewhere in the `com.macfaq` package, generally mirroring the `java` package hierarchy. For instance, Chapter 4's `SafePrintWriter` class is in the `com.macfaq.io` package. When working with these classes, don't forget that the compiled *.class* files must reside in directories matching their package structure inside your class path and that you'll have to import them in your own classes before you can use them. The book's web page at *http://metalab.unc.edu/javafaq/books/jnp2e/* includes a jar file containing all these classes that can be installed in your class path.

Request for Comments

I enjoy hearing from readers, whether with general comments about how this could be a better book, specific corrections, other topics you would like to see covered, or just war stories about your own network programming travails. You can reach me by sending email to *elharo@metalab.unc.edu*. Please realize, however, that I receive hundreds of email messages a day and cannot personally respond to each one. For the best chance of getting a personal response, please identify yourself as a reader of this book. If you have a question about a particular program that isn't working as you expect, try to reduce it to the simplest case that reproduces the bug, preferably a single class, and paste the text of the entire program into the *body* of your email. Unsolicited attachments will be deleted unopened. And please, please send the message from the account you want me to reply to and make sure that your Reply-to address is properly set! There's nothing quite so frustrating as spending an hour or more carefully researching the answer to an interesting question and composing a detailed response, only to have it bounce because my correspondent was sending from a public terminal and neglected to set the browser preferences to include an actual email address.

I also adhere to the old saying, "If you like this book, tell your friends. If you don't like it, tell me." I'm especially interested in hearing about mistakes. This is my eighth book. I've yet to publish a perfect one, but I keep trying. As hard as the editors at O'Reilly and I worked on this book, I'm sure that there are mistakes and typographical errors that we missed here somewhere. And I'm sure that at least one of them is a really embarrassing whopper of a problem. If you find a mistake or a typo, please let me know so that I can correct it. I'll post it on the web page for this book at *http://metalab.unc.edu/javafaq/books/jnp2e/* and on the O'Reilly web site at *http://www.oreilly.com/catalog/javanp2/errata/*. Before reporting errors, please check one of those pages to see if I already know about it and have posted a fix. Any errors that are reported will be fixed in future printings.

You can also send any errors you find, as well as suggestions for future editions, to:

O'Reilly & Associates, Inc.
101 Morris Street
Sebastopol, CA 95472
(800) 998-9938 (in the United States or Canada)
(707) 829-0515 (international/local)
(707) 829-0104 (fax)

To ask technical questions or comment on the book, send email to:

bookquestions@oreilly.com

For more information about O'Reilly books, conferences, software, Resource Centers, and the O'Reilly Network, see our web site at:

http://www.oreilly.com

Let me also preempt a couple of nonerrors that are often mistakenly reported. First, not all the method signatures given in this book exactly match the signatures given in Sun's javadoc API documentation. In particular, I often change argument names to make them clearer. For instance, Sun documents the `parse()` method in the `HTMLEditorKit.Parser` class like this:

```
public abstract void parse(Reader r, HTMLEditorKit.ParserCallback cb,
  boolean ignoreCharSet) throws IOException
```

I've rewritten that in this more intelligible form:

```
public abstract void parse(Reader input, HTMLEditorKit.ParserCallback
  callback, boolean ignoreCharSet) throws IOException
```

These are exactly equivalent, however. Method argument names are purely formal and have no effect on client programmers' code that invokes these methods. I could have rewritten them in Latin or Tuvan without really changing anything. The only difference is in their intelligibility to the reader.

Furthermore, I've occasionally added `throws` clauses to some methods that, while legal, are not required. For instance, when a method is declared to throw only an `IOException` but may actually throw `ConnectException`, `UnknownHost-Exception`, and `SSLException`, all subclasses of `IOException`, I sometimes declare all four possible exceptions. Furthermore, when a method seems likely to throw a particular runtime exception such as `NullPointerException`, `SecurityException`, or `IllegalArgumentException` under particular circumstances, I document that in the method signature as well. For instance, here's Sun's declaration of one of the `Socket` constructors:

```
public Socket(InetAddress address, int port) throws IOException
```

And here's mine for the same constructor:

```
public Socket(InetAddress address, int port)
  throws ConnectException, IOException, SecurityException
```

These aren't quite the same—mine's a little more complete—but they do produce identical compiled byte code.

Acknowledgments

Many people were involved in the production of this book. My editor, Mike Loukides, got this book rolling and provided many helpful comments along the way that substantially improved the book. Dr. Peter "Peppar" Parnes helped out immensely with the multicast chapter. The technical editors all provided·invaluable assistance in hunting down errors and omissions. Simon St. Laurent provided invaluable advice on which topics deserved more coverage. Scott Oaks lent his thread expertise to Chapter 5, proving once again by the many subtle bugs he hunted down that multithreading still requires the attention of an expert. Jim Farley provided many helpful comments on RMI (Chapter 18). Timothy F. Rohaly was unswerving in his commitment to making sure that I closed all my sockets and caught all possible exceptions and, in general, wrote the cleanest, safest, most exemplary code possible. John Zukowski found numerous errors of omission, all now filled thanks to him. And the eagle-eyed Avner Gelb displayed an astonishing ability to spot mistakes that had somehow managed to go unnoticed by me, all the other editors, and the tens of thousands of readers of the first edition.

It isn't customary to thank the publisher, but the publisher does set the tone for the rest of the company, authors, editors, and production staff alike; and I think Tim O'Reilly deserves special credit for making O'Reilly & Associates, Inc. absolutely one of the best houses an author can write for. If there's one person without whom this book would never have been written, it's him. If you, the reader, find O'Reilly books to be consistently better than most of the dreck on the market, the reason really can be traced straight back to Tim.

My agent, David Rogelberg, convinced me that it was possible to make a living writing books like this rather than working in an office. The entire crew at *metalab.unc.edu* over the last several years have really helped me to communicate better with my readers in a variety of ways. Every reader who sent in bouquets and brickbats about the first edition has been instrumental in helping me write this much improved edition. All these people deserve much thanks and credit. Finally, as always, I'd like to offer my largest thanks to my wife, Beth, without whose love and support this book would never have happened.

—Elliotte Rusty Harold
elharo@metalab.unc.edu
April 20, 2000

Why Networked Java?

Java is the first programming language designed from the ground up with networking in mind. As the global Internet continues to grow, Java is uniquely suited to build the next generation of network applications. Java provides solutions to a number of problems—platform independence, security, and international character sets being the most important—that are crucial to Internet applications, yet difficult to address in other languages. Together, these and other Java features allow web surfers to quickly download and execute untrusted programs from a web site without worrying that the program may spread a virus, steal their data, or crash their systems. Indeed, the intrinsic safety of a Java applet is far greater than that of shrink-wrapped software.

One of the biggest secrets about Java is that it makes writing network programs easy. In fact, it is far easier to write network programs in Java than in almost any other language. This book shows you dozens of complete programs that take advantage of the Internet. Some are simple textbook examples, while others are completely functional applications. One thing you'll note in the fully functional applications is just how little code is devoted to networking. Even in network-intensive programs like web servers and clients, almost all the code handles data manipulation or the user interface. The part of the program that deals with the network is almost always the shortest and simplest.

In short, it is easy for Java applications to send and receive data across the Internet. It is also possible for applets to communicate across the Internet, though they are limited by security restrictions. In this chapter, you'll learn about a few of the network-centric applets and applications that can be written in Java. In later chapters, you'll develop the tools you need to write these programs.

Networking adds a lot of power to simple programs. With networks, a single program can retrieve information stored in millions of computers located anywhere in the world. A single program can communicate with tens of millions of people. A single program can harness the power of many computers to work on one problem.

But that sounds like a Microsoft advertisement, not the start of a technical book. Let's talk more precisely about what network programs do. Network applications generally take one of several forms. The distinction you hear about most is between clients and servers. In the simplest case, clients retrieve data from a server and display it. More complex clients filter and reorganize data, repeatedly retrieve changing data, send data to other people and computers, and interact with peers in real time for chat, multiplayer games, or collaboration. Servers respond to requests for data. Simple servers merely look up some file and return it to the client, but more complex servers often do a lot of processing before answering an involved question. Beyond clients and servers, the next generation of Internet applications almost certainly includes mobile agents, which move from server to server, searching the Web for information and dragging their findings home. And that's only the beginning. Let's look a little more closely at the possibilities that open up when you add networking to your programs.

Retrieve Data and Display It

At the most basic level, a network client retrieves data from a server and shows it to a user. Of course, many programs did just this long before Java came along; after all, that's exactly what a web browser does. However, web browsers are limited. They can talk to only certain kinds of servers (generally web, FTP, gopher, and perhaps mail and news servers). They can understand and display certain kinds of data (generally text, HTML, and a few standard image formats). If you want to go further, you're in trouble: a web browser cannot send SQL commands to a database to ask for all books in print by Elliotte Rusty Harold published by O'Reilly & Associates, Inc. A web browser cannot check the time to within a hundredth of a second with the U.S. Naval Observatory's* super-accurate hydrogen maser clocks using the network time protocol. A web browser can't speak the custom protocol needed to remotely control the High Resolution Airborne Wideband Camera (HAWC) on the Stratospheric Observatory for Infrared Astronomy (SOFIA).†

---

* *http://tycho.usno.navy.mil/*

† SOFIA will be a 2.5-meter reflecting telescope mounted on a Boeing 747. When launched in 2001, it will be the largest airborne telescope in the world. Airborne telescopes have a number of advantages compared to ground-based telescopes—one is the ability to observe phenomena obscured by Earth's atmosphere. Furthermore, rather than being fixed at one latitude and longitude, they can fly anywhere to observe phenomenon. For information about Java-based remote control of telescopes, see *http://pioneer.gsfc.nasa.gov/public/irc/*. For information about SOFIA, see *http://www.sofia.usra.edu/*.

A Java program, however, can do all this and more. A Java program can send SQL queries to a database. Figure 1-1 shows part of a program that communicates with a remote database server to submit queries against the Books in Print database. While something similar could be done with HTML forms and CGI, a Java client is more flexible because it's not limited to single pages. When something changes, only the actual data needs to be sent across the network. A web server would have to send all the data as well as all the layout information. Furthermore, user requests that change only the appearance of data rather than which data is displayed (for example, hiding or showing a column of results) don't even require a connection back to the database server because presentation logic is incorporated in the client. HTML-based database interfaces tend to place fairly heavy loads on both web and database servers. Java clients move all the user interface processing to the client side, and let the database focus on the data.

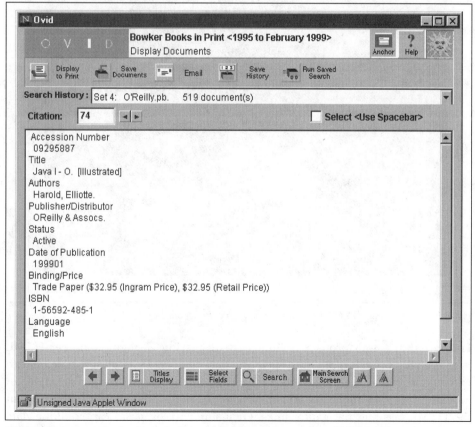

Figure 1-1. Access to Bowker Books in Print via a Java program at http://jclient.ovid.com/

A Java program can connect to a network time-server to synchronize itself with an atomic clock. Figure 1-2 shows an applet doing exactly this. A Java program can speak any custom protocols it needs to speak, including the one to control the HAWC. Figure 1-3 shows an early prototype of the HAWC controller. Even better: a Java program embedded into an HTML page (an applet) can give a Java-enabled web browser capabilities the browser didn't have to begin with.

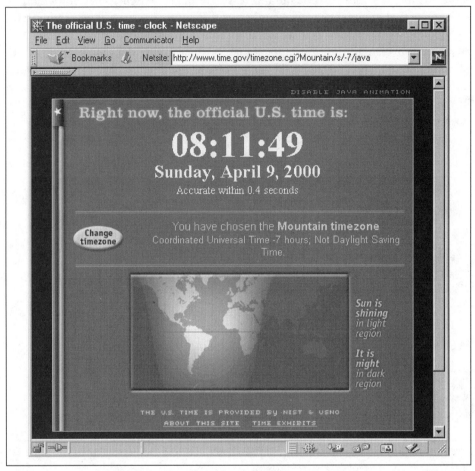

Figure 1-2. The Atomic Web Clock applet at http://www.time.gov/

Furthermore, a web browser is limited to displaying a single complete HTML page. A Java program can display more or less content as appropriate. It can extract and display the exact piece of information the user wants. For example, an indexing program might extract only the actual text of a page while filtering out the HTML tags and navigation links. Or a summary program can combine data from multiple sites and pages. For instance, a Java servlet can ask the user for the title of a book using an HTML form, then connect to 10 different online stores to

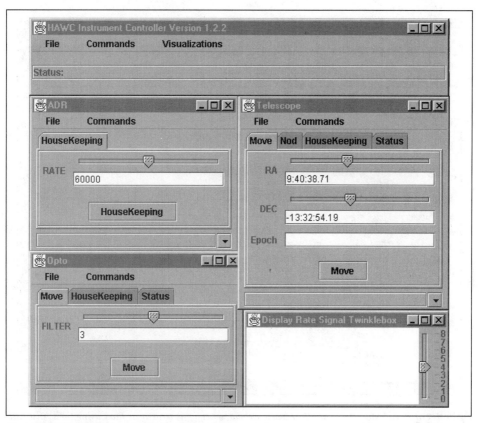

Figure 1-3. The HAWC controller prototype

check the prices for that book, then finally send the client an HTML page showing which stores have it in stock sorted by price. Figure 1-4 shows the Amazon.com (née Junglee) WebMarket site showing the results of exactly such a search for the lowest price for an Anne Rice novel. In both examples, what's shown to the user looks nothing like the original web page or pages would look in a browser. Java programs can act as filters that convert what the server sends into what the user wants to see.

Finally, a Java program can use the full power of a modern graphical user interface to show this data to the user and get a response to it. Although web browsers can create very fancy displays, they are still limited to HTML forms for user input and interaction.

Java programs are flexible because Java is a fully general programming language, unlike HTML. Java programs see network connections as streams of data, which can be interpreted and responded to in any way that's necessary. Web browsers see

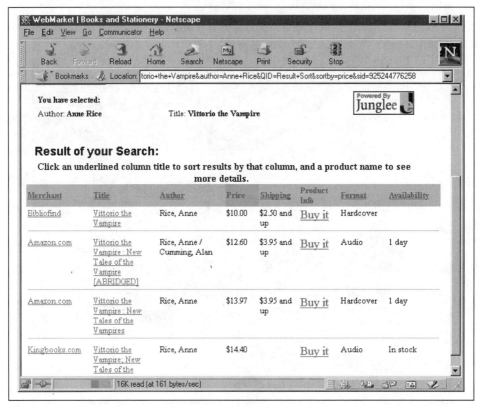

Figure 1-4. The WebMarket site at http://www.webmarket.com/ is written in Java using the servlet API

only certain kinds of data streams and can interpret them only in certain ways. If a browser sees a data stream that it's not familiar with (for example, a response to an SQL query), its behavior is unpredictable. Web sites can use CGI programs to provide some of these capabilities, but they're still limited to HTML for the user interface.

Writing Java programs that talk to Internet servers is easy. Java's core library includes classes for communicating with Internet hosts using the TCP and UDP protocols of the TCP/IP family. You just tell Java what IP address and port you want, and Java handles the low-level details. Java does not support NetWare IPX, Windows NetBEUI, AppleTalk, or other non-IP-based network protocols; but this is rapidly becoming a nonissue as TCP/IP becomes the *lingua franca* of networked applications. Slightly more of an issue is that Java does not provide direct access to the IP layer below TCP and UDP, so it can't be used to write programs such as *ping* or *traceroute*. However, these are fairly uncommon needs. Java certainly fills well over 90% of most network programmers' needs.

Once a program has connected to a server, the local program must understand the protocol that the remote server speaks and properly interpret the data the server sends back. In almost all cases, packaging data to send to a server and unpacking the data received is harder than simply making the connection. Java includes classes that help your programs communicate with certain types of servers, most notably web servers. It also includes classes to process some kinds of data, such as text, GIF images, and JPEG images. However, not all servers are web servers, and not all data is text, GIF, or JPEG. Therefore, Java lets you write protocol handlers to communicate with different kinds of servers and content handers that understand and display different kinds of data. A Java-enabled web browser can automatically download and install the software needed by a web site it visits. Java applets can perform tasks similar to those performed by Netscape plug-ins. However, applets are more secure and much more convenient than plug-ins. They don't require user intervention to download or install the software, and they don't waste memory or disk space when they're not in use.

Repeatedly Retrieve Data

Web browsers retrieve data on demand; the user asks for a page at a URL and the browser gets it. This model is fine as long as the user needs the information only once, and the information doesn't change often. However, continuous access to information that's changing constantly is a problem. There have been a few attempts to solve this problem with extensions to HTML and HTTP. For example, server push and client pull are fairly awkward ways of keeping a client up to date. There are even services that send email to alert you that a page you're interested in has changed.*

A Java client, however, can repeatedly connect to a server to keep an updated picture of the data. If the data changes very frequently—for example, a stock price—a Java application can keep a connection to the server open at all times, and display a running graph of the stock price on the desktop. Figure 1-5 shows only one of many such applets. A Java program can even respond in real time to changes in the data: a stock ticker applet might ring a bell if IBM's stock price goes over $100 so you know to call your broker and sell. A more complex program could even perform the sale without human intervention. It is easy to imagine considerably more complicated combinations of data that a client can monitor, data you'd be unlikely to find on any single web site. For example, you could get the stock price of a company from one server, the poll standings of candidates they've contributed to from another, and correlate that data to decide whether to buy or sell the company's stock. A stock broker would certainly not implement this scheme for the average small investor.

---

* See, for example, the URL-minder at *http://www.netmind.com/*.

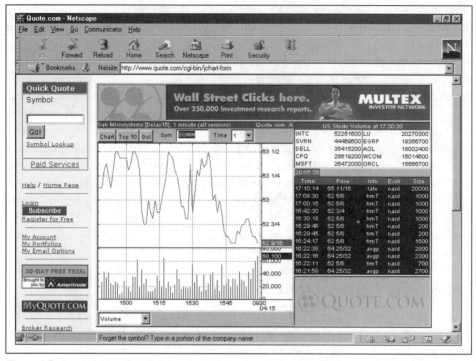

Figure 1-5. An applet-based stock ticker and information service

As long as the data is available via the Internet, a Java program can track it. Data available on the Internet ranges from weather conditions in Tuva to the temperature of soft drink machines in Pittsburgh to the stock price of Sun Microsystems to the sales status of this very book at amazon.com. Any or all of this information can be integrated into your programs in real time.

Send Data

Web browsers are optimized for retrieving data. They send only limited amounts of data back to the server, mostly via forms. Java programs have no such limitations. Once a connection between two machines is established, Java programs can send data across that connection just as easily as they can receive from it. This opens up many possibilities.

File storage

Applets often need to save data between runs; for example, to store the level a player has reached in a game. Untrusted applets aren't allowed to write files on local disks, but they can store data on a cooperating server. The applet just opens a network connection to the host it came from and sends the data to it. The host may accept the data through a CGI interface, *ftp*, SOAP, a custom server or servlet, or some other means.

Massively parallel computing

Since Java applets are secure, individual users can safely offer the use of their spare CPU cycles to scientific projects that require massively parallel machines. When part of the calculation is complete, the program makes a network connection to the originating host and adds its results to the collected data.

So far, efforts such as *SETI@home*'s* search for intelligent life in the universe and *distributed.net*'s† RC5/DES cracker have relied on native code programs written in C that have to be downloaded and installed separately, mostly because slow Java virtual machines have been at a significant competitive disadvantage on these CPU-intensive problems. However, Java applets performing the same work do make it more convenient for individuals to participate. With a Java applet version, all a user would have to do is point the browser at the page containing the applet that solves the problem.

The Charlotte project from New York University and Arizona State is currently developing a general architecture for using Java applets for supporting parallel calculations using Java applets running on many different clients all connected over the Internet. Figure 1-6 shows a Charlotte demo applet that calculates the Mandelbrot set relatively quickly by harnessing many different CPUs.

Smart forms

Java's AWT has all the user interface components available in HTML forms, including text fields, checkboxes, radio buttons, pop-up lists, buttons, and a few more besides. Thus with Java you can create forms with all the power of a regular HTML form. These forms can use network connections to send the data back to the server exactly as a web browser does.

However, because Java applets are real programs instead of mere displayed data, these forms can be truly interactive and respond immediately to user input. For instance, an order form can keep a running total including sales tax and shipping charges. Every time the user checks off another item to buy, the applet can update the total price. A regular HTML form would need to send the data back to the server, which would calculate the total price and send an updated version of the form—a process that's both slower and more work for the server.

---

* *http://setiathome.ssl.berkeley.edu/*

† *http://www.distributed.net/*

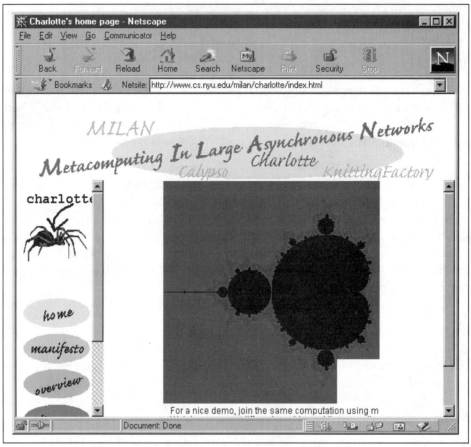

Figure 1-6. A multibrowser parallel computation of the Mandelbrot set

Furthermore, a Java applet can validate input. For example, an applet can warn users that they can't order 1.5 cases of jelly beans, that only whole cases are sent. When the user has filled out the form, the applet sends the data to the server over a new network connection. This can talk to the same CGI program that would process input from an HTML form, or it can talk to a more efficient custom server. Either way, it uses the Internet to communicate.

Peer-to-Peer Interaction

The previous examples all follow a client/server model. However, Java applications can also talk to each other across the Internet, opening up many new possibilities for group applications. Java applets can also talk to each other, though for security reasons they have to do it via an intermediary proxy program running on the server they were downloaded from. (Again, Java makes writing this proxy program relatively easy.)

Games

Combine the ability to easily include networking in your programs with Java's powerful graphics and you have the recipe for truly awesome multiplayer games. Some that have already been written are Backgammon, Battleship, Othello, Go, Mahjongg, Pong, Charades, Bridge, and even strip poker. Figure 1-7 shows a four-player game of Hearts in progress on Yahoo! Plays are made using the applet interface. Network sockets send the plays back to the central Yahoo!Yahoo! server, which copies them out to all the participants.

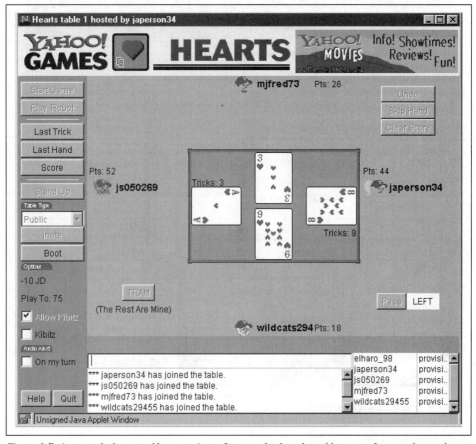

Figure 1-7. A networked game of hearts using a Java applet from http://games.yahoo.com/games/

Chat

Java lets you set up private or public chat rooms. Text that is typed in one applet can be echoed to other applets around the world. Figure 1-8 shows a basic chat applet like this on Yahoo! More interestingly, if you add a canvas with basic drawing ability to the applet, you can share a whiteboard between multiple locations.

And as soon as browsers support Version 2.0 of the Java Media Framework API, writing a network phone application or adding one to an existing applet will become trivial. Other applications of this type include custom clients for Multi-User Dungeons (MUDs) and Object-Oriented (MOOs), which could easily use Java's graphic capabilities to incorporate the pictures people have been imagining for years.

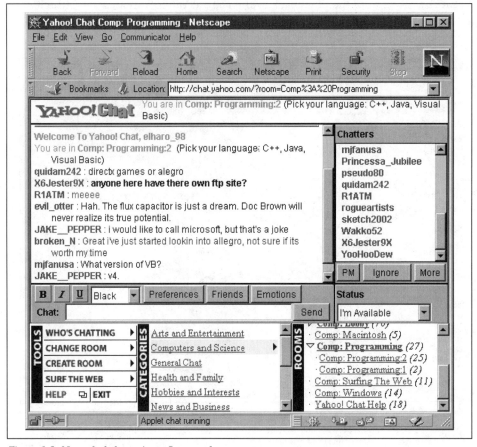

Figure 1-8. Networked chat using a Java applet

Whiteboards

Java programs aren't limited to sending text and data across the network. Graphics can be sent too. A number of programmers have developed whiteboard software that allows users in diverse locations to draw on their computers. For the most part, the user interfaces of these programs look like any simple drawing program with a canvas area and a variety of pencil, text, eraser, paintbrush, and other tools. However, when networking is added to a simple drawing program, many different people can collaborate on the same drawing at the same time. The final drawing may not be as polished or as artistic as the Warhol/Basquiat collaborations, but it doesn't require all the participants to be in the same New York loft either. Figure 1-9 shows several windows from a session of the IBM alphaWorks' WebCollab program.* WebCollab allows users in diverse locations to display and annotate slides during teleconferences. One participant runs the central WebCollab server that all the peers connect to while conferees participate using a Java applet loaded into their web browsers.

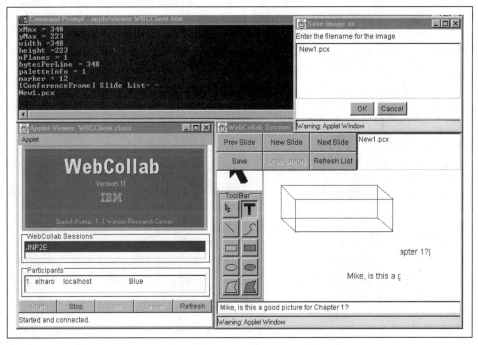

Figure 1-9. WebCollab

Servers

Java applications can listen for network connections and respond to them. This makes it possible to implement servers in Java. Both Sun and the W3C have written web servers in Java designed to be as fully functional and fast as servers written in C. Many other kinds of servers have been written in Java as well, including IRC servers, NFS servers, file servers, print servers, email servers, directory servers, domain name servers, FTP servers, TFTP servers, and more. In fact, pretty much any standard TCP or UDP server you can think of has probably been ported to Java.

---

* *http://www.alphaWorks.ibm.com/tech/webcollab*

More interestingly, you can write custom servers that fill your specific needs. For example, you might write a server that stored state for your game applet and had exactly the functionality needed to let the players save and restore their games, and no more. Or, since applets can normally communicate only with the host from which they were downloaded, a custom server could mediate between two or more applets that need to communicate for a networked game. Such a server could be very simple, perhaps just echoing what one applet sent to all other connected applets. The Charlotte project mentioned earlier uses a custom server written in Java to collect and distribute the computation performed by individual clients. WebCollab uses a custom server written in Java to collect annotations, notes, and slides from participants in the teleconference and distribute them to all other participants. It also stores the notes on the central server. It uses a combination of the normal HTTP and FTP protocols as well as its custom WebCollab protocol.

As well as classical servers that listen for and accept socket connections, Java provides several higher-level abstractions for client/server communication. Remote Method Invocation (RMI) allows objects located on a server to have their methods called by clients. Servers that support the Java Servlet API can load extensions written in Java called servlets that give them new capabilities. The easiest way to build your multiplayer game server might be to write a servlet, rather than writing an entire server.

Searching the Web

Java programs can wander through the Web, looking for crucial information. Search programs that run on a single client system are called *spiders*. A spider downloads a page at a particular URL, extracts the URLs from the links on that page, downloads the pages referred to by the URLs, and then repeats the process for each page it's downloaded. Generally, a spider does something with each page it sees, ranging from indexing it in a database to performing linguistic analysis to hunting for specific information. This is more or less how services like AltaVista build their indices. Building your own spider to search the Internet is a bad idea, because AltaVista and similar services have already done the work, and a few million private spiders would soon bring the Net to its knees. However, this doesn't mean that you shouldn't write spiders to index your own local intranet. In a company that uses the Web to store and access internal information, building a local index service might be very useful. You can use Java to build a program that indexes all your local servers and interacts with another server program (or acts as its own server) to let users query the index.

Agents have purposes similar to those of spiders (researching a stock, soliciting quotations for a purchase, bidding on similar items at multiple auctions, finding the lowest price for a CD, finding all links to a site, etc.). But whereas spiders run on a single host system to which they download pages from remote sites, agents actually move themselves from host to host and execute their code on each system they move to. When they find what they're looking for, they return to the originating system with the information, possibly even a completed contract for goods or services. People have been talking about mobile agents for years, but until now, practical agent technology has been rather boring. It hasn't come close to achieving the possibilities envisioned in various science fiction novels, like John Brunner's *Shockwave Rider* and William Gibson's *Neuromancer*. The primary reason for this is that agents have been restricted to running on a single system—and that's neither useful nor exciting. In fact until 2000, there's been only one widely successful (to use the term very loosely) true agent that ran on multiple systems, the Morris Internet worm of 1988.

The Internet worm demonstrates one reason developers haven't been willing to let agents go beyond a single host. It was destructive; after breaking into a system through one of several known bugs, it proceeded to overload the system, rendering it useless. Letting agents run on your system introduces the possibility that hostile or buggy agents may damage that system—and that's a risk most network managers haven't been willing to take. Java mitigates the security problem by providing a controlled environment for the execution of agents. This environment has a security manager that can ensure that, unlike the Morris worm, the agents won't do anything nasty. This allows systems to open their doors to these agents.

The second problem with agents has been portability. Agents aren't very interesting if they can run on only one kind of computer. That's like having a credit card for Nieman Marcus; it's somewhat useful and has a certain snob appeal, but it won't help as much as a Visa card if you want to buy something at Sears. Java provides a platform-independent environment in which agents can run; the agent doesn't care if it's visiting a Linux server, a Sun workstation, a Macintosh desktop, or a Windows PC.

An indexing program could be implemented in Java as a mobile agent: instead of downloading pages from servers to the client and building the index there, the agent could travel to each server and build the index locally, sending much less data across the network. Another kind of agent could move through a local network to inventory hardware, check software versions, update software, perform backups, and take care of other necessary tasks. Commercially oriented agents might let you check different record stores to find the best price for a CD, see whether opera tickets are available on a given evening, or more. A massively parallel computer could be implemented as a system that assigned small pieces of a problem to individual agents, which then searched out idle machines on the network to carry out parts of the computation. The same security features that allow clients to run untrusted programs downloaded from a server let servers run untrusted programs uploaded from a client.

Electronic Commerce

Shopping sites have proven to be one of the few real ways to make money from consumers on the Web. Although many sites accept credit cards through HTML forms, the mechanism is clunky. Shopping carts (pages that keep track of where users have been and what they have chosen) are at the outer limits of what's possible with HTML and forms. Building a server-based shopping cart is difficult, requires lots of CGI and database work, and puts a huge CPU load on the server. And it still limits the interface options. For instance, the user can't drag a picture of an item across the screen and drop it into a shopping cart. Java can move all this work to the client and offer richer user interfaces as well.

Applets can store state as the user moves from page to page, making shopping carts much easier to build. When the user finishes shopping, the applet sends the data back to the server across the network. Figure 1-10 shows one such shopping cart used on a Beanie Babies web site. To buy a doll, the user drags and drops its picture into the grocery bag.

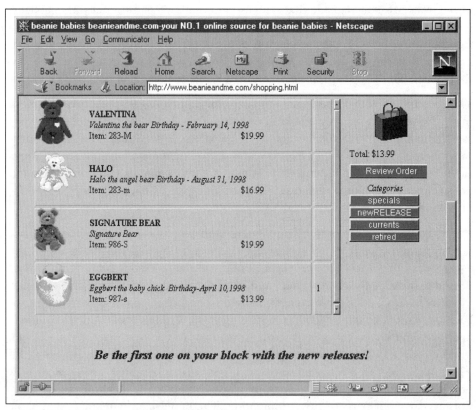

Figure 1-10. A shopping cart applet

Even this is too inconvenient and too costly for small payments of a couple of dollars or less. Nobody wants to fill out a form with name, address, billing address, credit card number, and expiration date every day just to pay $0.50 to read today's *Daily Planet*. Imagine how easy it would be to implement this kind of transaction in Java. The user clicks on a link to some information. The server downloads a small applet that pops up a dialog box saying, "Access to the information at *http://www. greedy.com/* costs $2. Do you wish to pay this?" The user can then click buttons that say "Yes" or "No". If the user clicks the No button, then he doesn't get into the site. Now let's imagine what happens if the user clicks "Yes".

The applet contains a small amount of information: the price, the URL, and the seller. If the client agrees to the transaction, then the applet adds the buyer's data to the transaction, perhaps a name and an account number, and signs the order with the buyer's private key. Then the applet sends the data back to the server over the network. The server grants the user access to the requested information using the standard HTTP security model. Then it signs the transaction with its private key and forwards the order to a central clearinghouse. Sellers can offer money-back guarantees or delayed purchase plans (No money down! Pay nothing until July!) by agreeing not to forward the transaction to the clearinghouse until a certain amount of time has elapsed.

The clearinghouse verifies each transaction with the buyer's and seller's public keys and enters the transaction in its database. The clearinghouse can use credit cards, checks, or electronic fund transfers to move money from the buyer to the seller. Most likely, the clearinghouse won't move the money until the accumulated total for a buyer or seller reaches a certain minimum threshold, keeping the transaction costs low.

Every part of this can be written in Java. An applet requests the user's permission. The Java Cryptography Extension authenticates and encrypts the transaction. The data moves from the client to the seller using sockets, URLs, CGI programs, servlets, and/or RMI. These can also be used for the host to talk to the central clearinghouse. The web server itself can be written in Java, as can the database and billing systems at the central clearinghouse; or JDBC can be used to talk to a traditional database such as Informix or Oracle.

The hard part of this is setting up a clearinghouse and getting users and sites to subscribe. The major credit card companies have a head start, though none of them yet use the scheme described here. In an ideal world you'd like the buyer and the seller to be able to use different banks or clearinghouses. However, this is a social problem, not a technological one; and it is solvable. You can deposit a check from any American bank at any other American bank where you have an account. The two parties to a transaction do not need to bank in the same place. Sun is currently developing a system somewhat like this as part of Java Wallet.

Applications of the Future

Java makes it possible to write many kinds of applications that have been imagined for years but haven't been practical until now. Many of these applications would require too much processing power if they were entirely server-based; Java moves the processing to the client, where it belongs. Other application types (for example, mobile agents) require extreme portability and some guarantees that the application can't do anything hostile to its host. While Java's security model has been criticized (and yes, some bugs have been found), it's a quantum leap beyond anything that has been attempted in the past and an absolute necessity for the mobile software we will want to write in the future.

Ubiquitous computing

Networked devices don't have to be tied to particular physical locations, subnets, or IP addresses. Jini is a framework that sits on top of Java for easily and instantly connecting all sorts of devices to a network. For example, when a group of coworkers gather for a meeting, they generally bring with them a random assortment of personal digital assistants, laptops, cell phones, pagers, and other electronic devices. The conference room where they meet may have one or two PCs, perhaps a Mac, a digital projector, a printer, a coffee machine, a speaker phone, an Ethernet router, and assorted other useful tools. If these devices include a Java virtual machine and Jini, they form an impromptu network as soon as they're turned on and plugged in. (With wireless connections, they may not even need to be plugged in.) Devices can join or leave the local network at any time without explicit reconfiguration. They can use one of the cell phones, the speaker phone, or the router to connect to hosts outside the room.

Participants can easily share files and trade data. Their computers and other devices can be configured to recognize and trust each other regardless of where in the network one happens to be at any given time. Trust can be restricted, though, so that, for example, all the laptops of company employees in the room are trusted, but those of outside vendors at the meeting aren't. Some devices, such as the printer and the digital projector, may be configured to trust anyone in the room to use their services but to not allow more than one person to use them at once. Most importantly of all, the coffee machine may not trust anyone, but it can notice that it's running out of coffee and email the supply room that it needs to be restocked.

Interactive television

Before the Web took the world by storm, Java was intended for the cable TV set-top box market. Five years after Java made its public debut, Sun's finally got back to its original plans, but this time those plans are even more network-centric.

PersonalJava is a stripped-down version of the rather large Java API that's useful for set-top boxes and other devices with restricted memory, CPU power, and user interfaces, such as Palm Pilots. The Java TV API adds some television-specific features such as channel changing, and audio and video streaming and synchronization. Although PersonalJava is missing a lot of things you may be accustomed to in the full JDK, it does include a complete complement of networking classes. TV stations can send applets down the data stream that allow channel surfers to interact with the shows. An infomercial for spray-on hair could include an applet that lets the viewer pick a color, enter his credit card number, and send the order through the cable modem, back over the Internet using his remote control. A news magazine could conduct a viewer poll in real time and report the responses after the commercial break. Ratings could be collected from every household with a cable modem instead of merely the 5,000 Nielsen families.

Collaboration

Peer-to-peer networked Java programs can allow multiple people to collaborate on a document at one time. Imagine a Java word processor that two people, perhaps in different countries, can pull up and edit simultaneously. Imagine the interaction that's possible when you attach an Internet phone. For example, two astronomers could work on a paper while one's in New Mexico and the other's in Moscow. The Russian could say, "I think you dropped the superscript in Equation 3.9", and then type the corrected equation so that it appears on both people's displays simultaneously. Then the astronomer in New Mexico might say, "I see, but doesn't that mean we have to revise Figure 3.2 like this?" and then use a drawing tool to make the change immediately. This sort of interaction isn't particularly hard to implement in Java (a word processor with a decent user interface for equations is probably the hardest part of the problem), but it does need to be built into the word processor from the start. It cannot be retrofitted onto a word processor that was not originally designed with networking in mind.

But Wait!—There's More!

Most of this book describes the fairly low-level APIs needed to write the kinds of programs discussed earlier. Some of these programs have already been written. Others are still only possibilities. Maybe you'll be the first to write them! This chapter has just scratched the surface of what you can do when you make your Java programs network-aware. The real advantage of a Java-powered web site is that anything you can imagine is now possible. You're going to come up with ideas others would never think of. For the first time you're not limited by the capabilities that other companies build into their browsers. You can give your users both the data you want them to see and the code they need to see that data at the same time. If you can imagine it, you can code it.

2

Basic Network Concepts

This chapter covers the fundamental networking concepts you need to understand before writing networked programs in Java (or, for that matter, in any language). Moving from the most general to the most specific, it explains what you need to know about networks in general, IP- and TCP/IP-based networks in particular, and the Internet. This chapter doesn't try to teach you how to wire a network or configure a router, but you will learn what you need to know to write applications that communicate across the Internet. Topics covered in this chapter include the definition of a network; the TCP/IP layer model; the IP, TCP, and UDP protocols; firewalls and proxy servers; the Internet; and the Internet standardization process. Experienced network gurus may safely skip this chapter.

Networks

A *network* is a collection of computers and other devices that can send data to and receive data from each other, more or less in real time. A network is normally connected by wires, and the bits of data are turned into electromagnetic waves that move through the wires. However, wireless networks that transmit data through infrared light or microwaves are beginning to appear; and many long-distance transmissions are now carried over fiber-optic cables that send visible light through glass filaments. There's nothing sacred about any particular physical medium for the transmission of data. Theoretically, data could be transmitted by coal-powered computers that sent smoke signals to each other. The response time (and environmental impact) of such a network, however, would be rather poor.

Each machine on a network is called a *node*. Most nodes are computers, but printers, routers, bridges, gateways, dumb terminals, and Coca-Cola machines can also be nodes. You might use Java to interface with a Coke machine (in the future, one major application for Java is likely to be embedded systems), but otherwise you'll mostly talk to other computers. Nodes that are fully functional computers are also called *hosts*. We will use the word *node* to refer to any device on the network, and the word *host* to refer to a node that is a general-purpose computer.

Every network node has an *address*: a series of bytes that uniquely identify it. You can think of this group of bytes as a number, but in general it is not guaranteed that the number of bytes in an address or the ordering of those bytes (big-endian or little-endian) matches any primitive numeric data type in Java. The more bytes there are in each address, the more addresses there are available and the more devices that can be connected to the network simultaneously.

Addresses are assigned differently on different kinds of networks. AppleTalk addresses are chosen randomly at startup by each host. The host then checks to see whether any other machine on the network is using that address. If another machine is using that address, then the host randomly chooses another, checks to see whether that address is already in use, and so on until it gets one that isn't being used. Ethernet addresses are attached to the physical Ethernet hardware. Manufacturers of Ethernet hardware use pre-assigned manufacturer codes to make sure there are no conflicts between the addresses in their hardware and the addresses of other manufacturers' hardware. Each manufacturer is responsible for making sure it doesn't ship two Ethernet cards with the same address. Internet addresses are normally assigned to a computer by the organization that is responsible for it. However, the addresses that an organization is allowed to choose for its computers are assigned to it by the organization's Internet Service Provider (ISP). ISPs get their Internet Protocol (IP) addresses from one of three regional Internet Registries (the registry for the Americas and Africa is ARIN, the American Registry for Internet Numbers, *http://www.arin.net/*), which are in turn assigned IP addresses by the Internet Assigned Numbers Authority (IANA, *http://www.iana. org/*).

On some kinds of networks, nodes also have names that help human beings identify them. At a set moment in time, a particular name normally refers to exactly one address. However, names are not locked to addresses. Names can change while addresses stay the same, or addresses can change while the names stay the same. It is not uncommon for one address to have several names; and it is possible, though somewhat less common, for one name to refer to several different addresses.

All modern computer networks are *packet-switched* networks. This means that data traveling on the network is broken into chunks called packets, and each packet is handled separately. Each packet contains information about who sent it and where it's going. The most important advantage of breaking data into individually addressed packets is that packets from many ongoing exchanges can travel on one wire, which makes it much cheaper to build a network: many computers can share the same wire without interfering. (In contrast, when you make a local telephone call within the same exchange, you have essentially reserved a wire from your phone to the phone of the person you're calling. When all the wires are in use, as sometimes happens during a major emergency or holiday, not everyone who picks up a phone will get a dial tone. If you stay on the line, you'll eventually get a dial tone when a line becomes free. In some countries with worse telephone service than the United States, it's not uncommon to have to wait half an hour or more for a dial tone.) Another advantage of packets is that checksums can be used to detect whether a packet was damaged in transit.

We're still missing one important piece: some notion of what computers need to say to pass data back and forth. A *protocol* is a precise set of rules defining how computers communicate: the format of addresses, how data is split into packets, etc. There are many different protocols defining different aspects of network communication. For example, the Hypertext Transfer Protocol (HTTP) defines how web browsers and servers communicate; at the other end of the spectrum, the IEEE 802.3 standard defines a protocol for how bits are encoded as electrical signals on a particular type of wire (among other protocols). Open, published protocol standards allow software and equipment from different vendors to communicate with each other: your web browser doesn't care whether any given server is a Unix workstation, a Windows box, or a Macintosh because the server and the browser both speak the same HTTP protocol regardless of platform.

The Layers of a Network

Sending data across a network is a complex operation that must be carefully tuned to the physical characteristics of the network as well as the logical character of the data being sent. Software that sends data across a network must understand how to avoid collisions between packets, how to convert digital data to analog signals, how to detect and correct errors, how to route packets from one host to another, and more. The process becomes even more complicated when the requirement to support multiple operating systems and heterogeneous network cabling is added.

To make this complexity manageable and to hide most of it from the application developer and end user, the different aspects of network communication are separated into multiple layers. Each layer represents a different level of abstraction between the physical hardware (e.g., wires and electricity) and the information being transmitted. Each layer has a strictly limited function. For instance, one layer may be responsible for routing packets, while the layer above it is responsible for detecting and requesting retransmission of corrupted packets. In theory, each layer talks only to the layers immediately above and immediately below it. Separating the network into layers lets you modify or even replace one layer without affecting the others as long as the interfaces between the layers stay the same.

There are several different layer models, each organized to fit the needs of a particular kind of network. This book uses the standard TCP/IP four-layer model appropriate for the Internet, shown in Figure 2-1. In this model, applications such as Netscape Navigator and Eudora run in the application layer and talk only to the transport layer. The transport layer talks only to the application layer and the internet layer. The internet layer in turn talks only to the host-to-network layer and the transport layer, never directly to the application layer. The host-to-network layer moves the data across the wires, fiber-optic cables, or other medium to the host-to-network layer on the remote system, which then moves the data up the layers to the application on the remote system.

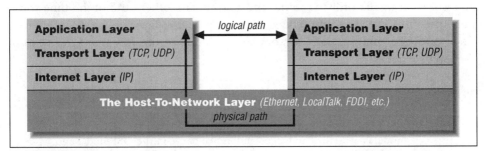

Figure 2-1. The layers of a network

For example, when a web browser sends a request to a web server to retrieve a page, it's actually talking only to the transport layer on the local client machine. The transport layer breaks up the request into TCP segments, adds some sequence numbers and checksums to the data, and then passes the request to the local internet layer. The internet layer fragments the segments into IP datagrams of the necessary size for the local network and passes them to the host-to-network layer for actual transmission onto the wire. The host-to-network layer encodes the digital data as analog signals appropriate for the particular physical medium and sends the request out the wire, where it will be read by the host-to-network layer of the remote system to which it's addressed.

The host-to-network layer on the remote system decodes the analog signals into digital data, then passes the resulting IP datagrams to the server's internet layer. The internet layer does some simple checks to see that the IP datagrams aren't corrupt, reassembles them if they've been fragmented, and passes them to the server's transport layer. The server's transport layer checks to see that all the data has arrived and requests retransmission of any missing or corrupt pieces. (This request actually goes back down through the server's internet layer, through the server's host-to-network layer, and back to the client system, where it bubbles up to the client's transport layer, which retransmits the missing data back down through the layers. This is all transparent to the application layer.) Once the datagrams composing all or part of the request have been received by the server's transport layer, it reassembles them into a stream and passes that stream up to the web server running in the server application layer. The server responds to the request and sends its response back down through the layers on the server system for transmission back across the Internet and delivery to the web client.

As you can guess, the real details are much more elaborate. The host-to-network layer is by far the most complex, and much has been deliberately hidden. For example, it's entirely possible that data sent across the Internet will actually be passed through various routers and their layers before reaching its final destination. However, 90% of the time your Java code will work in the application layer and will need to talk only to the transport layer. The other 10% of the time you'll be in the transport layer and talking to the application layer or the internet layer. The complexity of the host-to-network layer is hidden from you; that's the point of the layer model.

NOTE   If you read the network literature, you're also likely to encounter an alternative seven-layer model called the Open Systems Interconnection (OSI) Reference Model. For network programs in Java, the OSI model is overkill. The biggest difference between the OSI model and the TCP/IP model used in this book is that the OSI model splits the host-to-network layer into data link and physical layers and inserts presentation and session layers in between the application and transport layers. The OSI model is more general and better suited for non-TCP/IP networks, though most of the time it's still overly complex. In any case, Java's network classes work on only TCP/IP networks and always in the application or transport layers, so for purposes of this book, nothing is gained by using the more complicated OSI model.

To the application layer, it seems as if it is talking directly to the application layer on the other system; the network creates a logical path between the two application layers. It's easy to understand the logical path if you think about an IRC chat session. Most participants in an IRC chat would say that they're talking to another person. If you really push them, they might say that they're talking to the computer, (really the application layer), which is talking to the other person's computer which is talking to the other person. Everything more than one layer deep is effectively invisible, and that is exactly the way it should be. Let's consider each layer in more detail.

The Host-to-Network Layer

As a Java programmer, you're fairly high up in the network food chain. A lot happens below your radar. In the standard reference model for IP-based Internets (the only kind of network Java really understands), the hidden parts of the network belong to the host-to-network layer (also known as the link layer, data link layer, or network-interface layer). The host-to-network layer defines how a particular network interface, such as an Ethernet card or a PPP connection, sends IP datagrams over its physical connection to the local network and the world.

The part of the host-to-network layer made up of the hardware used to connect different computers (wires, fiber-optic cables, microwave relays, or smoke signals) is sometimes called the physical layer of the network. As a Java programmer you don't need to worry about this layer unless something goes wrong with it—the plug falls out of the back of your computer, or someone drops a backhoe through the T-1 line between you and the rest of the world. In other words, Java never sees the physical layer.

For computers to communicate with each other, it isn't sufficient to run wires between them and send electrical signals back and forth. The computers have to agree on certain standards for how those signals are interpreted. The first step is to determine how the packets of electricity or light or smoke map into bits and bytes of data. Since the physical layer is analog, and bits and bytes are digital, this involves a digital-to-analog conversion on the sending end and an analog-to-digital conversion on the receiving end.

Since all real analog systems have noise, error correction and redundancy need to be built into the way data is translated into electricity. This is done in the data link layer. The most common data link layer is Ethernet. Other popular data link layers include TokenRing and LocalTalk. A specific data link layer requires specialized hardware. Ethernet cards won't communicate on a TokenRing network, for example. Special devices called gateways convert information from one type of data link layer such as Ethernet to another such as LocalTalk. The data link layer does not affect you directly as a Java programmer. However, you can sometimes optimize the data you send in the application layer to match the native packet size of a particular data link layer, which can have some affect on performance. This is similar to matching disk reads and writes to the native block size of the disk. Whatever size you choose, the program will still run, but some sizes let the program run more efficiently than others, and which sizes these are can vary from one computer to the next.

The Internet Layer

The next layer of the network, and the first that you need to concern yourself with, is the internet layer. In the OSI model, the internet layer goes by the more generic name *network layer*. A network layer protocol defines how bits and bytes of data are organized into larger groups called *packets*, and the addressing scheme by which different machines find each other. The Internet Protocol is the most widely used network layer protocol in the world and the only network layer protocol Java understands. IP is almost exclusively the focus of this book. IPX is the second most popular protocol in the world and is used mostly by machines on NetWare networks. AppleTalk is a protocol used mostly by Macintoshes. NetBEUI is a Microsoft protocol used by Windows for Workgroups and Windows NT. Each network layer protocol is independent of the lower layers. AppleTalk, IP, IPX, and NetBEUI can each be used on Ethernet, TokenRing, and other data link layer protocol networks, each of which can themselves run across different kinds of physical layers.

Data is sent across the internet layer in packets called *datagrams*. Each IP datagram contains a header from 20 to 60 bytes long and a payload that contains up to 65,515 bytes of data. (In practice most IP datagrams are much smaller, ranging from a few dozen bytes to a little more than eight kilobytes.) The header of each IP datagram contains these 13 items in this order:

4-bit version number

> Always 0100 (decimal 4) for current IP; will be changed to 0110 (decimal 6) for IPv6, but the entire header format will also change in IPv6.

4-bit header length

> An unsigned integer between 0 and 15 specifying the number of 4-byte words in the header; since the maximum value of the header length field is 1111 (decimal 15), an IP header can be at most 60 bytes long.

1-byte type of service

> A 3-bit precedence field that is no longer used, 4 type-of-service bits (minimize delay, maximize throughput, maximize reliability, minimize monetary cost), and a 0 bit. Not all service types are compatible. Many computers and routers simply ignore these bits.

2-byte datagram length

> An unsigned integer specifying the length of the entire datagram, including both header and payload.

2-byte identification number .

> A unique identifier for each datagram sent by a host; allows duplicate datagrams to be detected and thrown away.

3-bit flags

> The first bit is 0; second bit is 0 if this datagram may be fragmented, 1 if it may not be; third bit is 0 if this is the last fragment of the datagram, 1 if there are more fragments.

13-bit fragment offset

> In the event that the original IP datagram is fragmented into multiple pieces, it identifies the position of this fragment in the original datagram.

1-byte time-to-live (TTL)

Number of nodes through which the datagram can pass before being discarded; used to avoid infinite loops.

1-byte protocol

Six for TCP, 17 for UDP, or a different number between 0 and 255 for each of more than one hundred different protocols (some quite obscure); see *http:// www.isi.edu/in-notes/iana/assignments/protocol-numbers* for the complete current list.

2-byte header checksum

A checksum of the header only (not the entire datagram) calculated using a 16-bit one's complement sum.

4-byte source address

The IP address of the sending node.

4-byte destination address

The IP address of the destination node.

In addition, an IP datagram header may contain from 0 to 40 bytes of optional information used for security options, routing records, timestamps, and other features Java does not support. Consequently, we will not discuss these here. The interested reader is referred to *TCP/IP Illustrated, Volume 1,* by W. Richard Stevens for more details on these fields. Figure 2-2 shows how these different quantities are arranged in an IP datagram. All bits and bytes are big-endian, from most significant to least significant from left to right.

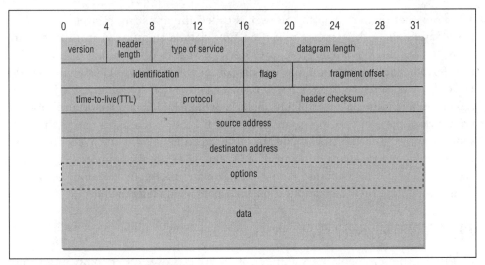

Figure 2-2. The structure of an IPv4 datagram

The Transport Layer

Raw datagrams have some drawbacks. Most notably, there's no guarantee that they will be delivered. Furthermore, even if they are delivered, they may have been corrupted in transit. The header checksum can detect corruption only in the header, not in the data portion of a datagram. Finally, even if the datagrams arrive uncorrupted, they do not necessarily arrive in the order in which they were sent. Individual datagrams may follow different routes from source to destination. Just because datagram A is sent before datagram B does not mean that datagram A will arrive before datagram B.

The transport layer is responsible for ensuring that packets are received in the order they were sent and making sure that no data is lost or corrupted. If a packet is lost, then the transport layer can ask the sender to retransmit the packet. IP networks implement this by adding an additional header to each datagram that contains more information. There are two primary protocols at this level. The first, the Transmission Control Protocol (TCP), is a high-overhead protocol that allows for retransmission of lost or corrupted data and delivery of bytes in the order they were sent. The second protocol, the User Datagram Protocol (UDP), allows the receiver to detect corrupted packets but does not guarantee that packets are delivered in the correct order (or at all). However, UDP is often much faster than TCP. TCP is called a *reliable* protocol; UDP is an *unreliable* protocol. Later we'll see that unreliable protocols are much more useful than they sound.

The Application Layer

The layer that delivers data to the user is called the application layer. The three lower layers all work together to define how data is transferred from one computer to another. The application layer decides what to do with that data after it's transferred. For example, an application protocol such as HTTP (for the World Wide Web) makes sure that your web browser knows to display a graphic image as a picture, not a long stream of numbers. The application layer is where most of the network parts of your programs spend their time. There is an entire alphabet soup of application layer protocols; in addition to HTTP for the Web, there are SMTP, POP, and IMAP for email; FTP, FSP, and TFTP for file transfer; NFS for file access; NNTP for news transfer; and many, many more. In addition, your programs can define their own application layer protocols as necessary.

IP, TCP, and UDP

IP, the Internet Protocol, has a number of advantages over other competing protocols such as AppleTalk and IPX, most stemming from its history. It was developed with military sponsorship during the Cold War, and ended up with a lot of features that the military was interested in. First, it had to be robust. The entire network couldn't stop functioning if the Soviets nuked a router in Cleveland; all messages still had to get through to their intended destinations (except those going to Cleveland, of course). Therefore, IP was designed to allow multiple routes between any two points and to route packets of data around damaged routers.

Second, the military had many different kinds of computers, and they needed all of them to be able to talk to each other. Therefore, the protocol had to be open and platform independent. It wasn't good enough to have one protocol for IBM mainframes and another for PDP-11s. The IBM mainframes needed to talk to the PDP-11s and any other strange computers that might be around.

Since there are multiple routes between two points and since the quickest path between two points may change over time as a function of network traffic and other factors (for example, the existence of Cleveland), the packets that make up a particular data stream may not all take the same route. Furthermore, they may not arrive in the order they were sent, if they even arrive at all. To improve on the basic scheme, the TCP was layered on top of IP to give each end of a connection the ability to acknowledge receipt of IP packets and request retransmission of lost or corrupted packets. Furthermore, TCP allows the packets to be put back together at the receiving end in the same order they were sent at the sending end.

TCP, however, carries a fair amount of overhead. Therefore, if the order of the data isn't particularly important and if the loss of individual packets won't completely corrupt the data stream, packets are sometimes sent without the guarantees that TCP provides. This is accomplished through the use of the UDP protocol. UDP is an unreliable protocol that does not guarantee that packets will arrive at their destination or that they will arrive in the same order they were sent. Although this would be a problem for some uses, such as file transfer, it is perfectly acceptable for applications where the loss of some data would go unnoticed by the end user. For example, losing a few bits from a video or audio signal won't cause much degradation; it would be a bigger problem if you had to wait for a protocol such as TCP to request a retransmission of missing data. Furthermore, error-correcting codes can be built into UDP data streams at the application level to account for missing data.

Besides TCP and UDP, there are a number of other protocols that can run on top of IP. The one most commonly asked for is ICMP, the Internet Control Message Protocol, which uses raw IP datagrams to relay error messages between hosts. The best known use of this protocol is in the *ping* program. Java does not support ICMP nor does it allow the sending of raw IP datagrams (as opposed to TCP segments or UDP datagrams). The only protocols Java supports are TCP and UDP and application layer protocols built on top of these. All other transport layer, internet layer, and lower-layer protocols such as ICMP, IGMP, ARP, RARP, RSVP, and others can be implemented in Java programs only by using native code.

IP Addresses and Domain Names

As a Java programmer, you don't need to worry about the inner workings of IP, but you do need to know about addressing. Every computer on an IP network is identified by a 4-byte number. This is normally written in a format like 199.1.32.90, where each of the four numbers is one unsigned byte ranging in value from 0 to 255. Every computer attached to an IP network has a unique 4-byte address. When data is transmitted across the network in packets, each packet's header includes the address of the machine for which the packet is intended (the destination address) and the address of the machine that sent the packet (the source address). Routers along the way choose the best route to send the packet along by inspecting the destination address. The source address is included so that the recipient will know who to reply to.

Although computers are comfortable with numbers, human beings aren't good at remembering them. Therefore, the Domain Name System (DNS) was developed to translate hostnames that humans can remember (like *http://www.oreilly.com*) into numeric Internet addresses (like 198.112.208.23). When Java programs access the network, they need to process both these numeric addresses and their corresponding hostnames. There are a series of methods for doing this in the `java.net.InetAddress` class, which is discussed in Chapter 6, *Looking Up Internet Addresses*.

Ports

Addresses would be all you needed if each computer did no more than one thing at a time. However, modern computers do many different things at once. Email needs to be separated from FTP requests, which need to be separated from web traffic. This is accomplished through *ports*. Each computer with an IP address has several thousand logical ports (65,535 per transport layer protocol, to be precise). These are purely abstractions in the computer's memory and do not represent anything physical like a serial or parallel port. Each port is identified by a number from 1 to 65,535. Each port can be allocated to a particular service.

For example, the HTTP service, which is used by the Web, generally runs on port 80: we say that a web server listens on port 80 for incoming connections. SMTP or email servers run on port 25. When data is sent to a web server on a particular machine at a particular IP address, it is also sent to a particular port (usually port 80) on that machine. The receiver checks each packet it sees for the port and sends the data to any programs that are listening to the specified port. This is how different types of traffic are sorted out.

Port numbers from 1 to 1023 are reserved for well-known services such as finger, FTP, HTTP, and email. On Unix systems, only programs running as root can receive data from these ports, but all programs may send data to them. On Windows and the Mac, including Windows NT, any program may use these ports without special privileges. Table 2-1 shows the well-known ports for the protocols that are discussed in this book. These assignments are not absolutely guaranteed; in particular, web servers often run on ports other than 80, either because multiple servers need to run on the same machine, or because the person who installed the server doesn't have the root privileges needed to run it on port 80. On Unix systems, a fairly complete listing of assigned ports is stored in the file */etc/services.*

Table 2-1. Well-known Port Assignments

Protocol	Port	Protocol	Purpose
echo	7	TCP/UDP	Echo is a test protocol used to verify that two machines are able to connect by having one echo back the other's input.
discard	9	TCP/UDP	Discard is a less useful test protocol in which all data received by the server is ignored.
daytime	13	TCP/UDP	Provides an ASCII representation of the current time on the server.
ftp-data	20	TCP	FTP uses two well-known ports. This port is used to transfer files.
FTP	21	TCP	This port is used to send FTP commands like put and get.
Telnet	23	TCP	Telnet is a protocol used for interactive, remote command-line sessions.
SMTP	25	TCP	The Simple Mail Transfer Protocol is used to send email between machines.
time	37	TCP/UDP	A time server returns the number of seconds that have elapsed on the server since midnight, January 1, 1900, as a 4-byte, signed, big-endian integer.
whois	43	TCP	Whois is a simple directory service for Internet network administrators.
finger	79	TCP	Finger is a service that returns information about a user or users on the local system.
HTTP	80	TCP	Hypertext Transfer Protocol is the underlying protocol of the World Wide Web.
POP3	110	TCP	Post Office Protocol Version 3 is a protocol for the transfer of accumulated email from the host to sporadically connected clients.
NNTP	119	TCP	Usenet news transfer is more formally known as the Network News Transfer Protocol.
RMI Registry	1099	TCP	This is the registry service for Java remote objects. This will be discussed in Chapter 18, *Remote Method Invocation.*

The Internet

The *Internet* is the world's largest IP-based network. It is an amorphous group of computers in many different countries on all seven continents (Antarctica included) that talk to each other using the IP protocol. Each computer on the Internet has at least one unique IP address by which it can be identified. Most of them also have at least one name that maps to that IP address. The Internet is not owned by anyone, though pieces of it are. It is not governed by anyone, which is not to say that some governments don't try. It is simply a very large collection of computers that have agreed to talk to each other in a standard way.

The Internet is not the only IP-based network, but it is the largest one. Other IP networks are called *internets* with a little *i:* for example, a corporate IP network that is not connected to the Internet. *Intranet* is a current buzzword that loosely describes corporate practices of putting lots of data on internal web servers. Since web browsers use IP, most intranets do too (though a few tunnel it through existing AppleTalk or IPX installations).

Almost certainly the internet that you'll be using is the Internet. To make sure that hosts on different networks on the Internet can communicate with each other, a few rules need to be followed that don't apply to purely internal internets. The most important rules deal with the assignment of addresses to different organizations, companies, and individuals. If everyone picked the Internet addresses she wanted at random, conflicts would arise almost immediately when different computers showed up on the Internet with the same address.

Internet Address Classes

To avoid this problem, Internet addresses are assigned to different organizations by the Internet Assigned Numbers Authority (IANA),* generally acting through intermediaries called ISPs. When a company or an organization wants to set up an IP-based network connected to the Internet, its ISP gives it a block of addresses. Currently, these blocks are available in two sizes called Class B and Class C. A Class C address block specifies the first 3 bytes of the address, for example, 199.1.32. This allows room for 254 individual addresses from 199.1.32.1 to 199.1.32.254.† A Class B address block specifies only the first 2 bytes of the addresses an organization may use, for instance, 167.1. Thus a Class B address has room for 65,024 different hosts (256 Class C-sized blocks times 254 hosts per Class C block).

---

* In the near future, this function will be assumed by the Internet Corporation for Assigned Names and Numbers (ICANN).

† Addresses with the last byte either .0 or .255 are reserved and should never actually be assigned to hosts.

Numeric addressing becomes important when you want to restrict access to your site. For instance, you may want to prevent a competing company from having access to your web site. In this case, you would find out your competitor's address block and throw away all requests that come from that block of addresses. More commonly, you might want to make sure that only people within your organization can access your internal web server. In this case, you would deny access to all requests except those that come from within your own address block.

There's no block with a size between a Class B and a Class C. This has become a problem because there are many organizations with more than 254 computers connected to the Internet but fewer than 65,024 of them. If each of these organizations gets a full Class B block, a lot of IP addresses are wasted. This is a problem since there's a limited number of addresses, about 4.2 billion to be precise. That sounds like a lot, but it gets crowded quickly when you can easily waste 50,000 or 60,000 addresses at a shot.

What About Class A Addresses?

When the Internet was originally designed, there was also room for 126 Class A addresses that specified only the first byte and allowed more than 16 million different hosts within one organization. However, almost no single organization needs this many addresses, and a large part of any Class A address tends to go unused. Since Internet addresses are a finite quantity, the IANA stopped giving out Class A addresses a long time ago, though a few more than three dozen are still in use.

There are also Class D and E addresses. Class D addresses are used for IP multicast group and will be discussed at length in Chapter 14, *Multicast Sockets*. Class D addresses all begin with the four bits 1110. Class E addresses begin with the five bits 11110 and are reserved for future extensions to the Internet.

There are also many networks, such as the author's own personal basement area network, that have a few to a few dozen computers but not 255 of them. To more efficiently allocate the limited address space, Classless Inter-Domain Routing (CIDR) was invented. CIDR mostly (though not completely) replaces the whole A, B, C addressing scheme with one based on a specified numbers of prefix bits. These are generally written as /24 or /19. The number after the / indicates the number of fixed prefix bits. Thus a /24 fixes the first 24 bits in the address, leaving 8 bits available to distinguish individual nodes. This allows 256 nodes and is equivalent to an old-style Class C. A /19 fixes 19 bits, leaving 13 for individual nodes within the network. It's equivalent to 32 separate Class C networks or an eighth of a Class B. A /28, generally the smallest you're likely to encounter in practice, leaves only four bits for identifying local nodes. It can handle networks with up to 16 nodes. CIDR also carefully specifies which address blocks are associated with which ISPs. This helps keep the Internet routing tables smaller and more manageable than they would be under the old system.

Several address blocks and patterns are special. All Internet addresses beginning with 10., 172.16. through 172.31., and 192.168. are deliberately unassigned. They can be used on internal networks, but no host using addresses in these blocks is allowed onto the global Internet. These *nonroutable* addresses are useful for building private networks that can't be seen from the rest of the Internet or for building a large network when you've been assigned only a Class C address block. Addresses beginning with 127 (most commonly 127.0.0.1) always mean the *local loopback address.* That is, these addresses always point to the local computer, no matter which computer you're running on. The hostname for this address is generally *localhost.* The address 0.0.0.0 always refers to the originating host but may be used only as a source address, not a destination. Similarly, any address that begins with 0.0 is assumed to refer to a host on the same local network.

Firewalls

There are some naughty people on the Internet. To keep them out, it's often helpful to set up one point of access to a local network and check all traffic into or out of that access point. The hardware and software that sits between the Internet and the local network, checking all the data that comes in or out to make sure it's kosher, is called a *firewall.*

The most basic firewall is a packet filter that inspects each packet coming into or out of a network and uses a set of rules to determine whether that traffic is allowed. Filtering is usually based on network addresses and ports. For example, all traffic coming from the Class C network 193.28.25 may be rejected because you had bad experiences with hackers from that net in the past. Outgoing Telnet connections may be allowed, but incoming Telnet connections may not be. Incoming connections on port 80 (Web) may be allowed but only to the corporate web server. The exact configuration of a firewall—which packets of data are and are not allowed to pass through—depends on the security needs of an individual site. Java doesn't have much to do with firewalls except insofar as they often get in your way.

Proxy Servers

Proxy servers are related to firewalls. If a firewall prevents hosts on a network from making direct connections to the outside world, a proxy server can act as a go-between. Thus a machine that is prevented from connecting to the external network by a firewall would make a request for a web page from the local proxy server instead of requesting the web page directly from the remote web server. The proxy server would then request the page from the web server and forward the response to the original requester. Proxies can also be used for FTP services and other connections. One of the security advantages of using a proxy server is that external hosts find out only about the proxy server. They do not learn the names and IP addresses of the internal machines, making it more difficult to hack into internal systems.

While firewalls generally operate at the level of the transport or internet layer, proxy servers operate at the application layer. A proxy server has detailed understanding of some application level protocols, like HTTP and FTP. Packets that pass through the proxy server can be examined to ensure that they contain data appropriate for their type. For instance, FTP packets that seem to contain Telnet data can be rejected. Figure 2-3 shows how proxy servers fit into the layer model.

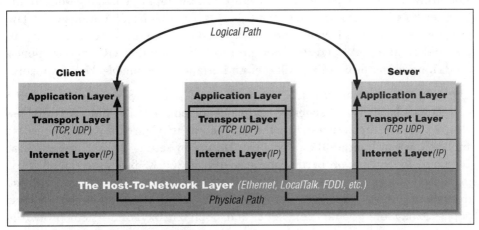

Figure 2-3. Layered connections through a proxy server

As long as all access to the Internet is forwarded through the proxy server, access can be tightly controlled. For instance, a company might choose to block access to *http://www.playboy.com* but allow access to *http://www.microsoft.com*. Some companies allow incoming FTP but disallow outgoing FTP so that confidential data cannot be as easily smuggled out of the company. Some companies have begun using proxy servers to track their employees' web usage so that they can see who's using the Internet to get tech support and who's using it to check out the Playmate of the Month. Such monitoring of employee behavior is controversial and not exactly an indicator of enlightened management techniques.

Proxy servers can also be used to implement local caching. When a file is requested from a web server, the proxy server will first check to see whether the file is in its cache. If the file is in the cache, then the proxy will serve the file from the cache rather than from the Internet. If the file is not in the cache, then the proxy server will retrieve the file, forward it to the requester, and store it in the cache for the next time it is requested. This scheme can significantly reduce load on an Internet connection and greatly improve response time. America Online (AOL) runs one of the largest farms of proxy servers in the world to speed the transfer of data to its users. If you look at a web server log file, you'll probably find some hits from clients with names like *http://www-d1.proxy.aol.com*, but not as many as you'd expect given the more than 20 million AOL subscribers. That's because AOL requests only pages they don't already have in their cache. Many other large ISPs do similarly.

The biggest problem with proxy servers is their inability to cope with all but a few protocols. Generally established protocols like HTTP, FTP, and SMTP are allowed to pass through, while newer protocols like Napster are not. (Some network administrators would consider that a feature.) In the rapidly changing world of the Internet, this is a significant disadvantage. It's a particular disadvantage for Java programmers because it limits the effectiveness of custom protocols. In Java, it's easy and often useful to create a new protocol that is optimized for your application. However, no proxy server will ever understand these one-of-a-kind protocols.

Applets that run in web browsers will generally use the proxy server settings of the web browser itself. This is generally set in a dialog box (possibly hidden several levels deep in the preferences) like the one shown in Figure 2-4. Standalone Java applications can indicate the proxy server to use by setting the socksProxyHost and socksProxyPort properties (if you're using a SOCKS proxy server), or http. proxySet, http.proxyHost, http.proxyPort, https.proxySet, https. proxyHost, https.proxyPort, ftpProxySet, ftpProxyHost, ftpProxyPort, gopherProxySet, gopherProxyHost, and gopherProxyPort system properties (if you're using protocol-specific proxies). You can set system properties from the command-line using the -D flag like this:

```
java -DsocksProxyHost=socks.cloud9.net -DsocksProxyPort=1080  MyClass
```

These can also be set by any other convenient means to set system properties, such as including them in the *appletviewer.properties* file like this:

```
ftpProxySet=true
ftpProxyHost=ftp.proxy.cloud9.net
ftpProxyPort=1000
gopherProxySet=true
gopherProxyHost=gopher.proxy.cloud9.net
gopherProxyPort=9800
http.proxySet=true
http.proxyHost=web.proxy.cloud9.net
http.proxyPort=8000
```

```
https.proxySet=true
https.proxyHost=web.proxy.cloud9.net
https.proxyPort=8001
```

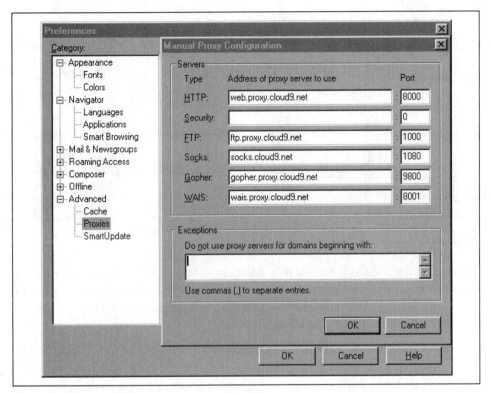

Figure 2-4. Netscape Navigator proxy server settings

The Client/Server Model

Most modern network programming is based on a client/server model. A client/
server application typically stores large quantities of data on an expensive, high-
powered server, while most of the program logic and the user interface is handled
by client software running on relatively cheap personal computers. In most cases, a
server primarily sends data, while a client primarily receives it, but it is rare for one
program to send or receive exclusively. A more reliable distinction is that a client
initiates a conversation, while a server waits for clients to start conversations with it.
Figure 2-5 illustrates both possibilities. In some cases, the same program may be
both a client and a server.

Some servers process and analyze the data before sending the results to the client.
Such servers are often referred to as "application servers" to distinguish them from
the more common file servers and database servers. A file or database server will

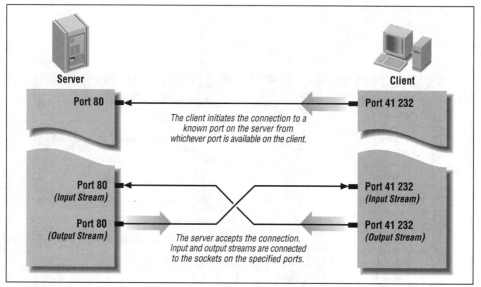

Figure 2-5. A client/server connection

retrieve information and send it to a client, but it won't process that information. In contrast, an application server might look at an order entry database and give the clients reports about monthly sales trends. An application server is not a server that serves files that happen to be applications.

You are already familiar with many examples of client/server systems. In 2000, the most popular client/server system on the Internet is the Web. Web servers such as Apache respond to requests from web clients such as Netscape. Data is stored on the web server and is sent out to the clients that request it. Aside from the initial request for a page, almost all data is transferred from the server to the client, not from the client to the server. Web servers that use CGI programs double as application and file servers. An older service that fits the client/server model is FTP. FTP uses different application protocols and different software but is still split into FTP servers, which send files, and FTP clients, which receive files. People often use FTP to upload files from the client to the server, so it's harder to say that the data transfer is primarily in one direction, but it is still true that an FTP client initiates the connection and the FTP server responds to it.

Java is a powerful environment in which to write GUI programs that access many different kinds of servers. The preeminent example of a client program written in Java is HotJava, the web browser from Sun, which is a general-purpose web client. Java makes it easy to write clients of all sorts, but it really shines when you start writing servers. Java does have some performance bottlenecks, mostly centered around GUIs and disk I/O. However, neither of these is a limiting factor for server programs where network bandwidth and robustness are far more important.

Not all applications fit easily into a client/server model. For instance, in networked games it seems likely that both players will send data back and forth roughly equally (at least in a fair game). These sorts of connections are called "peer-to-peer". The telephone system is the classic example of a peer-to-peer network. Each phone can either call another phone or be called by another phone. You don't have to buy one phone to send calls and another to receive them.

Java does not have explicit peer-to-peer communication in its networking API. However, applications can easily implement peer-to-peer communications in several ways, most commonly by acting as both a server and a client. Alternatively, the peers can communicate with each other through an intermediate server program that forwards data from one peer to the other peers. This is especially useful for applets whose security manager restricts them from talking directly to each other.

Internet Standards

This book discusses several application layer Internet protocols, most notably HTTP. However, this is not a book about those protocols, and it tries not to say more than the minimum you need to know. If you need detailed information about any protocol, the definitive source is the standards document for the protocol.

While there are many standards organizations in the world, the two that produce most of the standards relevant to network programming and protocols are the Internet Engineering Task Force (IETF) and the World Wide Web Consortium (W3C). The IETF is a relatively informal, democratic body open to participation by any interested party. Its standards are based on "rough consensus and running code" and tend to follow rather than lead implementations. IETF standards include TCP/IP, MIME, and SMTP. The W3C, by contrast, is a vendor organization, controlled by its dues-paying member corporations, that explicitly excludes participation by individuals. For the most part, the W3C tries to define standards in advance of implementation. W3C standards include HTTP, HTML, and XML.

IETF RFCs

IETF standards and near standards are published as Internet drafts and requests for comments (RFCs). RFCs and Internet drafts range from informational documents of general interest to detailed specifications of standard Internet protocols such as FTP. RFCs that document a standard or a proposed standard are published only with the approval of the Internet Engineering Steering Group (IESG) of the Internet Engineering Taskforce (IETF). All IETF-approved standards are RFCs, but not all RFCs are IETF standards. RFCs are available from many locations on the Internet, including *http://www.faqs.org/rfc/* and *http://www.ietf.org/rfc. html.*

For the most part, RFCs, particularly standards-oriented RFCs, are very technical, turgid, and nearly incomprehensible. Nonetheless, they are often the only complete and reliable source of information about a particular protocol.

Most proposals for a standard begin when a person or group gets an idea and builds a prototype. The prototype is incredibly important. Before something can become an IETF standard, it must actually exist and work. This requirement ensures that IETF standards are at least feasible, unlike the standards promulgated by some other standards bodies.

If the prototype becomes popular outside its original developers and if other organizations begin implementing their own versions of the protocol, then a working group may be formed under the auspices of the IETF. This working group attempts to document the protocol in an *Internet-Draft*. Internet-Drafts are working documents and change frequently to reflect experience with the protocol. The experimental implementations and the Internet-Draft evolve in rough synchronization, until eventually the working group agrees that the protocol is ready to become a formal standard. At this point, the proposed specification is submitted to the IESG.

At every step of the standardization track, the proposal is in one of six states or maturity levels:

- Experimental
- Proposed standard
- Draft standard
- Standard
- Informational
- Historic

For some time after the proposal is submitted, it is considered *experimental.* Being in an experimental stage does not imply that the protocol is not solid or that it is not widely used; unfortunately, the standards process usually lags behind *de facto* acceptance of the standard. If the IESG likes the experimental standard or it is in widespread use, the IESG will assign it an RFC number and publish it as an experimental RFC, generally after various changes.

If the experimental standard holds up well in further real-world testing, the IESG may advance it to the status of *proposed standard.* A proposed standard is fairly loose and is based on the experimental work of possibly as little as one organization. Changes may still be made to a protocol in this stage.

Once the bugs appear to have been worked out of a proposed standard and there are at least two independent implementations, the IESG may recommend that a proposed standard be promoted to a *draft standard*. A draft standard will probably not change too much before eventual standardization unless major flaws are found. The primary purpose of a draft standard is to clean up the RFC that documents the protocol and make sure the documentation conforms to actual practice, rather than to change the standard itself.

When a protocol completes this process, it has become an official Internet *standard*. It is assigned an STD number and is published as an STD in addition to an RFC. The absolute minimum time for a standard to be approved as such is 10 months, but in practice, the process almost always takes much longer. The commercial success of the Internet hasn't helped, since standards must now be worked out in the presence of marketers, vulture capitalists, lawyers, NSA spooks, and others with vested interests in seeing particular technologies succeed or fail. Therefore, many of the "standards" that this book references are in either the experimental, proposed, or draft stage. As of publication, there are almost 3,000 RFCs. Fewer than 100 of these have become STDs, and some of those that have are now obsolete. RFCs relevant to this book are detailed in Table 2-2.

Some RFCs that do not become standards are considered *informational*. These include RFCs that specify protocols that are widely used but weren't developed within the normal Internet standards track and haven't been through the formal standardization process. For example, NFS, originally developed by Sun, is described in the informational RFC 1813. Other informational RFCs provide useful information (such as users' guides) but don't document a protocol. For example, RFC 1635, *How to Use Anonymous FTP*, is an informational RFC.

Finally, changing technology and increasing experience renders some protocols and their associated RFCs obsolete. These are classified as *historic*. Historic protocols include IMAP3 (replaced by IMAP4), POP2 (replaced by POP3), and Remote Procedure Call Version 1 (replaced by Remote Procedure Call Version 2).

In addition to a protocol's maturity level, a protocol has a requirement level. The possible requirement levels are:

Required
> Must be implemented by all Internet hosts. There are very few required protocols. IP itself is one (RFC 791), but even protocols as important as TCP or UDP are only recommended. A standard is only required if it is absolutely essential to the proper functioning of a host on the Internet.

Recommended
> Should be implemented by Internet hosts that don't have a specific reason not to implement it. Most protocols that you are familiar with (for example, TCP and UDP, SMTP for email, Telnet for remote login, etc.) are recommended.

Elective

> Can be implemented by anyone who wants to use the protocol. For example, RFC 2045, *Multipurpose Internet Mail Extensions,* is a Draft Elective Standard. Given the importance of MIME these days, this protocol should probably be promoted to Recommended.

Limited Use

> May have to be implemented in certain unusual situations but won't be needed by most hosts. Mainly these are experimental protocols.

Not Recommended

> Should not be implemented by anyone.

Table 2-2 lists the RFCs and STDs that provide formal documentation for the protocols discussed in this book.

Table 2-2. Selected Internet RFCs

RFC	Title	Maturity Level	Requirement Level
RFC 2600 STD 1	Internet Official Protocol Standards	Standard	Required
Describes the standardization process and the current status of the different Internet protocols.			
RFC 1700 STD 2	Assigned Numbers	Standard	Required
This megalith of a document contains all of the information maintained by the Internet Assigned Numbers Authority, including MIME types and subtypes, port numbers for different services, the meanings of various numbers in IP headers, and more. As RFCs go, this one is rather unusual but absolutely essential.			
RFC 1122 RFC 1123 STD 3	Host Requirements	Standard	Required
Documents which protocols must be supported by all Internet hosts at different layers (data link layer, IP layer, transport layer, and application layer).			
RFC 791 RFC 919 RFC 922 RFC 950 STD 5	Internet Protocol	Standard	Required
The IP internet layer protocol.			
RFC 768 STD 6	User Datagram Protocol	Standard	Recommended
An unreliable, connectionless transport layer protocol.			
RFC 792 STD 5	Internet Control Message Protocol(ICMF)	Standard	Required
An internet layer protocol that uses raw IP datagrams but is not supported by Java. Its most familiar use is the *ping* program.			

Table 2-2. Selected Internet RFCs (continued)

RFC	Title	Maturity Level	Requirement Level
RFC 793 STD 7	Transmission Control Protocol	Standard	Recommended
A reliable, connection-oriented, streaming transport layer protocol.			
RFC 821 STD 10	Simple Mail Transfer Protocol	Standard	Recommended
The application layer protocol by which one host transfers email to another host. This standard doesn't say anything about email user interfaces; it covers the mechanism for passing email from one computer to another.			
RFC 822 STD 11	Format of Electronic Mail Messages	Standard	Recommended
The basic syntax for ASCII text email messages. MIME is designed to extend this to support binary data while ensuring that the messages transferred still conform to this standard.			
RFC 854 RFC 855 STD 8	Telnet Protocol	Standard	Recommended
An application-layer remote login service for command-line environments based around an abstract network virtual terminal (NVT) and TCP.			
RFC 862 STD 20	Echo Protocol	Standard	Recommended
An application-layer protocol that echoes back all data it receives over both TCP and UDP; useful as a debugging tool.			
RFC 863 STD 21	Discard Protocol	Standard	Elective
An application layer protocol that receives packets of data over both TCP and UDP and sends no response to the client; useful as a debugging tool.			
RFC 864 STD 22	Character Generator Protocol	Standard	Elective
An application layer protocol that sends an indefinite sequence of ASCII characters to any client that connects over either TCP or UDP; also useful as a debugging tool.			
RFC 865 STD 23	Quote of the Day	Standard	Elective
An application layer protocol that returns a quotation to any user who connects over either TCP or UDP and then closes the connection.			
RFC 867 STD 25	Daytime Protocol	Standard	Elective
An application layer protocol that sends a human-readable ASCII string indicating the current date and time at the server to any client that connects over TCP or UDP. This contrasts with the various NTP and Time Server protocols that do not return data that can be easily read by humans.			

Table 2-2. Selected Internet RFCs (continued)

RFC	Title	Maturity Level	Requirement Level
RFC 868 STD 26	Time Protocol	Standard	Elective
An application layer protocol that sends the time in seconds since midnight, January 1, 1900 to a client connecting over TCP or UDP. The time is sent as a machine-readable, 32-bit signed integer. The standard is incomplete in that it does not specify how the integer is encoded in 32 bits, but in practice a two's complement, big-endian integer is used.			
RFC 959 STD 9	File Transfer Protocol	Standard	Recommended
An optionally authenticated, two-socket application layer protocol for file transfer that uses TCP.			
RFC 977	Network News Transfer Protocol	Proposed Standard	Elective
The application layer protocol by which Usenet news is transferred from machine to machine over TCP; used by both news clients talking to news servers and news servers talking to each other.			
RFC 1034 RFC 1035 STD 13	Domain Name System	Standard	Recommended
The collection of distributed software by which hostnames that human beings can remember, like *www.oreilly.com*, are translated into numbers that computers can understand, like 198.112.208.11. This STD defines how domain name servers on different hosts communicate with each other using UDP.			
RFC 1112	Host Extensions for IP Multicasting	Standard	Recommended
The Internet layer methods by which conforming systems can direct a single packet of data to multiple hosts. This is called multicasting; Java's support for multicasting is discussed in Chapter 14.			
RFC 1153	Digest Message Format for Mail	Experimental	Limited use
A format for combining multiple postings to a mailing list into a single message.			
RFC 1288	Finger Protocol	Draft Standard	Elective
An application layer protocol for requesting information about a user at a remote site. It can be a security risk.			
RFC 1303	Network Time Protocol (Version 3)	Draft Standard	Elective
A more precise application layer protocol for synchronizing clocks between systems that attempts to account for network latency.			
RFC 1350 STD 33	Trivial File Transfer Protocol	Standard	Elective
An unauthenticated application layer protocol for file transfer that uses UDP; typically used by diskless workstations to retrieve files necessary for booting from a server.			

Table 2-2. Selected Internet RFCs (continued)

RFC	Title	Maturity Level	Requirement Level
RFC 1738	Uniform Resource Locators	Proposed Standard	Elective
Full URLs like *http://www.amnesty.org/* and *ftp://ftp.dnai.com/users/c/cityjava/javaio.htm.*			
RFC 1808	Relative Uniform Resource Locators	Proposed Standard	Elective
Partial URLs like */javafaq/books/* and *../examples/07/index.html* used as values of the HREF attribute of an HTML A element.			
RFC 1939 STD 53	Post Office Protocol, Version 3	Standard	Elective
An application layer protocol used by sporadically connected email clients such as Eudora to retrieve mail from a server over TCP.			
RFC 1945	Hypertext Transfer Protocol (HTTP 1.0)	Informational	N/A
Version 1.0 of the application layer protocol used by web browsers talking to web servers over TCP; developed by the W3C rather than the IETF.			
RFC 2045 RFC 2046 RFC 2047	Multipurpose Internet Mail Extensions	Draft Standard	Elective
A means of encoding binary data and non-ASCII text for transmission through Internet email and other ASCII-oriented protocols.			
RFC 2068	Hypertext Transfer Protocol (HTTP 1.1)	Proposed Standard	Elective
Version 1.1 of the application layer protocol used by web browsers talking to web servers over TCP.			
RFC 2141	Uniform Resource Names (URN) Syntax	Proposed Standard	Elective
Similar to URLs but intended to refer to actual resources in a persistent fashion rather than the transient location of those resources.			
RFC 2396	Uniform Resource Identifiers (URI): Generic Syntax	Proposed Standard	Elective
Similar to URLs but cut a broader path. For instance, ISBN numbers may be URIs even if the book cannot be retrieved over the Internet.			

The IETF has traditionally worked behind the scenes, codifying and standardizing existing practice. Although its activities are completely open to the public, it's traditionally been very low profile. There simply aren't that many people who get excited about the details of network arcana like the Internet Gateway Message Protocol (IGMP). The participants in the process have mostly been engineers and computer scientists, including many from academia as well as the profit-driven corporate world. Consequently, despite often vociferous debates about ideal implementations, most serious IETF efforts have produced reasonable standards.

Unfortunately, that can't be said of the IETF's efforts to produce Web (as opposed to Internet) standards. In particular, the IETF's early effort to standardize HTML was a colossal failure. The refusal of Netscape and other key vendors to participate in or even acknowledge the process was a crucial problem. That HTML was simple enough and high-profile enough to attract the attention of assorted market-droids and random flamers didn't help matters either. Thus in October 1994, the World Wide Web Consortium was formed as a vendor-controlled body that might be able to avoid the pitfalls that plagued the IETF's efforts to standardize HTML.

W3C Recommendations

Although the W3C standardization process is similar to the IETF process (a series of working drafts hashed out on mailing lists resulting in an eventual specification), the W3C is a fundamentally different organization from the IETF. Whereas the IETF is open to participation by anyone, only corporations and other organizations may become members of the W3C. Individuals are specifically excluded. Furthermore, although nonprofit organizations such as the World Wide Web Artists Consortium (WWWAC) may join the W3C, only the employees of these organizations may participate in W3C activities. Their volunteer members are not welcome. Specific individual experts are occasionally invited to participate in a particular working group even though they are not employees of a W3C member company. However, the number of such individuals is quite small relative to the number of interested experts in the broader community. Membership in the W3C costs $50,000 a year ($5,000 a year for nonprofits) with a minimum three-year commitment. Membership in the IETF costs nothing a year with no commitment beyond a willingness to participate. And although many people participate in developing W3C standards, each standard is ultimately approved or vetoed by one individual, W3C director Tim Berners-Lee. IETF standards are approved by a consensus of the people who worked on the standard. Clearly the IETF is a much more democratic (some would say anarchic) and open organization than the W3C.

Despite the W3C's strong bias toward the corporate members that pay its bills, it has so far managed to do a better job of navigating the politically tricky waters of Web standardization than the IETF. It has produced several HTML standards as well as a variety of others, such as HTTP, PICS, XML, CSS, MathML, and more. The W3C has had considerably less success in convincing vendors such as Netscape and Microsoft to fully and consistently implement its standards.

The W3C has five basic levels of standards:

Recommendation

A Recommendation is the highest level of W3C standard. However, the W3C is very careful not to actually call this a "standard" for fear of running afoul of antitrust statutes. The W3C describes a Recommendation as a "work that represents consensus within W3C and has the Director's stamp of approval. W3C considers that the ideas or technology specified by a Recommendation are appropriate for widespread deployment and promote W3C's mission."

Proposed Recommendation

A Proposed Recommendation is mostly complete and unlikely to undergo more than minor changes. The main purpose of a Proposed Recommendation is to work out bugs in the specification document rather than in the underlying technology being documented.

Candidate Recommendation

A Candidate Recommendation indicates that the working group has reached consensus on all major issues and is ready for third-party comment and implementations. If the implementations do not uncover any obstructions, the spec can be promoted to a Proposed Recommendation.

Working Drafts

A Working Draft is a reflection of the current thinking of some (not necessarily all) members of a working group. It should eventually lead to a Proposed Recommendation, but by the time it does so it may have changed substantially.

Note

A Note is generally one of two things, either an unsolicited submission by a W3C member (similar to an IETF Internet-Draft) or random musings by W3C staff or related parties that do not actually describe a full proposal (similar to an IETF informational RFC). Notes will not necessarily lead to the formation of a working group or a W3C Recommendation.

The W3C has not been around long enough to develop a need for a historical or informational standard status. Another difference is that the W3C process rarely fails to elevate a standard to full Recommendation status once work has actively commenced; that is, once a working group has been formed. This contrasts markedly with the IETF, which has more than a thousand proposed and draft standards but only a few dozen actual standards.

PR Standards

In recent years, both the W3C and IETF standards processes have been abused by companies seeking a little free press or perhaps a temporary boost to their stock price. The IETF will accept a submission from anyone, and the W3C will accept a submission from any W3C member. The IETF calls these Internet-Drafts and will publish them for six months before deleting them. The W3C refers to these as "acknowledged submissions" and will publish them indefinitely. However, neither organization actually promises to do more than acknowledge receipt of these documents. In particular, they do not promise to form a working group or begin the standardization process. Nonetheless, press releases invariably misrepresent the submission of such a document as a far more significant event than it actually is. PR reps can generally count on suckering at least a few clueless reporters who aren't up-to-speed on the intimate details of the standardization process. However, at least now you should be able to recognize these ploys for what they are.

3

Basic Web Concepts

By the time you finish this book, I hope you will realize that Java can do a lot more than create flashy web pages. Nonetheless, many of your programs will be applets on web pages or will need to talk to web servers to retrieve files or post data. Therefore, it's important to have a solid understanding of the interaction between web servers and web browsers.

The Hypertext Transfer Protocol (HTTP) is a standard that defines how a web client talks to a server and how data is transferred from the server back to the client. HTTP relies heavily on two other standards: the Multipurpose Internet Mail Extensions (MIME) and the Hypertext Markup Language (HTML). MIME is a way to encode different kinds of data, such as sound and text, to be transmitted over a 7-bit ASCII connection; it also lets the recipient know what kind of data has been sent, so that it can be displayed properly. As its name implies, MIME was originally designed to facilitate multimedia email and to provide an encoding that could get binary data past the most brain-damaged mail transfer programs. However, it is now used much more broadly. HTML is a simple standard for describing the semantic value of textual data. This means that you can say "this is a header", "this is a list item", "this deserves emphasis", and so on, but you can't specify how headers, lists, and other items are formatted: formatting is up to the browser. HTML is a "hypertext markup language" because it includes a way to specify links to other documents identified by URLs. A URL is a way to unambiguously identify the location of a resource on the Internet. To understand network programming, you'll need to understand URLs, HTML, MIME, and HTTP in somewhat more detail than the average web page designer.

URIs

A Uniform Resource Identifier (URI) is a string of characters in a particular syntax that identifies a resource. The resource identified may be a file on a server, but it may also be an email address, a news message, a book, a person's name, an Internet host, the current stock price of Sun Microsystems, or something else. An absolute URI is made up of a scheme for the URI and a scheme-specific part, separated by a colon like this:

    scheme:scheme-specific-part

The syntax of the scheme-specific part depends on the scheme being used. Many different schemes will eventually be defined, but current ones include:

data
    Base64-encoded data included directly in a link; see RFC 2397

file
    A file on a local disk

FTP
    An FTP server

HTTP
    A World Wide Web server using the Hypertext Transfer Protocol

gopher
    A Gopher server

mailto
    An email address

news
    A Usenet newsgroup

Telnet
    A connection to a Telnet-based service

urn
    A Uniform Resource Name

In addition, Java makes heavy use of nonstandard, custom schemes such as *rmi*, *jndi*, and *doc* for various purposes. We'll look at the mechanism behind this in Chapter 15, *The URLConnection Class,* when we discuss protocol handlers.

There is no specific syntax that applies to the scheme-specific parts of all URIs. However, many follow this form:

    //authority/path?query

The *authority* part of the URI names the authority responsible for resolving the rest of the URI. For instance, the URI *http://www.ietf.org/rfc/rfc2396.txt* has the scheme *http* and the authority *www.ietf.org*. This means that the server at *www.ietf.org* is responsible for mapping the path */rfc/rfc2396.txt* to an actual resource. This URI does not have a query part. The URI *http://www1.fatbrain.com/asp/bookinfo/bookinfo. asp?theisbn=1565924851* has the scheme *http*, the authority *www1.fatbrain.com*, the path */asp/bookinfo/bookinfo.asp*, and the query *theisbn=1565924851*. The URI *urn: isbn:1565924851* has the scheme *urn* but doesn't follow the `//authority/ path?query` form for scheme-specific parts.

Although current examples of URIs use an Internet host as an authority, this may not be true of all future schemes. However, if the authority is an Internet host, then optional usernames and ports may also be provided to make the authority more specific. For example, the URI *ftp://mp3:mp3@ci43198-a.ashvil1.nc.home.com: 33/VanHalen-Jump.mp3* has the authority *mp3:mp3@ci43198-a.ashvil1.nc.home.com: 33*. This authority has the username *mp3*, the password *mp3*, the host *ci43198-a. ashvil1.nc.home.com*, and the port *33*. It has the scheme *ftp* and the path */VanHalen-Jump.mp3*. (In most cases, including the password in the URI is a big security hole unless, as here, you really do want everyone in the universe to know the password.)

The path (which includes its initial /) is a string that the authority can use to determine which resource is identified. Different authorities may interpret the same path to refer to different resources. For instance, the path */index.html* means one thing when the authority is *www.georgewbush.com* and something very different when the authority is *www.gore2000.com*. The path may be hierarchical, in which case the individual parts are separated by forward slashes, and the . and .. operators are used to navigate the hierarchy. These are derived from the pathname syntax on the Unix operating systems where the Web and URLs were invented. They conveniently map to a filesystem stored on a Unix web server. However, there is no guarantee that the components of any particular path actually correspond to files or directories on any particular filesystem. For example, in the URI *http://www. amazon.com/exec/obidos/ISBN%3D1565924851/cafeaulaitA/002-3777605-3043449* all the pieces of the hierarchy are just used to pull information out of a database that's never stored in a filesystem. *ISBN%3D1565924851* selects the particular book from the database by its ISBN number. *cafeaulaitA* specifies who gets the referral fee if a purchase is made from this link. And *002-3777605-3043449* is a session key used to track this visitor's path through the site.

Of course, some URIs aren't at all hierarchical, at least in the filesystem sense. For example, *snews://secnews.netscape.com/netscape.devs-java* has a path of */netscape.devs-java*. Although there's some hierarchy to the newsgroup names indicated by the . between *netscape* and *netscape.devs-java*, it's not visible as part of the URI.

The scheme part is composed of lowercase letters, digits, and the plus sign, period, and hyphen. It must begin with a lowercase letter. The other three parts of a typical URI (authority, path, and query) should each be composed of the ASCII alphanumeric characters; that is, the letters A–Z, a–z, and the digits 0–9. In addition, the punctuation characters - _ . ! ~ * ' (and ,) may also be used. All other characters including non-ASCII alphanumerics such as á and π should be escaped by a percent sign (%) followed by the hexadecimal code for the character. For instance, á would be encoded as %E1 and π would be encoded %3C0. The latter assumes the underlying character set is 2-byte Unicode. The current draft of the URI specification does not yet provide a means of specifying the character set to be used. This is a deficiency that will be corrected in a future draft. A URL so transformed is said to have been "x-www-form-url-encoded".

Punctuation characters such as / and @ must also be encoded using percent escapes if they're used in any role other than what's specified for them in the scheme-specific part of a particular URL. For example, the forward slashes in the URI *http://metalab.unc.edu/javafaq/books/javaio/* do not need to be encoded as *%2F* because they serve to delimit the hierarchy as specified for the *http* URI scheme. However, if a filename included a / character—for instance, if the last directory were named *Java I/O* instead of *javaio* to more closely match the name of the book—then the URI would have to be written as *http://metalab.unc.edu/javafaq/books/Java%20I%2FO/*. This is not as farfetched as it might sound to Unix or Windows users. Mac filenames often include a forward slash. File names on many platforms often contain other characters that need to be encoded including @, $, +, =, and many more.

URNs

There are two types of URIs: Uniform Resource Locators (URLs) and Uniform Resource Names (URNs). A URL is a pointer to a particular resource on the Internet at a particular location. For example, *http://www.oreilly.com/catalog/javanp2/* is one of several URLs for the book *Java Network Programming*, 2nd edition. A URN is a name for a particular resource but without reference to a particular location. For instance, *urn:isbn:1565928709* is a URN referring to the same book. As this example shows, URNs, unlike URLs, are not limited to Internet resources.

The goal of URNs is to handle resources that are mirrored in many different locations or that have moved from one site to another; they identify the resource itself, not the place where the resource lives. For instance, when given a URN for a particular piece of software, an FTP program should get the file from the nearest mirror site. Given a URN for a book, a browser might reserve the book for you at the local library or order a copy from a bookstore.

A URN has the general form:

```
urn:namespace:resource_name
```

The *namespace* is the name of a collection of certain kinds of resources maintained by some authority. The *resource_name* is the name of a resource within that collection. For instance, the URN *urn:isbn:1565924851* identifies a resource in the *isbn* namespace with the identifier *1565924851*. Of all the books published, this one selects the first edition of *Java I/O*.

The exact syntax of resource names depends on the namespace. The ISBN namespace expects to see strings composed of 10 characters, all of which are digits with the single exception that the last character may be a capital letter *X* instead. Other namespaces will use very different syntaxes for resource names. The IANA is responsible for handing out namespaces to different organizations, but the procedure isn't really in place yet. URNs are still an area of active research and are not much used by current software. ISBN numbers are pretty much the only example established so far, and even those haven't been officially standardized as URNs. Consequently, the rest of this book will use URLs exclusively.

URLs

A URL identifies the location of a resource on the Internet. It specifies the protocol used to access a server (e.g., FTP, HTTP), the name of the server, and the location of a file on that server. A typical URL looks like *http://metalab.unc.edu/javafaq/javatutorial.html*. This specifies that there is a file called *javatutorial.html* in a directory called *javafaq* on the server *metalab.unc.edu*, and that this file can be accessed via the HTTP protocol. The syntax of a URL is:

```
protocol://username@hostname:port/path/filename#fragment?query
```

Here the protocol is another word for what was called the scheme of the URI. (*Scheme* is the word used in the URI RFC. *Protocol* is the word used in the Java documentation.) In a URL, the protocol part can be *file, ftp, http, https, gopher, news, Telnet, wais*, or various other strings (though not *urn*).

The *hostname* part of a URL is the name of the server that provides the resource you want, like *www.oreilly.com* or *utopia.poly.edu*. It can also be the server's IP address, like 204.148.40.9 or 128.238.3.21. The *username* is an optional username for the server. The *port* number is also optional. It's not necessary if the service is running on its default port (port 80 for HTTP servers).

The *path* points to a particular directory on the specified server. The path is relative to the document root of the server, not necessarily to the root of the filesystem on the server. As a rule, servers that are open to the public do not show their entire filesystem to clients. Rather, they show only the contents of a specified directory. This directory is called the document root, and all paths and filenames are relative to it. Thus on a Unix workstation all files that are available to the public may be in */var/public/html*, but to somebody connecting from a remote machine this directory looks like the root of the filesystem.

The filename points to a particular file in the directory specified by the path. It is often omitted, in which case it is left to the server's discretion what file, if any, to send. Many servers send an index file for that directory, often called *index.html* or *Welcome.html*. Others send a list of the files and folders in the directory as shown in Figure 3-1. Others may send a 403 forbidden error message as shown in Figure 3-2.

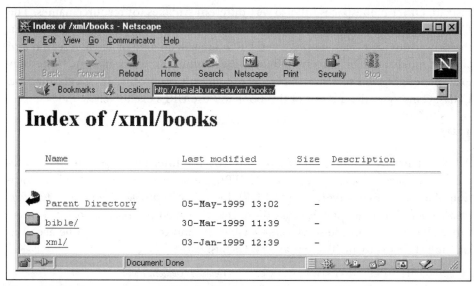

Figure 3-1. A web server configured to send a directory list when no index file exists

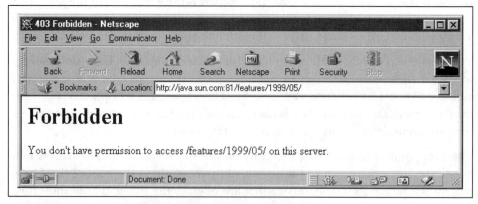

Figure 3-2. A web server configured to send a 403 error when no index file exists

The *fragment* is used to reference a named anchor in an HTML document. Some documents refer to the fragment part of the URL as a "section"; Java documents rather unaccountably refer to the section as a "Ref". A named anchor is created in an HTML document with a tag like this:

```
<A NAME="xtocid1902914">Comments</A>
```

This tag identifies a particular point in a document. To refer to this point, a URL includes not only the document's filename, but also the named anchor separated from the rest of the URL by a #:

```
http://metalab.unc.edu/javafaq/javafaq.html#xtocid1902914
```

Finally, the *query* string provides additional arguments for the server. It's commonly used only in *http* URLs, where it contains form data for input to CGI programs. This will be discussed further later on.

Relative URLs

A URL tells the web browser a lot about a document: the protocol used to retrieve the document, the name of the host where the document lives, and the path to that document on the host. Most of this information is likely to be the same for other URLs that are referenced in the document. Therefore, rather than requiring each URL to be specified in its entirety, a URL may inherit the protocol, hostname, and path of its parent document (i.e., the document in which it appears). URLs that aren't complete but inherit pieces from their parent are called *relative* URLs. In contrast, a completely specified URL is called an *absolute URL*. In a relative URL, any pieces that are missing are assumed to be the same as the corresponding pieces from the URL of the document in which the URL is found. For example, suppose that while browsing *http://metalab.unc.edu/javafaq/javatutorial. html* you click on this hyperlink:

```
<a href="javafaq.html">
```

Your browser cuts javatutorial.html off the end of *http://metalab.unc.edu/javafaq/ javatutorial.html* to get *http://metalab.unc.edu/javafaq/*. Then it attaches *javafaq.html* onto the end of *http://metalab.unc.edu/javafaq/* to get *http://metalab.unc.edu/javafaq/ javafaq.html*. Finally, it loads that document.

If the relative link begins with a /, then it is relative to the document root instead of relative to the current file. Thus, if you click on the following link while browsing *http://metalab.unc.edu/javafaq/javatutorial.html*:

```
<a href="/boutell/faq/www_faq.html">
```

your browser would throw away */javafaq/javatutorial.html* and attach */boutell/faq/ www_faq.html* to the end of *http://metalab.unc.edu* to get *http://metalab.unc.edu/ boutell/faq/www_faq.html*.

Relative URLs have a number of advantages. First and least, they save a little typing. More importantly, relative URLs allow a single document tree to be served by multiple protocols; for instance, both FTP and HTTP. The HTTP might be used for direct surfing while the FTP could be used for mirroring the site. Most importantly of all, relative URLs allow entire trees of HTML documents to be moved or copied from one site to another without breaking all the internal links.

HTML, SGML, and XML

HTML is the primary format used for Web documents. As I said earlier, HTML is a simple standard for describing the semantic content of textual data. The idea of describing a text's semantics rather than its appearance comes from an older standard called the Standard Generalized Markup Language (SGML). Standard HTML is an instance of SGML. SGML was invented beginning in the mid-1970s by Charles Goldfarb at IBM. SGML is now an International Standards Organization (ISO) standard, specifically ISO 8879:1986.

SGML and, by inheritance, HTML are based on the notion of design by meaning rather than design by appearance. You don't say that you want some text printed in 18-point type; you say that it is a top-level heading (<H1> in HTML). Likewise, you don't say that a word should be placed in italics. Rather you say it should be emphasized (<EM> in HTML). It is left to the browser to determine how to best display headings or emphasized text.

The tags used to mark up the text are case insensitive. Thus <STRONG> is the same as <strong> is the same as <Strong> is the same as <StrONg>. Some tags have a matching closing tag to define a region of text. A closing tag is the same as the opening tag except that the opening angle bracket is followed by a /. For example: <STRONG>this text is strong</STRONG>; <EM>this text is emphasized</EM>. The entire text from the beginning of the start tag to the end of the end tag is called an element. Thus <STRONG>this text is strong</STRONG> is a STRONG element.

HTML elements may nest but they should not overlap. The first line following is standard conforming. The second line is not, though many browsers accept it nonetheless:

```
<STRONG><EM>Jack and Jill went up the hill</EM></STRONG>
<STRONG><EM>to fetch a pail of water</STRONG></EM>
```

Some elements have additional attributes that are encoded as name-value pairs on the start tag. The <H1> tag and most other paragraph-level tags may have an ALIGN attribute that says whether the header should be centered, left aligned, or right aligned.

For example:

```
<H1 ALIGN=CENTER> This is a centered H1 heading </H1>
```

The value of an attribute may be enclosed in double or single quotes like this:

```
<H1 ALIGN="CENTER"> This is a centered H1 heading </H1>
<H2 ALIGN='LEFT'> This is a left-aligned H2 heading </H2>
```

Quotes are required only if the value contains embedded spaces. When processing HTML, you need to be prepared for attribute values that do and don't have quotes.

There have been several versions of HTML over the years. The current standard is HTML 4.0, most of which is supported by current web browsers with occasional exceptions. Furthermore, several companies, notably Netscape, Microsoft, and Sun, have added nonstandard extensions to HTML. These include blinking text, inline movies, frames, and, most importantly for this book, applets. Some of these extensions—for example, the <APPLET> tag—are allowed but deprecated in HTML 4.0. Others, such as Netscape's notorious <BLINK>, come out of left field and have no place in a semantically oriented language like HTML.

HTML 4.0 may be the end of the line, aside from minor fixes. The W3C has decreed that HTML is getting too bulky to layer more features on top of. Instead, new development will focus on XML, a semantic language that allows page authors to create the elements they need rather than relying on a few fixed elements such as P and LI. For example, if you're writing a web page with a price list, you would likely have an SKU element, a PRICE element, a MANUFACTURER element, a PRODUCT element, and so forth. That might look something like this:

```
<PRODUCT MANUFACTURER="LOTUS">
  <NAME>1-2-3</NAME>
  <VERSION>5.0</VERSION>
  <PLATFORM>Windows</PLATFORM>
  <PRICE CURRENCY="US">299.95</PRICE>
  <SKU>D05WGML</SKU>
</PRODUCT>
```

This looks a lot like HTML, in much the same way that Java looks like C. There are elements and attributes. Tags are set off by < and >. Attributes are enclosed in quotation marks, and so forth. However, instead of being limited to a finite set of tags, you can create all the new and different tags you need. Since no browser can know in advance all the different elements that may appear, a stylesheet is used to describe how each of the items should be displayed.

XML has another advantage over HTML that may not be obvious from this simple example. HTML can be quite sloppy. Elements are opened but not closed. Attribute values may or may not be enclosed in quotes. The quotes may or may not be closed.

XML tightens all this up. It lays out very strict requirements for the syntax of a well-formed XML document, and it requires that browsers reject all malformed documents. Browsers may not attempt to fix the problem and make a best-faith effort to display what they think the author meant. They must simply report the error. Furthermore, an XML document may have a Document Type Definition (DTD) which can impose additional constraints on valid documents. For example, a DTD may require that every PRODUCT element contain exactly one NAME element. This has a number of advantages, but the key one here is that XML documents are far easier to parse than HTML documents. As a programmer, you will find it much easier to work with XML than HTML.

XML can be used both for pure XML pages and for embedding new kinds of content in HTML. For example, the Mathematical Markup Language, MathML, is an XML application for including mathematical equations in web pages. SMIL, the Synchronized Multimedia Integration Language, is an XML application for including timed multimedia such as slide shows and subtitled videos on web pages. For a lot more information about XML, see my own *The XML Bible*, IDG Books, 1999.

HTTP

HTTP, the Hypertext Transfer Protocol, is the standard protocol for communication between web browsers and web servers. HTTP specifies how a client and server establish a connection, how the client requests data from the server, how the server responds to that request, and finally how the connection is closed. HTTP connections use the TCP/IP protocol for data transfer.

HTTP 1.0 is the currently accepted version of the protocol. It uses MIME to encode data. The basic protocol defines a sequence of four steps for each request from a client to the server:

1. **Making the connection**. The client establishes a TCP connection to the server, on port 80 by default; other ports may be specified in the URL.

2. **Making a request**. The client sends a message to the server requesting the page at a specified URL. The format of this request is typically something like:

   ```
   GET /index.html HTTP 1.0
   ```

   GET is a keyword. /index.html is a relative URL to a file on the server. The file is assumed to be on the machine that receives the request, so there is no need to prefix it with http://www.thismachine.com/. HTTP 1.0 is the version of the protocol that the client understands. The request is terminated with two carriage return/linefeed pairs (\r\n\r\n in Java parlance) regardless of how lines are terminated on the client or server platform.

Although the `GET` line is all that is required, a client request can include other information as well. This takes the following form:

```
Keyword: Value
```

The most common such keyword is `Accept`, which tells the server what kinds of data the client can handle (though servers often ignore this). For example, the following line says that the client can handle four MIME types, corresponding to HTML documents, plain text, and JPEG and GIF images:

```
Accept: text/html, text/plain, image/gif, image/jpeg
```

`User-Agent` is another common keyword that lets the server know what browser is being used. This allows the server to send files optimized for the particular browser type. The line below says that the request comes from Version 2.4 of the Lynx browser:

```
User-Agent: Lynx/2.4 libwww/2.1.4
```

Finally, the request is terminated with a blank line; that is, two carriage return/linefeed pairs, \r\n\r\n. A complete request might look like:

```
GET /index.html HTTP 1.0
Accept: text/html
Accept: text/plain
User-Agent: Lynx/2.4 libwww/2.1.4
```

In addition to `GET`, there are several other request types. `HEAD` retrieves only the header for the file, not the actual data. This is commonly used to check the modification date of a file, to see whether a copy stored in the local cache is still valid. `POST` sends form data to the server, and `PUT` uploads a file to the server.

3. **The response**. The server sends a response to the client. The response begins with a response code, followed by MIME header information, then a blank line, then the requested document or an error message. Assuming the requested file is found, a typical response looks like this:

```
HTTP 1.0 200 OK
Server: NCSA/1.4.2
MIME-version: 1.0
Content-type: text/html
Content-length: 107

<html>
<Head>
<Title>
A Sample HTML file
</Title>
</Head>
```

```
<body>
The rest of the document goes here
</body>
</html>
```

The first line indicates the protocol the server is using (HTTP 1.0), followed by a response code. 200 OK is the most common response code, indicating that the request was successful. Table 3-1 is a complete list of the response codes used by HTTP 1.0; HTTP 1.1 adds many more to this list. The other header lines identify the server software (the NCSA server, Version 1.4.2), the version of MIME in use, the MIME content type, and the length of the document delivered (not counting this header)—in this case, 107 bytes.

4. **Closing the connection.** Either the client or the server or both close the connection. Thus, a separate network connection is used for each request. If the client reconnects, the server retains no memory of the previous connection or its results. A protocol that retains no memory of past requests is called *stateless*; in contrast, a *stateful* protocol such as FTP can process many requests before the connection is closed. The lack of state is both a strength and a weakness of HTTP.

Table 3-1. HTTP 1.0 Response Codes

Response Code	Meaning
2xx Successful	Response codes between 200 and 299 indicate that the request was received, understood, and accepted.
200 OK	This is the most common response code. If the request used GET or POST, then the requested data is contained in the response, along with the usual headers. If the request used HEAD, then only the header information is included.
201 Created	The server has created a data file at a URL specified in the body of the response. The web browser should now attempt to load that URL. This is sent only in response to POST requests.
202 Accepted	This rather uncommon response indicates that a request (generally from POST) is being processed, but the processing is not yet complete so no response can be returned. The server should return an HTML page that explains the situation to the user, provides an estimate of when the request is likely to be completed, and, ideally, has a link to a status monitor of some kind.
204 No Content	The server has successfully processed the request but has no information to send back to the client. This is usually the result of a poorly written form-processing CGI program that accepts data but does not return a response to the user indicating that it has finished.
3xx Redirection	Response codes from 300 to 399 indicate that the web browser needs to go to a different page.

Table 3-1. HTTP 1.0 Response Codes (continued)

Response Code	Meaning
300 Multiple Choices	The page requested is available from one or more locations. The body of the response includes a list of locations from which the user or web browser can pick the most appropriate one. If the server prefers one of these choices, the URL of this choice is included in a Location header, which web browsers can use to load the preferred page.
301 Moved Permanently	The page has moved to a new URL. The web browser should automatically load the page at this URL and update any bookmarks that point to the old URL.
302 Moved Temporarily	This unusual response code indicates that a page is temporarily at a new URL but that the document's location will change again in the foreseeable future, so bookmarks should not be updated.
304 Not Modified	The client has performed a GET request but used the If-Modified-Since header to indicate that it wants the document only if it has been recently updated. This status code is returned because the document has not been updated. The web browser will now load the page from a cache.
4xx Client Error	Response codes from 400 to 499 indicate that the client has erred in some fashion, though this may as easily be the result of an unreliable network connection as it is of a buggy or nonconforming web browser. The browser should stop sending data to the server as soon as it receives a 4xx response. Unless it is responding to a HEAD request, the server should explain the error status in the body of its response.
400 Bad Request	The client request to the server used improper syntax. This is rather unusual, though it is likely to happen if you're writing and debugging a client.
401 Unauthorized	Authorization, generally username and password controlled, is required to access this page. Either the username and password have not yet been presented or the username and password are invalid.
403 Forbidden	The server understood the request but is deliberately refusing to process it. Authorization will not help. One reason this occurs is that the client asks for a directory listing but the server is not configured to provide it, as shown in Figure 3-1.
404 Not Found	This most common error response indicates that the server cannot find the requested page. It may indicate a bad link, a page that has moved with no forwarding address, a mistyped URL, or something similar.
5xx Server Error	Response codes from 500 to 599 indicate that something has gone wrong with the server, and the server cannot fix the problem.
500 Internal Server Error	An unexpected condition occurred that the server does not know how to handle.
501 Not Implemented	The server does not have the feature that is needed to fulfill this request. A server that cannot handle POST requests might send this response to a client that tried to POST form data to it.

Table 3-1. HTTP 1.0 Response Codes (continued)

Response Code	Meaning
502 Bad Gateway	This response is applicable only to servers that act as proxies or gateways. It indicates that the proxy received an invalid response from a server it was connecting to in an effort to fulfill the request.
503 Service Unavailable	The server is temporarily unable to handle the request, perhaps because overloading or maintenance.

HTTP 1.1 more than doubles the number of responses. However, a response code from 200 to 299 always indicates success; a response code from 300 to 399 always indicates redirection; one from 400 to 499 always indicates a client error; and one from 500 to 599 indicates a server error.

HTTP 1.0 is documented in the informational RFC 1945; it is not an official Internet standard because it was primarily developed outside the IETF by early browser and server vendors. HTTP 1.1 is a proposed standard being developed by the W3C and the HTTP working group of the IETF. It provides for much more flexible and powerful communication between the client and the server. It's also a lot more scalable.

The primary improvement in HTTP 1.1 is state. HTTP 1.0 opens a new connection for every request. In practice, the time taken to open and close all the connections opened in a typical web session can outweigh the time taken to transmit the data, especially for sessions with many small documents. HTTP 1.1 allows a browser to send many different requests over a single connection; the connection remains open until it is explicitly closed. The requests and responses are all asynchronous. A browser doesn't need to wait for a response to its first request before sending a second or a third. However, it remains tied to the basic pattern of a client request, followed by a server response that consists of a series of headers, followed by a blank line, followed by MIME-encoded data.

There are a lot of other smaller improvements in HTTP 1.1. Requests include a Host MIME header so that one web server can easily serve different sites at different URLs. Servers and browsers can exchange compressed files and particular byte ranges of a document, both of which can decrease network traffic. And HTTP 1.1 is designed to work much better with proxy servers. Although HTTP 1.1 isn't quite finished, it is relatively stable, and most major web servers implement at least some parts of it. Web clients (that is, browsers) are a little further behind, but the more recent browsers implement parts as well. HTTP 1.1 is a strict superset of HTTP 1.0, so HTTP 1.1 web servers have no trouble interacting with older browsers that speak only HTTP 1.0.

MIME

MIME is an open standard for sending multipart, multimedia data through Internet email.* The data may be binary, or it may use multiple ASCII and non-ASCII character sets. Although MIME was originally intended for email, it has become a widely used technique to describe a file's contents so that client software can tell the difference between different kinds of data. For example, a web browser uses MIME to tell whether a file is a GIF image or a printable PostScript file.

MIME supports almost a hundred predefined types of content. Content types are classified at two levels: a type and a subtype. The type shows very generally what kind of data is contained: is it a picture, is it text, is it a movie? The subtype identifies the specific type of data: GIF image, JPEG image, TIFF image. For example, HTML's content type is `text/html`; the type is `text`, and the subtype is `html`. The content type for a GIF image is `image/gif`; the type is `image`, and the subtype is `gif`. Table 3-2 lists the more common defined content types. On most systems, a simple text file maintains a mapping between MIME types and the application used to process that type of data; on Unix, this file is called *mime.types*. The most current list of registered MIME types is available from *ftp://ftp.isi.edu/in-notes/iana/assignments/media-types/media-types.*†

The data returned by an HTTP 1.0 or 1.1 web server is sent in MIME format. Most web servers and clients understand at least two MIME text content types, `text/html` and `text/plain`, and two image formats, `image/gif` and `image/jpeg`. The Web also uses MIME for posting forms to web servers, a common way for an applet to communicate with a server. Finally, Java relies on MIME types to pick the appropriate content handler for a particular stream of data.

Table 3-2. Predefined MIME Content Types

Type	Subtype	Description
text		The document represents printable text.
	calendar	Calendaring and scheduling information in the iCalendar format; see RFC 2445.
	css	A Cascading Style Sheet used for HTML and XML.

---

* Officially, MIME stands for Multipurpose Internet Mail Extensions, which is the expansion of the acronym used in RFC 2045. However, you will hear other versions—most frequently, Multipart Internet Mail Extensions and Multimedia Internet Mail Extensions.

† For more details on MIME, see Jerry Sweet, Ed Vielmetti, and Tim Goodwin, The *comp.mail.mime* FAQ, *http://www.cs.ruu.nl/wais/html/na-dir/mail/mime-faq/.html*; N. Borenstein, Bellcore, "Multimedia Mail From the Bottom Up or Teaching Dumb Mailers to Sing", *ConneXions*, pp. 10–16, Nov. 91; G. Vaudreuil, CNRI, "MIME: Multi-Media, Multi-Lingual Extensions for RFC 822 Based Electronic Mail", *ConneXions*, pp. 36–39, Sep. 92.

Table 3-2. Predefined MIME Content Types (continued)

Type	Subtype	Description
	directory	Address book information such as name, phone number, and email address; used by Netscape vCards; defined in RFCs 2425 and 2426.
	enriched	A very simple HTML-like language for adding basic font and paragraph-level formatting such as bold and italic to email; used by Eudora; defined in RFC 1896.
	html	Hypertext Markup Language as used by web browsers.
	plain	This is supposed to imply raw ASCII text. However, some web servers use text/plain as the default MIME type for any file they can't recognize. Therefore, anything and everything, most notably *.class* byte code files, can get identified as a text/plain file.
	richtext	This is an HTML-like markup for encoding formatting into pure ASCII text. It's never really caught on, in large part because of the popularity of HTML.
	rtf	An incompletely defined Microsoft format for word processing files.
	sgml	The Standard Generalized Markup Language; ISO standard 8879:1986.
	tab-separated-values	The interchange format used by many spreadsheets and databases; records are separated by line breaks, and fields by tabs.
	xml	The W3C standard Extensible Markup Language.
multipart		Multipart MIME messages encode several different files into one message.
	mixed	Several message parts intended for sequential viewing.
	alternative	The same message in multiple formats so a client may choose the most convenient one.
	digest	A popular format for merging many email messages into a single digest; used by many mailing lists and some FAQ lists.
	parallel	Several parts intended for simultaneous viewing.
	byteranges	Several separately contiguous byte ranges; used in HTTP 1.1.
	encrypted	One part for the body of the message and one part for the information necessary to decode the message.
	signed	One part for the body of the message and one part for the digital signature.
	related	Compound documents formed by aggregating several smaller parts.
	form-data	Form responses.
message		An email message.

Table 3-2. Predefined MIME Content Types (continued)

Type	Subtype	Description
	external-body	Just the headers of the email message; the message's body is not included but exists at some other location and is referenced, perhaps by a URL.
	http	An HTTP 1.1 request from a web client to a web server.
	news	A news article.
	partial	Part of a longer email message that has been split into multiple parts to allow transmission through email gateways.
	rfc822	A standard email message including headers.
image		Two-dimensional pictures.
	cgm	A Computer Graphics Metafile format image. CGM is ISO standard 8632:1992 for device-independent vector graphics and bitmap images.
	g3fax	The standard for bitmapped fax images.
	gif	A Graphics Interchange format image. The format was originally developed by CompuServe. It uses certain compression algorithms on which Unisys holds a patent.
	jpeg	The Joint Photographic Experts Group file format for bitmapped images with lossy compression.
	png	A Portable Network Graphics Format image. The format was developed at the W3C as a more modern replacement for GIF that supported 24-bit color and was not encumbered by patents.
	tiff	The Tagged Image File format from Adobe.
audio		Sound.
	basic	8-bit ISDN μ-law encoded audio with a single channel and a sample rate of eight kilohertz. This is the format used by *.au* and *.snd* files and supported by the `java.applet.AudioClip` class.
video		Video.
	mpeg	The Motion Picture Experts Group format for video data with lossy compression.
	quicktime	Apple's proprietary QuickTime movie format. Before being included in a MIME message, QuickTime files must be "flattened".
model		3-D images.
	vrml	A Virtual Reality Modeling Language file, an evolving standard for 3-D data on the Web.
	iges	The Initial Graphics Exchange Specification for interchanging documents between different CAD programs.
	mesh	The mesh structures used in finite element and finite difference methods.

Table 3-2. Predefined MIME Content Types (continued)

Type	Subtype	Description
application		Binary data specific to some application.
	octet-stream	Unspecified binary data, which is usually saved into a file for the user. This MIME type is sometimes used to serve *.class* byte code files.
	java	A not-yet-standard subtype sometimes used to serve *.class* byte code files.
	postscript	Adobe PostScript.
	dca-rft	IBM's Document Content Architecture-Richly Formatted Text.
	mac-BinHex40	A means of encoding the two forks of a Macintosh document into a single ASCII file.
	pdf	An Adobe Acrobat file.
	zip	A zip compressed file.
	macwriteii	A MacWrite II word processing document.
	msword	A Microsoft Word document.
	xml	An Extensible Markup Language document.

A MIME-compliant program is not required to understand all these different types of data; it just needs to recognize what it can and cannot handle. Many programs—Netscape Navigator, for example—use various helper programs to display types of content they themselves don't understand.

MIME allows you to define additional nonstandard subtypes by using the prefix `x-`. For example, the content type `application/x-tex` has the MIME type `application` and the nonstandard subtype `x-tex` for a TeX document. These x-types are not guaranteed to be understood by any program other than the one that created them. Indeed, two programs may use the same x-type to mean two completely different things; or different programs may use different x-types to mean the same thing. However, many nonstandard types have come into common use; some of the more common ones are listed in Table 3-3.

Table 3-3. X-types

Type	X-subtype	Description
application		Subtypes of an application; the name of the subtype is usually a file format name or an application name.
	x-aiff	SGI's AIFF audio data format.
	x-bitmap	An X Windows bitmap image.
	x-gzip	Data compressed in the GNU gzip format.
	x-dvi	A TeX DVI document.
	x-framemaker	A FrameMaker document.

Table 3-3. X-types (continued)

Type	X-subtype	Description
	x-latex	A LaTeX document.
	x-macBinHex40	Identical to `application/mac-BinHex40`, but older software may use this x-type instead.
	x-mif	A FrameMaker MIF document.
	x-sd	A session directory protocol announcement, used to announce MBONE events.
	x-shar	A shell archive; the Unix equivalent of a Windows or Macintosh self-extracting archive. Software shouldn't be configured to unpack shell archives automatically, because a shell archive can call any program the user who runs it has the rights to call.
	x-tar	A tar archive.
	x-gtar	A GNU tar archive.
	x-tcl	A tool command language (TCL) program. You should never configure your web browser or email program to automatically run programs you download from the web or receive in email messages.
	x-tex	A TeX document.
	x-texinfo	A GNU texinfo document.
	x-troff	A troff document.
	x-troff-man	A troff document written with the `man` macros.
	x-troff-me	A troff document that should be processed using the `me` macros.
	x-troff-ms	A troff document that should be processed using the `ms` macros.
	x-wais-source	A WAIS source.
	x-www-form-urlencoded	A CGI query string that has been encoded like a URL, with + replacing spaces and % escapes replacing non-alphanumeric characters that aren't separators.
audio		
	x-aiff	The same as `application/x-aiff`: an AIFF audio file.
	x-mpeg	The MP3 sound format.
	x-mpeg.mp3	The MP3 sound format.
	x-wav	The Windows WAV sound format.
image		
	x-fits	The FITS image format used primarily by astronomers.
	x-macpict	A Macintosh PICT image.
	x-pict	A Macintosh PICT image.
	x-macpaint	A MacPaint image.

Table 3-3. X-types (continued)

Type	X-subtype	Description
	x-pbm	A portable bitmap image.
	x-portable-bitmap	A portable bitmap image.
	x-pgm	A PGM image.
video		
	x-msvideo	A Microsoft AVI Video for Windows.
	x-sgi-movie	A Silicon Graphics movie.

CGI

CGI, the common gateway interface, is used to generate web pages dynamically; essentially, the browser invokes a program on the server that creates a new page on the fly. This web page may be based purely on server data, or it may process the results of a client form submission, the URL the client chose, or various environment variables. CGI programs can be written in almost any language, including Java, though currently most CGI programming is done in Perl, C, or AppleScript.

CGI programs run as independent processes, initiated by the HTTP server each time a request for services is received. This has three important consequences. First, CGI programs are relatively safe to run. A CGI program can crash without damaging the server, at least on preemptively multitasking memory-protected operating systems such as Unix and NT. Second, the CGI program has strictly limited access to the server. Third, CGI programs exact a performance penalty relative to serving a static file, because of the overhead of spawning a separate process for each request.

The simplest CGI programs run without any input from the user. From the viewpoint of the client, these are accessed like any other web page and aren't of much concern to this book. The difference between a web page produced by a CGI program that takes no input and a web page written in static HTML is all on the server side. What happens on the server side has been adequately covered in several other books. For more information about writing server programs that process CGI input and create dynamic web pages, see Shisir Gundavaram's *CGI Programming with Perl* (O'Reilly & Associates, Inc., 1999, ISBN 1-56592-419-3).

This book approaches CGI from an unusual direction: how to write a client that sends data to a CGI program. The most common use of CGI is to process user input from HTML forms. In this capacity, CGI provides a standard, well understood and well supported means for Java applets and applications to talk to remote systems; therefore, I will cover how to use Java to talk to a CGI program on the server. There are other ways for Java programs to talk to servers, including Remote Method Invocation (RMI) and servlets. However, RMI is slow and servlets are not supported by all web servers. By way of contrast, CGI is mature, robust, better supported across multiple platforms and web servers, and better understood in the web development community. Furthermore, the client-side interface to CGI is almost exactly like the client-side interface to servlets, so what I say about talking to CGI programs will apply equally to talking to servlets.

Example 3-1 and Figure 3-3 show a simple form with two fields that collects a name and an email address. The values the user enters in the form are sent back to the server when the user presses the "Submit Query" button. The CGI program to run when the form data is received is *cgi-bin/register.pl*; the program is specified in the ACTION attribute of the FORM element. The URL in this parameter is usually a relative URL, as it is in this example.

Example 3-1. A Simple Form with Input Fields for a Name and an Email Address

```
<HTML>
<HEAD>
<TITLE>Sample Form</TITLE>
</HEAD>
<BODY>

<FORM METHOD=GET ACTION="/cgi/register.pl">
<PRE>
Please enter your name:          <INPUT NAME="username" SIZE=40>
Please enter your email address: <INPUT NAME="email" SIZE=40>
</PRE>
<INPUT TYPE="SUBMIT">
</FORM>
</BODY>
</HTML>
```

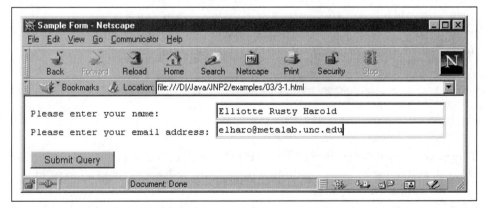

Figure 3-3. A simple form

The web browser reads the data the user enters and encodes it in a simple fashion. The name of each field is separated from its value by the equals sign (=). Different fields are separated from each other by an ampersand, &. Each field name and value is x-www-form-url-encoded; that is, any non-ASCII or nonalphanumeric characters are replaced by a percent sign followed by hexadecimal digits giving the value for that character in some character set. Spaces are a special case because they're so common. Instead of being encoded as %20, they become the + sign. The plus sign itself is encoded as %2b. For example, the data from the form in Figure 3-1 is encoded as:

```
username=Elliotte+Rusty+Harold&email=elharo%40metalab%2eunc%2eedu
```

This is called the *query string*.

There are two methods by which the query string can be sent to the server: GET and POST. If the form specifies the GET method, the browser attaches the query string to the URL it sends to the server. CGI programs that use POST send the query string on an output stream. The form in Example 3-1 uses GET to communicate with the server, so it connects to the server and sends the following command:

```
GET /cgi7/register.pl?username=Elliotte+Rusty+Harold&email=elharo%40metalab.unc.
edu HTTP 1.0
```

The server is responsible for recognizing that the URL contains the name of the CGI program plus input for the program; it passes the query string to the program, usually as an environment variable. Because of limitations in the lengths of environment variables on some platforms, the GET method is unreliable for sending more than about 200 characters of text. In these cases you're better off using POST.

With the POST method, the web browser sends the usual headers and follows them with a blank line (two successive carriage return/linefeed pairs) and then sends the query string. The query string is passed to the CGI program on standard input. If the form in Figure 3-1 used POST, it would send this to the server:

```
POST /cgi-bin/register.pl HTTP 1.0
Content-type: application/x-www-form-urlencoded
Content-length: 65

username=Elliotte+Rusty+Harold&email=elharo%40metalab.unc.edu
```

There are many different form tags in HTML that produce pop-up menus, radio buttons, and more. However, although these input widgets appear different to the user, the format of data they send to the server is the same. Each form element provides a name and an encoded string value.

Applets and Security

Now that you understand how files are transferred across the Web, you're ready to explore how applets are transferred. On one hand, applets are just more files that are transferred like any other. On the other hand, what an applet can do is closely related to where it came from. This isn't true of other data types such as HTML and GIF.

Where Do Applets and Classes Come from?

When a web browser sees an `applet` tag and decides to download and play the applet, it starts a long chain of events. Let's say your browser sees the following `applet` tag:

```
<applet codebase="http://metalab.unc.edu/javafaq/classes"
        code="Animation.class" width="200" height="100">
```

1. The web browser sets aside a rectangular area on the page 200 pixels wide and 100 pixels high. In most web browsers, this area has a fixed size and cannot be modified once created. The *appletviewer* in the JDK is a notable exception.

2. The browser opens a connection to the server specified in the `codebase` parameter, using port 80 unless another port is specified in the `codebase` URL. If there's no `codebase` parameter, then the browser connects to the same server that served the HTML page.

3. The browser requests the *.class* file from the web server as it requests any other file. If a `codebase` is present, it is prefixed to the requested filename. Otherwise, the document base (the directory that contains the HTML page) is used. For example:

```
GET /javafaq/classes/Animation.class HTTP 1.0
```

4. The server responds by sending a MIME header followed by a blank line (`\r\n`) followed by the binary data in the *.class* file. A properly configured server sends *.class* files with MIME type `application/octet-stream`. For example:

```
HTTP 1.0 200 OK
Date: Mon, 10 Jun 1999 17:11:43 GMT
Server: Apache/1.2.8
Content-type: application/octet-stream
Content-length: 2782
Last-modified: Fri, 08 Sep 1998 21:53:55 GMT
```

Not all web servers are configured to send *.class* files correctly. Some send them as `text/plain`, which, though technically incorrect, works in most cases.

5. The web browser receives the data and stores it in a byte array.

6. The byte code verifier goes over the byte codes that have been received to make sure they don't do anything forbidden, such as converting an integer into a pointer.

7. If the byte code verifier is satisfied with the bytes that were downloaded, then the raw data is converted into a Java class using the `defineClass()` and `loadClass()` methods of the current `ClassLoader` object.

8. The web browser instantiates the `Animation` class using its noargs constructor.

9. The web browser invokes the `init()` method of `Animation`.

10. The web browser invokes the `start()` method of `Animation`.

If the `Animation` class references another class, the Java interpreter first searches for the new class in the user's `CLASSPATH`. If the class is found in the user's `CLASSPATH`, then it is created from the *.class* file on the user's hard drive. Otherwise the web browser goes back to the site from which this class came and downloads the *.class* file for the new class. The same procedure is followed for the new class and any other class that is downloaded from the Net. If the new class cannot be found, a `ClassNotFoundException` is thrown.

Security: Who Can an Applet Talk to and What Can It Say?

There is much FUD (fear, uncertainty, and doubt) in the press about what Java applets can and cannot do. This is not a book about Java security, but I will mention a few things that applets loaded from the network are usually prohibited from doing.

• Applets cannot access arbitrary addresses in memory. Unlike the other restrictions in the list, which are enforced by the browser's `SecurityManager` instance, this restriction is a property of the Java language itself and the byte code verifier.

• Applets cannot access the local filesystem in any way. They cannot read from or write to the local filesystem nor can they find out any information about files. Therefore, they cannot find out whether a file exists or what its modification date may be.

• Applets cannot launch other programs on the client. In other words, they cannot call `System.exec()` or `Runtime.exec()`.

• Applets cannot load native libraries or define native method calls.

• Applets are not allowed to use `System.getProperty()` in a way that reveals information about the user or the user's machine, such as a username or home directory. They may use `System.getProperty()` to find out what version of Java is in use.

- Applets may not define any system properties.

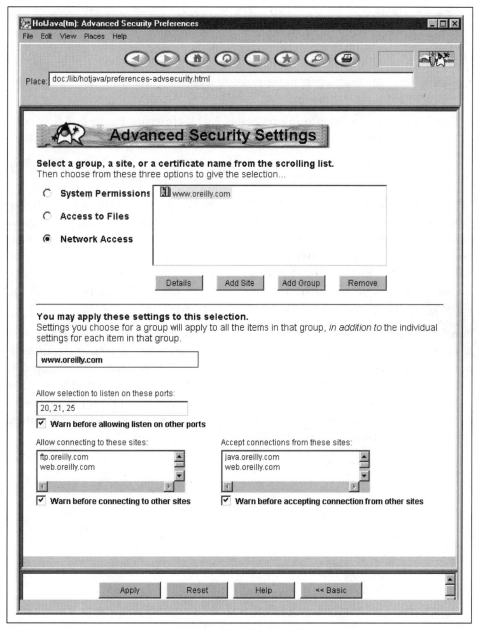

Figure 3-4. Applet network security preferences in HotJava 1.1.4

- In Java 1.1 and later, applets may not create or manipulate any `Thread` or `ThreadGroup` that is not in the applet's own `ThreadGroup`. They may do this in Java 1.0.

- Applets cannot define or use a new instance of `ClassLoader`, `SecurityManager`, `ContentHandlerFactory`, `SocketImplFactory`, or `URLStreamHandlerFactory`. They must use the ones already in place.

Finally, and most importantly for this book:

- An applet can only open network connections to the host from which the applet itself was downloaded.

- An applet cannot listen on ports below 1,024. (Internet Explorer 5.0 doesn't allow applets to listen on any ports.)

- Even if an applet can listen on a port, it can accept incoming connections only from the host from which the applet itself was downloaded.

Of these 11, only the second and ninth are serious inconveniences for a significant number of applets. These restrictions can be relaxed for digitally signed applets. Figure 3-4 shows the HotJava advanced applet security preferences window that allows the user to choose exactly which privileges she does and does not want to grant to which applets. Navigator and Internet Explorer 4.0 and later have similar options. Unfortunately, all three browsers have different procedures for allowing applets to ask the user for additional permissions.

However, even if you sign your applet, you should not expect that the user will choose to allow you to open connections to arbitrary hosts. If your program cannot live with these restrictions, it should be an application instead of an applet. Java applications are just like any other sort of application: they aren't restricted as to what they can do. If you are writing an application that will download and execute classes, you should consider carefully what restrictions you should put in place and design an appropriate security policy to implement those restrictions.

4

Java I/O

A large part of what network programs do is simple input and output, moving bytes from one system to another. Bytes are bytes; and to a large extent, reading data a server sends you is not all that different from reading a file. Sending text to a client is not all that different from writing a file. However, input and output (I/O) in Java is organized differently than it is in most other languages, such as C, Pascal, and C++. Consequently, I'd like to take one chapter to summarize Java's unique approach to I/O.

I/O in Java is built on streams. Input streams read data. Output streams write data. Different fundamental stream classes such as `java.io.FileInputStream` and `sun.net.TelnetOutputStream` read and write particular sources of data. However, all fundamental output streams have the same basic methods to write data and all fundamental input streams use the same basic methods to read data. After a stream is created, you can often ignore the details of exactly what it is you're reading or writing.

Filter streams can be chained to either an input stream or an output stream. Filters can modify the data as it's read or written—for instance, by encrypting or compressing it—or they can simply provide additional methods for converting the data that's read or written into other formats. For instance, the `java.io.DataOutputStream` class provides a method that converts an `int` to four bytes and writes those bytes onto its underlying output stream.

Finally, readers and writers can be chained to input and output streams to allow programs to read and write text (that is, characters) rather than bytes. Used properly, readers and writers can handle a wide variety of character encodings, including multibyte character sets such as SJIS and UTF-8.

Output Streams

Java's basic output class is `java.io.OutputStream`:

```
public abstract class OutputStream
```

This class provides the fundamental methods needed to write data. These are:

```
public abstract void write(int b) throws IOException
public void write(byte[] data) throws IOException
public void write(byte[] data, int offset, int length)
  throws IOException
public void flush() throws IOException
public void close() throws IOException
```

Subclasses of `OutputStream` use these methods to write data onto particular media. For instance, a `FileOutputStream` uses these methods to write data into a file. A `TelnetOutputStream` uses these methods to write data onto a network connection. A `ByteArrayOutputStream` uses these methods to write data into an expandable byte array. But whichever medium you're writing to, you mostly use only these same five methods. Sometimes you may not even know exactly what kind of stream you're writing onto. For instance, you won't find `TelnetOutputStream` in the Java class library documentation. It's deliberately hidden inside the sun packages. It's returned by various methods in various classes in `java.net`, like the `getOutputStream()` method of `java.net.Socket`. However, these methods are declared to return only `OutputStream`, not the more specific subclass `TelnetOutputStream`. That's the power of polymorphism. If you know how to use the superclass, you know how to use all the subclasses too.

`OutputStream`'s fundamental method is `write(int b)`. This method takes as an argument an integer from 0 to 255 and writes the corresponding byte to the output stream. This method is declared abstract because subclasses will need to change it to handle their particular medium. For instance, a `ByteArrayOutputStream` can implement this method with pure Java code that copies the byte into its array. However, a `FileOutputStream` will need to use native code that understands how to write data in files on the host platform.

Take special care to note that although this method takes an `int` as an argument, it actually writes an unsigned byte. Java doesn't have an unsigned byte data type, so an `int` has to be used here instead. The only real difference between an unsigned byte and a signed byte is the interpretation. They're both made up of eight bits, and when you write an `int` onto a network connection using `write(int b)`, only eight bits are placed on the wire. If an `int` outside the range 0–255 is passed to `write(int b)`, the least significant byte of the number is written, and the remaining three bytes are ignored. (This is the effect of casting an `int` to a `byte`.) On rare occasion, however, you may find a buggy third-party class that does something different, such as throwing an `IllegalArgumentException` or always writing 255, so it's best not to rely on this behavior if possible.

For example, the character generator protocol defines a server that sends out ASCII text. The most popular variation of this protocol sends 72-character lines containing printable ASCII characters. (The printable ASCII characters are those from 33 to 126 that exclude the various whitespace and control characters.) The first line contains characters 33 through 104 sorted. The second line contains characters 34 through 105. The third line contains characters 35 through 106. This continues through line 29, which contains characters 55 through 126. At that point, the characters wrap around so that line 30 contains characters 56 through 126 followed by character 33 again. Lines are terminated with a carriage return (ASCII 13) and a linefeed (ASCII 10). The output looks like this:

```
!"#$%&'()*+,-./0123456789:;<=>?@ABCDEFGHIJKLMNOPQRSTUVWXYZ[\]^_`abcdefgh
"#$%&'()*+,-./0123456789:;<=>?@ABCDEFGHIJKLMNOPQRSTUVWXYZ[\]^_`abcdefghi
#$%&'()*+,-./0123456789:;<=>?@ABCDEFGHIJKLMNOPQRSTUVWXYZ[\]^_`abcdefghij
$%&'()*+,-./0123456789:;<=>?@ABCDEFGHIJKLMNOPQRSTUVWXYZ[\]^_`abcdefghijk
%&'()*+,-./0123456789:;<=>?@ABCDEFGHIJKLMNOPQRSTUVWXYZ[\]^_`abcdefghijkl
&'()*+,-./0123456789:;<=>?@ABCDEFGHIJKLMNOPQRSTUVWXYZ[\]^_`abcdefghijklm
'()*+,-./0123456789:;<=>?@ABCDEFGHIJKLMNOPQRSTUVWXYZ[\]^_`abcdefghijklmn
```

Since ASCII is a 7-bit character set, each character is sent as a single byte. Consequently, this protocol is straightforward to implement using the basic `write()` methods as the next code fragment demonstrates:

```
public static void generateCharacters(OutputStream out)
  throws IOException {

    int firstPrintableCharacter    = 33;
    int numberOfPrintableCharacters = 94;
    int numberOfCharactersPerLine   = 72;

    int start = firstPrintableCharacter;
    while (true) { /* infinite loop */
      for (int i = start; i < start+numberOfCharactersPerLine; i++) {
        out.write((
          (i-firstPrintableCharacter) % numberOfPrintableCharacters)
          + firstPrintableCharacter);
      }
      out.write('\r'); // carriage return
      out.write('\n'); // linefeed
      start = ((start+1) - firstPrintableCharacter)
        % numberOfPrintableCharacters + firstPrintableCharacter;
    }
```

The character generator server class (the exact details of which will have to wait until we discuss server sockets in Chapter 11, *Sockets for Servers*) passes an

OutputStream named out to the generateCharacters() method. Bytes are written onto out one at a time. These bytes are given as integers in a rotating sequence from 33 to 126. Most of the arithmetic here is to make the loop rotate in that range. After each 72 characters are written, a carriage return and a linefeed are written onto the output stream. The next start character is calculated and the loop repeats. The entire method is declared to throw IOException. That's important because the character generator server will terminate only when the client closes the connection. The Java code will see this as an IOException.

Writing a single byte at a time is often inefficient. For example, every TCP segment that goes out your Ethernet card contains at least 40 bytes of overhead for routing and error correction. If each byte is sent by itself, then you may be filling the wire with 41 times more data than you think you are! Consequently, most TCP/IP implementations buffer data to some extent. That is, they accumulate bytes in memory and send them to their eventual destination only when a certain number have accumulated or a certain amount of time has passed. However, if you have more than one byte ready to go, it's not a bad idea to send them all at once. Using write(byte[] data) or write(byte[] data, int offset, int length) is normally much faster than writing all the components of the data array one at a time. For instance, here's an implementation of the generateCharacters() method that sends a line at a time by stuffing a complete line into a byte array:

```
public static void generateCharacters(OutputStream out)
  throws IOException {

  int firstPrintableCharacter = 33;
  int numberOfPrintableCharacters = 94;
  int numberOfCharactersPerLine = 72;
  int start = firstPrintableCharacter;
  byte[] line = new byte[numberOfCharactersPerLine+2];
  // the +2 is for the carriage return and linefeed

  while (true) { /* infinite loop */
    for (int i = start; i < start+numberOfCharactersPerLine; i++) {
      line[i-start] = (byte) ((i-firstPrintableCharacter)
        % numberOfPrintableCharacters + firstPrintableCharacter);
    }
    line[72] = (byte) '\r'; // carriage return
    line[73] = (byte) '\n'; // line feed
    out.write(line);
    start = ((start+1)-firstPrintableCharacter)
      % numberOfPrintableCharacters + firstPrintableCharacter;
  }

}
```

The algorithm for calculating which bytes to write when is the same as for the previous implementation. The crucial difference is that the bytes are all stuffed into a byte array before being written onto the network. Also notice that the int result of the calculation must be cast to a byte before being stored in the array. This wasn't necessary in the previous implementation because the single byte write() method is declared to take an int as an argument.

Streams can also be buffered in software, directly in the Java code as well as in the network hardware. Typically, this is accomplished by chaining a BufferedOutputStream or a BufferedWriter to the underlying stream, a technique we'll explore shortly. Consequently, if you are done writing data, it's important to flush the output stream. For example, suppose you've written a 300-byte request to an HTTP 1.1 server that uses HTTP Keep-Alive. You generally want to wait for a response before sending any more data. However, if the output stream has a 1,024-byte buffer, then the stream may be waiting for more data to arrive before it sends the data out of its buffer. No more data will be written onto the stream until after the server response arrives, but that's never going to arrive because the request hasn't yet been sent! The buffered stream won't send the data to the server until it gets more data from the underlying stream, but the underlying stream won't send more data until it gets data from the server, which won't send data until it gets the data that's stuck in the buffer! Figure 4-1 illustrates this Catch-22. The flush() method rescues you from this deadlock by forcing the buffered stream to send its data even if the buffer isn't yet full.

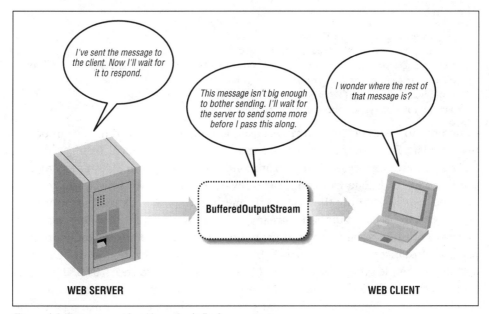

Figure 4-1. Data can get lost if you don't flush your streams

It's important to flush whether you think you need to or not. Depending on how you got hold of a reference to the stream, you may or may not know whether it's buffered. (For instance, System.out is buffered whether you want it to be or not.) If flushing isn't necessary for a particular stream, it's a very low cost operation. However, if it is necessary, it's very necessary. Failing to flush when you need to can lead to unpredictable, unrepeatable program hangs that are extremely hard to diagnose if you don't have a good idea of what the problem is in the first place. As a corollary to all this, you should flush all streams immediately before you close them. Otherwise, data left in the buffer when the stream is closed may get lost.

Finally, when you're done with a stream, you should close it by invoking its close() method. This releases any resources associated with the stream, such as file handles or ports. Once an output stream has been closed, further writes to it will throw IOExceptions. However, some kinds of streams may still allow you to do things with the object. For instance, a closed ByteArrayOutputStream can still be converted to an actual byte array and a closed DigestOutputStream can still return its digest.

Input Streams

Java's basic input class is java.io.InputStream:

```
public abstract class InputStream
```

This class provides the fundamental methods needed to read data as raw bytes. These are:

```
public abstract int read() throws IOException
public int read(byte[] input) throws IOException
public int read(byte[] input, int offset, int length) throws IOException
public long skip(long n) throws IOException
public int available() throws IOException
public void close() throws IOException
```

Concrete subclasses of InputStream use these methods to read data from particular media. For instance, a FileInputStream reads data from a file. A TelnetInputStream reads data from a network connection. A ByteArrayInputStream reads data from an array of bytes. But whichever source you're reading, you mostly use only these same six methods. Sometimes you may not even know exactly what kind of stream you're reading from. For instance, TelnetInputStream is an undocumented class hidden inside the sun.net package. Instances of it are returned by various methods in the java.net package; for example, the openStream() method of java.net.URL. However, these methods are declared to return only InputStream, not the more specific subclass TelnetInputStream. That's polymorphism at work once again. The instance of the subclass can be used transparently as an instance of its superclass. No specific knowledge of the subclass is required.

The basic method of InputStream is the noargs read() method. This method reads a single byte of data from the input stream's source and returns it as a number from 0 to 255. End of stream is signified by returning –1. Since Java doesn't have an unsigned byte data type, this number is returned as an int. The read() method waits and blocks execution of any code that follows it until a byte of data is available and ready to be read. Input and output can be slow, so if your program is doing anything else of importance you should try to put I/O in its own thread.

The read() method is declared abstract because subclasses need to change it to handle their particular medium. For instance, a ByteArrayInputStream can implement this method with pure Java code that copies the byte from its array. However, a TelnetInputStream will need to use a native library that understands how to read data from the network interface on the host platform.

The following code fragment reads 10 bytes from the InputStream in and stores them in the byte array input. However, if end of stream is detected, the loop is terminated early:

```
byte[] input = new byte[10];
for (int i = 0; i < input.length; i++) {
  int b = in.read();
  if (b  == -1) break;
  input[i] = (byte) b;
}
```

Although read() reads only a byte, it returns an int. Thus, a cast is necessary before storing the result in the byte array. Of course, this produces a signed byte from –128 to 127 instead of the unsigned byte from 0 to 255 returned by the read() method. However, as long as you keep clear which one you're working with, this is not a major problem. You can convert a signed byte to an unsigned byte like this:

```
int i = b >= 0 ? b : 256 + b;
```

Reading a byte at a time is as inefficient as writing data one byte at a time. Consequently, there are also two overloaded read() methods that fill a specified array with multiple bytes of data read from the stream, read(byte[] input) and read(byte[] input, int offset, int length). The first attempts to fill the specified array input. The second attempts to fill the specified subarray of input starting at offset and continuing for length bytes.

Notice that I said these methods *attempt* to fill the array, not necessarily that they succeed. An attempt may fail in several ways. For instance, it's not unheard of that while your program is reading data from a remote web server over a PPP dialup link, a bug in a switch in a phone company central office will disconnect you and several thousand of your neighbors from the rest of the world. This would throw an IOException. More commonly, however, a read attempt won't completely fail but won't completely succeed either. Some of the requested bytes may be read but not all of them. For example, you may try to read 1,024 bytes from a network connection, when only 512 have actually arrived from the server. The rest are still in transit. They'll arrive eventually, but they aren't available now. To account for this, the multibyte read methods return the number of bytes actually read. For example, consider this code fragment:

```
byte[] input  = new byte[1024];
int bytesRead = in.read(input);
```

It attempts to read 1,024 bytes from the InputStream in into the array input. However, if only 512 bytes are available, then that's all that will be read, and bytesRead will be set to 512. To guarantee that all the bytes you want are actually read, you must place the read in a loop that reads repeatedly until the array is filled. For example:

```
int bytesRead   = 0;
int bytesToRead = 1024;
byte[] input    = new byte[bytesToRead];
while (bytesRead < bytesToRead) {
   bytesRead += in.read(input, bytesRead, bytesToRead - bytesRead);
}
```

This technique is especially crucial for network streams. Chances are that if a file is available at all, then all the bytes of a file are also available. However, since networks move much more slowly than CPUs, it is very easy for a program to empty a network buffer before all the data has arrived. In fact, if one of these two methods tries to read from a temporarily empty but open network buffer, it will generally return 0, indicating that no data is available but the stream is not yet closed. This is often preferable to the behavior of the single-byte read() method, which in the same circumstances will block execution of the running program.

All three read() methods return –1 to signal the end of the stream. If the stream ends while there's still data that hasn't been read, then the multibyte read methods will return that data until the buffer has been emptied. The next call to any of the read methods will return –1. The –1 is never placed in the array. The array contains only actual data. The previous code fragment had a bug because it didn't consider the possibility that all 1,024 bytes might never arrive (as opposed to not being immediately available). Fixing that bug requires testing the return value of read() before adding it to bytesRead. For example:

```
int bytesRead=0;
int bytesToRead=1024;
byte[] input = new byte[bytesToRead];
```

```
while (bytesRead < bytesToRead) {
  int result = in.read(input, bytesRead, bytesToRead - bytesRead);
  if (result == -1) break;
  bytesRead += result;
}
```

If for some reason, you do not want to read until all the bytes you want are immediately available, you can use the `available()` method to determine how many bytes can be read without blocking. This is the minimum number of bytes you can read. You may in fact be able to read more, but you will be able to read at least as many bytes as `available()` suggests. For example:

```
int bytesAvailable = in.available();
byte[] input = new byte[bytesAvailable];
int bytesRead = in.read(input, 0, bytesAvailable);
// continue with rest of program immediately...
```

In this case, you can assert that `bytesRead` is exactly equal to `bytesAvailable`. You cannot, however, assert that `bytesRead` is greater than zero. It is possible that no bytes were available. On end of stream, `available()` returns 0. Generally, `read(byte[] input, int offset, int length)` returns –1 on end of stream; but if `length` is 0, then it will not notice the end of stream and will return 0 instead.

On rare occasions, you may want to skip over data without reading it. The `skip()` method accomplishes this. It's less useful on network connections than when reading from files. Network connections are sequential and overall quite slow so it's not significantly more time-consuming to read data than to skip over it. Files are random access so that skipping can be implemented simply by repositioning a file pointer rather than processing each byte to be skipped.

As with output streams, once your program has finished with an input stream, it should close it by invoking its `close()` method. This releases any resources associated with the stream, such as file handles or ports. Once an input stream has been closed, further reads from it will throw `IOExceptions`. However, some kinds of streams may still allow you to do things with the object. For instance, you generally won't want to get the message digest from a `java.security.DigestInputStream` until all the data has been read and the stream closed.

Marking and Resetting

The `InputStream` class also has three less commonly used methods that allow programs to back up and reread data they've already read. These are:

```
public void mark(int readAheadLimit)
public void reset() throws IOException
public boolean markSupported()
```

To do this, you mark the current position in the stream with the mark() method. At a later point, you can reset the stream back to the marked position using the reset() method. Subsequent reads then return data starting from the marked position. However, you may not be able to reset back as far as you like. The number of bytes you can read from the mark and still reset is determined by the readAheadLimit argument to mark(). If you try to reset back too far, an IOException will be thrown. Furthermore, there can be only one mark in a stream at any given time. Marking a second location erases the first mark.

Marking and resetting are usually implemented by storing every byte read from the marked position in an internal buffer. However, not all input streams support this. Thus, before trying to use marking and setting, you should check to see whether the markSupported() method returns true. If it does, the stream supports marking and resetting. Otherwise, mark() will do nothing and reset() will throw an IOException.

NOTE   In my opinion, this demonstrates very poor design. In practice, more streams *don't* support marking and resetting than *do*. Attaching functionality to an abstract superclass that is not available to many, probably most, subclasses is a very poor idea. It would be better to place these three methods in a separate interface that could be implemented by those classes that provided this functionality. The disadvantage of this approach is that you couldn't then invoke these methods on an arbitrary input stream of unknown type, but in practice you can't do that anyway because not all streams support marking and resetting. Providing a method such as markSupported() to check for functionality at runtime is a more traditional, non-object-oriented solution to the problem. An object-oriented approach would embed this in the type system through interfaces and classes so that it could all be checked at compile time.

The only two input stream classes in java.io that always support marking are BufferedInputStream and ByteArrayInputStream. However, other input streams such as TelnetInputStream may support marking if they're chained to a buffered input stream first.

Filter Streams

InputStream and OutputStream are fairly raw classes. They allow you to read and write bytes, either singly or in groups, but that's all. Deciding what those bytes mean—whether they're integers or IEEE 754 floating point numbers or Unicode text—is completely up to the programmer and the code. However, there are certain data formats that are extremely common and can benefit from a solid implementation in the class library. For example, many integers passed as parts of network protocols are 32-bit big-endian integers. Much text sent over the Web is either 7-bit ASCII or 8-bit Latin–1. Many files transferred by *ftp* are stored in the zip format. Java provides a number of filter classes you can attach to raw streams to translate the raw bytes to and from these and other formats.

The filters come in two versions: the filter streams and the readers and writers. The filter streams still work primarily with raw data as bytes, for instance, by compressing the data or interpreting it as binary numbers. The readers and writers handle the special case of text in a variety of encodings such as UTF-8 and ISO 8859-1. Filter streams are placed on top of raw streams such as a `TelnetInputStream` or a `FileOutputStream` or other filter streams. Readers and writers can be layered on top of raw streams, filter streams, or other readers and writers. However, filter streams cannot be placed on top of a reader or a writer, so we'll start here with filter streams and address readers and writers in the next section.

Filters are organized in a chain as shown in Figure 4-2. Each link in the chain receives data from the previous filter or stream and passes the data along to the next link in the chain. In this example, a compressed, encrypted text file arrives from the local network interface, where native code presents it to the undocumented `Telnet-InputStream`. A `BufferedInputStream` buffers the data to speed up the entire process. A `CipherInputStream` decrypts the data. A `GZIPInputStream` decompresses the deciphered data. An `InputStreamReader` converts the decompressed data to Unicode text. Finally, the text is read into the application and processed.

Every filter output stream has the same `write()`, `close()`, and `flush()` methods as `java.io.OutputStream`. Every filter input stream has the same `read()`, `close()`, and `available()` methods as `java.io.InputStream`. In some cases, such as `BufferedInputStream` and `BufferedOutputStream`, these may be the only methods they have. The filtering is purely internal and does not expose any new public interface. However, in most cases, the filter stream adds public methods with additional purposes. Sometimes these are intended to be used in addition to the usual `read()` and `write()` methods as with the `unread()` method of `PushbackInputStream`. At other times, they almost completely replace the original interface. For example, it's relatively rare to use the `write()` method of `PrintStream` instead of one of its `print()` and `println()` methods.

Chaining Filters Together

Filters are connected to streams by their constructor. For example, the following code fragment buffers input from the file *data.txt*. First a `FileInputStream` object `fin` is created by passing the name of the file as an argument to the

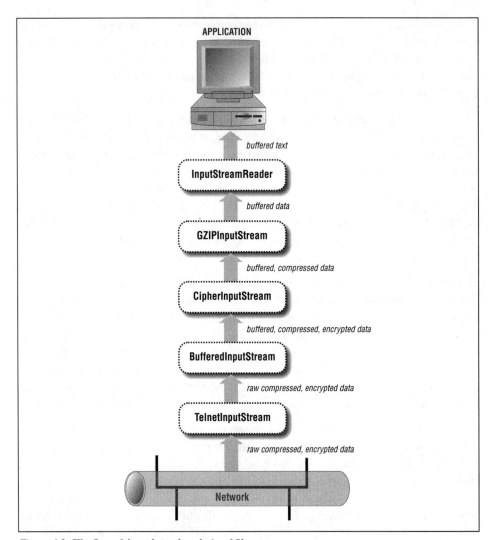

Figure 4-2. The flow of data through a chain of filters

FileInputStream constructor. Then a BufferedInputStream object bin is created by passing fin as an argument to the BufferedInputStream constructor:

```
FileInputStream     fin = new FileInputStream("data.txt");
BufferedInputStream bin = new BufferedInputStream(fin);
```

From this point forward, it's possible to use the read() methods of both fin and bin to read data from the file *data.txt*. However, intermixing calls to different streams connected to the same source may violate several implicit contracts of the filter streams. Consequently, most of the time you should use only the last filter in the chain to do the actual reading or writing. One way to write your code so that it's at least harder to introduce this sort of bug is to deliberately lose the reference to the underlying input stream. For example:

```
InputStream in = new FileInputStream("data.txt");
in = new BufferedInputStream(in);
```

After these two lines execute, there's no longer any way to access the underlying file input stream, so you can't accidentally read from it and corrupt the buffer. This example works because it's not necessary to distinguish between the methods of `InputStream` and those of `BufferedInputStream`. `BufferedInputStream` is simply used polymorphically as an instance of `InputStream` in the first place. In those cases where it is necessary to use the additional methods of the filter stream not declared in the superclass, you may be able to construct one stream directly inside another. For example:

```
DataOutputStream dout = new DataOutputStream(new BufferedOutputStream(
  new FileOutputStream("data.txt")));
```

Although these statements can get a little long, it's easy to split the statement across several lines like this:

```
DataOutputStream dout = new DataOutputStream(
                    new BufferedOutputStream(
                     new FileOutputStream("data.txt")
                    )
                   );
```

There are times when you may need to use the methods of multiple filters in a chain. For instance, if you're reading a Unicode text file, you may want to read the byte order mark in the first three bytes to determine whether the file is encoded as big-endian UCS-2, little-endian UCS-2, or UTF-8 and then select the matching `Reader` filter for the encoding. Or if you're connecting to a web server, you may want to read the MIME header the server sends to find the `Content-encoding` and then use that content encoding to pick the right `Reader` filter to read the body of the response. Or perhaps you want to send floating point numbers across a network connection using a `DataOutputStream` and then retrieve a `MessageDigest` from the `DigestOutputStream` that the `DataOutputStream` is chained to. In all these cases, you do need to save and use references to each of the underlying streams. However, under no circumstances should you ever read from or write to anything other than the last filter in the chain.

Buffered Streams

The `BufferedOutputStream` class stores written data in a buffer (a protected byte array field named `buf`) until the buffer is full or the stream is flushed. Then it writes the data onto the underlying output stream all at once. A single write of many bytes is almost always much faster than many small writes that add up to the same thing. This is especially true of network connections because each TCP segment or UDP packet carries a finite amount of overhead, generally about 40 bytes' worth. This means that sending 1 kilobyte of data 1 byte at a time actually requires sending 40 kilobytes over the wire whereas sending it all at once only requires sending a little more than 1K of data. Most network cards and TCP implementations provide some level of buffering themselves, so the real numbers aren't quite this dramatic. Nonetheless, buffering network output is generally a huge performance win.

The `BufferedInputStream` class also has a protected byte array named `buf` that servers as a buffer. When one of the stream's `read()` methods is called, it first tries to get the requested data from the buffer. Only when the buffer runs out of data does the stream read from the underlying source. At this point, it reads as much data as it can from the source into the buffer whether it needs all the data immediately or not. Data that isn't used immediately will be available for later invocations of `read()`. When reading files from a local disk, it's almost as fast to read several hundred bytes of data from the underlying stream as it is to read one byte of data. Therefore, buffering can substantially improve performance. The gain is less obvious on network connections where the bottleneck is often the speed at which the network can deliver data rather than either the speed at which the network interface delivers data to the program or the speed at which the program runs. Nonetheless, buffering input rarely hurts and will become more important over time as network speeds increase.

`BufferedInputStream` has two constructors, as does `BufferedOutputStream`:

```
public BufferedInputStream(InputStream in)
public BufferedInputStream(InputStream in, int bufferSize)
public BufferedOutputStream(OutputStream out)
public BufferedOutputStream(OutputStream out, int bufferSize)
```

The first argument is the underlying stream from which unbuffered data will be read or to which buffered data will be written. The second argument, if present, specifies the number of bytes in the buffer. Otherwise, the buffer size is set to 2,048 bytes for an input stream and 512 bytes for an output stream. The ideal size for a buffer depends on what sort of stream you're buffering. For network connections, you want something a little larger than the typical packet size. However, this can be hard to predict and varies depending on local network connections and protocols. Faster, higher bandwidth networks tend to use larger packets, though cight kilobytes is an effective maximum packet size for UDP on most networks today, and TCP segments are often no larger than a kilobyte.

BufferedInputStream does not declare any new methods of its own. It only over-rides methods from InputStream. It does support marking and resetting. For example:

```
public synchronized int read() throws IOException
public synchronized int read(byte[] input, int offset, int length)
  throws IOException
public synchronized long skip(long n) throws IOException
public synchronized int available() throws IOException
public synchronized void mark(int readLimit)
public synchronized void reset() throws IOException
public boolean markSupported()
```

Starting in Java 1.2, the two multibyte read() methods attempt to completely fill the specified array or subarray of data by reading from the underlying input stream as many times as necessary. They return only when the array or subarray has been completely filled, the end of stream is reached, or the underlying stream would block on further reads. Most input streams (including buffered input streams in Java 1.1.x and earlier) do not behave like this. They read from the underlying stream or data source only once before returning.

BufferedOutputStream also does not declare any new methods of its own. It overrides three methods from OutputStream:

```
public synchronized void write(int b) throws IOException
public synchronized void write(byte[] data, int offset, int length)
  throws IOException
public synchronized void flush() throws IOException
```

You call these methods exactly as you would for any output stream. The difference is that each write places data in the buffer rather than directly on the underlying output stream. Consequently, it is essential to flush the stream when you reach a point at which the data needs to be sent.

PrintStream

The PrintStream class is the first filter output stream most programmers encounter because System.out is a PrintStream. However, other output streams can also be chained to print streams, using these two constructors:

```
public PrintStream(OutputStream out)
public PrintStream(OutputStream out, boolean autoFlush)
```

By default, print streams should be explicitly flushed. However, if the autoFlush argument is true, then the stream will be flushed every time a byte array or line-feed is written or a println() method is invoked.

As well as the usual write(), flush(), and close() methods, PrintStream has 9 overloaded print() methods and 10 overloaded println() methods:

```
public void print(boolean b)
public void print(char c)
public void print(int i)
public void print(long l)
public void print(float f)
public void print(double d)
public void print(char[] text)
public void print(String s)
public void print(Object o)
public void println()
public void println(boolean b)
public void println(char c)
public void println(int i)
public void println(long l)
public void println(float f)
public void println(double d)
public void println(char[] text)
public void println(String s)
public void println(Object o)
```

Each print() method converts its argument to a string in a semipredictable fashion and writes the string onto the underlying output stream using the default encoding. The println() methods do the same thing, but they also append a platform-dependent line separator character to the end of the line they write. This is a linefeed (\n) on Unix, a carriage return (\r) on the Mac, and a carriage return/linefeed pair (\r\n) on Windows.

PrintStream is evil and network programmers should avoid it like the plague

The first problem is that the output from println() is platform-dependent. Depending on what system runs your code, your lines may sometimes be broken with a linefeed, a carriage return, or a carriage return/linefeed pair. This doesn't cause problems when writing to the console, but it's a disaster for writing network clients and servers that must follow a precise protocol. Most network protocols such as HTTP specify that lines should be terminated with a carriage return/linefeed pair. Using println() makes it easy to write a program that works on Windows but fails on Unix and the Mac. While many servers and clients are liberal in what they accept and can handle incorrect line terminators, there are occasional exceptions. In particular, in conjunction with the bug in readLine() discussed shortly, a client running on a Mac that uses println() may hang both the server and the client. To some extent, this could be fixed by using only print() and ignoring println(). However, PrintStream has other problems.

The second problem with PrintStream is that it assumes the default encoding of the platform on which it's running. However, this encoding may not be what the server or client expects. For example, a web browser receiving XML files will expect them to be encoded in UTF-8 or raw Unicode unless the server tells it otherwise. However, a web server that uses PrintStream may well send them encoded in CP1252 from a U.S.-localized Windows system or SJIS from a Japanese-localized system, whether the client expects or understands those encodings or not. PrintStream doesn't provide any mechanism to change the default encoding. This problem can be patched over by using the related PrintWriter class instead. But the problems continue.

The third problem is that PrintStream eats all exceptions. This makes PrintStream suitable for simple textbook programs such as HelloWorld, since simple console output can be taught without burdening students with first learning about exception handling and all that implies. However, network connections are much less reliable than the console. Connections routinely fail because of network congestion, phone company misfeasance, remote systems crashing, and many more reasons. Network programs must be prepared to deal with unexpected interruptions in the flow of data. The way to do this is by handling exceptions. However, PrintStream catches any exceptions thrown by the underlying output stream. Notice that the declaration of the standard five OutputStream methods in PrintStream does not have the usual throws IOException declaration:

```
public abstract void write(int b)
public void write(byte[] data)
public void write(byte[] data, int offset, int length)
public void flush()
public void close()
```

Instead, PrintStream relies on an outdated and inadequate error flag. If the underlying stream throws an exception, this internal error flag is set. The programmer is relied upon to check the value of the flag using the checkError() method:

```
public boolean checkError()
```

If programmers are to do any error checking at all on a PrintStream, they must explicitly check every call. Furthermore, once an error has occurred, there is no way to unset the flag so further errors can be detected. Nor is any additional information available about what the error was. In short, the error notification provided by PrintStream is wholly inadequate for unreliable network connections. At the end of this chapter, we'll introduce a class that fixes all these shortcomings.

PushbackInputStream

PushbackInputStream is a subclass of FilterInputStream that provides a push-back stack so that a program can "unread" bytes onto the input stream. The HTTP protocol handler in Java 1.2 uses PushbackInputStream. You might also use it when you need to check something a little way into the stream, then back up. For instance, if you were reading an XML document, you might want to read just far enough into the header to locate the encoding declaration that tells you what character set the document uses, then push all the read data back onto the input stream and start over with a reader configured for that character set.

The read() and available() methods of PushbackInputStream are invoked exactly as with normal input streams. However, they first attempt to read from the pushback buffer before reading from the underlying input stream. What this class adds is unread() methods that push bytes into the buffer:

```
public void unread(int b) throws IOException
```

This method pushes an unsigned byte given as an int between 0 and 255 onto the stream. Integers outside this range are truncated to this range as by a cast to byte. Assuming nothing else is pushed back onto this stream, the next read from the stream will return that byte. As multiple bytes are pushed onto the stream by repeated invocations of unread(), they are stored in a stack and returned in a last-in, first-out order. In essence, the buffer is a stack sitting on top of an input stream. Only when the stack is empty will the underlying stream be read.

There are two more unread() methods that push a specified array or subarray onto the stream:

```
public void unread(byte[] input) throws IOException
public void unread(byte[] input, int offset, int length) throws IOException
```

The arrays are stacked in last-in, first-out order. However, bytes popped from the same array will be returned in the order they appeared in the array. That is, the zeroth component of the array will be read before the first component of the array.

By default, the buffer is only one byte long, and trying to unread more than one byte throws an IOException. However, the buffer size can be changed with the second constructor as follows:

```
public PushbackInputStream(InputStream in)
public PushbackInputStream(InputStream in, int size)
```

Although PushbackInputStream and BufferedInputStream both use buffers, BufferedInputStream uses them for data read from the underlying input stream, while `PushbackInputStream` uses them for arbitrary data, which may or may not, have been read from the stream originally. Furthermore, `PushbackInputStream` does not allow marking and resetting. The `markSupported()` method of `PushbackInputStream` returns false.

Data Streams

The `DataInputStream` and `DataOutputStream` classes provide methods for reading and writing Java's primitive data types and strings in a binary format. The binary formats used are primarily intended for exchanging data between two different Java programs whether through a network connection, a data file, a pipe, or some other intermediary. What a data output stream writes, a data input stream can read. However, it happens that the formats used are the same ones used for most Internet protocols that exchange binary numbers. For instance, the time protocol uses 32-bit big-endian integers, just like Java's `int` data type. The controlled-load network element service uses 32-bit IEEE 754 floating point numbers, just like Java's `float` data type. (This is probably correlation rather than causation. Both Java and most network protocols were designed by Unix developers, and consequently both tend to use the formats common to most Unix systems.) However, this isn't true for all network protocols, so you should check details for any protocol you use. For instance, the Network Time Protocol (NTP) represents times as 64-bit unsigned fixed point numbers with the integer part in the first 32 bits and the fraction part in the last 32 bits. This doesn't match any primitive data type in any common programming language, though it is fairly straightforward to work with, at least as far as is necessary for NTP.

The `DataOutputStream` class offers these 11 methods for writing particular Java data types:

```
public final void writeBoolean(boolean b) throws IOException
public final void writeByte(int b) throws IOException
public final void writeShort(int s) throws IOException
public final void writeChar(int c) throws IOException
public final void writeInt(int i) throws IOException
public final void writeLong(long l) throws IOException
public final void writeFloat(float f) throws IOException
public final void writeDouble(double d) throws IOException
public final void writeChars(String s) throws IOException
public final void writeBytes(String s) throws IOException
public final void writeUTF(String s) throws IOException
```

All data is written in big-endian format. Integers are written in two's complement in the minimum number of bytes possible. Thus a `byte` is written as one two's-complement byte, a `short` as two two's-complement bytes, an `int` as four two's-complement bytes, and a `long` as eight two's-complement bytes. Floats and doubles are written in IEEE 754 form in 4 and 8 bytes, respectively. Booleans are written as a single byte with the value 0 for false and 1 for true. Chars are written as two unsigned bytes.

The last three methods are a little trickier. The writeChars() method simply iterates through the String argument, writing each character in turn as a 2-byte, big-endian Unicode character. The writeBytes() method iterates through the String argument but writes only the least significant byte of each character. Thus information will be lost for any string with characters from outside the Latin–1 character set. This method may be useful on some network protocols that specify the ASCII encoding, but it should be avoided most of the time.

Neither writeChars() nor writeBytes() encodes the length of the string in the output stream. Consequently, you can't really distinguish between raw characters and characters that make up part of a string. The writeUTF() method does include the length of the string. It encodes the string itself in a *variant* of UTF-8 rather than raw Unicode. Since writeUTF() uses a variant of UTF-8 that's subtly incompatible with most non-Java software, it should be used only for exchanging data with other Java programs that use a DataInputStream to read strings. For exchanging UTF-8 text with all other software, you should use an Input-StreamReader with the appropriate encoding. (There wouldn't be any confusion if Sun had just called this method and its partner writeString() and readString() rather than writeUTF() and readUTF().)

As well as these methods to write binary numbers, DataOutputStream also overrides three of the customary OutputStream methods:

```
public void write(int b)
public void write(byte[] data, int offset, int length)
public void flush()
```

These are invoked in the usual fashion with the usual semantics.

DataInputStream is the complementary class to DataOutputStream. Every format that DataOutputStream writes, DataInputStream can read. In addition, DataInputStream has the usual read(), available(), skip(), and close() methods as well as methods for reading complete arrays of bytes and lines of text.

There are 9 methods to read binary data that match the 11 methods in DataOutputStream (there's no exact complement for writeBytes() and writeChars(); these are handled by reading the bytes and chars one at a time):

```
public final boolean readBoolean() throws IOException
public final byte readByte() throws IOException
public final char readChar() throws IOException
public final short readShort() throws IOException
public final int readInt() throws IOException
public final long readLong() throws IOException
```

```
public final float readFloat() throws IOException
public final double readDouble() throws IOException
public final String readUTF() throws IOException
```

In addition, `DataInputStream` provides two methods to read unsigned bytes and unsigned shorts and return the equivalent `int`. Java doesn't have either of these data types, but you may encounter them when reading binary data written by a C program:

```
public final int readUnsignedByte() throws IOException
public final int readUnsignedShort() throws IOException
```

`DataInputStream` has the usual two multibyte `read()` methods that read data into an array or subarray and return the number of bytes read. It also has two `readFully()` methods that repeatedly read data from the underlying input stream into an array until the requested number of bytes have been read. If enough data cannot be read, then an `IOException` is thrown. These methods are especially useful when you know in advance exactly how many bytes you have to read. This might be the case when you've read the `Content-length` field out of an HTTP MIME header and thus know how many bytes of data there are:

```
public final int read(byte[] input) throws IOException
public final int read(byte[] input, int offset, int length)
  throws IOException
public final void readFully(byte[] input) throws IOException
public final void readFully(byte[] input, int offset, int length)
  throws IOException
```

Finally, `DataInputStream` provides the popular `readLine()` method that reads a line of text as delimited by a line terminator and returns a string:

```
public final String readLine() throws IOException
```

However, this method should not be used under any circumstances, both because it is deprecated and because it is buggy. It's deprecated because it doesn't properly convert non-ASCII characters to bytes in most circumstances. That task is now handled by the `readLine()` method of the `BufferedReader` class. However, both that method and this one share the same insidious bug: they do not always recognize a single carriage return as ending a line. Rather, `readLine()` recognizes only a linefeed or a carriage return/linefeed pair. When a carriage return is detected in the stream, `readLine()` waits to see whether the next character is a linefeed before continuing. If it is a linefeed, then both the carriage return and the linefeed are thrown away, and the line is returned as a `String`. If it isn't a linefeed, then the carriage return is thrown away, the line is returned as a `String`, and the extra character that was read becomes part of the next line. However, if the carriage return is the last character in the stream (a very likely occurrence if the stream originates from a Macintosh or a file created on a Macintosh), then readLine() hangs, waiting for the last character that isn't forthcoming.

This problem isn't so obvious when reading files because there will almost certainly be a next character, –1 for end of stream if nothing else. However, on persistent network connections such as those used for FTP and late-model HTTP, a server or client may simply stop sending data after the last character and wait for a response without actually closing the connection. If you're lucky, the connection may eventually time out on one end or the other and you'll get an IOException, though this will probably take at least a couple of minutes. If you're not lucky, the program will hang indefinitely.

Note that it is not enough for your program to merely be running on Windows or Unix to avoid this bug. It must also ensure that it does not send or receive text files created on a Macintosh and that it never talks to Macintosh clients or servers. These are very strong conditions in the heterogeneous world of the Internet. It is obviously much simpler to avoid readLine() completely.

Compressing Streams

The java.util.zip package contains filter streams that compress and decompress streams in zip, gzip, and deflate formats. Besides its better-known uses with respect to files, this allows your Java applications to easily exchange compressed data across the network. HTTP 1.1 explicitly includes support for compressed file transfer in which the server compresses and the browser decompresses files, in effect trading increasingly cheap CPU power for still-expensive network bandwidth. This is done completely transparently to the user. Of course, it's not at all transparent to the programmer who has to write the compression and decompression code. However, the java.util.zip filter streams make it a lot more transparent than it otherwise would be.

There are six stream classes that perform compression and decompression. The input streams decompress data and the output streams compress it. These are:

```
public class DeflaterOutputStream extends FilterOutputStream
public class InflaterInputStream extends FilterInputStream
public class GZIPOutputStream extends FilterOutputStream
public class GZIPInputStream extends FilterInputStream
public class ZipOutputStream extends FilterOutputStream
public class ZipInputStream extends FilterInputStream
```

All of these use essentially the same compression algorithm. They differ only in various constants and meta-information included with the compressed data. In addition, a zip stream may contain more than one compressed file.

Compressing and decompressing data with these classes is almost trivially easy. You simply chain the filter to the underlying stream and read or write it like normal. For example, suppose you want to read the compressed file *allnames.gz*. You simply open a `FileInputStream` to the file and chain a `GZIPInputStream` to that like this:

```
FileInputStream fin = new FileInputStream("allnames.gz");
GZIPInputStream gzin = new GZIPInputStream(fin);
```

From that point forward, you can read uncompressed data from `gzin` using merely the usual `read()`, `skip()`, and `available()` methods. For instance, this code fragment reads and decompresses a file named *allnames.gz* in the current working directory:

```
FileInputStream fin   = new FileInputStream("allnames.gz");
GZIPInputStream gzin  = new GZIPInputStream(fin);
FileOutputStream fout = new FileOutputStream("allnames");
int b = 0;
while ((b = gzin.read()) != -1) fout.write(b);
gzin.close();
out.flush();
out.close();
```

In fact, it isn't even necessary to know that `gzin` is a `GZIPInputStream` for this to work. A simple `InputStream` type would work equally well. For example:

```
InputStream in = new GZIPInputStream(new FileInputStream("allnames.gz"));
```

`DeflaterOutputStream` and `InflaterInputStream` are equally straightforward. `ZipInputStream` and `ZipOutputStream` are a little more complicated because a zip file is actually an archive that may contain multiple entries, each of which must be read separately. Each file in a zip archive is represented as a `ZipEntry` object whose `getName()` method returns the original name of the file. For example, this code fragment decompresses the archive *shareware.zip* in the current working directory:

```
FileInputStream fin = new FileInputStream("shareware.zip");
ZipInputStream zin = new ZipInputStream(fin);
ZipEntry ze = null;
int b = 0;
while ((ze = zin.getNextEntry()) != null) {
  FileOutputStream fout = new FileOutputStream(ze.getName());
  while ((b = zin.read()) != -1) fout.write(b);
  zin.closeEntry();
  fout.flush();
  fout.close();
}
zin.close();
```

Digest Streams

The `java.util.security` package contains two filter streams that can calculate a message digest for a stream. They are `DigestInputStream` and `DigestOutputStream`. A message digest, represented in Java by the `java.util.security.MessageDigest` class, is a strong hash code for the stream; that is, it is a large integer (typically 20 bytes long in binary format) that can easily be calculated from a stream of any length in such a fashion that no information about the stream is available from the message digest. Message digests can be used for digital signatures and for detecting data that has been corrupted in transit across the network.

In practice, the use of message digests in digital signatures is more important. Mere data corruption can be detected with much simpler, less computationally expensive algorithms. However, the digest filter streams are so easy to use that at times it may be worth paying the computational price for the corresponding increase in programmer productivity. To calculate a digest for an output stream, you first construct a `MessageDigest` object that uses a particular algorithm, such as the Secure Hash Algorithm (SHA). You pass both the `MessageDigest` object and the stream you want to digest to the `DigestOutputStream` constructor. This chains the digest stream to the underlying output stream. Then you write data onto the stream as normal, flush it, close it, and invoke the `getMessageDigest()` method to retrieve the `MessageDigest` object. Finally you invoke the `digest()` method on the `MessageDigest` object to finish calculating the actual digest. For example:

```
MessageDigest sha = MessageDigest.getInstance("SHA");
DigestOutputStream dout = new DigestOutputStream(out, sha);
byte[] buffer = new byte[128];
while (true) {
   int bytesRead = in.read(buffer);
   if (bytesRead < 0) break;
   dout.write(buffer, 0, bytesRead);
}
dout.flush();
dout.close();
byte[] result = dout.getMessageDigest().digest();
```

Calculating the digest of an input stream you read is equally simple. It still isn't quite as transparent as some of the other filter streams because you do need to be at least marginally conversant with the methods of the `MessageDigest` class. Nonetheless, it's still far easier than writing your own secure hash function and manually feeding it each byte you write.

Of course, you also need a way of associating a particular message digest with a particular stream. In some circumstances, the digest may be sent over the same channel used to send the digested data. The sender can calculate the digest as it sends data, while the receiver calculates the digest as it receives the data. When the sender is done, it sends some signal that the receiver recognizes as indicating end of stream and then sends the digest. The receiver receives the digest, checks that the digest received is the same as the one calculated locally, and closes the connection. If the digests don't match, the receiver may instead ask the sender to send the message again. Alternatively, both the digest and the files it digests may be stored in the same zip archive. And there are many other possibilities. Situations like this generally call for the design of a relatively formal custom protocol. However, while the protocol may be complicated, the calculation of the digest is straightforward, thanks to the `DigestInputStream` and `DigestOutputStream` filter classes.

Encrypting Streams

Not all filter streams are part of the core Java API. For legal reasons, the filters for encrypting and decrypting data, `CipherInputStream` and `CipherOutputStream`, are part of a standard extension to Java called the Java Cryptography Extension, JCE for short. This is in the `javax.crypto` package. Sun provides an implementation of this API in the U.S. and Canada available from *http://java.sun.com/products/jce/*, and various third parties have written independent implementations that are available worldwide. Of particular note is the more or less Open Source Cryptix package, which can be retrieved from *http://www.cryptix.org/*.

The `CipherInputStream` and `CipherOutputStream` classes are both powered by a `Cipher` engine object that encapsulates the algorithm used to perform encryption and decryption. By changing the `Cipher` engine object, you change the algorithm that the streams use to encrypt and decrypt. Most ciphers also require a key that's used to encrypt and decrypt the data. Symmetric or secret key ciphers use the same key for both encryption and decryption. Asymmetric or public key ciphers use the different keys for encryption and decryption. The encryption key can be distributed as long as the decryption key is kept secret. Keys are specific to the algorithm in use, and are represented in Java by instances of the `java.security.Key` interface. The `Cipher` object is set in the constructor. Like all filter stream constructors, these constructors also take another input stream as an argument:

```
public CipherInputStream(InputStream in, Cipher c)
public CipherOutputStream(InputStream in, Cipher c)
```

To get a properly initialized `Cipher` object, you use the static `Cipher.getInstance()` factory method. This `Cipher` object must be initialized for either encryption or decryption with `init()` before being passed into one of the previous constructors. For example, this code fragment prepares a `CipherInput-`

Stream for decryption using the password "two and not a fnord" and the Data Encryption Standard (DES) algorithm:

```
byte[] desKeyData = "two and not a fnord".getBytes();
DESKeySpec desKeySpec = new DESKeySpec(desKeyData);
SecretKeyFactory keyFactory = SecretKeyFactory.getInstance("DES");
SecretKey desKey = keyFactory.generateSecret(desKeySpec);
Cipher des = Cipher.getInstance("DES");
des.init(Cipher.DECRYPT_MODE, desKey);
CipherInputStream cin = new CipherInputStream(fin, des);
```

This fragment uses classes from the java.security, java.security.spec, javax.crypto, and javax.crypto.spec packages. Different implementations of the JCE support different groups of encryption algorithms. Common algorithms include DES, RSA, and Blowfish. The construction of a key is generally algorithm specific. Consult the documentation for your JCE implementation for more details.

CipherInputStream overrides most of the normal InputStream methods like read() and available(). CipherOutputStream overrides most of the usual OutputStream methods like write() and flush(). These methods are all invoked much as they would be for any other stream. However, as the data is read or written, the stream's Cipher object either decrypts or encrypts the data. (Assuming your program wants to work with unencrypted data as is most commonly the case, a cipher input stream will decrypt the data, and a cipher output stream will encrypt the data.) For example, this code fragment encrypts the file *secrets.txt* using the password "Mary had a little spider":

```
String infile   = "secrets.txt";
String outfile  = "secrets.des";
String password = "Mary had a little spider";

try {

  FileInputStream fin = new FileInputStream(infile);
  FileOutputStream fout = new FileOutputStream(outfile);

  // register the provider that implements the algorithm
  Provider sunJce = new com.sun.crypto.provider.SunJCE();
  Security.addProvider(sunJce);

  // create a key
  char[] pbeKeyData = password.toCharArray();
  PBEKeySpec pbeKeySpec = new PBEKeySpec(pbeKeyData);
  SecretKeyFactory keyFactory =
  SecretKeyFactory.getInstance("PBEWithMD5AndDES");
  SecretKey pbeKey = keyFactory.generateSecret(pbeKeySpec);
```

```
    // use Data Encryption Standard
    Cipher pbe = Cipher.getInstance("PBEWithMD5AndDES");
    pbe.init(Cipher.ENCRYPT_MODE, pbeKey);
    CipherOutputStream cout = new CipherOutputStream(fout, pbe);

    byte[] input = new byte[64];
    while (true) {
      int bytesRead = fin.read(input);
      if (bytesRead == -1) break;
      cout.write(input, 0, bytesRead);
    }

    cout.flush();
    cout.close();
    fin.close();


  }
  catch (Exception e) {
    System.err.println(e);
    e.printStackTrace();
  }
```

I admit that this is more complicated than it needs to be. There's a lot of setup work involved in creating the Cipher object that actually performs the encryption. Partly that's a result of key generation involving quite a bit more than a simple password. However, a large part of it is also due to inane U.S. export laws that prevent Sun from fully integrating the JCE with the JDK and JRE. To a large extent, the complex architecture used here is driven by a need to separate the actual encrypting and decrypting code from the cipher stream classes.

Readers and Writers

Most programmers have a bad habit of writing code as if all text were ASCII or, at the least, in the native encoding of the platform. While some older, simpler network protocols, such as daytime, quote of the day, and chargen, do specify ASCII encoding for text, this is not true of HTTP and many other more modern protocols, which allow a wide variety of localized encodings, such as KOI8-R Cyrillic, Big-5 Chinese, and ISO 8859-2, for most Central European languages. When the encoding is no longer ASCII, the assumption that bytes and chars are essentially the same things also breaks down. Java's native character set is the 2-byte Unicode character set. Consequently, Java provides an almost complete mirror of the input and output stream class hierarchy that's designed for working with characters instead of bytes.

In this mirror image hierarchy, two abstract superclasses define the basic API for reading and writing characters. The java.io.Reader class specifies the API by which characters are read. The java.io.Writer class specifies the API by which characters are written. Wherever input and output streams use bytes, readers and writers use Unicode characters. Concrete subclasses of `Reader` and `Writer` allow particular sources to be read and targets to be written. Filter readers and writers can be attached to other readers and writers to provide additional services or interfaces.

The most important concrete subclasses of `Reader` and `Writer` are the `InputStreamReader` and the `OutputStreamWriter` classes. An `InputStream-Reader` contains an underlying input stream from which it reads raw bytes. It translates these bytes into Unicode characters according to a specified encoding. An `OutputStreamWriter` receives Unicode characters from a running program. It then translates those characters into bytes using a specified encoding and writes the bytes onto an underlying output stream.

In addition to these two classes, the `java.io` package also includes several raw reader and writer classes that read characters without directly requiring an underlying input stream. These include:

- `FileReader`
- `FileWriter`
- `StringReader`
- `StringWriter`
- `CharArrayReader`
- `CharArrayWriter`

The first two work with files and the last four work internally to Java, so they won't be of great use for network programming. However, aside from different constructors, they do have pretty much the same public interface as all the other reader and writer classes.

Writers

The `Writer` class mirrors the `java.io.OutputStream` class. It's abstract and has two protected constructors. Like `OutputStream`, the `Writer` class is never used directly, only polymorphically through one of its subclasses. It has five `write()` methods as well as a `flush()` and a `close()` method:

```
protected Writer()
protected Writer(Object lock)
public abstract void write(char[] text, int offset, int length)
  throws IOException
public void write(int c) throws IOException
public void write(char[] text) throws IOException
public void write(String s) throws IOException
public void write(String s, int offset, int length) throws IOException
public abstract void flush() throws IOException
public abstract void close() throws IOException
```

The write(char[] text, int offset, int length) method is the base method in terms of which the other four write() methods are implemented. A subclass must override at least this method as well as flush() and close(), though most will override some of the other write() methods as well to provide more efficient implementations. For example, given a Writer object w, you can write the string "Network" like this:

```
char[] network = {'N', 'e', 't', 'w', 'o', 'r', 'k'};
w.write(network, 0, network.length);
```

The same task can be accomplished with these other methods as well:

```
w.write(network);
for (int i = 0;  i < network.length;  i++) w.write(network[i]);
w.write("Network");
w.write("Network", 0, 7);
```

Assuming that they use the same Writer object w, all of these are different ways of expressing the same thing. Which you use in any given situation is mostly a matter of convenience and taste. However, how many and which bytes are written by these lines depends on the encoding w uses. If it's using big-endian Unicode, then it will write these 14 bytes (shown here in hexadecimal) in this order:

```
00 4E 00 65 00 74 00 77 00 6F 00 72 00 6B
```

On the other hand, if w uses little-endian Unicode, this sequence of 14 bytes is written:

```
4E 00 65 00 74 00 77 00 6F 00 72 00 6B 00
```

If w uses Latin–1, UTF-8, or MacRoman, this sequence of seven bytes is written:

```
4E 65 74 77 6F 72 6B
```

Other encodings may write still different sequences of bytes. The exact output depends on the encoding.

Writers may be buffered, either directly by being chained to a BufferedWriter or indirectly because their underlying output stream is buffered. To force a write to be committed to the output medium, invoke the flush() method:

```
w.flush();
```

The close() method behaves similarly to the close() method of OutputStream. This flushes the writer, then closes the underlying output stream and releases any resources associated with it:

```
public abstract void close() throws IOException
```

Once a writer has been closed, further writes will throw IOExceptions.

OutputStreamWriter

OutputStreamWriter is the most important concrete subclass of Writer. An OutputStreamWriter receives Unicode characters from a Java program. It converts these into bytes according to a specified encoding and writes them onto an underlying output stream. Its constructor specifies the output stream to write to and the encoding to use:

```
public OutputStreamWriter(OutputStream out, String encoding)
  throws UnsupportedEncodingException
public OutputStreamWriter(OutputStream out)
```

Valid encodings are listed in the documentation for Sun's native2ascii tool included with the JDK and available from *http://java.sun.com/products/jdk/1.2/docs/tooldocs/win32/native2ascii.html*. If no encoding is specified, the default encoding for the platform is used. (In the United States, the default encoding is ISO Latin–1 on Solaris and Windows, MacRoman on the Mac.) For example, this code fragment writes the string ἦμος δ'ἠριγένεια φάνη ῥοδοδάκτυλος Ἡώς in the Cp1253 Windows Greek encoding:

```
OutputStreamWriter w = new OutputStreamWriter(
  new FileOutputStream("OdysseyB.txt"), "Cp1253");
w.write("ἦμος δ'ἠριγένεια φάνη ῥοδοδάκτυλος Ἡώς");
```

Other than the constructors, OutputStreamWriter has only the usual Writer methods (which are used exactly as they are for any Writer class) and one method to return the encoding of the object:

```
public String getEncoding()
```

Readers

The Reader class mirrors the java.io.InputStream class. It's abstract with two protected constructors. Like InputStream and Writer, the Reader class is never used directly, only polymorphically through one of its subclasses. It has three read() methods as well as skip(), close(), ready(), mark(), reset(), and markSupported() methods:

```
protected Reader()
protected Reader(Object lock)
public abstract int read(char[] text, int offset, int length)
  throws IOException
public int read() throws IOException
public int read(char[] text) throws IOException
public long skip(long n) throws IOException
public boolean ready()
public boolean markSupported()
public void mark(int readAheadLimit) throws IOException
```

```
public void reset() throws IOException
public abstract void close() throws IOException
```

The read(char[] text, int offset, int length) method is the fundamental method through which the other two read() methods are implemented. A subclass must override at least this method as well as close(), though most will override some of the other read() methods as well in order to provide more efficient implementations.

Most of these methods are easily understood by analogy with their InputStream counterparts. The read() method returns a single Unicode character as an int with a value from 0 to 65,535 or –1 on end of stream. The read(char[] text) method tries to fill the array text with characters and returns the actual number of characters read or –1 on end of stream. The read(char[] text, int offset, int length) method attempts to read length characters into the subarray of text beginning at offset and continuing for length characters. It also returns the actual number of characters read or –1 on end of stream. The skip(long n) method skips n characters. The mark() and reset() methods allow some readers to reset back to a marked position in the character sequence. The markSupported() method tells you whether this reader supports marking and resetting. The close() method closes the reader and any underlying input stream so that further attempts to read from it will throw IOExceptions.

The exception to the rule of similarity is ready(), which has the same general purpose as available() but not quite the same semantics, even modulo the byte-to-char conversion. Whereas available() returns an int specifying a minimum number of bytes that may be read without blocking, ready() returns only a boolean indicating whether the reader may be read without blocking. The problem is that some character encodings such as UTF-8 use different numbers of bytes for different characters. Thus it's hard to tell how many characters are waiting in the network or filesystem buffer without actually reading them out of the buffer.

InputStreamReader is the most important concrete subclass of Reader. An InputStreamReader reads bytes from an underlying input stream such as a FileInputStream or TelnetInputStream. It converts these into characters according to a specified encoding and returns them. The constructor specifies the input stream to read from and the encoding to use:

```
public InputStreamReader(InputStream in)
public InputStreamReader(InputStream in, String encoding)
  throws UnsupportedEncodingException
```

If no encoding is specified, the default encoding for the platform is used. If an unknown encoding is specified, then an UnsupportedEncodingException is thrown.

For example, this method reads an input stream and converts it all to one Unicode string using the MacCyrillic encoding:

```
public static String getMacCyrillicString(InputStream in)
 throws IOException {

  InputStreamReader r = new InputStreamReader(in, "MacCyrillic");
  StringBuffer sb = new StringBuffer();
  int c;
  while ((c = r.read()) != -1) sb.append((char) c);
  r.close();
  return sb.toString();

}
```

Filter Readers and Writers

The InputStreamReader and OutputStreamWriter classes act as decorators on top of input and output streams that change the interface from a byte-oriented interface to a character-oriented interface. Once this is done, additional character-oriented filters can be layered on top of the reader or writer using the java.io.FilterReader and java.io.FilterWriter classes. As with filter streams, there are a variety of subclasses that perform specific filtering, including:

- BufferedReader

- BufferedWriter

- LineNumberReader

- PushbackReader

- PrintWriter

Buffered readers and writers

The BufferedReader and BufferedWriter classes are the character-based equivalents of the byte-oriented BufferedInputStream and BufferedOutputStream classes. Where BufferedInputStream and BufferedOutputStream use an internal array of bytes as a buffer, BufferedReader and BufferedWriter use an internal array of chars.

When a program reads from a BufferedReader, text is taken from the buffer rather than directly from the underlying input stream or other text source. When the buffer empties, it is filled again with as much text as possible, even if not all of it is immediately needed. This will make future reads much faster.

When a program writes to a BufferedWriter, the text is placed in the buffer. The text is moved to the underlying output stream or other target only when the buffer fills up or when the writer is explicitly flushed. This can make writes much faster than would otherwise be the case.

Both `BufferedReader` and `BufferedWriter` have the usual methods associated with readers and writers, like `read()`, `ready()`, `write()`, and `close()`. They each have two constructors used to chain the `BufferedReader` or `BufferedWriter` to an underlying reader or writer and to set the size of the buffer. If the size is not set, then the default size of 8,192 characters is used:

```
public BufferedReader(Reader in, int bufferSize)
public BufferedReader(Reader in)
public BufferedWriter(Writer out)
public BufferedWriter(Writer out, int bufferSize)
```

For example, the earlier `getMacCyrillicString()` example was less than efficient because it read characters one at a time. Since MacCyrillic is a 1-byte character set, this also meant it read bytes one at a time. However, it's straightforward to make it run faster by chaining a `BufferedReader` to the `InputStreamReader` like this:

```
public static String getMacCyrillicString(InputStream in)
  throws IOException {

  Reader r = new InputStreamReader(in, "MacCyrillic");
  r = new BufferedReader(r, 1024);
  StringBuffer sb = new StringBuffer();
  int c;
  while ((c = r.read()) != -1) sb.append((char) c);
  r.close();
  return sb.toString();

}
```

All that was needed to buffer this method was one additional line of code. None of the rest of the algorithm had to change, since the only `InputStreamReader` methods used were the `read()` and `close()` methods declared in the `Reader` superclass and shared by all `Reader` subclasses, including `BufferedReader`.

The `BufferedReader` class also has a `readLine()` method that reads a single line of text and returns it as a string:

```
public String readLine() throws IOException
```

This method is supposed to replace the deprecated `readLine()` method in `DataInputStream`, and it has mostly the same behavior as that method. The big difference is that by chaining a `BufferedReader` to an `InputStreamReader`, you can correctly read lines in character sets other than the default encoding for the platform. Unfortunately, this method shares the same bugs as the `readLine()` method in `DataInputStream`, discussed before. That is, it will tend to hang its thread when reading streams where lines end in carriage returns, such as is commonly the case when the streams derive from a Macintosh or a Macintosh text file. Consequently, you should scrupulously avoid this method in network programs.

It's not all that difficult, however, to write a safe version of this class that correctly implements the readLine() method. Example 4-1 is such a Safe-BufferedReader class. It has exactly the same public interface as Buffered-Reader. It just has a slightly different private implementation. I'll use this class in future chapters in situations where it's extremely convenient to have a readLine() method.

Example 4-1. The SafeBufferedReader Class

```
package com.macfaq.io;

import java.io.*;

public class SafeBufferedReader extends BufferedReader {

  public SafeBufferedReader(Reader in) {
    this(in, 1024);
  }

  public SafeBufferedReader(Reader in, int bufferSize) {
    super(in, bufferSize);
  }

  private boolean lookingForLineFeed = false;

  public String readLine() throws IOException {
    StringBuffer sb = new StringBuffer("");
    while (true) {
      int c = this.read();
      if (c == -1) { // end of stream
        return null;
      }
      else if (c == '\n') {
        if (lookingForLineFeed) {
          lookingForLineFeed = false;
          continue;
        }
        else {
          return sb.toString();
        }
      }
      else if (c == '\r') {
        lookingForLineFeed = true;
        return sb.toString();
      }
```

Example 4-1. The SafeBufferedReader Class (continued)

```
    else {
      lookingForLineFeed = false;
      sb.append((char) c);
    }
  }
 }

}
```

The `BufferedWriter()` class also adds one new method not included in its superclass, and this method is also geared toward writing lines. That method is `newLine()`:

```
    public void newLine() throws IOException
```

This method inserts a platform-dependent line-separator string into the output. The `line.separator` system property determines exactly what this string is. It will probably be a linefeed on Unix, a carriage return on the Macintosh, and a carriage return/linefeed pair on Windows. Since network protocols generally specify the required line terminator, you should not use this method for network programming. Instead, you should explicitly write the line terminator the protocol requires.

LineNumberReader

The `LineNumberReader` class replaces the deprecated `LineNumberInputStream` class from Java 1.0. It's a subclass of `BufferedReader` that keeps track of the current line number being read. This can be retrieved at any time with the `getLineNumber()` method:

```
    public int getLineNumber()
```

By default, the first line number is 0. However, the number of the current line and all subsequent lines can be changed with the `setLineNumber()` method:

```
    public void setLineNumber(int lineNumber)
```

This method adjusts only the line numbers that `getLineNumber()` reports. It does not change the point at which the stream is read.

The `LineNumberReader`'s `readLine()` method shares the same bug as `BufferedReader`'s and `DataInputStream`'s, and thus is not suitable for network programming. However, the line numbers are also tracked if you use only the regular `read()` methods, and these do not share that bug. Besides these methods and the usual `Reader` methods, `LineNumberReader` has only these two constructors:

```
    public LineNumberReader(Reader in)
    public LineNumberReader(Reader in, int bufferSize)
```

Since LineNumberReader is a subclass of BufferedReader, it does have an internal character buffer whose size can be set with the second constructor. The default size is 8,192 characters.

PushbackReader

The PushbackReader class is the mirror image of the PushbackInputStream class. As usual, the main difference is that it pushes back chars rather than bytes. It provides three unread() methods that push characters onto the reader's input buffer:

```
public void unread(int c) throws IOException
public void unread(char[] cbuf) throws IOException
public void unread(char[] cbuf, int offset, int length)
  throws IOException
```

The first unread() method pushes a single character onto the reader. The second pushes an array of characters. The third pushes the specified subarray of characters starting with cbuf[offset] and continuing through cbuf [offset+length-1].

By default, the size of the pushback buffer is only one character. However, this can be adjusted in the second constructor:

```
public PushbackReader(Reader in)
public PushbackReader(Reader in, int bufferSize)
```

Trying to unread more characters than the buffer will hold throws an IOException.

PrintWriter

The PrintWriter class is a replacement for Java 1.0's PrintStream class that properly handles multibyte character sets and international text. Sun originally planned to deprecate PrintStream in favor of PrintWriter but backed off when it realized this would invalidate too much existing code, especially code that depended on System.out. Nonetheless, new code should use PrintWriter instead of PrintStream.

Aside from the constructors, the PrintWriter class has an almost identical collection of methods to PrintStream. These include:

```
public PrintWriter(Writer out)
public PrintWriter(Writer out, boolean autoFlush)
public PrintWriter(OutputStream out)
public PrintWriter(OutputStream out, boolean autoFlush)
public void flush()
public void close()
```

```
public boolean checkError()
protected void setError()
public void write(int c)
public void write(char[] text, int offset, int length)
public void write(char[] text)
public void write(String s, int offset, int length)
public void write(String s)
public void print(boolean b)
public void print(char c)
public void print(int i)
public void print(long l)
public void print(float f)
public void print(double d)
public void print(char[] text)
public void print(String s)
public void print(Object o)
public void println()
public void println(boolean b)
public void println(char c)
public void println(int i)
public void println(long l)
public void println(float f)
public void println(double d)
public void println(char[] text)
public void println(String s)
public void println(Object o)
```

Most of these methods behave the same for `PrintWriter` as they do for `PrintStream`. The exceptions are that the four `write()` methods write characters rather than bytes and that if the underlying writer properly handles character set conversion, then so do all the methods of the `PrintWriter`. This is an improvement over the noninternationalizable `PrintStream` class, but it's still not good enough for network programming. `PrintWriter` still has the problems of platform dependency and minimal error reporting that plague `PrintStream`.

It isn't hard to write a `PrintWriter` class that does work for network programming. You simply have to require the programmer to specify a line separator and let the `IOExceptions` fall where they may. Example 4-2 demonstrates. Notice that all the constructors require an explicit line-separator string to be provided.

Example 4-2. SafePrintWriter

```
/*
 * @(#)SafePrintWriter.java 1.0 99/07/10
 *
 * Written 1999 by Elliotte Rusty Harold,
 * Placed in the public domain
 * No rights reserved.
 */
```

Example 4-2. SafePrintWriter (continued)

```java
package com.macfaq.io;

import java.io.*;

/**
 * @version   1.0, 99/07/10
 * @author  Elliotte Rusty Harold
 * @since Java Network Programming, 2nd edition
 */

public class SafePrintWriter extends Writer {

  protected Writer out;

  private boolean autoFlush = false;
  private String lineSeparator;
  private boolean closed = false;

  public SafePrintWriter(Writer out, String lineSeparator) {
    this(out, false, lineSeparator);
  }

  public SafePrintWriter(Writer out, char lineSeparator) {
    this(out, false, String.valueOf(lineSeparator));
  }

  public SafePrintWriter(Writer out, boolean autoFlush, String lineSeparator) {
    super(out);
    this.out = out;
    this.autoFlush = autoFlush;
    this.lineSeparator = lineSeparator;
  }

  public SafePrintWriter(OutputStream out, boolean autoFlush,
   String encoding, String lineSeparator)
   throws UnsupportedEncodingException {
    this(new OutputStreamWriter(out, encoding), autoFlush, lineSeparator);
  }

  public void flush() throws IOException {

    synchronized (lock) {
      if (closed) throw new IOException("Stream closed");
      out.flush();
    }
```

Example 4-2. SafePrintWriter (continued)

```
  }

  public void close() throws IOException {

    try {
      this.flush();
    }
    catch (IOException e) {
    }

    synchronized (lock) {
      out.close();
      this.closed = true;
    }

  }

  public void write(int c) throws IOException {
    synchronized (lock) {
      if (closed) throw new IOException("Stream closed");
      out.write(c);
    }
  }

  public void write(char[] text, int offset, int length) throws IOException {
    synchronized (lock) {
      if (closed) throw new IOException("Stream closed");
      out.write(text, offset, length);
    }
  }

  public void write(char[] text) throws IOException {
    synchronized (lock) {
      if (closed) throw new IOException("Stream closed");
      out.write(text, 0, text.length);
    }
  }

  public void write(String s, int offset, int length) throws IOException {

    synchronized (lock) {
      if (closed) throw new IOException("Stream closed");
      out.write(s, offset, length);
    }

  }

  public void print(boolean b) throws IOException {
```

Example 4-2. SafePrintWriter (continued)

```
      if (b) this.write("true");
      else this.write("false");
  }

  public void println(boolean b) throws IOException {
    if (b) this.write("true");
    else this.write("false");
    this.write(lineSeparator);
    if (autoFlush) out.flush();
  }

  public void print(char c) throws IOException {
    this.write(String.valueOf(c));
  }

  public void println(char c) throws IOException {
    this.write(String.valueOf(c));
    this.write(lineSeparator);
    if (autoFlush) out.flush();
  }

  public void print(int i) throws IOException {
    this.write(String.valueOf(i));
  }

  public void println(int i) throws IOException {
    this.write(String.valueOf(i));
    this.write(lineSeparator);
    if (autoFlush) out.flush();
  }

  public void print(long l) throws IOException {
    this.write(String.valueOf(l));
  }

  public void println(long l) throws IOException {
    this.write(String.valueOf(l));
    this.write(lineSeparator);
    if (autoFlush) out.flush();
  }

  public void print(float f) throws IOException {
    this.write(String.valueOf(f));
  }

  public void println(float f) throws IOException {
    this.write(String.valueOf(f));
    this.write(lineSeparator);
```

Example 4-2. SafePrintWriter (continued)

```
    if (autoFlush) out.flush();
  }

  public void print(double d) throws IOException {
    this.write(String.valueOf(d));
  }

  public void println(double d) throws IOException {
    this.write(String.valueOf(d));
    this.write(lineSeparator);
    if (autoFlush) out.flush();
  }

  public void print(char[] text) throws IOException {
    this.write(text);
  }

  public void println(char[] text) throws IOException {
    this.write(text);
    this.write(lineSeparator);
    if (autoFlush) out.flush();
  }

  public void print(String s) throws IOException {
    if (s == null) this.write("null");
    else this.write(s);
  }

  public void println(String s) throws IOException {
    if (s == null) this.write("null");
    else this.write(s);
    this.write(lineSeparator);
    if (autoFlush) out.flush();
  }

  public void print(Object o) throws IOException {
    if (o == null) this.write("null");
    else this.write(o.toString());
  }

  public void println(Object o) throws IOException {
    if (o == null) this.write("null");
    else this.write(o.toString());
    this.write(lineSeparator);
    if (autoFlush) out.flush();
  }

  public void println() throws IOException {
```

Example 4-2. SafePrintWriter (continued)

```
    this.write(lineSeparator);
    if (autoFlush) out.flush();
  }


}
```

This class actually extends `Writer` rather than `FilterWriter`, as does `PrintWriter`. It could extend `FilterWriter` instead. However, this would save only one field and one line of code, since this class needs to override every single method in `FilterWriter` (`close()`, `flush()`, and all three `write()` methods). The reason for this is twofold. First, the `PrintWriter` class has to be much more careful about synchronization than the `FilterWriter` class is. Second, some of the classes that may be used as an underlying `Writer` for this class, notably `CharArrayWriter`, do not implement the proper semantics for `close()` and allow further writes to take place even after the writer is closed. Consequently, we have to handle the checks for whether the stream is closed in this class rather than relying on the underlying `Writer` out to do it for us.

NOTE   This chapter has been a whirlwind tour of the `java.io` package, covering the bare minimum you need to know to write network, programs. For a more detailed and comprehensive look, with many more examples, you should check out my previous book, *Java I/O* (O'Reilly & Associates, Inc., 1999).

5

In this chapter:
- *Running Threads*
- *Returning Information from a Thread*
- *Synchronization*
- *Deadlock*
- *Thread Scheduling*
- *Thread Pools*

Threads

Back in the good old days of the Net, circa the early 1990s, we didn't have the Web and HTTP and graphical browsers. Instead, we had Usenet news and FTP and command-line interfaces, and we liked it that way! But as good as the good old days were, there were some problems. For instance, when we were downloading kilobytes of free software from a popular FTP site over our 2400bps modems using Kermit, we would often encounter error messages like this one:

```
% ftp eunl.java.sun.com
Connected to eunl.javasoft.com.
220 softwarenl FTP server (wu-2.4.2-academ[BETA-16]+opie-2.32(1) 981105) ready.
Name (eunl.java.sun.com:elharo): anonymous
530-
530-    Server is busy.  Please try again later or try one of our other
530-    ftp servers at ftp.java.sun.com.  Thank you.
530-
530 User anonymous access denied.
Login failed.
ftp>
```

In fact, in the days when the Internet had only a few million users instead of a few hundred million, we were far more likely to come across an overloaded and congested site than we are today. The problem was that both the FTP servers bundled with most Unixes and the third-party FTP servers, such as *wu-ftpd*, forked a new process for each connection. One hundred simultaneous users meant 100 additional processes to handle. Since processes are fairly heavyweight items, too many of them could rapidly bring a server to its knees. The problem wasn't that the machines weren't powerful enough or the network fast enough; it was that the FTP servers were (and many still are) poorly implemented. Many more simultaneous users could be served if a new process wasn't needed for each connection.

Early web servers suffered from this problem as well, though the problem was masked a little by the transitory nature of HTTP connections. Since web pages and their embedded images tend to be small (at least compared to the software archives commonly retrieved by FTP) and since web browsers "hang up" the connection after each file is retrieved instead of staying connected for minutes or hours at a time, web users don't put nearly as much load on a server as FTP users do. Nonetheless, if the pages are large or are dynamically generated through CGI (which spawns a process for each new connection), then web server performance can also degrade rapidly as usage grows. The fundamental problem is that while it's easy to write code that handles each incoming connection and each new task as a separate process (at least on Unix), this solution doesn't scale. By the time a server is attempting to handle a thousand or more simultaneous connections, performance slows to a crawl.

There are at least two solutions to this problem. The first is to reuse processes rather than spawning new ones. When the server starts up, a fixed number of processes (say, 300) are spawned to handle requests. Incoming requests are placed in a queue. Each process removes one request from the queue, services the request, then returns to the queue to get the next request. There are still 300 separate processes running, but because all the overhead of building up and tearing down the processes is avoided, these 300 processes can now do the work of a thousand.*

The second solution to this problem is to use lightweight threads to handle connections instead of using heavyweight processes. Whereas each separate process has its own block of memory, threads are easier on resources because they share memory. Using threads instead of processes can buy you another factor of three in server performance. By combining this with a pool of reusable threads (as opposed to a pool of reusable processes), your server can run nine times faster, all on the same hardware and network connection! While it's still the case that most Java virtual machines keel over somewhere between 700 and 2,000 simultaneous threads, the impact of running many different threads on the server hardware is relatively minimal since they all run within one process. Furthermore, by using a thread pool instead of spawning new threads for each connection, your server can use fewer than a hundred threads to handle thousands of connections per minute.

Unfortunately, this increased performance doesn't come for free. There's a cost in terms of program complexity. In particular, multithreaded servers (and other multithreaded programs) require programmers to address concerns that aren't issues for single-threaded programs, particularly issues of safety and liveness. Because different threads share the same memory, it's entirely possible for one

---

* These numbers are rough estimates. Your exact mileage may vary, especially if your server hasn't yet reached the hit volume where scalability issues come into play. Still, whatever mileage you get out of spawning new processes, you should be able to do much better by reusing old processes.

thread to stomp all over the variables and data structures used by another thread. This is much the same as how one program running on a non-memory–protected operating system such as the Mac or Windows 95 can crash the entire system. Consequently, different threads have to be extremely careful about which resources they use when. Generally, each thread must agree to use certain resources only when it's sure either that those resources can't change or that it has exclusive access to them. However, it's also possible for two threads to be too careful, each waiting for exclusive access to resources it will never get. This can lead to deadlock, where two threads are each waiting for resources the other possesses. Neither thread can proceed without the resources that the other thread has reserved, but neither is willing to give up the resources it has already.

Running Threads

A thread with a little *t* is a separate independent path of execution in the virtual machine. A `Thread` with a capital *T* is an instance of the `java.lang.Thread` class. There is a one-to-one relationship between threads executing in the virtual machine and `Thread` objects constructed by the virtual machine. Most of the time it's obvious from the context which is meant if the difference is really important. To start a new thread running in the virtual machine, you construct an instance of the `Thread` class and invoke its `start()` method, like this:

```
Thread t = new Thread();
t.start();
```

Of course, this thread isn't very interesting because it doesn't have anything to do. To give a thread something to do, you either subclass the `Thread` class and override its `run()` method, or implement the `Runnable` interface and pass the `Runnable` object to the `Thread` constructor. I generally prefer the second option since it more cleanly separates the task that the thread performs from the thread itself, but you will see both techniques used in this book and elsewhere. In both cases, the key is the `run()` method, which has this signature:

```
public void run()
```

You're going to put all the work the thread does in this one method. This method may invoke other methods; it may construct other objects; it may even spawn other threads. However, the thread starts here and it stops here. When the `run()` method completes, the thread dies. In essence, the `run()` method is to a thread what the `main()` method is to a traditional nonthreaded program. A single-threaded program exits when the `main()` method returns. A multithreaded program exits when both the `main()` method and the `run()` methods of all nondaemon threads return. (Daemon threads perform background tasks such as garbage collection and don't prevent the virtual machine from exiting.)

Subclassing Thread

For example, suppose you want to write a program that calculates the Secure Hash Algorithm (SHA) digest for many files. To a large extent, this program is I/O-bound; that is, its speed is limited by the amount of time it takes to read the files from the disk. If you write it as a standard program that processes the files in series, the program's going to spend a lot of time waiting for the hard drive to return the data. This is characteristic of a lot of network programs; they have a tendency to execute faster than the network can supply input. Consequently, they spend a lot of time blocked. This is time that other threads can use, either to process other input sources or to do something that doesn't rely on slow input. (Not all threaded programs will share this characteristic. Sometimes even if none of the threads have a lot of spare time to allot to other threads, it's simply easier to design a program by breaking it into multiple threads that perform independent operations.) Example 5-1 is a subclass of **Thread** whose **run()** method calculates an SHA message digest for a specified file.

Example 5-1. FileDigestThread

```
import java.io.*;
import java.security.*;


public class DigestThread extends Thread {

  private File input;

  public DigestThread(File input) {
   this.input = input;
  }

  public void run() {
    try {
      FileInputStream in = new FileInputStream(input);
      MessageDigest sha = MessageDigest.getInstance("SHA");
      DigestInputStream din = new DigestInputStream(in, sha);
      int b;
      while ((b = din.read()) != -1) ;
      din.close();
      byte[] digest = sha.digest();
      StringBuffer result = new StringBuffer(input.toString());
      result.append(": ");
      for (int i = 0; i < digest.length; i++) {
        result.append(digest[i] + " ");
      }
      System.out.println(result);
    }
```

Example 5-1. FileDigestThread (continued)

```
    catch (IOException e) {
      System.err.println(e);
    }
    catch (NoSuchAlgorithmException e) {
      System.err.println(e);
    }

  }

  public static void main(String[] args) {

    for (int i = 0; i < args.length; i++) {
      File f = new File(args[i]);
      Thread t = new DigestThread(f);
      t.start();
    }

  }

}
```

The `main()` method reads filenames from the command-line and starts a new `DigestThread` for each one. The work of the thread is actually performed in the `run()` method. Here a `DigestInputStream` reads the file. Then the resulting digest is printed on `System.out`. Notice that the entire output from this thread is first built in a local `StringBuffer` variable `result`. This is then printed on the console with one method invocation. The more obvious path of printing the pieces one at a time using `System.out.print()` is not taken. There's a reason for that, which we'll discuss soon.

Since the signature of the `run()` method is fixed, you can't pass arguments to it or return values from it. Consequently, you need different ways to pass information into the thread and get information out of it. The simplest way to pass information in is to pass arguments to the constructor, which set fields in the `Thread` subclass, as done here.

Getting information out of a thread back into the original calling thread is trickier because of the asynchronous nature of threads. Example 5-1 sidesteps that problem by never passing any information back to the calling thread and simply printing the results on `System.out`. Most of the time, however, you'll want to pass the information to other parts of the program. You can store the result of the calculation in a field and provide a getter method to return the value of that field. However, how do you know when the calculation of that value is complete? What do you return if somebody calls the getter method before the value has been calculated? This is quite tricky, and we'll discuss it more later in this chapter.

If you subclass Thread, you should override run() **and nothing else!** The various other methods of the Thread class, start(), stop(), interrupt(), join(), sleep(), etc., all have very specific semantics and interactions with the virtual machine that are difficult to reproduce in your own code. You should override run(), and you should provide additional constructors and other methods as necessary, but you should not replace any of the other standard Thread methods.

Implementing the Runnable Interface

One way to avoid overriding the standard Thread methods is not to subclass Thread. Instead, you can write the task you want the thread to perform as an instance of the Runnable interface. This interface declares the run() method, exactly the same as the Thread class:

```
public void run()
```

Other than this method, which any class implementing this interface must provide, you are completely free to create any other methods with any other names you choose, all without any possibility of unintentionally interfering with the behavior of the thread. This also allows you to place the thread's task in a subclass of some other class such as Applet or HTTPServlet. To start a thread that performs the Runnable's task, you pass the Runnable object to the Thread constructor. For example:

```
Thread t = new Thread(myRunnableObject);
t.start();
```

It's easy to recast most problems that subclass Thread into Runnable forms. Example 5-2 demonstrates by rewriting Example 5-1 to use the Runnable interface rather than subclassing Thread. Aside from the name change, the only modifications that were necessary were changing extends Thread to implements Runnable and passing a DigestRunnable object to the Thread constructor in the main() method. The essential logic of the program is unchanged.

Example 5-2. DigestRunnable

```
import java.io.*;
import java.security.*;


public class DigestRunnable implements Runnable {

  private File input;

  public DigestRunnable(File input) {
   this.input = input;
  }
```

Example 5-2. DigestRunnable (continued)

```
public void run() {
  try {
    FileInputStream in = new FileInputStream(input);
    MessageDigest sha = MessageDigest.getInstance("SHA");
    DigestInputStream din = new DigestInputStream(in, sha);
    int b;
    while ((b = din.read()) != -1) ;
    din.close();
    byte[] digest = sha.digest();
    StringBuffer result = new StringBuffer(input.toString());
    result.append(": ");
    for (int i = 0; i < digest.length; i++) {
      result.append(digest[i] + " ");
    }
    System.out.println(result);
  }
  catch (IOException e) {
    System.err.println(e);
  }
  catch (NoSuchAlgorithmException e) {
    System.err.println(e);
  }

}

public static void main(String[] args) {

  for (int i = 0; i < args.length; i++) {
    File f = new File(args[i]);
    DigestRunnable dr = new DigestRunnable(f);
    Thread t = new Thread(dr);
    t.start();
  }

}

}
```

There's no strong reason to prefer implementing Runnable to extending Thread or vice versa in the general case. In a few special cases such as Example 5-14 later in this chapter, it may be useful to invoke some methods of the Thread class for the specific thread from within the constructor. This would require using a subclass. Subclassing Thread does allow hostile applets some attacks they might not otherwise have available. In some specific cases, it may be necessary to place the run() method in a class that extends some other class such as Applet, so the Runnable interface is essential. Finally, some object-oriented purists argue that the task that a thread undertakes is not really a kind of Thread, and therefore should be placed in a separate class or interface such as Runnable rather than in a subclass of Thread. I half agree with them, though I don't think the argument's as strong as it's sometimes made out to be. Consequently, I'll mostly use the Runnable interface in this book, but you should feel free to do whatever seems most convenient to you.

Returning Information from a Thread

One of the hardest things for programmers accustomed to traditional, single-threaded procedural models to grasp when moving to a multithreaded environment is how to return information from a thread. Getting information out of a finished thread is one of the most commonly misunderstood aspects of multithreaded programming. The run() method and the start() method don't return any values. For example, suppose that instead of simply printing out the SHA digest as in Example 5-1 and Example 5-2, the digest thread needs to return the digest to the main thread of execution. Most people's first reaction is to store the result in a field, then provide a getter method, as shown in Example 5-3 and Example 5-4. Example 5-3 is a Thread subclass that calculates a digest for a specified file. Example 5-4 is a simple command-line user interface that receives filenames and spawns threads to calculate digests for them.

Example 5-3. A Thread That Uses an Accessor Method to Return the Result

```
import java.io.*;
import java.security.*;


public class ReturnDigest extends Thread {

  private File input;
  private byte[] digest;

  public ReturnDigest(File input) {
   this.input = input;
  }

  public void run() {
    try {
      FileInputStream in = new FileInputStream(input);
      MessageDigest sha = MessageDigest.getInstance("SHA");
      DigestInputStream din = new DigestInputStream(in, sha);
      int b;
      while ((b = din.read()) != -1) ;
      din.close();
      digest = sha.digest();
```

Example 5-3. A Thread That Uses an Accessor Method to Return the Result (continued)

```
    }
    catch (IOException e) {
      System.err.println(e);
    }
    catch (NoSuchAlgorithmException e) {
      System.err.println(e);
    }


  }


  public byte[] getDigest() {
    return digest;
  }

}
```

Example 5-4. A Main Program That Uses the Accessor Method to Get the Output of the Thread

```
import java.io.*;


public class ReturnDigestUserInterface {

  public static void main(String[] args) {

    for (int i = 0; i < args.length; i++) {

      // Calculate the digest
      File f = new File(args[i]);
      ReturnDigest dr = new ReturnDigest(f);
      dr.start();

      // Now print the result
      StringBuffer result = new StringBuffer(f.toString());
      result.append(": ");
      byte[] digest = dr.getDigest();
      for (int j = 0; j < digest.length; j++) {
        result.append(digest[j] + " ");
      }
      System.out.println(result);

    }

  }

}
```

The `ReturnDigest` class stores the result of the calculation in the private field `digest`, which is accessed via the accessor method `getDigest()`. The `main()` method in `ReturnDigestUserInterface` loops through a list of files from the command line. It starts a new `ReturnDigest` thread for each file, then tries to retrieve the result using `getDigest()`. However, when you run this program, the result is not what you expect:

```
D:\JAVA\JNP2\examples\05>java ReturnDigestUserInterface *.java
Exception in thread "main" java.lang.NullPointerException
        at ReturnDigestUserInterface.main(ReturnDigestUserInterface.java,
        Compiled Code)
```

The problem is that the main program gets the digest and uses it before the thread has had a chance to initialize it. Although this flow of control would work in a single-threaded program in which `dr.start()` simply invoked the `run()` method in the same thread, that's not what happens here. The calculations that `dr.start()` kicks off may or may not finish before the `main()` method reaches the call to `dr.getDigest()`. If they haven't finished, then `dr.getDigest()` returns `null`, and the first attempt to access `digest` throws a `NullPointerException`.

Race Conditions

One possibility is to move the call to `dr.getDigest()` later in the `main()` method like this:

```
public static void main(String[] args) {

  ReturnDigest[] digests = new ReturnDigest[args.length];

  for (int i = 0; i < args.length; i++) {

    // Calculate the digest
    File f = new File(args[i]);
    digests[i] = new ReturnDigest(f);
    digests[i].start();

  }

  for (int i = 0; i < args.length; i++) {

    // Now print the result
    StringBuffer result = new StringBuffer(args[i]);
    result.append(": ");
    byte[] digest = digests[i].getDigest();
    for (int j = 0; j < digest.length; j++) {
      result.append(digest[j] + " ");
    }
```

```
    System.out.println(result);

  }


}
```

If you're lucky, this may work, and you'll get the expected output like this:

```
D:\JAVA\JNP2\examples\05>java ReturnDigest2 *.java
BadDigestRunnable.java: 73 -77 -74 111 -75 -14 70 13 -27 -28 32 68 -126
43 -27 55 -119 26 -77 6
BadDigestThread.java: 69 101 80 -94 -98 -113 29 -52 -124 -121 -38 -82 39
-4 8 -38 119 96 -37 -99
DigestRunnable.java: 61 116 -102 -120 97 90 53 37 -14 111 -60 -86 -112
124 -54 111 114 -42 -36 -111
DigestThread.java: 69 101 80 -94 -98 -113 29 -52 -124 -121 -38 -82 39
-4 8 -38 119 96 -37 -99
```

But let me emphasize that point about being lucky. You may not get this output. In fact, you may still get a `NullPointerException`. Whether this code works is completely dependent on whether every one of the `ReturnDigest` threads finishes before its `getDigest()` method is called. If the first `for` loop is too fast, and the second `for` loop is entered before the threads spawned by the first loop start finishing, then you're back where we started:

```
D:\JAVA\JNP2\examples\05>java ReturnDigest2 ReturnDigest.java
Exception in thread "main" java.lang.NullPointerException
        at ReturnDigest2.main(ReturnDigest2.java, Compiled Code)
```

Whether you get the correct results, or this exception, depends on many factors, including how many threads you're spawning, the relative speeds of the CPU and disk on the system where this is run, and the algorithm the Java virtual machine uses to allot time to different threads. This is called a *race condition*. Getting the correct result depends on the relative speeds of different threads, and you can't control those! You need a better way to guarantee that the `getDigest()` method isn't called until the digest is ready.

Polling

The solution most novices adopt is to have the getter method return a flag value (or perhaps throw an exception) until the result field is set. Then the main thread periodically polls the getter method to see whether it's returning something other than the flag value. In this example, that would mean repeatedly testing whether the digest is null and using it only if it isn't. For example:

```
public static void main(String[] args) {

  ReturnDigest[] digests = new ReturnDigest[args.length];
```

```
for (int i = 0; i < args.length; i++) {

  // Calculate the digest
  File f = new File(args[i]);
  digests[i] = new ReturnDigest(f);
  digests[i].start();

}

for (int i = 0; i < args.length; i++) {
  while (true) {
    // Now print the result
    byte[] digest = digests[i].getDigest();
    if (digest != null) {
      StringBuffer result = new StringBuffer(args[i]);
      result.append(": ");
      for (int j = 0; j < digest.length; j++) {
        result.append(digest[j] + " ");
      }
      System.out.println(result);
      break;
    }
  }
}

}
```

This solution works. It gives the correct answers in the correct order, and it works irrespective of how fast the individual threads run relative to each other. However, it's doing a lot more work than it needs to.

Callbacks

In fact, there's a much simpler, more efficient way to handle the problem. The infinite loop that repeatedly polls each ReturnDigest object to see whether it's finished can be eliminated. The trick is that rather than having the main program repeatedly ask each ReturnDigest thread whether it's finished (like a five-year-old repeatedly asking, "Are we there yet?" on a long car trip, and almost as annoying), we let the thread tell the main program when it's finished. It does this by invoking a method in the main class that started it. This is called a *callback* because the thread calls back its creator when it's done. This way, the main program can go to sleep while waiting for the threads to finish and not steal time from the running threads.

When the thread's run() method is nearly done, the last thing it does is invoke a known method in the main program with the result. Rather than the main program asking each thread for the answer, each thread tells the main program the answer. For instance, Example 5-5 shows a `CallbackDigest` class that is much the same as before. However, at the end of the `run()` method, it passes off the `digest` to the static `CallbackDigestUserInterface.receiveDigest()` method in the class that originally started the thread.

Example 5-5. CallbackDigest

```
import java.io.*;
import java.security.*;


public class CallbackDigest implements Runnable {

  private File input;

  public CallbackDigest(File input) {
   this.input = input;
  }

  public void run() {
    try {
      FileInputStream in = new FileInputStream(input);
      MessageDigest sha = MessageDigest.getInstance("SHA");
      DigestInputStream din = new DigestInputStream(in, sha);
      int b;
      while ((b = din.read()) != -1) ;
      din.close();
      byte[] digest = sha.digest();
      CallbackDigestUserInterface.receiveDigest(digest,
       input.getName());
    }
    catch (IOException e) {
      System.err.println(e);
    }
    catch (NoSuchAlgorithmException e) {
      System.err.println(e);
    }

  }

}
```

The `CallbackDigestUserInterface` class shown in Example 5-6 provides the `main()` method. However, unlike the `main()` methods in the other variations of this program in this chapter, this one only starts the threads for the files named on the command line. It does not attempt to actually read, print out, or in any other way work with the results of the calculation. That is handled by a separate method, `receiveDigest()`. This method is not invoked by the `main()` method or by any

method that can be reached by following the flow of control from the `main()`
method. Instead, it is invoked by each thread separately. In effect, it runs inside
the digesting threads rather than inside the main thread of execution.

Example 5-6. CallbackDigestUserInterface

```
import java.io.*;


public class CallbackDigestUserInterface {

  public static void receiveDigest(byte[] digest, String name) {

    StringBuffer result = new StringBuffer(name);
    result.append(": ");
    for (int j = 0; j < digest.length; j++) {
      result.append(digest[j] + " ");
    }
    System.out.println(result);

  }

  public static void main(String[] args) {

    for (int i = 0; i < args.length; i++) {
      // Calculate the digest
      File f = new File(args[i]);
      CallbackDigest cb = new CallbackDigest(f);
      Thread t = new Thread(cb);
      t.start();
    }

  }

}
```

Example 5-5 and Example 5-6 use static methods for the callback so that
`CallbackDigest` needs to know only the name of the method in
`CallbackDigestUserInterface` to call. However, it's not much harder (and
considerably more common) to call back to an instance method. In this case, the
class making the callback must have a reference to the object it's calling back.
Generally, this reference is provided as an argument to the thread's constructor.
When the `run()` method is nearly done, the last thing it does is invoke the
instance method on the callback object to pass along the result. For instance,
Example 5-7 shows a `CallbackDigest` class that is much the same as before. However, it now has one additional field, a `CallbackDigestUserInterface` object
called `callback`. At the end of the `run()` method, the digest is passed to call-

back's `receiveDigest()` method. The `CallbackDigestUserInterface` object itself is set in the constructor.

Example 5-7. InstanceCallbackDigest

```
import java.io.*;
import java.security.*;


public class InstanceCallbackDigest implements Runnable {

  private File input;
  private InstanceCallbackDigestUserInterface callback;

  public InstanceCallbackDigest(File input,
   InstanceCallbackDigestUserInterface callback) {
    this.input = input;
    this.callback = callback;
  }

  public void run() {
    try {
      FileInputStream in = new FileInputStream(input);
      MessageDigest sha = MessageDigest.getInstance("SHA");
      DigestInputStream din = new DigestInputStream(in, sha);
      int b;
      while ((b = din.read()) != -1) ;
      din.close();
      byte[] digest = sha.digest();
      callback.receiveDigest(digest);
    }
    catch (IOException e) {
      System.err.println(e);
    }
    catch (NoSuchAlgorithmException e) {
      System.err.println(e);
    }

  }

}
```

The `CallbackDigestUserInterface` class shown in Example 5-8 holds the `main()` method as well as the `receiveDigest()` method used to handle an incoming digest. Example 5-8 just prints out the digest, but a more expansive class could do other things as well, such as storing the digest in a field, using it to start another thread, or performing further calculations on it.

Example 5-8. InstanceCallbackDigestUserInterface

```java
import java.io.*;


public class InstanceCallbackDigestUserInterface {

  private File input;
  private byte[] digest;

  public InstanceCallbackDigestUserInterface(File input) {
    this.input = input;
  }

  public void calculateDigest() {
    InstanceCallbackDigest cb = new InstanceCallbackDigest(input, this);
    Thread t = new Thread(cb);
    t.start();
  }

  void receiveDigest(byte[] digest) {
    this.digest = digest;
    System.out.println(this);
  }

  public String toString() {
    String result = input.getName() + ": ";
    if (digest != null) {
      for (int i = 0; i < digest.length; i++) {
        result += digest[i] + " ";
      }
    }
    else {
      result += "digest not available";
    }
    return result;
  }

  public static void main(String[] args) {

    for (int i = 0; i < args.length; i++) {
      // Calculate the digest
      File f = new File(args[i]);
      InstanceCallbackDigestUserInterface d
       = new InstanceCallbackDigestUserInterface(f);
      d.calculateDigest();
    }

  }

}
```

Using instance methods instead of static methods for callbacks is a little more complicated but has a number of advantages. First, each instance of the main class, `InstanceCallbackDigestUserInterface` in this example, maps to exactly one file and can keep track of information about that file in a natural way without needing extra data structures. Furthermore, the instance can easily recalculate the digest for a particular file if necessary. In practice, this scheme proves a lot more flexible. However, there is one caveat. Notice the addition of the `calculateDigest()` method to start the thread. You might logically think that this belongs in a constructor. However, starting threads in a constructor is dangerous, especially threads that will call back to the originating object. There's a race condition here that may allow the new thread to call back before the constructor is finished and the object is fully initialized. It's unlikely in this case, because starting the new thread is the last thing this constructor does. Nonetheless, it's at least theoretically possible. Therefore, it's good form to avoid launching threads from constructors.

The first advantage of the callback scheme over the polling scheme is that it doesn't waste so many CPU cycles on polling. But a much more important advantage is that callbacks are more flexible and can handle more complicated situations involving many more threads, objects, and classes. For instance, if more than one object is interested in the result of the thread's calculation, the thread can keep a list of objects to call back. Particular objects can register their interest by invoking a method in the Thread or Runnable class to add themselves to the list. If instances of more than one class are interested in the result, then a new `interface` can be defined that all these classes implement. The `interface` would declare the callback methods. If you're experiencing déjà vu right now, that's probably because you have seen this scheme before. This is *exactly* how events are handled in the AWT and JavaBeans™. The AWT runs in a separate thread from the rest of your program. Components and beans inform you of events by calling back to methods declared in particular interfaces, such as `ActionListener` and `PropertyChangeListener`. Your listener objects register their interests in events fired by particular components using methods in the `Component` class, such as `addActionListener()` and `addPropertyChange-Listener()`. Inside the component, the registered listeners are stored in a linked list built out of `java.awt.AWTEventMulticaster` objects. It's easy to duplicate this pattern in your own classes. Example 5-9 shows one very simple possible interface class called `DigestListener` that declares the `digestCalculated()` method.

Example 5-9. DigestListener Interface

```
public interface DigestListener {

  public void digestCalculated(byte[] digest);

}
```

Example 5-10 shows the Runnable class that calculates the digest. Several new methods and fields are added for registering and deregistering listeners. For convenience and simplicity, a java.util.Vector manages the list. The run() method no longer directly calls back the object that created it. Instead, it communicates with the private sendDigest() method, which sends the digest to all registered listeners. The run() method neither knows nor cares who's listening to it. This class no longer knows anything about the user interface class. It has been completely decoupled from the classes that may invoke it. This is one of the strengths of this approach.

Example 5-10. The ListCallbackDigest Class

```java
import java.io.*;
import java.security.*;
import java.util.*;


public class ListCallbackDigest implements Runnable {

  private File input;
  List listenerList = new Vector();

  public ListCallbackDigest(File input) {
   this.input = input;
  }

  public synchronized void addDigestListener(DigestListener l) {
    listenerList.add(l);
  }

  public synchronized void removeDigestListener(DigestListener l) {
    listenerList.remove(l);
  }

  private void synchronized sendDigest(byte[] digest) {

    ListIterator iterator = listenerList.listIterator();
    while (iterator.hasNext()) {
      DigestListener dl = (DigestListener) iterator.next();
      dl.digestCalculated(digest);
    }

  }

  public void run() {

    try {
      FileInputStream in = new FileInputStream(input);
```

Example 5-10. The ListCallbackDigest Class (continued)

```
      MessageDigest sha = MessageDigest.getInstance("SHA");
      DigestInputStream din = new DigestInputStream(in, sha);
      int b;
      while ((b = din.read()) != -1) ;
      din.close();
      byte[] digest = sha.digest();
      this.sendDigest(digest);
    }
    catch (IOException e) {
      System.err.println(e);
    }
    catch (NoSuchAlgorithmException e) {
      System.err.println(e);
    }


  }


}
```

Finally, Example 5-11 is a main program that implements the `DigestListener` interface and exercises the `ListCallbackDigest` class by calculating digests for all the files named on the command line. However, this is no longer the only possible main program. There are now many more possible ways the digest thread could be used.

Example 5-11. ListCallbackDigestUserInterface Interface

```
import java.io.*;


public class ListCallbackDigestUserInterface implements DigestListener {

  private File input;
  private byte[] digest;

  public ListCallbackDigestUserInterface(File input) {
    this.input = input;
  }

  public void calculateDigest() {
    ListCallbackDigest cb = new ListCallbackDigest(input);
    cb.addDigestListener(this);
    Thread t = new Thread(cb);
    t.start();
  }

  public void digestCalculated(byte[] digest) {
    this.digest = digest;
```

Example 5-11. ListCallbackDigestUserInterface Interface (continued)

```
    System.out.println(this);
  }

  public String toString() {
    String result = input.getName() + ": ";
    if (digest != null) {
      for (int i = 0; i < digest.length; i++) {
        result += digest[i] + " ";
      }
    }
    else {
      result += "digest not available";
    }
    return result;
  }

  public static void main(String[] args) {

    for (int i = 0; i < args.length; i++) {
      // Calculate the digest
      File f = new File(args[i]);
      ListCallbackDigestUserInterface d
        = new ListCallbackDigestUserInterface(f);
      d.calculateDigest();
    }

  }

}
```

Synchronization

My shelves are overflowing with books, including many duplicate books, out-of-date books, and books I haven't looked at for ten years and probably never will again. Over the years, these books have cost me tens of thousands of dollars, maybe more, to acquire. By contrast, two blocks down the street from my apartment, you'll find the Central Brooklyn Public Library. Its shelves are also overflowing with books, and over its 150 years, it's spent millions on its collection. But the difference is that its books are shared among all the residents of Brooklyn, and consequently the books have very high turnover. Most books in the collection are used several times a year. Although the public library spends a lot more on buying and storing books than I do, the cost per page read is much lower at the library than for my personal shelves. That's the advantage of a shared resource.

Of course, there are disadvantages to shared resources too. If I need a book from the library, I have to walk over there. I have to find the book I'm looking for on the shelves. I have to stand in line to check the book out, or else I have to use it right there in the library rather than bringing it home with me. Sometimes, somebody else has checked the book out, and I have to fill out a reservation slip requesting that the book be saved for me when it's returned. And I can't write notes in the margins, highlight paragraphs, or tear pages out to paste on my bulletin board. (Well, I can, but if I do, it significantly reduces the usefulness of the book for future borrowers, and if the library catches me, I may lose my borrowing privileges.) There's a significant time and convenience penalty associated with borrowing a book from the library rather than purchasing my own copy, but it does save me money and storage space.

A thread is like a borrower at a library. It's borrowing from a central pool of resources. Threads make programs more efficient by sharing memory, file handles, sockets, and other resources. As long as two threads don't want to use the same resource at the same time, a multithreaded program is much more efficient than the multiprocess alternative in which each process would have to keep its own copy of every resource. The downside of this is that if two threads do want the same resource at the same time, one of them will have to wait for the other one to finish. If one of them doesn't wait, then the resource may get corrupted. Let's look at a specific example. Consider the run() method of Example 5-1 and Example 5-2. As previously mentioned, the method builds the result as a String, and then prints the String on the console using one call to System.out. println(). The output looks like this:

```
DigestThread.java: 69 101 80 -94 -98 -113 29 -52 -124 -121 -38 -82 39
-4 8 -38 119 96 -37 -99
DigestRunnable.java: 61 116 -102 -120 97 90 53 37 -14 111 -60 -86 -112
124 -54 111 114 -42 -36 -111
DigestThread.class: -62 -99 -39 -19 109 10 -91 25 -54 -128 -101 17 13
-66 119 25 -114 62 -21 121
DigestRunnable.class: 73 15 7 -122 96 66 -107 -45 69 -36 86 -43 103
-104 25 -128 -97 60 14 -76
```

Four threads run in parallel to produce this output. Each writes one line to the console. The order in which the lines are written is unpredictable because thread scheduling is unpredictable. But each line is written as a unified whole. Suppose, however, we used this variation of the run() method, which, rather than storing intermediate parts of the result in the String variable result, simply prints them on the console as they become available:

```
public void run() {

  try {
    FileInputStream in = new FileInputStream(input);
    MessageDigest sha = MessageDigest.getInstance("SHA");
    DigestInputStream din = new DigestInputStream(in, sha);
```

```
    int b;
    while ((b = din.read()) != -1) ;
    din.close();
    byte[] digest = sha.digest();
    System.out.print(input + ": ");
    for (int i = 0; i < digest.length; i++) {
      System.out.print(digest[i] + " ");
    }
    System.out.println();
  }
  catch (IOException e) {
    System.err.println(e);
  }
  catch (NoSuchAlgorithmException e) {
    System.err.println(e);
  }


}
```

When you run the program on the same input, you get output that looks something like this:

```
DigestRunnable.class: 73 15 7 -122 96 66 -107 -45 69 -36 86 -43 103 -104 25
-128 DigestRunnable.java: DigestThread.class: DigestThread.java:
61 -62 69 116 -99 101 -102 -39 80 -120 -19 -94 97 109 -98 90 -97 10 -113 53 60
-91 29 37 14 25 -52 -14 -76 -54 -124 111
-128 -121 -60 -101 -38 -86 17 -82 -112 13 39 124 -66 -4 -54 119 8 111 25 -38 114
-114 119 -42 62 96 -36 -21 -37 -111 121 -99
```

The digests of the different files are all mixed up! There's no telling which number belongs to which digest. Clearly, this is a problem.

The reason this occurs is that `System.out` is shared between the four different threads. When one thread starts writing to the console through several `System.out.print()` statements, it may not finish all its writes before another thread breaks in and starts writing its output. The exact order in which one thread preempts the other threads is indeterminate. You'll probably see slightly different output every time you run this program.

What's needed is a way to assign exclusive access to a shared resource to one thread for a specific series of statements. In this example, that shared resource is `System.out`, and the statements that need exclusive access are:

```
System.out.print(input + ": ");
for (int i = 0; i < digest.length; i++) {
  System.out.print(digest[i] + " ");
}
System.out.println();
```

Synchronized Blocks

Java's means of assigning exclusive access to an object is the synchronized keyword. To indicate that these five lines of code should be executed together, wrap them in a synchronized block that synchronizes on the System.out object, like this:

```
synchronized (System.out) {
  System.out.print(input + ": ");
  for (int i = 0; i < digest.length; i++) {
    System.out.print(digest[i] + " ");
  }
  System.out.println();
}
```

This means that once one thread starts printing out the values, all other threads will have to stop and wait for it to finish before they can print out their values. Synchronization is only a partial lock on an object. Other methods can use the synchronized object if they do so blindly, without attempting to synchronize on the object. For instance, in this case, there's nothing to prevent an unrelated thread from printing on System.out if it doesn't also try to synchronize on System.out.* Java provides no means to stop all other threads from using a shared resource. It can only prevent other threads that synchronize on the same object from using the shared resource.

Synchronization must be considered any time multiple threads share resources. These threads may be instances of the same Thread subclass or use the same Runnable class, or they may be instances of completely different classes. The key is what resources they share, not what classes they are. In Java, all resources are represented by objects that are instances of particular classes. Synchronization becomes an issue only when two threads both possess references to the same object. In the previous example, the problem was that several threads had access to the same PrintStream object System.out. In this case, it was a static class variable that led to the conflict. However, instance variables can also have problems.

For example, suppose your web server keeps a log file. The log file may be represented by a class something like the one shown in Example 5-12. This class itself doesn't use multiple threads. However, if the web server uses multiple threads to handle incoming connections, then each of those threads will need access to the same log file and consequently to the same LogFile object.

---

* In fact, the PrintStream class internally synchronizes most methods on the PrintStream object, System.out in this example. This means that every other thread that calls System.out.println( ) will be synchronized on System.out and will have to wait for this code to finish. PrintStream is unique in this respect. Most other OutputStream subclasses do not synchronize themselves.

Example 5-12. LogFile

```java
import java.io.*;
import java.util.*;

public class LogFile {

  private Writer out;

  public LogFile(File f) throws IOException {
    FileWriter fw = new FileWriter(f);
    this.out = new BufferedWriter(fw);
  }

  public void writeEntry(String message) throws IOException {
    Date d = new Date();
    out.write(d.toString());
    out.write('\t');
    out.write(message);
    out.write("\r\n");
  }

  public void close() throws IOException {
    out.flush();
    out.close();
  }

  protected void finalize() {
    try {
      this.close();
    }
    catch (IOException e) {
    }
  }

}
```

In this class, the `writeEntry()` method finds the current date and time, then writes into the underlying file using four separate invocations of `out.write()`. A problem occurs if two or more threads each have a reference to the same `LogFile` object, and one of those threads interrupts another one while it's in the process of writing the data. One thread may write the date and a tab, then the next thread might write three complete entries, then the first thread could write the message, a carriage return, and a linefeed. The solution, once again, is synchronization. However, here there are two good choices for which object to synchronize on. The first choice is to synchronize on the `Writer` object out.

For example:

```
public void writeEntry(String message) throws IOException {

    synchronized (out) {
        Date d = new Date();
        out.write(d.toString());
        out.write('\t');
        out.write(message);
        out.write("\r\n");
    }


}
```

This works because all the threads that use this `LogFile` object are also using the same `out` object that's part of that `LogFile`. It doesn't matter that `out` is private. Although it is used by the other threads and objects, it's referenced only within the `LogFile` class. Furthermore, although we're synchronizing here on the `out` object, it's the `writeEntry()` method that needs to be protected from interruption. The `Writer` classes all have their own internal synchronization that protects one thread from interfering with a `write()` method in another thread. (This is not true of input and output streams, with the exception of `PrintStream`. It is possible for a write to an output stream to be interrupted by another thread.) Each `Writer` class has a `lock` field that specifies the object on which writes to that writer synchronize.

The second possibility is to synchronize on the `LogFile` object itself. This is simple enough to arrange with the `this` keyword. For example:

```
public void writeEntry(String message) throws IOException {

    synchronized (this) {
        Date d = new Date();
        out.write(d.toString());
        out.write('\t');
        out.write(message);
        out.write("\r\n");
    }


}
```

Synchronized Methods

However, since synchronizing the entire method body on the object itself is such a common thing to do, Java provides a shortcut for this. You can synchronize an entire method on the current object (the `this` reference) by adding the

synchronized modifier to the method declaration. This synchronizes on the
Class object for the class if a static method is being synchronized. For example:

```
public synchronized void writeEntry(String message)
  throws IOException {

    Date d = new Date();
    out.write(d.toString());
    out.write('\t');
    out.write(message);
    out.write("\r\n");


}
```

Simply adding the synchronized modifier to all methods is not a catchall solution for synchronization problems. For one thing, it exacts a severe performance
penalty in many VMs (though HotSpot is much better in this respect than most),
potentially slowing down your code by a factor of three or more. Second, it dramatically increases the chances of deadlock. Third, and most importantly, it's not
always the object itself you need to protect from simultaneous modification or
access, and synchronizing on the instance of the method's class may not protect
the object you really need to protect. For instance, in this example, what we're
really trying to prevent is two threads simultaneously writing onto out. If some
other class had a reference to out completely unrelated to the LogFile, then this
attempt would have failed. However, in this example, synchronizing on the
LogFile object is sufficient because out is a private instance variable. Since we
never expose a reference to this object, there's no way for any other object to
invoke its methods except through the LogFile class. Therefore, synchronizing
on the LogFile object has the same effect as synchronizing on out.

Alternatives to Synchronization

Synchronization is not always the best possible solution to the problem of inconsistent behavior as a result of thread scheduling. There are a number of techniques
you can use to avoid the need for synchronization. The first is to use local variables
instead of fields wherever possible. Local variables do not have synchronization
problems. Every time a method is entered, the virtual machine creates a completely new set of local variables for the method. These variables are destroyed
when the method exits. This means there is no possibility for one local variable to
be used in two different threads. Every thread has its own separate set of local
variables.

Method arguments of primitive types are also safe from modification in separate
threads because Java passes arguments by value rather than by reference. A

corollary of this is that methods such as `Math.sqrt()` that simply take zero or more primitive data type arguments, perform some calculation, and return a value without ever interacting with the fields of any class are inherently thread safe. These methods often either are or should be declared static.

Method arguments of object types are a little trickier because the actual argument passed by value is a reference to the object. Suppose, for example, you pass a reference to an array into a `sort()` method. While the method is sorting the array, there's nothing to stop some other thread that also has a reference to the array from changing the values in the array.

`String` arguments are safe because they're *immutable*; that is, once a `String` object has been created, it cannot be changed by any thread. An immutable object never changes state. The values of its fields are set once when the constructor runs and then never altered. `StringBuffer` arguments are not safe because they're *not immutable*; they can be changed after they're created.

A constructor normally does not have to worry about issues of thread safety because until the constructor returns, no thread has a reference to the object, and so it's impossible for two threads to have a reference to the object. (The most likely issue is if a constructor depends on another object in another thread that may change while the constructor runs, but that's uncommon. There's also a potential problem if a constructor somehow passes a reference to the object into a different thread, but this is also uncommon.)

You can take advantage of immutability in your own classes. This is often the easiest way to make a class thread safe, often much easier than determining exactly which methods or code blocks to synchronize. To make an object immutable, you simply declare all its fields private, and don't write any methods that can change them. A lot of classes in the core Java library are immutable, for instance, `java.lang.String`, `java.lang.Integer`, `java.lang.Double`, and many more. This makes these classes less useful for some purposes, but it does make them a lot more thread-safe.

A third technique is to use a thread unsafe class but only as a private field of a class that is thread-safe. As long as the containing class accesses the unsafe class only in a thread-safe fashion, and as long as it never lets a reference to the private field leak out into another object, the class is safe. An example of this might be a web server that used an unsynchronized `LogFile` class but gave each separate thread its own separate log so that no resources were shared between the individual threads.

Deadlock

Synchronization can lead to another possible problem with your code: deadlock. Deadlock occurs when two threads each need exclusive access to the same set of resources, but each thread possesses a different subset of those resources. If neither thread is willing to give up the resources it has, both threads will come to an indefinite halt. This can bring your program to a halt. This isn't quite a hang in the classical sense, because the program is still active and behaving normally from the perspective of the OS, but to a user the difference is insignificant.

To return to the library example, deadlock is what occurs when Jack and Jill are each writing a term paper on Thomas Jefferson and each needs the two books *Thomas Jefferson and Sally Hemings: An American Controversy* and *Sally Hemings and Thomas Jefferson: History, Memory and Civic Culture*. If Jill has checked out the first book, while Jack has checked out the second, then neither can finish the paper. Eventually the deadline expires, and they both get an F. That's the problem of deadlock.

Worse yet, deadlock can be a sporadic and hard-to-detect bug. Deadlock closely depends on unpredictable issues of timing. Most of the time, either Jack or Jill will get to the library first and get both books. In this case, the one who gets the books writes his paper and returns the books; then the other one gets the books and writes her paper. Only rarely will they arrive at the same time and each get one of the two books. Ninety-nine times out of 100 or 999 times out of 1,000, a program may run to completion perfectly normally. Only rarely will it hang for no apparent reason. Of course, if a multithreaded server is handling hundreds or thousands of connections a minute, then even a problem that occurs only once every million requests can hang the server in short order.

The most important technique to prevent deadlock is to avoid unnecessary synchronization. If there's an alternative approach for ensuring thread safety, such as using immutable objects or a local copy of an object, then use that. Synchronization should be a last resort for ensuring thread safety. If you do need to synchronize, keep your synchronized blocks small and try not to synchronize on more than one object at a time. This can be tricky though because many of the methods from the Java class library that your code may invoke synchronize on objects you aren't aware of. Consequently, you may in fact be synchronizing on many more objects than you expect.

The best you can do in the general case is carefully consider whether deadlock is likely to be a problem and architect your code around it. If multiple objects need the same set of shared resources to operate, then make sure they request them in the same order. For instance, if Class A and Class B both need exclusive access to Object X and Object Y, then make sure that both classes request X first and Y second. If neither requests Y unless it already possesses X, then deadlock is not a problem.

Thread Scheduling

When multiple threads are running at the same time (more properly, when multiple threads are available to be run at the same time), you have to consider issues of thread scheduling. You need to make sure that all important threads get at least some time to run and that the more important threads get more time. Furthermore, you want to ensure that the threads execute in a reasonable order. If your web server has 10 queued requests, each of which requires 5 seconds to process, you don't want to process them in series. If you do that, the first request will be finished in 5 seconds, but the second will take 10, the third 15, and so on until the last request, which will have to wait almost a minute to be serviced. By that point, the user has likely gone to another page. By running threads in parallel, you might be able to process all 10 requests in only 10 seconds total. The reason is that there's a lot of dead time in servicing a typical web request, time in which the thread is simply waiting for the network to catch up with the CPU, and this is time that the VM's thread scheduler can be put to good use by other threads. However, CPU bound threads (as opposed to the I/O-bound threads more common in network programs) may never reach a point where they have to wait for more input. It is possible for such a thread to starve all other threads by taking all the available CPU resources. But with a little thought, it's generally straightforward to avoid this problem. In fact, starvation is a considerably easier problem to avoid than either mis-synchronization or deadlock.

Priorities

Not all threads are created equal. Each thread has a priority that's specified as an integer from 1 to 10. When multiple threads are able to run, generally the VM will run only the highest-priority thread, though that's not a hard-and-fast rule. In Java, 10 is the highest priority and 1 is the lowest. The default priority is 5, and this is the priority that your threads will have unless you deliberately set them otherwise.

WARNING   This is exactly opposite to the normal Unix way of prioritizing processes, where the higher the priority number of a process, the less CPU time the process gets.

These three priorities are often specified as the three named constants `Thread.MIN_PRIORITY`, `Thread.NORM_PRIORITY`, and `Thread.MAX_PRIORITY`:

```
public static final int MIN_PRIORITY  = 1;
public static final int NORM_PRIORITY = 5;
public static final int MAX_PRIORITY  = 10;
```

Sometimes you want to give one thread more time than another. Threads that interact with the user should get very high priorities so that perceived

responsiveness will be very quick. On the other hand, threads that calculate in the
background should get low priorities. Tasks that will complete quickly should have
high priorities. Tasks that take a long time should have low priorities so that they
won't get in the way of other tasks. The priority of a thread can be changed using
the setPriority() method:

```
public final void setPriority(int newPriority)
```

Attempting to exceed the maximum priority or set a nonpositive priority throws an
IllegalArgumentException.

The getPriority() method returns the current priority of the thread:

```
public final int getPriority()
```

For instance, in Example 5-11, you might want to give higher priorities to the
threads that do the calculating than the main program that spawns the threads.
This is easily achieved by changing the calculateDigest() method to set the
priority of each spawned thread to 8:

```
public void calculateDigest() {

    ListCallbackDigest cb = new ListCallbackDigest(input);
    cb.addDigestListener(this);
    Thread t = new Thread(cb);
    t.setPriority(8);
    t.start();

}
```

In general, though, try to avoid using too high a priority for threads, since you run
the risk of starving other, lower-priority threads.

Preemption

Every virtual machine has a thread scheduler that determines which thread to run
at any given time. There are two kinds of thread scheduling, preemptive and cooperative. A preemptive thread scheduler determines when a thread has had its fair
share of CPU time, pauses that thread, and then hands off control of the CPU to a
different thread. A cooperative thread scheduler waits for the running thread to
pause itself before handing off control of the CPU to a different thread. A virtual
machine that uses cooperative thread scheduling is much more susceptible to
thread starvation than a virtual machine that uses preemptive thread scheduling,
since one high-priority, uncooperative thread can hog an entire CPU.

All Java virtual machines are guaranteed to use preemptive thread scheduling
between priorities. That is, if a lower-priority thread is running when a higher-

priority thread becomes able to run, the virtual machine will sooner or later (and probably sooner) pause the lower-priority thread to allow the higher-priority thread to run. The higher-priority thread *preempts* the lower-priority thread.

The situation when multiple threads of the same priority are able to run is trickier. A preemptive thread scheduler will occasionally pause one of the threads to allow the next one in line to get some CPU time. However, a cooperative thread scheduler will not. It will wait for the running thread to explicitly give up control or come to a stopping point. If the running thread never gives up control and never comes to a stopping point and if no higher-priority threads preempt the running thread, then all other threads will starve. This is a bad thing. Consequently, it's important to make sure that all your threads periodically pause themselves so that other threads have an opportunity to run.

WARNING   A starvation problem can be hard to spot if you're developing on a VM that uses preemptive thread scheduling. Just because the problem doesn't arise on your machine doesn't mean it won't arise on your customers' machines if their VMs use cooperative thread scheduling. Most Windows virtual machines use preemptive thread scheduling. Most Mac virtual machines use cooperative thread scheduling. Unix virtual machines are a mix of preemptively and cooperatively scheduled VMs and, in a few cases, don't precisely fit into either category. Any Unix virtual machine that uses the green threads model (on Solaris, this is Sun's reference implementation of the VM) is cooperatively scheduled. Any Unix virtual machine that uses native threads (on Solaris, this is Sun's production implementation of the VM) is more or less preemptively scheduled.

There are 10 ways a thread can pause in favor of other threads or indicate that it is ready to pause. These are:

*   It can block on I/O.
*   It can block on a synchronized object.
*   It can yield.
*   It can go to sleep.
*   It can join another thread.
*   It can wait on an object.
*   It can finish.
*   It can be preempted by a higher-priority thread.
*   It can be suspended.
*   It can stop.

You should inspect every run() method you write to make sure that one of these conditions will occur with reasonable frequency. The last two possibilities are deprecated because they have the potential to leave objects in inconsistent states, so let's look at the other eight ways a thread can be a cooperative citizen of the virtual machine.

Blocking

Blocking occurs any time a thread has to stop and wait for a resource it doesn't have. The most common way a thread in a network program will voluntarily give up control of the CPU is by blocking on I/O. Since CPUs are much faster than networks and disks, a network program will often block while waiting for data to arrive from the network or be sent out to the network. Even though it may block for only a few milliseconds, this is enough time for other threads to do significant work.

Threads can also block when they enter a synchronized method or block. If the thread does not already possess the lock for the object being synchronized on and some other thread does possess that lock, then the thread will pause until the lock is released. If the lock is never released, then the thread is permanently stopped.

Neither blocking on I/O nor blocking on a lock will release any locks the thread already possesses. For I/O blocks, this is not such a big deal since eventually the I/O will either unblock and the thread will continue or an IOException will be thrown and the thread will thereby exit the synchronized block or method and release its locks. However, a thread blocking on a lock that it doesn't possess will never give up its own locks. If one thread is waiting for a lock that a second thread owns and the second thread is waiting for a lock that the first thread owns, then deadlock results.

Yielding

The second way for a thread to give up control is to explicitly yield. A thread does this by invoking the static Thread.yield() method:

```
public static void yield()
```

This signals the virtual machine that it can run another thread if another one is ready to run. Some virtual machines, particularly on real-time operating systems, may ignore this hint.

Before yielding, a thread should make sure that it or its associated Runnable object is in a consistent state that can be used by other objects. Yielding does not release any locks the thread holds. Therefore, ideally, a thread should not be synchronized on anything when it yields. If the only other threads waiting to run when a thread yields are blocked because they need the synchronized resources that the yielding thread possesses, then the other threads won't be able to run. Instead, control will return to the only thread that can run, the one that just yielded, which pretty much defeats the purpose of yielding.

Making a thread yield is quite simple in practice. If the thread's `run()` method simply consists of an infinite loop, just put a call to `Thread.yield()` at the end of the loop. For example:

```
public void run() {

  while (true) {
    // Do the thread's work...
    Thread.yield();
  }


}
```

As long as the `run()` method isn't synchronized (normally, a very bad idea anyway), this should give other threads of the same priority the opportunity to run.

If each iteration of the loop takes a significant amount of time, you may want to intersperse more calls to `Thread.yield()` in the rest of the code. This should have minimal effect in the event that yielding isn't necessary.

Sleeping

Sleeping is a more powerful form of yielding. Whereas yielding indicates only that a thread is willing to pause and let other equal-priority threads have a turn, a thread that goes to sleep will pause whether any other thread is ready to run or not. This can give not only other threads of the same priority but also threads of lower priorities an opportunity to run. However, a thread that goes to sleep does hold onto all the locks it's grabbed. Consequently, other threads that need the same locks will be blocked even if the CPU is available. Therefore, you should try to avoid threads sleeping inside a synchronized method or block.

Sometimes sleeping is useful even if you don't need to yield to other threads. Putting a thread to sleep for a specified period of time lets you write code that executes once every second, every minute, every ten minutes, and so forth. For instance, if you were to write a network monitor program that retrieved a page from a web server every five minutes and emailed the webmaster if the server had crashed, then you would implement it as a thread that slept for five minutes between retrievals.

A thread goes to sleep by invoking one of two overloaded static `Thread.sleep()` methods. The first takes the number of milliseconds to sleep as an argument. The second takes both the number of milliseconds and the number of nanoseconds:

```
public static void sleep(long milliseconds) throws InterruptedException
public static void sleep(long milliseconds, int nanoseconds)
  throws InterruptedException
```

While most modern computer clocks have at least close-to-millisecond accuracy, nanosecond accuracy is rarer. There's no guarantee on any particular virtual machine that you can actually time the sleep to within a nanosecond or even within a millisecond. If the local hardware can't support that level of accuracy, the sleep time is simply rounded to the nearest value that can be measured. For example:

```
public void run() {

  while (true) {
    if (!getPage("http://metalab.unc.edu/javafaq/")) {
      mailError("elharo@metalab.unc.edu");
    }
    try {
      Thread.sleep(300000); // 300,000 milliseconds == 5 minutes
    }
    catch (InterruptedException e) {
      break;
    }
  }

}
```

It is not absolutely guaranteed that a thread will sleep for as long as it wants to. On occasion, the thread may not be woken up until some time after its requested wake-up call, simply because the VM is busy doing other things. It is also possible that some other thread will do something to wake up the sleeping thread before its time. Generally, this is accomplished by invoking the sleeping thread's `interrupt()` method.

```
public void interrupt()
```

This is one of those cases where the distinction between the thread and the `Thread` object is important. Just because the thread is sleeping doesn't mean that other awake threads can't be working with the corresponding `Thread` object through its methods and fields. In particular, another thread can invoke the sleeping `Thread` object's `interrupt()` method, which the sleeping thread experiences as an `InterruptedException`. From that point forward, it's awake and executes as normal, at least until it goes to sleep again. In the previous example, an `InterruptedException` is used to terminate a thread that would otherwise run forever. When the `InterruptedException` is thrown, the infinite loop is broken, the `run()` method finishes, and the thread dies. The user interface thread can invoke this thread's `interrupt()` method when the user selects Exit from a menu or otherwise indicates that he wants the program to quit.

Joining threads

It's not uncommon for one thread to need the result of another thread. For example, a web browser loading an HTML page in one thread might spawn a separate thread to retrieve every image embedded in the page. If the IMG elements don't have HEIGHT and WIDTH attributes, then the main thread might have to wait for all the images to load before it can finish by displaying the page. Java provides three join() methods to allow one thread to wait for another thread to finish before continuing. These are:

```
public final void join() throws InterruptedException
public final void join(long milliseconds) throws InterruptedException
public final void join(long milliseconds, int nanoseconds)
  throws InterruptedException
```

The first variant waits indefinitely for the joined thread to finish. The second two variants wait for the specified amount of time, after which they continue even if the joined thread has not finished. As with the sleep() method, nanosecond accuracy is not guaranteed.

The joining thread—that is, the one that invokes the join() method—waits for the joined thread—that is, the one whose join() method is invoked—to finish. For instance, consider this code fragment. We want to find the minimum, maximum, and median of a random array of doubles. It's quicker to do this with a sorted array. We spawn a new thread to sort the array, then join to that thread to await its results. Only when it's done do we read out the desired values.

```
double[] array = new double[10000];                            // 1
for (int i = 0; i < array.length; i++) {                       // 2
  array[i] = Math.random();                                    // 3
}                                                              // 4
SortThread t = new SortThread(array);                          // 5
t.start();                                                     // 6
try {                                                          // 7
  t.join();                                                    // 8
  System.out.println("Minimum: " + array[0]);                 // 9
  System.out.println("Median: " + array[array.length/2]);    // 10
  System.out.println("Maximum: " + array[array.length-1]);   // 11
}                                                             // 12
catch (InterruptedException e) {                              // 13
}                                                             // 14
```

First lines 1 through 4 execute, filling the array with random numbers. Then line 5 creates a new SortThread. Line 6 starts the thread that will sort the array. Before we can find the minimum, median, and maximum of the array, we need to wait for the sorting thread to finish. Therefore, line 8 joins the current thread to the sorting thread. At this point, the thread executing these lines of code stops in its tracks. It waits for the sorting thread to finish running. The minimum, median,

and maximum are not retrieved in lines 9 through 10 until the sorting thread has
finished running and died. Notice that at no point is there a reference to the
thread that pauses. It's not the Thread object on which the join() method is
invoked. It's not passed as an argument to that method. It exists implicitly only as
the current thread. If this is within the normal flow of control of the main()
method of the program, there may well not be any Thread variable anywhere that
points to this thread.

A thread that's joined to another thread can be interrupted just like a sleeping
thread if some other thread invokes its interrupt() method. The thread experiences this invocation as an InterruptedException. From that point forward, it
executes as normal, starting from the catch block that caught the exception. In
the preceding example, if the thread is interrupted, it skips over the calculation of
the minimum, median, and maximum because they won't be available if the sorting thread was interrupted before it could finish.

We can use join() to fix up Example 5-4. That example's problem was that the
main() method tended to outrace the threads whose results the main() method
was using. It's straightforward to fix this by joining to each thread before trying to
use its result. Example 5-13 demonstrates.

Example 5-13. Avoiding a Race Condition by Joining to the Thread Whose Result You Need

```
import java.io.*;


public class JoinDigestUserInterface {

  public static void main(String[] args) {

    ReturnDigest[] digestThreads = new ReturnDigest[args.length];

    for (int i = 0; i < args.length; i++) {

      // Calculate the digest
      File f = new File(args[i]);
      digestThreads[i] = new ReturnDigest(f);
      digestThreads[i].start();

    }

    for (int i = 0; i < args.length; i++) {

      try {
        digestThreads[i].join();
        // Now print the result
        StringBuffer result = new StringBuffer(args[i]);
```

Example 5-13. Avoiding a Race Condition by Joining to the Thread Whose Result You Need (continued)

```
    result.append(": ");
    byte[] digest = digestThreads[i].getDigest();
    for (int j = 0; j < digest.length; j++) {
      result.append(digest[j] + " ");
    }
    System.out.println(result);
  }
  catch (InterruptedException e) {
    System.err.println("Thread Interrupted before completion");
  }


  }


}
```

Since Example 5-13 joins to threads in the same order as the threads are started, this also has the side effect of printing the output in the same order as the arguments used to construct the threads, rather than in the order the threads finish. This doesn't make the program any slower, but it may occasionally be an issue if you want to get the output of a thread as soon as it's done, without waiting for other unrelated threads to finish first.

Waiting on an object

A thread can wait on an object it has locked. While waiting, it releases the lock on the object and pauses until it is notified by some other thread. Another thread changes the object in some way, notifies the thread waiting on that object, and then continues. This differs from joining in that neither the waiting nor the notifying thread has to finish before the other thread can continue. Waiting is used to pause execution until an object or resource reaches a certain state. Joining is used to pause execution until a thread finishes.

Waiting on an object is one of the lesser-known ways a thread can pause. That's because it doesn't involve any methods in the Thread class. Instead, to wait on a particular object, the thread that wants to pause must first obtain the lock on the object using synchronized and then invoke one of the object's three overloaded wait() methods:

```
public final void wait() throws InterruptedException
public final void wait(long milliseconds) throws InterruptedException
public final void wait(long milliseconds, int nanoseconds)
  throws InterruptedException
```

These methods are not in the `Thread` class. Rather, they are in the `java.lang.Object` class. Consequently, they can be invoked on any object of any class. When one of these methods is invoked, the thread that invoked it releases its lock on the object it's waiting on (though not any locks it may possess on other objects) and goes to sleep. It remains asleep until one of three things happens:

- The timeout expires.
- The thread is interrupted.
- The object is notified.

The timeout is the same as for the `sleep()` and `join()` methods; that is, the thread wakes up after the specified amount of time has passed (within the limits of the local hardware clock accuracy). When the timeout expires, execution of the thread resumes with the statement immediately following the invocation of `wait()`. However, if the thread can't immediately regain the lock on the object it was waiting on, it may still be blocked for some time.

Interruption is also the same as for `sleep()` and `join()`; that is, some other thread invokes this thread's `interrupt()` method. This causes an `InterruptedException`, and execution resumes in the `catch` block that catches the exception. The thread regains the lock on the object it was waiting on before the exception is thrown, however, so the thread may still be blocked for some time after the `interrupt()` method is invoked.

The third possibility, notification, is new. Notification occurs when some other thread invokes the `notify()` or `notifyAll()` method on the object on which the thread is waiting. Both of these methods are in the `java.lang.Object` class:

```
public final void notify()
public final void notifyAll()
```

These must be invoked on the object the thread was waiting on, not generally on the `Thread` itself. Before notifying an object, a thread must first obtain the lock on the object using a synchronized method or block. The `notify()` method selects one thread more or less at random from the list of threads waiting on the object and wakes it up. The `notifyAll()` method wakes up every thread waiting on the given object.

Once a waiting thread is notified, it attempts to regain the lock of the object it was waiting on. If it succeeds, its execution resumes with the statement immediately following the invocation of `wait()`. If it fails, it blocks on the object until its lock becomes available, and then execution resumes with the statement immediately following the invocation of `wait()`.

For example, suppose one thread is reading a JAR archive from a network connection. The first entry in the archive is the manifest file. Another thread might be interested in the contents of the manifest file even before the rest of the archive was available. The interested thread could create a custom `ManifestFile` object. It could then pass a reference to this `ManifestFile` object to the thread that would read the JAR archive. Then it would wait on the `ManifestFile` object. The thread reading the archive would first fill the `ManifestFile` with entries from the stream, then notify the `ManifestFile`, then continue reading the rest of the JAR archive. When the reader thread notified the `ManifestFile`, the original thread would wake up and do whatever it planned to do with the now fully prepared `ManifestFile` object. The first thread would work something like this:

```
ManifestFile m = new ManifestFile();
JarThread     t = new JarThread(m, in);
synchronized (m) {
  t.start();
  try {
    m.wait();
    // work with the manifest file...
  }
  catch (InterruptedException e) {
    // handle exception...
  }
}
```

The `JarThread` class would work like this:

```
ManifestFile theManifest;
InputStream in;

public JarThread(Manifest m, InputStream in) {
  theManifest = m;
  this.in= in;
}

public void run() {

  synchronized (theManifest) {
    // read the manifest from the stream in...
    theManifest.notify();
  }
  // read the rest of the stream...

}
```

Waiting and notification are more commonly used when multiple threads want to wait on the same object. For example, one thread may be reading a web server log file in which each line contains one entry to be processed. Each line is placed in a `java.util.Vector` as it's read. Several threads wait on the `Vector` to process

entries as they're added. Every time an entry is added, the waiting threads are notified using the notifyAll() method. If more than one thread is waiting on an
object, then notifyAll() is preferred since there's no way to select which thread
to notify. When all threads waiting on one object are notified, all will wake up and
try to get the lock on the object. However, only one can succeed immediately.
That one continues. The rest are blocked until the first one releases the lock. If
several threads are all waiting on the same object, a significant amount of time
may pass before the last one gets its turn at the lock on the object and continues.
It's entirely possible that in this time the object on which the thread was waiting
will once again have been placed in an unacceptable state. Thus you'll generally
put the call to wait() in a loop that checks the current state of the object. Do not
assume that just because the thread was notified, the object is now in the correct
state. Check it explicitly if you can't guarantee that once the object reaches a correct state it will never again reach an incorrect state. For example, this is how the
client threads waiting on the log file entries might look:

```
private Vector entries;

public void processEntry() {

  synchronized (entries) { // must synchronize on the object we wait on
    while (entries.size() == 0) {
      try {
        entries.wait();
        // We stopped waiting because entries.size() became non-zero
        // However we don't know that it's still non-zero so we
        // pass through the loop again to test its state now.
      }
      catch (InterruptedException e) {
        // If interrupted, the last entry has been processed so
        return;
      }
    }
    String entry = (String) entries.remove(entries.size()-1);
    // process this entry...
  }

}
```

The code reading the log file and adding entries to the vector might look something like this:

```
public void readLogFile() {

  String entry;

  while (true) {
    entry = log.getNextEntry();
```

```
      if (entry == null) {
        // There are no more entries to add to the vector so
        // we have to interrupt all threads that are still waiting.
        // Otherwise, they'll wait forever.
        for (int i = 0; i < threads.length; i++) threads[i].interrupt();
        break;
      }
      synchronized (entries) {
        entries.add(0, entry);
        entries.notifyAll();
      }
    }
  }
```

```
  }
```

Priority-based preemption

Since threads are preemptive between priorities, you do not need to worry about giving up time to higher-priority threads. A high-priority thread will preempt lower-priority threads when it's ready to run. However, when the high-priority thread finishes running or blocks, it generally won't be the same low-priority thread that runs next. Instead, most non-real-time VMs use a round-robin scheduler so that the lower-priority thread that hasn't run for the longest time will be run next.

For example, suppose there are three threads with priority 5 named A, B, and C running in a cooperatively scheduled virtual machine. None of them will yield or block. Thread A starts running first. It runs for a while, and is then preempted by thread D, which has priority 6, so A stops running. Eventually, thread D blocks, and the thread scheduler looks for the next highest-priority thread to run. It finds three: A, B, and C. Thread A has already had some time to run, so it picks B (or perhaps C; this doesn't have to go in alphabetical order). B runs for a while when thread D suddenly unblocks. Thread D still has higher priority so the virtual machine pauses thread B and lets D run for a while. Eventually, D blocks again, and the thread scheduler looks for another thread to run. Again, it finds A, B, and C, but at this point, A has had some time and B has had some time, but C hasn't had any. So the thread scheduler picks thread C to run. Thread C runs until it is once again preempted by thread D. When thread D blocks again, the thread scheduler finds three threads ready to run. Of the three, however, A ran the longest ago, so the scheduler picks thread A. From this point forward, every time D preempts and blocks and the scheduler needs a new thread to run, it will run the threads A, B, and C in that order, circling back around to A after C.

If you'd rather avoid explicit yielding, you can use a higher-priority thread to force the lower-priority threads to give up time to each other. In essence, you can use a high-priority thread scheduler of your own devising to make all threading preemptive. The trick is to run a high-priority thread that does nothing but sleep and wake up periodically, say every 100 milliseconds. This will split the lower-priority threads into 100-millisecond time slices. It isn't necessary for the thread that's doing the splitting to know anything about the threads it's preempting. It's simply enough that it exists and is running. Example 5-14 demonstrates with a TimeSlicer class that allows you to guarantee preemption of threads with priorities less than a fixed value every timeslice milliseconds.

Example 5-14. A Thread That Forces Preemptive Scheduling for Lower-Priority Threads

```
public class TimeSlicer extends Thread {

  private long timeslice;

  public TimeSlicer(long milliseconds, int priority) {

    this.timeslice = milliseconds;
    this.setPriority(priority);
    // If this is the last thread left, it should not
    // stop the VM from exiting
    this.setDaemon(true);

  }

  // Use maximum priority
  public TimeSlicer(long milliseconds) {
    this(milliseconds, 10);
  }

  // Use maximum priority and 100ms timeslices
  public TimeSlicer() {
    this(100, 10);
  }

  public void run() {

    while (true) {
      try {
        Thread.sleep(timeslice);
      }
      catch (InterruptedException e) {
      }
    }

  }

}
```

Finish

The final way a thread can give up control of the CPU in an orderly fashion is by finishing. When the run() method returns, the thread dies and other threads can take over. In network applications, this tends to occur with threads that wrap a single blocking operation, like downloading a file from a server, so that the rest of the application won't be blocked.

Otherwise, if your run() method is really so simple that it always finishes quickly enough without blocking, then there's a very real question of whether you should spawn a thread at all. There's a nontrivial amount of overhead for the virtual machine in setting up and tearing down threads. If a thread is finishing in a small fraction of a second anyway, chances are it would finish even faster if you used a simple method call rather than a separate thread.

Thread Pools

Adding multiple threads to a program dramatically improves performance, especially for I/O-bound programs such as most network programs. However, threads are not without overhead of their own. Starting a thread and cleaning up after a thread that has died takes a noticeable amount of work from the virtual machine, especially if a program spawns thousands of threads, not an unusual occurrence for even a low- to medium-volume network server. Even if the threads finish quickly, this can overload the garbage collector or other parts of the VM, and hurt performance, just like allocating thousands of any other kind of object every minute. Even more importantly, switching between running threads carries overhead. If the threads are blocking naturally—for instance, by waiting for data from the network—then there's no real penalty to this, but if the threads are CPU bound then the total task may finish more quickly if you can avoid a lot of switching between threads. Finally, and most importantly, although threads help make more efficient use of a computer's limited CPU resources, there's still only a finite amount of resources to go around. Once you've spawned enough threads to use all the computer's available idle time, spawning more threads just wastes MIPS and memory on thread management.

Fortunately, you can get the best of both worlds by reusing threads. You cannot restart a thread once it's died, but you can engineer your threads so that they don't die as soon as they've finished one task. Instead, you put all the tasks you need to accomplish in a queue or other data structure and have each thread retrieve a new task from the queue when it's completed its previous task. This is called *thread pooling*, and the data structure in which the tasks are kept is called the *pool*.

The simplest way to implement a thread pool is by using a fixed number of threads set when the pool is first created. When the pool is empty, each thread waits on the pool. When a task is added to the pool, all waiting threads are notified. When a thread finishes its assigned task, it goes back to the pool for a new task. If it doesn't get one, it waits until a new task is added to the pool.

An alternative is to put the threads themselves in the pool and have the main program pull threads out of the pool and assign them tasks. If no thread is in the pool when a task becomes necessary, the main program can spawn a new thread. As each thread finishes a task, it returns to the pool. (Imagine this scheme as a union hall in which new workers join the union only when full employment of current members is achieved.)

There are many data structures you can use for a pool, though a queue is probably the most reasonable so that tasks are performed in a first-in, first-out order. Whichever data structure you use to implement the pool, however, you have to be extremely careful about synchronization, since many threads will be interacting with it very close together in time. The simplest way to avoid problems is to use either a `java.util.Vector` (which is fully synchronized) or a synchronized `Collection` from the Java Collections API.

Let's look at an example. Suppose you want to gzip every file in the current directory using a `java.util.zip.GZIPOutputStream`. On the one hand, this is an I/O-heavy operation because all the files have to be read and written. On the other hand, data compression is a very CPU-intensive operation, so you don't want too many threads running at once. This is a good opportunity to use a thread pool. Each client thread will compress files while the main program will determine which files to compress. In this example, the main program is likely to significantly outpace the compressing threads since all it has to do is list the files in a directory. Therefore, it's not out of the question to fill the pool first, then start the threads that compress the files in the pool. However, to make this example as general as possible, we'll allow the main program to run in parallel with the zipping threads.

Example 5-15 shows the `GZipThread` class. It contains a private field called `pool` containing a reference to the pool. Here that field is declared to have `List` type, but it's always accessed in a strictly queue-like first-in, first-out order. The `run()` method removes `File` objects from the pool and gzips each one. If the pool is empty when the thread is ready to get something new from the pool, then the thread waits on the `pool` object.

Example 5-15. The GZipThread Class

```
import java.io.*;
import java.util.*;
import java.util.zip.*;
```

Example 5-15. The GZipThread Class (continued)

```java
public class GZipThread extends Thread {

  private List pool;
  private static int filesCompressed = 0;

  public GZipThread(List pool) {
    this.pool = pool;
  }

  private static synchronized void incrementFilesCompressed() {
    filesCompressed++;
  }

  public void run() {

    while (filesCompressed
     != GZipAllFiles.getNumberOfFilesToBeCompressed()) {

      File input = null;

      synchronized (pool) {
        while (pool.isEmpty()) {
          if (filesCompressed
           == GZipAllFiles.getNumberOfFilesToBeCompressed()) return;
          try {
            pool.wait();
          }
          catch (InterruptedException e) {
          }
        }

        input = (File) pool.remove(pool.size()-1);

      }

      // don't compress an already compressed file
      if (!input.getName().endsWith(".gz")) {

        try {
          InputStream in = new FileInputStream(input);
          in = new BufferedInputStream(in);

          File output = new File(input.getParent(), input.getName() + ".gz");
          if (!output.exists()) { // Don't overwrite an existing file
            OutputStream out = new FileOutputStream(output);
            out = new GZIPOutputStream(out);
            out = new BufferedOutputStream(out);
```

Example 5-15. The GZipThread Class (continued)

```
            int b;
            while ((b = in.read()) != -1) out.write(b);
            out.flush();
            out.close();
            incrementFilesCompressed();
            in.close();
          }
        }
        catch (IOException e) {
          System.err.println(e);
        }

      } // end if

    } // end while

  } // end run

} // end ZipThread
```

Example 5-16 is the main program. It constructs the pool as a `Vector` object, passes this to four newly constructed `GZipThread` objects, starts all four threads, and then iterates through all the files and directories listed on the command line. Those files and files in those directories are added to the pool for eventual processing by the four threads.

Example 5-16. The GZipThread User Interface Class

```
import java.io.*;
import java.util.*;


public class GZipAllFiles {

  public final static int THREAD_COUNT = 4;
  private static int filesToBeCompressed = -1;

  public static void main(String[] args) {

    Vector pool = new Vector();
    GZipThread[] threads = new GZipThread[THREAD_COUNT];

    for (int i = 0; i < threads.length; i++) {
      threads[i] = new GZipThread(pool);
      threads[i].start();
    }

    int totalFiles = 0;
```

Example 5-16. The GZipThread User Interface Class (continued)

```
    for (int i = 0; i < args.length; i++) {

      File f = new File(args[i]);
      if (f.exists()) {
        if (f.isDirectory()) {
          File[] files = f.listFiles();
          for (int j = 0; j < files.length; j++) {
            if (!files[j].isDirectory()) { // don't recurse directories
              totalFiles++;
              synchronized (pool) {
                pool.add(files[j]);
                pool.notifyAll();
              }
            }
          }
        }
        else {
          totalFiles++;
          synchronized (pool) {
            pool.add(0, f);
            pool.notifyAll();
          }
        }

      } // end if

    } // end for

    filesToBeCompressed = totalFiles;

    // make sure that any waiting thread knows that no
    // more files will be added to the pool
    for (int i = 0; i < threads.length; i++) {
      threads[i].interrupt();
    }

  }

  public static int getNumberOfFilesToBeCompressed() {
    return filesToBeCompressed;
  }

}
```

The big question here is how to tell the program that it's done and should exit.
You can't simply exit when all files have been added to the pool, because at that
point most of the files won't have been processed yet. Neither can you exit when

the pool is empty, because that may occur both at the start of the program (before any files have been placed in the pool) and at various intermediate times when not all files have yet been put in the pool but all files that have been put there are processed. The latter possibility also prevents the use of a simple counter scheme.

The solution adopted here is to separately track the number of files that need to be processed (GZipAllFiles.filesToBeCompressed) and the number of files actually processed (GZipThread.filesCompressed). When these two values match, all threads' run() methods return. Checks are made at the start of each of the while loops in the run() method to see whether it's necessary to continue. This scheme is preferred to the deprecated stop() method, because it won't suddenly stop the thread while it's halfway through compressing a file. This gives us much more fine-grained control over exactly when and where the thread stops.

Initially, GZipAllFiles.filesToBeCompressed is set to the impossible value –1. Only when the final number is known is it set to its real value. This prevents early coincidental matches between the number of files processed and the number of files to be processed. It's possible that when the final point of the main() method is reached, one or more of the threads is waiting. Thus we interrupt each of the threads (which has no effect if the thread is merely processing and not waiting or sleeping) to make sure it checks one last time.

The final note about this program is the private GZipThread. incrementFilesCompressed() method. This is synchronized to ensure that if two threads try to update the filesCompressed field at the same time, one will wait. Otherwise, the GZipThread.filesCompressed field could end up one short of the true value and the program would never exit. Since the method is static, all threads synchronize on the same Class object. A synchronized instance method wouldn't be sufficient here.

The complexity of determining when to stop this program is mostly atypical of the more heavily threaded programs you'll write because it does have such a definite ending point, the point at which all files are processed. Most network servers will continue indefinitely until such time as some part of the user interface shuts them down. Thus the real solution here is to provide some sort of simple user interface such as typing a period on a line by itself that ends the program.

NOTE   This chapter has been a whirlwind tour of threading in Java, covering the bare minimum you need to know to write multithreaded network programs. For a more detailed and comprehensive look with many more examples, you should check out *Java Threads*, by Scott Oaks and Henry Wong (O'Reilly & Associates, Inc., 1999). Once you've mastered that book, Doug Lea's *Concurrent Programming in Java* (Addison Wesley, 1999) provides a comprehensive look at the traps and pitfalls of concurrent programming from a design patterns perspective.

6

Looking Up Internet Addresses

DNS, IP Addresses, and All That

Devices connected to the Internet are called *nodes*. Nodes that are computers are called *hosts*. Each node or host is identified by at least one unique 32-bit number called an Internet address, an IP address, or a host address, depending on who you talk to. This takes up exactly four bytes of memory. An IP address is normally written as four unsigned bytes, each ranging from 0 to 255, with the most significant byte first. Bytes are separated by periods for the convenience of human eyes. For example, the address for *hermes.oit.unc.edu* is 152.2.21.1. This is called the *dotted quad* format.

IP addresses are great for computers, but they are a problem for humans, who have a hard time remembering long numbers. In the 1950s, it was discovered that most people could remember about seven digits per number; some can remember as many as nine, while others remember as few as five. This is why phone numbers are broken into three- and four-digit pieces with three-digit area codes.[*] Obviously an IP address, which can have as many as 12 decimal digits, is beyond the capacity of most humans to remember. I can remember about two IP addresses, and then only if I use both daily and the second is a simple permutation of the first.

To avoid the need to carry around Rolodexes full of IP addresses, the designers of the Internet invented the Domain Name System (DNS). DNS associates hostnames that humans can remember (like *hermes.oit.unc.edu*) with IP addresses that computers can remember (such as 152.2.21.1).[†] Most hosts have at least one

---

[*] G.A. Miller, "The Magic Number Seven, Plus or Minus Two: Some Limits on Our Capacity for Processing Information", *Psychological Review*, vol. 63, pp. 81-97.

[†] Colloquially, people often use "Internet address" to mean a hostname (or even an email address). In a book about network programming, it is crucial to be precise about addresses and hostnames. In this book, an address is always a numeric IP address, never a human-readable hostname.

hostname. An exception is made for computers that don't have a permanent IP address (like many PCs); since these computers don't have a permanent address, they can't be used as servers and therefore don't need a name, since nobody will need to refer to them.

Some machines have multiple names. For instance, *www.oreilly.com* and *helio.ora. com* are really the same SPARCstation in California. The name *www.oreilly.com* really refers to a web site rather than a particular machine. In the past, when this web site has moved from one machine to another, the name has been reassigned to the new machine so that it always points to the site's current server. This way, URLs around the Web don't need to be updated just because the site has moved to a new host. Some common names like *www* and *news* are often aliases for the machines providing those services. For example, *news.cloud9.net* is an alias for my ISP's news server. Since the server may change over time, the alias can move with the service.

On occasion, one name maps to multiple IP addresses. It is then the responsibility of the DNS server to randomly choose machines to respond to each request. This feature is most frequently used for very high traffic web sites, where it splits the load across multiple systems.

Every computer connected to the Internet should have access to a machine called a domain name server, generally a Unix box running special DNS software that knows the mappings between different hostnames and IP addresses. Most domain name servers know the addresses of only the hosts on their local network, plus the addresses of a few domain name servers at other sites. If a client asks for the address of a machine outside the local domain, then the local domain name server asks a domain name server at the remote location and relays the answer to the requester.*

Most of the time, you can use hostnames and let DNS handle the translation to IP addresses. As long as you can connect to a domain name server, you don't need to worry about the details of how names and addresses are passed between your machine, the local domain name server, and the rest of the Internet. However, you will need to have access to at least one domain name server to use the examples in this chapter and most of the rest of this book. These programs will not work on a standalone Mac or PC. Your machine must be connected to the Internet.

---

* For more information about DNS, see Albitz, Paul and Cricket Liu, *DNS and BIND*, 3rd edition (O'Reilly & Associates, Inc., 1998).

IPv6 and 128-bit Addresses

The current IP address standard uses 32 bits, which is enough to address more than four billion computers, almost one for every person on Earth. You'd think it would be enough to handle even the explosive growth of the Internet for some time. However, we're currently in the middle of an address shortage. The cause of the address shortage is that the available addressees aren't allocated very efficiently. Because of the way addresses are parceled out, many organizations possess at least 256 numbers even though they need only a few dozen. Other organizations have blocks of 65,536 even if they need only a few thousand. And a few dozen organizations have blocks of more than 16 million, even though they don't use anywhere near that many. Consequently, there's a lot of waste, and the addresses are beginning to run out.

Don't worry too much, though. A series of stopgap measures have been put in place to allocate addresses more efficiently; this should get the Internet through the next couple of years. After that, a new standard called IPv6 will begin using 16-byte, 128-bit addresses. This expands the available address space to 2^{128} or 1.6043703E32 different addresses. It's not enough to address every molecule in the universe, but it should be enough to get us well into the 21st century. IPv6 has been designed to be backward compatible with 32-bit IP addresses to ease the transition.

Java 1.3 and earlier versions don't yet support 128-bit IP addresses, nor are these addresses in common use. However, Java's networking classes have been designed with 128-bit addresses in mind. When IPv6 does begin moving out of the labs and into the real world, it will be easy for Sun to modify the `java.net` classes to support the new address format, and almost everything in this book will continue to work.

The InetAddress Class

The `java.net.InetAddress` class is Java's encapsulation of an IP address. It is used by most of the other networking classes, including `Socket`, `ServerSocket`, `URL`, `DatagramSocket`, `DatagramPacket`, and more.

```
public final class InetAddress extends Object implements Serializable
```

This class represents an Internet address as two fields: `hostName` (a `String`) and `address` (an `int`). `hostName` contains the name of the host; for example, *www. oreilly.com*. `address` contains the 32-bit IP address. These fields are not public, so you can't access them directly. It will probably be necessary to change this representation to a byte array when 16-byte IPv6 addresses come into use. However, if you always use the `InetAddress` class to represent addresses, the changeover should not affect you; the class shields you from the details of how addresses are implemented.

Creating New InetAddress Objects

There are no public constructors in the `InetAddress` class. However, `InetAddress` has three static methods that return suitably initialized `InetAddress` objects, given a little information. They are:

```
public static InetAddress InetAddress.getByName(String hostName)
  throws UnknownHostException
public static InetAddress[] InetAddress.getAllByName(String hostName)
  throws UnknownHostException
public static InetAddress InetAddress.getLocalHost()
  throws UnknownHostException
```

All three of these may make a connection to the local DNS server to fill out the information in the `InetAddress` object. This has a number of possibly unexpected implications, among them that these methods may throw security exceptions if the connection to the DNS server is prohibited. Furthermore, invoking one of these methods may cause a host that uses a dialup PPP or SLIP connection to dial into its provider if it isn't already connected. The key thing to remember is that these are not constructors; they do not simply use their arguments to set the internal fields. They actually make network connections to retrieve all the information they need. The other methods in this class such as **getAddress()** and **getHostName()** mostly work with the information provided by one of these three methods. They do not make network connections; and on the rare occasions they do, they do not throw any exceptions. Only these three methods have to go outside Java and the local system to get their work done.

public static InetAddress InetAddress.getByName(String hostName) throws UnknownHostException

The method you'll use most frequently is **InetAddress.getByName()**. This is a static method that takes the hostname you're looking for as its argument. It looks up the host's IP address using DNS. Call **getByName()** like this:

```
java.net.InetAddress address =
  java.net.InetAddress.getByName("www.oreilly.com");
```

If you have already imported the **java.net.InetAddress** class, which will almost always be the case, you can call **getByName()** like this:

```
InetAddress address = InetAddress.getByName("www.oreilly.com");
```

In the rest of this book, I will assume that there is an `import java.net.*;` statement at the top of the program containing each code fragment, as well as any other necessary `import` statements.

The `InetAddress.getByName()` method throws an `UnknownHostException` if the host can't be found, so you need to declare that the method making the call throws `UnknownHostException` (or its superclass, `IOException`) or wrap it in a `try` block like this:

```
try {
  InetAddress address = InetAddress.getByName("www.oreilly.com");
  System.out.println(address);
}
catch (UnknownHostException e) {
  System.out.println("Could not find www.oreilly.com");
}
```

Example 6-1 is a complete program that creates an `InetAddress` object for *www. oreilly.com* and prints it out.

Example 6-1. A Program That Prints the Address of www.oreilly.com

```
import java.net.*;

public class OReillyByName {

  public static void main (String[] args) {

    try {
      InetAddress address = InetAddress.getByName("www.oreilly.com");
      System.out.println(address);
    }
    catch (UnknownHostException e) {
      System.out.println("Could not find www.oreilly.com");
    }

  }

}
```

Here's the result:

```
% java OReillyByName
www.oreilly.com/204.148.40.9
```

On rare occasions, you will need to connect to a machine that does not have a hostname. In this case, you can pass a `String` containing the dotted quad form of the IP address to `InetAddress.getByName()`:

```
InetAddress address = InetAddress.getByName("204.148.40.9");
```

Example 6-2 uses the IP address for *www.oreilly.com* instead of the name.

Example 6-2. A Program That Prints the Address of 204.148.40.9

```
import java.net.*;

public class OReillyByAddress {

  public static void main (String[] args) {

    try {
      InetAddress address = InetAddress.getByName("204.148.40.9");
      System.out.println(address);
    }
    catch (UnknownHostException e) {
      System.out.println("Could not find 204.148.40.9");
    }

  }

}
```

Here's the result:

```
% java OReillyByAddress
helio.ora.com/204.148.40.9
```

In Java 1.1 and later, when you call getByName() with an IP address as an argument, it creates an InetAddress object for the requested IP address without checking with DNS. This means it's possible to create InetAddress objects for hosts that don't really exist and that you can't connect to. The hostname of an InetAddress object created from a dotted quad string is initially set to that dotted quad string. A DNS lookup for the actual hostname is performed only when the hostname is requested, either explicitly via getAddress() or implicitly through toString(). That's how *helio.ora.com* is determined from the dotted quad address 204.148.40.9. If at the time the hostname is requested and a DNS lookup is finally performed, the host with the specified IP address can't be found, then the hostname remains the original dotted quad string. However, no UnknownHostException is thrown.

Hostnames are much more stable than IP addresses. Some services such as the MIT FAQ archives have lived at the same hostname (*rtfm.mit.edu*) for years but switched IP addresses several times. If you have a choice between using a hostname like *www.oreilly.com* or an IP address like 204.148.40.9, always choose the hostname. Use an IP address only when a hostname is not available.

public static InetAddress[ ] InetAddress.getAllByName
(String hostName) throws UnknownHostException

Some computers have more than one Internet address. Given a hostname, `InetAddress.getAllByName()` returns an array that contains all the addresses corresponding to that name. Its use is straightforward:

```
InetAddress[] addresses = InetAddress.getAllByName("www.apple.com");
```

Like `InetAddress.getByName()`, `InetAddress.getAllByName()` can throw an `UnknownHostException`, so you need to enclose it in a `try` block or declare that your method throws `UnknownHostException`. Example 6-3 demonstrates by returning a complete list of the IP addresses for *www.microsoft.com.*

Example 6-3. A Program That Prints All the Addresses of www.microsoft.com

```java
import java.net.*;

public class AllAddressesOfMicrosoft {

  public static void main (String[] args) {

    try {
      InetAddress[] addresses =
       InetAddress.getAllByName("www.microsoft.com");
      for (int i = 0; i < addresses.length; i++) {
        System.out.println(addresses[i]);
      }
    }
    catch (UnknownHostException e) {
      System.out.println("Could not find www.microsoft.com");
    }

  }

}
```

Here's the result:

```
% java AllAddressesOfMicrosoft
www.microsoft.com/207.46.131.15
www.microsoft.com/207.46.131.137
www.microsoft.com/207.46.130.14
www.microsoft.com/207.46.130.149
www.microsoft.com/207.46.130.150
www.microsoft.com/207.46.131.13
```

It appears that *www.microsoft.com* has six IP addresses. Hosts with more than one address are the exception rather than the rule. Most hosts with multiple IP addresses are, like *www.microsoft.com,* very high volume web servers. Even in those cases, you rarely need to know more than one address.

public static InetAddress InetAddress.getLocalHost( ) throws UnknownHostException

The `InetAddress` class contains one final means of getting an `InetAddress` object. The static method `InetAddress.getLocalHost()` returns the `Inet-Address` of the machine on which it's running. Like `InetAddress.getByName()` and `InetAddress.getAllByName()`, it throws an `UnknownHostException` when it can't find the address of the local machine. Its use is straightforward:

```
InetAddress thisComputer = InetAddress.getLocalHost();
```

Example 6-4 prints the address of the machine it's run on.

Example 6-4. Find the Address of the Local Machine

```
import java.net.*;

public class MyAddress {

  public static void main (String[] args) {

    try {
      InetAddress address = InetAddress.getLocalHost();
      System.out.println(address);
    }
    catch (UnknownHostException e) {
      System.out.println("Could not find this computer's address.");
    }

  }

}
```

Here's the output; I ran the program on *titan.oit.unc.edu:*

```
% java MyAddress
titan.oit.unc.edu/152.2.22.14
```

Whether you see a fully qualified name like *titan.oit.unc.edu* or a partial name like *titan* depends on what the local DNS server returns for hosts in the local domain.

Security issues

Creating a new `InetAddress` object from a hostname is considered a potentially insecure operation because it requires a DNS lookup. An untrusted applet under the control of the default security manager will be allowed to get only the IP address of the host it came from (its codebase) and possibly the local host. (Netscape 4.6 allows untrusted applets to get the name and IP address of the local host, while IE5 allows applets to get only the loopback address and name local-host/127.0.0.1 for the local host.) An untrusted applet is not allowed to create an `InetAddress` object from any other hostname. This is true whether it uses the `InetAddress.getByName()` method, the `InetAddress.getAllByName()` method, the `InetAddress.getLocalHost()` method, or something else. Netscape 4.6 does allow untrusted applets to construct `InetAddress` objects from arbitrary dotted quad strings, though it will not perform a DNS lookup for such an address. IE5 does not allow even this.

An untrusted applet is not allowed to perform arbitrary DNS lookups for third-party hosts because of the prohibition against making network connections to hosts other than the codebase. Arbitrary DNS lookups would open a covert channel by which an applet could talk to third-party hosts. For instance, suppose an applet downloaded from *www.bigisp.com* wants to send the message "macfaq.dialup.cloud9.net is vulnerable" to *crackersinc.com*. All it has to do is request DNS information for *macfaq.dialup.cloud9.net.is.vulnerable.crackersinc.com*. To resolve that hostname, the applet would contact the local DNS server. The local DNS server would contact the DNS server at *crackersinc.com*. Even though these hosts don't exist, the cracker can inspect the DNS error log for *crackersinc.com* to retrieve the message. This scheme could be considerably more sophisticated with compression, error correction, encryption, custom DNS servers that email the messages to a fourth site, and more, but this is good enough for a proof of concept. Arbitrary DNS lookups are prohibited because arbitrary DNS lookups leak information.

An untrusted applet is allowed to call `InetAddress.getLocalHost()`. However, this should always return a hostname of localhost and an IP address of 127.0.0.1. This is a special hostname and IP address called the loopback address. No matter which machine you use this hostname or IP address on, it always refers to the current machine. No specific DNS resolution is necessary. The reason for prohibiting the applet from finding out the true hostname and address is that the computer on which the applet is running may be deliberately hidden behind a firewall and a proxy server. In this case, an applet should not be a channel for information the web server doesn't already have. (Netscape 4.6 does allow a little more information about the local host to leak out, including its IP address, but only if no DNS lookup is required to get this information.)

Like all security checks, prohibitions against DNS resolutions can be relaxed for trusted applets. The specific `SecurityManager` method used to test whether a host can be resolved is `checkConnect()`:

```
public void checkConnect(String host, int port)
```

When the `port` argument is –1, this method checks whether DNS may be invoked to resolve the specified host. (If the `port` argument is greater than –1, this method checks whether a connection to the named host on the specified port is allowed.) The `host` argument may be either a hostname like *www.oreilly.com* or a dotted quad IP address like 204.148.40.9.

In Java 1.2 and later, you can grant an applet permission to resolve a host by using the Policy Tool to add a `java.net.SocketPermission` with the action connect and the target being the name of the host you want to allow the applet to resolve. You can use the asterisk wildcard (*) to allow all hosts in particular domains to be resolved. For example, setting the target to *.oreilly.com allows the applet to resolve the hosts *www.oreilly.com, java.oreilly.com, perl.oreilly.com,* and all others in the *oreilly.com* domain. Although you'll generally use a hostname to set permissions, Java checks against the actual IP addresses. In this example, that also allows hosts in the *ora.com* domain to be resolved because this is simply an alias for *oreilly.com* with the same range of IP addresses. To allow all hosts in all domains to be resolved, just set the target to *. Figure 6-1 demonstrates.

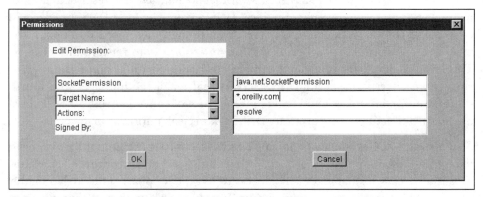

Figure 6-1. Using the Policy Tool to grant DNS resolution permission to all applets

Other sources of InetAddress objects

Several other methods in the `java.net` package also return `InetAddress` objects. These include the `getAddress()` method of `DatagramPacket`, the `getLocalAddress()` method of `DatagramPacket`, the `getInetAddress()` method of `Socket`, the `getLocalAddress()` method of `Socket`, the `getInetAddress()` method of `SocketImpl`, the `getInetAddress()` method of `ServerSocket`, and the `getInterface()` method of `MulticastSocket`. Each of these will be discussed, along with its respective class, in later chapters.

Getter Methods

The `InetAddress` class contains three getter methods that return the hostname as a string and the IP address as both a string and a byte array. These are:

```
public String getHostName()
public byte[] getAddress()
public String getHostAddress()
```

There are no corresponding `setHostName()` and `setAddress()` methods, which means that packages outside of `java.net` can't change an `InetAddress` object's fields behind its back. Therefore, Java can guarantee that the hostname and the IP address match each other.

public String getHostName( )

The `getHostName()` method returns a `String` that contains the name of the host with the IP address represented by this `InetAddress` object. If the machine in question doesn't have a hostname or if applet security prevents the name from being determined, then a dotted quad format of the numeric IP address is returned. For example:

```
InetAddress machine = InetAddress.getLocalHost();
String localhost = machine.getHostName();
```

In some cases, you may only see a partially qualified name like *titan* instead of the full name like *titan.oit.unc.edu*. The details depend on how the local DNS behaves when resolving local hostnames.

The `getHostName()` method is particularly useful when you're starting with a dotted quad IP address rather than the hostname. Example 6-5 converts the dotted quad address 152.2.22.3 into a hostname by using `InetAddress.getByName()` and then applying `getHostName()` on the resulting object.

Example 6-5. Given the Address, Find the Hostname

```
import java.net.*;


public class ReverseTest {

  public static void main (String[] args) {

    try {
      InetAddress ia = InetAddress.getByName("152.2.22.3");
      System.out.println(ia.getHostName());
    }
```

Example 6-5. Given the Address, Find the Hostname (continued)

```
  catch (Exception e) {
    System.err.println(e);
  }


 }


}
```

Here's the result:

```
% java ReverseTest
helios.oit.unc.edu
```

public String getHostAddress( )

The getHostAddress() method returns a string containing the dotted quad format of the IP address. Example 6-6 uses this method to print the IP address of the local machine in the customary format.

Example 6-6. Find the IP Address of the Local Machine

```
import java.net.*;


public class MyDottedQuadAddress {

  public static void main (String[] args) {

    try {
      InetAddress me = InetAddress.getLocalHost();
      String dottedQuad = me.getHostAddress();
      System.out.println("My address is " + dottedQuad);
    }
    catch (UnknownHostException e) {
      System.out.println("I'm sorry. I don't know my own address.");
    }

  }

}
```

Here's the result:

```
% java MyDottedQuadAddress
My address is 152.2.22.14.
```

Of course, the exact output depends on where the program is run.

public byte[ ] getAddress( )

If you want to know the IP address of a machine (and you rarely do), getAddress() lsreturns an IP address as an array of bytes in network byte order. The most significant byte (i.e., the first byte in the address's dotted quad form) is the first byte in the array, or element zero—remember, Java array indices start with zero. To be ready for 128-bit IP addresses, try not to assume anything about the length of this array. While currently this array has a length of 4 bytes, future implementations are likely to return arrays with 16 bytes. If you need to know the length of the array, use the array's length field:

```
InetAddress me = InetAddress.getLocalHost();
byte[] address = me.getAddress());
```

The bytes returned are unsigned, which poses a problem. Unlike C, Java doesn't have an unsigned byte primitive data type. Bytes with values higher than 127 are treated as negative numbers. Therefore, if you want to do anything with the bytes returned by getAddress(), you need to promote the bytes to ints and make appropriate adjustments. Here's one way to do it:

```
int unsignedByte = signedByte < 0 ? signedByte + 256 : signedByte;
```

Here signedByte may be either positive or negative. The conditional operator ? tests whether signedByte is negative. If it is, 256 is added to signedByte to make it positive. Otherwise, it's left alone. signedByte is automatically promoted to an int before the addition is performed so wraparound is not a problem.

One reason to look at the raw bytes of an IP address is to determine the type of the address. As mentioned in Chapter 2, *Basic Network Concepts*, Class A addresses always begin with a 0 bit. Class B addresses begin with the two bits 10. Class C addresses begin with the three bits 110. Class D addresses begin with the four bits 1110, and Class E addresses begin with the five bits 11110. Figure 6-2 summarizes.

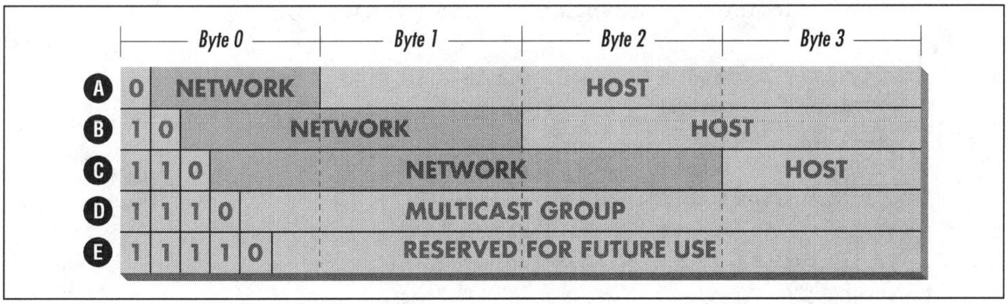

Figure 6-2. The five address classes as divided into class ID, network ID, and host ID

Class D addresses are multicast addresses, used to refer not to a particular host but rather to a group of hosts that have chosen to join a particular multicast group.

This will be discussed further in Chapter 14, *Multicast Sockets*. The `InetAddress` class contains a method that tells you whether a particular address is a multicast address:

```
public boolean isMulticastAddress()
```

It operates merely by using the bitwise operators to compare the first 4 bits of the address to 1110 and returning true if they match, false otherwise. To retrieve the other information that's implicit in the address, you'll have to do your own comparisons. For example, you can test the first byte of the address to determine the address class. You can test the number of bytes in the array returned by `getAddress()` to determine whether you're dealing with an IPv4 or IPv6 address. Example 6-7 demonstrates.

Example 6-7. Print the IP Address of the Local Machine

```java
import java.net.*;


public class AddressTests {

  public static int getVersion(InetAddress ia) {

    byte[] address = ia.getAddress();
    if (address.length == 4) return 4;
    else if (address.length == 16) return 6;
    else return -1;

  }


  public static char getClass(InetAddress ia) {

    byte[] address = ia.getAddress();
    if (address.length != 4) {
      throw new IllegalArgumentException("No IPv6 addresses!");
    }

    int firstByte = address[0];
    if ((firstByte & 0x80) == 0) return 'A';
    else if ((firstByte & 0xC0) == 0x80) return 'B';
    else if ((firstByte & 0xE0) == 0xC0) return 'C';
    else if ((firstByte & 0xF0) == 0xE0) return 'D';
    else if ((firstByte & 0xF8) == 0xF0) return 'E';
    else return 'F';

  }

}
```

Object Methods

Like every other class, `java.net.InetAddress` inherits from `java.lang.Object`. Thus it has access to all the methods of that class. It overrides three methods to provide more specialized behavior:

```
public boolean equals(Object o)
public int hashCode()
public String toString()
```

public boolean equals(Object o)

An object is equal to an `InetAddress` object only if it is itself an instance of the `InetAddress` class and it has the same IP address. It does not need to have the same hostname. Thus an `InetAddress` object for *www.oreilly.com* is equal to an `InetAddress` object for *helio.ora.com* since both names refer to the same IP address. Example 6-8 creates `InetAddress` objects for *www.oreilly.com* and *helio.ora.com* and then tells you whether they're the same machine.

Example 6-8. Are www.oreilly.com and helio.ora.com the Same?

```
import java.net.*;

public class OReillyAliases {

  public static void main (String args[]) {

    try {
      InetAddress oreilly = InetAddress.getByName("www.oreilly.com");
      InetAddress helio = InetAddress.getByName("helio.ora.com");
      if (oreilly.equals(helio)) {
        System.out.println
          ("www.oreilly.com is the same as helio.ora.com");
      }
      else {
        System.out.println
          ("www.oreilly.com is not the same as helio.ora.com");
      }
    }
    catch (UnknownHostException e) {
      System.out.println("Host lookup failed.");
    }

  }

}
```

When you run this program, you discover:

```
% java OReillyAliases
www.oreilly.com is the same as helio.ora.com
```

public int hashCode( )

The `hashCode()` method returns an `int` that is needed when `InetAddress` objects are used as keys in hash tables. This is called by the various methods of `java.util.Hashtable`. You will almost certainly not need to call this method directly.

Currently, the `int` that `hashCode()` returns is simply the four bytes of the IP address converted to an `int`. This is different for every two unequal `InetAddress` objects (where unequal has the meaning provided by the `equals()` method). If two `InetAddress` objects have the same address, then they have the same hash code, even if their hostnames are different. Therefore, if you try to store two objects in a `Hashtable` using equivalent `InetAddress` objects as a key (for example, the `InetAddress` objects for *www.oreilly.com* and *helio.ora.com*), the second will overwrite the first. If this is a problem, use the `String` returned by `getHostName()` as the key instead of the `InetAddress` itself.

The `hashCode()` method is the single method in the `InetAddress` class that can't be easily modified to work with 16-byte addresses. The algorithm to calculate hash codes may become considerably more complex when 16-byte addresses are supported. Do not write code that depends on the `hashCode()` method returning the IP address.

public String toString( )

Like all good classes, `java.net.InetAddress` has a `toString()` method that returns a short text representation of the object. Example 6-1 through Example 6-4 all implicitly called this method when passing `InetAddress` objects to `System.out.println()`. As you saw, the string produced by `toString()` has the form:

> *host name/dotted quad address*

Not all `InetAddress` objects have hostnames. If one doesn't, then the dotted quad format of the IP address will be substituted. This format isn't particularly useful, so you'll probably never call `toString()` explicitly. If you do, the syntax is simple:

```
InetAddress thisComputer = InetAddress.getLocalHost();
String address = thisComputer.toString();
```

Some Useful Programs

You now know everything there is to know about the `java.net.InetAddress` class. The tools in this class alone let you write some genuinely useful programs. Here we'll look at two: one that queries your domain name server interactively and another that can improve the performance of your web server by processing log files offline.

HostLookup

nslookup is a Unix utility that converts hostnames to IP addresses and IP addresses to hostnames. It has two modes: interactive and command line. If you enter a host-name on the command line, *nslookup* prints the IP address of that host. If you enter an IP address on the command line, *nslookup* prints the hostname. If no hostname or IP address is entered on the command line, *nslookup* enters interactive mode, in which it reads hostnames and IP addresses from standard input and echoes back the corresponding IP addresses and hostnames until you type "exit". Example 6-9 is a simple character mode application called `HostLookup`, which emulates *nslookup*. It doesn't implement any of *nslookup*'s more complex features, but it does enough to be useful.

Example 6-9. An nslookup Clone

```
import java.net.*;
import java.io.*;

public class HostLookup {

  public static void main (String[] args) {

    if (args.length > 0) { // use command line
      for (int i = 0; i < args.length; i++) {
        System.out.println(lookup(args[i]));
      }
    }
    else {
      BufferedReader in = new BufferedReader(
                          new InputStreamReader(System.in));
      System.out.println(
        "Enter names and IP addresses. Enter \"exit\" to quit.");
      try {
        while (true) {
          String host = in.readLine();
          if (host.equals("exit")) break;
          System.out.println(lookup(host));
        }
      }
    }
```

Example 6-9. An nslookup Clone (continued)

```
    catch (IOException e) {
      System.err.println(e);
    }

  }

} /* end main */


private static String lookup(String host) {

  InetAddress thisComputer;
  byte[] address;

  // get the bytes of the IP address
  try {
    thisComputer = InetAddress.getByName(host);
    address = thisComputer.getAddress();
  }
  catch (UnknownHostException e) {
    return "Cannot find host " + host;
  }

  if (isHostName(host)) {
    // Print the IP address
    String dottedQuad = "";
    for (int i = 0; i < address.length; i++) {
      int unsignedByte = address[i] < 0 ? address[i] + 256 : address[i];
      dottedQuad += unsignedByte;
      if (i != address.length-1) dottedQuad += ".";
    }
    return dottedQuad;
  }
  else {  // this is an IP address
    return thisComputer.getHostName();
  }

}  // end lookup

private static boolean isHostName(String host) {

  char[] ca = host.toCharArray();
  // if we see a character that is neither a digit nor a period
  // then host is probably a host name
  for (int i = 0; i < ca.length; i++) {
    if (!Character.isDigit(ca[i])) {
      if (ca[i] != '.') return true;
    }
```

Example 6-9. An nslookup Clone (continued)

```
    }

    // Everything was either a digit or a period
    // so host looks like an IP address in dotted quad format
    return false;

  }  // end isHostName

} // end HostLookup
```

Here's some sample output; input typed by the user is in bold:

```
% java HostLookup utopia.poly.edu
128.238.3.21
% java HostLookup 128.238.3.21
utopia.poly.edu
% java HostLookup
Enter names and IP addresses. Enter "exit" to quit.
cs.nyu.edu
128.122.80.78
199.1.32.90
star.blackstar.com
localhost
127.0.0.1
cs.cmu.edu
128.2.222.173
rtfm.mit.edu
18.181.0.29
star.blackstar.com
199.1.32.90
cs.med.edu
Cannot find host cs.med.edu
exit
```

The HostLookup program is built using three methods: main(), lookup(), and isHostName(). The main() method determines whether there are command-line arguments. If there are command-line arguments, main() calls lookup() to process each one. If there are no command-line arguments, it chains a BufferedReader to an InputStreamReader chained to System.in and reads input from the user with the readLine() method. (The warning in Chapter 4, *Java I/O*, about this method doesn't apply here because we're reading from the console, not a network connection.) If the line is "exit", then the program exits. Otherwise, the line is assumed to be a hostname or IP address, and is passed to the lookup() method.

The lookup() method uses InetAddress.getByName() to find the requested host, regardless of the input's format; remember that getByName() doesn't care if its argument is a name or a dotted quad address. If getByName() fails, then lookup() returns a failure message. Otherwise, it gets the address of the requested system. Then lookup() calls isHostName() to determine whether the input string host is a hostname like *cs.nyu.edu* or a dotted quad format IP address like 128.122.153.70. isHostName() looks at each character of the string; if all the characters are digits or periods, isHostName() guesses that the string is a numeric IP address and returns false. Otherwise, isHostName() guesses that the string is a hostname and returns true. What if the string is neither? That is very unlikely, since if the string is neither a hostname nor an address, getByName() won't be able to do a lookup and will throw an exception. However, it would not be difficult to add a test making sure that the string looks valid; this is left as an exercise for the reader. If the user types a hostname, lookup() returns the corresponding dotted quad address; we have already saved the address in the byte array address[], and the only complication is making sure that we don't treat byte values from 128 to 255 as negative numbers. If the user types an IP address, then we use the getHostName() method to look up the hostname corresponding to the address, and return it.

Processing Web Server Log Files

Web server logs track the hosts that access a web site. By default, the log reports the IP addresses of the sites that connect to the server. However, you can often get more information from the names of those sites than from their IP addresses. Most web servers have an option to store hostnames instead of IP addresses, but this can hurt performance because the server needs to make a DNS request for each hit. It is much more efficient to log the IP addresses and convert them to hostnames at a later time. This task can be done when the server isn't busy or even on another machine completely. Example 6-10 is a program called Weblog that reads a web server log file and prints each line with IP addresses converted to hostnames.

Most web servers have standardized on the common log file format, although there are exceptions; if your web server is one of those exceptions, you'll have to modify this program. A typical line in the common log file format looks like this:

```
205.160.186.76 unknown - [17/Jun/1999:22:53:58 -0500] "GET /bgs/greenbg.gif HTTP
1.0" 200 50
```

This means that a web browser at IP address 205.160.186.76 requested the file */bgs/greenbg.gif* from this web server at 11:53 P.M. (and 58 seconds) on June 17, 1999. The file was found (response code 200), and 50 bytes of data were successfully transferred to the browser.

The first field is the IP address or, if DNS resolution is turned on, the hostname from which the connection was made. This is followed by a space. Therefore, for our purposes, parsing the log file is easy: everything before the first space is the IP address, and everything after it does not need to be changed.

The Common Log File Format

If you want to expand Weblog into a more general web server log processor, you need a little more information about the common log file format. A line in the file has the format:

```
remotehost rfc931 authuser [date] "request" status bytes
```

remotehost
> remotehost is either the hostname or IP address from which the browser connected.

rfc931
> rfc931 is the username of the user on the remote system, as specified by Internet protocol RFC 931. Very few browsers send this information, so it's almost always either unknown or a dash. This is followed by a space.

authuser
> authuser is the authenticated username as specified by RFC 931. Once again, this is not supported by most popular browsers or client systems; this field usually is filled in with a dash, followed by a space.

[date]
> The date and time of the request are given in brackets. This is the local system time when the request was made. Days are a two-digit number ranging from 01 to 31. The month is Jan, Feb, Mar, Apr, May, Jun, Jul, Aug, Sep, Oct, Nov, or Dec. The year is given by four digits. This is followed by a colon, then the hour (from 00 to 23), another colon, then two digits signifying the minute (00 to 59), then a colon, then two digits signifying the seconds (00 to 59). Then comes the closing bracket and another space.

"request"
> This is the request line exactly as it came from the client. It is enclosed in quotation marks because it may contain embedded spaces. It is not guaranteed to be a valid HTTP request since client software may misbehave.

status
> This is a numeric HTTP status code returned to the client. A list of HTTP 1.0 status codes is given in Chapter 3, *Basic Web Concepts*. The most common response is 200, which means the request was successfully processed.

bytes
> This is the number of bytes of data that was sent to the client as a result of this request.

The dotted quad format IP address is converted into a hostname using the usual methods of `java.net.InetAddress`. Example 6-10 shows the code.

Example 6-10. Process Web Server Log Files

```java
import java.net.*;
import java.io.*;
import java.util.*;
import com.macfaq.io.SafeBufferedReader;


public class Weblog {

  public static void main(String[] args) {

    Date start = new Date();
    try {
      FileInputStream fin =  new FileInputStream(args[0]);
      Reader in = new InputStreamReader(fin);
      SafeBufferedReader bin = new SafeBufferedReader(in);

      String entry = null;
      while ((entry = bin.readLine()) != null) {

        // separate out the IP address
        int index = entry.indexOf(' ', 0);
        String ip = entry.substring(0, index);
        String theRest = entry.substring(index, entry.length());

        // find the host name and print it out
        try {
          InetAddress address = InetAddress.getByName(ip);
          System.out.println(address.getHostName() + theRest);
        }
        catch (UnknownHostException e) {
          System.out.println(entry);
        }

      } // end while
    }
    catch (IOException e) {
      System.out.println("Exception: " + e);
    }

    Date end = new Date();
    long elapsedTime = (end.getTime()-start.getTime())/1000;
    System.out.println("Elapsed time: " + elapsedTime + " seconds");

  } // end main


}
```

The name of the file to be processed is passed to `Weblog` as the first argument on the command line. A `FileInputStream fin` is opened from this file, and an `InputStreamReader` is chained to `fin`. This `InputStreamReader` is buffered by chaining it to an instance of the `SafeBufferedReader` class developed in Chapter 4. The file is processed line by line in a `while` loop.

Each pass through the loop places one line in the `String` variable `entry`. `entry` is then split into two substrings: `ip`, which contains everything before the first space, and `theRest`, which is everything after the first space. The position of the first space is determined by `entry.indexOf(" ", 0)`. `ip` is converted to an `InetAddress` object using `getByName()`. The hostname is then looked up by `getHostName()`. Finally, the hostname, a space, and everything else on the line (`theRest`) are printed on `System.out`. Output can be sent to a new file through the standard means for redirecting output.

`Weblog` is more efficient than you might expect. Most web browsers generate multiple log file entries per page served, since there's an entry in the log not just for the page itself but for each graphic on the page. And many web browsers request multiple pages while visiting a site. DNS lookups are expensive, and it simply doesn't make sense to look up each of those sites every time it appears in the log file. The `InetAddress` class caches requested addresses. If the same address is requested again, it can be retrieved from the cache much more quickly than from DNS.

Nonetheless, this program could certainly be faster. In my initial tests, it took more than a second per log entry. (Exact numbers depend on the speed of your network connection, the speed of both local and remote DNS servers you access, and network congestion when the program is run.) It spends a huge amount of time just sitting and waiting for DNS requests to return. Of course, this is exactly the problem multithreading is designed to solve. One main thread can read the log file and pass off individual entries to other threads for processing.

A thread pool is absolutely necessary here. Over the space of a few days, even low volume web servers can easily generate a log file with hundreds of thousands of lines. Trying to process such a log file by spawning a new thread for each entry would rapidly bring even the strongest virtual machine to its knees, especially since the main thread can read log file entries much faster than individual threads can resolve domain names and die. Consequently, reusing threads is essential here. The number of threads is stored in a tunable parameter, `numberOfThreads`, so that it can be adjusted to fit the VM and network stack. (Launching too many simultaneous DNS requests can also cause problems.)

This program is now divided into two classes. The first class, `PooledWeblog`, shown in Example 6-11, contains the `main()` method and the `processLogFile()`

method. It also holds the resources that need to be shared among the threads. These are the pool, implemented as a synchronized `LinkedList` from the Java Collections API, and the output log, implemented as a `BufferedWriter` named out. Individual threads will have direct access to the pool but will have to pass through `PooledWeblog`'s `log()` method to write output.

The key method is `processLogFile()`. As before, this method reads from the underlying log file. However, each entry is placed in the `entries` pool rather than being immediately processed. Because this method is likely to run much more quickly than the threads that have to access DNS, it yields after reading each entry. Furthermore, it goes to sleep if there are more entries in the pool than threads available to process them. The amount of time it sleeps depends on the number of threads. This will avoid using excessive amounts of memory for very large log files. When the last entry is read, the `finished` flag is set to `true` to tell the threads that they can die once they've completed their work.

Example 6-11. PooledWebLog

```
import java.io.*;
import java.util.*;
import com.macfaq.io.SafeBufferedReader;


public class PooledWeblog {

  private BufferedReader in;
  private BufferedWriter out;
  private int numberOfThreads;
  private List entries = Collections.synchronizedList(new LinkedList());
  private boolean finished = false;
  private int test = 0;


  public PooledWeblog(InputStream in, OutputStream out,
    int numberOfThreads) {
    this.in = new BufferedReader(new InputStreamReader(in));
    this.out = new BufferedWriter(new OutputStreamWriter(out));
    this.numberOfThreads = numberOfThreads;
  }

  public boolean isFinished() {
    return this.finished;
  }

  public int getNumberOfThreads() {
    return numberOfThreads;
  }
```

Example 6-11. PooledWebLog (continued)

```
public void processLogFile() {

  for (int i = 0; i < numberOfThreads; i++) {
    Thread t = new LookupThread(entries, this);
    t.start();
  }

  try {

    String entry = null;
    while ((entry = in.readLine()) != null) {

      if (entries.size() > numberOfThreads) {
        try {
          Thread.sleep((long) (1000.0/numberOfThreads));
        }
        catch (InterruptedException e) {}
        continue;
      }

      synchronized (entries) {
        entries.add(0, entry);
        entries.notifyAll();
      }

      Thread.yield();

    } // end while

  }
  catch (IOException e) {
    System.out.println("Exception: " + e);
  }

  this.finished = true;

  // finish any threads that are still waiting
  synchronized (entries) {
    entries.notifyAll();
  }

}

public void log(String entry) throws IOException {
  out.write(entry + System.getProperty("line.separator", "\r\n"));
  out.flush();
}
```

Example 6-11. PooledWebLog (continued)

```
  public static void main(String[] args) {

    try {
      PooledWeblog tw = new PooledWeblog(new FileInputStream(args[0]),
       System.out, 100);
      tw.processLogFile();
    }
    catch (FileNotFoundException e) {
      System.err.println("Usage: java PooledWeblog logfile_name");
    }
    catch (ArrayIndexOutOfBoundsException e) {
      System.err.println("Usage: java PooledWeblog logfile_name");
    }
    catch (Exception e) {
      System.err.println(e);
      e.printStackTrace();
    }

  }  // end main


}
```

The detailed work of converting IP addresses to hostnames in the log entries is handled by the LookupThread class, shown in Example 6-12. The constructor provides each thread with a reference to the entries pool it will retrieve work from and a reference to the PooledWeblog object it's working for. The latter reference allows callbacks to the PooledWeblog so that the thread can log converted entries and check to see when the last entry has been processed. It does so by calling the isFinished() method in PooledWeblog when the entries pool is empty (has size 0). Neither an empty pool nor isFinished() returning true is sufficient by itself. isFinished() returns true after the last entry is placed in the pool, which is, at least for a small amount of time, before the last entry is removed from the pool. And entries may be empty while there are still many entries remaining to be read, if the lookup threads outrun the main thread reading the log file.

Example 6-12. LookupThread

```
import java.net.*;
import java.io.*;
import java.util.*;

public class LookupThread extends Thread {

  private List entries;
  PooledWeblog log;   // used for callbacks

  public LookupThread(List entries, PooledWeblog log) {
```

Example 6-12. LookupThread (continued)

```
    this.entries = entries;
    this.log = log;
  }

 public void run() {

    String entry;

    while (true) {

      synchronized (entries) {
        while (entries.size() == 0) {
          if (log.isFinished()) return;
          try {
            entries.wait();
          }
          catch (InterruptedException e) {
          }
        }
        entry = (String) entries.remove(entries.size()-1);
      }

      int index = entry.indexOf(' ', 0);
      String remoteHost = entry.substring(0, index);
      String theRest = entry.substring(index, entry.length());

      try {
        remoteHost = InetAddress.getByName(remoteHost).getHostName();
      }
      catch (Exception e) {
        // remoteHost remains in dotted quad format
      }

      try {
        log.log(remoteHost + theRest);
      }
      catch (IOException e) {
      }
      this.yield();

    }

  }

}
```

Using threads like this lets the same log files be processed in parallel. This is a huge time savings. In my unscientific tests, the threaded version is 10 to 50 times faster than the sequential version.

The biggest disadvantage to the multithreaded approach is that it reorders the log file. The output statistics aren't necessarily in the same order as the input statistics. For simple hit counting, this doesn't matter. However, there are some log analysis tools that can mine a log file to determine paths users followed through a site. These could well get confused if the log is out of sequence. If that's an issue, you'd need to attach a sequence number to each log entry. As the individual threads returned log entries to the main program, the log() method in the main program would store any that arrived out of order until their predecessors appeared. This is in some ways reminiscent of how network software reorders TCP packets that arrive out of order.

7

Retrieving Data with URLs

The simplest way for a Java program to locate and retrieve data from the network is to use the URL class. You do not need to worry about the details of the protocol being used, the format of the data being retrieved, or how to communicate with the server; you simply tell Java the URL, and it gets the data for you. Although Java can handle only a few protocols and content types out of the box, in later chapters you'll learn how to write and install new content and protocol handlers that extend Java's capabilities to include new protocols and new kinds of data. You'll also learn how to open sockets and communicate directly with different kinds of servers. But that's later; for now, let's see how much you can do with a minimum of work.

The URL Class

The java.net.URL class is an abstraction of a Uniform Resource Locator like *http://www.hamsterdance.com/* or *ftp://ftp.redhat.com/pub/*. It extends java.lang.Object, and it is a final class that cannot be subclassed. Rather than relying on inheritance to configure instances for different kinds of URLs, it uses the strategy design pattern. Protocol handlers are the strategies, and the URL class itself forms the context through which the different strategies are selected:

```
public final class URL extends Object implements Serializable
```

Although storing a URL as a string would be trivial, it is helpful to think of URLs as objects with fields that include the protocol, hostname, port, path, query string, and ref, each of which may be set independently. Indeed, this is almost exactly how the java.net.URL class is organized, though the details vary a little between different versions of Java.

The fields of `java.net.URL` are visible only to other members of the `java.net` package; classes that aren't in `java.net` can't access a URL's fields directly. However, you can set these fields using the URL constructors, and retrieve their values using the various getter methods (`getHost()`, `getPort()`, etc.). The URL class has a single method for setting the fields of a URL after it has been created, but this method is protected, and you won't need it unless you're implementing a new protocol handler. URLs are effectively immutable. After a URL object has been constructed, its fields do not change.

Creating New URLs

Unlike the `InetAddress` objects of Chapter 6, *Looking Up Internet Addresses*, you can construct instances of `java.net.URL`. There are six constructors, differing in the information they require. Which constructor you use depends on what information you have and the form it's in. All these constructors throw a `MalformedURLException` if you try to create a URL for an unsupported protocol.

Exactly which protocols are supported is implementation dependent. The only protocols that have been available in all major virtual machines are http and file, and the latter isn't very useful for applets. Sun's Java Development Kit 1.1 and Apple's Macintosh Runtime for Java 2.1 support HTTP, file, FTP, mailto, and gopher as well as some custom protocols like doc, netdoc, systemresource, and verbatim used internally by HotJava for special purposes like help files. JDK 1.2 adds the jar protocol to this list. Netscape Navigator 4.x supports the HTTP, file, FTP, mailto, Telnet, idap, and gopher protocols. Internet Explorer 5 supports HTTP, file, FTP, HTTPS, mailto, gopher, doc, and systemresource, but not Telnet, netdoc, jar, or verbatim. HotJava 3.0 supports all the JDK protocols plus NFS. Of course, support for all these protocols is limited in applets by the security policy. For example, just because an untrusted applet can construct a file URL object does not mean that the applet can actually read the file the URL refers to. Just because an untrusted applet can construct a URL object from an HTTP URL that points to a third-party web site does not mean that the applet can connect to that site.

If the protocol you want to use isn't supported by a particular VM, you may be able to install a protocol handler for that scheme. This is subject to a number of security checks in applets and is really practical only for applications. Other than verifying that it recognizes the protocol part of the URL, Java does not make any checks about the correctness of the URLs it constructs. The programmer is responsible for making sure that URLs created are valid. For instance, Java does not check that the hostname in an HTTP URL does not contain spaces or that the query string is x www-form-URL-encoded. It does not check that a mailto URL actually contains an email address. Java does not check the URL to make sure that it points at an existing host or that it meets any other requirements for URLs. You can create

URLs for hosts that don't exist and for hosts that do exist but that you won't be allowed to connect to.

Constructing a URL from a string

The simplest URL constructor just takes an absolute URL in string form as its single argument:

```
public URL(String url) throws MalformedURLException
```

Like all constructors, this may only be called after the new operator; and, like all URL constructors, it can throw a MalformedURLException. The following code constructs a URL object from a String, catching the exception that might be thrown:

```
try {
  URL u = new URL("http://www.macfaq.com/personal.html");
}
catch (MalformedURLException e)  {
  System.err.println(e);
}
```

Example 7-1 is a simple program for determining which protocols a virtual machine does and does not support. It attempts to construct a URL object for each of 14 protocols (8 standard ones, 3 custom protocols for various Java APIs, and 4 undocumented protocols used internally by HotJava). If the constructor succeeds, you know the protocol is supported. Otherwise, a MalformedURLException is thrown, and you know the protocol is not supported.

Example 7-1. ProtocolTester

```
/* Which protocols does a virtual machine support? */
import java.net.*;


public class ProtocolTester {

  public static void main(String[] args) {

    // hypertext transfer protocol
    testProtocol("http://www.adc.org");

    // secure http
    testProtocol("https://www.amazon.com/exec/obidos/order2/");

    // file transfer protocol
    testProtocol("ftp://metalab.unc.edu/pub/languages/java/javafaq/");

    // Simple Mail Transfer Protocol
    testProtocol("mailto:elharo@metalab.unc.edu");
```

Example 7-1. ProtocolTester (continued)

```
    // telnet
    testProtocol("telnet://dibner.poly.edu/");

    // local file access
    testProtocol("file:///etc/passwd");

    // gopher
    testProtocol("gopher://gopher.anc.org.za/");

    // Lightweight Directory Access Protocol
    testProtocol(
     "ldap://ldap.itd.umich.edu/o=University%20of%20Michigan,c=US?postalAddress");

    // Jar
    testProtocol(
     "jar:http://metalab.unc.edu/java/books/javaio/ioexamples/javaio.jar!"
        +"/com/macfaq/io/StreamCopier.class");

    // NFS, Network File System
    testProtocol("nfs://utopia.poly.edu/usr/tmp/");

    // a custom protocol for JDBC
    testProtocol("jdbc:mysql://luna.metalab.unc.edu:3306/NEWS");

    // rmi, a custom protocol for remote method invocation
    testProtocol("rmi://metalab.unc.edu/RenderEngine");

    // custom protocols for HotJava
    testProtocol("doc:/UsersGuide/release.html");
    testProtocol("netdoc:/UsersGuide/release.html");
    testProtocol("systemresource://www.adc.org/+/index.html");
    testProtocol("verbatim:http://www.adc.org/");

  }

  private static void testProtocol(String url) {

    try {
      URL u = new URL(url);
      System.out.println(u.getProtocol() + " is supported");
    }
    catch (MalformedURLException e) {
      String protocol = url.substring(0, url.indexOf(':'));
      System.out.println(protocol + " is not supported");
    }


  }


}
```

The results of this program depend on which virtual machine runs it. Here are the results from Sun's JDK 1.2.2 on Windows NT, which turns out to support all the protocols except Telnet, HTTPS, LDAP, RMI, NFS, and JDBC:

```
D:\JAVA\JNP2\examples\07>java ProtocolTester
http is supported
https is not supported
ftp is supported
mailto is supported
telnet is not supported
file is supported
gopher is supported
ldap is not supported
jar is supported
nfs is not supported
jdbc is not supported
rmi is not supported
doc is supported
netdoc is supported
systemresource is supported
verbatim is supported
```

The nonsupport of RMI and JDBC is actually a little deceptive since in fact the JDK does support these protocols. However, that support is through various parts of the `java.rmi` and `java.sql` packages, respectively. These protocols are not accessible through the URL class like the other supported protocols (although I have no idea why Sun chose to wrap up RMI and JDBC parameters in URL clothing if it wasn't intending to interface with these via Java's quite sophisticated mechanism for handling URLs).

Constructing a URL from its component parts

The second constructor builds a URL from three strings specifying the protocol, the hostname, and the file:

```
public URL(String protocol, String hostname, String file)
  throws MalformedURLException
```

This constructor sets the port to −1 so the default port for the protocol will be used. The `file` argument should begin with a slash, and include a path, a filename, and optionally a reference to a named anchor. Forgetting the initial slash is a common mistake, and one that is not easy to spot. Like all URL constructors, it can throw a `MalformedURLException`. For example:

```
try {
  URL u = new URL("http", "www.eff.org", "/blueribbon.html#intro");
}
catch (MalformedURLException e) {
  // All VMs should recognize http
}
```

This creates a URL object that points to *http://www.eff.org/blueribbon.html#intro*, using the default port for the HTTP protocol (port 80). The file specification includes a reference to a named anchor. The code catches the exception that would be thrown if the virtual machine did not support the HTTP protocol. However, this shouldn't happen in practice.

For those rare occasions when the default port isn't correct, the next constructor lets you specify the port explicitly, as an int:

```
public URL(String protocol, String host, int port, String file)
  throws MalformedURLException
```

The other arguments are the same as for the URL(String protocol, String host, String file) constructor and carry the same caveats. For example:

```
try {
  URL u = new URL("http", "lcsaxp.lcs.psu.edu", 1212, "/%3b&db=psu");
}
catch (MalformedURLException e)  {
  System.err.println(e);
}
```

This code creates a URL object that points to *http://lcsaxp.lcs.psu.edu:1212/ %3b&db=psu*, specifying port 1,212 explicitly.

Example 7-2 is an alternative protocol tester that can run as an applet, making it useful for testing support of browser virtual machines. It uses the three-argument constructor rather than the one-argument constructor of Example 7-1. It also stores the schemes to be tested in an array and uses the same host and file for each scheme. This produces seriously malformed URLs like *mailto://www.peacefire.org/ bypass/SurfWatch/*, once again demonstrating that all Java checks for at object construction is whether it recognizes the scheme, not whether the URL is appropriate.

Example 7-2. A Protocol Tester Applet

```
import java.net.*;
import java.applet.*;
import java.awt.*;


public class ProtocolTesterApplet extends Applet {

  TextArea results = new TextArea();

  public void init() {
    this.setLayout(new BorderLayout());
    this.add("Center", results);
  }

  public void start() {
```

Example 7-2. A Protocol Tester Applet (continued)

```
    String host = "www.peacefire.org";
    String file = "/bypass/SurfWatch/";

    String[] schemes = {"http",    "https",   "ftp",   "mailto",
                        "telnet", "file",     "ldap", "gopher",
                        "jdbc",   "rmi",      "jndi", "jar",
                        "doc",    "netdoc",   "nfs",  "verbatim",
                        "finger", "daytime", "systemresource"};

    for (int i = 0; i < schemes.length; i++) {
      try {
        URL u = new URL(schemes[i], host, file);
        results.append(schemes[i] + " is supported\r\n");
      }
      catch (MalformedURLException e) {
        results.append(schemes[i] + " is not supported\r\n");
      }
    }

  }

}
```

Figure 7-1 shows the results in HotJava 3.0. This browser supports HTTP, FTP, mailto, file, gopher, doc, netdoc, verbatim, systemresource, jar, finger, and daytime but not HTTPS, ldap, Telnet, jdbc, rmi, or jndi. In fact, the last two protocols supported by HotJava in this list are provided by custom protocol handlers I'll introduce in Chapter 16. They are not part of the default installation of HotJava 3.0.

Constructing relative URLs

This constructor builds an absolute URL from a relative URL and a base URL:

```
    public URL(URL base, String relative) throws MalformedURLException
```

For instance, you may be parsing an HTML document at *http://metalab.unc.edu/javafaq/index.html* and encounter a link to a file called *mailinglists.html* with no further qualifying information. In this case, you use the URL to the document that contains the link to provide the missing information. The constructor computes the new URL as *http://metalab.unc.edu/javafaq/mailinglists.html.* For example:

```
    try {
      URL u1 = new URL("http://metalab.unc.edu/javafaq/index.html");
      URL u2 = new URL (u1, "mailinglists.html");
    }
    catch (MalformedURLException e) {
      System.err.println(e);
    }
```

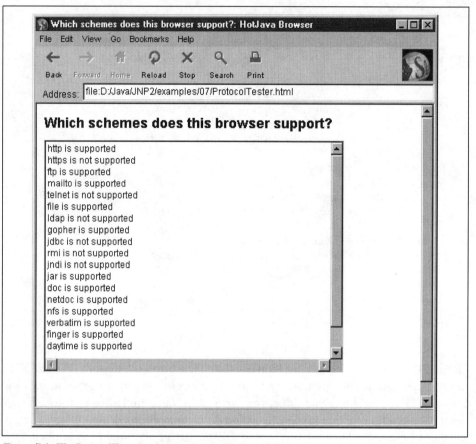

Figure 7-1. The ProtocolTesterApplet running in HotJava 3.0

The filename is removed from the path of u1, and the new filename *mailinglists. html* is appended to make u2. This constructor is particularly useful when you want to loop through a list of files that are all in the same directory. You can create a URL for the first file and then use this initial URL to create URL objects for the other files by substituting their filenames. You also use this constructor when you want to create a URL relative to the applet's document base or codebase, which you retrieve using the getDocumentBase() or getCodeBase() methods of the java. applet.Applet class. Example 7-3 is a very simple applet that uses get DocumentBase() to create a new URL object:

Example 7-3. A URL Relative to the Web Page

```
import java.net.*;
import java.applet.*;
import java.awt.*;
```

Example 7-3. A URL Relative to the Web Page (continued)

```
public class RelativeURLTest extends Applet {

  public void init () {

    try {
      URL base = this.getDocumentBase();
      URL relative = new URL(base, "mailinglists.html");
      this.setLayout(new GridLayout(2,1));
      this.add(new Label(base.toString()));
      this.add(new Label(relative.toString()));
    }
    catch (MalformedURLException e) {
      this.add(new Label("This shouldn't happen!"));
    }


  }


}
```

Of course, the output from this applet depends on the document base. In the run shown in Figure 7-2, the original URL (the document base) refers to the file *RelativeURL.html*; the constructor creates a new URL that points to the file *mailinglists.html* in the same directory.

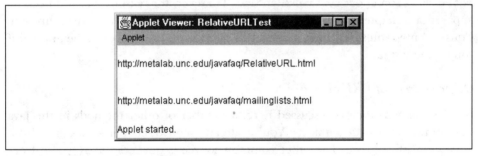

Figure 7-2. A base and a relative URL

When using this constructor with `getDocumentBase()`, you frequently put the call to `getDocumentBase()` inside the constructor, like this:

```
URL relative = new URL(this.getDocumentBase(), "mailinglists.html");
```

Specifying a URLStreamHandler

Java 1.2 adds two URL constructors that allow you to specify the protocol handler used for the URL. The first constructor builds a relative URL from a base URL and a relative part, then uses the specified handler to do the work for the URL. The

second builds the URL from its component pieces, then uses the specified handler
to do the work for the URL:

```
public URL(URL base, String relative, URLStreamHandler handler) // 1.2
  throws MalformedURLException
public URL(String protocol, String host, int port, String file, // 1.2
  URLStreamHandler handler) throws MalformedURLException
```

All URL objects have URLStreamHandler objects to do their work for them. These
two constructors allow you to change from the default URLStreamHandler subclass for a particular protocol to one of your own choosing. This is useful for working with URLs whose schemes aren't supported in a particular virtual machine as
well as for adding functionality that the default stream handler doesn't provide,
like asking the user for a username and password. For example:

```
URL u = new URL("finger", "utopia.poly.edu", 79, "/marcus",
  new com.macfaq.net.www.protocol.finger.Handler());
```

The com.macfaq.net.www.protocol.finger.Handler class used here will be
developed in Chapter 16.

While the other four constructors raise no security issues in and of themselves,
these two do because class loader security is closely tied to the various
URLStreamHandler classes. Consequently, untrusted applets are not allowed to
specify a URLSreamHandler. Trusted applets can do so if they have the
NetPermission specifyStreamHandler. However, for reasons that will become
apparent in Chapter 16, this is a security hole big enough to drive a truck through.
Consequently, you should not request this permission or expect it to be granted if
you do request it.

Other sources of URL objects

Besides the constructors discussed here, a number of other methods in the Java
class library return URL objects. You've already seen getDocumentBase() from
java.applet.Applet. The other common source is getCodeBase(), also from
java.applet.Applet. This works just like getDocumentBase(), except it
returns the URL of the applet itself instead of the URL of the page that contains
the applet. Both getDocumentBase() and getCodeBase() come from the java.
applet.AppletStub interface, which java.applet.Applet implements. You're
unlikely to implement this interface yourself unless you're building a web browser
or applet viewer.

In Java 1.2 and later, the java.io.File class has a toURL() method that returns
a file URL matching the given file. The exact format of the URL returned by this
method is platform dependent. For example, on Windows it may return something like *file:/D:/JAVA/JNP2/07/ToURLTest.java*.

From Java 1.1 on, class loaders are used not only to load classes but also to load resources such as images and audio files. The static `ClassLoader.getSystemResource(String name)` method returns a URL from which a single resource can be read. The `ClassLoader.getSystemResources(String name)` method returns an `Enumeration` containing a list of URLs from which the named resource can be read. In Java 1.1, these two methods use the virtual machine's default class loader. In Java 1.2 and later, they use the system class loader. Finally, the instance method `getResource(String name)` will search the path used by the referenced class loader for a URL to the named resource. The URLs returned by these methods may be file URLs, HTTP URLs, or some other scheme. The name of the resource is a slash-separated list of Java identifiers like */com/macfaq/ sounds/swale.au* or *com/macfaq/images/headshot.jpg*. The Java implementation will attempt to find the requested resource in the class path, potentially including parts of the class path on the web server that an applet was loaded from, or inside a JAR archive.

There are a few other methods that return URL objects here and there throughout the class library, but most of these are simple getter methods that return only a URL you probably already know because you used it to construct the object in the first place; for instance, the `getPage()` method of `java.swing.JEditorPane`, and the `getURL()` method of `java.net.URLConnection`.

Splitting a URL into Pieces

URLs can be thought of as composed of five pieces:

*   The scheme, also known as the protocol
*   The authority
*   The path
*   The ref, also known as the section or named anchor
*   The query string

For example, given the URL *http://metalab.unc.edu/javafaq/books/jnp/index. html?isbn=1565922069#toc,* the scheme is *http;* the authority is *metalab.unc.edu;* the path is */javafaq/books/jnp/index.html;* the ref is *toc;* and the query string is *isbn=1565922069.* However, not all URLs have all these pieces. For instance, the URL *http://www.faqs.org/rfcs/rfc2396.html* has a scheme, an authority, and a path but no ref or query string.

The authority may further be divided into the user info, the host, and the port. For example, in the URL *http://admin@www.blackstar.com:8080/,* the authority is *admin@www.blackstar.com:8080.* This has the user info *admin,* the host *www.black- star.com,* and the port *8080.*

Read-only access to these parts of a URL is provided by five public methods: getFile(), getHost(), getPort(), getProtocol(), and getRef(). Java 1.3 adds four more methods: getQuery(), getPath(), getUserInfo(), and getAuthority().

public String getProtocol( )

The getProtocol() method returns a String containing the scheme of the URL: for example, "http", "https", or "file". For example:

```
URL page = this.getCodeBase();
System.out.println("This applet was downloaded via "
  + page.getProtocol());
```

public String getHost( )

The getHost() method returns a String containing the hostname of the URL. For example:

```
URL page = this.getCodeBase();
System.out.println("This applet was downloaded from " + page.getHost());
```

The host string is not necessarily a valid hostname or address. In particular, URLs that incorporate usernames, like *ftp://anonymous:anonymous@wuarchive.wustl.edu/*, include the user info in the host. For example, consider this code fragment:

```
try {
  URL u = new URL("ftp://anonymous:anonymous@wuarchive.wustl.edu/");
  String host = u.getHost();
}
catch (MalformedURLException e) {
  // should never happen
}
```

This sets host to anonymous:anonymous@wuarchive.wustl.edu, not simply wuarchive.wustl.edu. Java 1.3 provides a method to get the user info, anonymous:anonymous in this example. However, for reasons of backward compatibility, Java 1.3 did not change the semantics of the getHost() method to return only the host rather than the host plus the user info.

public int getPort( )

The getPort() method returns the port number specified in the URL as an int. If no port was specified in the URL, then getPort() returns −1 to signify that the URL does not specify the port explicitly, and will use the default port for the protocol. For example, if the URL is *http://www.userfriendly.org/*, getPort() returns −1; if the URL is *http://www.userfriendly.org:80/*, getPort() returns 80. The following code prints –1 for the port number, because it isn't specified in the URL:

```
try {
  URL u = new URL("http://www.ncsa.uiuc.edu/demoweb/html-primer.html");
  System.out.println("The port part of " + u + " is " + u.getPort());
}
catch (MalformedURLException e) {
  System.err.println(e);
}
```

public String getFile( )

The getFile() method returns a String that contains the path and file portion of a URL; remember that Java does not break a URL into separate path and file parts. Everything from the first / after the hostname until the character preceding the # sign that begins a section is considered to be part of the file. For example:

```
URL page = this.getDocumentBase();
System.out.println("This page's path is " + page.getFile());
```

If the URL does not have a file part, Java 1.0, 1.1, and 1.2 append a slash (/) to the URL and return the slash as the filename. For example, if the URL is *http://www.slashdot.org* (rather than something like *http://www.slashdot.org/index.html*), getFile() returns /. Java 1.3 simply sets the file to the empty string.

public String getPath( )   // Java 1.3

The getPath() method, available only in JDK 1.3 and later, is a synonym for getFile(); that is, it returns a String containing the path and file portion of a URL and has exactly the same semantics as getFile(). The reason for this duplicate method is to sync up Java's terminology with the URI specification in RFC 2396. RFC 2396 calls what we and Java have been calling the "file" the "path" instead. The getFile() method isn't yet deprecated as of Java 1.3, but it may become so in future releases. Note especially that the getPath() method does not return only the directory path and getFile() does not return only the filename as you might naively expect. Both getPath() and getFile() return exactly the same thing, the full path and filename.

public string getRef( )

The getRef() method returns the named anchor part of the URL. If the URL doesn't have a named anchor, the method returns null. In the following code, getRef() returns the string xtocid1902914:

```
try {
  URL u = new URL(
```

```
        "http://metalab.unc.edu/javafaq/javafaq.html#xtocid1902914");
      System.out.println("The ref of " + u + " is " + u.getRef());
    }
    catch (MalformedURLException e) {
      System.err.println(e);
    }
```

public string getQuery( )   // Java 1.3

The getQuery() method returns the query string of the URL. If the URL doesn't have a query string, the method returns null. In the following code, getQuery() returns the string category=Piano:

```
    try {
      URL u = new URL(
        "http://metalab.unc.edu/nywc/compositions.phtml?category=Piano");
      System.out.println("The query string of " + u + " is " + u.getQuery());
    }
    catch (MalformedURLException e) {
      System.err.println(e);
    }
```

public string getUserInfo( )   // Java 1.3

Some URLs include usernames and occasionally even password information. This comes after the scheme and before the host. An @ symbol delimits it. For instance, in the URL *http://elharo@java.oreilly.com/*, the user info is *elharo*. Some URLs also include passwords in the user info. For instance, in the URL *ftp://mp3: mp3@138.247.121.61:21000/c%3a/stuff/mp3/mp3s/Organized_kinda/Quarterflash/ Quarterflash%20-%20Harden%20My%20Heart.mp3*, the user info is *mp3:mp3*. However, most of the time including a password in a URL is a security risk. If the URL doesn't have any user info, getUserInfo() returns null. Mailto URLs may not behave like you expect. In a URL like *mailto:elharo@metalab.unc.edu*, *elharo@metalab.unc.edu* is the path, not the user info and the host. That's because the URL specifies the remote recipient of the message rather than the username and host that's sending the message.

public string getAuthority( )   // Java 1.3

Between the scheme and the path of a URL, you'll find the authority. The term authority is taken from the Uniform Resource Identifier specification (RFC 2396), where this part of the URI indicates the authority that's resolving the resource. In the most general case, this includes the user info, the host, and the port. For example, in the URL *ftp://mp3:mp3@138.247.121.61:21000/c%3a/*, the authority is *mp3:mp3@138.247.121.61:21000*. However, not all URLs have all parts. For instance, in the URL *http://conferences.oreilly.com/java/speakers/*, the authority is simply the hostname *conferences.oreilly.com*. The `getAuthority()` method returns the authority as it exists in the URL, with or without the user info and port.

Example 7-4 uses all eight methods to split URLs entered on the command-line into their component parts. This program requires Java 1.3, though it's easy to port to Java 1.2.

Example 7-4. The Parts of a URL

```
import java.net.*;

public class URLSplitter {

  public static void main(String args[]) {

    for (int i = 0; i < args.length; i++) {
      try {
        URL u = new URL(args[i]);
        System.out.println("The URL is " + u);
        System.out.println("The scheme is " + u.getProtocol());
        System.out.println("The user info is " + u.getUserInfo());

        String host = u.getHost();
        if (host != null) {
          int atSign = host.indexOf('@');
          if (atSign != -1) host = host.substring(atSign+1);
          System.out.println("The host is " + host);
        }
        else {
          System.out.println("The host is null.");
        }

        System.out.println("The port is " + u.getPort());
        System.out.println("The path is " + u.getPath());
        System.out.println("The ref is " + u.getRef());
        System.out.println("The query string is " + u.getQuery());
      }  // end try
      catch (MalformedURLException e) {
        System.err.println(args[i] + " is not a URL I understand.");
      }
      System.out.println();
    }  // end for

  }  // end main

}  // end URLSplitter
```

Here's the result of running this against several of the URL examples in this chapter:

```
% java URLSplitter     \
 http://www.ncsa.uiuc.edu/demoweb/html-primer.html#A1.3.3.3     \
 ftp://mp3:mp3@138.247.121.61:21000/c%3a/                       \
 http://www.oreilly.com                                         \
 http://metalab.unc.edu/nywc/compositions.phtml?category=Piano     \
 http://admin@www.blackstar.com:8080/                           \
The URL is http://www.ncsa.uiuc.edu/demoweb/html-primer.html#A1.3.3.3
The scheme is http
The user info is null
The host is www.ncsa.uiuc.edu
The port is -1
The path is /demoweb/html-primer.html
The ref is A1.3.3.3
The query string is null

The URL is ftp://mp3:mp3@138.247.121.61:21000/c%3a/
The scheme is ftp
The user info is mp3:mp3
The host is 138.247.121.61
The port is 21000
The path is /c%3a/
The ref is null
The query string is null

The URL is http://www.oreilly.com
The scheme is http
The user info is null
The host is www.oreilly.com
The port is -1
The path is
The ref is null
The query string is null

The URL is http://metalab.unc.edu/nywc/compositions.phtml?category=Piano
The scheme is http
The user info is null
The host is metalab.unc.edu
The port is -1
The path is /nywc/compositions.phtml
The ref is null
The query string is category=Piano

The URL is http://admin@www.blackstar.com:8080/
The scheme is http
The user info is admin
The host is www.blackstar.com
```

```
The port is 8080
The path is /
The ref is null
The query string is null
```

Retrieving Data from a URL

Naked URLs aren't very exciting. What's exciting is the data contained in the documents they point to. The URL class has three methods (four in Java 1.3) to retrieve data from a URL; they are:

```
public final InputStream openStream() throws IOException
public URLConnection openConnection() throws IOException
public final Object getContent() throws IOException
public final Object getContent(Class[] classes)                // 1.3
  throws IOException
```

These methods differ in that they return the data at the URL as an instance of different classes.

public final InputStream openStream( ) throws IOException

The openStream( ) method connects to the resource referenced by the URL, performs any necessary handshaking between the client and the server, and then returns an InputStream from which data can be read. The data you get from this InputStream is the raw (i.e., uninterpreted) contents of the file the URL references: ASCII if you're reading an ASCII text file, raw HTML if you're reading an HTML file, binary image data if you're reading an image file, and so forth. It does not include any of the HTTP headers or any other protocol-related information. You can read from this InputStream as you would read from any other InputStream. For example:

```
try {
  URL u  = new URL("http://www.hamsterdance.com");
  InputStream in = u.openStream();
  int c;
  while ((c = in.read()) != -1) System.out.write(c);
}
catch (IOException e) {
  System.err.println(e);
}
```

This code fragment catches an IOException, which also catches the MalformedURLException that the URL constructor can throw, since MalformedURLException subclasses IOException.

Example 7-5 reads a URL from the command line, opens an `InputStream` from that URL, chains the resulting `InputStream` to an `InputStreamReader` using the default encoding, and then uses `InputStreamReader`'s `read()` method to read successive characters from the file, each of which is printed on `System.out`. That is, it prints the raw data located at the URL: if the URL references an HTML file, the program's output is raw HTML.

Example 7-5. Download a Web Page

```
import java.net.*;
import java.io.*;

public class SourceViewer {

  public static void main (String[] args) {

    if  (args.length > 0) {
      try {
        //Open the URL for reading
        URL u = new URL(args[0]);
        InputStream in = u.openStream();
        // buffer the input to increase performance
        in = new BufferedInputStream(in);
        // chain the InputStream to a Reader
        Reader r = new InputStreamReader(in);
        int c;
        while ((c = r.read()) != -1) {
          System.out.print((char) c);
        }
      }
      catch (MalformedURLException e) {
        System.err.println(args[0] + " is not a parseable URL");
      }
      catch (IOException e) {
        System.err.println(e);
      }

    } //  end if

  } // end main

} // end SourceViewer
```

Here are the first few lines of output when `SourceViewer` downloads *http://www. oreilly.com*:

```
% java SourceViewer http://www.oreilly.com
<HTML>
<HEAD>
```

```
<TITLE>www.oreilly.com -- Welcome to O'Reilly &amp; Associates! -- computer
books, software, online publishing</TITLE>
<META name="keywords" content="computer books, technical books, UNIX, unix,
Perl, Java, Linux, Internet, Web, C, C++, Windows, Windows NT, Security,
Sys Admin, System Administration, Oracle, design, graphics, online books,
online courses, Perl Conference, Web-based training, Software, open source,
free software">
<META name="description" content="O'Reilly is a leader in technical and
computer book documentation for UNIX, Perl, Java, Linux, Internet,
Web, C, C++, Windows, Windows NT, Security, Sys Admin, System
Administration, Oracle, Design & Graphics, Online Books, Online Courses,
Perl Conference, Web-based training, and Software">
</HEAD>
```

There are quite a few more lines in that web page; if you want to see them, you can
fire up your web browser.

The shakiest part of this program is that it blithely assumes that the remote URL is
in fact text data, and that its encoding is the same as the default encoding of the
client system. That's not necessarily true. The remote URL could be binary data;
and even if it's not, the remote host and local client may not have the same default
character set. As a general rule, for web pages that use a character set radically different from ASCII, the HTML page will include a META tag in the header that
specifies the character set in use. For instance, this META tag specifies the Big-5
encoding for Chinese:

```
<meta http-equiv="Content-Type" content="text/html; charset=big5">
```

In practice, there's no easy way to get at this information other than by parsing the
file and looking for a header like this one, and even that's limited. Many HTML
files hand-coded in Latin alphabets don't have such a META tag. Since Windows,
the Mac, and most Unixes have somewhat different interpretations of the characters from 128 to 255, the extended characters in these documents are messed up
on platforms other than the one on which they were created.

public URLConnection openConnection( ) throws IOException

The openConnection( ) method opens a socket to the specified URL and returns
a URLConnection object. A URLConnection represents an open connection to a
network resource. If the call fails, openConnection( ) throws an IOException.
For example:

```
try {
  URL u = new URL("http://www.jennicam.org/");
  try {
    URLConnection uc = u.openConnection();
    InputStream in = uc.getInputStream();
    // read from the connection...
```

```
    } // end try
    catch (IOException e) {
      System.err.println(e);
    }
  } // end try
  catch (MalformedURLException e) {
    System.err.println(e);
  }
```

This method is used when you want to communicate directly with the server. The URLConnection gives you access to everything sent by the server: in addition to the document itself, in its raw form (i.e., HTML, plain text, binary image data), you can access all the headers used by the protocol in use. For example, if you are retrieving an HTML document, the URLConnection will let you access the HTTP headers as well as the raw HTML. The URLConnection class also lets you write data to as well as read from a URL—for instance, to send email to a mailto URL or post form data for a CGI. The URLConnection class will be the primary subject of Chapter 15, *The URLConnection Class.*

public final Object getContent( ) throws IOException

The getContent() method is the third and final way to download data referenced by a URL. The getContent() method retrieves the data referenced by the URL and tries to make it into some type of object. If the URL refers to some kind of text object, such as an ASCII or HTML file, the object returned is usually some sort of InputStream. If the URL refers to an image, such as a GIF or a JPEG file, then getContent() usually returns a java.awt.ImageProducer (more specifically, an instance of a class that implements the ImageProducer interface). What unifies these two disparate classes is that they are not the thing itself but a means by which a program can construct the thing:

```
  try {
    URL u = new URL("http://mesola.obspm.fr/");
    Object o = u.getContent();
    // cast the Object to the appropriate type
    // work with the Object...
  }
  catch (Exception e) {
    System.err.println(e);
  }
```

getContent() operates by looking at the Content-type field in the MIME header of data it gets from the server. If the server does not use MIME headers or sends an unfamiliar Content-type, then getContent() returns some sort of InputStream with which the data can be read. An IOException is thrown if the object can't be retrieved. Example 7-6 demonstrates this.

Example 7-6. Download an Object

```
import java.net.*;
import java.io.*;

public class ContentGetter {

  public static void main (String[] args) {

    if  (args.length > 0) {

      //Open the URL for reading
      try {
        URL u = new URL(args[0]);
        try {
          Object o = u.getContent();
          System.out.println("I got a " + o.getClass().getName());
        } // end try
        catch (IOException e) {
          System.err.println(e);
        }
      } // end try
      catch (MalformedURLException e) {
        System.err.println(args[0] + " is not a parseable URL");
      }
    } //  end if

  } // end main

}  // end ContentGetter
```

Here's the result of trying to get the content of *http://www.oreilly.com/*:

```
% java ContentGetter http://www.oreilly.com/
I got a java.io.PushbackInputStream
```

On the other hand, here's what you get when you try to load a header image from that page:

```
% java ContentGetter http://www.oreilly.com/graphics_new/animation.gif
I got a sun.awt.image.URLImageSource
```

Here's what happens when you try to load a Java applet using getContent():

```
% java ContentGetter http://metalab.unc.edu/java/RelativeURLTest.class
I got a sun.net.www.MeteredStream
```

Here's what happens when you try to load an audio file using getContent():

```
% java ContentGetter http://metalab.unc.edu/javafaq/course/week9/spacemusic.au
I got a sun.applet.AppletAudioClip
```

The last result is the most unusual because it is as close as the Java core API gets to a class that represents a sound file. It's not just an interface through which you can load the sound data.

This example demonstrates the biggest problems with using getContent(): it's hard to predict what kind of object you'll get. You get either some kind of InputStream or an ImageProducer or perhaps an AudioClip; it's easy to check what you get by using the instanceof operator. This should be enough knowledge to let you read a text file or display an image.

public final Object getContent(Class[ ] classes)
throws IOException   // Java 1.3

Starting with JDK 1.3, it is possible for a content handler to provide different views of an object. This overloaded variant of the getContent() method lets you choose what class you'd like the content returned as. The method will attempt to return the URL's content in the order used in the array. For instance, if you'd prefer an HTML file to be returned as a String, but your second choice is a Reader and your third choice is an InputStream, you would write:

```
URL u = new URL("http://www.nwu.org");
Class[] types = new Class[3];
types[0] = String.class;
types[1] = Reader.class;
types[2] = InputStream.class;
Object o = u.getContent(types);
```

You would then have to test for the type of the returned object using instanceof. For example:

```
if (o instanceof String) {
  System.out.println(o);
}
else if (o instanceof Reader) {
  int c;
  Reader r = (Reader) o;
  while ((c = r.read()) != -1) System.out.print((char) c);
}
else if (o instanceof InputStream) {
  int c;
  InputStream in = (InputStream) o;
  while ((c = in.read()) != -1) System.out.write(c);
}
else {
  System.out.println("Error: unexpected type " + o.getClass());
}
```

Utility Methods

The URL class contains a couple of utility methods that perform common operations on URLs. The sameFile() method determines whether two URLs point to the same document. The toExternalForm() method converts a URL object to a string that can be used in an HTML link or a web browser's Open URL dialog.

public boolean sameFile(URL other)

The sameFile() method tests whether two URL objects point to the same file. If they do, sameFile() returns true; otherwise, it returns false. The test that sameFile() performs is quite shallow; all it does is compare the corresponding fields for equality. It will detect whether the two hostnames are really just aliases for each other. For instance, it can tell that *http://helio.oreilly.com/* and *http://www.oreilly.com/* are the same file. However, it cannot tell that *http://www.oreilly.com:80/* and *http://www.oreilly.com/* are the same file or that *http://www.oreilly.com/* and *http://www.oreilly.com/index.html* are the same file. sameFile() is smart enough to ignore the ref part of a URL, however. Here's a fragment of code that uses sameFile() to compare two URLs:

```
try {
  URL u1 = new URL("http://www.ncsa.uiuc.edu/HTMLPrimer.html#GS");
  URL u2 = new URL("http://www.ncsa.uiuc.edu/HTMLPrimer.html#HD");
  if (u1.sameFile(u2)) {
    System.out.println(u1 + " is the same file as \n" + u2);
  }
  else {
    System.out.println(u1 + " is not the same file as \n" + u2);
  }
}
catch (MalformedURLException e) {
  System.err.println(e);
}
```

The output is:

```
http://www.ncsa.uiuc.edu/HTMLPrimer.html#GS is the same file as
http://www.ncsa.uiuc.edu/HTMLPrimer.html#HD
```

The sameFile() method is similar to the equals() method of the URL class. The main difference between sameFile() and equals() is that equals() considers the ref (if any), whereas sameFile() does not. The two URLs shown here do not compare equal although they are the same file. Also, any object may be passed to equals(); only URL objects can be passed to sameFile().

public String toExternalForm( )

The `toExternalForm()` method returns a human-readable `String` representing the URL. It is identical to the `toString()` method. In fact, all the `toString()` method does is return `toExternalForm()`. Therefore, this method is currently redundant and rarely used.

The Object Methods

URL inherits from `java.lang.Object`, so it has access to all the methods of the `Object` class. It overrides three to provide more specialized behavior: `equals()`, `hashCode()`, and `toString()`.

public String toString( )

Like all good classes, `java.net.URL` has a `toString()` method. Example 7-1 through Example 7-5 all implicitly called this method when URLs were passed to `System.out.println()`. As those examples demonstrated, the `String` produced by `toString()` is an absolute URL, like *http://metalab.unc.edu/javafaq/javatutorial.html*.

It's uncommon to call `toString()` explicitly; in print statements, you can just print the URL, which calls `toString()` implicitly. Outside of print statements, it's usually more convenient to retrieve the individual pieces of the URL using the `get` methods. If you do call `toString()`, the syntax is simple:

```
URL codeBase = this.getCodeBase();
String appletURL = codeBase.toString();
```

public boolean equals(Object o)

An object is equal to a URL only if it is also a URL, both URLs point to the same file as determined by the `sameFile()` method, and both URLs have the same ref (or both URLs have null refs). Since `equals()` depends on `sameFile()`, `equals()` has the same limitations as `sameFile()`. For example, *http://www.oreilly.com/* is not equal to *http://www.oreilly.com/index.html*, and *http://www.oreilly.com:80/* is not equal to *http://www.oreilly.com/*. Whether this makes sense depends on whether you think of a URL as a string or as a reference to a particular Internet resource.

Example 7-7 creates URL objects for *http://www.oreilly.com/* and *http://www.ora.com/* and then tells you whether or not they're the same by using the `equals()` method.

Example 7-7. Are http://www.oreilly.com/ and http://www.ora.com/ the same?

```java
import java.net.*;

public class URLEquality {

  public static void main (String[] args) {

    try {
      URL oreilly = new URL ("http://www.oreilly.com/");
      URL ora = new URL("http://www.ora.com/");
      if (oreilly.equals(ora)) {
        System.out.println(oreilly + " is the same as " + ora);
      }
      else {
        System.out.println(oreilly + " is not the same as " + ora);
      }
    }
    catch (MalformedURLException e) {
      System.err.println(e);
    }

  }

}
```

When you run this program, you discover:

```
% java URLEquality
http://www.oreilly.com/ is the same as http://www.ora.com/
```

public int hashCode( )

The hashCode() method returns an int that is used when URL objects are used as keys in hash tables. Thus, it is called by the various methods of java.util. Hashtable; you rarely need to call this method directly, if ever. Hash codes for two different URL objects are unlikely to be the same, but it is certainly possible; there are far more conceivable URLs than there are 4-byte integers.

Methods for Protocol Handlers

The last two methods in the URL class I'll just mention briefly here for the sake of completeness. These are setURLStreamHandlerFactory() and set(). They're primarily used by protocol handlers that are responsible for new schemes, not by programmers who just want to retrieve data from a URL. We'll discuss them both in more detail in Chapter 16.

public static synchronized void
setURLStreamHandlerFactory (URLStreamHandlerFactory factory)

This method sets the `URLStreamHandlerFactory` for the application and throws a generic `Error` if the factory has already been set. A `URLStreamHandler` is responsible for parsing the URL, and then constructing the appropriate `URLConnection` object to handle the connection to the server. Most of the time this happens behind the scenes.

protected void set(String protocol, String host, int port, String file,
String ref)

The `set()` method is used by subclasses of `URL` that need to parse a string into its component parts differently than the default. This method allows those subclasses to do their custom parsing, then set the standard fields in the superclass.

This method is deprecated in JDK 1.3 because it doesn't fill in the new properties of the URL. Instead, JDK 1.3 provides this overloaded variant:

```
protected void set(String protocol, String host, int port,
  String authority, String userInfo, String path, String query,
  String ref)
```

The URLEncoder and URLDecoder Classes

One of the problems that the designers of the Web faced was differences between local operating systems. These differences can cause problems with URLs: for example, some operating systems allow spaces in filenames; some don't. Most operating systems won't complain about a # sign in a filename; in a URL, a # sign means that the filename has ended, and a named anchor follows. Similar problems are presented by other special characters, nonalphanumeric characters, etc., all of which may have a special meaning inside a URL or on another operating system. To solve these problems, characters used in URLs must come from a fixed subset of ASCII, in particular:

- The capital letters A–Z
- The lowercase letters a–z
- The digits 0–9
- The punctuation characters - _ . ! ~ * ' (and ,)

The characters : / & ? @ # ; $ + = % and , may also be used, but only for their specified purposes. If these characters occur as part of a filename, then they and all other characters should be encoded.

The encoding used is very simple. Any characters that are not ASCII numerals, letters, or the punctuation marks specified earlier are represented by a percent sign followed by two hexadecimal digits giving the value for that character. Spaces are a special case because they're so common. Besides being encoded as %20, they can be encoded as a plus sign (+). The plus sign itself is encoded as %2B. The / # = & and ? characters should be encoded when they are used as part of a name, and not as a separator between parts of the URL.

NOTE   This scheme doesn't work well (or really at all) for multibyte character sets. This is a distinct shortcoming of the current URI specification that should be addressed in the future.

Java 1.0 and later provides a URLEncoder class to encode strings in this format. Java 1.2 adds a URLDecoder class that can decode strings in this format. Neither of these classes will be instantiated. Both provide a single static method to do their work:

```
public class URLDecoder extends Object
public class URLEncoder extends Object
```

URLEncoder

The java.net.URLEncoder class contains a single static method called encode() that encodes a String according to these rules:

```
public static String encode(String s)
```

URLEncoder.encode() changes any nonalphanumeric characters except the space, underscore, hyphen, period, and asterisk characters into % sequences. The space is converted into a plus sign. This method is a little overly aggressive in that it also converts tildes, single quotes, exclamation points, and parentheses to percent escapes even though they don't absolutely have to be. (In Java 1.0, URLEncoder was even more aggressive and also encoded asterisks and periods.) However, this isn't forbidden by the URL specification, so web browsers will deal reasonably with these excessively encoded URLs. There's no reason encode() couldn't have been included in the URL class, but it wasn't. The signature of encode() is:

```
public static String encode(String s)
```

It returns a new String suitably encoded. Example 7-8 uses this method to print various encoded strings.

Example 7-8. x-www-form-urlencoded Strings

```
import java.net.*;


public class EncodeTest {

  public static void main(String[] args) {

      System.out.println(URLEncoder.encode("This string has spaces"));
      System.out.println(URLEncoder.encode("This*string*has*asterisks"));
      System.out.println(URLEncoder.encode(
          "This%string%has%percent%signs"));
      System.out.println(URLEncoder.encode("This+string+has+pluses"));
      System.out.println(URLEncoder.encode("This/string/has/slashes"));
      System.out.println(URLEncoder.encode(
          "This\"string\"has\"quote\"marks"));
      System.out.println(URLEncoder.encode(This:string:has:colons"));
      System.out.println(URLEncoder.encode("This~string~has~tildes"));
      System.out.println(URLEncoder.encode(
          "This(string)has(parentheses)"));
      System.out.println(URLEncoder.encode("This.string.has.periods"));
      System.out.println(URLEncoder.encode(
          "This=string=has=equals=signs"));
      System.out.println(URLEncoder.encode("This&string&has&ampersands"));


  }


}
```

Here is the output:

```
% java EncodeTest
This+string+has+spaces
This*string*has*asterisks
This%25string%25has%25percent%25signs
This%2Bstring%2Bhas%2Bpluses
This%2Fstring%2Fhas%2Fslashes
This%22string%22has%22quote%22marks
This%3Astring%3Ahas%3Acolons
This%7Estring%7Ehas%7Etildes
This%28string%29has%28parentheses%29
This.string.has.periods
This%3Dstring%3Dhas%3Dequals%3Dsigns
This%26string%26has%26ampersands
```

Notice in particular that this method does encode the forward slash, the ampersand, the equals sign, and the colon. It does not attempt to determine how these characters are being used in a URL. Consequently, you have to encode your URLs piece by piece, rather than encoding an entire URL in one method call. This is an important point, because the primary use of URLEncoder is in preparing query strings for communicating with CGI programs that use GET. For example, suppose you want to encode this query string used for an AltaVista search:

```
pg=q&kl=XX&stype=stext&q=+"Java+I/O"&search.x=38&search.y=3
```

This code fragment encodes it:

```
String query = URLEncoder.encode(
  "pg=q&kl=XX&stype=stext&q=+\"Java+I/O\"&search.x=38&search.y=3");
System.out.println(query);
```

Unfortunately, the output is:

```
pg%3Dq%26kl%3DXX%26stype%3Dstext%26q%3D%2B%22Java%2BI%2FO%22%26search
.x%3D38%26search.y%3D3
```

The problem is that URLEncoder.encode() encodes blindly. It can't distinguish between special characters used as part of the URL or query string, like & and = in the previous string, and characters that need to be encoded. Consequently, URLs need to be encoded a piece at a time like this:

```
String query = URLEncoder.encode("pg");
query += "=";
query += URLEncoder.encode("q");
query += "&";
query += URLEncoder.encode("kl");
query += "=";
query += URLEncoder.encode("XX");
query += "&";
query += URLEncoder.encode("stype");
query += "=";
query += URLEncoder.encode("stext");
query += "&";
query += URLEncoder.encode("q");
query += "=";
query += URLEncoder.encode("\"Java I/O\"");
query += "&";
query += URLEncoder.encode("search.x");
query += "=";
query += URLEncoder.encode("38");
query += "&";
query += URLEncoder.encode("search.y");
query += "=";
query += URLEncoder.encode("3");
System.out.println(query);
```

The output of this is what you actually want:

```
pg=q&kl=XX&stype=stext&q=%2B%22Java+I%2FO%22&search.x=38&search.y=3
```

Example 7-9 is a `QueryString` class that uses the `URLEncoder` to encode successive name and value pairs in a Java object, which will be used for sending data to CGI programs. When you create a `QueryString`, you can supply the first name-value pair to the constructor; the arguments are a pair of objects, which are converted to strings using their `toString()` methods and then encoded. To add further pairs, call the `add()` method, which also takes two objects as arguments, converts them to `Strings`, and encodes them. The `QueryString` class supplies its own `toString()` method, which simply returns the accumulated list of name-value pairs. `toString()` is called implicitly whenever you add a `QueryString` to another string or print it on an output stream.

Example 7-9. The QueryString Class

```
package com.macfaq.net;

import java.net.URLEncoder;

public class QueryString {

  private String query;

  public QueryString(Object name, Object value) {
    query = URLEncoder.encode(name.toString()) + "=" +
      URLEncoder.encode(value.toString());
  }

  public QueryString() {
    query = "";
  }

  public synchronized void add(Object name, Object value) {

    if (!query.trim().equals("")) query += "&" ;
    query += URLEncoder.encode(name.toString()) + "=" +
      URLEncoder.encode(value.toString());

  }

  public String toString() {
    return query;
  }

}
```

Using this class, we can now encode the previous example like this:

```
QueryString qs = new QueryString("pg", "q");
qs.add("kl", "XX");
```

```
qs.add("stype", "stext");
qs.add("q", "+\"Java I/O\"");
qs.add("search.x", "38");
qs.add("search.y", "3");
String url = "http://www.altavista.com/cgi-bin/query?" + qs;
System.out.println(url);
```

URLDecoder

Java 1.2 adds a corresponding URLDecoder class. This has a single static method that decodes any string encoded in x-www-form-url-encoded format. That is, it converts all plus signs to spaces and all percent escapes to their corresponding character. Its signature is:

```
public static String decode(String s) throws Exception
```

An IllegalArgumentException is thrown if the string contains a percent sign that isn't followed by two hexadecimal digits. Since this method passes all non-escaped characters along as is, you can pass an entire URL to it, rather than splitting it into pieces first. For example:

```
String input = "http://www.altavista.com/cgi-bin/" +
"query?pg=q&kl=XX&stype=stext&q=%2B%22Java+I%2FO%22&search.x=38&search.y=3";
 try {
  String output = URLDecoder.decode(input);
  System.out.println(output);
 }
```

Communicating with CGIs and Servlets Through GET

The URL class makes it easy for Java applets and applications to communicate with server-side CGI programs and servlets that use the GET method. (CGI programs and servlets that use the POST method require the URLConnection class and will be discussed in Chapter 15.) All you need to do is determine what combination of names and values the program expects to receive, then cook up a URL with a query string that provides the requisite names and values. All names and values must be x-www-form-url-encoded as by the URLEncoder.encode() method discussed in the last section.

There are a number of ways to determine the exact syntax for a query string that talks to a particular CGI or servlet. If you've written the server-side program yourself, you already know what name-value pairs it expects. If you've installed a third-party program on your own server, the documentation for that program should tell you what it expects.

On the other hand, if you're talking to a program on a third-party server, matters are a little trickier. You can always ask people at the remote server to provide you with the specifications for talking to their CGI programs. However, even if they don't mind you doing this, there's probably no one person whose job description includes "telling third-party hackers with whom we have no business relationship exactly how to access our servers". Thus, unless you happen upon a particularly friendly or bored individual who has nothing better to do with her time except write long emails detailing exactly how to access her server, you're going to have to do a little reverse engineering.

Many CGI programs are designed to process form input. If this is the case, it's straightforward to figure out what input the CGI program expects. The method the form uses should be the value of the METHOD attribute of the FORM element. This value should be either GET, in which case you use the process described here for talking to CGIs, or POST, in which case you use the process described in Chapter 15. The part of the URL that precedes the query string is given by the value of the ACTION attribute of the FORM element. Note that this may be a relative URL, in which case you'll need to determine the corresponding absolute URL. Finally, the name-value pairs are simply the NAME attributes of the INPUT elements, except for any INPUT elements whose TYPE attribute has the value submit.

For example, consider this HTML form for the local search engine on my Cafe con Leche site. You can see that it uses the GET method. The CGI program that processes the form is found at the URL *http://search.metalab.unc.edu:8765/query. html*. It has 20 separate name-value pairs, most of which have default values:

```
<FORM NAME="seek" METHOD="GET"
 ACTION="http://search.metalab.unc.edu:8765/query.html">
<INPUT TYPE="hidden" NAME="col" VALUE="metalab"></INPUT>
<INPUT TYPE="hidden" NAME="op0" VALUE="+"></INPUT>
<INPUT TYPE="hidden" NAME="fl0" VALUE="url:"></INPUT>
<INPUT TYPE="hidden" NAME="ty0" VALUE="w"></INPUT>
<INPUT TYPE="hidden" NAME="tx0" size="50" VALUE="xml/"></INPUT>
<INPUT TYPE="hidden" NAME="op1" VALUE="+"></INPUT>
<INPUT TYPE="hidden" NAME="fl1" VALUE=""></INPUT>
<INPUT TYPE="hidden" NAME="ty1" VALUE="w"></INPUT>
<INPUT TYPE="text" NAME="tx1" size="20" VALUE=""
        max length="2047"><INPUT>
INPUT TYPE="hidden" NAME="qp" VALUE=""></INPUT>
<INPUT TYPE="hidden" NAME="qs" VALUE=""></INPUT>
<INPUT TYPE="hidden" NAME="qc" VALUE=""></INPUT>
<INPUT TYPE="hidden" NAME="ws" VALUE="0"></INPUT>
<INPUT TYPE="hidden" NAME="qm" VALUE="0"></INPUT>
<INPUT TYPE="hidden" NAME="st" VALUE="1"></INPUT>
<INPUT TYPE="hidden" NAME="nh" VALUE="10"></INPUT>
<INPUT TYPE="hidden" NAME="lk" VALUE="1"></INPUT>
```

```
<INPUT TYPE="hidden" NAME="rf" VALUE="0"></INPUT>
<INPUT TYPE="hidden" NAME="oq" VALUE=""></INPUT>
<INPUT TYPE="hidden" NAME="rq" VALUE="0"></INPUT>
<br />
<INPUT TYPE="submit" VALUE="Search"></input>
</FORM>
```

The type of the INPUT field doesn't matter—for instance, whether it's a set of checkboxes or a pop-up list or a text field—only the name of each INPUT field and the value you give it. The single exception is a submit input that tells the web browser only when to send the data but does not give the server any extra information. In some cases, you may find hidden INPUT fields that must have particular required default values. This form is almost nothing but hidden INPUT fields.

In some cases, the CGI may not be able to handle arbitrary text strings for values of particular inputs. However, since the form is meant to be read and filled in by human beings, it should provide sufficient clues to figure out what input is expected; for instance, that a particular field is supposed to be a two-letter state abbreviation or a phone number.

A CGI that doesn't respond to a form is much harder to reverse engineer. For example, at *http://metalab.unc.edu/nywc/bios.phtml*, you'll find a lot of links to a CGI that talks to a database to retrieve a list of musical works by a particular named composer. However, there's no form anywhere that corresponds to this CGI. It's all done by hardcoded URLs. In this case, the best you can do is look at as many of those URLs as possible and see whether you can guess what the server expects. If the designer hasn't tried to be too devious, this generally isn't all that hard. For example, these URLs are all found on that page:

```
http://metalab.unc.edu/nywc/compositionsbycomposer.phtml?last=Anderson
     &first=Beth&middle=
http://metalab.unc.edu/nywc/compositionsbycomposer.phtml?last=Austin
     &first=Dorothea&middle=
http://metalab.unc.edu/nywc/compositionsbycomposer.phtml?last=Bliss
     &first=Marilyn&middle=
http://metalab.unc.edu/nywc/compositionsbycomposer.phtml?last=Hart
     &first=Jane&middle=Smith
```

Looking at these, you can probably guess that this particular CGI programs expects three inputs named first, middle, and last whose values are the first, middle, and last names of a composer, respectively. Sometimes the inputs may not have such obvious names. In this case, you'll just have to do some experimenting, first copying some existing values and then tweaking them to see what values are and aren't accepted. You don't need to do this in a Java program. You can do it simply by editing the URL in the Address or Location bar of your web browser window.

NOTE   The likelihood that other hackers may experiment with your own
                  CGIs and servlets in such a fashion is a good reason to make them
                  extremely robust against unexpected input.

Regardless of how you determine the set of name-value pairs the CGI or servlet
expects, actually communicating with the program once you know them is simple.
All you have to do is create a query string that includes the necessary name-value
pairs, then form a URL that includes that query string. You send the query string to
the server and read its response using the same methods you use to connect to a
server and retrieve a static HTML page. There's no special protocol to follow once
the URL is constructed. (There is a special protocol to follow for the POST
method, which is why discussion of that method will have to wait until Chapter 15.)

Let's demonstrate this procedure by writing a very simple command-line program
to look up topics in the Netscape Open Directory (*http://dmoz.org/*). This is shown
in Figure 7-3 and has the advantage of being really simple.

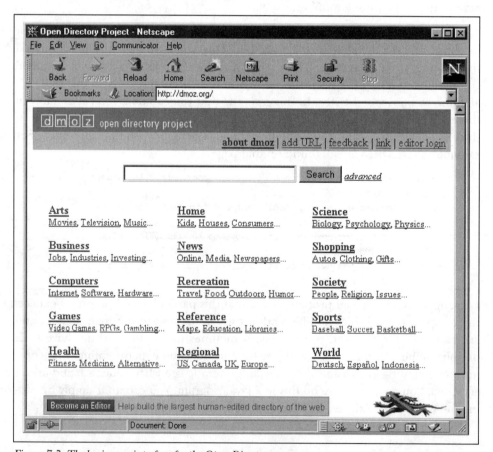

Figure 7-3. The basic user interface for the Open Directory

The basic Open Directory interface is a simple form with one input field named search; input typed in this field is sent to a CGI program at *http://search.dmoz.org/ cgi-bin/search*, which does the actual search. The HTML for the form looks like this:

```
<form method=get action="http://search.dmoz.org/cgi-bin/search">
          <input size=30 name=search>
<input type=submit value="Search">
<a href="http://search.dmoz.org/cgi-bin/search?a.x=0"><small><i>advanced</i>
    </small></a>
</form>
```

Thus, to submit a search request to the Open Directory, you just need to collect the search string, encode that in a query string, and send it to *http://search.dmoz. org/cgi-bin/search*. For example, to search for "java", you would open a connection to the URL *http://search.dmoz.org/cgi-bin/search?search=java* and read the resulting input stream. Example 7-10 does exactly this.

Example 7-10. Do an Open Directory Search

```
import com.macfaq.net.*;
import java.net.*;
import java.io.*;


public class DMoz {

  public static void main(String[] args) {

    String target = "";

    for (int i = 0; i < args.length; i++) {
      target += args[i] + " ";
    }
    target = target.trim();
    QueryString query = new QueryString("search", target);
    try {
      URL u = new URL("http://search.dmoz.org/cgi-bin/search?" + query);
      InputStream in = new BufferedInputStream(u.openStream());
      InputStreamReader theHTML = new InputStreamReader(in);
      int c;
      while ((c = theHTML.read()) != -1) {
        System.out.print((char) c);
      }
    }
    catch (MalformedURLException e) {
      System.err.println(e);
    }
```

Example 7-10. Do an Open Directory Search (continued)

```
    catch (IOException e) {
      System.err.println(e);
    }


  }


}
```

Of course, a lot more effort could be expended if you actually want to parse or display the results. But notice how simple the code was to talk to this CGI. Aside from the funky-looking URL, and the slightly greater likelihood that some pieces of it need to be x-www-form-url-encoded, talking to a CGI that uses GET is no harder than retrieving any other HTML page.

Accessing Password-Protected Sites

Many popular sites, such as *The Wall Street Journal*, require a username and password for access. Some sites, such as Oracle TechNet, implement this through HTTP authentication. Others, such as the Java Developer Connection, implement it through cookies and HTML forms. Java's URL class can access sites that use HTTP authentication, though you'll of course need to tell it what username and password to use. Java does not provide support for sites that use nonstandard, cookie-based authentication, partially because Java doesn't really support cookies and partially because this requires parsing and submitting HTML forms. You can provide this support yourself using the URLConnection class to read and write the HTTP headers where cookies are set and returned. However, doing so is decidedly nontrivial, and often requires custom code for each site you want to connect to. It's really hard to do short of implementing a complete web browser with full HTML forms and cookie support. Accessing sites protected by standard, HTTP authentication is much easier.

The Authenticator Class

Starting in Java 1.2 (but not available in Java 1.1), the `java.net` package includes an `Authenticator` class you can use to provide a username and password for sites that protect themselves using HTTP authentication:

```
    public abstract class Authenticator extends Object
```

Since `Authenticator` is an abstract class, you must subclass it. Different subclasses may retrieve the information in different ways. For example, a character mode program might just ask the user to type the username and password on

`System.in`. A GUI program would likely put up a dialog box like the one shown in Figure 7-4. An automated robot might read it out of an encrypted file.

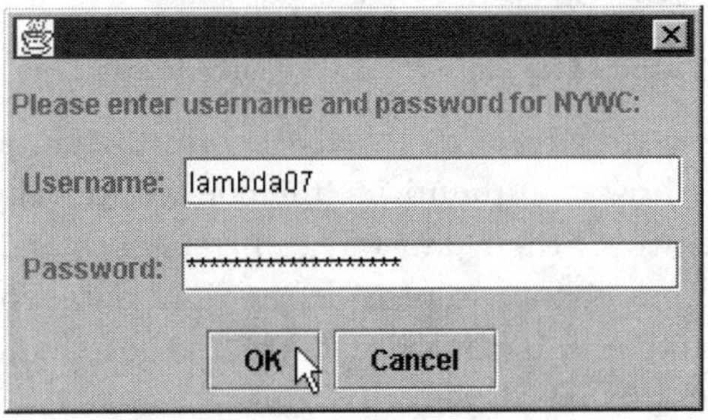

Figure 7-4. An authentication dialog

To make the `URL` class use your subclass, you install it as the default authenticator by passing it to the static `Authenticator.setDefault()` method:

```
public static void setDefault(Authenticator a)
```

For example, if you've written an `Authenticator` subclass named `DialogAuthenticator`, you'd install it like this:

```
Authenticator.setDefault(new DialogAuthenticator());
```

You only need to do this once. From this point forward, when the `URL` class needs a username and password, it will ask the `DialogAuthenticator` for it using the static `Authenticator.requestPasswordAuthentication()` method:

```
public static PasswordAuthentication requestPasswordAuthentication(InetAddress
address, int port, String protocol, String prompt, String scheme) throws
SecurityException
```

The `address` argument is the host for which authentication is required. The `port` argument is the port on that host, and the `protocol` argument is the application layer protocol by which the site is being accessed. The `prompt` is provided by the HTTP server. It's typically the name of the realm for which authentication is required. (Some large web servers such as *metalab.unc.edu* have multiple realms, each of which requires different usernames and passwords.) The `scheme` is the authentication scheme being used. (Here the word *scheme* is not being used as a synonym for *protocol*. Rather it is an HTTP authentication scheme, typically basic.)

Untrusted applets may not be allowed to ask the user for a name and password. Trusted applets can do so, but only if they possess the `requestPass-wordAuthentication NetPermission`. Otherwise, `Authenticator.request-Password Authentication()` throws a `SecurityException`.

Your Authenticator subclass must override the getPasswordAuthentication()
method. Inside this method, you collect the username and password from the user
or some other source and return it as an instance of the java.net.
PasswordAuthentication class.

```
protected PasswordAuthentication getPasswordAuthentication()
```

If you don't want to authenticate this request, return null, and Java will tell the
server it doesn't know how to authenticate the connection. If you submit an incorrect username or password, then Java will call getPasswordAuthentication()
again to give you another chance to provide the right data. You normally have five
tries to get the username and password correct; after that, openStream() will
throw a ProtocolException.

Usernames and passwords are cached within the same virtual machine session.
Once you set the correct password for a realm, you shouldn't be asked for it again
unless you've explicitly deleted the password by zeroing out the char array that
contains it.

You can get more details about the request by invoking any of these methods
inherited from the Authenticator superclass:

```
protected final InetAddress getRequestingSite()
protected final int getRequestingPort()
protected final String getRequestingProtocol()
protected final String getRequestingPrompt()
protected final String getRequestingScheme()
```

These methods either return the information as given in the last call to
requestPasswordAuthentication() or return null if that information is not
available. (getRequestingPort() returns –1 if the port isn't available.)

The PasswordAuthentication Class

PasswordAuthentication is a very simple final class that supports two read-only
properties: username and password. The username is a String. The password is a
char array so that the password can be erased when no longer needed. A String
would have to wait to be garbage collected before it could be erased, and even
then it might still exist somewhere in memory on the local system, possibly even
on disk if the block of memory that contained it had been swapped out to virtual
memory at one point. Both username and password are set in the constructor:

```
public PasswordAuthentication(String userName, char[] password)
```

Each is accessed via a get method:

```
public String getUserName()
public char[] getPassword()
```

The JPasswordField Class

One useful tool for asking users for their passwords in a more or less secure fashion is the JPasswordField component from Swing:

```
public class JPasswordField extends JTextField
```

This lightweight component behaves almost exactly like a text field. However, anything the user types into it is echoed as an asterisk. This way, the password is safe from anyone looking over the user's shoulder at what he's typing on the screen.

JPasswordField also stores the passwords as a char array so that when you're done with the password you can overwrite it with zeroes. It provides the getPassword() method to return this:

```
public char[] getPassword()
```

Otherwise, you mostly use the methods it inherits from the JTextField superclass. Example 7-11 demonstrates a Swing-based Authenticator subclass that brings up a dialog to ask the user for his username and password. Most of this code handles the GUI. A JPasswordField collects the password, and a simple JTextField retrieves the username. Figure 7-4 showed the rather simple dialog box this produces.

Example 7-11. A GUI Authenticator

```java
package com.macfaq.net;

import java.net.*;
import javax.swing.*;
import java.awt.*;
import java.awt.event.*;


public class DialogAuthenticator extends Authenticator {

  private JDialog passwordDialog;
  private JLabel mainLabel
    = new JLabel("Please enter username and password: ");
  private JLabel userLabel = new JLabel("Username: ");
  private JLabel passwordLabel = new JLabel("Password: ");
  private JTextField usernameField = new JTextField(20);
  private JPasswordField passwordField = new JPasswordField(20);
  private JButton okButton = new JButton("OK");
  private JButton cancelButton = new JButton("Cancel");

  public DialogAuthenticator() {
    this("", new JFrame());
  }
```

Example 7-11. A GUI Authenticator (continued)

```java
public DialogAuthenticator(String username) {
  this(username, new JFrame());
}

public DialogAuthenticator(JFrame parent) {
  this("", parent);
}

public DialogAuthenticator(String username, JFrame parent) {

  this.passwordDialog = new JDialog(parent, true);
  Container pane = passwordDialog.getContentPane();
  pane.setLayout(new GridLayout(4, 1));
  pane.add(mainLabel);
  JPanel p2 = new JPanel();
  p2.add(userLabel);
  p2.add(usernameField);
  usernameField.setText(username);
  pane.add(p2);
  JPanel p3 = new JPanel();
  p3.add(passwordLabel);
  p3.add(passwordField);
  pane.add(p3);
  JPanel p4 = new JPanel();
  p4.add(okButton);
  p4.add(cancelButton);
  pane.add(p4);
  passwordDialog.pack();

  ActionListener al = new OKResponse();
  okButton.addActionListener(al);
  usernameField.addActionListener(al);
  passwordField.addActionListener(al);
  cancelButton.addActionListener(new CancelResponse());

}

private void show() {

  String prompt = this.getRequestingPrompt();
  if (prompt == null) {
    String site     = this.getRequestingSite().getHostName();
    String protocol = this.getRequestingProtocol();
    int    port     = this.getRequestingPort();
    if (site != null & protocol != null) {
      prompt = protocol + "://" + site;
      if (port > 0) prompt += ":" + port;
    }
```

Example 7-11. A GUI Authenticator (continued)

```
    else {
      prompt = "";
    }


  }

  mainLabel.setText("Please enter username and password for "
    + prompt + ": ");
  passwordDialog.pack();
  passwordDialog.show();

}


PasswordAuthentication response = null;

class OKResponse implements ActionListener {

  public void actionPerformed(ActionEvent e) {

    passwordDialog.hide();
    // The password is returned as an array of
    // chars for security reasons.
    char[] password = passwordField.getPassword();
    String username = usernameField.getText();
    // Erase the password in case this is used again.
    passwordField.setText("");
    response = new PasswordAuthentication(username, password);

  }

}

class CancelResponse implements ActionListener {

  public void actionPerformed(ActionEvent e) {

    passwordDialog.hide();
    // Erase the password in case this is used again.
    passwordField.setText("");
    response = null;

  }

}

public PasswordAuthentication getPasswordAuthentication() {

  this.show();
```

Example 7-11. A GUI Authenticator (continued)

```
    return this.response;

  }

}
```

Example 7-12 is a revised `SourceViewer` program that can ask the user for a name and password by using the `DialogAuthenticator` class.

Example 7-12. A Program to Download Password-Protected Web Pages

```java
import java.net.*;
import java.io.*;
import com.macfaq.net.DialogAuthenticator;


public class SecureSourceViewer {

  public static void main (String args[]) {

    Authenticator.setDefault(new DialogAuthenticator());

    for (int i = 0; i < args.length; i++) {

      try {
        //Open the URL for reading
        URL u = new URL(args[i]);
        InputStream in = u.openStream();
        // buffer the input to increase performance
        in = new BufferedInputStream(in);
        // chain the InputStream to a Reader
        Reader r = new InputStreamReader(in);
        int c;
        while ((c = r.read()) != -1) {
          System.out.print((char) c);
        }
      }
      catch (MalformedURLException e) {
        System.err.println(args[0] + " is not a parseable URL");
      }
      catch (IOException e) {
        System.err.println(e);
      }

      // print a blank line to separate pages
      System.out.println();

    } // end for
```

Example 7-12. A Program to Download Password-Protected Web Pages (continued)

```
    // Since we used the AWT, we have to explicitly exit.
    System.exit(0);

  } // end main

} // end SecureSourceViewer
```

8

HTML in Swing

As anyone who has ever tried to write code to read HTML can tell you, it's a painful experience. The problem is that although there is an HTML specification, no web designer or browser vendor actually follows it. And the specification itself is extremely loose. Element names may be uppercase, lowercase, or mixed case. Attribute values may or may not be quoted. If they are quoted, either single or double quotes may be used. The < sign may be escaped as < or it may just be left raw in the file. The <P> tag may be used to begin or end a paragraph. Closing </P>, </LI>, and </TD> tags may or may not be used. Tags may or may not overlap. There are just too many different ways of doing the same thing to make parsing HTML an easy task. In fact, the difficulties encountered in parsing real-world HTML were one of the prime motivators for inventing the much more strict XML, in which what is and is not allowed is precisely specified and all browsers are strictly prohibited from accepting documents that don't measure up to the standard (as opposed to HTML, where most browsers try to fix up bad HTML, thereby leading to the proliferation of nonconformant HTML on the Web, which all browsers must then try to parse).

Fortunately, as of JFC 1.1.1 (included in Java 1.2.2), Sun provides classes for basic HTML parsing and display that shield Java programmers from most of the tribulations of working with raw HTML. The `javax.swing.text.html.parser` package can be used to read HTML documents, in more or less their full nonstandard atrocity, while the `javax.swing.text.html` package allows you to display basic HTML in your JFC-based applications.

HTML on Components

Starting with JFC 1.1.1, most text-based Swing components, such as labels, buttons, menu items, tabbed panes, and ToolTips, can have their text specified as

236

HTML. The component will display it appropriately. If you want the label on your JButton to include bold, italic, and plain text, the simplest way is to add HTML:

```
JButton jb = new JButton("<html><b><i>Hello World!</i></b></html>");
```

WARNING   For reasons I've never quite understood, Sun seems to have a grudge against uppercase HTML tags going back to the earliest alphas of HotJava. This technique fails if you use completely legal uppercase HTML tags like this:

```
    JButton jb = new JButton("<HTML><B><I>Hello World!</I></B>
      </HTML>");
```

On the other hand, Sun has no qualms about malformed HTML that omits the end tags like this:

```
    JButton jb = new JButton("<html><b><i>Hello World!</i>
      </b>");
```

The same technique works for JFC-based labels, menu items, tabbed panes, and Tool Tips. Future releases may add HTML support to checkboxes and radio buttons as well. Example 8-1 and Figure 8-1 show an applet with a multiline JLabel that uses HTML. This is running in the applet viewer because HTML on components is available out of the box only in the latest release of the JDK. It does work in Internet Explorer 5.0, though not particularly well, if the javax.swing classes are included in the applet's codebase so that they can be downloaded by the browser. No version of Netscape Navigator I tested could run this applet at all, though perhaps the Java Plug-In would help.

Example 8-1. Including HTML in a JLabel

```
import javax.swing.*;


public class HTMLLabelApplet extends JApplet {

  public void init() {

    JLabel theText = new JLabel(
      "<html>Hello! This is a multiline label with <b>bold</b> "
    + "and <i>italic</i> text. <P> "
    + "It can use paragraphs, horizontal lines, <hr> "
    + "<font color=red>colors</font> "
    + "and most of the other basic features of HTML 3.2</html>");

    this.getContentPane().add(theText);


  }


}
```

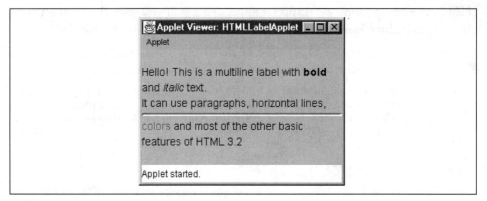

Figure 8-1. An HTML label

You can actually go pretty far with this. Almost all tags are supported, at least partially, including IMG and the various table tags. The only completely unsupported
HTML 3.2 tags are <APPLET>, <PARAM>, <MAP>, <AREA>, <LINK>, <SCRIPT>, and
<STYLE>. The various frame tags (technically not part of HTML 3.2 though widely
used and implemented) are also unsupported. In addition, the various new tags
introduced in HTML 4.0 such as BDO, BUTTON, LEGEND, and TFOOT, are unsupported. If you try to use unrecognized or unsupported tags on your components,
Java will throw a ClassCastException.

Furthermore, there are some limitations on other common tags. First of all, relative URLs in attribute values are not resolved because there's no page for them to
be relative to. This most commonly affects the SRC attribute of the IMG element.
The simplest way around this is to store the images in the same JAR archive as the
applet or application and load them from an absolute *jar* URL. Links will appear
as blue underlined text as most users are accustomed to, but nothing happens
when you click on one. Forms are rendered, but users can't type in them or submit them. Some CSS Level 1 properties such as font-size are supported through
the style attribute, but STYLE tags and external stylesheets are not. In brief, the
HTML support is limited to static text and images. After all, we're only talking
about labels, menu items, and other simple components.

JEditorPane

If you need a more interactive, complete implementation of HTML 3.2, you can
use a javax.swing.JEditorPane. This class provides an even more complete
HTML 3.2 renderer that can handle frames, forms, hyperlinks, and parts of CSS
Level 1. The JEditorPane class also supports plain text and basic RTF, though
the emphasis in this book will be on using it to display HTML.

JEditorPane supports HTML in a fairly intuitive way. You simply feed its constructor a URL or a large string containing HTML, then display it like any other component. There are four constructors in this class:

```
public JEditorPane()
public JEditorPane(URL initialPage) throws IOException
public JEditorPane(String url)  throws IOException
public JEditorPane(String mimeType, String text)
```

The noargs constructor simply creates a JEditorPane with no initial data. You can change this later with the setPage() or setText() methods:

```
public void setPage(URL page) throws IOException
public void setPage(String url) throws IOException
public void setText(String html)
```

Example 8-2 shows how to use this constructor to display a web page. JEditorPane is placed inside a JScrollPane to add scrollbars; JFrame provides a home for the JScrollPane. Figure 8-2 shows this program displaying the O'Reilly home page.

Example 8-2. Using a JEditorPane to Display a Web Page

```java
import javax.swing.text.*;
import javax.swing.*;
import java.io.*;
import java.awt.*;

public class OReillyHomePage {

  public static void main(String[] args) {

    JEditorPane jep = new JEditorPane();
    jep.setEditable(false);

    try {
      jep.setPage("http://www.oreilly.com");
    }
    catch (IOException e) {
      jep.setContentType("text/html");
      jep.setText("<html>Could not load http://www.oreilly.com </html>");
    }

    JScrollPane scrollPane = new JScrollPane(jep);
    JFrame f = new JFrame("O'Reilly & Associates");
    f.setDefaultCloseOperation(WindowConstants.DISPOSE_ON_CLOSE);
    f.setContentPane(scrollPane);
    f.setSize(512, 342);
    f.show();

  }

}
```

Figure 8-2. The O'Reilly home page shown in a JEditorPane

Figure 8-2 shows just how good Swing really is at displaying HTML. It correctly renders this page containing tables, images, animated GIFs, links, colors, fonts, and more with almost no effort from the programmer. There's very little noticeable difference between the page as displayed by Swing and by Netscape Navigator or Internet Explorer. Although not used on this particular page, frames and CSS Level 1 are also supported.

What is missing, though, is precisely what's not obvious from this static image: the activity. The links are blue and underlined, but clicking on one won't change the page that's displayed. JavaScript and applets will not run. Shockwave animations and QuickTime movies won't play. Password-protected web pages will be off limits because there's no way to provide a username and password. You can add all this yourself, but it will require extra code to recognize the relevant parts of the HTML and behave accordingly. Different active content requires different levels of support. Supporting hypertext linking, for example, is fairly straightforward, as we'll explore later. Applets aren't that hard to add either, mostly requiring you to simply parse the HTML to find the tags and parameters and provide an instance of the `AppletContext` interface. We'll discuss this in the next chapter. Adding JavaScript is only a little harder, provided that someone has already written a JavaScript interpreter you can use. Fortunately, the Mozilla Project has written the

Open Source Rhino (*http://www.mozilla.org/rhino/*) JavaScript interpreter, which you can use in your own work. Apple's QuickTime for Java (*http://www.apple.com/quicktime/qtjava/index.html*) makes QuickTime support almost a no-brainer on Mac and Windows. (A Unix version is sorely lacking though.) Macromedia has likewise written a Shockwave Flash player entirely in Java (*http://www.macromedia.com/*). I'm not going to discuss all (or even most) of these in this chapter or this book. Nonetheless, you should be aware that they're available if you need them.

The second constructor accepts a URL object as an argument. It connects to the specified URL, downloads the page it finds, and attempts to display it. If this attempt fails, an IOException is thrown. For example:

```
JFrame f = new JFrame("O'Reilly & Associates");
f.setDefaultCloseOperation(WindowConstants.DISPOSE_ON_CLOSE);

try {
  URL u = new URL("http://www.oreilly.com");
  JEditorPane jep = new JEditorPane(u);
  jep.setEditable(false);
  JScrollPane scrollPane = new JScrollPane(jep);
  f.setContentPane(scrollPane);
}
catch (IOException e) {
  f.getContentPane().add(
   new Label("Could not load http://www.oreilly.com"));
}

f.setSize(512, 342);
f.show();
```

The third constructor is almost identical to the second except that it takes a String form of the URL rather than a URL object as an argument. One of the IOExceptions it can throw is a MalformedURLException if it doesn't recognize the protocol. Otherwise, its behavior is the same as the second constructor. For example:

```
try {
  JEditorPane jep = new JEditorPane("http://www.oreilly.com");
  jep.setEditable(false);
  JScrollPane scrollPane = new JScrollPane(jep);
  f.setContentPane(scrollPane);
}
catch (IOException e) {
  f.getContentPane().add(
   new Label("Could not load http://www.oreilly.com"));
}
```

Neither of these constructors requires you to call setText() or setPage() since that information is provided in the constructor. However, you can still call these methods to change the page or text that's displayed.

Constructing HTML User Interfaces on the Fly

The fourth JEditorPane constructor does not connect to a URL. Rather, it gets its data directly from the second argument. The MIME type of the data is determined by the first argument. For example:

```
JEditorPane jep = new JEditorPane("text/html",
  "<html><h1>Hello World!</h1> <h2>Goodbye World!</h2></html>");
```

This may be useful when you want to display HTML created programmatically or read from somewhere other than a URL. Example 8-3 shows a program that calculates the first 50 Fibonacci numbers and then displays them in an HTML ordered list. Figure 8-3 shows the output.

Example 8-3. Fibonacci Sequence Displayed in HTML

```
import javax.swing.text.*;
import javax.swing.*;
import java.net.*;
import java.io.*;
import java.awt.*;

public class Fibonacci {

 public static void main(String[] args) {

     StringBuffer result =
      new StringBuffer("<html><body><h1>Fibonacci Sequence</h1><ol>");

     long f1 = 0;
     long f2 = 1;

     for (int i = 0; i < 50; i++) {
       result.append("<li>");
       result.append(f1);
       long temp = f2;
       f2 = f1 + f2;
       f1 = temp;
     }

     result.append("</ol></body></html>");

     JEditorPane jep = new JEditorPane("text/html", result.toString());
     jep.setEditable(false);
```

Example 8-3. Fibonacci Sequence Displayed in HTML (continued)

```
JScrollPane scrollPane = new JScrollPane(jep);
JFrame f = new JFrame("Fibonacci Sequence");
f.setDefaultCloseOperation(WindowConstants.DISPOSE_ON_CLOSE);
f.setContentPane(scrollPane);
f.setSize(512, 342);
f.show();

    }

}
```

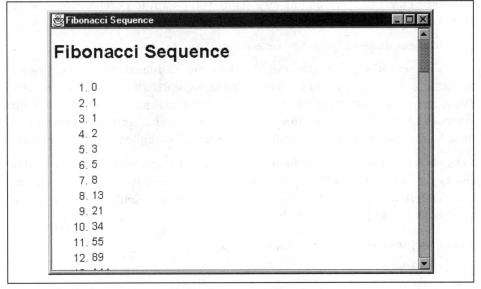

Figure 8-3. The Fibonacci sequence displayed as HTML using a JEditorPane

The significance of this should be apparent. Your programs now have access to a very powerful styled text engine. That the format used on the back end is HTML is a nice fringe benefit. It means that you can use a familiar, easy-to-write format to create a user interface that uses styled text. You don't have quite all the power of QuarkXPress here (nor should you, since HTML doesn't have it), but this is more than adequate for 99% of your text display needs, whether those needs are simple program output, help files, database reports, or something more complex.

Handling Hyperlinks

When the user clicks on a link in a noneditable `JEditorPane`, the pane fires a `HyperlinkEvent`. As you might guess, this is responded to by any registered

HyperlinkListener objects. This follows the same callback pattern used for AWT events and JavaBeans. The `javax.swing.event.HyperlinkListener` interface defines a single method, `hyperlinkUpdate()`:

```
public void hyperlinkUpdate(HyperlinkEvent e)
```

Inside this method, you'll place the code that responds to the HyperlinkEvent. The HyperlinkEvent object passed to this method contains the URL of the event, which is returned by its getURL() method:

```
public URL getURL()
```

HyperlinkEvents are fired not just when the user clicks the link, but also when the mouse enters or exits the link area. Thus, you'll want to check the type of the event before changing the page with the getEventType() method:

```
public HyperlinkEvent.EventType getEventType()
```

This will return one of the three mnemonic constants HyperlinkEvent. EventType.EXITED, HyperlinkEvent.EventTypeENTERED, or Hyperlink- Event.EventType.ACTIVATED. Notice that these are not numbers but static instances of the EventType inner class in the HyperlinkEvent class. Using these instead of integer constants allows more careful compile-time type checking.

Example 8-4 is an implementation of the HyperLinkListener interface that checks the event fired and, if it's an activated event, switches to the page in the link. A reference to the JEditorPane is stored in a private field in the class so that a callback to make the switch can be made.

Example 8-4. A Basic HyperlinkListener Class

```
import javax.swing.*;
import javax.swing.event.*;


public class LinkFollower implements HyperlinkListener {

  private JEditorPane pane;

  public LinkFollower(JEditorPane pane) {
    this.pane = pane;
  }

  public void hyperlinkUpdate(HyperlinkEvent evt) {

    if (evt.getEventType() == HyperlinkEvent.EventType.ACTIVATED) {
      try {
        pane.setPage(evt.getURL());
      }
```

Example 8-4. A Basic HyperlinkListener Class (continued)

```
        catch (Exception e) {
        }
    }


    }


}
```

Example 8-5 is a very simple web browser. It registers an instance of the `LinkFollower` class of Example 8-4 to handle any `HyperlinkEvents`. It doesn't have a Back button, a Location bar, bookmarks, or any frills at all. But it does let you surf the Web by following links. The remaining aspects of the user interface you'd want in a real browser are mostly just exercises in GUI programming, so I'll omit them. But it really is amazing just how easy Swing makes it to write a web browser.

Example 8-5. SimpleWebBrowser

```
import javax.swing.text.*;
import javax.swing.*;
import java.net.*;
import java.io.*;
import java.awt.*;

public class SimpleWebBrowser {

  public static void main(String[] args) {

    // get the first URL
    String initialPage = "http://metalab.unc.edu/javafaq/";
    if (args.length > 0) initialPage = args[0];

    // set up the editor pane
    JEditorPane jep = new JEditorPane();
    jep.setEditable(false);
    jep.addHyperlinkListener(new LinkFollower(jep));

    try {
      jep.setPage(initialPage);
    }
    catch (IOException e) {
      System.err.println("Usage: java SimpleWebBrowser url");
      System.err.println(e);
      System.exit(-1);
    }
```

Example 8-5. SimpleWebBrowser (continued)

```
  // set up the window
  JScrollPane scrollPane = new JScrollPane(jep);
  JFrame f = new JFrame("Simple Web Browser");
  f.setDefaultCloseOperation(WindowConstants.DISPOSE_ON_CLOSE);
  f.setContentPane(scrollPane);
  f.setSize(512, 342);
  f.show();

  }


}
```

The one thing this browser doesn't do is follow links to named anchors inside the body of a particular HTML page. There is a protected `scrollToReference()` method in `JEditorPane` that can find the specified named anchor in the currently displayed HTML document and reposition the pane at that point that you can use to add this functionality if you so desire:

```
protected void scrollToReference(String reference)
```

Reading HTML Directly

The `JEditorPane` class mostly assumes that you're going to provide either a URL or the string form of a URL and let it handle all the details of retrieving the data from the network. However, it contains one method that allows you to read HTML directly from an input stream. That method is `read()`:

```
public void read(InputStream in, Object document) throws IOException
```

This may be useful if you need to read HTML from a chain of filter streams; for instance, unzipping it before you read it. It could also be used when you need to perform some custom handshaking with the server, such as providing a username and password, rather than simply letting the default connection take place.

The first argument is the stream from which the HTML will be read. The second argument should be an instance of `javax.swing.text.html.HTMLDocument`. (You can use another type, but if you do, the `JEditorPane` will treat the stream as plain text rather than HTML.) Although you could use the `HTMLDocument()` noargs constructor to create the `HTMLDocument` object, the document it creates is missing a lot of style details. You're better off letting a `javax.swing.text.html.HTMLEditorKit` create the document for you. You get an `HTMLEditorKit` by passing the MIME type you want to edit (`text/html` in this case) to the `JEditorPane` `getEditorKitForContentType()` method like this:

```
EditorKit htmlKit = jep.getEditorKitForContentType("text/html");
```

Finally, before reading from the stream, you have to use the `JEditorPane`'s `setEditorKit()` method to install a `javax.swing.text.html.HTMLEditorKit`. For example:

```
jep.setEditorKit(htmlKit);
```

This code fragment uses these techniques to load the web page at *http://www.macfaq.com*. Here the stream comes from a URL anyway, so this is really more trouble than it's worth compared to the alternative. However, this approach would also allow you to read from a gzipped file, a file on the local drive, data written by another thread, a byte array, or anything else you can hook a stream to:

```
JEditorPane jep = new JEditorPane();
jep.setEditable(false);
EditorKit htmlKit = jep.getEditorKitForContentType("text/html");
HTMLDocument doc = (HTMLDocument) htmlKit.createDefaultDocument();
jep.setEditorKit(htmlKit);

try {
  URL u = new URL("http://www.macfaq.com");
  InputStream in = u.openStream();
  jep.read(in, doc);
}
catch (IOException e) {
  System.err.println(e);
}

JScrollPane scrollPane = new JScrollPane(jep);
JFrame f = new JFrame("Macfaq");
f.setDefaultCloseOperation(WindowConstants.DISPOSE_ON_CLOSE);
f.setContentPane(scrollPane);
f.setSize(512, 342);
f.show();
```

This would also be useful if you need to interpose yourself in the stream to perform some sort of filtering. For example, you might want to remove IMG tags from the file before displaying it. The methods of the next section would help you do this.

Parsing HTML

Sometimes you want to read HTML, looking for information without actually displaying it on the screen. For instance, more than one author I know has written a "book ticker" program to track the hour-by-hour progress of her book in the Amazon.com bestseller list. The hardest part of this program isn't retrieving the raw HTML. It's reading through the raw HTML to find the one line that contains the book's ranking. As another example, consider a Web Whacker–style program that

downloads a web site or part thereof to a local PC with all links intact. Downloading the files once you have the URLs is easy. But reading through the document to
find the URLs of the linked pages is considerably more complex.

Both of these examples are parsing problems. While parsing a clearly defined language that doesn't allow syntax errors, such as Java or XML, is relatively straightforward, parsing a flexible language that attempts to recover from errors, like
HTML, is extremely difficult. It's easier to write in HTML than it is to write in a
strict language like XML, but it's much harder to read such a language. Ease of
use for the page author has been favored at the cost of ease of development for
the programmer.

Fortunately, the `javax.swing.text.html` and `javax.swing.text.html.`
`parser` packages include classes that do most of the hard work for you. They're
primarily intended for the internal use of HotJava and the `JEditorPane` class discussed in the last section. Consequently, they can be a little tricky to get at. The
constructors are often not public or hidden inside inner classes, and the classes
themselves aren't very well documented. But once you've seen a few examples,
they aren't very hard to use.

HTMLEditorKit.Parser

The main HTML parsing class is the inner class `javax.swing.html.`
`HTMLEditorKit.Parser`:

```
public abstract static class HTMLEditorKit.Parser extends Object
```

Since this is an abstract class, the actual parsing work is performed by an instance
of its concrete subclass `javax.swing.text.html.parser.ParserDelegator`:

```
public class ParserDelegator extends HTMLEditorKit.Parser
```

An instance of this class reads an HTML document from a `Reader`. It looks for five
things in the document: start tags, end tags, empty tags, text, and comments. That
covers all the important parts of a common HTML file. (Document type declara-
tions and processing instructions are omitted, but they're rare and not very important in most HTML files, even when they are included.) Every time the parser sees
one of these five items, it invokes the corresponding callback method in a particular instance of the `javax.swing.text.html.HTMLEditorKit.ParserCallback`
class. To parse an HTML file, you write a subclass of `HTMLEditorKit.`
`ParserCallback` that responds to text and tags as you desire. Then you pass an
instance of your subclass to the `HTMLEditorKit.Parser`'s `parse()` method,
along with the `Reader` from which the HTML will be read:

```
public void parse(Reader in, HTMLEditorKit.ParserCallback callback,
  boolean ignoreCharacterSet) throws IOException
```

The third argument indicates whether you want to be notified of the character set of the document, assuming one is found in a META tag in the HTML header. This will normally be true. If it's false, then the parser will throw a javax.swing.text. ChangedCharSetException when a META tag in the HTML header is used to change the character set. This would give you an opportunity to switch to a different Reader that understands that character set and reparse the document (this time, setting ignoreCharSet to true since you already know the character set).

parse() is the only public method in the HTMLEditorKit.Parser class. All the work is handled inside the callback methods in the HTMLEditorKit. ParserCallback subclass. The parse() method simply reads from the Reader in until it's read the entire document. Every time it sees a tag, comment, or block of text, it invokes the corresponding callback method in the HTMLEditorKit. ParserCallback instance. If the Reader throws an IOException, that excep tion is passed along. Since neither the HTMLEditorKit.Parser nor the HTMLEditorKit.ParserCallback instance is specific to one reader, it can be used to parse multiple files, simply by invoking parse() multiple times. If you do this, your HTMLEditorKit.ParserCallback class must be fully thread-safe, because parsing takes place in a separate thread and the parse() method normally returns before parsing is complete.

Before you can do any of this, however, you have to get your hands on an instance of the HTMLEditorKit.Parser class, and that's harder than it should be. HTMLEditorKit.Parser is an abstract class, so it can't be instantiated directly. Its subclass, javax.swing.text.html.parser.ParserDelegator, is concrete. However, before you can use it, you have to configure it with a DTD, using the protected, static methods ParserDelegator.setDefaultDTD() and Parser Delegator.createDTD():

```
protected static void setDefaultDTD()
protected static DTD createDTD(DTD dtd, String name)
```

So to create a ParserDelegator, you first need to have an instance of javax. swing.text.html.parser.DTD. This class represents a Standardized General Markup Language (SGML) Document Type Definition. The DTD class has a protected constructor and many protected methods that subclasses can use to build a DTD from scratch, but this is an API that only an SGML expert could be expected to use. The normal way DTDs are created is by reading the text form of a standard DTD published by someone like the W3C. You should be able to get a DTD for HTML by using the DTDParser class to parse the W3C's published HTML DTD. Unfortunately, the DTDParser class didn't make the cut for JFC 1.1.1, so you can't. Thus, we're going to need to go through the back door to create an HTMLEditorKit.Parser instance. What we'll do is use the HTMLEditorKit.

Parser getParser() method instead, which ultimately returns a Parser-Delegator after properly initializing the DTD for HTML 3.2:

```
protected HTMLEditorKit.Parser getParser()
```

Since this method is protected, we'll simply subclass HTMLEditorKit and override it with a public version, as Example 8-6 demonstrates:

Example 8-6. This Subclass Just Makes the getParser( ) Method Public

```
import javax.swing.text.html.*;

public class ParserGetter extends HTMLEditorKit {

  // purely to make this method public
  public HTMLEditorKit.Parser getParser(){
    return super.getParser();
  }

}
```

Now that we've got a way to get a parser, we're ready to parse some documents. This is accomplished through the parse() method of HTMLEditorKit.Parser:

```
public abstract void parse(Reader input, HTMLEditorKit.ParserCallback
  callback, boolean ignoreCharSet) throws IOException
```

The Reader is straightforward. We simply chain an InputStreamReader to the stream reading the HTML document, probably one returned by the openStream() method of java.net.URL. For the third argument, you can pass true to ignore encoding issues (this generally works only if you're pretty sure you're dealing with ASCII text) or false if you want to receive a ChangedCharSetException when the document has a META tag indicating the character set. The second argument is where the action is. You're going to write a subclass of HTMLEditorKit.ParserCallback that is notified of every start tag, end tag, empty tag, text, comment, and error that the parser encounters.

HTMLEditorKit.ParserCallback

The ParserCallback class is a public inner class inside javax.swing.text.html.HTMLEditorKit:

```
public static class HTMLEditorKit.ParserCallback extends Object
```

It has a single, public noargs constructor:

```
public HTMLEditorKit.ParserCallback()
```

However, you probably won't use this directly because the standard implementation of this class does nothing. It exists to be subclassed. It has six callback methods that do nothing. You will override these methods to respond to specific items seen in the input stream as the document is parsed:

```
public void handleText(char[] text, int position)
public void handleComment(char[] text, int position)
public void handleStartTag(HTML.Tag tag,
  MutableAttributeSet attributes, int position)
public void handleEndTag(HTML.Tag tag, int position)
public void handleSimpleTag(HTML.Tag tag,
  MutableAttributeSet attributes, int position)
public void handleError(String errorMessage, int position)
```

There's also a `flush()` method you use to perform any final cleanup. The parser invokes this method once after it's finished parsing the document:

```
public void flush() throws BadLocationException
```

WARNING   More accurately, the parser is supposed to invoke this method after it's finished parsing the document. In practice, it doesn't do that, at least in JFC 1.1.1. This should probably be classified as a bug.

Let's begin with a simple example. Suppose you want to write a program that strips out all the tags and comments from an HTML document and leaves only the text. You would write a subclass of `HTMLEditorKit.ParserCallback` that overrides the `handleText()` method to write the text on a `Writer`. You would leave the other methods alone. Example 8-7 demonstrates.

Example 8-7. TagStripper

```
import javax.swing.text.html.*;
import java.io.*;


public class TagStripper extends HTMLEditorKit.ParserCallback {

  private Writer out;

  public TagStripper(Writer out) {
    this.out = out;
  }

  public void handleText(char[] text, int position) {
    try {
      out.write(text);
      out.flush();
    }
    catch (IOException e) {
      System.err.println(e);
```

Example 8-7. TagStripper (continued)

```
    }
  }

}
```

Now let's suppose you want to use this class to actually strip the tags from a URL. You begin by retrieving a parser using Example 8-5's `ParserGetter` class:

```
ParserGetter kit = new ParserGetter();
HTMLEditorKit.Parser parser = kit.getParser();
```

Next, you construct an instance of your callback class like this:

```
HTMLEditorKit.ParserCallback callback
  = new TagStripper(new OutputStreamWriter(System.out));
```

Then you get a stream you can read the HTML document from. For example:

```
try {
  URL u = new URL("http://www.oreilly.com");
  InputStream in = new BufferedInputStream(u.openStream());
  InputStreamReader r = new InputStreamReader(in);
```

Finally, you pass the `Reader` and the `HTMLEditorKit.ParserCallback` to the `HTMLEditorKit.Parser`'s `parse()` method, like this:

```
  parser.parse(r, callback, false);
}
catch (IOException e) {
  System.err.println(e);
}
```

There are a couple of details about the parsing process that are not obvious. First, the parser parses in a separate thread. Therefore, you should not assume that the document has been parsed when the `parse()` method returns. If you're using the same `HTMLEditorKit.ParserCallback` object for two separate parses, you need to make all your callback methods thread-safe.

Second, the parser actually skips some of the data in the input. In particular, it normalizes and strips whitespace. If the input document contains seven spaces in a row, the parser will convert that to a single space. Carriage returns, linefeeds, and tabs are all converted to a single space, so you lose line breaks. Furthermore, most text elements are stripped of *all* leading and trailing whitespace. Elements that contain nothing but space are eliminated completely. Thus, suppose the input document contains this content:

```
<H1> Here's   the   Title </H1>

<P> Here's the text </P>
```

What actually comes out of the tag stripper is:

```
Here's the TitleHere's the text
```

The single exception is the PRE element, which maintains all whitespace in its contents unedited. Short of implementing your own parser, I don't know of any way to retain all the stripped space. But you can include the minimum necessary line breaks and whitespace by looking at the tags as well as the text. Generally, you expect a single break in HTML when you see one of these tags:

```
<BR>
<LI>
<TR>
```

You expect a double break (paragraph break) when you see one of these tags:

```
<P>
</H1> </H2> </H3> </H4> </H5> </H6>
<HR>
<DIV>
</UL> </OL> </DL>
```

To include line breaks in the output, you have to look at each tag as it's processed and determine whether it falls in one of these sets. This is straightforward because the first argument passed to each of the tag callback methods is an HTML.Tag object.

HTML.Tag

Tag is a public inner class in the javax.swing.text.html.HTML class.

```
public static class HTML.Tag extends Object
```

It has these four methods:

```
public boolean isBlock()
public boolean breaksFlow()
public boolean isPreformatted()
public String toString()
```

The breaksFlow() method returns true if the tag should cause a single line break. The isBlock() method returns true if the tag should cause a double line break. The isPreformatted() method returns true if the tag indicates that whitespace should be preserved. This makes it easy to provide the necessary breaks in the output.

Chances are you'll see more tags than you'd expect when you parse a file. The parser inserts missing closing tags. In other words, if a document contains only a <P> tag, then the parser will report both the <P> tag and the implied </P> tag at the appropriate points in the document. Example 8-8 is a program that does the best job yet of converting HTML to pure text. It looks for the empty and end tags, explicit or implied, and, if the tag indicates that line breaks are called for, inserts the necessary number of line breaks.

Example 8-8. LineBreakingTagStripper

```java
import javax.swing.text.*;
import javax.swing.text.html.*;
import javax.swing.text.html.parser.*;
import java.io.*;
import java.net.*;


public class LineBreakingTagStripper
 extends HTMLEditorKit.ParserCallback {

  private Writer out;
  private String lineSeparator;

  public LineBreakingTagStripper(Writer out) {
    this(out, System.getProperty("line.separator", "\r\n"));
  }

  public LineBreakingTagStripper(Writer out, String lineSeparator) {
    this.out = out;
    this.lineSeparator = lineSeparator;
  }

  public void handleText(char[] text, int position) {
    try {
      out.write(text);
      out.flush();
    }
    catch (IOException e) {
      System.err.println(e);
    }
  }

  public void handleEndTag(HTML.Tag tag, int position) {

    try {
      if (tag.isBlock()) {
        out.write(lineSeparator);
        out.write(lineSeparator);
      }
      else if (tag.breaksFlow()) {
        out.write(lineSeparator);
      }
    }
```

Example 8-8. LineBreakingTagStripper (continued)

```
    catch (IOException e) {
      System.err.println(e);
    }


  }
  public void handleSimpleTag(HTML.Tag tag,
   MutableAttributeSet attributes, int position) {

    try {
      if (tag.isBlock()) {
        out.write(lineSeparator);
        out.write(lineSeparator);
      }
      else if (tag.breaksFlow()) {
        out.write(lineSeparator);
      }
      else {
        out.write(' ');
      }
    }
    catch (IOException e) {
      System.err.println(e);
    }


  }


}
```

Most of the time, of course, you want to know considerably more than whether a tag breaks a line. You want to know what tag it is, and behave accordingly. For instance, if you were writing a full-blown HTML-to-TeX or HTML-to-RTF converter, you'd want to handle each tag differently. You test the type of tag by comparing it against these 73 mnemonic constants from the HTML.Tag class:

HTML.Tag.A	HTML.Tag.FRAMESET	HTML.Tag.PARAM
HTML.Tag.ADDRESS	HTML.Tag.H1	HTML.Tag.PRE
HTML.Tag.APPLET	HTML.Tag.H2	HTML.Tag.SAMP
HTML.Tag.AREA	HTML.Tag.H3	HTML.Tag.SCRIPT
HTML.Tag.B	HTML.Tag.H4	HTML.Tag.SELECT
HTML.Tag.BASE	HTML.Tag.H5	HTML.Tag.SMALL
HTML.Tag.BASEFONT	HTML.Tag.H6	HTML.Tag.STRIKE
HTML.Tag.BIG	HTML.Tag.HEAD	HTML.Tag.S
HTML.Tag.BLOCKQUOTE	HTML.Tag.HR	HTML.Tag.STRONG
HTML.Tag.BODY	HTML.Tag.HTML	HTML.Tag.STYLE
HTML.Tag.BR	HTML.Tag.I	HTML.Tag.SUB
HTML.Tag.CAPTION	HTML.Tag.IMG	HTML.Tag.SUP
HTML.Tag.CENTER	HTML.Tag.INPUT	HTML.Tag.TABLE

```
HTML.Tag.CITE           HTML.Tag.ISINDEX        HTML.Tag.TD
HTML.Tag.CODE           HTML.Tag.KBD            HTML.Tag.TEXTAREA
HTML.Tag.DD             HTML.Tag.LI             HTML.Tag.TH
HTML.Tag.DFN            HTML.Tag.LINK           HTML.Tag.TR
HTML.Tag.DIR            HTML.Tag.MAP            HTML.Tag.TT
HTML.Tag.DIV            HTML.Tag.MENU           HTML.Tag.U
HTML.Tag.DL             HTML.Tag.META           HTML.Tag.UL
HTML.Tag.DT             HTML.Tag.NOFRAMES       HTML.Tag.VAR
HTML.Tag.EM             HTML.Tag.OBJECT         HTML.Tag.IMPLIED
HTML.Tag.FONT           HTML.Tag.OL             HTML.Tag.COMMENT
HTML.Tag.FORM           HTML.Tag.OPTION
HTML.Tag.FRAME          HTML.Tag.P
```

These are not `int` constants. They are object constants to allow compile-time type checking. You saw this trick once before in the `javax.swing.event.HyperlinkEvent` class. All `HTML.Tag` elements passed to your callback methods by the `HTMLEditorKit.Parser` will be one of these 73 constants. They are not just *the same as* these 73 objects; they *are* these 73 objects. There are exactly 73 objects in this class; no more, no less. You can test against them with == rather than `equals()`.

For example, let's suppose you need a program that outlines HTML pages by extracting their H1 through H6 headings while ignoring the rest of the document. It organizes the outline as nested lists in which each H1 heading is at the top level, each H2 heading is one level deep, and so on. You would write an `HTMLEditorKit.ParserCallback` subclass that extracted the contents of all H1, H2, H3, H4, H5, and H6 elements while ignoring all others, as Example 8-9 demonstrates.

Example 8-9. Outliner

```
import javax.swing.text.*;
import javax.swing.text.html.*;
import javax.swing.text.html.parser.*;
import java.io.*;
import java.net.*;
import java.util.*;

public class Outliner extends HTMLEditorKit.ParserCallback {

  private Writer out;
  private int level = 0;
  private boolean inHeader=false;
  private static String lineSeparator
    = System.getProperty("line.separator", "\r\n");

  public Outliner(Writer out) {
```

Example 8-9. Outliner (continued)

```
    this.out = out;
  }

  public void handleStartTag(HTML.Tag tag,
   MutableAttributeSet attributes, int position) {

    int newLevel = 0;
    if (tag == HTML.Tag.H1) newLevel = 1;
    else if (tag == HTML.Tag.H2) newLevel = 2;
    else if (tag == HTML.Tag.H3) newLevel = 3;
    else if (tag == HTML.Tag.H4) newLevel = 4;
    else if (tag == HTML.Tag.H5) newLevel = 5;
    else if (tag == HTML.Tag.H6) newLevel = 6;
    else return;

    this.inHeader = true;
    try {
      if (newLevel > this.level) {
        for (int i =0; i < newLevel-this.level; i++) {
          out.write("<ul>" + lineSeparator + "<li>");
        }
      }
      else if (newLevel < this.level) {
        for (int i =0; i < this.level-newLevel; i++) {
          out.write(lineSeparator + "</ul>" + lineSeparator);
        }
        out.write(lineSeparator + "<li>");
      }
      else {
        out.write(lineSeparator + "<li>");
      }
      this.level = newLevel;
      out.flush();
    }
    catch (IOException e) {
      System.err.println(e);
    }

  }


  public void handleEndTag(HTML.Tag tag, int position) {

    if (tag == HTML.Tag.H1 || tag == HTML.Tag.H2
      || tag == HTML.Tag.H3 || tag == HTML.Tag.H4
      || tag == HTML.Tag.H5 || tag == HTML.Tag.H6) {
      inHeader = false;
    }
```

Example 8-9. Outliner (continued)

```
    // work around bug in the parser that fails to call flush
    if (tag == HTML.Tag.HTML) this.flush();

  }


  public void handleText(char[] text, int position) {

    if (inHeader) {
      try {
        out.write(text);
        out.flush();
      }
      catch (IOException e) {
        System.err.println(e);
      }
    }

  }

  public void flush() {
    try {
      while (this.level-- > 0) {
        out.write(lineSeparator + "</ul>");
      }
      out.flush();
    }
    catch (IOException e) {
      System.err.println(e);
    }
  }

  public static void main(String[] args) {

    ParserGetter kit = new ParserGetter();
    HTMLEditorKit.Parser parser = kit.getParser();

    try {
      URL u = new URL(args[0]);
      InputStream in = u.openStream();
      InputStreamReader r = new InputStreamReader(in);
      HTMLEditorKit.ParserCallback callback = new Outliner
        (new OutputStreamWriter(System.out));
      parser.parse(r, callback, false);
    }
    catch (IOException e) {
      System.err.println(e);
    }
```

Example 8-9. Outliner (continued)

```
  catch (ArrayIndexOutOfBoundsException e) {
    System.out.println("Usage: java Outliner url");
  }


  }


}
```

When a heading start tag is encountered by the `handleStartTag()` method, the necessary number of `<ul>`, `</ul>`, and `<li>` tags is emitted. Furthermore, the `inHeading` flag is set to true so that the `handleText()` method will know to output the contents of the heading. All start tags except the six levels of headers are simply ignored. The `handleEndTag()` method likewise considers heading tags only by comparing the tag it receives with the seven tags it's interested in. If it sees a heading tag, it sets the `inHeading` flag to false again so that body text won't be emitted by the `handleText()` method. If it sees the end of the document via an `</html>` tag, it flushes out the document. Otherwise, it does nothing. The end result is a nicely formatted group of nested, unordered lists that outlines the document. For example, here's the output of running it against *http://metalab.unc.edu/ xml/*:

```
D:\JAVA\JNP2\examples\08>java Outliner http://metalab.unc.edu/xml/
<ul>
<li> Cafe con Leche XML News and Resources<ul>
<li><ul>
<li>XML Overview
<li>Random Notes
<li>Specifications
<li>Books
<li>XML Resources
<li>Development Tools<ul>
<li>Validating Parsers
<li>Non-validating Parsers
<li>Online Validators and Syntax Checkers
<li>Formatting Engines
<li>Browsers
<li>Class Libraries
<li>Editors
<li>XLL
<li>XML Applications
<li>External Sites
</ul>

</ul>

<li>Quote of the Day
```

```
<li>Today's News
<li>Recommended Reading
<li>Recent News</ul>
</ul>
```

Attributes

When processing an HTML file, you often need to look at the attributes as well
as the tags. The second argument to the `handleStartTag()` and
`handleSimpleTag()` callback methods is an instance of the `javax.swing.text.`
`MutableAttributeSet` class. This object allows you to see what attributes are
attached to a particular tag. `MutableAttributeSet` is a subinterface of the
`javax.swing.text.AttributeSet` interface:

```
public abstract interface MutableAttributeSet extends AttributeSet
```

Both `AttributeSet` and `MutableAttributeSet` represent a collection of
attributes on an HTML tag. The difference is that the `MutableAttributeSet`
interface declares methods to add attributes to and remove attributes from, as well
as inspect, the attributes in the set. The attributes themselves are represented as
pairs of `java.lang.Object` objects, one for the name of the attribute and one for
the value. The `AttributeSet` interface declares these methods:

```
public int         getAttributeCount()
public boolean     isDefined(Object name)
public boolean     containsAttribute(Object name, Object value)
public boolean     containsAttributes(AttributeSet attributes)
public boolean     isEqual(AttributeSet attributes)
public AttributeSet copyAttributes()
public Enumeration getAttributeNames()
public Object      getAttribute(Object name)
public AttributeSet getResolveParent()
```

Most of these methods are self-explanatory. The `getAttributeCount()` method
returns the number of attributes in the set. The `isDefined()` method returns
true if an attribute with the specified name is in the set, false otherwise. The
`containsAttribute(Object name, Object value)` method returns true if
an attribute with the given name and value is in the set. The
`containsAttributes(AttributeSet attributes)` method returns true if all
the attributes in the specified set are in this set with the same values; in other
words, if the argument is a subset of the set on which this method is invoked. The
`isEqual()` method returns true if the invoking `AttributeSet` is the same as the
argument. The `copyAttributes()` method returns a clone of the current
`AttributeSet`. The `getAttributeNames()` method returns a `java.util.`
`Enumeration` of all the names of the attributes in the set. Once you know the
name of one of the elements of the set, the `getAttribute()` method returns

its value. Finally, the `getResolveParent()` method returns the parent
`AttributeSet`, which will be searched for attributes that are not found in the current set. For example, given an `AttributeSet`, this method prints the attributes
in name-value format:

```
private void listAttributes(AttributeSet attributes) {
  Enumeration e = attributes.getAttributeNames();
  while (e.hasMoreElements()) {
    Object name = e.nextElement();
    Object value = attributes.getAttribute(name);
    System.out.println(name + "=" + value);
  }
}
```

Although the argument and return types of these methods are mostly declared in
terms of `java.lang.Object`, in practice, all values are instances of `java.lang.`
`String`, while all names are instances of the public inner class `javax.swing.`
`text.html.HTML.Attribute`. Just as the `HTML.Tag` class predefines 73 HTML
tags and uses a private constructor to prevent the creation of others, so too does
the `HTML.Attribute` class predefine 80 standard HTML attributes (`HTML.`
`Attribute.ACTION`, `HTML.Attribute.ALIGN`, `HTML.Attribute.ALINK`, `HTML.`
`Attribute.ALT`, etc.) and prohibits the construction of others via a nonpublic
constructor. Generally, this isn't an issue, since you mostly use `getAttribute()`,
`containsAttribute()`, and so forth only with names returned by
`getAttributeNames()`. The 80 predefined attributes are:

HTML.Attribute.ACTION	HTML.Attribute.DUMMY	HTML.Attribute.PROMPT
HTML.Attribute.ALIGN	HTML.Attribute.ENCTYPE	HTML.Attribute.REL
HTML.Attribute.ALINK	HTML.Attribute.ENDTAG	HTML.Attribute.REV
HTML.Attribute.ALT	HTML.Attribute.FACE	HTML.Attribute.ROWS
HTML.Attribute.ARCHIVE	HTML.Attribute.FRAMEBORDER	HTML.Attribute.ROWSPAN
HTML.Attribute.BACKGROUND	HTML.Attribute.HALIGN	HTML.Attribute.SCROLLING
HTML.Attribute.BGCOLOR	HTML.Attribute.HEIGHT	HTML.Attribute.SELECTED
HTML.Attribute.BORDER	HTML.Attribute.HREF	HTML.Attribute.SHAPE
HTML.Attribute.CELLPADDING	HTML.Attribute.HSPACE	HTML.Attribute.SHAPES
HTML.Attribute.CELLSPACING	HTML.Attribute.HTTPEQUIV	HTML.Attribute.SIZE
HTML.Attribute.CHECKED	HTML.Attribute.ID	HTML.Attribute.SRC
HTML.Attribute.CLASS	HTML.Attribute.ISMAP	HTML.Attribute.STANDBY
HTML.Attribute.CLASSID	HTML.Attribute.LANG	HTML.Attribute.START
HTML.Attribute.CLEAR	HTML.Attribute.LANGUAGE	HTML.Attribute.STYLE
HTML.Attribute.CODE	HTML.Attribute.LINK	HTML.Attribute.TARGET
HTML.Attribute.CODEBASE	HTML.Attribute.LOWSRC	HTML.Attribute.TEXT
HTML.Attribute.CODETYPE	HTML.Attribute.MARGINHEIGHT	HTML.Attribute.TITLE
HTML.Attribute.COLOR	HTML.Attribute.MARGINWIDTH	HTML.Attribute.TYPE
HTML.Attribute.COLS	HTML.Attribute.MAXLENGTH	HTML.Attribute.USEMAP
HTML.Attribute.COLSPAN	HTML.Attribute.METHOD	HTML.Attribute.VALIGN
HTML.Attribute.COMMENT	HTML.Attribute.MULTIPLE	HTML.Attribute.VALUE

```
HTML.Attribute.COMPACT        HTML.Attribute.N          HTML.Attribute.VALUETYPE
HTML.Attribute.CONTENT        HTML.Attribute.NAME       HTML.Attribute.VERSION
HTML.Attribute.COORDS         HTML.Attribute.NOHREF     HTML.Attribute.VLINK
HTML.Attribute.DATA           HTML.Attribute.NORESIZE   HTML.Attribute.VSPACE
HTML.Attribute.DECLARE        HTML.Attribute.NOSHADE    HTML.Attribute.WIDTH
HTML.Attribute.DIR            HTML.Attribute.NOWRAP
```

The `MutableAttributeSet` interface adds six methods to add attributes to and remove attributes from the set:

```
public void addAttribute(Object name, Object value)
public void addAttributes(AttributeSet attributes)
public void removeAttribute(Object name)
public void removeAttributes(Enumeration names)
public void removeAttributes(AttributeSet attributes)
public void setResolveParent(AttributeSet parent)
```

Again, the values are strings and the names are `HTML.Attribute` objects.

One possible use for all these methods is to modify documents before saving or displaying them. For example, most web browsers let you save a page on your hard drive as either HTML or text. However, both these formats lose track of images and relative links. The problem is that most pages are full of relative URLs, and these all break when you move the page to your local machine. Example 8-10 is an application called `PageSaver` that downloads a web page to a local hard drive while keeping all links intact by rewriting all relative URLs as absolute URLs.

The `PageSaver` class reads a series of URLs from the command line. It opens each one in turn and parses it. Every tag, text block, comment, and attribute is copied into a local file. However, all link attributes, such as SRC, LOWSRC, CODEBASE, and HREF, are remapped to an absolute URL. Note particularly the extensive use to which the URL and `javax.swing.text` classes were put; `PageSaver` could be rewritten with string replacements, but that would be considerably more complicated.

Example 8-10. PageSaver

```
import javax.swing.text.*;
import javax.swing.text.html.*;
import javax.swing.text.html.parser.*;
import java.io.*;
import java.net.*;
import java.util.*;

public class PageSaver extends HTMLEditorKit.ParserCallback {

  private Writer out;
  private URL base;

  public PageSaver(Writer out, URL base) {
```

Example 8-10. PageSaver (continued)

```
    this.out = out;
    this.base = base;
  }

  public void handleStartTag(HTML.Tag tag,
   MutableAttributeSet attributes, int position) {
    try {
      out.write("<" + tag);
      this.writeAttributes(attributes);
      // for the <APPLET> tag we may have to add a codebase attribute
      if (tag == HTML.Tag.APPLET
        && attributes.getAttribute(HTML.Attribute.CODEBASE) == null) {
        String codebase = base.toString();
        if (codebase.endsWith(".htm") || codebase.endsWith(".html")) {
          codebase = codebase.substring(0, codebase.lastIndexOf('/'));
        }
        out.write(" codebase=\"" + codebase + "\"");
      }
      out.write(">");
      out.flush();
    }
    catch (IOException e) {
      System.err.println(e);
      e.printStackTrace();
    }
  }

  public void handleEndTag(HTML.Tag tag, int position) {
    try {
      out.write("</" + tag + ">");
      out.flush();
    }
    catch (IOException e) {
      System.err.println(e);
    }
  }

  private void writeAttributes(AttributeSet attributes)
   throws IOException {

    Enumeration e = attributes.getAttributeNames();
    while (e.hasMoreElements()) {
      Object name = e.nextElement();
      String value = (String) attributes.getAttribute(name);
      try {
        if (name == HTML.Attribute.HREF || name == HTML.Attribute.SRC
          || name == HTML.Attribute.LOWSRC
          || name == HTML.Attribute.CODEBASE ) {
          URL u = new URL(base, value);
```

Example 8-10. PageSaver (continued)

```
                out.write(" " + name + "=\"" + u + "\"");
            }
            else {
                out.write(" " + name + "=\"" + value + "\"");
            }
        }
        catch (MalformedURLException ex) {
            System.err.println(ex);
            System.err.println(base);
            System.err.println(value);
            ex.printStackTrace();
        }
    }
}


public void handleComment(char[] text, int position) {

    try {
        out.write("<!-- ");
        out.write(text);
        out.write(" -->");
        out.flush();
    }
    catch (IOException e) {
        System.err.println(e);
    }

}


public void handleText(char[] text, int position) {

    try {
        out.write(text);
        out.flush();
    }
    catch (IOException e) {
        System.err.println(e);
        e.printStackTrace();
    }

}

public void handleSimpleTag(HTML.Tag tag,
  MutableAttributeSet attributes, int position) {
    try {
        out.write("<" + tag);
        this.writeAttributes(attributes);
        out.write(">");
    }
```

Example 8-10. PageSaver (continued)

```java
      catch (IOException e) {
        System.err.println(e);
        e.printStackTrace();
      }
    }

  public static void main(String[] args) {

    for (int i = 0; i < args.length; i++) {

      ParserGetter kit = new ParserGetter();
      HTMLEditorKit.Parser parser = kit.getParser();

      try {
        URL u = new URL(args[i]);
        InputStream in = u.openStream();
        InputStreamReader r = new InputStreamReader(in);
        String remoteFileName = u.getFile();
        if (remoteFileName.endsWith("/")) {
          remoteFileName += "index.html";
        }
        if (remoteFileName.startsWith("/")) {
          remoteFileName = remoteFileName.substring(1);
        }
        File localDirectory = new File(u.getHost());
        while (remoteFileName.indexOf('/') > -1) {
          String part = remoteFileName.substring(0, remoteFileName.indexOf('/'));
          remoteFileName =
                  remoteFileName.substring(remoteFileName.indexOf('/')+1);
          localDirectory = new File(localDirectory, part);
        }
        if (localDirectory.mkdirs()) {
          File output = new File(localDirectory, remoteFileName);
          FileWriter out = new FileWriter(output);
          HTMLEditorKit.ParserCallback callback = new PageSaver(out, u);
          parser.parse(r, callback, false);
        }
      }
      catch (IOException e) {
        System.err.println(e);
        e.printStackTrace();
      }

    }

  }

}
```

The `handleEndTag()`, `handleText()`, and `handleComment()` methods simply copy their content from the input into the output. The `handleStartTag()` and `handleSimpleTag()` methods write their respective tags onto the output but also invoke the private `writeAttributes()` method. This method loops through the attributes in the set and mostly just copies them onto the output. However, for a few select attributes, such as `SRC` and `HREF`, that typically have URL values, it rewrites the values as absolute URLs. Finally, the `main()` method reads URLs from the command line, calculates reasonable names and directories for corresponding local files, and starts a new `PageSaver` for each URL.

In the first edition of this book, I included a similar program that downloaded the raw HTML using the `URL` class and parsed it manually. That program was about a third longer than this one and much less robust. For instance, it did not support frames or the `LOWSRC` attributes of `IMG` tags. It went to great effort to handle both quoted and unquoted attribute values and still didn't recognize attribute values enclosed in single quotes. By contrast, this program needs only one extra line of code to support each additional attribute. It is much more robust, much easier to understand since there's not a lot of detailed string manipulation, and much easier to extend.

This is just one example of the various HTML filters that the `javax.swing.text.html` package makes easy to write. You could, for example, write a filter that pretty prints the HTML by indenting the different levels of tags. You could write a program to convert HTML to TeX, XML, RTF, or many other formats. You could write a program that spidered a web site, downloading all linked pages—and this is just the beginning. All of these programs are much easier to write because Swing provides a simple-to-use HTML parser. All you have to do is respond to the individual elements and attributes that the parser discovers in the HTML document. The much harder problem of parsing the document is removed.

9

The Network Methods of java.applet.Applet

Undoubtedly you're familiar with applets, Java programs that can be embedded on a web page and run in a secure environment within a browser. All applets extend the `java.applet.Applet` class, which includes a number of methods that perform network-related operations. These methods allow an applet to find out where it came from, download images and sounds from a web server, and track the progress of the download. This chapter discusses the interaction between applets and the network. It doesn't provide an introduction to the `Applet` class as a whole; for that, see an introductory book such as Niemeyer and Peck's *Learning Java* (O'Reilly & Associates, Inc., 2000).

Using java.applet.Applet to Download Data

The methods of the `Applet` class discussed in this section are really just thin veneers over equivalent methods in the `java.applet.AppletStub` and `java.applet.AppletContext` interfaces. These interfaces describe services that the web browser or applet viewer provides to applets. The exact classes that implement these interfaces are undocumented and vary from implementation to implementation. Applets that you instantiate yourself (for example, an applet that also runs as an application by supplying a `main()` method that calls the applet's `init()` and `start()` methods) will generally have null `AppletStub` and `AppletContext` members. Therefore, if you try to use these methods in such an applet, a `NullPointerException` will be thrown.

267

Figuring Out Where the Applet Came from

Most often, applets retrieve image files or other data from one of two directories: the directory the applet came from, or the directory the HTML page in which the applet was embedded came from. These directories are called the *codebase* and the *document base*, respectively. To make it easy to find other files, the Applet class has methods that return URL objects referring to the current page and the current applet. These methods are called getDocumentBase() and getCodeBase() respectively.

public URL getDocumentBase( )

The getDocumentBase() method returns the URL of the page containing the applet. Example 9-1 is a simple applet that displays the URL of the document in which it is embedded.

Example 9-1. An Applet That Shows Its Document Base

```
import java.applet.*;
import java.awt.*;

public class WhereAmI extends Applet {

  public void paint (Graphics g) {
    g.drawString(this.getDocumentBase().toString(), 25, 50);
  }

}
```

public URL getCodeBase( )

The getCodeBase() method returns the URL of the directory where the applet is located. If the applet is in a JAR archive, then the codebase is the URL of the directory where the JAR archive is. If the applet is in a package (e.g., com.macfaq.applets.MyApplet instead of just MyApplet), then the codebase is the directory or JAR archive containing the outermost package such as com. Security restrictions in applets are calculated relative to the codebase, not the document base. Example 9-2 is an applet that displays its document base and its codebase.

Example 9-2. An Applet That Displays Its Document Base and Its Codebase

```
import java.applet.*;
import java.awt.*;

public class AppletBases extends Applet {

  public void paint(Graphics g) {
```

Example 9-2. An Applet That Displays Its Document Base and Its Codebase (continued)

```
    g.drawString("Codebase:       "
      + this.getCodeBase().toString(), 10, 40);
    g.drawString("Document base: "
      + this.getDocumentBase().toString(), 10, 65);


  }


}
```

Figure 9-1 shows what happens when the applet runs; the result depends on the URLs of the applet and the document. It's worth noting that getCodeBase() always returns the URL of a directory, not the URL of the applet itself, while getDocumentBase() always returns the URL of a file.

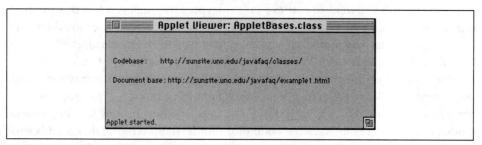

Figure 9-1. An applet that shows its document base and its codebase

Downloading Images

In Chapter 7, *Retrieving Data with URLs*, you learned how to download data from an HTTP URL by using the getContent() and openStream() methods of the URL class. These methods are useful for text data such as an HTML file, but they don't work as well for binary data, which usually requires some knowledge of the data's structure. The Applet class includes several methods that understand more about what they're downloading. The getImage() methods download image files and convert them into java.awt.Image objects:

```
    public Image getImage(URL url)
    public Image getImage(URL url, String name)
```

Like the other methods in this chapter, the two getImage() methods in the Applet class rely on an AppletContext field that is null for applets you instantiate yourself rather than being instantiated by a web browser or an applet viewer. However, the java.awt.Toolkit class includes identical getImage() methods that do not rely on an AppletContext. You can always get a Toolkit object by calling the static java.awt.Toolkit.getDefaultToolkit() method or the getToolkit() instance method of any subclass of java.awt.Component. Then you can use its `getImage()` methods just as you use the `getImage()` methods described here. The one difference is that you'll need to prefix the calls to `getImage()` with a variable that refers to the `Toolkit` object. For example:

```
Toolkit t = java.awt.Toolkit.getDefaultToolkit();
URL u = new URL("http://metalab.unc.edu/javafaq/cup.gif")
Image theImage = t.getImage(u);
```

public Image getImage(URL u)

This method retrieves the image data at the specified URL and puts it in a `java.awt.Image` object. For example:

```
Image myLogo = getImage(new URL("http://metalab.unc.edu/java/cup.gif"));
```

The `getImage()` method relies on the `AppletContext` (provided by the web browser or applet viewer) to retrieve and interpret the image. Thus this method can get images only in formats understood by the `AppletContext` in which the applet is running. Currently, all contexts that run in a graphical environment understand the GIF format. (IBM's Java environment for some of its mainframes and minicomputers is completely nongraphical because those platforms don't support graphics.) Most contexts also understand JPEG though JPEG support was omitted from some vendors' early alpha and beta releases. Finally, Java implementations derived from Sun's source code often understand XBM. JDK 1.3 adds support for PNG. Example 9-3 is a complete applet that loads and displays the image referenced by the IMAGE parameter, which comes from a <PARAM> tag in the HTML file.

Example 9-3. Display an Image via a URL

```
import java.applet.*;
import java.awt.*;
import java.net.*;

public class ImageView extends Applet {

  Image picture;

  public void init() {

    try {
      URL u = new URL(this.getCodeBase(), this.getParameter("IMAGE"));
      this.picture = this.getImage(u);
      System.err.println(u);
    }
    catch (MalformedURLException e) {
      // shouldn't happen, the codebase is never malformed
```

Example 9-3. Display an Image via a URL (continued)

```
    }

  }

  public void paint (Graphics g) {
    g.drawImage(this.picture, 0, 0, this);
  }

}
```

The `getImage()` method returns immediately, even before it knows whether the image actually exists. The image isn't loaded until some other part of the program actually tries to draw it, or you explicitly force the image to start loading— you'll see how to do that shortly. At that point, the virtual machine starts a separate thread to download and process the image file.

public Image getImage(URL path, String filename)

This is similar to the previous method, except that it uses the `path` argument (a URL) to find the image's directory and the `filename` argument (a `String`) to get the name of the image file. For example:

```
Image logo = this.getImage(new URL("http://metalab.unc.edu/java/"),
  "cup.gif");
```

This version of `getImage()` is frequently used with `getCodeBase()` or `getDocumentBase()`. You would use `getCodeBase()` in an applet that might be used on many different web servers but whose images would always be in the same directory as the applet. For example:

```
Image logo = this.getImage(this.getCodeBase(), "logo.gif"));
```

If the applet exists on only one web server but is embedded on many different pages, each of which loads different images, you would use `getDocumentBase()` to locate the images:

```
Image logo = this.getImage( this.getDocumentBase(), "logo.gif"));
```

This technique would be useful in an animator applet; the applet would probably read the names of some image files from parameters included in the HTML. You can use the `filename` argument to add to the path you get from the URL component. For example, if the pictures are in a directory called *images*, which is in the same directory as the HTML page, you would load the file *logo.gif* like this:

```
Image logo = this.getImage(this.getDocumentBase(), "images/logo.gif"));
```

Downloading Sounds

The `Applet` class has five methods that download sounds from the web. The two `play()` methods download a sound file and play it immediately. The two `getAudioClip()` methods and the static `Applet.newAudioClip()` method save a sound for later playing. The `AppletContext`, which is provided by the web browser or applet viewer, does the actual work of downloading and playing the sound file. Most Java 1.1 and earlier virtual machines support only Sun's *.au* format and a very restricted form at that (8-bit sampling, 8 kilohertz, mono, μ-law encoded). Java 1.2 adds many more formats, including AIFF, WAV, MIDI Type 0, MIDI Type 1, and Rich Music Format (RMF). Furthermore, it supports 8- and 16-bit sampling, in both mono and stereo, with sampling rates from 8 kHz to 48 kHz in linear, a-law, or μ-law encoding. For pre-1.2 VMs, there are a number of freeware, shareware, and payware tools that convert sounds to the *.au* format, including SoX on Linux and Unix systems (*http://home.sprynet.com/~cbagwell/sox.html*); SoundHack (*http://shoko.calarts.edu/~tre/SndHckDoc/*), Ulaw (*http://www.kagi.com/rod/*), and SoundEdit 16 (*http://www.macromedia.com/software/sound/*) on the Mac; and GoldWave on Windows (*http://www.goldwave.com/*).

public void play(URL u)

The `play()` method looks for a sound file at the `URL u`. If the sound file is found, then it is downloaded and played. Otherwise, nothing happens. For example:

```
try {
  URL soundLocation = new URL(
    "http://metalab.unc.edu/java/course/week9/spacemusic.au" );
  play(soundLocation);
}
catch (MalformedURLException e) {
  System.err.println(e);
}
```

Example 9-4 is a simple applet that plays a sound file. The name of the file is taken from the parameter sound, which is supplied by a <PARAM> tag in the HTML file. The sound file should be in the same directory as the applet.

Example 9-4. Play a Sound

```
import java.applet.*;
import java.awt.*;
import java.net.*;

public class PlaySound extends Applet {

  public void init() {
```

Example 9-4. Play a Sound (continued)

```
  try {
    URL u = new URL(this.getCodeBase(), this.getParameter("sound"));
    this.play(u);
  }
  catch (MalformedURLException e) {
  }


  }


}
```

public void play(URL url, String filename)

This is similar to the presious method, except that it uses the `url` argument to find the sound file's directory and the `filename` argument to get the actual filename. For example:

```
    play(new URL("http://www.macfaq.com/", "gong.au"));
```

The URL argument is frequently a call to `getCodeBase()` or `getDocument-Base()`. You use `getCodeBase()` if you know that the sound files will always be in the same directory as the applet, even if you don't know in advance where the applet will be located. For example:

```
    this.play(this.getCodeBase(), "gong.au"));
```

If the sound files are always located in the same directory as the HTML file that loads the applet, you would use `getDocumentBase()`. In this scenario, one applet, residing in one directory, might be used by several web pages located in different directories on that server; each page might use a <PARAM> tag to specify its own sound file. Such an applet might call `play()` like this:

```
    this.play(this.getDocumentBase(), this.getParameter("sound")));
```

You can use the `filename` argument to add to the path you get from the URL argument. For example, if the sounds are in a directory called *sounds*, which is a subdirectory of the directory containing the HTML page, you would call `play()`:

```
    this.play(this.getDocumentBase(), "sounds/gong.au"));
```

public AudioClip getAudioClip(URL u)

The `java.applet.AudioClip` interface represents a sound. You can download a sound from a web site with the `getAudioClip()` method. Once you have an `AudioClip` object, play it at your leisure by calling the clip's `play()` and `loop()` methods; `play()` plays the file once, and `loop()` plays it repeatedly. Both of these methods let you keep the audio clip around for future use—unlike the `play()` method of the last section, which discarded the audio data after it had finished.

Using the `AudioClip` interface is simple. Make sure you've imported `java.applet.AudioClip` (many programmers, out of habit, import only `java.applet.Applet`); declare an `AudioClip` variable, and call `getAudioClip()` to retrieve the sound file. As usual, the URL constructor needs to be wrapped in a `try` block because of a potential `MalformedURLException`. For example:

```
AudioClip theGong;

try {
  URL u = new URL(http://metalab.unc.edu/javafaq/gong.au);
  theGong = this.getAudioClip(u);
}
catch (MalformedURLException e) {
  System.err.println(e);
}
```

public AudioClip getAudioClip(URL url, String filename)

This is similar to the previous method, except that it uses `url` to find the directory in which the sound file is located and `filename` to supply the name of the audio file. For example:

```
AudioClip ac = getAudioClip(new URL("http://www.macfaq.com/", "gong.au"));
```

This version of `getAudioClip()` is frequently used with `getCodeBase()` or `getDocumentBase()`. For example, if you are writing an applet that will be stored on many different servers but whose sound files will always be in the same directory as the applet, you would call `getAudioClip()` like this:

```
AudioClip ac = this.getAudioClip(this.getCodeBase(), "gong.au"));
```

Or, if you're writing an applet that will reside on one server but be used by many web pages with different sound files, you might call `getAudioClip()` like this:

```
String filename = this.getParameter("sound");
if (filename != null) {  // HTML included necessary PARAM tag
  AudioClip ac = this.getAudioClip(this.getDocumentBase(), filename);
}
```

In this case, `getDocumentBase()` returns the location of the HTML file, and `getParameter()` retrieves the name of an audio file from a <PARAM> tag in the HTML. You can use the `filename` argument to `getAudioClip()` to add to the path supplied by the URL. For example, in the following code, the sound file is located in the directory *sounds*, which is a subdirectory of the document's directory:

```
this.getAudioClip(this.getDocumentBase(), "sounds/gong.au"));
```

Example 9-5 is a complete applet that downloads a sound file called *gong.au*, which is located in the same directory as the applet, and then spawns a `Thread` to play the sound every five seconds.

Example 9-5. Download a Sound via a Relative URL and Play It at Five-Second Intervals

```
import java.applet.*;
import java.awt.*;

public class RelativeBeep extends Applet implements Runnable {

  private AudioClip beep;
  private boolean stopped = false;

  public void init() {

    beep = this.getAudioClip(this.getDocumentBase(), "sounds/beep.au");
    if (beep != null) {
      Thread t = new Thread(this);
      t.start();
    }

  }

  public void start() {
    this.stopped = false;
  }

  public void stop() {
    this.stopped = true;
  }

  public void run() {

    Thread.currentThread().setPriority(Thread.MIN_PRIORITY);
    while (true) {
      if (!stopped) beep.play();
      try {
        Thread.sleep(5000);
      }
      catch (InterruptedException e) {
      }
    }

  }

}
```

public static final AudioClip newAudioClip(URL url) // Java 1.2

Java 1.2 adds the static `Applet.newAudioClip()` method so that applications can download audio clips too. Why, you may ask, if this method is intended for the use of standalone applications, is it in the `Applet` class? The only answer I can suggest is that it was a quick hack designed to answer a long-standing request and that nobody gave a lot of thought to exactly what a sensible API for this would look like. Perhaps the underlying, undocumented infrastructure on which the `play()` and `getAudioClip()` methods depend was easily accessible only from inside the `Applet` class. Regardless of the reason, the `Applet` class is where the `newAudioClip()` method resides, and you'll need to use that class even in non-applets that want to load audio clips.

The `Applet.newAudioClip()` method returns an `AudioClip`, just like `getAudioClip()`. Therefore, you can invoke the same `loop()` and `play()` methods on it. For example, this code fragment loads the sound file at *http://metalab. unc.edu/java/course/week9/spacemusic.au* and plays it continuously. It can do this from an applet or an application. It does not need a web browser or `AppletContext`:

```
try {
  URL sound
    = new URL("http://metalab.unc.edu/java/course/week9/spacemusic.au");
  AudioClip ac = new AudioClip(sound);
  ac.loop();
}
catch (MalformedURLException e) {
  // shouldn't happen
}
```

The ImageObserver Interface

It is sometimes said, only half in jest, that WWW stands for "World Wide Wait", primarily because of the amount of time it takes for graphics-heavy pages to load. Although reading large files off a hard drive can be time-consuming, most users have trained themselves not to notice the time it takes; file loading seems to happen instantaneously. However, this is not the case when files are loaded from a network, particularly when that network is the Internet. It is not uncommon for even small images to take several minutes to load. Since Java loads images in a different thread than the main execution of a program, a program can do something while the pictures are downloaded. However, programs don't get impatient; users do. It is a good idea to keeps users informed about how much of an image has been loaded and how much longer they can expect to wait. The `java.awt. image.ImageObserver` interface allows you to monitor the loading process so that you can keep the user informed and use the image as quickly as possible once it does load.

When discussing `getImage()`, I said that the method returned immediately, before downloading the image. Downloading begins when you try to display the image or do something else that forces loading to start (for example, passing the `Image` object to the `prepareImage()` method of `java.awt.Component`). Because loading takes place in a separate thread, programs don't have to spin their wheels while lots of pictures are downloaded; they can continue doing something useful, even if that's limited to keeping the user informed. However, loading an image asynchronously creates a new problem: how do you know when it's ready? An `Image` object exists as soon as `getImage()` returns, long before anything is known about the image it represents. You can call an `Image`'s methods before it has finished loading, but the results are rarely what you want or expect. For example, the `getWidth()` and `getHeight()` methods return −1 until enough data has been loaded for these values to be known.

The `ImageObserver` interface allows an object to monitor the progress of loading and to take action (such as drawing the `Image`) when the `Image` is ready for use. You can also use `ImageObserver` objects to track the progress of an image that is being created from scratch, using `java.awt.image.MemoryImageSource` or some other instance of the `java.awt.image.ImageProducer` interface. This interface consists of a group of constants and a single method, `imageUpdate()`:

```
public boolean imageUpdate(Image image, int infoflags, int x, int y,
  int width, int height)
```

`java.awt.Component` implements `ImageObserver`, so all its subclasses (including `java.applet.Applet`, `java.awt.Canvas`, `java.awt.Panel`, `javax.swing.JButton`, and many more) do as well.

If you've done much programming in Java, you've probably used the `ImageObserver` class without thinking about it: the `this` that you stick at the end of a call to `drawImage()` says to use the current component as an `ImageObserver`:

```
g.drawImage(theImage, 0, 0, this);
```

If the image is complete, then it's drawn and that's that. On the other hand, if the image is not ready, then the component's `imageUpdate()` method will be called periodically, giving it the chance to check the status of the image and respond accordingly. Other methods that take `ImageObserver` objects as arguments include the `getWidth()`, `getHeight()`, and `getProperty()` methods of `java.awt.Image`; the `checkImage()` and `prepareImage()` methods of `java.awt.Component`; and the `setImageObserver()` method of `javax.swing.ImageIcon`. Passing an `ImageObserver` to any of these methods signals that the object is

interested in the image and should be notified through the `imageUpdate()`
method when the image's status changes. Variables that are set using a method
such as `getWidth()` or `getHeight()`, and pictures that are drawn on the screen
using `drawImage()`, are not updated automatically when `imageUpdate()` is
called. It's your job to update them when the image changes.

If you want to create your own `ImageObserver`, you first create a subclass of any
`Component` or create your own class that implements the `ImageObserver`
interface. Be sure to import `java.awt.image.ImageObserver` or `java.awt.`
`image.*` Importing `java.awt.*` does not automatically import `java.awt.`
`image.ImageObserver`. Your new class, or your `Component` subclass, must
include an `imageUpdate()` method. As you'll see in the next section, there are a
series of tests that `imageUpdate()` can perform to determine the current status
of the image.

Example 9-6 is an applet that loads an image from the Net. It supplies its own
`imageUpdate()` method (overriding the `imageUpdate()` method `Applet` inherits from `Component`) to see whether the image has loaded. Until the image has finished loading, the applet displays the words "Loading Picture. Please hang on".
Once the image has fully loaded, the applet displays it.

Example 9-6. Load an Image

```
import java.awt.*;
import java.applet.*;
import java.awt.image.*;

public class DelayedImageView extends Applet {

  private Image picture;

  public void init() {
    this.picture = this.getImage(this.getDocumentBase(), "cup.gif");
  }

  public void paint(Graphics g) {

    if(!g.drawImage(this.picture, 0, 0, this)) {
      g.drawString("Loading Picture. Please hang on", 25, 50);
    }

  }

public boolean imageUpdate(Image image, int infoflags, int x, int y,
  int width, int height) {

    if ((infoflags & ImageObserver.ALLBITS) == ImageObserver.ALLBITS) {
      this.repaint();
      return false;
```

Example 9-6. Load an Image (continued)

```
    }
    else {
      return true;
    }


  }


}
```

There are a couple of things to note about this example. First, the `drawImage()` method returns a `boolean`. Many programmers don't realize this, since the return value of `drawImage()` is often ignored. However, that `boolean` tells you whether the image was drawn successfully. If it was, `drawImage()` returns `true`. Otherwise, `drawImage()` returns `false`.

Second, the `imageUpdate()` method is called by the `ImageObserver` when necessary; you do not call it explicitly. It returns `false` if the image is complete and no longer needs to be updated. It returns `true` if the image still needs to be updated.

TIP   Let's repeat that point, since it's easy to get backwards. The `imageUpdate()` method should return `false` if the image is complete and `true` if the image is not complete. The `imageUpdate()` method answers the question "Does this image need to be updated?" It does not answer the question "Is this image complete?"

Now, let's look at what `imageUpdate()` does. The `Image` being loaded is passed into `imageUpdate()` through the `image` argument. Various mnemonic constants are combined to form the `infoflags` argument, which indicates what information about the image is now available. For instance, `ImageObserver.ALLBITS` is 32, and means that the `Image` is complete. You test whether the `ALLBITS` flag is set in `infoflags` by logically *and*ing it with the mnemonic constant `ImageObserver.ALLBITS` and then seeing if the result is equal to `ImageObserver.ALLBITS`. This chunk of Boolean algebra looks complicated but is more efficient than the alternatives.

The precise meaning of the `x`, `y`, `width`, and `height` arguments depends on the contents of the `infoflags` argument. The flags used in this argument are described in the next section.

The `imageUpdate()` method needs to do three things:

1. Check to see what has changed in this `Image`, using `infoflags`.

2. Perform any action needed to update the state of the running program.

3. Return `true` if further updates are needed and `false` if all necessary information is available.

The ImageObserver Constants

The `ImageObserver` interface defines eight mnemonic constants, which are used as flags to report the image's status in calls to `imageUpdate()`. Table 9-1 lists the constants and their meanings.

Table 9-1. ImageObserver Constants

Flag	Meaning If the Flag Is Set
ImageObserver.WIDTH	The width of the image is available in the `width` argument to `imageUpdate()`. Until this flag is set, `getWidth()` returns –1.
ImageObserver.HEIGHT	The height of the image is available in the `height` argument to `imageUpdate()`. Until this flag is set, calls to `getHeight()` return –1.
ImageObserver.PROPERTIES	The properties of the image are now available and can be accessed with the `getProperty()` method of the `Image` object.
ImageObserver.SOMEBITS	Some portion of the data needed to draw the image has been delivered. The bounding box of the available pixels is given by the `x`, `y`, `width`, and `height` arguments to the `imageUpdate()` method.
ImageObserver.FRAMEBITS	Another complete frame of a multiframe image is now available. The `x`, `y`, `width`, and `height` arguments to `imageUpdate()` have no meaning.
ImageObserver.ALLBITS	The image is now complete. The `x`, `y`, `width`, and `height` arguments to `imageUpdate()` have no meaning. At this point, the `imageUpdate()` method should return false, to indicate that the image requires no further monitoring.
ImageObserver.ERROR	The image encountered an error while loading. No further information will be forthcoming, and attempts to draw the image will fail. The `ImageObserver.ABORT` flag is set at the same time to indicate that image loading was aborted.
ImageObserver.ABORT	Loading aborted before the image was complete. No more information will become available without further action to reload the `Image`. If the `ImageObserver.ERROR` bit is not also set in `infoflags`, then attempting to access any of the data in the image restarts the loading process.

For example, to test whether the width and the height of the image are known, you would put the following code in the `imageUpdate()` method:

```
if ((infoflags & ImageObserver.WIDTH) == ImageObserver.WIDTH  &&
    (infoflags & ImageObserver.HEIGHT) == ImageObserver.HEIGHT) {...}
```

The difference between the `ImageObserver.ERROR` and `ImageObserver.ABORT` flags can be confusing. You would get an `ImageObserver.ERROR` if the image data was incorrect—for example, you tried to download a mangled file. If you try to load the image again, you'll get the same bad data. `ImageObserver.ABORT` usually indicates some kind of network error, such as a timeout; if you try to load the image again, you might succeed.

The MediaTracker Class

The `ImageObserver` interface is useful for monitoring a single image, but it starts to fall apart when faced with multiple images. The `java.awt.MediaTracker` class can track the loading status of many different images and organize them into logical groups. In future versions of Java, it may even be able to monitor the loading of audio clips and other kinds of multimedia content. However, Sun's been promising this since Java 1.0 and still hasn't delivered, so I'm not holding my breath.

To use `java.awt.MediaTracker`, simply create an instance of `MediaTracker` and then use the `MediaTracker`'s `addImage()` method to place each `Image` you care about under the `MediaTracker`'s control. When you add an `Image` to a `MediaTracker`, you give it a numeric ID. This ID does not have to be unique; it is really a group ID that is used to organize different images into groups. Before using the image, you call a method such as `checkID()` to see whether the image is ready. Other methods let you force loading to start, discover which images in a group have failed to load successfully, wait for images to finish loading, and so on.

NOTE   One difference between a `MediaTracker` and an `ImageObserver` is that the `MediaTracker` is called before the `Image` is used, while an `ImageObserver` is called after the `Image` is used.

Example 9-7 is an applet that loads an image from the Net. As usual, the image is loaded from the document base, and the name of the image file is read from a <PARAM> tag; the name of the parameter is `imagefile`. The applet uses a `MediaTracker` to see whether the image has loaded. The applet displays the words "Loading Picture. Please hang on" until the image has finished loading.

Example 9-7. Load an Image

```
import java.awt.*;
import java.applet.*;

public class TrackedImage extends Applet implements Runnable {

    private Image picture;
    private MediaTracker tracker;
```

Example 9-7. Load an Image (continued)

```
public void init() {

  this.picture = this.getImage(this.getCodeBase(),
   this.getParameter("imagefile"));
  this.tracker = new MediaTracker(this);
  this.tracker.addImage(this.picture, 1);

  Thread play = new Thread(this);
  play.start();

}

public void run() {

  try {
    this.tracker.waitForID(1);
    this.repaint();
  }
  catch (InterruptedException ie) {
  }

}

public void paint(Graphics g) {

  if (this.tracker.checkID(1, true)) {
    g.drawImage(this.picture, 0, 0, this);
  }
  else {
    g.drawString("Loading Picture. Please hang on", 25, 50);
  }

}

}
```

The `init()` method reads the name of the image to be loaded; prepares an Image object, `picture`, to hold it by calling `getImage()`; constructs a new MediaTracker called `tracker`; and then adds `picture` to `tracker` with an ID of 1. Next it constructs a new Thread and starts it.

The Thread that's spawned just makes sure that the applet is repainted as soon as the image has finished loading. It calls `tracker.waitForID(1)`, which blocks until all media with ID number 1 have finished loading. When that's true, the method returns and `repaint()` is called. I used a separate thread so the call to `waitForID()` won't block the rest of the applet.

The paint() method calls tracker.checkID(1, true) to see whether the media with ID 1 is available. If this method returns true, the image is available, and the applet calls drawImage() to render the image on the screen. Otherwise, the picture is not available, so the applet displays the string "Loading Picture. Please hang on". A more sophisticated applet could put up a progress bar that showed the percentage of the Image that had been loaded and the approximate time remaining.

The Constructor

The MediaTracker class has one constructor:

```
public MediaTracker(Component comp)
```

This constructor creates a MediaTracker object that tracks images for a specified Component. It's usually invoked like this:

```
MediaTracker tracker = new MediaTracker(this);
```

The constructor's argument is the component on which the images you want to track will be displayed, generally a Panel or an Applet or a Canvas. You often call the constructor within the subclass defining the component that will be rendering the images; therefore, the argument to MediaTracker() is often this.

Adding Images to MediaTrackers

The two overloaded addImage() methods each add one Image to the list of images being tracked by this MediaTracker object. When an image is added, it is assigned an ID number by which it can later be referred to. Images are loaded in order of their IDs; that is, image 1 is loaded before image 2, and so on. If multiple images have the same ID, there's no guarantee which will be loaded first. Adding an Image to a MediaTracker does not start loading the image data. You have to call checkID(ID, true), checkAll(true), or one of the four wait methods first.

public void addImage(Image image, int id)

This addImage() method adds image to the list of images being tracked by this MediaTracker object and assigns it the ID number id. The image will eventually be displayed at its normal (unscaled) size. For example, the following code fragment from an applet sets up a tracker for an image called *logo.gif* that's in the same directory as the web page—it's given the ID number 1:

```
Image picture = this.getImage(this.getDocumentBase(), "logo.gif");
MediaTracker tracker = new MediaTracker(this);
tracker.addImage(picture, 1);
```

If you are going to scale the image, you must use the next version of addImage().

public void addImage(Image image, int id, int width, int height)

This version of `addImage()` adds `image` to the list of `Image` objects being tracked by this `MediaTracker` with the ID number `id`. The image will eventually be displayed scaled to the width `width` and the height `height`. The following code fragment sets up a tracker for an image called *logo.gif* that's in the same directory as the web page. This image will be scaled into a 30-pixel × 30-pixel square when it's displayed:

```
Image picture = this.getImage(this.getDocumentBase(), "logo.gif");
MediaTracker tracker = new MediaTracker(this);
tracker.addImage(picture, 1, 30, 30);
```

Checking Whether Media Has Loaded

There are four check methods that tell you whether particular images tracked by a `MediaTracker` have loaded. These are:

```
public boolean checkID(int id)
public boolean checkID(int id, boolean load)
public boolean checkAll()
public boolean checkAll(boolean load)
```

public boolean checkID(int id)

This method checks whether all the images with the indicated ID that are tracked by this `MediaTracker` have finished loading. If they have, it returns true; otherwise, it returns false. Multiple `Image` objects may have the same ID. Merely checking the status of an image with this method will not make it start loading if it is not already loading. For example, the following `paint()` method draws `thePicture` only if all the `Image` objects with ID 1 have finished loading:

```
public void paint(Graphics g) {

    if (theTracker.checkID(1)) {
      g.drawImage(thePicture, 0, 0, this);
    }
    else {
      g.drawString("Loading Picture. Please hang on", 25, 50);
    }

}
```

WARNING   There's something a little funny about how this operates. The `Image` with ID 1 is not necessarily the same `Image` as `thePicture`. There may be zero or more `Image` objects with ID 1, and none of them are necessarily `thePicture`. It's up to the programmer to make sure the ID you check is the ID of the `Image` you want to load. Although there are occasions when you want to check one picture and display another, this is rare. There probably should be a `MediaTracker` method with the signature check(`Image img`), but there isn't.

public boolean checkID(int id, boolean load)

This method checks whether all the `Image` objects with the indicated ID that are tracked by this `MediaTracker` have finished loading. If they have, it returns true; otherwise, it returns false. Multiple `Image` objects may have the same ID. If the `boolean` argument `load` is true, all images with that ID that are not yet being loaded will begin loading.

The following `paint()` method checks whether the `Image` objects with ID 1 have finished loading. If they have, then `thePicture` is drawn. Otherwise, the `Image` objects with ID 1 start loading (if they aren't already), and the message "Loading Picture. Please hang on" is displayed:

```
public void paint(Graphics g) {

    if (theTracker.checkID(1, true)) {
      g.drawImage(thePicture, 0, 0, this);
    }
    else {
      g.drawString("Loading Picture. Please hang on", 25, 50);
    }


  }
```

public boolean checkAll( )

This method checks whether all the `Image` objects that are tracked by this object have finished loading. ID numbers are not considered. If all images are loaded, it returns true; otherwise, it returns false. It does not start loading images that are not already loading.

public boolean checkAll(boolean load)

This version of `checkAll()` checks whether all the `Image` objects that are tracked by this `MediaTracker` have finished loading. If they have, it returns true; otherwise, it returns false. If the `boolean` argument `load` is true, then it also starts loading any `Image` objects that are not already being loaded.

Waiting for Media to Load

MediaTracker is often used in conjunction with the getImage() methods of Applet or java.awt.Toolkit. The getImage() method is called as many times as necessary to load images. Then the MediaTracker makes sure the images have finished loading before the program continues. You could do this yourself by loading images in separate threads, then waiting on the threads loading the images. However, the MediaTracker class shields you from the details and is substantially easier to use correctly.

The next four methods start loading images tracked by the MediaTracker and then block while waiting for the images to load. For performance reasons, each method loads four images at a time in four separate threads. If more than four images need to be loaded, then some of them will have to wait for others to finish first. After invoking one of these methods, the calling thread will not continue until all the requested images have finished loading. If you don't want your program to block while you wait for images to download, you can call these methods inside a separate thread.

public void waitForID(int id) throws InterruptedException

This method forces the images with the ID number id that are tracked by this MediaTracker to start loading and then waits until each one has either finished loading, aborted, or received an error. An InterruptedException is thrown if another thread interrupts this thread. For example, to begin loading Image objects with ID 1 and then wait for them to finish loading, you would write:

```
try {
  tracker.waitForID(1);
}
catch (InterruptedException e) {
}
```

Let's look at a longer example. Netscape may be infamous for foisting the <BLINK> tag on the world, but it made some solid contributions to HTML as well. Two of the best are the HEIGHT and WIDTH attributes of the <IMG> tag. To the user, it seems much faster to load a page that includes HEIGHT and WIDTH attributes for all its images than one that doesn't. Actually, the time it takes to load the page is the same either way; but browsers can start displaying text and partial images as soon as they know how much space to reserve for each image. Consequently, if the width and height of each image is specified in the HTML, the browser can lay out the page and display the text immediately, without forcing the user to wait for everything to load. However, it takes a lot of time to measure every image on a page manually and rewrite the HTML, especially for pages that include many different size images.

Example 9-8 is a program that gets a URL from the user, reads the requested page
using an HTMLEditorKit.Parser, and outputs the HTML with HEIGHT and
WIDTH attributes added to all the <IMG> tags that didn't have them. It uses the
default Toolkit object's getImage() method to retrieve the Image objects, the
Image's getWidth() and getHeight() methods to measure them, and a
MediaTracker to make sure that the height and width are available. Before the
height and the width of a particular image are read, the MediaTracker's
waitForID() method is invoked to let the image finish loading first.

Example 9-8. A Program That Adds Height and Width Tags to the IMGs on a Web Page

```java
import javax.swing.text.*;
import javax.swing.text.html.*;
import javax.swing.text.html.parser.*;
import java.io.*;
import java.net.*;
import java.util.*;
import java.awt.*;
import java.awt.image.*;


public class ImageSizer extends HTMLEditorKit.ParserCallback {

  private Writer out;
  private URL base;

  public ImageSizer(Writer out, URL base) {
    this.out = out;
    this.base = base;
  }

  public void handleStartTag(HTML.Tag tag,
   MutableAttributeSet attributes, int position) {
    try {
      out.write("<" + tag);
      this.writeAttributes(tag, attributes);
      out.write(">");
      out.flush();
    }
    catch (IOException e) {
      System.err.println(e);
      e.printStackTrace();
    }

  }

  public void handleEndTag(HTML.Tag tag, int position) {
    try {
```

Example 9-8. A Program That Adds Height and Width Tags to the IMGs on a Web Page (continued)

```java
      out.write("</" + tag + ">");
      if (tag.breaksFlow()) out.write("\r\n");
      out.flush();
    }
    catch (IOException e) {
      System.err.println(e);
    }
  }


  private void writeAttributes(HTML.Tag tag, AttributeSet attributes)
   throws IOException {

    Enumeration e = attributes.getAttributeNames();
    while (e.hasMoreElements()) {
      Object name = e.nextElement();
      String value = (String) attributes.getAttribute(name);
      out.write(" " + name + "=\"" + value + "\"");
    }
    // for the IMG tag we may have to add HEIGHT and WIDTH attributes
    if (tag == HTML.Tag.IMG) {
      try {
        if (attributes.getAttribute(HTML.Attribute.HEIGHT) == null
          || attributes.getAttribute(HTML.Attribute.WIDTH) == null) {
          URL u = new URL(base,
            (String) attributes.getAttribute(HTML.Attribute.SRC));
          Image img = Toolkit.getDefaultToolkit().getImage(u);
          Component temp = new Label();
          MediaTracker tracker = new MediaTracker(temp);
          tracker.addImage(img, 1);
          try {
            tracker.waitForID(1);
            if (attributes.getAttribute(HTML.Attribute.WIDTH) == null) {
              out.write(" WIDTH=\"" + img.getWidth(temp) + "\"");
            }
            if (attributes.getAttribute(HTML.Attribute.HEIGHT) == null) {
              out.write(" HEIGHT=\"" + img.getHeight(temp) + "\"");
            }
          }
          catch (InterruptedException ex) {
          }
        }
      }
      catch (MalformedURLException ex) {
        // SRC attribute is malformed
      }
    }


  }
```

Example 9-8. A Program That Adds Height and Width Tags to the IMGs on a Web Page (continued)

```java
public void handleComment(char[] text, int position) {

  try {
    out.write("<!-- ");
    out.write(text);
    out.write(" -->");
    out.flush();
  }
  catch (IOException e) {
    System.err.println(e);
  }

}


public void handleText(char[] text, int position) {

  try {
    out.write(text);
    out.flush();
  }
  catch (IOException e) {
    System.err.println(e);
    e.printStackTrace();
  }

}

public void handleSimpleTag(HTML.Tag tag,
 MutableAttributeSet attributes, int position) {
  try {
    out.write("<" + tag);
    this.writeAttributes(tag, attributes);
    out.write(">");
  }
  catch (IOException e) {
    System.err.println(e);
    e.printStackTrace();
  }
}

public static void main(String[] args) {

  for (int i = 0; i < args.length; i++) {

    // The ParserGetter class is from Chapter 8
    ParserGetter kit = new ParserGetter();
    HTMLEditorKit.Parser parser = kit.getParser();
```

Example 9-8. A Program That Adds Height and Width Tags to the IMGs on a Web Page (continued)

```
    try {
      URL u = new URL(args[0]);
      InputStream in = u.openStream();
      InputStreamReader r = new InputStreamReader(in);
      HTMLEditorKit.ParserCallback callback
        = new ImageSizer(new OutputStreamWriter(System.out), u);
      parser.parse(r, callback, false);
    }
    catch (IOException e) {
      System.err.println(e);
      e.printStackTrace();
    }


  }


}
```

This is a standalone application that extends `HTMLEditorKit.ParserCallback`. It's very similar to Example 8-10, `PageSaver`, in the last chapter. The only real difference is that it adds `HEIGHT` and `WIDTH` attributes to the `IMG` tags rather than rewriting attribute values. Consequently, the only significantly different part of this example is the `writeAttributes()` method. If this method sees that it's dealing with an `IMG` tag, it checks to see whether that tag has both `HEIGHT` and `WIDTH` attributes. If it does, then the tag is simply copied from the input onto the output. However, if either is missing, the method then constructs the full URL for the image and retrieves it with `Toolkit.getDefaultToolkit().getImage()`. Next, a `MediaTracker` is created. The `MediaTracker()` constructor requires an `ImageObserver` as an argument, so a blank `java.awt.Label` is constructed to fill that role. This will also be used later as the `ImageObserver` for the `getWidth()` and `getHeight()` methods. The image is added to the tracker, and the tracker's `waitForID()` method is used to pause execution until the image has actually finished loading. At this point, the image's `getWidth()` and `getHeight()` methods are invoked, and their results are written in the output as the value of the `HEIGHT` and `WIDTH` attributes.

public boolean waitForID(int id, long milliseconds)
throws InterruptedException

This version of `waitForID()` begins loading all the images that are tracked by this `MediaTracker` with the ID number `id` and then waits until each one has either finished loading, aborted, or received an error or until the specified number of milliseconds has passed. An `InterruptedException` is thrown if another thread interrupts this thread. For example, to begin loading all `Image` objects with ID 1 and wait no longer than 2 minutes (120,000 milliseconds) for them to finish loading, you would write:

```
try {
  tracker.waitForID(1, 120000);
}
catch (InterruptedException e) {
}
```

public boolean waitForAll( ) throws InterruptedException

The `waitForAll()` method starts loading all the images that are tracked by this `MediaTracker` in up to four separate threads while pausing the thread that invoked it until each tracked image has either finished loading, aborted, or received an error. An `InterruptedException` is thrown if another thread interrupts the waiting thread.

This method might be used by an animation applet that wants to load all frames before it begins playing. The applet would add each frame to the `MediaTracker` and then call `waitForAll()` before starting the animation. Example 9-9 is a simple applet that does exactly this. To play an animation, an applet must download a series of images, each of which will be one cell of the animation. Downloading the images is easy using the `URL` class: just create `URL` objects that point to each image, and call `getImage()` with each `URL`. Use a `MediaTracker` to force the images to load; then use `waitForAll()` to make sure all frames have loaded. Finally, call `drawImage()` to display the images in sequence.

Example 9-9 reads a list of filenames from <PARAM> tags in the applet; the parameter names are `Cell1`, `Cell2`, `Cell3`, and so on. The value of the parameter `Celln` should be the name of the nth file in the animation sequence. This makes it easy to retrieve an indefinite number of images; the `init()` method continues reading parameters until it finds a parameter name that doesn't exist. The applet builds URLs from the filenames and the document base and uses `getImage()` to retrieve each image. The `Image` objects are stored in a `Vector` since it's not known in advance how many there will be. The applet assumes that the files reside in the same directory as the HTML page; therefore, one applet on a site can play many different animations just by changing the <PARAM> tags and the image files. When an image is retrieved, it's added to the `MediaTracker` tracker, and `tracker`'s `checkID()` method starts loading the image. Then the `start()` method spawns a new thread to display the images in sequence. `tracker`'s `waitForAll()` method pauses the animation thread until the images have finished loading.

Example 9-9. A Very Simple Animator Applet

```java
import java.awt.*;
import java.awt.image.*;
import java.awt.event.*;
import java.applet.*;
import java.util.*;

public class Animator extends Applet
 implements Runnable, MouseListener {

  private boolean running = false;
  private int      currentCell = 0;
  private Vector  cells = new Vector();
  private MediaTracker tracker;

  public void init() {

    this.addMouseListener(this);

    String nextCell;
    this.tracker = new MediaTracker(this);
    for (int i = 0; (nextCell = this.getParameter("Cell" + i)) != null;  i++) {
      Image img = this.getImage(this.getDocumentBase(), nextCell);
      cells.addElement(img);
      tracker.addImage(img, i);
      // start loading the image in a separate thread
      tracker.checkID(i, true);
    }

  }

  public void run() {

    // wait for all images to finish loading
    try {
      this.tracker.waitForAll();
    }
    catch (InterruptedException e) {
    }

    for (currentCell-0; currentCell < cells.size(); currentCell++) {
      if (!running) return;
        // paint the cell
        this.repaint();
        // sleep for a tenth of a second
        // i.e. play ten frames a second
      try {
        Thread.sleep(100);
```

Example 9-9. A Very Simple Animator Applet (continued)

```
      }
      catch (InterruptedException ie) {
      }
    }

  }

  public void stop() {
    this.running = false;
  }

  public void start() {
    this.running = true;
    Thread play = new Thread(this);
    play.start();
  }

  public void paint(Graphics g) {
    g.drawImage((Image) cells.elementAt(currentCell), 0, 0, this);
  }

  // The convention is that a mouseClick starts
  // a stopped applet and stops a running applet.
  public void mouseClicked(MouseEvent e) {

    if (running) {
      this.stop();
    }
    else {
      this.start();
    }

  }


  // do-nothing methods required to implement the MouseListener interface
  public void mousePressed(MouseEvent e) {}
  public void mouseReleased(MouseEvent e) {}
  public void mouseEntered(MouseEvent e) {}
  public void mouseExited(MouseEvent e) {}


}
```

It's easy to imagine ways to enhance this applet. One possibility would be sprites that follow a path across a constant background. But whatever extensions you add, they won't require any changes to the applet's networking code.

public boolean waitForAll(long milliseconds)
throws InterruptedException

This method is similar to the previous `waitForAll()` method. It too starts loading all the images that are tracked by this `MediaTracker` and waits until each one has either finished loading, aborted, or received an error. However, this method times out if the specified number of milliseconds has passed before all images are complete. It throws an `InterruptedException` if another thread interrupts this thread. The following code fragment begins loading all `Image` objects tracked by the `MediaTracker` tracker and waits not more than 2 minutes (120,000 milliseconds) for them to finish loading:

```
try {
  tracker.waitForAll(120000);
}
catch (InterruptedException e) {
}
```

As with any time-consuming operation, you should display some sort of progress bar so that the user has an idea how long the operation is likely to take and give the user an option to cancel the download.

Error Checking

If there is an error as an `Image` is loaded or scaled, then that `Image` is considered "complete"; no further loading of that image's data takes place. The following methods let you check whether an error has occurred and find out which image is at fault. However, there are no methods that tell you what sort of error has occurred.

public boolean isErrorAny( )

This method checks whether an error occurred while loading any image tracked by this object:

```
if (tracker.isErrorAny()) {
  System.err.println("There was an error while loading media");
}
```

This method does not tell you which image failed or why. If there was an error, you can use `getErrorsAny()` to find out which objects returned errors. Do not assume that a single `Image` caused the error; it is common for an entire group of images to fail to load as a result of a single error, such as a broken network connection. Consequently, if one image failed to load, chances are others did too.

public Object[ ] getErrorsAny( )

This method returns an array containing all the objects tracked by this MediaTracker that encountered an error while loading. If there were no errors, it returns null:

```
if (tracker.isErrorAny()) {
  System.err.println("The following media failed to load:");
  Object[] failedMedia = tracker.getErrorsAny();
  for (int i = 0; i < failedMedia.length; i++) {
    System.err.println(failedMedia[i]);
  }
}
```

public boolean isErrorID(int id)

This method returns true if any of the media with the specified ID encountered an error while loading; otherwise, it returns false. If there was an error, use getErrorsID() to find out which objects returned errors. Remember, a single ID may refer to several Image objects, any of which may have encountered errors:

```
if (tracker.isErrorID(2)) {
  System.err.println("An error occurred loading media with ID 2");
}
```

public Object[ ] getErrorsID(int id)

This method returns an array containing all the objects with this ID that encountered an error while loading. If there were no errors, it returns null:

```
if (tracker.isErrorID(2)) {
  System.err.println("The following media failed to load:");
  Object[] failedMedia = tracker.getErrorsID(2);
  for (int i = 0; i < failedMedia.length; i++) {
    System.err.println(failedMedia[i]);
  }
}
```

Checking the Status of Media

MediaTracker has a number of methods that report the status of image groups. Unfortunately, MediaTracker only lets you check the status of image groups, not individual images—which is a good argument for keeping image groups small. To report the status, the MediaTracker class defines four flag constants that are combined to tell you whether the images in question are loading, aborted, errored out, or completed. These constants are shown in Table 9-2.

Table 9-2. Media Status Constants

Constant	Value	Meaning
MediaTracker.LOADING	1	At least one image in the group is still being downloaded.
MediaTracker.ABORTED	2	The loading process aborted for at least one image in the group.
MediaTracker.ERRORED	4	An error occurred during loading for at least one image in the group.
MediaTracker.COMPLETE	8	At least one image in the group was downloaded successfully.

These constants are compared to the values returned by the status methods to determine whether particular conditions or combinations of conditions are true. Since each constant is an integral power of two, each has exactly one set bit, and thus the different constants can be easily combined with the bitwise operators to test combinations of conditions.

public int statusAll(boolean load)

This method returns the status of all the media tracked by this `MediaTracker` object. Thus to test whether any of the media tracked by `MediaTracker` m have finished loading, you would write:

```
if ((m.statusAll(false) & MediaTracker.COMPLETE)
        == MediaTracker.COMPLETE) {
```

If the argument `load` is true, any media that have not yet begun loading will start loading. If it is false, they will not.

public int statusID(int id, boolean load)

This method returns the status of the media sharing the ID `id` that are tracked by this `MediaTracker`. If the `load` argument is true, the media with the given `id` will begin loading if they haven't already started. If `load` is false, they won't. Thus, to test whether any of the media tracked by `MediaTracker` m with ID 2 have finished loading, you would write:

```
if ((m.statusAll(2, false) & MediaTracker.COMPLETE)
        == MediaTracker.COMPLETE) {...}
```

Because of the nature of the flags, if any of the images with ID 2 have finished loading, this will be true. Similarly, if any of the images with ID 2 have errored out, then the following expression will also be true:

```
(m.statusAll(2, false) & MediaTracker.ABORTED)
        == MediaTracker.ABORTED)
```

The same is true for the `MediaTracker.LOADING` and `MediaTracker.ERRORED` flags. Because there isn't any way to check a single image (other than putting the image into a group by itself), `statusID()` and `statusAll()` can return apparently contradictory results. For example, if there are four images in the group, it's entirely possible that `statusID()` will return the value:

```
MediaTracker.LOADING | MediaTracker.ABORTED | MediaTracker.ERRORED
  | MediaTracker.COMPLETE
```

This means that, of the four images, one is still loading, one aborted, an error occurred in another, and one loaded successfully. A single group of images can appear to simultaneously have completed loading, still be loading, have aborted, and have encountered an error. There is no way to test the status of a single `Image` if it shares an ID with another `Image`. For this reason, it's probably not a good idea to let too many images share the same ID.

Removing Images from MediaTrackers

Starting in Java 1.1, it is possible to remove an image from a `MediaTracker` using one of the three overloaded `removeImage()` methods:

```
public void removeImage(Image image)
public void removeImage(Image image, int id)
public void removeImage(Image image, int id, int width, int height)
```

The first method removes all instances of the `Image` argument from the `MediaTracker`. Most of the time, there'll be only one of these. The second variant removes the specified image if it has the given ID. The third removes the specified image if it has the given ID and width and height.

Network Methods of java.applet.AppletContext

`AppletContext` is an interface that lets an applet manipulate the environment in which it is running. Every applet has an `AppletContext` field, which is a reference to an object implementing `AppletContext`. In some sense, this object represents the web browser or applet viewer that is running the applet. (In rare cases, mostly applets started from the command line and instantiated in the `main()` method, the `AppletContext` may be `null`.) To access the applet's context, call the applet's `getAppletContext()` method:

```
public AppletContext getAppletContext()
```

The `AppletContext` must provide several methods for the use of the applet, including `getAudioClip()` and `getImage()` methods; the `getAudioClip()` and `getImage()` methods of `java.applet.Applet` merely call the corresponding method in the applet's `AppletContext`. However, there are two overloaded `showDocument()` methods in `java.applet.AppletContext` that are relevant to network programming and are not mirrored in `java.applet.Applet`. The first takes as an argument a single URL:

```
public void showDocument(URL url)
```

This method shows the document at URL `url` in the `AppletContext`'s window. It is not supported by all web browsers and applet viewers, but it is supported by Netscape, HotJava, and Internet Explorer. This method is most useful in fancy image map applets, where it is used to send the user to a new page after clicking on a hot button. For example, to send the user to the O'Reilly home page, you would write:

```
AppletContext ac = this.getAppletContext();
try {
  URL oreillyHomePage = new URL("http://www.oreilly.com/");
  ac.showDocument(oraHomePage);
}
catch (MalformedURLException e) {
}
```

Most web servers allow you to redirect requests from one URL to another; this feature can save you a lot of work when a site moves. For example, "The Well Connected Mac" began its life at *http://rever.nmsu.edu/~elharo/faq/* but eventually went commercial at *http://www.macfaq.com/*. When this happened, a redirector was set up to redirect requests for files in *http://rever.nmsu.edu/~elharo/faq/* to *http://www.macfaq.com/*. That way, I didn't have to update thousands of links and references to the old site overnight. Fortunately, the old site had an exceedingly friendly system administrator, who was willing to modify his server configuration files to perform the necessary redirection. However, some administrators aren't so friendly or willing to help you leave their site. In these cases, if you don't have the privileges to modify the server configuration, you can use `showDocument()` to write a simple redirector in Java that will send people along their merry way.

Example 9-10 is an applet that reads the new URL from the `newhost` parameter in the HTML and sends the browser from the old site to the new site. For maximum effect, place any text that should appear on the page between the opening and closing <APPLET> tags. This way, people with Java-capable browsers will be redirected without realizing they took a roundabout route.

Example 9-10. Redirector

```
import java.applet.*;
import java.net.*;

public class Redirector extends Applet {
```

Example 9-10. Redirector (continued)

```
public void init() {

  AppletContext ac = getAppletContext();
  URL oldURL = this.getDocumentBase();
  try {
    URL newURL = new URL(this.getParameter("newhost")
      + oldURL.getFile());
    ac.showDocument(newURL);
  }
  catch (MalformedURLException e) {
  }


}

}
```

The Redirector class is extremely simple. It reads the newhost parameter from a <PARAM> tag in the HTML file, adds the name of the file being requested, and constructs a new URL. It then calls showDocument() to jump to the new URL.

The second overloaded variant of the showDocument() method lets you pick where you want the document to be shown:

```
public void showDocument(URL url, String frameName)
```

This method displays the document at the URL url in the HTML frame with the specified name. If no such frame exists, then Java looks for another browser window with that name. If no such window exists, then a new window is created with the specified name. The name given as an argument here is not the title of the browser window but the name given to it by Java when it created the window the first time. This method is not supported by all web browsers and applet viewers. However, it is supported by Netscape, HotJava, and Internet Explorer. Here's a typical use:

```
AppletContext ac = this.getAppletContext();
ac.showDocument(new URL("http://www.oreilly.com/"), "main");
```

There are four special strings you can use for the frameName argument. These define where the document is shown rather than the title of the window. Table 9-3 lists the different possible target strings.

Table 9-3. Targets for showDocument( )

String	Target
_self	Show the document in the current frame (the frame containing the applet).
_parent	Show the document in the parent of the current frame; that is, the FRAME element whose SRC attribute points to the document containing this frame's FRAMESET element; this is the same as _top in a page that doesn't use frames.

Table 9-3. Targets for showDocument( ) (continued)

String	Target
_top	Show the document in the current window, replacing all existing frames and documents in that window.
_blank	Show the document in a new, unnamed, top-level window.

For example, to send the browser to the O'Reilly home page in a new window, you might write:

```
AppletContext ac = getAppletContext();
try {
  URL oreillyHomePage = new URL("http://www.oreilly.com/");
  ac.showDocument(oreillyHomePage, "_blank");
}
catch (Exception e) {
}
```

There are many uses for the showDocument() methods. Programmers have written fancy image map applets that respond to cursor position by showing ToolTips, highlighting the current selection, or displaying menus of sub-pages. When an actual selection is made, the applet uses showDocument() to send the browser to the requested page. Applet-based slide shows move from page to page automatically under the control of a timing thread. One of the more notorious uses of these applets is to pop up multiple windows on porn sites even after the user has closed the original window. Some of the more basic uses of redirection can now be handled with JavaScript, but Java applets do allow much more sophisticated user interfaces for these programs and do make it much easier to store state in the applet as the browser moves from page to page.

In this chapter:
- *Socket Basics*
- *Investigating
  Protocols with Telnet*
- *The Socket Class*
- *Socket Exceptions*
- *Examples*

10

Sockets for Clients

Data is transmitted across the Internet in packets of finite size called *datagrams*. Each datagram contains a *header* and a *payload*. The header contains the address and port to which the packet is going, the address and port from which the packet came, and various other housekeeping information used to ensure reliable transmission. The payload contains the data itself. However, since datagrams have finite length, it's often necessary to split the payload across multiple packets and reassemble it at the destination. It's also possible that one or more packets may be lost or corrupted in transit and need to be retransmitted or that packets will arrive out of order. Keeping track of this—splitting the payload into packets, generating headers, parsing the headers of incoming packets, keeping track of what packets have and haven't been received, etc.—is a lot of work and requires a lot of intricate code.

Fortunately, you don't have to do the work yourself. Sockets are an innovation of Berkeley Unix that allow the programmer to treat a network connection as just another stream onto which bytes can be written and from which bytes can be read. Historically, sockets are an extension of one of Unix's most important ideas: that all I/O should look like file I/O to the programmer, whether you're working with a keyboard, a graphics display, a regular file, or a network connection. Sockets shield the programmer from low-level details of the network, such as media types, packet sizes, packet retransmission, network addresses, and more. This abstraction has proved to be immensely useful and has long since traveled from its origins in Berkeley Unix to all breeds of Unix, plus Windows, the Macintosh, and of course Java.

Socket Basics

A socket is a connection between two hosts. It can perform seven basic operations:

- Connect to a remote machine
- Send data
- Receive data
- Close a connection
- Bind to a port
- Listen for incoming data
- Accept connections from remote machines on the bound port

Java's Socket class, which is used by both clients and servers, has methods that correspond to the first four of these operations. The last three operations are needed only by servers, which wait for clients to connect to them. They are implemented by the ServerSocket class, which is discussed in the next chapter. Java programs normally use client sockets in the following fashion:

1. The program creates a new socket with a Socket() constructor.

2. The socket attempts to connect to the remote host.

3. Once the connection is established, the local and remote hosts get input and output streams from the socket and use those streams to send data to each other. This connection is *full-duplex*; both hosts can send and receive data simultaneously. What the data means depends on the protocol; different commands are sent to an FTP server than to an HTTP server. There will normally be some agreed-upon hand-shaking followed by the transmission of data from one to the other.

4. When the transmission of data is complete, one or both sides close the connection. Some protocols, such as HTTP 1.0, require the connection to be closed after each request is serviced. Others, such as FTP, allow multiple requests to be processed in a single connection.

Investigating Protocols with Telnet

In this chapter, you'll see clients that use sockets to communicate with a number of well-known Internet services such as HTTP, echo, and more. The sockets themselves are simple enough; however, the protocols to communicate with different servers make life complex.

To get a feel for how a protocol operates, you can use Telnet to connect to a server, type different commands to it, and watch its responses. By default, Telnet attempts to connect to port 23. To connect to servers on different ports, specify the port you want to connect to like this:*

```
% telnet localhost 25
```

This example requests a connection to port 25, the SMTP port, on the local machine; SMTP is the protocol used to transfer email between servers or between a mail client and a server. If you know the commands to interact with an SMTP server, you can send email without going through a mail program. This trick can be used to forge email. For example, a few years ago, the summer students at the National Solar Observatory in Sunspot, New Mexico, made it appear that the party that one of the scientists was throwing after the annual volleyball match between the staff and the students was in fact a victory party for the students. (Of course, the author of this book had absolutely nothing to do with such despicable behavior. ;-)) The interaction with the SMTP server went something like this; input that you type is shown in bold (the names have been changed to protect the gullible):

```
flare% telnet localhost 25
Trying 127.0.0.1 ...
Connected to localhost.sunspot.noao.edu.
Escape character is '^]'.
220 flare.sunspot.noao.edu Sendmail 4.1/SMI-4.1 ready at Fri, 5 Jul 93 13:13:01
MDT
HELO sunspot.noao.edu
250 flare.sunspot.noao.edu Hello localhost [127.0.0.1], pleased to meet you
MAIL FROM: bart
250 bart... Sender ok
RCPT TO: local@sunspot.noao.edu
250 local@sunspot.noao.edu... Recipient ok
DATA
354 Enter mail, end with "." on a line by itself

In a pitiful attempt to reingratiate myself with the students
after their inevitable defeat of the staff on the volleyball
court at 4:00 P.M., July 24, I will be throwing a victory
party for the students at my house that evening at 7:00.
Everyone is invited.

Beer and Ben-Gay will be provided so the staff may drown
their sorrows and assuage their aching muscles after their
public humiliation.

Sincerely,
```

---

* This example and the other examples using Telnet assume that you're using a Unix system. However, Telnet clients are available for all common operating systems, and they are all pretty similar; for example, on Windows, you might have to type the hostname and the port into a dialog box rather than on the command-line, but otherwise, the clients work the same.

```
Bart
.
250 Mail accepted
QUIT
221 flare.sunspot.noao.edu delivering mail
Connection closed by foreign host.
```

Several members of the staff asked Bart why he, a staff member, was throwing a victory party for the students. The moral of this story is that you should never trust email, especially patently ridiculous email like this, without independent verification. The other moral of this story is that you can use Telnet to simulate a client, see how the client and the server interact, and thus learn what your Java program needs to do. Although this session doesn't demonstrate all the features of the SMTP protocol, it's sufficient to enable you to deduce how a simple email client talks to a server.

The Socket Class

The `java.net.Socket` class is Java's fundamental class for performing client-side TCP operations. Other client-oriented classes that make TCP network connections, such as `URL`, `URLConnection`, `Applet`, and `JEditorPane`, all ultimately end up invoking the methods of this class. This class itself uses native code to communicate with the local TCP stack of the host operating system. The methods of the `Socket` class set up and tear down connections and set as various socket options. Because TCP sockets are more or less reliable connections, the interface that the `Socket` class provides to the programmer is streams. The actual reading and writing of data over the socket is accomplished via the familiar stream classes.

The Constructors

The four nondeprecated public `Socket` constructors are simple. Each lets you specify the host and the port you want to connect to. Hosts may be specified as an `InetAddress` or a `String`. Ports are always specified as `int` values from 0 to 65,535. Two of the constructors also specify the local address and local port from which data will be sent. You might need to do this when you want to select one particular network interface from which to send data on a multihomed host.

In Java 1.1 and later, the `Socket` class also has two protected constructors. Network clients and servers will probably never need to use these; they become important if you're creating a subclass of `Socket` (perhaps to implement a new type of socket that automatically performs encryption, authentication, or data compression).

public Socket(String host, int port)
throws UnknownHostException, IOException

This constructor creates a TCP socket to the specified port on the specified host and attempts to connect to the remote host. For example:

```
try {
  Socket toOReilly = new Socket("www.oreilly.com", 80);
  // send and receive data...
}
catch (UnknownHostException e) {
  System.err.println(e);
}
catch (IOException e) {
  System.err.println(e);
}
```

In this constructor, the `host` argument is just a hostname—expressed as a `String`, not a URL such as *http://www.oreilly.com*—or an `InetAddress` object. If the domain-name server cannot resolve the hostname or is not functioning, the constructor throws an `UnknownHostException`. If the socket cannot be opened for some other reason, the constructor throws an `IOException`. There are many reasons a connection attempt might fail: the host you're trying to reach may not be accepting connections, a dialup Internet connection may be down, or routing problems may be preventing your packets from reaching their destination.

Since this constructor doesn't just create a `Socket` object but also tries to connect the socket to the remote host, you can use the object to determine whether connections to a particular port are allowed, as in Example 10-1:

Example 10-1. Find Out Which of the First 1,024 Ports Seem to Be Hosting TCP Servers on a Specified Host (the Local Host by Default)

```
import java.net.*;
import java.io.*;


public class LowPortScanner {

  public static void main(String[] args) {

    String host = "localhost";

    if (args.length > 0) {
      host = args[0];
    }
    for (int i = 1; i < 1024; i++) {
      try {
        Socket s = new Socket(host, i);
```

Example 10-1. Find Out Which of the First 1,024 Ports Seem to Be Hosting TCP Servers on a Specified Host (the Local Host by Default) (continued)

```
        System.out.println("There is a server on port " + i + " of "
          + host);
      }
      catch (UnknownHostException e) {
        System.err.println(e);
        break;
      }
      catch (IOException e) {
        // must not be a server on this port
      }
    } // end for

  } // end main

} // end PortScanner
```

Here's the output this program produces on my local host. Your results will vary, depending on which ports are occupied. As a rule, more ports will be occupied on a Unix workstation than on a PC or a Mac:

```
% java LowPortScanner
There is a server on port 21 of localhost
There is a server on port 22 of localhost
There is a server on port 23 of localhost
There is a server on port 25 of localhost
There is a server on port 37 of localhost
There is a server on port 111 of localhost
There is a server on port 139 of localhost
There is a server on port 210 of localhost
There is a server on port 515 of localhost
There is a server on port 873 of localhost
```

If you're curious about what servers are running on these ports, try experimenting with Telnet. On a Unix system, you may be able to find out which services reside on which ports by looking in the file */etc/services*. If LowPortScanner finds any ports that are running servers but are not listed in */etc/services*, then that's interesting.

Although this program looks simple, it's not without its uses. The first step to securing a system is understanding it. This program helps you understand what your system is doing so that you can find (and close) possible entrance points for attackers. You may also find rogue servers: for example, LowPortScanner might tell you that there's a server on port 800, which, on further investigation, turns out to be an HTTP server somebody is running to serve erotic GIFs, and which is saturating your T1. However, like most security tools, this program can be misused. Don't use LowPortScanner to probe a machine you do not own; most system administrators would consider that a hostile act.

public Socket(InetAddress host, int port) throws IOException

Like the previous constructor, this constructor creates a TCP socket to the specified port on the specified host and tries to connect. It differs by using an `InetAddress` object (discussed in Chapter 6, *Looking Up Internet Addresses*) to specify the host rather than a hostname. It throws an `IOException` if it can't connect, but does not throw an `UnknownHostException`; if the host is unknown, you will find out when you create the `InetAddress` object. For example:

```
try {
  InetAddress OReilly = InetAddress.getByName("www.oreilly.com");
  Socket OReillySocket = new Socket(OReilly, 80);
  // send and receive data...
}
catch (UnknownHostException e) {
  System.err.println(e);
}
catch (IOException e) {
  System.err.println(e);
}
```

In the rare case where you open many sockets to the same host, it is more efficient to convert the hostname to an `InetAddress` and then repeatedly use that `InetAddress` to create sockets. Example 10-2 uses this technique to improve on the efficiency of Example 10-1.

Example 10-2. Find Out Which of the Ports at or Above 1,024 Seem to Be Hosting TCP Servers

```
import java.net.*;
import java.io.*;


public class HighPortScanner {

  public static void main(String[] args) {

    String host = "localhost";

    if (args.length > 0) {
      host = args[0];
    }

    try {
      InetAddress theAddress = InetAddress.getByName(host);
      for (int i = 1024; i < 65536; i++) {
        try {
          Socket theSocket = new Socket(theAddress, i);
          System.out.println("There is a server on port "
```

Example 10-2. Find Out Which of the Ports at or Above 1,024 Seem to Be Hosting
TCP Servers (continued)

```
            + i + " of " + host);
        }
        catch (IOException e) {
          // must not be a server on this port
        }
      } // end for
    } // end try
    catch (UnknownHostException e) {
      System.err.println(e);
    }


  }  // end main


}  // end HighPortScanner
```

The results are much the same as before, except that `HighPortScanner` checks
ports above 1023.

public Socket(String host, int port, InetAddress interface, int localPort) throws IOException

This constructor creates a socket to the specified port on the specified host and
tries to connect. It connects *to* the host and port specified in the first two arguments. It connects *from* the local network interface and port specified by the last
two arguments. The network interface may be either physical (e.g., a different
Ethernet card) or virtual (a multihomed host). If 0 is passed for the `localPort`
argument, Java chooses a random available port between 1024 and 65,535. For
example, if I were running a program on *metalab.unc.edu* and wanted to make sure
that my connection went over its 100 megabit-per-second (Mbps) fiber-optic interface (*fddisunsite.oit.unc.edu*) instead of the 10Mbps Ethernet interface (*helios.oit.*
unc.edu), I would open a socket like this:

```
try {
  InetAddress fddi = InetAddress.getByName("fddisunsite.oit.unc.edu");
  Socket OReillySocket = new Socket("www.oreilly.com", 80, fddi, 0);
  // work with the sockets...
}
catch (UnknownHostException e) {
  System.err.println(e);
}
catch (IOException e) {
  System.err.println(e);
}
```

By passing 0 for the local port number, I say that I don't care which port is used but I do want to use the FDDI network interface.

This constructor can throw an IOException for all the usual reasons given in the previous constructors. Furthermore, an IOException (specifically, an UnknownHostException, though that's not declared in the throws clause of this constructor) will also be thrown if the String host cannot be located.

Finally, an IOException (probably a BindException, though again that's just a subclass of IOException and not specifically declared in the throws clause of this method) will be thrown if the socket is unable to bind to the requested local network interface. This tends to limit the portability of applications that use this constructor. You could take deliberate advantage of this to restrict a compiled program to run on only a predetermined host. This would require customizing distributions for each computer and is certainly overkill for cheap products. Furthermore, Java programs are so easy to disassemble, decompile, and reverse engineer that this scheme is far from foolproof. Nonetheless, it might be part of a scheme to enforce a software license or to prevent disgruntled employees from emailing your proprietary software to your competitors.

public Socket(InetAddress host, int port, InetAddress interface, int localPort) throws IOException

This constructor is identical to the previous one except that the host to connect to is passed as an InetAddress, not a String. It creates a TCP socket to the specified port on the specified host from the specified interface and local port, and tries to connect. If it fails, it throws an IOException. For example:

```
try {
  InetAddress metalab = InetAddress.getByName("metalab.unc.edu");
  InetAddress oreilly = InetAddress.getByName("www.oreilly.com");
  Socket oreillySocket = new Socket(oreilly, 80, metalab, 0);
}
catch (UnknownHostException e) {
  System.err.println(e);
}
catch (IOException e) {
  System.err.println(e);
}
```

protected Socket( )

The Socket class also has two protected constructors that initialize the superclass without connecting the socket. You use these if you're subclassing Socket, perhaps to implement a special kind of socket that encrypts transactions or understands your local proxy server. Most of your implementation of a new socket class will be written in a `SocketImpl` object.

The noargs `Socket()` constructor, available only in Java 1.1, installs the default `SocketImpl` (from either the factory or a `java.net.PlainSocketImpl`). It creates a new `Socket` without connecting it, and is usually called by subclasses of `java.net.Socket`. In Java 1.0, `java.net.Socket` is declared `final` so it cannot be subclassed, and this constructor does not exist.

protected Socket(SocketImpl impl)

This constructor, available only in Java 1.1 and later, installs the `SocketImpl` object `impl` when it creates the new `Socket` object. The `Socket` object is created but is not connected. This constructor is usually called by subclasses of `java.net.Socket`. In Java 1.0, `java.net.Socket` is final so it cannot be subclassed, and this constructor does not exist. You can pass `null` to this constructor if you don't need a `SocketImpl`. However, in this case, you must override all the base class methods that depend on the underlying `SocketImpl`.

NOTE   Java also has two `Socket` constructors that were deprecated starting in Java 1.1:

```
public Socket(String host, int port,
  boolean useStreams) throws IOException
public Socket(InetAddress host, int port,
  boolean useStreams) throws IOException
```

These constructors allowed the programmer to specify whether the socket was to be used for reliable, connection-oriented TCP stream traffic or unreliable UDP datagram traffic. If the `useStreams` argument is true, then the TCP datagrams are combined into a reliable stream of data, just as is done by all the other `Socket` constructors. However, if `useStreams` is false, then the socket transmits data as UDP datagrams instead.

These constructors have been deprecated starting with Java 1.1, and their inclusion in Java 1.0 was probably a mistake in the first place. Sockets are normally thought of as applying to TCP traffic only, and there are two entire other Java classes to handle UDP traffic (which will be discussed in Chapter 13, *UDP Datagrams and Sockets*). This constructor was always on the flaky side. The documentation for these constructors was never very clear. Different versions of the Java 1.0 documentation said different things about how this constructor was used, and you had to dig into the source code to figure out what was really happening.

Getting Information About a Socket

To the programmer, Socket objects appear to have several private fields that are accessible through various getter methods. Actually, sockets have only one field, a SocketImpl; the fields that appear to belong to the Socket actually reflect native code in the SocketImpl. This way, socket implementations can be changed without disturbing the program; for example, to support firewalls and proxy servers. The actual SocketImpl in use is almost completely transparent to the programmer.

public InetAddress getInetAddress( )

Given a Socket object, the getInetAddress() method tells you which remote host the Socket is connected to or, if the connection is now closed, which host the Socket was connected to when it was connected. For example:

```
try {
  Socket theSocket = new Socket("java.sun.com", 80);
  InetAddress host = theSocket.getInetAddress();
  System.out.println("Connected to remote host " + host);
} // end try
catch (UnknownHostException e) {
  System.err.println(e);
}
catch (IOException e) {
  System.err.println(e);
}
```

public int getPort( )

The getPort() method tells you which port the Socket is (or was or will be) connected to on the remote host. For example:

```
try {
  Socket theSocket = new Socket("java.sun.com", 80);
  int port = theSocket.getPort();
  System.out.println("Connected on remote port " + port);
} // end try
catch (UnknownHostException e) {
  System.err.println(e);
}
catch (IOException e) {
  System.err.println(e);
}
```

public int getLocalPort( )

There are two ends to a connection: the remote host and the local host. To find the port number for the local end of a connection, call `getLocalPort()`. For example:

```
try {
  Socket theSocket = new Socket("java.sun.com", 80, true);
  int localPort = theSocket.getLocalPort();
  System.out.println("Connecting from local port " + localPort);
}  // end try
catch (UnknownHostException e) {
  System.err.println(e);
}
catch (IOException e) {
  System.err.println(e);
}
```

Unlike the remote port, which (for a client socket) is usually a "well-known port" that has been preassigned by a standards committee, the local port is usually chosen by the system at runtime from the available unused ports. This way, many different clients on a system can access the same service at the same time. The local port is embedded in outbound IP packets along with the local host's IP address, so the server can send data back to the right port on the client.

public InetAddress getLocalAddress( )

The `getLocalAddress()` method tells you which network interface a socket is bound to. You normally use this on a multihomed host, or one with multiple network interfaces. For example:

```
try {
  Socket theSocket = new Socket(hostname, 80);
  InetAddress localAddress = theSocket.getLocalAddress();
  System.out.println("Connecting from local address " + localAddress);
}  // end try
catch (UnknownHostException e) {
  System.err.println(e);
}
catch (IOException e) {
  System.err.println(e);
}
```

Example 10-3 reads a list of hostnames from the command-line, attempts to open a socket to each one, and then uses these four methods to print the remote host, the remote port, the local address, and the local port.

Example 10-3. Get a Socket's Information

```
import java.net.*;
import java.io.*;

public class SocketInfo {

  public static void main(String[] args) {

    for (int i = 0; i < args.length; i++) {
      try {
        Socket theSocket = new Socket(args[i], 80);
        System.out.println("Connected to " + theSocket.getInetAddress()
          + " on port "  + theSocket.getPort() + " from port "
          + theSocket.getLocalPort() + " of "
          + theSocket.getLocalAddress());
      } // end try
      catch (UnknownHostException e) {
        System.err.println("I can't find " + args[i]);
      }
      catch (SocketException e) {
        System.err.println("Could not connect to " + args[i]);
      }
      catch (IOException e) {
        System.err.println(e);
      }

    } // end for

  } // end main

} // end SocketInfo
```

Here's the result. I included *www.oreilly.com* on the command-line twice to demonstrate that each connection was assigned a different local port, regardless of the remote host; the local port assigned to any connection is unpredictable and depends mostly on what other ports are in use. The connection to *shock.njit.edu* failed because that machine does not run any servers on port 80:

```
% java SocketInfo www.oreilly.com www.oreilly.com www.macfaq.com shock.njit.edu
Connected to www.oreilly.com/198.112.208.23 on port 80 from port 46770 of calzone.
oit.unc.edu/152.2.22.81
Connected to www.oreilly.com/198.112.208.23 on port 80 from port 46772 of calzone.
oit.unc.edu/152.2.22.81
Connected to www.macfaq.com/204.162.81.201 on port 80 from port 46773 of calzone.
oit.unc.edu/152.2.22.81
Could not connect to shock.njit.edu
```

public InputStream getInputStream( ) throws IOException

The `getInputStream( )` method returns an input stream that can read data from the socket into a program. You usually chain this `InputStream` to a filter stream or reader that offers more functionality—`DataInputStream` or `InputStream-Reader`, for example—before reading input. It's also extremely helpful to buffer the input by chaining it to a `BufferedInputStream` or a `BufferedReader` for performance reasons.

Now that we can get an input stream, we can read data from a socket and start experimenting with some actual Internet protocols. One of the simplest protocols is called "daytime", and is defined in RFC 867. There's almost nothing to it. The client opens a socket to port 13 on the daytime server. In response, the server sends the time in a human-readable format and closes the connection. You can test the daytime server with Telnet like this:

```
% telnet tock.usno.navy.mil 13
Trying 198.116.61.158...
Connected to tock.usno.navy.mil.
Escape character is '^]'.
Thu Sep  9 16:09:00 1999
Connection closed by foreign host.
```

The line "Thu Sep 9 16:09:00 1999" is sent by the daytime server; when you read your `Socket`'s `InputStream`, this is what you will get. The other lines are produced either by the Unix shell or by the Telnet program. Example 10-4 uses the `InputStream` returned by `getInputStream( )` to read the time sent by the daytime server.

TIP   The daytime protocol doesn't specify the format for the time it returns. Therefore, it is difficult to convert the character data that the server returns to a Java `Date` in a reliable fashion. If you want to create a `Date` object based on the time at the server, it's easier to use the time protocol from RFC 868 instead, which does specify a format for the time.

Example 10-4. A Daytime Protocol Client

```
import java.net.*;
import java.io.*;

public class DaytimeClient {

  public static void main(String[] args) {

    String hostname;
```

Example 10-4. A Daytime Protocol Client (continued)

```
    if (args.length > 0) {
      hostname = args[0];
    }
    else {
      hostname = "tock.usno.navy.mil";
    }

    try {
      Socket theSocket = new Socket(hostname, 13);
      InputStream timeStream = theSocket.getInputStream();
      StringBuffer time = new StringBuffer();
      int c;
      while ((c = timeStream.read()) != -1) time.append((char) c);
      String timeString = time.toString().trim();
      System.out.println("It is " + timeString + " at " + hostname);
    } // end try
    catch (UnknownHostException e) {
      System.err.println(e);
    }
    catch (IOException e) {
      System.err.println(e);
    }

  } // end main

} // end DaytimeClient
```

DaytimeClient reads the hostname of a daytime server from the command-line and uses it to construct a new Socket that connects to port 13 on the server. If the hostname is omitted, then the U.S. Naval Observatory's standard time server at *tock.usno.navy.mil* is used. The client then calls theSocket.getInputStream() to get theSocket's input stream, which is stored in the variable timeStream. Since the daytime protocol specifies ASCII, DaytimeClient doesn't bother chaining a reader to the stream. Instead, it just reads the bytes into a StringBuffer one at a time, breaking when the server closes the connection as the protocol requires it to do. Here's what happens:

```
% java DaytimeClient
It is Thu Sep  9 17:08:47 1999 at tock.usno.navy.mil
% java DaytimeClient vision.poly.edu
It is Thu Sep  9 13:04:55 1999 at vision.poly.edu
```

You can see that the clocks on the *tock.usno.navy.mil* and *vision.poly.edu* aren't synchronized, even after accounting for time zone differences. Differences of a few seconds can also be caused by the time it takes packets to travel across the Internet. For more details about network timekeeping, see *http://tycho.usno.navy.mil/*.

When reading data from the network, it's important to keep in mind that not all protocols use ASCII or even text. For example, the time protocol specified in RFC 868 specifies that the time be sent as the number of seconds since midnight, January 1, 1900 Greenwich Mean Time. However, this is not sent as an ASCII string like "2,524,521,600" or "–1297728000". Rather, it is sent as a 32-bit, unsigned, big-endian binary number.[*] Since this isn't text, you can't easily use Telnet to test such a service, and your program can't read the server response with a `Reader` or any sort of `readLine()` method. A Java program that connects to time servers must read the raw bytes and interpret them appropriately. In this example that's complicated by Java's lack of a 32-bit unsigned integer type. Consequently, you have to read the bytes one at a time and manually convert them into a `long` using the bitwise operators `<<` and `|`. Example 10-5 demonstrates. When speaking other protocols, you may encounter data formats even more alien to Java. For instance, a few network protocols use 64-bit fixed point numbers. There's no shortcut to handle all possible cases. You simply have to grit your teeth and code the math you need to handle the data in whatever format the server sends.

Example 10-5. A Time Protocol Client

```
import java.net.*;
import java.io.*;
import java.util.*;

public class TimeClient {

  public final static int DEFAULT_PORT = 37;

  public static void main(String[] args) {

    String hostname;
    int port = DEFAULT_PORT;

    if (args.length > 0) {
      hostname = args[0];
    }
    else {
      hostname = "tock.usno.navy.mil";
    }
```

---

[*] The RFC never actually comes out and says that this is the format used. It specifies 32 bits and assumes you know that all network protocols use big-endian numbers. That the number is unsigned can be determined only by calculating the wraparound date for signed and unsigned integers and comparing it to the date given in the specification (2036). To make matters worse, the specification actually gives an example of a negative time that can't actually be sent by time servers that follow the protocol. Time is a fairly old protocol, standardized in the early 1980s before the IETF was as careful about such issues as it is today. Nonetheless, if you find yourself implementing a not particularly well-specified protocol, you may have to do a significant amount of testing against existing implementations to figure out what you need to do. In the worst case, different existing implementations may behave differently.

Example 10-5. A Time Protocol Client (continued)

```
if (args.length > 1) {
  try {
    port = Integer.parseInt(args[1]);
  }
  catch (NumberFormatException e) {
  }
}

// The time protocol sets the epoch at 1900,
// the java Date class at 1970. This number
// converts between them.

long differenceBetweenEpochs = 2208988800L;

// If you'd rather not use the magic number uncomment
// the following section which calculates it directly.

/*
TimeZone gmt = TimeZone.getTimeZone("GMT");
Calendar epoch1900 = Calendar.getInstance(gmt);
epoch1900.set(1900, 01, 01, 00, 00, 00);
long epoch1900ms = epoch1900.getTime().getTime();
Calendar epoch1970 = Calendar.getInstance(gmt);
epoch1970.set(1970, 01, 01, 00, 00, 00);
long epoch1970ms = epoch1970.getTime().getTime();

long differenceInMS = epoch1970ms - epoch1900ms;
long differenceBetweenEpochs = differenceInMS/1000;
*/

InputStream raw = null;
try {
  Socket theSocket = new Socket(hostname, port);
  raw = theSocket.getInputStream();

  long secondsSince1900 = 0;
  for (int i = 0; i < 4; i++) {
    secondsSince1900 = (secondsSince1900 << 8) | raw.read();
  }

  long secondsSince1970
    = secondsSince1900 - differenceBetweenEpochs;
  long msSince1970 = secondsSince1970 * 1000;
  Date time = new Date(msSince1970);

  System.out.println("It is " + time + " at " + hostname);
```

Example 10-5. A Time Protocol Client (continued)

```
    }  // end try
    catch (UnknownHostException e) {
      System.err.println(e);
    }
    catch (IOException e) {
      System.err.println(e);
    }
    finally {
      try {
        if (raw != null) raw.close();
      }
      catch (IOException e) {}
    }

  }  // end main

} // end TimeClient
```

Here's the output of this program from a couple of sample runs. Since the time protocol specifies Greenwich Mean Time, the previous differences between time zones are eliminated. Most of the difference that's left simply reflects the clock drift between the two machines:

```
% java TimeClient
It is Thu Sep 09 10:20:47 PDT 1999 at tock.usno.navy.mil
% java TimeClient vision.poly.edu
It is Thu Sep 09 10:16:55 PDT 1999 at vision.poly.edu
```

Like DaytimeClient, TimeClient reads the hostname of the server and an optional port from the command-line and uses it to construct a new Socket that connects to that server. If the user omits the hostname, then TimeClient defaults to *tock.usno.navy.mil*. The default port is 37. The client then calls theSocket. getInputStream() to get theSocket's input stream, which is stored in the variable raw. Four bytes are read from this stream and used to construct a long that represents the value of those four bytes interpreted as a 32-bit unsigned integer. This gives the number of seconds that have elapsed since 12:00 A.M., January 1, 1900 GMT (the time protocol's epoch); 2,208,988,800 seconds are subtracted from this number to get the number of seconds since 12:00 A.M., January 1, 1970 GMT (the Java Date class epoch). This number is multiplied by 1,000 to convert it into milliseconds. Finally, that number of milliseconds is converted into a Date object, which can be printed to show the current time and date.

public OutputStream getOutputStream( ) throws IOException

The getOutputStream( ) method returns a raw OutputStream for writing data from your application to the other end of the socket. You usually chain this stream to a more convenient class like `DataOutputStream` or `OutputStreamWriter` before using it. For performance reasons, it's a good idea to buffer it as well. For example:

```
OutputStreamWriter out;
try {
  Socket http = new Socket("www.oreilly.com", 80)
  OutputStream raw = http.getOutputStream();
  OutputStream buffered = new BufferedOutputStream(raw);
  out = new OutputStreamWriter(buffered, "ASCII");
  out.write("GET / HTTP 1.0\r\n\r\n");
  // read the server response...
}
catch (Exception e) {
  System.err.println(e);
}
finally {
  try {
    out.close();
  }
  catch (Exception e) {}
}
```

The echo protocol, defined in RFC 862, is one of the simplest interactive TCP services. The client opens a socket to port 7 on the echo server and sends data. The server sends the data back. This continues until the client closes the connection. The echo protocol is useful for testing the network to make sure that data is not mangled by a misbehaving router or firewall. You can test echo with Telnet like this:

```
% telnet localhost 7
Trying 127.0.0.1...
Connected to localhost.
Escape character is '^]'.
This is a test
This is a test
This is another test
This is another test
9876543210
9876543210
^]
telnet> close
Connection closed.
%
```

Example 10-6 uses `getOutputStream()` and `getInputStream()` to implement a simple echo client. The user types input on the command-line, which is then sent to the server. The server echoes it back. The program exits when the user types a period on a line by itself. The echo protocol does not specify a character encoding. Indeed, what it specifies is that the data sent to the server is exactly the data returned by the server. The server echoes the raw bytes, not the characters they represent. Thus this program uses the default character encoding and line separator of the client system for reading the input from `System.in`, sending the data to the remote system, and typing the output on `System.out`. Since an echo server echoes exactly what is sent, it's as if the server dynamically adjusts itself to the client system's conventions for character encoding and line breaks. Consequently, we can use convenient classes and methods like `PrintWriter` and `readLine()` that would normally be too unreliable.

Example 10-6. An Echo Client

```
import java.net.*;
import java.io.*;

public class EchoClient {

  public static void main(String[] args) {

    String hostname = "localhost";

    if (args.length > 0) {
      hostname = args[0];
    }

    PrintWriter out = null;
    BufferedReader networkIn = null;
    try {
      Socket theSocket = new Socket(hostname, 7);
      networkIn = new BufferedReader(
       new InputStreamReader(theSocket.getInputStream()));
      BufferedReader userIn = new BufferedReader(
       new InputStreamReader(System.in));
      out = new PrintWriter(theSocket.getOutputStream());
      System.out.println("Connected to echo server");

      while (true) {
        String theLine = userIn.readLine();
        if (theLine.equals(".")) break;
        out.println(theLine);
        out.flush();
        System.out.println(networkIn.readLine());
      }

    } // end try
    catch (IOException e) {
      System.err.println(e);
    }
```

Example 10-6. An Echo Client (continued)

```
    finally {
      try {
        if (networkIn != null) networkIn.close();
        if (out != null) out.close();
      }
      catch (IOException e) {}
    }

  }  // end main

}  // end EchoClient
```

As usual, EchoClient reads the host to connect to from the command line. The hostname is used to create a new Socket object on port 7, called theSocket. The socket's InputStream is returned by getInputStream() and chained to an InputStreamReader, which is chained to a BufferedReader called networkIn. This reader reads the server responses. Since this client also needs to read input from the user, it creates a second BufferedReader, this one called userIn, which reads from System.in. Next, EchoClient calls theSocket.getOutputStream() to get theSocket's output stream, which is used to construct a new PrintWriter called out.

Now that the three streams have been created, it's simply a matter of reading from userIn and writing whatever the user types to out. Once data has been sent to the echo server, networkIn waits for a response. When networkIn receives a response, it's printed on System.out. In theory, this client could get hung waiting for a response that never comes. However, this is unlikely if the connection can be made in the first place, since the TCP protocol checks for bad packets and automatically asks the server for replacements. When we implement a UDP echo client in Chapter 13, we will need a different approach because UDP does no error checking. Here's a sample run:

```
% java EchoClient photon.poly.edu
Connected to echo server
Hello
Hello
How are you?
How are you?
I'm fine thank you.
I'm fine thank you.
Goodbye
Goodbye
.
```

Example 10-7 is line-oriented. It reads a line of input from the console, sends it to the server, then waits to read a line of output it gets back. However, the echo protocol doesn't require this. It echoes each byte as it receives it. It doesn't really care whether those bytes represent characters in some encoding or are divided into lines. Java does not allow you to put the console into "raw" mode, where each character is read as soon as it's typed instead of waiting for the user to press the Enter key. Consequently, if you want to explore the more immediate echo responses, you must provide a nonconsole interface. You also have to separate the network input from user input and network output. This is because the connection is full duplex but may be subject to some delay. If the Internet's running slow, the user may be able to type and send several characters before the server returns the first one. Then the server may return several bytes all at once. Unlike many protocols, echo does not specify lockstep behavior where the client sends a request but then waits for the full server response before sending any more data. The simplest way to handle such a protocol in Java is to place network input and output in separate threads.

Closing the Socket

That's almost everything you need to know about client-side sockets. When you're writing a client application, almost all the work goes into handling the streams and interpreting the data. The sockets themselves are very easy to work with; all the hard parts are hidden. That is one reason sockets are such a popular paradigm for network programming. After we cover a couple of remaining methods, you'll know everything you need to know to write TCP clients.

public synchronized void close( ) throws IOException

Until now, our examples have assumed that sockets close on their own; they haven't done anything to clean up after themselves. It is true that a socket is closed automatically when one of its two streams is closed, when the program ends, or when it's garbage collected. However, it is a bad practice to assume that the system will close sockets for you, especially for programs that may run for an indefinite period of time. In a socket-intensive program like a web browser, the system may well hit its maximum number of open sockets before the garbage collector kicks in. The port scanner programs of Example 10-1 and Example 10-2 are particularly bad offenders in this respect, since it may take a long time for the program to run through all the ports. Shortly, we'll write a new version that doesn't have this problem.

When you're through with a socket, you should call its close() method to disconnect. Ideally, you put this in a finally block so that the socket is closed whether or not an exception is thrown. The syntax is straightforward:

```
Socket connection = null;
try {
```

```
      Socket connection = new Socket("www.oreilly.com", 13);
      // interact with the socket
    }  // end try
    catch (UnknownHostException e) {
      System.err.println(e);
    }
    catch (IOException e) {
      System.err.println(e);
    }
    finally {
      if (connection != null) connection.close();
    }
```

Once a `Socket` has been closed, its `InetAddress`, port number, local address, and local port number are still accessible through the `getInetAddress()`, `getPort()`, `getLocalAddress()`, and `getLocalPort()` methods. However, although you can still call `getInputStream()` or `getOutputStream()`, attempting to read data from the `InputStream` or write data to the `OutputStream` throws an `IOException`.

Example 10-7 is a revision of the `PortScanner` program that closes each socket once it's through with it. It does not close sockets that fail to connect. Since these are never opened, they don't need to be closed. In fact, if the constructor failed, `connection` is actually `null`.

Example 10-7. Look for Ports with Socket Closing

```
import java.net.*;
import java.io.*;


public class PortScanner {

  public static void main(String[] args) {

    String host = "localhost";

    if (args.length > 0) {
      host = args[0];
    }

    try {
      InetAddress theAddress = InetAddress.getByName(host);
      for (int i = 1; i < 65536; i++) {
        Socket connection = null;
        try {
          connection = new Socket(host, i);
          System.out.println("There is a server on port "
            + i + " of " + host);
```

Example 10-7. Look for Ports with Socket Closing (continued)

```
      }
      catch (IOException e) {
        // must not be a server on this port
      }
      finally {
        try {
          if (connection != null) connection.close();
        }
        catch (IOException e) {}
      }
    } // end for
  } // end try
  catch (UnknownHostException e) {
    System.err.println(e);
  }

  } // end main

} // end PortScanner
```

Half-closed sockets   // Java 1.3

The close() method shuts down both input and output from the socket. On occasion, you may want to shut down only half of the connection, either input or output. Starting in Java 1.3, the shutdownInput() and shutdownOutput() methods let you close only half of the connection:

```
public void shutdownInput() throws IOException    // Java 1.3
public void shutdownOutput() throws IOException   // Java 1.3
```

This doesn't actually close the socket. However, it does adjust the stream connected to it so that it thinks it's at the end of the stream. Further reads from the input stream will return –1. Further writes to the output stream will throw an IOException. In practice, though, there's not a lot to be gained by this approach.

Many protocols, such as finger, whois, and HTTP, begin with the client sending a request to the server, then reading the response. It would be possible to shut down the output after the client has sent the request. For example, this code fragment sends a request to an HTTP server, then shuts down the output, since it won't need to write anything else over this socket:

```
Socket connection = null;
try {
  connection = new Socket("www.oreilly.com", 80);
  Writer out = new OutputStreamWriter(
    connection.getOutputStream(), "8859_1");
  out.write("GET / HTTP 1.0\r\n\r\n");
```

```
      out.flush();
      connection.shutdownOutput();
      // read the response...
    }
    catch (IOException e) {
    }
    finally {
      try {
        if (connection != null) connection.close();
      }
      catch (IOException e) {}
    }
```

Notice that even though you shut down half or even both halves of a connection, you still need to close the socket when you're through with it. The shutdown methods simply affect the socket's streams. They don't release the resources associated with the socket such as the port it occupies.

The Object Methods

The Socket class overrides only one of the standard methods from java.lang. Object, toString(). Since sockets are transitory objects that typically last only as long as the connection they represent, there's not much need or purpose to storing them in hash tables or comparing them to each other.

public String toString( )

The toString() method produces a string that looks like this:

```
Socket[addr=www.oreilly.com/198.112.208.11,port=80,localport=50055]
```

This is ugly and useful primarily for debugging. You should not rely on this format; it may (and probably should) change in the future. All parts of this string are accessible directly through other methods (specifically getInetAddress(), getPort(), and getLocalPort()).

Setting Socket Options

Socket options specify how the native sockets on which the Java Socket class relies send and receive data. You can set four options in Java 1.1, six in Java 1.2, and seven in Java 1.3:

- TCP_NODELAY
- SO_BINDADDR
- SO_TIMEOUT
- SO_LINGER

- SO_SNDBUF (Java 1.2 and later)

- SO_RCVBUF (Java 1.2 and later)

- SO_KEEPALIVE (Java 1.3 and later)

The funny-looking names for these options are taken from the named constants in the C header files used in Berkeley Unix where sockets were invented. Thus they follow classic Unix C naming conventions rather than the more legible Java naming conventions. For instance, SO_SNDBUF really means "Socket Option Send Buffer Size".

TCP_NODELAY

```
public void setTcpNoDelay(boolean on) throws SocketException
public boolean getTcpNoDelay() throws SocketException
```

Setting TCP_NODELAY to true ensures that packets are sent as quickly as possible regardless of their size. Normally small (1-byte) packets are combined into larger packets before being sent. Before sending another packet, the local host waits to receive acknowledgement of the previous packet from the remote system. This is known as *Nagle's algorithm*. The problem with Nagle's algorithm is that if the remote system doesn't send acknowledgements back to the local system fast enough, then applications that depend on the steady transfer of small bits of information may slow down. This is especially problematic for GUI programs such as games or network computer applications where the server needs to track client-side mouse movement in real time. On a really slow network, even simple typing can be too slow because of the constant buffering. Setting TCP_NODELAY to true defeats this buffering scheme, so that all packets are sent as soon as they're ready.

`setTcpNoDelay(true)` turns off buffering for the socket. `setTcpNoDelay(false)` turns it back on. `getTcpNoDelay()` returns `true` if buffering is off and `false` if buffering is on. For example, the following fragment turns off buffering (that is, it turns on TCP_NODELAY) for the socket `s` if it isn't already off:

```
if (!s.getTcpNoDelay()) s.setTcpNoDelay(true);
```

These two methods are each declared to throw a `SocketException`. These will be thrown only if the underlying socket implementation doesn't support the TCP_NODELAY option.

SO_LINGER

```
public void setSoLinger(boolean on, int seconds) throws SocketException
public int getSoLinger() throws SocketException
```

The SO_LINGER option specifies what to do with datagrams that have not yet been sent when a socket is closed. By default, the close() method returns immediately, but the system still tries to send any remaining data. If the linger time is set to zero, then any unsent packets are thrown away when the socket is closed. If the linger time is any positive value, then the close() method blocks while waiting the specified number of seconds for the data to be sent and the acknowledgments to be received. When that number of seconds has passed, the socket is closed and any remaining data is not sent, acknowledgment or no.

These two methods each throw a SocketException if the underlying socket implementation does not support the SO_LINGER option. The setSoLinger() method can also throw an IllegalArgumentException if you try to set the linger time to a negative value. However, the getSoLinger() method may return –1 to indicate that this option is disabled, and as much time as is needed is taken to deliver the remaining data; for example, to set the linger timeout for the Socket s to four minutes, if it's not already set to some other value:

```
if (s.getTcpSoLinger() == -1) s.setSoLinger(true, 240);
```

The maximum linger time is 65,535 seconds. Times larger than that will be reduced to 65,535 seconds. Frankly, 65,535 seconds is much longer than you actually want to wait. Generally, the platform default value is more appropriate.

SO_TIMEOUT

```
public synchronized void setSoTimeout(int milliseconds)
  throws SocketException
public synchronized int getSoTimeout() throws SocketException
```

Normally when you try to read data from a socket, the read() call blocks as long as necessary to get enough bytes. By setting SO_TIMEOUT, you ensure that the call will not block for more than a fixed number of milliseconds. When the timeout expires, an InterruptedIOException is thrown, and you should be prepared to catch it. However, the socket is still connected. Although this read() call failed, you can try to read from the socket again. The next call may succeed.

Timeouts are given in milliseconds. Zero is interpreted as an infinite timeout, and is the default value. For example, to set the timeout value of the Socket object s to three minutes if it isn't already set, specify 180,000 milliseconds:

```
if (s.getSoTimeout() == 0) s.setSoTimeout(180000);
```

These two methods each throw a SocketException if the underlying socket implementation does not support the SO_TIMEOUT option. The setSoTimeout() method also throws an IllegalArgumentException if the specified timeout value is negative.

SO_RCVBUF

Most TCP stacks use buffers to improve network performance. Larger buffers tend to improve performance for reasonably fast (say, 10Mbps and up) connections while slower, dialup connections do better with smaller buffers. Generally, transfers of large, continuous blocks of data, as is common in file transfer protocols such as FTP and HTTP, benefit from large buffers, while the smaller transfers of interactive sessions, such as Telnet and many games do not. Relatively old operating systems designed in the age of small files and slow networks, such as BSD 4.2, use 2-kilobyte buffers. Somewhat newer systems, such as SunOS 4.1.3, use larger 4-kilobyte buffers by default. Still newer systems, such as Solaris, use 8- or even 16-kilobyte buffers. Starting in Java 2 (but not Java 1.1), there are methods to get and set the suggested receive buffer size used for network input:

```
public void setReceiveBufferSize(int size)  // Java 1.2
  throws SocketException, IllegalArgumentException
public int getReceiveBufferSize() throws SocketException    // Java 1.2
```

The `getReceiveBufferSize()` method returns the number of bytes in the buffer that can be used for input from this socket. It throws a `SocketException` if the underlying socket implementation does not recognize the SO_RCVBUF option. This might happen on a non-POSIX operating system.

The `setReceiveBufferSize()` method suggests a number of bytes to use for buffering output on this socket. However, the underlying implementation is free to ignore this suggestion. The `setReceiveBufferSize()` method throws an `IllegalArgumentException` if its argument is less than or equal to zero. Although it's declared to also throw `SocketException`, it probably won't in practice since a `SocketException` is thrown for the same reason as `IllegalArgumentException` and the check for the `IllegalArgument Exception` is made first.

SO_SNDBUF

Starting in Java 1.2 (but not Java 1.1), there are methods to get and set the suggested send buffer size used for network output:

```
public void setSendBufferSize(int size)                // Java 1.2
  throws SocketException, IllegalArgumentException
public int getSendBufferSize() throws SocketException    // Java 1.2
```

The `getSendBufferSize()` method returns the number of bytes in the buffer used for output on this socket. It throws a `SocketException` if the underlying socket implementation doesn't understand the SO_SNDBUF option.

The `setSendBufferSize()` method suggests a number of bytes to use for buffering output on this socket. However, again the client is free to ignore this suggestion. The `setSendBufferSize()` method also throws a `SocketException` if the underlying socket implementation doesn't understand the SO_SNDBUF option. However, it throws an `IllegalArgumentException` if its argument is less than or equal to zero.

SO_KEEPALIVE

If SO_KEEPALIVE is turned on, then the client will occasionally send a data packet over an idle connection, (most commonly once every two hours) just to make sure the server hasn't crashed. If the server fails to respond to this packet, the client will keep trying for a little more than 11 minutes until it receives a response. If it doesn't receive a response within 12 minutes, then the client will close the socket. Without SO_KEEPALIVE, an inactive client could live more or less forever without noticing that the server had crashed.

Java 1.3 adds methods to turn SO_KEEPALIVE on and off and to determine its current state:

```
public void setKeepAlive(boolean on) throws SocketException   // Java 1.3
public boolean getKeepAlive() throws SocketException   // Java 1.3
```

The default for SO_KEEPALIVE is false. This code fragment turns SO_KEEP-ALIVE off, if it's turned on:

```
if (s.getKeepAlive()) s.setKeepAlive(false);
```

Socket Exceptions

In Java 1.0, a problem with a socket method is likely to throw a `java.net.SocketException`, which is a subclass of `IOException`:

```
public class SocketException extends IOException
```

Indeed, even in Java 1.1 and later, many methods are declared to throw only `SocketException` or even `IOException` rather than the more specific subclasses. However, knowing that a problem occurred is often not sufficient to deal with the problem. Did the remote host refuse the connection because it was busy? Did the remote host refuse the connection because no service was listening on the port? Did the connection attempt timeout because of network congestion or because the host was down? Java 1.1 added three new subclasses of `SocketException` that provide more information about what went wrong: `BindException`, `ConnectException`, and `NoRouteToHostException`:

```
public class BindException extends SocketException
public class ConnectException extends SocketException
public class NoRouteToHostException extends SocketException
```

A BindException is thrown if you try to construct a Socket or ServerSocket object on a local port that is in use or that you do not have sufficient privileges to use. A ConnectException is thrown when a connection is refused at the remote host, which usually happens because the host is busy or no process is listening on that port. Finally, a NoRouteToHostException indicates that the connection has timed out.

Code that you write in Java 1.0 should catch SocketException and IOException. Since all three of these new exceptions are subclasses of SocketException, that code should continue to work in Java 1.1. New code that you write in Java 1.1 and later can take advantage of these three subclasses to provide more informative error messages or to decide whether retrying the offending operation is likely to be successful.

Examples

One of the first large-scale Java programs was HotJava, a web browser that was easily the equal of the early versions of Mosaic. Today's HotJava is easily comparable to Netscape Navigator, Opera, or Internet Explorer. It is completely possible to write commercial-quality applications in Java, and it is especially possible to write network-aware applications, both clients and servers. This section shows two network clients, finger and whois, to prove this point. I stop short of what could be done, but only in the user interface. All the necessary networking code is present. Indeed, once again we find out that network code is easy; it's user interfaces that are hard.

Finger

Finger is a straightforward protocol described in RFC 1288. The client makes a TCP connection to the server on port 79 and sends a one-line query; the server responds to the query and closes the connection. The format of the query is precisely defined, the format of the response somewhat less so. All data transferred should probably be pure printable ASCII text, though unfortunately the specification contradicts itself repeatedly on this point. The specification also recommends that clients filter out any non-ASCII data they do receive, at least by default.* All lines must end with a carriage return/linefeed pair (\r\n in Java parlance).

---

* Failure to filter non-printable characters allows mischievous users to configure their *.plan* files to reset people's terminals, switch them into graphics mode, or play other tricks accessible to those with intimate knowledge of VT-terminal escape sequences. While amusing to experienced users who recognize what's going on and appreciate the hack value of such *.plan* files, these tricks do confuse and terrify the uninitiated.

The simplest allowable request from the client is a bare carriage return/linefeed pair, which is usually interpreted as a request to show a list of the currently logged-in users.* For example:

```
% telnet rama.poly.edu 79
Trying 128.238.10.212...
Connected to rama.poly.edu.
Escape character is '^]'.

Login       Name            TTY      Idle   When     Where
jacola      Jane Colaginae  *pts/7          Tue 08:01 208.34.37.104
marcus      Marcus Tullius   pts/15  13d Tue 17:33 farm-dialup11.poly.e
matewan     Sepin Matewan   *pts/17  17: Thu 15:32 128.238.10.177
hengpi      Heng Pin        *pts/10      Tue 10:36 128.238.18.119
nadats      Nabeel Datsun    pts/12   56 Mon 10:38 128.238.213.227
matewan     Sepin Matewan   *pts/8    4 Sun 18:39 128.238.10.177
Connection closed by foreign host.
```

It is also possible to request information about a specific user or username by including that user or username on the query line:

```
% telnet rama.poly.edu 79
Trying 128.238.10.212...
Connected to rama.poly.edu.
Escape character is '^]'.
marcus
Login       Name            TTY      Idle   When     Where
marcus      Marcus Tullius   pts/15  13d Tue 17:33 farm-dialup11.poly.e
```

The information that finger servers return typically includes the user's full name, where he's connected from, how long he has been connected, and any other information he has chosen to make available in his *.plan* file.† A few servers put finger to other uses; for example, several sites give you a list of recent earthquake activity. It is possible to request information about users via their first name, last name, or login name. You can also request information about more than one user at a time like this:

```
% telnet rama.poly.edu 79
Trying 128.238.10.212...
Connected to rama.poly.edu.
Escape character is '^]'.
marcus nadats matewan
Login       Name            TTY      Idle   When     Where
marcus      Marcus Tullius   pts/15  13d Tue 17:33 farm-dialup11.poly.e
nadats      Nabeel Datsun    pts/12   59 Mon 10:38 128.238.213.227
matewan     Sepin Matewan   *pts/17  17: Thu 15:32 128.238.10.177
```

---

* Vending machines connected to the Internet return a list of items available for purchase instead.

† The *.plan* file is a peculiarity of Unix; you won't find this file on other operating systems.

```
matewan   Sepin Matewan     *pts/8      8 Sun 18:39   128.238.10.177
Connection closed by foreign host.
```

In this section, we'll develop a Java finger client that allows users to specify a host-name on the command-line, followed by zero or more usernames. For example, a typical command-line will look like:

```
% java FingerClient hostname user1 user2 ...
```

FingerClient connects to port 79 on the specified host. The socket's OutputStream is chained to an OutputStreamWriter using the ISO 8859-1 encoding, which is used to send a line consisting of all the names on the command-line, followed by a carriage return and a linefeed. Next, the output from the server (which is input to the program) is taken from theSocket. getInputStream() and chained first to a BufferedInputStream for performance and then to an InputStreamReader so that the server response can be read as text. The server's output is presented to the user on System.out. Example 10-8 shows the code.

Example 10-8. A Java Command-line Finger Client

```
import java.net.*;
import java.io.*;

public class FingerClient {

  public final static int DEFAULT_PORT = 79;

  public static void main(String[] args) {

    String hostname = "localhost";

    try {
      hostname = args[0];
    }
    catch (ArrayIndexOutOfBoundsException e) {
      hostname = "localhost";
    }

    Socket connection = null;
    try {
      connection = new Socket(hostname, DEFAULT_PORT);
      Writer out = new OutputStreamWriter(
       connection.getOutputStream(), "8859_1");
      for (int i = 1; i < args.length; i++) out.write(args[i] + " ");
      out.write("\r\n");
      out.flush();
      InputStream raw = connection.getInputStream();
      BufferedInputStream buffer = new BufferedInputStream(raw);
```

Example 10-8. A Java Command-line Finger Client (continued)

```
    InputStreamReader in = new InputStreamReader(buffer, "8859_1");
    int c;
    while ((c = in.read()) != -1) {
     // filter non-printable and non-ASCII as recommended by RFC 1288
     if ((c >= 32 && c < 127) || c == '\t' || c == '\r' || c == '\n')
      {
        System.out.write(c);
      }
     }
    }
   }
   catch (IOException e) {
     System.err.println(e);
   }
   finally {
     try {
       if (connection != null) connection.close();
     }
     catch (IOException e) {}
   }

  }

}
```

Here are some samples of this program running:

```
D:\JAVA\JNP2\examples\10>java FingerClient rama.poly.edu
Login    Name            TTY       Idle    When        Where
jacolag  Jane Colaginae  *pts/7            Tue 08:01   208.34.37.104
hengpi   Heng Pin        pts/9     5       Tue 14:09   128.238.18.119
marcus   Marcus Tullius  pts/15    13d     Tue 17:33   farm-dialup11.poly.e
matewan  Sepin Matewan   *pts/17   17:     Thu 15:32   128.238.10.177
hengpi   Heng Pin        *pts/10           Tue 10:36   128.238.18.119
nadats   Nabeel Datsun   pts/12    1:05    Mon 10:38   128.238.213.227
nadats   Nabeel Datsun   pts/12    1:05    Mon 10:38   128.238.213.227
matewan  Sepin Matewan   *pts/8    14      Sun 18:39   128.238.10.177

D:\JAVA\JNP2\examples\10>java FingerClient rama.poly.edu marcus
Login    Name            TTY       Idle    When        Where
Marcus   Marcus Tullius  pts/15    13d     Tue 17:33   farm-dialup11.poly.e
```

Whois

Whois is a simple directory service protocol defined in RFC 954; it was originally designed to keep track of administrators responsible for Internet hosts and domains. A whois client connects to one of several central servers and requests directory information for a person or persons; it can usually give you a phone number, an email address, and a U.S. mail address (not necessarily current ones

though). With the explosive growth of the Internet, flaws have become apparent
in the whois protocol, most notably its centralized nature. A more complex
replacement called whois++ is documented in RFCs 1913 and 1914 but is not yet
widely implemented.

Let's begin with a simple client to connect to a whois server. The basic structure of
the whois protocol is:

1. The client opens a TCP socket to port 43 on the server *whois.internic.net*. When
   you're using whois, you almost always connect to this server; there are a few
   other servers, but these are relatively rare; there's also a separate whois server
   for the U.S. Department of Defense. This is actually the protocol's biggest
   problem: all the information is concentrated in one place. Not only is it inefficient and subject to network outages, but when the one company maintaining
   the central server decides to unilaterally change the protocol for its own private benefit, as Network Solutions has indeed done several times, everybody
   else's client software breaks instantaneously.

2. The client sends a search string terminated by a carriage return/linefeed pair
   (\r\n). The search string can be a name, a list of names, or a special command, as discussed below. You can also search for domain names, like *oreilly.
   com* or *netscape.com*, which give you information about a network.

3. The server sends an unspecified amount of human-readable information in
   response to the command and closes the connection.

4. The client displays this information to the user.

The search string the client sends has a fairly simple format. At its most basic, it's
just the name of the person you're searching for. Here's a simple whois search for
"Harold". The phone numbers have been changed, and about two-thirds of the
hits have been deleted. If this is what you get with a search for "Harold", imagine a
search for "John" or "Smith":

```
% telnet whois.internic.net 43
Trying 198.41.0.10-..
Connected to rs.internic.net.
Escape character is '^]'.
Harold
The Data in Network Solutions' WHOIS database is provided by Network
Solutions for information purposes, and to assist persons in obtaining
information about or related to a domain name registration record.
Network Solutions does not guarantee its accuracy.  By submitting a
WHOIS query, you agree that you will use this Data only for lawful
purposes and that, under no circumstances will you use this Data to:
(1) allow, enable, or otherwise support the transmission of mass
unsolicited, commercial advertising or solicitations via e-mail
(spam); or  (2) enable high volume, automated, electronic processes
```

```
that apply to Network Solutions (or its systems).  Network Solutions
reserves the right to modify these terms at any time.  By submitting
this query, you agree to abide by this policy.
Aborting search 50 records found .....
Harold (SAGECAT-DOM)                                        SAGECAT.COM
Harold (ANYTHING-GETS-DOM)                            ANYTHING-GETS.COM
Harold (CAJUNGLORY-DOM)                                  CAJUNGLORY.COM
Harold (BONITAMENSCLUB-DOM)                          BONITAMENSCLUB.ORG
Harold (HA793-ORG)       hphoto@DIGITALWEB.NET       780-555-4032
Harold (HA1305-ORG)      moacollect@AOL.COM          (408)555-7698
Harold (MYSTICSINTHEWORKPLACE-DOM)          MYSTICSINTHEWORKPLACE.COM
Harold (KOC-COLORADO-DOM)                            KOC-COLORADO.ORG
Harold (PSYCHRESOURCES3-DOM)                        PSYCHRESOURCES.NET
Harold (PHONESECURE-DOM)                                PHONESECURE.COM
Harold  Adams (HJADAMS3-DOM)                                HJADAMS.NET
Harold  E.  Fields (LOWSURF-DOM)                           LOWSURF.COM
Harold  E., Fortner (FH3120)      Fortnerh@ATT.COM   828-555-0597


To single out one record, look it up with "!xxx", where xxx is the
handle, shown in parenthesis following the name, which comes first.
Connection closed by foreign host.
```

Although the previous input has a pretty clear format, that format is regrettably nonstandard. Different whois servers can and do send decidedly different output. For example, here are some results from the same search at the main French whois server, *whois.nic.fr*:

```
% telnet whois.nic.fr 43
telnet whois.nic.fr 43
Trying 192.134.4.18...
Connected to winter.nic.fr.
Escape character is '^]'.
Harold


Rights restricted by copyright.
See http://www.ripe.net/db/dbcopyright.html
Tous droits reserves par copyright.
Voir http://www.nic.fr/info/whois/dbcopyright.html



person:    Harold Schilmper
address:   Toshiba Elec. Europe GmbH
address:   Elitinger Str. 61
address:   D-W-7250 Leonberg
address:   Germany
phone:     +49 7152 555530
fax-no:    +49 7152 555545
e-mail:    hs%asicsan.uucp@Germany.EU.net
nic-hdl:   HS6091-RIPE
```

```
changed:        ar@deins.Informatik.Uni-Dortmund.DE 19920422
changed:        ripe-dbm@ripe.net 19920424
changed:        ripe-dbm@ripe.net 19990615
source:         RIPE

person:         Harold Cawood
address:        N G Bailey and Co Ltd
address:        Heathcote, Kings Road
address:        Ilkley
address:        West Yorkshire LS29 9AS
address:        United Kingdom
phone:          +44 943 555234
fax-no:         +44 943 555391
nic-hdl:        HC744-RIPE
changed:        hostmaster@nosc.ja.net 19930913
changed:        ripe-dbm@ripe.net 19990615
source:         RIPE
```

Here each complete record is returned rather than just a summary. Other whois servers may use still other formats. This protocol is not at all designed for machine processing. You pretty much have to write new code to handle the output of each different whois server. However, regardless of the output format, each response likely contains a *handle*, which in the Internic output is in parentheses, and in the nic.fr output is in the nic-hdl field. Handles are guaranteed to be unique, and are used to get more specific information about a person or a network. If you search for a handle, you will get at most one match. If your search only has one match, either because you're lucky or you're searching for a handle, then the server returns a more detailed record. Here's a search for *oreilly.com*. Because there is only one *oreilly.com* in the database, the server returns all the information it has on this domain:

```
% telnet whois.internic.net 43
Trying 198.41.0.6...
Connected to rs.internic.net.
Escape character is '^]'.
oreilly.com
The Data in Network Solutions' WHOIS database is provided by Network
Solutions for information purposes, and to assist persons in obtaining
information about or related to a domain name registration record.
Network Solutions does not guarantee its accuracy.  By submitting a
WHOIS query, you agree that you will use this Data only for lawful
purposes and that, under no circumstances will you use this Data to:
(1) allow, enable, or otherwise support the transmission of mass
unsolicited, commercial advertising or solicitations via e-mail
(spam); or  (2) enable high volume, automated, electronic processes
that apply to Network Solutions (or its systems).  Network Solutions
reserves the right to modify these terms at any time.  By submitting
this query, you agree to abide by this policy.
```

```
Registrant:
O'Reilly & Associates (OREILLY6-DOM)
    101 Morris Street
    Sebastopol, CA 95472


    Domain Name: OREILLY.COM


    Administrative Contact, Technical Contact, Zone Contact:
        Pearce, Eric  (EP86)  eap@ORA.COM
        707-829-0515 x221
    Billing Contact:
        Johnston, Rick  (RJ724)  rick@ORA.COM
        707-829-0515 x331


    Record last updated on 05-Jan-99.
    Record created on 27-May-97.
    Database last updated on 30-Aug-99 04:05:23 EDT.


    Domain servers in listed order:

    NS.ORA.COM                    207.25.97.8
    NS1.SONIC.NET                 208.201.224.11
```

```
Connection closed by foreign host.
```

It's easy to implement a simple whois client that connects to *whois.internic.net* and searches for names entered on the command line. Example 10-9 is just such a client. It would not be hard to expand this client to allow searching other servers. You'd simply have to provide a command-line flag like -h to allow the user to choose a different host.

Example 10-9. A Command-line Whois Client

```java
import java.net.*;
import java.io.*;

public class WhoisClient {

  public final static int DEFAULT_PORT = 43;
  public final static String DEFAULT_HOST = "whois.internic.net";

  public static void main(String[] args) {

    InetAddress server;

    try {
      server = InetAddress.getByName(DEFAULT_HOST);
    }
```

Example 10-9. A Command-line Whois Client (continued)

```
catch (UnknownHostException e) {
  System.err.println("Error: Could not locate default host "
   + DEFAULT_HOST);
  System.err.println(
    "Check to make sure you're connected to the Internet and that DNS is "
    + "funtioning");
  System.err.println("Usage: java WhoisClient host port");
  return;
}

int port = DEFAULT_PORT;

try {
  Socket theSocket = new Socket(server, port);
  Writer out = new OutputStreamWriter(theSocket.getOutputStream(),
   "8859_1");
  for (int i = 0; i < args.length; i++) out.write(args[i] + " ");
  out.write("\r\n");
  out.flush();
  InputStream raw = theSocket.getInputStream();
  InputStream in  = new BufferedInputStream(theSocket.getInputStream());
  int c;
  while ((c = in.read()) != -1) System.out.write(c);
}
catch (IOException e) {
  System.err.println(e);
}

  }

}
```

The class has two **final static** fields: the **port**, 43, and the **hostname**, *whois. internic.net*. This client always connects to this host and port; it doesn't give the user a choice because there are few situations in which you need to use another server. The main() method begins by opening a socket to *whois.internic.net* on port 43. The Socket's OutputStream is chained to an OutputStreamWriter. Then each argument on the command-line is written on this stream and thus sent out over the socket to the whois server. A carriage return/linefeed is written, and the writer is flushed.

Next, the Socket's InputStream is stored in the variable raw and this is buffered using the BufferedInputStream in. Since whois is known to use ASCII, bytes are read from this stream with read() and copied onto System.out until read() returns –1, which signals the end of the server's response. Each character is simply copied onto System.out.

The whois protocol supports several flags you can use to restrict or expand your search. For example, if you know you want to search for a person named "Elliott" but you aren't sure whether he spells his name "Elliot", "Elliott", or perhaps even something as unlikely as "Elliotte", you would type:

```
% whois Person Partial Elliot
```

This tells the whois server that you want only matches for people (not domains, gateways, groups, or the like) whose name begins with the letters "Elliot". Unfortunately, you need to do a separate search if you want to find someone who spells his name "Eliot". The rules for modifying a search are summarized in Table 10-1. Each prefix should be placed before the search string on the command line.

Table 10-1. Whois Prefixes

Prefix	Meaning
Domain	Find only domain records.
Gateway	Find only gateway records.
Group	Find only group records.
Host	Find only host records.
Network	Find only network records.
Organization	Find only organization records.
Person	Find only person records.
ASN	Find only autonomous system number records.
Handle or !	Search only for matching handles.
Mailbox or @	Search only for matching email addresses.
Name or :	Search only for matching names.
Expand or *	Search only for group records and show all individuals in that group.
Full or =	Show complete record for each match.
Partial or suffix	Match records that start with the given string.
Summary or $	Show just the summary, even if there's only one match.
SUBdisplay or %	Show the users of the specified host, the hosts on the specified network, etc.

These keywords are all useful, and you could use them with the command-line client of Example 10-10, but they're way too much trouble to remember. In fact, most people don't even know that they exist. They just type "whois Harold" at the command-line and sort through the mess that comes back. A good whois client doesn't rely on users remembering arcane keywords. Rather, it shows them the options they have to choose from. This requires a graphical user interface for end users and a better API for client programmers.

Example 10-11 is a more reusable `Whois` class. The state of each `Whois` object is defined by two fields: `host`, an `InetAddress` object, and `port`, an `int`. Together

these define the server that this particular `Whois` object will connect to. Five constructors set these fields from various combinations of arguments. The `getPort()`
and `getHost()` accessor methods return the values of these fields. However, there
are no setter methods so that these objects will be immutable and thread safety will
not be a large concern.

The main functionality of the class is in one method, `lookUpNames()`. The
`lookUpNames()` method returns a `String` containing the whois response to a
given query. The arguments specify the string to search for, what kind of record to
search for, which database to search in, and whether an exact match is required.
We could have used strings or `int` constants to specify the kind of record to search
for and the database to search in, but since there are only a small number of valid
values, we define public inner classes with a fixed number of members instead.
This provides much stricter compile-time type checking and guarantees we won't
have to handle an unexpected value.

Example 10-10. The Whois Class

```
import java.net.*;
import java.io.*;
import com.macfaq.io.SafeBufferedReader; // see Chapter 4


public class Whois {

  public final static int DEFAULT_PORT = 43;
  public final static String DEFAULT_HOST = "whois.internic.net";

  private int port = DEFAULT_PORT;
  private InetAddress host;

  public Whois(InetAddress host, int port) {
    this.host = host;
    this.port = port;
  }

  public Whois(InetAddress host) {
    this(host, DEFAULT_PORT);
  }

  public Whois(String hostname, int port) throws UnknownHostException

    this(InetAddress.getByName(hostname), port);
  }

  public Whois(String hostname) throws UnknownHostException {
    this(InetAddress.getByName(hostname), DEFAULT_PORT);
  }
```

Example 10-10. The Whois Class (continued)

```java
public Whois() throws UnknownHostException {
  this(DEFAULT_HOST, DEFAULT_PORT);
}

// Items to search for
public static class SearchFor {

  public static SearchFor ANY = new SearchFor();
  public static SearchFor NETWORK = new SearchFor();
  public static SearchFor PERSON = new SearchFor();
  public static SearchFor HOST = new SearchFor();
  public static SearchFor DOMAIN = new SearchFor();
  public static SearchFor ORGANIZATION = new SearchFor();
  public static SearchFor GROUP = new SearchFor();
  public static SearchFor GATEWAY = new SearchFor();
  public static SearchFor ASN = new SearchFor();

  private SearchFor() {};

}

// Categories to search in
public static class SearchIn {

  public static SearchIn ALL = new SearchIn();
  public static SearchIn NAME = new SearchIn();
  public static SearchIn MAILBOX = new SearchIn();
  public static SearchIn HANDLE = new SearchIn();

  private SearchIn() {};

}

public String lookUpNames(String target, SearchFor category,
  SearchIn group, boolean exactMatch) throws IOException {

  String suffix = "";
  if (!exactMatch) suffix = ".";

  String searchInLabel  = "";
  String searchForLabel = "";

  if (group == SearchIn.ALL) searchInLabel = "";
  else if (group == SearchIn.NAME) searchInLabel = "Name ";
  else if (group == SearchIn.MAILBOX) searchInLabel = "Mailbox ";
  else if (group == SearchIn.HANDLE) searchInLabel = "!";

  if (category == SearchFor.NETWORK) searchForLabel = "Network ";
```

Example 10-10. The Whois Class (continued)

```
    else if (category == SearchFor.PERSON) searchForLabel = "Person ";
    else if (category == SearchFor.HOST) searchForLabel = "Host ";
    else if (category == SearchFor.DOMAIN) searchForLabel = "Domain ";
    else if (category == SearchFor.ORGANIZATION) {
      searchForLabel = "Organization ";
    }
    else if (category == SearchFor.GROUP) searchForLabel = "Group ";
    else if (category == SearchFor.GATEWAY) {
      searchForLabel = "Gateway ";
    }
    else if (category == SearchFor.ASN) searchForLabel = "ASN ";

    String prefix = searchForLabel + searchInLabel;
    String query = prefix + target + suffix;

    Socket theSocket = new Socket(host, port);
    Writer out
      = new OutputStreamWriter(theSocket.getOutputStream(), "ASCII");
    SafeBufferedReader in = new SafeBufferedReader(new
      InputStreamReader(theSocket.getInputStream(), "ASCII"));
    out.write(query + "\r\n");
    out.flush();
    StringBuffer response = new StringBuffer();
    String theLine = null;
    while ((theLine = in.readLine()) != null) {
      response.append(theLine);
      response.append("\r\n");
    }
    theSocket.close();

    return response.toString();

  }

  public InetAddress getHost() {
    return this.host;
  }

  public int getPort() {
    return this.port;
  }

}
```

Figure 10-1 shows one possible interface for a graphical whois client that depends on Example 10-11 for the actual network connections. This interface has a text field to enter the name to be searched for and a checkbox to determine whether the match should be exact or partial. A group of radio buttons lets users specify which group of records they want to search. Another group of radio buttons chooses the fields that should be searched. By default, this client searches all fields of all records for an exact match.

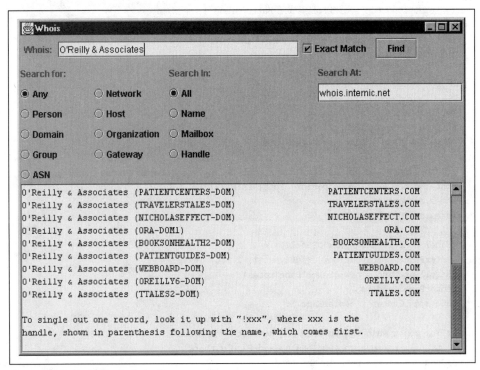

Figure 10-1. A graphical whois client

When a user enters a string in the Whois: text field and presses Enter or the Find button, the program makes a connection to the whois server and retrieves records that match that string. These are placed in the text area in the bottom of the window. Initially, the server is set to *whois.internic.net*, but the user is free to change this. Example 10-11 is the program that produces this interface.

Example 10-11. A Graphical Whois Client Interface

```
import javax.swing.*;
import java.awt.*;
import java.awt.event.*;
import java.io.*;
import java.net.*;


public class WhoisGUI extends JFrame {
```

Example 10-11. A Graphical Whois Client Interface (continued)

```java
  private JTextField searchString = new JTextField(30);
  private JTextArea names = new JTextArea(15, 80);
  private JButton findButton = new JButton("Find");;
  private ButtonGroup searchIn = new ButtonGroup();
  private ButtonGroup searchFor = new ButtonGroup();
  private JCheckBox exactMatch = new JCheckBox("Exact Match", true);
  private JTextField chosenServer = new JTextField();
  private Whois server;

public WhoisGUI(Whois whois) {

  super("Whois");
  this.server = whois;
  Container pane = this.getContentPane();

  // whois.internic.net assumes a monospaced font, 72 columns across
  Font f = new Font("Monospaced", Font.PLAIN, 12);
  names.setFont(f);
  names.setEditable(false);

  JPanel centerPanel = new JPanel();
  centerPanel.setLayout(new GridLayout(1, 1, 10, 10));
  JScrollPane jsp = new JScrollPane(names);
  centerPanel.add(jsp);
  pane.add("Center", centerPanel);

  // You don't want the buttons in the south and north
  // to fill the entire sections so add Panels there
  // and use FlowLayouts in the Panel
  JPanel northPanel = new JPanel();
  JPanel northPanelTop = new JPanel();
  northPanelTop.setLayout(new FlowLayout(FlowLayout.LEFT));
  northPanelTop.add(new JLabel("Whois: "));
  northPanelTop.add("North", searchString);
  northPanelTop.add(exactMatch);
  northPanelTop.add(findButton);
  northPanel.setLayout(new BorderLayout(2,1));
  northPanel.add("North", northPanelTop);
  JPanel northPanelBottom = new JPanel();
  northPanelBottom.setLayout(new GridLayout(1,3,5,5));
  northPanelBottom.add(initRecordType());
  northPanelBottom.add(initSearchFields());
  northPanelBottom.add(initServerChoice());
  northPanel.add("Center", northPanelBottom);

  pane.add("North", northPanel);

  ActionListener al = new LookupNames();
```

Example 10-11. A Graphical Whois Client Interface (continued)

```
      findButton.addActionListener(al);
      searchString.addActionListener(al);

   }

   private JPanel initRecordType() {

      JPanel p = new JPanel();
      p.setLayout(new GridLayout(6, 2, 5, 2));
      p.add(new JLabel("Search for:"));
      p.add(new JLabel(""));

      JRadioButton any = new JRadioButton("Any", true);
      any.setActionCommand("Any");
      searchFor.add(any);
      p.add(any);

      p.add(this.makeRadioButton("Network"));
      p.add(this.makeRadioButton("Person"));
      p.add(this.makeRadioButton("Host"));
      p.add(this.makeRadioButton("Domain"));
      p.add(this.makeRadioButton("Organization"));
      p.add(this.makeRadioButton("Group"));
      p.add(this.makeRadioButton("Gateway"));
      p.add(this.makeRadioButton("ASN"));

      return p;

   }

   private JRadioButton makeRadioButton(String label) {

      JRadioButton button = new JRadioButton(label, false);
      button.setActionCommand(label);
      searchFor.add(button);
      return button;

   }

   private JRadioButton makeSearchInRadioButton(String label) {

      JRadioButton button = new JRadioButton(label, false);
      button.setActionCommand(label);
      searchIn.add(button);
      return button;

   }
```

Example 10-11. A Graphical Whois Client Interface (continued)

```
  private JPanel initSearchFields() {

    JPanel p = new JPanel();
    p.setLayout(new GridLayout(6, 1, 5, 2));
    p.add(new JLabel("Search In: "));

    JRadioButton all = new JRadioButton("All", true);
    all.setActionCommand("All");
    searchIn.add(all);
    p.add(all);

    p.add(this.makeSearchInRadioButton("Name"));
    p.add(this.makeSearchInRadioButton("Mailbox"));
    p.add(this.makeSearchInRadioButton("Handle"));

    return p;

  }

  private JPanel initServerChoice() {

    JPanel p = new JPanel();
    p.setLayout(new GridLayout(6, 1, 5, 2));
    p.add(new JLabel("Search At: "));

    chosenServer.setText(server.getHost().getHostName());
    p.add(chosenServer);
    chosenServer.addActionListener( new ActionListener() {
      public void actionPerformed(ActionEvent evt) {
        try {
          InetAddress newHost
            = InetAddress.getByName(chosenServer.getText());
          Whois newServer = new Whois(newHost);
          server = newServer;
        }
        catch (Exception e) {
          // should use an error dialog here, but that
          // doesn't teach much about networking
          chosenServer.setText(server.getHost().getHostName());
        }
      }
    } );

    return p;

  }

  class LookupNames implements ActionListener {
```

Example 10-11. A Graphical Whois Client Interface (continued)

```java
public void actionPerformed(ActionEvent evt) {

  Whois.SearchIn group = Whois.SearchIn.ALL;
  Whois.SearchFor category = Whois.SearchFor.ANY;

  String searchForLabel = searchFor.getSelection().getActionCommand();
  String searchInLabel = searchIn.getSelection().getActionCommand();
  if (searchInLabel.equals("Name")) group = Whois.SearchIn.NAME;
  else if (searchInLabel.equals("Mailbox")) {
    group = Whois.SearchIn.MAILBOX;
  }
  else if (searchInLabel.equals("Handle")) {
    group = Whois.SearchIn.HANDLE;
  }

  if (searchForLabel.equals("Network")) {
    category = Whois.SearchFor.NETWORK;
  }
  else if (searchForLabel.equals("Person")) {
    category = Whois.SearchFor.PERSON;
  }
  else if (searchForLabel.equals("Host")) {
    category = Whois.SearchFor.HOST;
  }
  else if (searchForLabel.equals("Domain")) {
    category = Whois.SearchFor.DOMAIN;
  }
  else if (searchForLabel.equals("Organization")) {
    category = Whois.SearchFor.ORGANIZATION;
  }
  else if (searchForLabel.equals("Group")) {
    category = Whois.SearchFor.GROUP;
  }
  else if (searchForLabel.equals("Gateway")) {
    category = Whois.SearchFor.GATEWAY;
  }
  else if (searchForLabel.equals("ASN")) {
    category = Whois.SearchFor.ASN;
  }

  try {
    names.setText("");
    String result = server.lookUpNames(searchString.getText(),
      category, group, exactMatch.isSelected());
    names.setText(result);
  }
  catch (IOException e) {
    names.setText("Lookup failed due to " + e);
```

Example 10-11. A Graphical Whois Client Interface (continued)

```
    }
  }

}

public static void main(String[] args) {

  try {
    Whois server = new Whois();
    WhoisGUI a = new WhoisGUI(server);
    a.addWindowListener(new WindowAdapter() {
      public void windowClosing(WindowEvent e) {
        System.exit(0);
      }
    });
    a.pack();
    a.show();
  }
  catch (UnknownHostException e) {
    System.err.println("Error: Could not locate default host "
      + Whois.DEFAULT_HOST);
    System.err.println("Check to make sure you're connected to the"
      + " Internet and that DNS is" funtioning");
    System.err.println("Usage: java WhoisGUI");
    return;
  }

}

}
```

The `main()` method is the usual block of code to start up a standalone application. It constructs a `Whois` object, then uses that to construct a `WhoisGUI` object. Then the `WhoisGUI ()` constructor sets up the graphical user interface. There's a lot of redundant code here, so it's broken out into the private methods `initSearchFields()`, `initServerChoice()`, `makeSearchInRadioButton()`, and `makeSearchForRadioButton()`. As usual with `LayoutManager`-based interfaces, the setup is fairly involved. Since you'd probably use a visual designer to build such an application, I won't describe it in detail here.

When the constructor returns, the `main()` method attaches an anonymous inner class to the window that will close the application when the window is closed. (This isn't in the constructor because other programs that use this class may not want to exit the program when the window closes.) It then packs and shows the window. From that point on, all activity takes place in the AWT thread.

The first event this program must respond to is the user's typing a name in the Whois: text field and either pressing the Find button or hitting Enter. In this case, the LookupNames inner class passes the information in the text field and the various radio buttons and checkboxes to the server.lookUpNames() method. This method returns a String, which is placed in the names text area.

The second event this program must respond to is the user typing a new host in the server text field. In this case, an anonymous inner class tries to construct a new Whois object and store it in the server field. If it fails (e.g., because the user mistyped the hostname), then the old server is restored. It would be a good idea to tell the user this by putting up an alert box, but I omitted that to keep this example a more manageable size.

This is not a perfect client by any means. The most glaring omission is that it doesn't provide a way to save the data and quit the program. Less obvious until you run the program is that responsiveness suffers because the network connection is made inside the AWT thread. It would be better to place the connections to the server in their own thread, then use callbacks to place the data in the GUI as the data is received. However, implementing these would take us too far afield from the topic of network programming, so I leave them as exercises for the reader.

11

Sockets for Servers

The last chapter discussed sockets from the standpoint of clients: programs that open a socket to a server that's listening for connections. However, client sockets themselves aren't enough; clients aren't much use unless they can talk to a server, and if you think about it, the sockets we discussed in the last chapter aren't sufficient for writing servers. To create a Socket, you need to know the Internet host to which you want to connect. When you're writing a server, you don't know in advance who will contact you, and even if you did, you wouldn't know when that host wanted to contact you. In other words, servers are like receptionists who sit by the phone and wait for incoming calls. They don't know who will call or when, only that when the phone rings, they have to pick it up and talk to whoever is there. We can't program that behavior with the Socket class alone. Granted, there's no reason that clients written in Java have to talk to Java servers—in fact, a client doesn't care what language the server was written in or what platform it runs on. However, if Java didn't let us write servers, there would be a glaring hole in its capabilities.

Fortunately, there's no such hole. Java provides a ServerSocket class to allow programmers to write servers. Basically, a server socket's job is to sit by the phone and wait for incoming calls. More technically, a ServerSocket runs on the server and listens for incoming TCP connections. Each ServerSocket listens on a particular port on the server machine. When a client Socket on a remote host attempts to connect to that port, the server wakes up, negotiates the connection between the client and the server, and opens a regular Socket between the two hosts. In other words, server sockets wait for connections while client sockets initiate connections. Once the server socket has set up the connection, the server uses a regular Socket object to send data to the client. Data always travels over the regular socket.

The ServerSocket Class

The ServerSocket class contains everything you need to write servers in Java. It has constructors that create new ServerSocket objects, methods that listen for connections on a specified port, and methods that return a Socket object when a connection is made so that you can send and receive data. In addition, it has methods to set various options and the usual miscellaneous methods such as toString().

The basic life cycle of a server is:

1. A new ServerSocket is created on a particular port using a ServerSocket() constructor.

2. The ServerSocket listens for incoming connection attempts on that port using its accept() method. accept() blocks until a client attempts to make a connection, at which point accept() returns a Socket object connecting the client and the server.

3. Depending on the type of server, either the Socket's getInputStream() method, getOutputStream() method, or both are called to get input and output streams that communicate with the client.

4. The server and the client interact according to an agreed-upon protocol until it is time to close the connection.

5. The server, the client, or both close the connection.

6. The server returns to step 2 and waits for the next connection.

If step 4 is likely to take a long or indefinite amount of time, traditional Unix servers such as wu-ftpd create a new process to handle each connection so that multiple clients can be serviced at the same time. Java programs should spawn a thread to interact with the client so that the server can be ready to process the next connection sooner. A thread places a far smaller load on the server than a complete child process. In fact, the overhead of forking too many processes is why the typical Unix FTP server can't handle more than roughly 400 connections without slowing to a crawl. On the other hand, if the protocol is simple and quick and allows the server to close the connection when it's through, then it will be more efficient for the server to process the client request immediately without spawning a thread.

The operating system stores incoming connection requests addressed to a particular port in a first-in, first-out queue. The default length of the queue is normally 50, though this can vary from operating system to operating system. Some operating systems (though not Solaris) have a maximum queue length, typically five. On these systems, the queue length will be the largest possible value less than or equal to 50. After the queue fills to capacity with unprocessed connections, the host refuses additional connections on that port until slots in the queue open up. Many (though not all) clients will try to make a connection multiple times if their initial attempt is refused. Managing incoming connections and the queue is a service provided by the operating system; your program does not need to worry about it. Several ServerSocket constructors allow you to change the length of the queue if its default length isn't large enough; however, you won't be able to increase the queue beyond the maximum size that the operating system supports:

The Constructors

There are three public ServerSocket constructors:

```
public ServerSocket(int port) throws IOException, BindException
public ServerSocket(int port, int queueLength)
  throws IOException, BindException
public ServerSocket(int port, int queueLength, InetAddress bindAddress)
  throws IOException
```

These constructors let you specify the port, the length of the queue used to hold incoming connection requests, and the local network interface to bind to. They pretty much all do the same thing, though some use default values for the queue length and the address to bind to. Let's explore these in order.

public ServerSocket(int port) throws IOException, BindException

This constructor creates a server socket on the port specified by the argument. If you pass 0 for the port number, the system selects an available port for you. A port chosen for you by the system is sometimes called an *anonymous port* since you don't know its number. For servers, anonymous ports aren't very useful because clients need to know in advance which port to connect to; however, there are a few situations (which we will discuss later) in which an anonymous port might be useful.

For example, to create a server socket that would be used by an HTTP server on port 80, you would write:

```
try {
  ServerSocket httpd = new ServerSocket(80);
}
catch (IOException e) {
  System.err.println(e);
}
```

The constructor throws an IOException (specifically, a BindException) if the socket cannot be created and bound to the requested port. An IOException when creating a ServerSocket almost always means one of two things. Either another server socket, possibly from a completely different program, is already using the requested port, or you're trying to connect to a port from 1 to 1023 on Unix without root (superuser) privileges.

You can use this constructor to write a variation on the `PortScanner` programs of the previous chapter. Example 11-1 checks for ports on the local machine by attempting to create `ServerSocket` objects on them and seeing on which ports that fails. If you're using Unix and are not running as root, this program works only for ports 1,024 and above.

Example 11-1. Look for Local Ports

```java
import java.net.*;
import java.io.*;

public class LocalPortScanner {

  public static void main(String[] args) {

    for (int port = 1; port <= 65535; port++) {

      try {
        // the next line will fail and drop into the catch block if
        // there is already a server running on the port
        ServerSocket server = new ServerSocket(port);
      }
      catch (IOException e) {
        System.out.println("There is a server on port " + port + ".");
      } // end try

    } // end for

  }

}
```

Here's the output I got when running `LocalPortScanner` on my NT workstation:

```
D:\JAVA\JNP2\examples\11>java LocalPortScanner
There is a server on port 135.
There is a server on port 1025.
There is a server on port 1026.
There is a server on port 1027.
There is a server on port 1028.
```

public ServerSocket(int port, int queueLength) throws IOException, BindException

This constructor creates a `ServerSocket` on the specified port with a queue length of your choosing. If the machine has multiple network interfaces or IP

addresses, then it listens on this port on all those interfaces and IP addresses. The
queueLength argument sets the length of the queue for incoming connection
requests—that is, how many incoming connections can be stored at one time
before the host starts refusing connections. Some operating systems have a maximum queue length, typically five. If you try to expand the queue past that maximum number, the maximum queue length is used instead. If you pass 0 for the
port number, the system selects an available port.

For example, to create a server socket on port 5,776 that would hold up to 100
incoming connection requests in the queue, you would write:

```
try {
  ServerSocket httpd = new ServerSocket(5776, 100);
}
catch (IOException e) {
  System.err.println(e);
}
```

The constructor throws an IOException (specifically, a BindException) if the
socket cannot be created and bound to the requested port. An IOException
when creating a ServerSocket almost always means one of two things. Either the
specified port is already in use, or you do not have root privileges on Unix and
you're trying to connect to a port from 1 to 1,023.

public ServerSocket(int port, int queueLength, InetAddress bindAddress) throws BindException, IOException

This constructor, which is available only in Java 1.1 and later, creates a
ServerSocket on the specified port with the specified queue length. This
ServerSocket binds only to the specified local IP address. This constructor is useful for servers that run on systems with several IP addresses (a common practice at
web server farms) because it allows you to choose the address to which you'll listen. That is, this ServerSocket listens only for incoming connections on the specified address; it won't listen for connections that come in through the host's other
addresses. The other constructors bind to all local IP addresses by default.

For example, *metalab.unc.edu* is a particular SPARCstation in North Carolina. It's
connected to the Internet with the IP address 152.2.254.81. The same SPARCstation is also called *www.gigabit-ethernet.org*, but with a different IP address (152.2.254.
82). To create a server socket that listens on port 5,776 of *metalab.unc.edu* but not
on port 5,776 of *www.gigabit-ethernet.org*, you would write:

```
try {
  ServerSocket httpd = new ServerSocket(5776, 10,
    InetAddress.getByName("metalab.unc.edu"));
}
catch (IOException e) {
```

```
      System.err.println(e);
  }
```

The constructor throws an IOException (again, really a BindException) if the socket cannot be created and bound to the requested port. A BindException when creating a ServerSocket almost always means one of two things. Either the specified port is already in use, or you do not have root privileges on Unix and you're trying to connect to a port from 1 to 1,023.

Accepting and Closing Connections

A ServerSocket generally operates in a loop that repeatedly accepts connections. Each pass through the loop invokes the accept() method. This returns a Socket object representing the connection between the remote client and the local server. Interaction with the client takes place through this Socket object. When the transaction is finished, the server should invoke the Socket object's close() method and get ready to process the next incoming connection. However, when the server needs to shut down and not process any further incoming connections, you should invoke the ServerSocket object's close() method.

public Socket accept( ) throws IOException

When server setup is done and you're ready to accept a connection, call the ServerSocket's accept() method. This method "blocks": it stops the flow of execution and waits until a client connects. When a client does connect, the accept() method returns a Socket object. You use the streams returned by this Socket's getInputStream() and getOutputStream() methods to communicate with the client. For example:

```
ServerSocket server = new ServerSocket(5776);
while (true) {
  Socket connection = server.accept();
  OutputStreamWriter out
    = new OutputStreamWriter(connection.getOutputStream());
  out.write("You've connected to this server. Bye-bye now.\r\n");
  connection.close();
}
```

If you don't want your program to halt while it waits for a connection, put the call to accept() in a separate thread.

When you add exception handling, the code becomes somewhat more convoluted. It's important to distinguish between exceptions thrown by the ServerSocket, which should probably shut down the server and log an error message, and exceptions thrown by a Socket, which should just close that active connection. Exceptions thrown by the accept() method are an intermediate case that can go either way. To do this, you'll need to nest your try blocks. Finally,

most servers will want to make sure that all sockets they accept are closed when
they're finished. Even if the protocol specifies that clients are responsible for closing connections, clients do not always strictly adhere to the protocol. The call to
close() also has to be wrapped in a try block that catches an IOException.
However, if you do catch an IOException when closing the socket, ignore it. It
just means that the client closed the socket before the server could. Here's a
slightly more realistic example:

```
try {
  ServerSocket server = new ServerSocket(5776);
  while (true) {
    Socket connection = server.accept();
    try {
      OutputStreamWriter out
        = new OutputStreamWriter(connection.getOutputStream());
      out.write("You've connected to this server. Bye-bye now.\r\n");
      connection.close();
    }
    catch (IOException e) {
      // This tends to be a transitory error for this one connection;
      // e.g. the client broke the connection early. Consequently,
      // we don't want to break the loop or print an error message.
      // However, you might choose to log this exception in an error log.
    }
    finally {
      // Most servers will want to guarantee that sockets are closed
      // when complete.
      try {
        if (connection != null) connection.close();
      }
      catch (IOException e) {}
    }
  }
}
catch (IOException e) {
  System.err.println(e);
}
```

Example 11-2 implements a simple daytime server, as per RFC 867. Since this
server just sends a single line of text in response to each connection, it processes
each connection immediately. More complex servers should spawn a thread to
handle each request. In this case, the overhead of spawning a thread would be
greater than the time needed to process the request.

NOTE   If you run this program on a Unix box, you need to run it as root in
                order to connect to port 13. If you don't want to or can't run it as
                root, change the port number to something above 1024, say 1313.

Example 11-2. A Daytime Server

```java
import java.net.*;
import java.io.*;
import java.util.Date;

public class DaytimeServer {

  public final static int DEFAULT_PORT = 13;

  public static void main(String[] args) {

    int port = DEFAULT_PORT;
    if (args.length > 0) {
      try {
        port = Integer.parseInt(args[0]);
        if (port < 0 || port >= 65536) {
          System.out.println("Port must between 0 and 65535");
          return;
        }
      }
      catch (NumberFormatException e) {
        // use default port
      }

    }

    try {

      ServerSocket server = new ServerSocket(port);

      Socket connection = null;
      while (true) {

        try {
          connection = server.accept();
          OutputStreamWriter out
           = new OutputStreamWriter(connection.getOutputStream());
          Date now = new Date();
          out.write(now.toString() +"\r\n");
          out.flush();
          connection.close();
        }
        catch (IOException e) {}
        finally {
          try {
            if (connection != null) connection.close();
          }
          catch (IOException e) {}
        }
```

Example 11-2. A Daytime Server (continued)

```
    }  // end while

  }  // end try
  catch (IOException e) {
    System.err.println(e);
  } // end catch

 } // end main

} // end DaytimeServer
```

Example 11-2 is straightforward. The first three lines import the usual packages, `java.io` and `java.net`, as well as `java.util.Date` so we can get the time. There is a single `public  final  static  int` field (i.e., a constant) in the class `DEFAULT_PORT`, which is set to the well-known port for a daytime server (port 13). The class has a single method, `main()`, which does all the work. If the port is specified on the command-line, then it's read from `args[0]`. Otherwise, the default port is used.

The outer `try` block traps any `IOExceptions` that may arise while the `ServerSocket` server is constructed on the daytime port or when it accepts connections. The inner `try` block watches for exceptions thrown while the connections are accepted and processed. The `accept()` method is called within an infinite loop to watch for new connections; like many servers, this program never terminates but continues listening until an exception is thrown or you stop it manually.*

When a client makes a connection, `accept()` returns a `Socket`, which is stored in the local variable `connection`, and the program continues. We call `getOutputStream()` to get the output stream associated with that `Socket` and then chain that output stream to a new `OutputStreamWriter`, `out`. To get the current date, we construct a new `Date` object and send it to the client by writing its string representation on `out` with `write()`.

Finally, after the data is sent or an exception has been thrown, we close `connection` inside the `finally` block. Always close a socket when you're finished with it. In the previous chapter, we said that a client shouldn't rely on the other side of a connection to close the socket. That goes triple for servers. Clients can time out or crash; users can cancel transactions; networks can go down in high-traffic periods. For any of these or a dozen more reasons, you cannot rely on clients to close sockets, even when the protocol requires them to (which it doesn't in this case).

---

* The command for stopping a program manually depends on your system; under Unix, NT, and many other systems, CTRL-C will do the job. If you are running the server in the background on a Unix system, stop it by finding the server's process ID and killing it with the kill command (**kill** *pid*).

Sending binary, nontext data is not significantly harder. Example 11-3 demonstrates with a time server. This follows the time protocol outlined in RFC 868. When a client connects, the server sends a 4-byte, big-endian, unsigned integer specifying the number of seconds that have passed since 12:00 A.M., January 1, 1900 GMT (the epoch). The current time can be retrieved simply by creating a new Date object. However, since the Date class counts milliseconds since 12:00 A.M., January 1, 1970 GMT rather than seconds since 12:00 A.M., January 1, 1900 GMT, some conversion is necessary.

Example 11-3. A Time Server

```
import java.net.*;
import java.io.*;
import java.util.Date;


public class TimeServer {

  public final static int DEFAULT_PORT = 37;

  public static void main(String[] args) {

    int port = DEFAULT_PORT;
    if (args.length > 0) {
      try {
        port = Integer.parseInt(args[0]);
        if (port < 0 || port >= 65536) {
          System.out.println("Port must between 0 and 65535");
          return;
        }
      }
      catch (NumberFormatException e) {}
    }

    // The time protocol sets the epoch at 1900,
    // the java Date class at 1970. This number
    // converts between them.

    long differenceBetweenEpochs = 2208988800L;

    try {
      ServerSocket server = new ServerSocket(port);
        while (true) {
          Socket connection = null;
          try {
            connection = server.accept();
            OutputStream out = connection.getOutputStream();
            Date now = new Date();
            long msSince1970 = now.getTime();
```

Example 11-3. A Time Server (continued)

```
          long secondsSince1970 = msSince1970/1000;
          long secondsSince1900 = secondsSince1970
            + differenceBetweenEpochs;
          byte[] time = new byte[4];
          time[0]
            = (byte) ((secondsSince1900 & 0x00000000FF000000L) >> 24);
          time[1]
            = (byte) ((secondsSince1900 & 0x0000000000FF0000L) >> 16);
          time[2]
            = (byte) ((secondsSince1900 & 0x000000000000FF00L) >> 8);
          time[3] = (byte) (secondsSince1900 & 0x00000000000000FFL);
          out.write(time);
          out.flush();
        } // end try
        catch (IOException e) {
        } // end catch
        finally {
          if (connection != null) connection.close();
        }
      } // end while
    } // end try
    catch (IOException e) {
      System.err.println(e);
    } // end catch

  } // end main

} // end TimeServer
```

As with the `TimeClient` of the previous chapter, most of the effort here goes into working with a data format (32-bit unsigned integers) that Java doesn't natively support.

public void close( ) throws IOException

If you're finished with a server socket, you should close it, especially if your program is going to continue to run for some time. This frees up the port for other programs that may wish to use it. Closing a `ServerSocket` should not be confused with closing a `Socket`. Closing a `ServerSocket` frees a port on the local host, allowing another server to bind to the port; closing a `Socket` breaks the connection between the local and the remote hosts.

Server sockets are closed automatically when a program dies, so it's not absolutely necessary to close them in programs that terminate shortly after the `ServerSocket` is no longer needed. Nonetheless, it doesn't hurt. For example, the main loop of the `LocalPortScanner` program might be better written like this so that it doesn't temporarily occupy most of the ports on the system:

```
for (int port = 1; port <= 65535; port++) {

  try {
    // the next line will fail and drop into the catch block if
    // there is already a server running on the port
    ServerSocket server = new ServerSocket(port);
    server.close();
  }
  catch (IOException e) {
    System.out.println("There is a server on port " + port + ".");
  } // end try

} // end for
```

The get Methods

The `ServerSocket` class provides two getter methods to tell you the local address and port occupied by the server socket. These are useful if you've opened a server socket on an anonymous port and/or an unspecified network interface. This would be the case, for one example, in the data connection of an FTP session.

public InetAddress getInetAddress()

This method returns the address being used by the server (the local host). If the local host has a single IP address (as most do), then this is the address returned by `InetAddress.getLocalHost()`. If the local host has more than one IP address, then the specific address returned is one of the host's IP addresses. You can't predict which address you will get. For example:

```
try {
  ServerSocket httpd = new ServerSocket(80);
  InetAddress ia = httpd.getInetAddress();
}
catch (IOException e) {
}
```

public int getLocalPort()

The `ServerSocket` constructors allow you to listen on an unspecified port by passing 0 for the port number. This method lets you find out what port you're listening on. You might use this in a peer-to-peer multisocket program where you already have a means to inform other peers of your location. Or a server might spawn several smaller servers to perform particular operations. The well-known server could inform clients what ports they can find the smaller servers on. Of course, you can also use getLocalPort() to find a non-anonymous port, but why would you need to? Example 11-4 demonstrates.

Example 11-4. A Random Port

```
import java.net.*;
import java.io.*;

public class RandomPort {

  public static void main(String[] args) {

    try {
      ServerSocket server = new ServerSocket(0);
      System.out.println("This server runs on port "
        + server.getLocalPort());
    }
    catch (IOException e) {
      System.err.println(e);
    }

  }

}
```

Here's the output of several runs:

```
D:\JAVA\JNP2\examples\11>java RandomPort
This server runs on port 1154
D:\JAVA\JNP2\examples\11>java RandomPort
This server runs on port 1155
D:\JAVA\JNP2\examples\11>java RandomPort
This server runs on port 1156
```

At least on this VM, the ports aren't really random; but they are at least indeterminate until runtime.

Socket Options

The only socket option supported for server sockets is SO_TIMEOUT. SO_TIME-OUT is the amount of time, in milliseconds, that accept() waits for an incoming connection before throwing a java.io.InterruptedIOException. If SO_TIME-OUT is 0, then accept() will never time out. The default is to never time out.

Using SO_TIMEOUT is rather rare. You might need it if you were implementing a complicated and secure protocol that required multiple connections between the client and the server where some responses needed to occur within a fixed amount of time. Most servers are designed to run for indefinite periods of time and therefore use the default timeout value, which is 0 (never time out).

public void setSoTimeout(int timeout) throws SocketException

The setSoTimeout() method sets the SO_TIMEOUT field for this server socket
object. The countdown starts when accept() is invoked. When the timeout
expires, accept() throws an InterruptedIOException. You should set this
option before calling accept(); you cannot change the timeout value while
accept() is waiting for a connection. The timeout argument must be
greater than or equal to zero; if it isn't, the method throws an Illegal-
ArgumentException. For example:

```
try {
  ServerSocket server = new ServerSocket(2048);
  server.setSoTimeout(30000); // block for no more than 30 seconds
  try {
    Socket s = server.accept();
    // handle the connection
    // ...
  }
  catch (InterruptedIOException e) {
    System.err.println("No connection within 30 seconds");
  }
  finally {
    server.close();
  }
catch (IOException e) {
  System.err.println("Unexpected IOException: " + e);
}
```

public int getSoTimeout() throws IOException

The getSoTimeout() method returns this server socket's current SO_TIMEOUT
value. For example:

```
public void printSoTimeout(ServerSocket server) {

  int timeout = server.getSoTimeOut();
  if (timeout > 0) {
    System.out.println(server + " will time out after "
      + timeout + "milliseconds.");
  }
  else if (timeout == 0) {
    System.out.println(server + " will never time out.");
  }
  else {
    System.out.println("Impossible condition occurred in " + server);
    System.out.println("Timeout cannot be less than zero." );
  }

}
```

The Object Methods

jServerSocket overrides only one of the standard methods from java.lang. Object, toString(). Thus, equality comparisons test for strict identity, and server sockets are problematic in hash tables. Normally, this isn't a large problem.

public String toString( )

A String returned by ServerSocket's toString() method looks like this:

```
ServerSocket[addr=0.0.0.0,port=0,localport=5776]
```

In current implementations, addr is always 0.0.0.0 and port is always 0. Presumably, these may become something more interesting in the future. The localport is the local port on which the server is listening for connections.

Implementation

The ServerSocket class provides two methods for changing the default implementation of server sockets. I'll describe them only briefly here, since they're primarily intended for implementers of Java virtual machines rather than application programmers.

public static synchronized void setSocketFactory (SocketImpl Factory fac) throws IOException

This method sets the *system's* server SocketImplFactory, which is the factory used to create ServerSocket objects. This is not the same factory that is used to create client Socket objects, though the syntax is similar; you can have one factory for Socket objects and a different factory for ServerSocket objects. You can set this factory only once in a program, however. A second attempt to set the SocketImplFactory throws a SocketException.

Protected final void implAccept(Socket s) throws IOException

Subclasses of ServerSocket use this method to implement accept(). You pass an unconnected Socket object to implAccept(). (Doing this requires you to subclass Socket as well since the standard java.net.Socket class doesn't provide a means to create unconnected sockets.) When the method returns, the Socket argument s is connected to a client.

Some Useful Servers

This section shows several servers you can build with server sockets. It starts with a server you can use to test client responses and requests, much as you use Telnet to test server behavior. Then we present three different HTTP servers, each with a different special purpose and each slightly more complex than the previous one.

Client Tester

In the previous chapter, you learned how to use Telnet to experiment with servers. There's no equivalent program to test clients, so let's create one. Example 11-5 is a program called `ClientTester` that runs on a port specified on thecommand-line, shows all data sent by the client, and allows you to send a response to the client by typing it on the command line. For example, you can use this program to see the commands that Netscape Navigator sends to a server.

NOTE　　Clients are rarely as forgiving about unexpected server responses as servers are about unexpected client responses. If at all possible, try to run the clients that connect to this program on a Unix system or some other platform that is moderately crash-proof. Don't run them on a Mac or Windows 98, which are less stable.

This program uses two threads: one to handle input from the client and the other to send output from the server. Using two threads allows the program to handle input and output simultaneously: it can be sending a response to the client while receiving a request—or, more to the point, it can send data to the client while waiting for the client to respond. This is convenient because different clients and servers talk in unpredictable ways. With some protocols, the server talks first; with others, the client talks first. Sometimes the server sends a one-line response; often, the response is much larger. Sometimes the client and the server talk at each other simultaneously. Other times, one side of the connection waits for the other to finish before it responds. The program must be flexible enough to handle all these cases. Example 11-5 shows the code.

Example 11-5. A Client Tester

```
import java.net.*;
import java.io.*;
import com.macfaq.io.SafeBufferedReader; // from Chapter 4


public class ClientTester {

  public static void main(String[] args) {

    int port;

    try {
      port = Integer.parseInt(args[0]);
```

Example 11-5. A Client Tester (continued)

```
      }
    catch (Exception e) {
      port = 0;
    }

    try {
      ServerSocket server = new ServerSocket(port, 1);
      System.out.println("Listening for connections on port "
       + server.getLocalPort());

      while (true) {
        Socket connection = server.accept();
        try {
          System.out.println("Connection established with "
           + connection);
          Thread input = new InputThread(connection.getInputStream());
          input.start();
          Thread output
           = new OutputThread(connection.getOutputStream());
          output.start();
          // wait for output and input to finish
          try {
            input.join();
            output.join();
          }
          catch (InterruptedException e) {
          }
        }
        catch (IOException e) {
          System.err.println(e);
        }
        finally {
          try {
            if (connection != null) connection.close();
          }
          catch (IOException e) {}
        }
      }
    }
    catch (IOException e) {
      e.printStackTrace();
    }

  }

}

class InputThread extends Thread {
```

Example 11-5. A Client Tester (continued)

```
  InputStream in;

  public InputThread(InputStream in) {
    this.in = in;
  }

  public void run()  {

    try {
      while (true) {
        int i = in.read();
        if (i == -1) break;
        System.out.write(i);
      }
    }
    catch (SocketException e) {
      // output thread closed the socket
    }
    catch (IOException e) {
      System.err.println(e);
    }
    try {
      in.close();
    }
    catch (IOException e) {
    }

  }

}

class OutputThread extends Thread {

  Writer out;

  public OutputThread(OutputStream out) {
    this.out = new OutputStreamWriter(out);
  }

  public void run() {

    String line;
    BufferedReader in
      = new SafeBufferedReader(new InputStreamReader(System.in));
    try {
      while (true) {
        line = in.readLine();
        if (line.equals(".")) break;
```

Example 11-5. A Client Tester (continued)

```
      out.write(line +"\r\n");
      out.flush();
    }
  }
  catch (IOException e) {
  }
  try {
    out.close();
  }
  catch (IOException e) {
  }


  }


}
```

The client tester application is split into three classes: `ClientTester`, `InputThread`, and `OutputThread`. The `ClientTester` class reads the port from the command-line, opens a `ServerSocket` on that port, and listens for incoming connections. Only one connection is allowed at a time, because this program is designed for experimentation, and a slow human being has to provide all responses. Consequently, we set an unusually short queue length of 1. Further connections will be refused until the first one has been closed.

An infinite `while` loop waits for connections with the `accept()` method. When a connection is detected, its `InputStream` is used to construct a new `InputThread`, and its `OutputStream` is used to construct a new `OutputThread`. After starting these threads, we wait for them to finish by calling their `join()` methods.

The `InputThread` is contained almost entirely in the `run()` method. It has a single field, `in`, which is the `InputStream` from which data will be read. Data is read from `in` one byte at a time. Each `byte` read is written on `System.out`. The `run()` method ends when the end of stream is encountered or an `IOException` is thrown. The most likely exception here is a `SocketException` thrown because the corresponding `OutputThread` closed the connection.

The `OutputThread` reads input from the local user sitting at the terminal and sends that data to the client. Its constructor has a single argument, an output stream for sending data to the client. `OutputThread` reads input from the user on `System.in`, which is chained to an instance of the `SafeBufferedReader` class developed in Chapter 4, *Java I/O*. The `OutputStream` that was passed to the constructor is chained to an `OutputStreamWriter` for convenience. The `run()` method for `OutputThread` reads lines from the `SafeBufferedReader`, and copies them onto the `OutputStreamWriter`, which sends them to the client. A period typed on a line by itself signals the end of user input. When this occurs, `run()`

exits the loop and out is closed. This has the effect of also closing the socket, so that a `SocketException` is thrown in the input thread, which also exits.

For example, here's the output when Netscape Communicator 4.6 for Windows connected to this server:

```
D:\JAVA\JNP2\examples\11>java ClientTester 80
Listening for connections on port 80
Connection established with
Socket[addr=localhost/127.0.0.1,port=1033,localport=80]
GET / HTTP 1.0
Connection: Keep-Alive
User-Agent: Mozilla/4.6 [en] (WinNT; I)
Host: localhost
Accept: image/gif, image/x-xbitmap, image/jpeg, image/pjpeg, image/png, */*
Accept-Encoding: gzip
Accept-Language: en
Accept-Charset: iso-8859-1,*,utf-8

<html><body><h1>Hello Client!</h1></body></html>
```

Even minimal exploration of clients can reveal some surprising things. For instance, I didn't know until I wrote this example that Netscape Navigator 4.6 can read *.gz* files just as easily as it can read HTML files. That may be useful for serving large text files full of redundant data.

HTTP Servers

HTTP is a large protocol. As you saw in Chapter 3, *Basic Web Concepts*, a full-featured HTTP server must respond to requests for files, convert URLs into file-names on the local system, respond to POST and GET requests, handle requests for files that don't exist, interpret MIME types, launch CGI programs, and much, much more. However, many HTTP servers don't need all of these features. For example, many sites simply display an "under construction" message. Clearly, Apache is overkill for a site like this. Such a site is a candidate for a custom server that does only one thing. Java's network class library makes writing simple servers like this almost trivial.

Custom servers aren't useful only for small sites. High-traffic sites like Yahoo! are also candidates for custom servers because a server that does only one thing can often be much faster than a general purpose server such as Apache or Netscape. It is easy to optimize a special purpose server for a particular task; the result is often much more efficient than a general purpose server that needs to respond to many different kinds of requests. For instance, icons and images that are used repeatedly across many pages or on high-traffic pages might be better handled by a server that read all the image files into memory on startup, and then served them straight out of RAM rather than having to read them off disk for each request. Furthermore, this server could avoid wasting time on logging if you didn't want to track the image request separately from the requests for the pages they were included in.

Finally, Java isn't a bad language for feature-full web servers meant to compete with the likes of Apache or AOLServer. Although CPU-intensive Java programs are demonstrably slower than CPU-intensive C and C++ programs, even when run under a JIT, most HTTP servers are limited by bandwidth, not by CPU speed. Consequently, Java's other advantages, such as its half-compiled/half-interpreted nature, dynamic class loading, garbage collection, and memory protection, really get a chance to shine. In particular, sites that make heavy use of dynamic content through CGI scripts, PHP pages, or other mechanisms can often run much faster when reimplemented on top of a pure or mostly pure Java web server. Indeed, there are several production web servers written in Java such as the W3C's testbed server Jigsaw (*http://www.w3.org/Jigsaw/*). Many other web servers written in C now include substantial Java components to support the Java Servlet API and Java Server Pages. On many sites, these are replacing the traditional CGIs, ASPs, and server-side includes, mostly because the Java equivalents are faster and less resource-intensive. I'm not going to explore these technologies here since they easily deserve a book of their own. I refer interested readers to Jason Hunter's *Java Servlet Programming* (O'Reilly & Associates, Inc., 1998). However, it is important to note that servers in general and web servers in particular are one area where Java really is competitive with C.

A single-file server

Our investigation of HTTP servers begins with a server that always sends out the same file, no matter who or what the request. This is shown in Example 11-6, `SingleFileHTTPServer`. The filename, local port, and content encoding are read from the command line. If the port is omitted, port 80 is assumed. If the encoding is omitted, ASCII is assumed.

Example 11-6. An HTTP Server That Chunks Out the Same File

```
import java.net.*;
import java.io.*;
import java.util.*;

public class SingleFileHTTPServer extends Thread {

  private byte[] content;
  private byte[] header;
  private int port = 80;
```

Example 11-6. An HTTP Server That Chunks Out the Same File (continued)

```
public SingleFileHTTPServer(String data, String encoding,
 String MIMEType, int port) throws UnsupportedEncodingException {
  this(data.getBytes(encoding), encoding, MIMEType, port);
}

public SingleFileHTTPServer(byte[] data, String encoding,
 String MIMEType, int port) throws UnsupportedEncodingException {

  this.content = data;
  this.port = port;
  String header = "HTTP 1.0 200 OK\r\n"
   + "Server: OneFile 1.0\r\n"
   + "Content-length: " + this.content.length + "\r\n"
   + "Content-type: " + MIMEType + "\r\n\r\n";
  this.header = header.getBytes("ASCII");

}


public void run() {

  try {
    ServerSocket server = new ServerSocket(this.port);
    System.out.println("Accepting connections on port "
      + server.getLocalPort());
    System.out.println("Data to be sent:");
    System.out.write(this.content);
    while (true) {

      Socket connection = null;
      try {
        connection = server.accept();
        OutputStream out = new BufferedOutputStream(
                            connection.getOutputStream()
                          );
        InputStream in   = new BufferedInputStream(
                            connection.getInputStream()
                          );
        // read the first line only; that's all we need
        StringBuffer request = new StringBuffer(80);
        while (true) {
          int c = in.read();
          if (c == '\r' || c == '\n' || c == -1) break;
          request.append((char) c);
          // If this is HTTP 1.0 or later send a MIME header

        }
        if (request.toString().indexOf("HTTP/") != -1) {
```

Example 11-6. An HTTP Server That Chunks Out the Same File (continued)

```
          out.write(this.header);
        }
        out.write(this.content);
        out.flush();
      }  // end try
      catch (IOException e) {
      }
      finally {
        if (connection != null) connection.close();
      }

    } // end while
  } // end try
  catch (IOException e) {
    System.err.println("Could not start server. Port Occupied");
  }

} // end run


public static void main(String[] args) {

  try {

    String contentType = "text/plain";
    if (args[0].endsWith(".html") || args[0].endsWith(".htm")) {
      contentType = "text/html";
    }

    InputStream in = new FileInputStream(args[0]);
    ByteArrayOutputStream out = new ByteArrayOutputStream();
    int b;
    while ((b = in.read()) != -1) out.write(b);
    byte[] data = out.toByteArray();

    // set the port to listen on
    int port;
    try {
      port = Integer.parseInt(args[1]);
      if (port < 1 || port > 65535) port = 80;
    }
    catch (Exception e) {
      port = 80;
    }

    String encoding = "ASCII";
    if (args.length >= 2) encoding = args[2];
```

Example 11-6. An HTTP Server That Chunks Out the Same File (continued)

```
      Thread t = new SingleFileHTTPServer(data, encoding,
       contentType, port);
      t.start();

    }
    catch (ArrayIndexOutOfBoundsException e) {
      System.out.println(
        "Usage: java SingleFileHTTPServer filename port encoding");
    }
    catch (Exception e) {
      System.err.println(e);
    }


  }


}
```

The constructors set up the data to be sent along with an HTTP header that includes information about content length and content encoding. The header and the body of the response are stored in byte arrays in the desired encoding so that they can be blasted to clients very quickly.

The `SingleFileHTTPServer` class itself is a subclass of `Thread`. Its `run()` method processes incoming connections. Chances are this server will serve only small files and will support only low-volume web sites. Since all the server needs to do for each connection is check whether the client supports HTTP 1.0 and spew one or two relatively small byte arrays over the connection, chances are this will be sufficient. On the other hand, if you find clients are getting refused, you could use multiple threads instead. A lot depends on the size of the file being served, the peak number of connections expected per minute, and the thread model of Java on the host machine. Using multiple threads would be a clear win for a server that was even slightly more sophisticated than this one.

The `run()` method creates a `ServerSocket` on the specified port. Then it enters an infinite loop that continually accepts connections and processes them. When a socket is accepted, an `InputStream` reads the request from the client. It looks at the first line to see whether it contains the string `HTTP`. If it sees this, the server assumes that the client understands HTTP 1.0 or later and therefore sends a MIME header for the file; then it sends the data. If the client request doesn't contain the string `HTTP`, the server omits the header, sending the data by itself. Finally, the server closes the connection and tries to accept the next connection.

The `main()` method just reads parameters from the command line. The name of the file to be served is read from the first command-line argument. If no file is specified or the file cannot be opened, an error message is printed and the program exits. Assuming the file can be read, its contents are read into the byte array data. A reasonable guess is made about the content type of the file, and that guess is stored in the contentType variable. Next, the port number is read from the second command-line argument. If no port is specified, or if the second argument is not an integer from 0 to 65,535, then port 80 is used. The encoding is read from the third command-line argument if present. Otherwise, ASCII is assumed. (Surprisingly, some VMs don't support ASCII, so you might want to pick 8859-1 instead.) Then these values are used to construct a SingleFileHTTPServer object and start it running. This is only one possible interface. You could easily use this class as part of some other program. If you added a setter method to change the content, you could easily use it to provide simple status information about a running server or system. However, that would raise some additional issues of thread safety that Example 11-5 doesn't have to address because it's immutable.

Here's what you see when you connect to this server via Telnet; the specifics depend on the exact server and file:

```
% telnet macfaq.dialup.cloud9.net 80
Trying 168.100.203.234...
Connected to macfaq.dialup.cloud9.net.
Escape character is '^]'.
GET / HTTP 1.0
HTTP 1.0 200 OK
Server: OneFile 1.0
Content-length: 959
Content-type: text/html

<!DOCTYPE HTML PUBLIC "-//W3C//DTD HTML 3.2//EN">
<HTML>
<HEAD>
<TITLE>Under Construction</TITLE>
</HEAD>

<BODY>
...
```

A redirector

Another simple but useful application for a special-purpose HTTP server is redirection. In this section, we develop a server that redirects users from one web site to another—for example, from *cnet.com* to *home.cnet.com*. Example 11-7 reads a URL and a port number from the command-line, opens a server socket on the port, then redirects all requests that it receives to the site indicated by the new URL, using a 302 FOUND code. Chances are this server is fast enough not to require multiple threads. Nonetheless, threads might be mildly advantageous, especially on a high-volume site on a slow network connection. And this server does a lot of string processing, one of Java's most notorious performance bottle-necks. But really for purposes of example more than anything, I've made the server multithreaded. In this example, I chose to use a new thread rather than a thread pool for each connection. This is perhaps a little simpler to code and understand but somewhat less efficient. In Example 11-8, we'll look at an HTTP server that uses a thread pool.

Example 11-7. An HTTP Redirector

```
import java.net.*;
import java.io.*;
import java.util.*;

public class Redirector implements Runnable {

  private int port;
  private String newSite;

  public Redirector(String site, int port) {
    this.port = port;
    this.newSite = site;
  }

  public void run() {

    try {

      ServerSocket server = new ServerSocket(this.port);
      System.out.println("Redirecting connections on port "
        + server.getLocalPort() + " to " + newSite);

      while (true) {

        try {
          Socket s = server.accept();
          Thread t = new RedirectThread(s);
          t.start();
        }  // end try
        catch (IOException e) {
        }

      } // end while

    } // end try
    catch (BindException e) {
      System.err.println("Could not start server. Port Occupied");
    }
    catch (IOException e) {
      System.err.println(e);
```

Example 11-7. An HTTP Redirector (continued)

```java
    }

  } // end run

class RedirectThread extends Thread {

  private Socket connection;

  RedirectThread(Socket s) {
    this.connection = s;
  }

  public void run() {

    try {

      Writer out = new BufferedWriter(
                   new OutputStreamWriter(
                    connection.getOutputStream(), "ASCII"
                   )
                  );
      Reader in = new InputStreamReader(
                   new BufferedInputStream(
                    connection.getInputStream()
                   )
                  );

      // read the first line only; that's all we need
      StringBuffer request = new StringBuffer(80);
      while (true) {
        int c = in.read();
        if (c == '\r' || c == '\n' || c == -1) break;
        request.append((char) c);
      }
      // If this is HTTP 1.0 or later send a MIME header
      String get = request.toString();
      int firstSpace = get.indexOf(' ');
      int secondSpace = get.indexOf(' ', firstSpace+1);
      String theFile = get.substring(firstSpace+1, secondSpace);
      if (get.indexOf("HTTP") != -1) {
        out.write("HTTP1.0 302 FOUND\r\n");
        Date now = new Date();
        out.write("Date: " + now + "\r\n");
        out.write("Server: Redirector 1.0\r\n");
        out.write("Location: " + newSite + theFile + "\r\n");
        out.write("Content-type: text/html\r\n\r\n");
        out.flush();
      }
```

Example 11-7. An HTTP Redirector (continued)

```
        // Not all browsers support redirection so we need to
        // produce HTML that says where the document has moved to.
        out.write("<HTML><HEAD><TITLE>Document moved</TITLE></HEAD>\r\n");
        out.write("<BODY><H1>Document moved</H1>\r\n");
        out.write("The document " + theFile
          + " has moved to\r\n<A HREF=\"" + newSite + theFile + "\">"
          + newSite  + theFile
          + "</A>.\r\n Please update your bookmarks<P>");
        out.write("</BODY></HTML>\r\n");
        out.flush();

      } // end try
      catch (IOException e) {
      }
      finally {
        try {
          if (connection != null) connection.close();
        }
        catch (IOException e) {}
      }

    }  // end run

  }

  public static void main(String[] args) {

    int thePort;
    String theSite;

    try {
      theSite = args[0];
      // trim trailing slash
      if (theSite.endsWith("/")) {
        theSite = theSite.substring(0, theSite.length()-1);
      }
    }
    catch (Exception e) {
      System.out.println(
        "Usage: java Redirector http://www.newsite.com/ port");
      return;
    }

    try {
      thePort = Integer.parseInt(args[1]);
    }
    catch (Exception e) {
      thePort = 80;
```

Example 11-7. An HTTP Redirector (continued)

```
    }

    Thread t = new Thread(new Redirector(theSite, thePort));
    t.start();

  }  // end main

}
```

To start the redirector on port 80 and redirect incoming requests to *http://metalab. unc.edu/xml,* you would type:

```
D:\JAVA\JNP2\examples\11>java Redirector http://metalab.unc.edu/xml
Redirecting connections on port 80 to http://metalab.unc.edu/xml
```

If you connect to this server via Telnet, this is what you'll see:

```
% telnet macfaq.dialup.cloud9.net 80
Trying 168.100.203.234...
Connected to macfaq.dialup.cloud9.net.
Escape character is '^]'.
GET / HTTP 1.0
HTTP 1.0 302 FOUND
Date: Wed Sep 08 11:59:42 PDT 1999
Server: Redirector 1.0
Location: http://metalab.unc.edu/xml/
Content-type: text/html

<HTML><HEAD><TITLE>Document moved</TITLE></HEAD>
<BODY><H1>Document moved</H1>
The document / has moved to
<A HREF="http://metalab.unc.edu/xml/">http://metalab.unc.edu/xml/</A>.
 Please update your bookmarks<P></BODY></HTML>
Connection closed by foreign host.
```

If, however, you connect with a reasonably modern web browser, you should be sent to *http://metalab.unc.edu/xml* with only a slight delay. You should never see the HTML added after the response code; this is provided to support older browsers that don't do redirection automatically.

The main() method provides a very simple interface that reads the URL of the new site to redirect connections to and the local port to listen on. It uses this information to construct a Redirector object. Then it uses the resulting Runnable object (Redirector implements Runnable) to spawn a new thread and start it. If the port is not specified, Redirector listens on port 80. If the site is omitted, Redirector prints an error message and exits.

The run() method of Redirector binds the server socket to the port, prints a brief status message, and then enters an infinite loop in which it listens for connections. Every time a connection is accepted, the resulting Socket object is used to construct a RedirectThread. This RedirectThread is then started. All further interaction with the client takes place in this new thread. The run() method of Redirector then simply waits for the next incoming connection.

The run() method of RedirectThread does most of the work. It begins by chaining a Writer to the Socket's output stream, and a Reader to the Socket's input stream. Both input and output are buffered. Then the run() method reads the first line the client sends. Although the client will probably send a whole MIME header, we can ignore that. The first line contains all the information we need. This line looks something like this:

```
GET /directory/filename.html HTTP 1.0
```

It is possible that the first word will be POST or PUT instead or that there will be no HTTP version. The second "word" is the file the client wants to retrieve. This *must* begin with a slash (/). Browsers are responsible for converting relative URLs to absolute URLs that begin with a slash; the server does not do this. The third word is the version of the HTTP protocol the browser understands. Possible values are nothing at all (pre-HTTP 1.0 browsers), HTTP 1.0 (most current browsers), or HTTP 1.1.

To handle a request like this, Redirector ignores the first word. The second word is attached to the URL of the target server (stored in the field newSite) to give a full redirected URL. The third word is used to determine whether to send a MIME header; MIME headers are not used for old browsers that do not understand HTTP 1.0. If there is a version, a MIME header is sent; otherwise, it is omitted.

Sending the data is almost trivial. The Writer out is used. Since all the data we send is pure ASCII, the exact encoding isn't too important. The only trick here is that the end-of-line character for HTTP requests is \r\n—a carriage return followed by a linefeed.

The next lines each send one line of text to the client. The first line printed is:

```
HTTP 1.0 302 FOUND
```

This is an HTTP 1.0 response code that tells the client to expect to be redirected. The second line is a Date: header that gives the current time at the server. This line is optional. The third line is the name and version of the server; this is also optional but is used by spiders that try to keep statistics about the most popular web servers. (It would be very surprising to ever see Redirector break into single digits in lists of the most popular servers.) The next line is the Location: header, which is required for this server. It tells the client where it is being redirected to.

Last is the standard Content-type: header. We send the content type text/html to indicate that the client should expect to see HTML. Finally, a blank line is sent to signify the end of the header data.

Everything after this will be HTML, which is processed by the browser and displayed to the user. The next several lines print a message for browsers that do not support redirection, so those users can manually jump to the new site. That message looks like:

```
<HTML><HEAD><TITLE>Document moved</TITLE></HEAD>
<BODY><H1>Document moved</H1>
The document / has moved to
<A HREF="http://metalab.unc.edu/xml/">http://metalab.unc.edu/xml/</A>.
 Please update your bookmarks<P></BODY></HTML>
```

Finally, the connection is closed and the thread dies.

A full-fledged HTTP server

Enough with special-purpose HTTP servers. This section develops a full-blown HTTP server, called JHTTP, that can serve an entire document tree, including images, applets, HTML files, text files, and more. It will be very similar to the SingleFileHTTPServer, except that it pays attention to the GET requests. This server is still fairly lightweight; after looking at the code, we'll discuss other features you might want to add.

Since this server may have to read and serve large files from the filesystem over potentially slow network connections, we'll change its approach. Rather than processing each request as it arrives in the main thread of execution, we'll place incoming connections in a pool. Separate instances of a RequestProcessor class will remove the connections from the pool and process them. Example 11-8 shows the main JHTTP class. As in the previous two examples, the main() method of JHTTP handles initialization, but other programs could use this class themselves to run basic web servers.

Example 11-8. The JHTTP Web Server

```
import java.net.*;
import java.io.*;
import java.util.*;

public class JHTTP extends Thread {

  private File documentRootDirectory;
  private String indexFileName = "index.html";
  private ServerSocket server;
  private int numThreads = 50;
```

Example 11-8. The JHTTP Web Server (continued)

```java
public JHTTP(File documentRootDirectory, int port,
 String indexFileName) throws IOException {

  if (!documentRootDirectory.isDirectory()) {
    throw new IOException(documentRootDirectory
      + " does not exist as a directory");
  }
  this.documentRootDirectory = documentRootDirectory;
  this.indexFileName = indexFileName;
  this.server = new ServerSocket(port);
}

public JHTTP(File documentRootDirectory, int port)
 throws IOException {
  this(documentRootDirectory, port, "index.html");
}

public JHTTP(File documentRootDirectory) throws IOException {
  this(documentRootDirectory, 80, "index.html");
}

public void run() {

  for (int i = 0; i < numThreads; i++) {
    Thread t = new Thread(
     new RequestProcessor(documentRootDirectory, indexFileName));
    t.start();
  }
  System.out.println("Accepting connections on port "
   + server.getLocalPort());
  System.out.println("Document Root: " + documentRootDirectory);
  while (true) {
    try {
      Socket request = server.accept();
      RequestProcessor.processRequest(request);
    }
    catch (IOException e) {
    }
  }

}

public static void main(String[] args) {

  // get the Document root
  File docroot;
  try {
    docroot = new File(args[0]);
```

Example 11-8. The JHTTP Web Server (continued)

```
    }
    catch (ArrayIndexOutOfBoundsException e) {
      System.out.println("Usage: java JHTTP docroot port indexfile");
      return;
    }

    // set the port to listen on
    int port;
    try {
      port = Integer.parseInt(args[1]);
      if (port < 0 || port > 65535) port = 80;
    }
    catch (Exception e) {
      port = 80;
    }

    try {
      JHTTP webserver = new JHTTP(docroot, port);
      webserver.start();
    }
    catch (IOException e) {
      System.out.println("Server could not start because of an "
        + e.getClass());
      System.out.println(e);
    }

  }

}
```

The `main()` method of the `JHTTP` class sets the document root directory from `args[0]`. The port is read from `args[1]`, or 80 is used for a default. Then a new `JHTTP` thread is constructed and started. The `JHTTP` thread spawns 50 `RequestProcessor` threads to handle requests, each of which will retrieve incoming connection requests from the `RequestProcessor` pool as they become available. The JHTTP thread repeatedly accepts incoming connections and puts them in the `RequestProcessor` pool.

Each connection is handled by the `run()` method of the `RequestProcessor` class shown in Example 11-9. This method waits until it can get a `Socket` out of the pool. Once it does that, it gets input and output streams from the socket and chains them to a reader and a writer. The reader reads the first line of the client request to determine the version of HTTP that the client supports—we want to send a MIME header only if this is HTTP 1.0 or later—and what file is requested. Assuming the method is `GET`, the file that is requested is converted to a filename on the local filesystem. If the file requested was a directory (i.e., its name ended with a slash), we add the name of an index file. We use the canonical path to make sure that the requested file doesn't come from outside the document root directory. Otherwise, a sneaky client could walk all over the local filesystem by including .. in URLs to walk up the directory hierarchy. This is all we'll need from the client, though a more advanced web server, especially one that logged hits, would read the rest of the MIME header the client sends.

Next the requested file is opened and its contents are read into a byte array. If the HTTP version is 1.0 or later, we write the appropriate MIME headers on the output stream. To figure out the content type, we call the guessContentTypeFromName() method to map file extensions such as *.html* onto MIME types such as text/html. The byte array containing the file's contents is written onto the output stream, and the connection is closed. Exceptions may be thrown at various places if, for example, the file cannot be found or opened. If an exception occurs, we send an appropriate HTTP error message to the client instead of the file's contents.

Example 11-9. The Thread Pool That Handles HTTP Requests

```
import java.net.*;
import java.io.*;
import java.util.*;

public class RequestProcessor implements Runnable {

  private static List pool = new LinkedList();
  private File documentRootDirectory;
  private String indexFileName = "index.html";

  public RequestProcessor(File documentRootDirectory,
    String indexFileName) {

    if (documentRootDirectory.isFile()) {
      throw new IllegalArgumentException(
      "documentRootDirectory must be a directory, not a file");
    }
    this.documentRootDirectory = documentRootDirectory;
    try {
      this.documentRootDirectory
        = documentRootDirectory.getCanonicalFile();
    }
    catch (IOException e) {
    }
    if (indexFileName != null) this.indexFileName = indexFileName;
  }

  public static void processRequest(Socket request) {
```

Example 11-9. The Thread Pool That Handles HTTP Requests (continued)

```java
    synchronized (pool) {
      pool.add(pool.size(), request);
      pool.notifyAll();
    }

  }

  public void run() {

    // for security checks
    String root = documentRootDirectory.getPath();

    while (true) {
      Socket connection;
      synchronized (pool) {
        while (pool.isEmpty()) {
          try {
            pool.wait();
          }
          catch (InterruptedException e) {
          }
        }
        connection = (Socket) pool.remove(0);
      }

      try {
        String filename;
        String contentType;
        OutputStream raw = new BufferedOutputStream(
                           connection.getOutputStream()
                          );
        Writer out = new OutputStreamWriter(raw);
        Reader in = new InputStreamReader(
                    new BufferedInputStream(
                     connection.getInputStream()
                    ),"ASCII"
                   );
        StringBuffer requestLine = new StringBuffer();
        int c;
        while (true) {
          c = in.read();
          if (c == '\r' || c == '\n') break;
          requestLine.append((char) c);
        }

        String get = requestLine.toString();

        // log the request
```

Example 11-9. The Thread Pool That Handles HTTP Requests (continued)

```
System.out.println(get);

StringTokenizer st = new StringTokenizer(get);
String method = st.nextToken();
String version = "";
if (method.equals("GET")) {
  filename = st.nextToken();
  if (filename.endsWith("/")) filename += indexFileName;
  contentType = guessContentTypeFromName(filename);
  if (st.hasMoreTokens()) {
    version = st.nextToken();
  }

  File theFile = new File(documentRootDirectory,
   filename.substring(1,filename.length()));
  if (theFile.canRead()
      // Don't let clients outside the document root
    && theFile.getCanonicalPath().startsWith(root)) {
    DataInputStream fis = new DataInputStream(
                           new BufferedInputStream(
                             new FileInputStream(theFile)
                           )
                          );
    byte[] theData = new byte[(int) theFile.length()];
    fis.readFully(theData);
    fis.close();
    if (version.startsWith("HTTP ")) {  // send a MIME header
      out.write("HTTP 1.0 200 OK\r\n");
      Date now = new Date();
      out.write("Date: " + now + "\r\n");
      out.write("Server: JHTTP 1.0\r\n");
      out.write("Content-length: " + theData.length + "\r\n");
      out.write("Content-type: " + contentType + "\r\n\r\n");
      out.flush();
    } // end if

    // send the file; it may be an image or other binary data
    // so use the underlying output stream
    // instead of the writer
    raw.write(theData);
    raw.flush();
  } // end if
  else {  // can't find the file
    if (version.startsWith("HTTP ")) {  // send a MIME header
      out.write("HTTP 1.0 404 File Not Found\r\n");
      Date now = new Date();
      out.write("Date: " + now + "\r\n");
      out.write("Server: JHTTP 1.0\r\n");
```

Example 11-9. The Thread Pool That Handles HTTP Requests (continued)

```
                out.write("Content-type: text/html\r\n\r\n");
              }
              out.write("<HTML>\r\n");
              out.write("<HEAD><TITLE>File Not Found</TITLE>\r\n");
              out.write("</HEAD>\r\n");
              out.write("<BODY>");
              out.write("<H1>HTTP Error 404: File Not Found</H1>\r\n");
              out.write("</BODY></HTML>\r\n");
              out.flush();
            }
          }
          else {  // method does not equal "GET"
            if (version.startsWith("HTTP ")) {  // send a MIME header
              out.write("HTTP 1.0 501 Not Implemented\r\n");
              Date now = new Date();
              out.write("Date: " + now + "\r\n");
              out.write("Server: JHTTP 1.0\r\n");
              out.write("Content-type: text/html\r\n\r\n");
            }
            out.write("<HTML>\r\n");
            out.write("<HEAD><TITLE>Not Implemented</TITLE>\r\n");
            out.write("</HEAD>\r\n");
            out.write("<BODY>");
            out.write("<H1>HTTP Error 501: Not Implemented</H1>\r\n");
            out.write("</BODY></HTML>\r\n");
            out.flush();
          }
        }
        catch (IOException e) {
        }
        finally {
          try {
            connection.close();
          }
          catch (IOException e) {}
        }

      } // end while

  } // end run

  public static String guessContentTypeFromName(String name) {
    if (name.endsWith(".html") || name.endsWith(".htm")) {
      return "text/html";
    }
    else if (name.endsWith(".txt") || name.endsWith(".java")) {
      return "text/plain";
    }
```

Example 11-9. The Thread Pool That Handles HTTP Requests (continued)

```
    else if (name.endsWith(".gif")) {
      return "image/gif";
    }
    else if (name.endsWith(".class")) {
      return "application/octet-stream";
    }
    else if (name.endsWith(".jpg") || name.endsWith(".jpeg")) {
      return "image/jpeg";
    }
    else return "text/plain";
  }

} // end RequestProcessor
```

This server is functional but still rather austere. Here are a few features you might want to think about adding:

- A server administration interface
- Support for CGI programs and/or the Java Servlet API
- Support for other request methods, such as **POST**, **HEAD**, and **PUT**
- A log file in the common web log file format
- Server-side includes and/or Java Server Pages
- Support for multiple document roots, so that individual users can have their own sites

Finally, you should spend a little time thinking about ways to optimize this server. If you really want to use JHTTP to run a high-traffic site, there are a couple of things you can do to speed this server up. The first and most important is to use a Just-in-Time (JIT) compiler such as HotSpot. JITs can improve program performance by as much as an order of magnitude or more. The second thing you should do is implement smart caching. Keep track of the requests you've received, and store the data from the most frequently requested files in a Hashtable so that they're kept in memory. Use a low-priority thread to update this cache.

12

In this chapter:
• *Secure Communications*
• *Creating Secure Client Sockets*
• *Methods of the SSLSocket Class*
• *Creating Secure Server Sockets*
• *Methods of the SSLServerSocket Class*

Secure Sockets

One of the perennial fears of consumers buying goods over the Internet is that some hacker will steal their credit card number and run up a several-thousand-dollar bill by calling phone sex lines. In reality, it's far more likely that a clerk at a department store will steal their credit card number from a store receipt than that some hacker will grab it in transit across the Internet. In fact, as of early 2000, all the major online thefts of credit card numbers have been accomplished by stealing the information from poorly secured databases and text files *after* the information has been safely transmitted across the Internet. Nonetheless, to make Internet connections more fundamentally secure, sockets can be encrypted. This allows transactions to be confidential, authenticated, and accurate.

However, encryption is a complex subject. Performing it properly requires a detailed understanding not only of the mathematical algorithms used to encrypt data but also of the protocols used to exchange keys and encrypted data. Even a small mistake can open a large hole in your armor and reveal your communications to an eavesdropper. Consequently, writing encryption software is a task best left to experts. Fortunately, nonexperts with only a layperson's understanding of the underlying protocols and algorithms can secure their communications with software designed by experts. Every time you order something from an online store from within Netscape Navigator, chances are the transaction is encrypted and authenticated using protocols and algorithms you need to know next to nothing about. As a programmer who wants to write network client software that talks to online stores, you need to know a little more about the protocols and algorithms involved but not a lot more, provided you can use a class library written by experts who do understand the details. If you want to write the server software that runs the online store, then you need to know a little bit more but still not as much as you would if you were designing all this from scratch without reference to other work.

Unfortunately, such software is still subject to the arms control laws of the United States and various other countries and consequently cannot be freely imported or exported. (Details depend on jurisdiction.) Consequently, such capabilities are not built into the standard `java.net` classes in the JDK. Instead, they are provided as a standard extension to the JDK called the Java Secure Sockets Extension (JSSE). This is an add-on for the JDK that secures network communications using the Secure Sockets Layer (SSL) Version 3 and Transport Layer Security (TLS) protocols and their associated algorithms. SSL is a security protocol to allow web browsers to talk to web servers using various levels of confidentiality and authentication. SSL was originally developed at and patented by Netscape (building on the work of many previous cryptographers). Its successor, TLS, is being developed under the auspices of the IETF.

Secure Communications

Confidential communication through an open channel such as the public Internet that nonetheless resists eavesdropping absolutely requires that the data be encrypted. Most encryption schemes that lend themselves to computer implementation are based around the notion of a key, a slightly more general kind of password that's not limited to text. The clear text message is combined with the bits of the key according to a mathematical algorithm to produce the encrypted cipher text. Using keys with more bits makes messages exponentially more difficult to decrypt by brute-force guessing of the keys.

In traditional secret key (or symmetric) encryption, the same key is used both to encrypt and decrypt the data. Both the sender and the receiver have to possess the single key. Suppose Angela wants to send Gus a secret message. She first sends Gus the key they'll use to exchange the secret. But the key can't be encrypted because Gus doesn't have the key yet, so Angela has to send the key unencrypted. Now suppose Edgar is eavesdropping on the connection between Angela and Gus. He will get the key at the same time that Gus does. From that point forward, he can read anything Angela and Gus say to each other using that key.

In public key (or asymmetric) encryption, different keys are used to encrypt and decrypt the data. One key, called the public key, is used to encrypt the data. This key can be given to anyone. A different key, called the private key, is used to decrypt the data. This must be kept secret but needs to be possessed by only one of the correspondents. If Angela wants to send a message to Gus, she asks Gus for his public key. Gus sends it to her over an unencrypted connection. Angela uses Gus's public key to encrypt her message and sends it to him. If Edgar is eavesdropping when Gus sends Angela his key, Edgar also gets Gus's public key. However, this doesn't allow Edgar to decrypt the message Angela sends Gus, since decryption requires Gus's private key. The message is safe even if the public key is detected in transit.

Asymmetric encryption can also be used for authentication and message integrity checking. For this use, Angela would encrypt a message with her private key before sending it. When Gus received it, he'd decrypt it with Angela's public key. If the decryption succeeded, then Gus would know that the message came from Angela. After all, no one else could have produced a message that would decrypt properly with her public key. Gus would also know that the message wasn't changed en route, either maliciously by Edgar or unintentionally by buggy software or network noise, since any such change would have screwed up the decryption. With a little more effort, Angela can double-encrypt the message, once with her private key, once with Gus's public key, thus getting all three benefits of privacy, authentication, and integrity.

In practice, public key encryption is much more CPU-intensive and much slower than secret key encryption. Therefore, instead of encrypting the entire transmission with Gus's public key, Angela encrypts a traditional secret key and sends it to Gus. Gus decrypts it with his private key. Now Angela and Gus both know the secret key, but Edgar doesn't. Therefore, Gus and Angela can now use faster secret-key encryption to communicate privately without Edgar being able to listen in.

Edgar still has one good attack on this protocol, however. (Very important: the attack is on the protocol used to send and receive messages, *not* on the encryption algorithms used. This attack does not require Edgar to break Gus and Angela's encryption and is completely independent of key length.) Edgar not only can read Gus's public key when he sends it to Angela, but also can replace it with his own public key! Then when Angela thinks she's encrypting a message with Gus's public key, she's really using Edgar's. When she sends a message to Gus, Edgar intercepts it, decrypts it using his private key, encrypts it using Gus's public key, and sends it on to Gus. This is called a *man-in-the-middle attack*. Working alone on an insecure channel, Gus and Angela have no easy way to protect against this. The solution used in practice is for both Gus and Angela to store and verify their public keys with a trusted third-party certification authority. Rather than sending each other their public keys, Gus and Angela retrieve each other's public key from the certification authority. This scheme still isn't perfect—Edgar may be able to place himself in between Gus and the certification authority, Angela and the certification authority, and Gus and Angela—but it is making life harder for Edgar.

NOTE   This discussion has been necessarily brief. Many interesting details
            have been skimmed over or omitted entirely. If you want to know
            more, the Crypt Cabal's Cryptography FAQ at *http://www.faqs.org/*
            faqs/cryptography-faq/ is a good place to start. For in-depth analysis of
            protocols and algorithms for confidentiality, authentication, and
            message integrity, Bruce Schneier's *Applied Cryptography* (John Wiley
            & Sons, 1996) is the standard introductory text. Finally, Jonathan
            Knudsen's *Java Cryptography* (O'Reilly & Associates, Inc., 1998) and
            Scott Oak's *Java Security* (O'Reilly & Associates, Inc., 1998) cover the
            underlying cryptography and authentication packages on which the
            JSSE rests.

As this example should indicate, the theory and practice of encryption and
authentication, both algorithms and protocols, is a challenging field that's fraught
with minefields to surprise the amateur cryptographer. It is much easier to design
a bad encryption algorithm or protocol than a good one. And it's not always obvious which algorithms and protocols are good and which aren't. Fortunately, you
don't have to be a cryptography expert to use strong cryptography in your Java
network programs. JSSE is the standard extension to Java 1.2 and later that shields
you from the low-level details of how algorithms are negotiated, keys are
exchanged, correspondents are authenticated, and data is encrypted. JSSE allows
you to create sockets and server sockets that transparently handle the negotiations
and encryption necessary for secure communication. All you have to do is send
your data over the same streams and sockets you're familiar with from previous
chapters. The Java Secure Socket Extension is divided into four packages:

javax.net.ssl
    The abstract classes that define Java's API for secure network communication.

javax.net
    The abstract socket factory classes used instead of constructors to create
    secure sockets.

javax.security.cert
    A minimal set of classes for handling public key certificates that's needed for
    SSL in Java 1.1. (In Java 1.2 and later, the java.security.cert package
    should be used instead.)

com.sun.net.ssl
    The concrete classes that implement the encryption algorithms and protocols
    in Sun's reference implementation of the JSSE. Technically, these are not part
    of the JSSE standard. Other implementers may replace this package with one
    of their own; for instance, one that uses native code to speed up the CPU-
    intensive key generation and encryption process.

None of these are included as a standard part of the JDK. Before you can use any of these classes, you'll have to download the JSSE (either global or domestic version) from *http://java.sun.com/products/jsse/* (as always, the URL is subject to change). In the future, third parties may also implement this API, though no such third-party implementations are available as of July 2000.

Sun's reference implementation is distributed as a zip file, which you can unpack and place anywhere on your system. In the *lib* directory of this zip file, you'll find three JAR archives: *jcert.jar*, *jnet.jar*, and *jsse.jar*. These need to be placed in your class path. In Java 1.2 and later, you can simply move them to your *jre/lib/ext* directory. In Java 1.1, you'll need to include the paths to each archive in the CLASS-PATH environment variable.

Next you need to register the cryptography provider by editing your *jre/lib/ext/ security/java.security* file. Open this file in a text editor and look for a line like these:

```
security.provider.1=sun.security.provider.Sun
security.provider.2=com.sun.rsajca.Provider
```

You may have more or fewer providers than this. However many you have, add one more line like this:

```
security.provider.3=com.sun.net.ssl.internal.ssl.Provider
```

You may have to change the "3" to 2 or 4 or 5 or whatever the next number is in the security provider sequence. If you install a third-party JSSE implementation, you'll add another line like this with the class name as specified by your JSSE implementation's documentation.

NOTE   If you use multiple copies of the JRE, you'll need to repeat this pro-
            cedure for each one you use. For reasons that have never been com-
            pletely clear to me, Sun installed separate copies of the JRE 1.3 on
            my filesystem: one for compiling and one for running. I had to make
            these changes to both copies to get JSSE programs to run.

If you don't get this right, you'll see exceptions like "java.net.SocketException: SSL implementation not available" when you try to run programs that use the JSSE. Alternatively, instead of editing the *java.policy* file, you can add this line to classes that use Sun's implementation of the JSSE:

```
java.security.Security.addProvider(
  new com.sun.net.ssl.internal.ssl.Provider());
```

This may be useful if you're writing software to run on someone else's system and don't want to ask her to modify her *java.policy* file.

Creating Secure Client Sockets

If you don't care very much about the underlying details, using an encrypted SSL socket to talk to an existing secure server is truly straightforward. Rather than constructing a `java.net.Socket` object with a constructor, you get one from a `javax.net.ssl.SSLSocketFactory` by using its `createSocket()` method. SSL-SocketFactory is an abstract class that follows the abstract factory design pattern:

```
public abstract class SSLSocketFactory extends SocketFactory
```

Since the `SSLFactorySocket` class is itself abstract, you get an instance of it by invoking the static `SSLSocketFactory.getDefault()` method:

```
public static SocketFactory getDefault() throws InstantiationException
```

This either returns an instance of `SSLSocketFactory` or throws an `InstantiationException` if no concrete subclass can be found. Once you have a reference to the factory, use one of the five overloaded `createSocket()` methods to build an `SSLSocket`:

```
public abstract Socket createSocket(String host, int port)
  throws IOException, UnknownHostException
public abstract Socket createSocket(InetAddress host, int port)
  throws IOException
public abstract Socket createSocket(String host, int port,
  InetAddress interface, int localPort)
  throws IOException, UnknownHostException
public abstract Socket createSocket(InetAddress host, int port,
  InetAddress interface, int localPort)
  throws IOException, UnknownHostException
public abstract Socket createSocket(Socket proxy, String host, int port,
  boolean autoClose) throws IOException
```

The first two methods create and return a socket that's connected to the specified host and port or throw an `IOException` if they can't connect. The third and fourth methods connect and return a socket that's connected to the specified host and port from the specified local network interface and port. The last `createSocket()` method, however, is a little different. It begins with an existing `Socket` object that's connected to a proxy server. It returns a `Socket` that tunnels through this proxy server to the specified host and port. The `autoClose` argument determines whether the underlying proxy socket should be closed when this socket is closed. If `autoClose` is true, the underlying socket will be closed; if false, it won't be.

The `Socket` that all these methods return will really be a `javax.net.ssl.SSLSocket`, a subclass of `java.net.Socket`. However, you don't need to know that. Once the secure socket has been created, you use it just like any other socket, through its `getInputStream()`, `getOutputStream()`, and other methods. For

example, let's suppose there's a server running on *login.metalab.unc.edu* on port
7,000 that accepts orders. Each order is sent as an ASCII string using a single TCP
connection. The server accepts the order and closes the connection. (I'm leaving
out a *lot* of details that would be necessary in a real-world system, such as the server
sending a response code telling the client whether the order was accepted.) The
orders that clients send look like this:

```
Name: John Smith
Product-ID: 67X-89
Address: 1280 Deniston Blvd, NY NY 10003
Card number: 4000-1234-5678-9017
Expires: 08/05
```

There's enough information in this message to let someone snooping packets figure out John Smith's credit card number and use it for nefarious purposes. Consequently, before sending this order, you should encrypt it, and the simplest way to
do that, without burdening either the server or the client with a lot of complicated, error-prone encryption code, is to use a secure socket. The following code
sends the order over a secure socket:

```
try {

  // This statement is only needed if you didn't add
  // security.provider.3=com.sun.net.ssl.internal.ssl.Provider
  // to your java.security file.
  Security.addProvider(new com.sun.net.ssl.internal.ssl.Provider());

  SSLSocketFactory factory
   = (SSLSocketFactory) SSLSocketFactory.getDefault();
  Socket socket = factory.createSocket("login.metalab.unc.edu", 7000);

  Writer out = new OutputStreamWriter(socket.getOutputStream(),
   "ASCII");
  out.write("Name: John Smith\r\n");
  out.write("Product-ID: 67X-89\r\n");
  out.write("Address: 1280 Deniston Blvd, NY NY 10003\r\n");
  out.write("Card number: 4000-1234-5678-9017\r\n");
  out.write("Expires: 08/05\r\n");
  out.flush();
  out.close();
  socket.close();

}
catch (IOException e) {
  e.printStackTrace();
}
```

Only the first three statements are noticeably different from what you'd do with an insecure socket. The rest of the code just uses the normal methods of the Socket, OutputStream, and Writer classes.

Reading input is no harder. Example 12-1 is a simple program that connects to a secure HTTP server, sends a simple GET request, and prints out the response.

Example 12-1. HTTPSClient

```
import java.net.*;
import java.io.*;
import java.security.*;
import javax.net.ssl.*;

public class HTTPSClient {

  public static void main(String[] args) {

    if (args.length == 0) {
      System.out.println("Usage: java HTTPSClient host");
      return;
    }

    int port = 443; // default https port
    String host = args[0];

    try {

     Security.addProvider(new com.sun.net.ssl.internal.ssl.Provider());
      SSLSocketFactory factory
       = (SSLSocketFactory) SSLSocketFactory.getDefault();

      SSLSocket socket = (SSLSocket) factory.createSocket(host, port);

      Writer out = new OutputStreamWriter(socket.getOutputStream());
      // https requires the full URL in the GET line
      out.write("GET http://" + host + "/ HTTP 1.1\r\n");
      out.write("\r\n");
      out.flush();

      // read response
      BufferedReader in = new BufferedReader(
       new InputStreamReader(socket.getInputStream()));
      int c;
      while ((c = in.read()) != -1) {
        System.out.write(c);
      }

      out.close();
```

Example 12-1. HTTPSClient (continued)

```
      in.close();
      socket.close();

    }
    catch (IOException e) {
      System.err.println(e);
    }

  }

}
```

Here are the first few lines of output you get when you connect to the U.S. Postal
Service's web site:

```
D:\JAVA\JNP2\examples\19>java HTTPSClient www.usps.gov
HTTP 1.1 200 OK
Server: Netscape-Enterprise/4.0
Date: Mon, 10 Jan 2000 19:35:40 GMT
Content-type: text/html
Etag: "34ad7c5d-1-491-3867bec9"
Last-modified: Mon, 27 Dec 1999 19:32:25 GMT
Content-length: 1169
Accept-ranges: bytes
Connection: keep-alive

<HTML>
<Head>
<META NAME="Description" CONTENT="The United States Postal Service
 (USPS).  This Post Office is open 7 days a week, 24 hours a day.
 USPS - for your mailing and shipping needs.">
```

On the other hand, here's what happens when you try to connect to Verisign's
secure web server:

```
D:\JAVA\JNP2\examples\19>java HTTPSClient www.verisign.com
javax.net.ssl.SSLException: untrusted server cert chain
```

This is a little surprising. What's apparently happened is that Java has decided it
doesn't trust that Verisign really is who it says it is. This may be because Verisign is
authenticating itself. In most cases, it would be Verisign that would be authenticating someone else.

One thing you may notice when you run this program is that it's slower to respond
than you might expect. There's a noticeable amount of both CPU and network
overhead involved in generating and exchanging the public keys. Even over a fast
connection, it can easily take 10 seconds or more for the connection to be

established. Consequently, you probably don't want to serve all your content over HTTPS, only that which really needs to be private.

Methods of the SSLSocket Class

Besides the methods we've already discussed and those it inherits from `java.net.Socket`, the `SSLSocket` class has a number of methods for configuring exactly how much and what kind of authentication and encryption is performed. For instance, you can choose weaker or stronger algorithms, require clients to prove their identity, force reauthentication of both sides, and more.

Choosing the Cipher Suites

Different implementations of the JSSE support different combinations of authentication and encryption algorithms. For instance, although so far I've been talking about Sun's reference implementation as though it were one thing, it's actually two: one for domestic use within the U.S. and Canada that allows for encryption with key lengths up to 128 bits, and one for global use that allows only 40-bit encryption. The `getSupportedCipherSuites()` method tells you which combination of algorithms are available on a given socket:

```
public abstract String[] getSupportedCipherSuites()
```

However, not all cipher suites that are understood are necessarily allowed on the connection. Some may be too weak and consequently disabled. The `getEnabledCipherSuites()` method tells you which suites this socket is willing to use:

```
public abstract String[] getEnabledCipherSuites()
```

The actual suite used is negotiated between the client and server at connection time. It's possible that the client and the server won't agree on any suite. It's also possible that although a suite is enabled on both client and server, one or the other or both won't have the keys and certificates needed to use the suite. In either case, the `createSocket()` method will throw an `SSLException`, a subclass of `IOException`. You can change which suites the client will attempt to use via the `setEnabledCipherSuites()` method:

```
public abstract void setEnabledCipherSuites(String[] suites)
```

The argument to this method should be a list of the suites you want to use. Each name must be one of the suites listed by `getSupportedCipherSuites()`.

CHAPTER 12: SECURE SOCKETS

Otherwise, an `IllegalArgumentException` will be thrown. The export version of Sun's reference implementation of the JSSE supports the cipher suites in the following list:

SSL_DH_anon_EXPORT_WITH_DES40_CBC_SHA
> Secure Sockets Layer Version 3; Diffie-Hellman method for key agreement; no authentication; Data Encryption Standard block encryption with 40-bit keys; Cipher Block Chaining, and the Secure Hash Algorithm checksum

SSL_DHE_DSS_EXPORT_WITH_DES40_CBC_SHA
> Secure Sockets Layer Version 3; Diffie-Hellman method for key agreement; Digital Signature algorithm authentication; Data Encryption Standard 40-bit block encryption with Cipher Block Chaining, and the Secure Hash Algorithm checksum

SSL_RSA_EXPORT_WITH_RC4_40_MD5
> Secure Sockets Layer Version 3 with RSA authentication; RC4 stream encryption with 40-bit keys; and an MD5 checksum

SSL_RSA_WITH_NULL_MD5
> Secure Sockets Layer Version 3 with RSA authentication; no encryption; and an MD5 checksum

SSL_RSA_WITH_NULL_SHA
> Secure Sockets Layer Version 3 with RSA authentication; no encryption; and a Secure Hash Algorithm checksum

SSL_DH_anon_EXPORT_WITH_RC4_40_MD5
> Secure Sockets Layer Version 3 with Diffie-Hellman key agreement, no authentication; RC4 stream encryption with 40-bit keys, and an MD5 checksum

By default, the export version enables SSL_DHE_DSS_EXPORT_WITH_DES40_CBC_SHA and SSL_RSA_EXPORT_WITH_RC4_40_MD5. The domestic version enables these two as well as the stronger ones that perform authentication. You can change this with the `setEnabledCipherSuites()` method. Besides key lengths, there's an important difference between DES- and RC4-based ciphers. DES is a block cipher; that is, it encrypts 64 bits at a time. If 64 bits aren't available, then it has to pad the input with extra bits. This isn't a problem for file transfer applications such as secure HTTP and FTP where more or less all the data is available at once. However, it's problematic for user-centered protocols such as chat and Telnet. RC4 is a stream cipher that can encrypt one byte at a time and is more appropriate for protocols that may need to send a single byte at a time. For more details on the individual algorithms and their strengths and weaknesses, see *Applied Cryptography* by Bruce Schneier (John Wiley & Sons, 1996).

The domestic version of Sun's reference implementation of the JSSE supports the cipher suites in the following list (as well as the suites in the previous list):

SSL_DH_anon_WITH_DES_CBC_SHA
Secure Sockets Layer Version 3; Diffie-Hellman method for key agreement; no authentication; Data Encryption Standard block encryption with 56-bit keys; Cipher Block Chaining, and the Secure Hash Algorithm checksum

SSL_DH_anon_WITH_3DES_EDE_CBC_SHA
Same as previous but with 112-bit strong keys

SSL_DHE_DSS_WITH_DES_CBC_SHA
Secure Sockets Layer Version 3; Diffie-Hellman method for key agreement; Digital Signature algorithm authentication; Data Encryption Standard block encryption with 56-bit keys; Cipher Block Chaining, and the Secure Hash Algorithm checksum

SSL_DHE_DSS_WITH_3DES_EDE_CBC_SHA
Same as previous but with 112-bit strong keys

SSL_RSA_WITH_RC4_128_MD5
Secure Sockets Layer Version 3 with RSA authentication; RC4 stream encryption with 128-bit keys; and an MD5 checksum

SSL_RSA_WITH_RC4_128_SHA
Secure Sockets Layer Version 3 with RSA authentication; RC4 stream encryption with 128-bit keys; and a Secure Hash Algorithm checksum

SSL_RSA_WITH_DES_CBC_SHA
Secure Sockets Layer Version 3 with RSA authentication; 56-bit DES block encryption; and a Secure Hash Algorithm checksum

SSL_RSA_WITH_3DES_EDE_CBC_SHA
Secure Sockets Layer Version 3 with RSA authentication; triple DES (112-bit strong) block encryption; Cipher Block Chaining, and a Secure Hash Algorithm checksum

SSL_DH_anon_WITH_RC4_128_MD5
Secure Sockets Layer Version 3 with Diffie-Hellman key agreement, no authentication; RC4 stream encryption with 128-bit keys, and an MD5 checksum

For example, let's suppose that Edgar has some fairly powerful parallel computers at his disposal and can quickly break any encryption that's 64 bits or fewer and that Gus and Angela know this. Furthermore, they suspect that Edgar can black-mail one of their ISPs or the phone company into letting him tap the line, so they want to avoid anonymous connections that are vulnerable to man-in-the-middle attacks. To be safe, Gus and Angela decide they want to use at least 112-bit, authenticated encryption. It then behooves them to enable only the strongest available algorithms. This code fragment accomplishes that:

```
String[] strongSuites = {"SSL_DHE_DSS_WITH_3DES_EDE_CBC_SHA",
 "SSL_RSA_WITH_RC4_128_MD5", "SSL_RSA_WITH_RC4_128_SHA",
 "SSL_RSA_WITH_3DES_EDE_CBC_SHA"};
socket.setEnabledCipherSuites(strongSuites);
```

If the other side of the connection doesn't support strong encryption, the socket will throw an exception when they try to read from or write to it, thus ensuring that no confidential information is accidentally transmitted over too weak a channel.

Event Handlers

Network communications are slow compared to the speed of most computers. Authenticated network communications are even slower. The necessary key generation and setup for a secure connection can easily take 10 seconds or more. Consequently, you may want to deal with the connection asynchronously. JSSE uses the standard event model introduced in Java 1.1 to notify programs when the handshaking between client and server is complete. The pattern is a familiar one. To get notifications of handshake-complete events, you simply implement the HandshakeCompletedListener interface:

```
public interface HandshakeCompletedListener
  extends java.util.EventListener
```

This interface declares the handshakeCompleted() method:

```
public void handshakeCompleted(HandshakeCompletedEvent event)
```

This method receives as an argument a `javax.net.ssl.Handshake-CompletedEvent`:

```
public class HandshakeCompletedEvent extends java.util.EventObject
```

The HandshakeCompletedEvent class provides four methods for getting information about the event:

```
public SSLSession getSession()
public String getCipherSuite()
public X509Certificate[] getPeerCertificateChain()
  throws SSLPeerUnverifiedException
public SSLSocket getSocket()
```

Particular HandshakeCompletedListener objects register their interest in handshake-completed events from a particular SSLSocket via its

addHandshakeCompletedListener() and removeHandshakeCompleted-
Listener() methods:

```
public abstract void addHandshakeCompletedListener(
  HandshakeCompletedListener listener)
public abstract void removeHandshakeCompletedListener(
  HandshakeCompletedListener listener) throws IllegalArgumentException
```

Session Management

SSL is most commonly used on web servers. Web connections tend to be transitory. Every page requires a separate socket. For instance, checking out of Amazon.
com on its secure server requires seven separate page loads, more if you have to
edit an address or choose gift wrapping. Imagine if every one of those pages took
an extra 10 seconds or more to negotiate a secure connection. Because of the high
overhead involved in handshaking between two hosts for secure communications,
SSL allows *sessions* to be established that extend over multiple sockets. Different
sockets within the same session use the same set of public and private keys. If the
secure connection to Amazon.com takes seven sockets, all seven will be established within the same session and use the same keys. Only the first socket within
that session will have to endure the overhead of key generation and exchange.

As a programmer using JSSE, you don't need to do anything extra to take advantage of sessions. If you open multiple secure sockets to one host on one port
within a reasonably short period of time, JSSE will reuse the session's keys automatically. However, in high-security applications, you may want to disallow session
sharing between sockets or force reauthentication of a session. In the JSSE, sessions are represented by instances of the SSLSession interface, and you can use
the methods of this interface to check the times the session was created and last
accessed, to invalidate the session, and to get various information about the session:

```
public byte[] getId()
public SSLSessionContext getSessionContext()
public long getCreationTime()
public long getLastAccessedTime()
public void invalidate()
public void putValue(String name, Object value)
public Object getValue(String name)
public void removeValue(String name)
public String[] getValueNames()
public X509Certificate[] getPeerCertificateChain()
  throws SSLPeerUnverifiedException
public String getCipherSuite()
public String getPeerHost()
```

The getSession() method of SSLSocket returns the Session of which this socket is a part:

```
public abstract SSLSession getSession()
```

In some circumstances, however, a session can be a security risk. Consequently, you can prevent a socket from creating a session by passing false to setEnableSessionCreation():

```
public abstract void setEnableSessionCreation(boolean allowSessions)
```

The getEnableSessionCreation() method returns true if multisocket sessions are allowed, false if they're not:

```
public abstract boolean getEnableSessionCreation()
```

On the rare occasion, you may even want to reauthenticate a connection; that is, throw away all the certificates and keys that have previously been agreed to and start over with a new session. The startHandshake() method does this:

```
public abstract void startHandshake() throws IOException
```

Client Mode

As a general rule, in a secure communication, the server is required to authenticate itself using the appropriate certificate. However, the client is not. That is, when I buy a book from Fatbrain using its secure server, it has to prove to my browser's satisfaction that it is indeed Fatbrain and not Joe Random Hacker. However, I do not have to prove to Fatbrain that I am Elliotte Rusty Harold. For the most part, this is as it should be, since purchasing and installing the trusted certificates necessary for authentication is a fairly user-hostile experience that readers shouldn't have to go through just to buy the latest Nutshell handbook. However, this asymmetry leads to a little credit card fraud. To avoid problems like this, sockets can be required to authenticate themselves. This wouldn't work for a service open to the general public. However, it might be reasonable in certain internal, high-security applications.

The setUseClientMode() method determines whether this socket will need to use authentication in its first handshake. The name of the method is a little misleading. It can be used for both client- and server-side sockets. However, when true is passed in, that means the socket is in client mode (whether it's on the client side or not) and will not offer to authenticate itself. When false is passed, it will try to authenticate itself:

```
public abstract void setUseClientMode(boolean mode)
  throws IllegalArgumentException
```

This property can be set only once for any given socket. Attempting to set it a second time throws an `IllegalArgumentException`.

The `getUseClientMode()` method simply tells you whether this socket will use authentication in its first handshake:

```
public abstract boolean getUseClientMode()
```

The `setNeedClientAuth()` method is used by a secure socket on the server side (that is, one returned by the `accept()` method of an `SSLServerSocket`) to require that all clients connecting to it authenticate themselves (or not):

```
public abstract void setNeedClientAuth(boolean needsAuthentication)
  throws IllegalArgumentException
```

This method throws an `IllegalArgumentException` if this socket is not on the server side.

The `getNeedClientAuth()` returns true if the socket will require authentication from the client side, false otherwise:

```
public abstract boolean getNeedClientAuth()
```

Creating Secure Server Sockets

Secure client sockets are only half of the equation. The other half is SSL-enabled server sockets. These are instances of the `javax.net.SSLServerSocket` class:

```
public abstract class SSLServerSocket extends ServerSocket
```

Like `SSLSocket`, all the constructors in this class are protected. Like `SSLSocket`, instances of `SSLServerSocket` are created by an abstract factory class, `javax.net.SSLServerSocketFactory`:

```
public abstract class SSLServerSocketFactory
  extends ServerSocketFactory
```

Also like `SSLSocketFactory`, an instance of `SSLServerSocketFactory` is returned by a static `SSLServerSocketFactory.getDefault()` method:

```
public static ServerSocketFactory getDefault()
```

And like `SSLSocketFactory`, `SSLServerSocketFactory` has three overloaded `createServerSocket()` methods that return instances of `SSLServerSocket` and are easily understood by analogy with the `java.net.ServerSocket` constructors:

```
public abstract ServerSocket createServerSocket(int port)
  throws IOException
public abstract ServerSocket createServerSocket(int port,
  int queueLength) throws IOException
public abstract ServerSocket createServerSocket(int port,
  int queueLength, InetAddress interface) throws IOException
```

If that were all there was to creating secure server sockets, then they would be quite straightforward and simple to use. Unfortunately, that's not all there is to it. The factory that `SSLServerSocketFactory.getDefault()` returns generally supports only server authentication. It does not support encryption. To get encryption as well, server-side secure sockets require more initialization and setup. Exactly how this is performed is implementation-dependent. In Sun's reference implementation, a `com.sun.net.ssl.SSLContext` object is responsible for creating fully configured and initialized secure server sockets. The details will vary from JSSE implementation to JSSE implementation, but to create a secure server socket in the reference implementation, you have to:

- Generate public keys and certificates using *keytool*.

- Pay money to have your certificates authenticated by a trusted third party such as Verisign.

- Create an `SSLContext` for the algorithm you'll use.

- Create a `TrustManagerFactory` for the source of certificate material you'll be using.

- Create a `KeyManagerFactory` for the type of key material you'll be using.

- Create a `KeyStore` object for your key and certificate database. (Sun's default is JKS.)

- Fill the `KeyStore` object with keys and certificates; for instance, by loading them from the filesystem using the pass phrase they're encrypted with.

- Initialize the `KeyManagerFactory` with the `KeyStore` and its pass phrase.

- Initialize the context with the necessary key managers from the `KeyManagerFactory`, trust managers from the `TrustManagerFactory`, and a source of randomness. (The last two may be null if you're willing to accept the defaults.)

Example 12-2 demonstrates this procedure with a complete `SecureOrderTaker` for accepting orders and printing them on `System.out`. Of course, in a real application, you'd do something more interesting with the orders.

Example 12-2. SecureOrderTaker

```
import java.net.*;
import java.io.*;
import java.util.*;
import java.security.*;
import javax.net.ssl.*;
import javax.net.*;
import com.sun.net.ssl.*;
```

Example 12-2. SecureOrderTaker (continued)

```java
public class SecureOrderTaker {

  public final static int DEFAULT_PORT = 7000;
  public final static String algorithm = "SSL";

  public static void main(String[] args) {

    int port = DEFAULT_PORT;
    if (args.length > 0) {
      try {
        port = Integer.parseInt(args[0]);
        if (port <= 0 || port >= 65536) {
          System.out.println("Port must between 1 and 65535");
          return;
        }
      }
      catch (NumberFormatException e) {}
    }

    try {

      SSLContext context = SSLContext.getInstance(algorithm);

      // The reference implementation only supports X.509 keys
      KeyManagerFactory kmf = KeyManagerFactory.getInstance("SunX509");

      // Sun's default kind of key store
      KeyStore ks = KeyStore.getInstance("JKS");

      // For security, every key store is encrypted with a
      // pass phrase that must be provided before we can load
      // it from disk. The pass phrase is stored as a char[] array
      // so it can be wiped from memory quickly rather than
      // waiting for a garbage collector. Of course using a string
      // literal here completely defeats that purpose.
      char[] password = "2andnotafnord".toCharArray();
      ks.load(new FileInputStream("jnp2e19.keys"), password);
      kmf.init(ks, password);

      //
      context.init(kmf.getKeyManagers(), null, null);

      SSLServerSocketFactory factory
        = context.getServerSocketFactory();

      SSLServerSocket server
        = (SSLServerSocket) factory.createServerSocket(port);
```

Example 12-2. SecureOrderTaker (continued)

```
          // Now all the set up is complete and we can focus
          // on the actual communication.
          try {
            while (true) {
              // This socket will be secure,
              // but there's no indication of that in the code!
              Socket theConnection = server.accept();
              InputStream in = theConnection.getInputStream();
              int c;
              while ((c = in.read()) != -1) {
                System.out.write(c);
              }
              theConnection.close();
            }  // end while
          }  // end try
          catch (IOException e) {
            System.err.println(e);
          }  // end catch

      }  // end try
      catch (IOException e) {
        e.printStackTrace();
      }  // end catch
      catch (KeyManagementException e) {
        e.printStackTrace();
      }  // end catch
      catch (KeyStoreException e) {
        e.printStackTrace();
      }  // end catch
      catch (NoSuchAlgorithmException e) {
        e.printStackTrace();
      }  // end catch
      catch (java.security.cert.CertificateException e) {
        e.printStackTrace();
      }  // end catch
      catch (UnrecoverableKeyException e) {
        e.printStackTrace();
      }  // end catch

  }  // end main

}  // end server
```

This example loads the necessary keys and certificates from a file named *jnp2e19.
keys* in the current working directory protected with the password

"2andnotafnord". What this example doesn't show you is how that file was created. It was built with the *keytool* program that's bundled with the JDK like this:

```
D:\JAVA>keytool -genkey -alias ourstore -keystore jnp2e19.keys
Enter keystore password:  2andnotafnord
What is your first and last name?
  [Unknown]:  Elliotte
What is the name of your organizational unit?
  [Unknown]:  Me, Myself, and I
What is the name of your organization?
  [Unknown]:  Cafe au Lait
What is the name of your City or Locality?
  [Unknown]:  Brooklyn
What is the name of your State or Province?
  [Unknown]:  New York
What is the two-letter country code for this unit?
  [Unknown]:  NY
Is <CN=Elliotte, OU="Me, Myself, and I", O=Cafe au Lait, L=Brooklyn,
ST=New York, C=NY> correct?
  [no]:  y

Enter key password for <ourstore>
        (RETURN if same as keystore password):
```

When this is finished, you'll have the file *jnp2e19.keys*, which contains your public
keys. However, no one will believe that these are your public keys unless you have
them certified by a trusted third party such as Verisign (*http://www.verisign.com/*).
Unfortunately, this certification costs money. The cheapest option is $14.95 per
year for a Class 1 Digital ID. Verisign hides the sign-up form for this kind of ID
deep within its web site, apparently to get you to sign up for much more expensive
options that are much more prominently featured on its home page. At the time
of this writing, the sign-up form was at *https://www.verisign.com/client/*. Verisign has
changed this URL several times in the past, making it much harder to find than its
more expensive options. In the more expensive options, Verisign goes to greater
lengths to guarantee that you are who you say you are. Before signing up for any
kind of digital ID, you should be aware that purchasing one has potentially severe
legal consequences. In many jurisdictions, poorly thought-out laws make digital ID
owners liable for all purchases made and contracts signed using their digital ID,
regardless of whether the ID was stolen or forged. If you just want to explore the
JSSE before deciding whether you want to go through the hassle, expense, and lia-
bility of purchasing a verified certificate, Sun includes a verified keystore file called
testkeys protected with the password "passphrase", with some JSSE samples at *http://
java.sun.com/products/jsse/*. However, this isn't good enough for real work.

For more information about exactly what's going on here, and what the various
options are as well as other ways to create key and certificate files, you can consult

the online documentation for the *keytool* utility that came with your JDK, the Java Cryptography Architecture guide at *http://java.sun.com/products/jdk/1.2/docs/guide/security/CryptoSpec.html*, or the previously mentioned books *Java Cryptography*, by Jonathan Knudsen, or *Java Security*, by Scott Oaks (both from O'Reilly & Associates, Inc., 1998).

Another approach is to use cipher suites that don't require authentication. There are two of these in Sun's export reference implementation: SSL_DH_anon_EXPORT_WITH_DES40_CBC_SHA and SSL_DH_anon_EXPORT_WITH_RC4_40_MD5; and three more in the domestic implementation: SSL_DH_anon_WITH_DES_CBC_SHA, SSL_DH_anon_WITH_3DES_EDE_CBC_SHA, and SSL_DH_anon_WITH_RC4_128_MD5. These are not enabled by default because they're vulnerable to the man-in-the-middle attack discussed earlier, but at least they allow you to write simple programs without paying Verisign money.

Methods of the SSLServerSocket Class

Once you've successfully created and initialized an SSLServerSocket, there are a lot of applications you can write using nothing more than the methods inherited from java.net.ServerSocket. However, there are times when you need to adjust its behavior a little. Like SSLSocket, SSLServerSocket provides methods to choose the cipher suites it uses, to manage sessions, and to establish whether clients are required to authenticate themselves. Most of these methods are very similar to the methods of the same name in SSLSocket. The difference is that they work on the server side and set the defaults for sockets accepted by an SSLServerSocket. In some cases, once an SSLSocket has been accepted, you can still use the methods of SSLSocket to configure that one socket rather than all sockets accepted by this SSLServerSocket.

Choosing the Cipher Suites

The SSLServerSocket class has the same three methods for determining which cipher suites are supported and enabled as SSLSocket does:

```
public abstract String[] getSupportedCipherSuites()
public abstract String[] getEnabledCipherSuites()
public abstract void     setEnabledCipherSuites(String[] suites)
```

These use the same suite names as the similarly named methods in SSLSocket. The difference is that these apply to all sockets accepted by the SSLServerSocket rather than to just one SSLSocket. For example, this code fragment has the effect of enabling anonymous, unauthenticated connections on the SSLServerSocket server. It relies on the names of these suites containing the string "_anon_". This is true for Sun's reference implementations, though there's no guarantee that other implementers will follow this convention:

```
String[] supported = server.getSupportedCipherSuites();
String[] anonCipherSuitesSupported = new String[supported.length];
int numAnonCipherSuitesSupported = 0;
for (int i = 0; i < supported.length; i++) {
  if (supported[i].indexOf("_anon_") > 0) {
     anonCipherSuitesSupported[numAnonCipherSuitesSupported++]
      = supported[i];
  }
}

String[] oldEnabled = server.getEnabledCipherSuites();
String[] newEnabled = new String[oldEnabled.length
 + numAnonCipherSuitesSupported];
System.arraycopy(oldEnabled, 0, newEnabled, 0, oldEnabled.length);
System.arraycopy(anonCipherSuitesSupported, 0, newEnabled,
 oldEnabled.length, numAnonCipherSuitesSupported);

server.setEnabledCipherSuites(newEnabled);
```

This fragment retrieves the list of both supported and enabled cipher suites using `getSupportedCipherSuites()` and `getEnabledCipherSuites()`. It looks at the name of every supported suite to see whether it contains the substring "_anon_". If it does, it's added to a list of anonymous cipher suites. Once the list of anonymous cipher suites is built, it's combined in a new array with the previous list of enabled cipher suites. This new array is then passed to `set-EnabledCipherSuites()` so that both the previously enabled and the anonymous cipher suites can now be used.

Session Management

Both client and server must agree to establish a session for multisocket secure sessions to be allowed. The server side uses the `setEnableSessionCreation()` method to specify whether this will be allowed and the `getEnable-SessionCreation()` method to determine whether this is currently allowed:

```
public abstract void setEnableSessionCreation(boolean allowSessions)
public abstract boolean getEnableSessionCreation()
```

Session creation is enabled by default. If the server disallows session creation, then a client that wants a session will still be able to connect. It just won't get a session and will have to handshake again for every socket. Similarly, if the client refuses sessions, but the server allows them, then they'll still be able to talk to each other but without sessions.

Client Mode

The SSLServerSocket class has two methods for determining and specifying whether client sockets are required to authenticate themselves to the server. By passing true to the setNeedClientAuth() method, you specify that only connections where the client is able to authenticate itself will be accepted. By passing false, you specify that authentication is not required of clients. The default is false. If for some reason you need to know what the current state of this property is, the getNeedClientAuth() method will tell you:

```
public abstract void setNeedClientAuth(boolean flag)
public abstract boolean getNeedClientAuth()
```

The setUseClientMode() method allows a program to indicate that even though it has created an SSLServerSocket, it is and should be treated as a client in the communication with respect to authentication and other negotiations. For example, in an FTP session, the client program opens a server socket to receive data from the server, but that doesn't make it less of a client. The getUseClientMode() method returns true if the SSLServerSocket is in client mode, false otherwise:

```
public abstract void setUseClientMode(boolean flag)
public abstract boolean getUseClientMode()
```

13

UDP Datagrams and Sockets

Previous chapters discussed network applications that used the TCP protocol. TCP is designed for reliable transmission of data. If data is lost or damaged in transmission, TCP ensures that the data is resent; if packets of data arrive out of order, TCP puts them back in the correct order; if the data is coming too fast for the connection, TCP throttles the speed back so that packets won't be lost. A program never needs to worry about receiving data that is out of order or incorrect. However, this reliability comes at a price. That price is speed. Establishing and tearing down TCP connections can take a fair amount of time, particularly for protocols such as HTTP, which tend to require many short transmissions.

The User Datagram Protocol (UDP) is an alternative protocol for sending data over IP that is very quick, but not reliable. That is, when you send UDP data, you have no way of knowing whether it arrived, much less whether different pieces of data arrived in the order in which you sent them. However, the pieces that do arrive generally arrive much more quickly.

The UDP Protocol

The obvious question to ask is why anyone would ever use an unreliable protocol. Surely, if you have data worth sending, you care about whether the data arrives correctly. Clearly, UDP isn't a good match for applications like FTP that require reliable transmission of data over potentially unreliable networks. However, there are many kinds of applications in which raw speed is more important than getting every bit right. For example, in real-time audio or video, lost or swapped packets of data simply appear as static. Static is tolerable, but awkward pauses in the audio stream, when TCP requests a retransmission or waits for a wayward packet to arrive, are unacceptable. In other applications, reliability tests can be implemented in the application layer. For example, if a client sends a short UDP request to a server, it may assume that the packet is lost if no response is returned within an established period of time; this is one way the Domain Name System (DNS) works.* In fact, you could implement a reliable file transfer protocol using UDP, and many people have: Network File System (NFS), Trivial FTP (TFTP), and FSP, a more distant relative of FTP, all use UDP.† In these protocols, the application is responsible for reliability; UDP doesn't take care of it. That is, the application must handle missing or out-of-order packets. This is a lot of work, but there's no reason it can't be done—though if you find yourself writing this code, you should think carefully about whether you might be better off with TCP.

The difference between TCP and UDP is often explained by analogy with the phone system and the post office. TCP is like the phone system. When you dial a number, the phone is answered and a connection is established between the two parties. As you talk, you know that the other party hears your words in the order in which you say them. If the phone is busy or no one answers, you find out right away. UDP, by contrast, is like the postal system. You send packets of mail to an address. Most of the letters arrive, but some may be lost on the way. The letters probably arrive in the order in which you sent them, but that's not guaranteed. The farther away you are from your recipient, the more likely it is that mail will be lost on the way or arrive out of order. If this is a problem, you can write sequential numbers on the envelopes, then ask the recipients to arrange them in the correct order and send you mail telling you which letters arrived so that you can resend any that didn't get there the first time. However, you and your correspondent need to agree on this protocol in advance. The post office will not do it for you.

Both the phone system and the post office have their uses. Although either one could be used for almost any communication, in some cases one is definitely superior to the other. The same is true of UDP and TCP. The last several chapters have all focused on TCP applications, which are far more common than UDP applications. However, UDP also has its place; in this chapter, we'll look at what you can do with UDP in Java. If you want to go further, look at Chapter 14, *Multicast Sockets*. Multicasting relies on UDP; a multicast socket is a fairly simple variation on a UDP socket.

Java's implementation of UDP is split into two classes: `DatagramPacket` and `DatagramSocket`. The `DatagramPacket` class stuffs bytes of data into UDP packets called datagrams and lets you unstuff datagrams that you receive. A `DatagramSocket` sends as well as receives UDP datagrams. To send data, you put the data in a `DatagramPacket` and send the packet using a `DatagramSocket`. To receive data, you receive a `DatagramPacket` object from a `DatagramSocket` and

---

* DNS can also use TCP.

† The latest version of NFS can use either UDP or TCP.

then read the contents of the packet. The sockets themselves are very simple crea-tures. In UDP, everything about a datagram, including the address to which it is directed, is included in the packet itself; the socket needs to know only the local port on which to listen or send.

This division of labor contrasts with the Socket and ServerSocket classes used by TCP. First, UDP doesn't have any notion of a server socket. You use the same kind of socket to send data and to receive data. Second, TCP sockets allow you to treat a network connection as a stream: you send and receive with input and out-put streams that you get from the socket. UDP doesn't allow this; you always work with individual datagram packets. All the data you stuff into a single datagram is sent as a single packet and is either received or lost as a group. One packet is not necessarily related to the next. Given two packets, there is no way to determine which packet was sent first and which was sent second. Instead of the orderly queue of data that's necessary for a stream, datagrams try to crowd into the recipi-ent as quickly as possible, like a crowd of people pushing their way onto a bus. A third difference, which is really a consequence of the first two, is that a single DatagramSocket can send data to and receive data from many independent hosts. The socket isn't dedicated to a single connection, as it is in TCP. In fact, UDP doesn't have any concept of a connection between two hosts; it only knows about individual datagrams. Figuring out who sent what data is the application's responsibility.

The DatagramPacket Class

UDP datagrams add very little to the IP datagrams they sit on top of. Figure 13-1 shows a typical UDP datagram. The UDP header adds only eight bytes to the IP header. The UDP header includes source and destination port numbers, the length of everything that follows the IP header, and an optional checksum. Since port numbers are given as a 2-byte unsigned integer, 65,536 different possible UDP ports are available per host. These are distinct from the 65,536 different TCP ports per host. Since the length is also a 2-byte unsigned integer, the number of bytes in a datagram is limited to 65,536 minus the 8 bytes for the header. How-ever, this is redundant with the datagram length field of the IP header, which lim-its datagrams to from 65,467 to 65,507 bytes. (The exact number depends on the size of the IP header.) The checksum field is optional and not used in or accessi-ble from application layer programs. If the checksum for the data fails, the native network software will silently discard the datagram; neither the sender nor the receiver is notified. UDP is an unreliable protocol, after all.

Although the theoretical maximum amount of data in a UDP datagram is 65,507 bytes, in practice there is almost always much less. On many platforms, the actual limit is more likely to be 8,192 bytes (8K). And implementations are not required

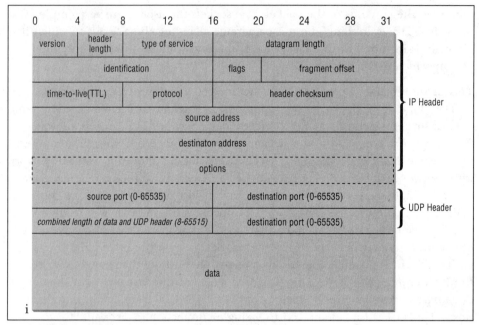

Figure 13-1. The structure of a UDP datagram

to accept datagrams with more than 576 total bytes including data and headers. Consequently, I would be extremely wary of any program that depended on sending or receiving UDP packets with more than 8K of data. Most of the time, larger packets are simply truncated to 8K of data. For maximum safety, the data portion of a UDP packet should be kept to 512 bytes or fewer, though this can negatively affect performance compared to larger packet sizes. (This is a problem for TCP datagrams too, but the stream-based API provided by `Socket` and `ServerSocket` completely shields programmers from these details.)

In Java, a UDP datagram is represented by an instance of the `DatagramPacket` class:

```
public final class DatagramPacket extends Object
```

This class provides methods to get and set the source or destination address from the IP header, to get and set the source or destination port, to get and set the data, and to get and set the length of the data. The remaining header fields are inaccessible from pure Java code.

The Constructors

There are two constructors for `DatagramPacket` objects in Java 1.1. The first constructor is used to receive data from the Net; the second is for data that you will send to the Net. (Java 1.2 adds two more constructors, one each for sending and receiving, though these don't differ in a major way.)

This is a little unusual. Normally, constructors are overloaded to let you provide different kinds of information when you create an object, not to create objects of the same class that will be used in different contexts. In this case, all four constructors take as arguments a `byte` array that holds the datagram's data, and the number of bytes in that array to use for the datagram's data. When you want to receive a datagram, these are the only arguments you provide; in addition, the array should be empty. When the socket receives a datagram from the network, it store's the datagram's data in the `DatagramPacket` object's buffer array, up to the length you specified.

The second pair of `DatagramPacket` constructors is used to create datagrams you will send to the Net. Like the first, these constructors require a buffer array and a length, but they also require the `InetAddress` and port to which the packet is to be sent. In this case, you will pass to the constructor a byte array containing the data you want to send and the destination address and port to which the packet is to be sent. The `DatagramSocket` reads the destination address and port from the packet; the address and port aren't stored within the socket, as they are in TCP.

Constructors for receiving datagrams

These two constructors create new `DatagramPacket` objects for receiving data from the network:

```
public DatagramPacket(byte[] buffer, int length)
public DatagramPacket(byte[] buffer, int offset, int length)  // Java 1.2
```

When a socket receives a datagram, it stores the datagram's data part in `buffer` beginning at `buffer[0]` and continuing until the packet is completely stored or until `length` bytes have been written into the `buffer`. If the second constructor is used, storage begins at `buffer[offset]` instead. Otherwise, these two constructors are identical. `length` must be less than or equal to `buffer.length-offset`. If you try to construct a `DatagramPacket` with a length that will overflow the `buffer`, the constructor throws an `IllegalArgumentException`. This is a `RuntimeException`, so your code is not required to catch it. It is okay to construct a `DatagramPacket` with a length less than `buffer.length-offset`. In this case, at most the first `length` bytes of `buffer` will be filled when the datagram is received. For example, this code fragment creates a new `DatagramPacket` for receiving a datagram of up to 8,192 bytes:

```
byte[] buffer = new byte[8192];
DatagramPacket dp = new DatagramPacket(buffer, buffer.length);
```

The constructor doesn't care how large the buffer is, and would happily let you create a DatagramPacket with megabytes of data. However, the underlying native network software is less forgiving, and most native UDP implementations don't support more than 8,192 bytes of data per datagram. The theoretical limit for an IPv4 datagram is 65,507 bytes of data, and a DatagramPacket with a 65,507-byte buffer can receive any possible IPv4 datagram without losing data. IPv6 datagrams raise the theoretical limit to 65,536 bytes. In practice, however, many UDP-based protocols such as DNS and TFTP use packets with 512 bytes of data per datagram or fewer. The largest data size in common usage is 8,192 bytes for NFS. Almost all UDP datagrams you're likely to encounter will have 8K of data or fewer. In fact, many operating systems don't support UDP datagrams with more than 8K of data and either truncate, split, or discard larger datagrams. If a large datagram is too big and as a result the network truncates or drops it, your Java program won't be notified of the problem. (UDP is an unreliable protocol, after all.) Consequently, you shouldn't create DatagramPacket objects with more than 8,192 bytes of data.

Constructors for sending datagrams

These two constructors create new DatagramPacket objects for sending data across the network:

```
public DatagramPacket(byte[] data, int length,
  InetAddress destination, int port)
public DatagramPacket(byte[] data, int offset, int length,
  InetAddress destination, int port)  // Java 1.2
```

Each constructor creates a new DatagramPacket to be sent to another host. The packet is filled with length bytes of the data array starting at offset or 0 if offset is not used. If you try to construct a DatagramPacket with a length that is greater than data.length, the constructor throws an Illegal-ArgumentException. It's okay to construct a DatagramPacket object with an offset and a length that will leave extra, unused space at the end of the data array. In this case, only length bytes of data will be sent over the network. The InetAddress object destination points to the host you want the packet delivered to; the int argument port is the port on that host.

It's customary to convert the data to a byte array and place it in data *before* creating the DatagramPacket, but it's not absolutely necessary. Changing data *after* the datagram has been constructed and *before* it has been sent changes the data in the datagram; the data isn't copied into a private buffer. In some applications, you can take advantage of this. For example, you could store data that changes over time in data and send out the current datagram (with the most recent data) every minute. However, it's more important to make sure that your data doesn't change when you don't want it to. This is especially true if your program is multithreaded,

---

Choosing a Datagram Size

The amount of data to stuff into one packet depends on the situation. Some protocols dictate the size of the packet. For example, *rlogin* transmits each character to the remote system almost as soon as the user types it. Therefore, packets tend to be short: a single byte of data, plus a few bytes of headers. Other applications aren't so picky. For example, file transfer is more efficient with large buffers; the only requirement is that you split files into packets no larger than the maximum allowable packet size.

Several factors are involved in choosing the optimal packet size. If the network is highly unreliable, such as a packet radio network, smaller packets are preferable since they're less likely to be corrupted in transit. On the other hand, very fast and reliable LANs should use the largest packet size possible. Newer technologies such as gigabit Ethernet will probably require a revision of the IP protocol to allow for packets larger than 64K in order to achieve maximum efficiency. Eight kilobytes—that is, 8,192 bytes—is a good compromise for many types of networks.

---

and different threads may write into the data buffer. If this is the case, synchronize the `data` variable or copy the data into a temporary buffer before you construct the `DatagramPacket`.

For instance, this code fragment creates a new `DatagramPacket` filled with the data "This is a test" in ASCII. The packet is directed at port 7 (the echo port) of the host *metalab.unc.edu*:

```
String s = "This is a test";
byte[] data = s.getBytes("ASCII");

try {
  InetAddress ia = InetAddress.getByName("metalab.unc.edu");
  int port = 7;
  DatagramPacket dp = new DatagramPacket(data, data.length, ia, port);
  // send the packet...
}
catch (IOException e) {
}
```

Most of the time, the hardest part of creating a new `DatagramPacket` is translating the data into a `byte` array. Since this code fragment wants to send an ASCII string, it uses the `getBytes()` method of `java.lang.String` to do this. The `java.io.ByteArrayOutputStream` class can also be very useful for preparing data for inclusion in datagrams.

The get Methods

`DatagramPacket` has five methods that retrieve different parts of a datagram: the actual data plus several fields from its header. These methods are mostly used for datagrams you receive from the network.

public InetAddress getAddress( )

The `getAddress()` method returns an `InetAddress` object containing the address of the remote host. If the datagram was received from the Internet, the address returned is the address of the machine that sent it (the source address). On the other hand, if the datagram was created locally to be sent to a remote machine, this method returns the address of the host to which the datagram is addressed (the destination address). This method is most commonly used to determine the address of the host that sent a UDP datagram, so that the recipient can reply.

public int getPort( )

The `getPort()` method returns an integer specifying the remote port. If this datagram was received from the Internet, this is the port on the host that sent the packet. If the datagram was created locally to be sent to a remote host, this is the port to which this packet is addressed on the remote machine.

public byte[ ] getData( )

The `getData()` method returns a byte array containing the data from the datagram. It's often necessary to convert the bytes into some other form of data before they'll be useful to your program. One way to do this is to change the byte array into a `String` using the following `String` constructor:

```
public String(byte[] buffer, String encoding)
```

The first argument, `buffer`, is the array of bytes that contains the data from the datagram. The second argument contains the name of the encoding used for this string such as ASCII or ISO-8859-1. Thus, given a `DatagramPacket` `dp` received from the network, you can convert it to a `String`, like this:

```
String s = new String(dp.getData(), "ASCII");
```

If the datagram does not contain text, converting it to Java data is more difficult. One approach is to convert the `byte` array returned by `getData()` into a `ByteArrayInputStream` using this constructor:

```
public ByteArrayInputStream(byte[] buffer, int offset, int length)
```

buffer is the byte array to be used as an InputStream. It's important to specify the portion of the buffer that you want to use as an InputStream using the offset and length arguments. When converting datagram data into InputStream objects, offset is either 0 (Java 1.1) or given by the DatagramPacket object's getOffset() method (Java 2), and length is given by the DatagramPacket object's getLength() method. For example:

```
InputStream in = new ByteArrayInputStream(packet.getData(),
  packet.getOffset(), packet.getLength());
```

You *must* specify the offset and the length when constructing the ByteArrayInputStream. Do not use the ByteArrayInputStream() constructor that takes only an array as an argument. The array returned by packet.getData() probably has extra space in it that was not filled with data from the network. This space will contain whatever random values those components of the array had when the DatagramPacket was constructed.

The ByteArrayInputStream can then be chained to a DataInputStream:

```
DataInputStream din = new DataInputStream(in);
```

The data can then be read using the DataInputStream's readInt(), readLong(), readChar(), and other methods. Of course, this assumes that the datagram's sender uses the same data formats as Java; this is probably the case when the sender is written in Java, and is often (though not necessarily) the case otherwise. (Most modern computers use the same floating point format as Java, and most network protocols specify two's complement integers in network byte order, which also matches Java's formats.)

public int getLength( )

The getLength() method returns the number of bytes of data in the datagram. This is *not* necessarily the same as the length of the array returned by getData(), i.e., getData().length. The int returned by getLength() may be less than the length of the array returned by getData().

public int getOffset( )   // Java 1.2

This method simply returns the point in the array returned by getData() where the data from the datagram begins.

Example 13-1 uses all the methods covered in this section to print the information in the DatagramPacket. This example is a little artificial; because you create the DatagramPacket, you already know what's in it. More often, you'll use these methods on a DatagramPacket received from the network, but that will have to wait for the introduction of the DatagramSocket class in the next section.

Example 13-1. Construct a DatagramPacket to Receive Data

```java
import java.net.*;

public class DatagramExample {

  public static void main(String[] args) {

    String s = "This is a test.";

    byte[] data = s.getBytes();
    try {
      InetAddress ia = InetAddress.getByName("metalab.unc.edu");
      int port = 7;
      DatagramPacket dp
       = new DatagramPacket(data, data.length, ia, port);
      System.out.println("This packet is addressed to "
       + dp.getAddress() + " on port " + dp.getPort());
      System.out.println("There are " + dp.getLength()
       + " bytes of data in the packet");
      System.out.println(
        new String(dp.getData(), dp.getOffset(), dp.getLength()));
    }
    catch (UnknownHostException e) {
      System.err.println(e);
    }

  }

}
```

Here's the output:

```
% java DatagramExample
This packet is addressed to metalab.unc.edu/152.2.254.81 on port 7
There are 15 bytes of data in the packet
This is a test.
```

The set Methods

Most of the time, the four constructors are sufficient for creating datagrams. However, Java also provides four (five in Java 1.2 and later) methods for changing the data, remote address, and remote port after the datagram has been created. These might be important in a situation where the time to create and garbage collect new DatagramPacket objects was a significant performance hit. In some situations, reusing objects can be significantly faster than constructing new ones. This might be the case in a networked twitch game like Quake that sends a datagram for every bullet fired or every centimeter of movement, for example. However, you would have to use a very speedy connection for this to be noticeable relative to the slowness of the network itself.

public void setData(byte[ ] data)

The `setData()` method changes the payload of the UDP datagram. You might use this method if you were sending a large file (where large is defined as "bigger than can comfortably fit in one datagram") to a remote host. You could repeatedly send the same `DatagramPacket` object, just changing the data each time.

public void setData(byte[ ] data, int offset, int length)   // Java 1.2

This overloaded variant of the `setData()` method available only in Java 1.2 and later provides an alternative approach to sending a large quantity of data. Instead of sending lots of new arrays, you can put all the data in one array and send it a piece at a time. For instance, this loop sends a large array in 512-byte chunks:

```
int offset = 0;
DatagramPacket dp = new DatagramPacket(bigarray, offset, 512);
int bytesSent = 0;
while (bytesSent < bigarray.length) {
    socket.send(dp);
    bytesSent += dp.getLength();
    int bytesToSend = bigarray.length - bytesSent;
    int size = (bytesToSend > 512) ? 512 : bytesToSend;
    dp.setData(bigarray, bytesSent, 512);
}
```

On the other hand, this requires either a lot of confidence that the data will in fact arrive, or alternatively, a disregard for the consequences of its not arriving. It's relatively difficult to attach sequence numbers or other reliability tags to the individual packets when you take this approach.

public void setAddress(InetAddress remote)

The `setAddress()` method lets you change the address a datagram packet is sent to. This might allow you to send the same datagram to many different recipients. For example:

```
String s = "Really Important Message";
byte[] data = s.getBytes("ASCII");
DatagramPacket dp = new DatagramPacket(data, data.length);
dp.setPort(2000);
int network = "128.238.5.";
for (int host = 1; host < 255; host++) {
  try {
    InetAddress remote = InetAddress.getByName(network + host);
    dp.setAddress(remote);
```

```
    socket.send(dp);
  }
  catch (Exception e) {}
}
```

Whether or not this is sensible depends on your application. If you're trying to send to all the stations on a network segment, as in this fragment, you'd probably be better off using the local broadcast address and letting the network do the work. The local broadcast address is determined by setting all bits of the IP address after the network and subnet IDs to 1. For example, Polytechnic University's network address is 128.238.0.0. Consequently, its broadcast address is 128.238.255.255. Sending a datagram to 128.238.255.255 will copy it to every host on that network (though some routers and firewalls may block it, depending on its origin).

For more widely separated hosts, you'd probably be better off using multicasting. Multicasting actually uses the same `DatagramPacket` class described here. However, it uses different IP addresses and a `MulticastSocket` instead of a `DatagramSocket`. This will be explored in Chapter 14.

public void setPort(int port)

The `setPort()` method changes the port a datagram is addressed to. I honestly can't think of many uses for this method. It could be used in a port scanner application that tried to find open ports running particular UDP-based services such as FSP. Another possibility would be some sort of networked game or conferencing server where the clients that needed to receive the same information were all running on different ports as well as different hosts. In this case, it could be used in conjunction with `setAddress()` to change the destination before sending out the same datagram again.

public void setLength(int length)

The `setLength()` method changes the number of bytes of data in the internal buffer that are considered to be part of the datagram's data as opposed to merely unfilled space. This method is useful when receiving datagrams, as we'll explore later in this chapter. When a datagram is received, its length is set to the length of the incoming data. This means that if you try to receive another datagram into the same `DatagramPacket`, then it's limited to no more than the number of bytes in the first. That is, once you've received a 10-byte datagram, all subsequent datagrams will be truncated to 10 bytes; once you've received a 9-byte datagram, all subsequent datagrams will be truncated to 9 bytes; and so on. This method lets you reset the length of the buffer so that subsequent datagrams aren't truncated.

The DatagramSocket Class

To send or receive a `DatagramPacket`, you need to open a datagram socket. In Java, a datagram socket is created and accessed through the `DatagramSocket` class:

```
public class DatagramSocket extends Object
```

All datagram sockets are bound to a local port, on which they listen for incoming data and which they place in the header of outgoing datagrams. If you're writing a client, you don't care what the local port is, so you call a constructor that lets the system assign an unused port (an anonymous port). This port number is placed in any outgoing datagrams and will be used by the server to address any response datagrams. If you're writing a server, clients need to know on which port the server is listening for incoming datagrams; therefore, when a server constructs a `DatagramSocket`, it must specify the local port on which it will listen. However, the sockets used by clients and servers are otherwise identical: they differ only in whether they use an anonymous (system-assigned) or a well-known port. There's no distinction between client sockets and server sockets, as there is with TCP; there is no such thing as a `DatagramServerSocket`.

The Constructors

The `DatagramSocket` class has three constructors that are used in different situations, much like the `DatagramPacket` class. The first constructor opens a datagram socket on an anonymous local port. The second constructor opens a datagram socket on a well-known local port that listens to all local network interfaces. The third constructor opens a datagram socket on a well-known local port on a specific network interface. All three constructors deal only with the local address and port. The remote address and port are stored in the `DatagramPacket`, not the `DatagramSocket`. Indeed, one `DatagramSocket` can send and receive datagrams from multiple remote hosts and ports.

public DatagramSocket( ) throws SocketException

This constructor creates a socket that is bound to an anonymous port. For example:

```
try {
  DatagramSocket client = new DatagramSocket();
  // send packets...
}
catch (SocketException e) {
  System.err.println(e);
}
```

You would use this constructor in a client that initiates a conversation with a server. In this scenario, you don't care what port you are using, because the server will send its response to the port from which the datagram originated. Letting the system assign a port means that you don't have to worry about finding an unused port. If for some reason you need to know the local port, you can find out with the `getLocalPort()` method described later in this chapter.

The same socket may be used to receive the datagrams that a server sends back to it. A `SocketException` is thrown if the socket can't be created. It's unusual for this constructor to throw an exception; it's hard to imagine situations in which the socket could not be opened, since the system gets to choose the local port.

public DatagramSocket(int port) throws SocketException

This constructor creates a socket that listens for incoming datagrams on a specific port, specified by the `port` argument. You would use this constructor to write a server that has to listen on a well-known port; if servers listened on anonymous ports, clients would not be able to contact them. A `SocketException` is thrown if the socket can't be created. There are two common reasons for the constructor to fail: the specified port is already occupied, or you are trying to connect to a port below 1,024 and you don't have sufficient privileges (i.e., you are not root on a Unix system; for better or worse, other platforms allow anyone to connect to low-numbered ports).

TCP ports and UDP ports are not related. Two unrelated servers or clients can use the same port number if one uses UDP and the other uses TCP. Example 13-2 is a port scanner that looks for UDP ports in use on the local host. It decides that the port is in use if the `DatagramSocket` constructor throws an exception. As written, it looks at ports from 1,024 up to avoid Unix's requirement that it run as root to bind to ports below 1,024. You can easily extend it to check ports below 1,024, however, if you have root access or are running it on Windows or a Mac.

Example 13-2. Look for Local UDP Ports

```
import java.net.*;

public class UDPPortScanner {

  public static void main(String[] args) {

    for (int port = 1024; port <= 65535; port++) {
      try {
        // the next line will fail and drop into the catch block if
        // there is already a server running on port i
        DatagramSocket server = new DatagramSocket(port);
        server.close();
```

Example 13-2. Look for Local UDP Ports (continued)

```
    }
    catch (SocketException e) {
      System.out.println("There is a server on port " + port + ".");
    } // end try
  } // end for


  }

}
```

The speed at which UDPPortScanner runs depends strongly on the speed of your machine and its UDP implementation. I've clocked Example 13-2 at as little as two minutes on a moderately powered SPARCstation and as long as an hour on a PowerBook 5300. Here are the results from one SPARCstation:

```
% java UDPPortScanner
There is a server on port 2049.
There is a server on port 4045.
There is a server on port 32771.
There is a server on port 32773.
There is a server on port 32778.
There is a server on port 32779.
There is a server on port 32787.
There is a server on port 32788.
There is a server on port 32790.
There is a server on port 32793.
There is a server on port 32797.
There is a server on port 32804.
There is a server on port 32812.
There is a server on port 32822.
There is a server on port 32834.
There is a server on port 32852.
There is a server on port 32857.
There is a server on port 32858.
There is a server on port 32860.
There is a server on port 32871.
There is a server on port 32877.
There is a server on port 33943.
There is a server on port 34955.
There is a server on port 35977.
There is a server on port 35982.
There is a server on port 36000.
There is a server on port 36159.
There is a server on port 36259.
```

The high-numbered UDP ports in the 30,000 range are Remote Procedure Call (RPC) services. Aside from RPC, some common protocols that use UDP are NFS, TFTP, and FSP.

It's much harder to scan UDP ports on a remote system than to scan for remote TCP ports. Whereas there's always some indication that your TCP packet has been received by a listening port regardless of application layer protocol, UDP provides no such guarantees. To determine that a UDP server is listening, you have to send it a packet it will recognize and respond to.

public DatagramSocket(int port, InetAddress address)
throws SocketException

This constructor is primarily used on multihomed hosts; it creates a socket that listens for incoming datagrams on a specific port and network interface. The `port` argument is the port on which this socket listens for datagrams. As with TCP sockets, you need to be root on a Unix system to create a `DatagramSocket` on a port below 1,024. The `address` argument is an `InetAddress` object matching one of the host's network addresses. A `SocketException` is thrown if the socket can't be created. There are three common reasons for this constructor to fail: the specified port is already occupied, you are trying to connect to a port below 1,024 and you don't have sufficient privileges (i.e., you are not root on a Unix system), or `address` is not the address of one of the system's network interfaces.

Sending and Receiving Datagrams

The primary task of the `DatagramSocket` class is to send and receive UDP datagrams. One socket can both send and receive. Indeed, it can send and receive to and from multiple hosts at the same time.

public void send(DatagramPacket dp) throws IOException

Once a `DatagramPacket` is created and a `DatagramSocket` is constructed, you send the packet by passing it to the socket's `send()` method. For example, if `theSocket` is a `DatagramSocket` object and `theOutput` is a `DatagramPacket` object, you send `theOutput` using `theSocket` like this:

```
theSocket.send(theOutput);
```

If there's a problem sending the data, an `IOException` may be thrown. However, this is less common with `DatagramSocket` than `Socket` or `ServerSocket`, since the unreliable nature of UDP means you won't get an exception just because the packet doesn't arrive at its destination. You may get an `IOException` if you're trying to send a larger datagram than your host's native networking software supports, but then again you may not. This depends heavily on the native UDP software in the OS and the native code that interfaces between this and Java's `DatagramSocketImpl` class. This method may also throw a `SecurityException` if the `SecurityManager` won't let you communicate with the host to which the packet is addressed. This is primarily a problem for applets.

Example 13-3 is a UDP-based discard client. It reads lines of user input from `System.in`, and sends them to a discard server, which simply discards all the data. Each line is stuffed in a `DatagramPacket`. Many of the simpler Internet protocols such as discard have both TCP and UDP implementations.

Example 13-3. A UDP Discard Client

```
import java.net.*;
import java.io.*;

public class UDPDiscardClient {

  public final static int DEFAULT_PORT = 9;

  public static void main(String[] args) {

    String hostname;
    int port = DEFAULT_PORT;

    if (args.length > 0) {
      hostname = args[0];
      try {
      port = Integer.parseInt(args[1]);
      }
      catch (Exception e) {
      }
    }
    else {
      hostname = "localhost";
    }

    try {
      InetAddress server = InetAddress.getByName(hostname);
      BufferedReader userInput
        = new BufferedReader(new InputStreamReader(System.in));
      DatagramSocket theSocket = new DatagramSocket();
      while (true) {
        String theLine = userInput.readLine();
        if (theLine.equals(".")) break;
        byte[] data = theLine.getBytes();
        DatagramPacket theOutput
          = new DatagramPacket(data, data.length, server, port);
        theSocket.send(theOutput);
      } // end while
    } // end try
    catch (UnknownHostException e) {
```

Example 13-3. A UDP Discard Client (continued)

```
    System.err.println(e);
  }
  catch (SocketException se) {
    System.err.println(se);
  }
  catch (IOException e) {
    System.err.println(e);
  }

 } // end main


}
```

The UDPDiscardClient class should look familiar. It has a single static field, DEFAULT_PORT, which is set to the standard port for the discard protocol (port 9), and a single method, main(). The main() method reads a hostname from the command-line and converts that hostname to the InetAddress object called server. A BufferedReader is chained to System.in to read user input from the keyboard. Next, a DatagramSocket object called theSocket is constructed. After creating the socket, the program enters an infinite while loop that reads user input line by line using readLine(). We are careful, however, to use only readLine() to read data from the console, the one place where it is guaranteed to work as advertised. Since the discard protocol deals only with raw bytes, we can ignore character encoding issues.

In the while loop, each line is converted to a byte array using the getBytes() method, and the bytes are stuffed in a new DatagramPacket, theOutput. Finally, theOutput is sent over theSocket, and the loop continues. If at any point the user types a period on a line by itself, the program exits. The DatagramSocket constructor may throw a SocketException, so that needs to be caught. Because this is a discard client, we don't need to worry about data coming back from the server.

public void receive(DatagramPacket dp) throws IOException

This method receives a single UDP datagram from the network and stores it in the pre-existing DatagramPacket object dp. Like the accept() method in the ServerSocket class, this method blocks the calling thread until a datagram arrives. If your program does anything besides wait for datagrams, you should call receive() in a separate thread.

The datagram's buffer should be large enough to hold the data received. If not, receive() places as much data in the buffer as it can hold; the rest is lost. It may be useful to remember that the maximum size of the data portion of a UDP datagram is 65,507 bytes. (That's the 65,536-byte maximum size of an IP datagram minus the 20-byte size of the IP header and the 8-byte size of the UDP header.) Some application protocols that use UDP further restrict the maximum number of bytes in a packet; for instance, NFS uses a maximum packet size of 8,192 bytes.

If there's a problem receiving the data, an IOException may be thrown. In practice, this is rare. Unlike send(), this method does not throw a SecurityException if an applet receives a datagram from other than the applet host. However, it will silently discard all such packets. (This behavior prevents a denial-of-service attack against applets that receive UDP datagrams.)

Example 13-4 shows a UDP discard server that receives incoming datagrams. Just for fun, it logs the data in each datagram to System.out so that you can see who's sending what to your discard server.

Example 13-4. The UDPDiscardServer

```
import java.net.*;
import java.io.*;

public class UDPDiscardServer {

  public final static int DEFAULT_PORT = 9;
  public final static int MAX_PACKET_SIZE = 65507;

  public static void main(String[] args) {

    int port = DEFAULT_PORT;
    byte[] buffer = new byte[MAX_PACKET_SIZE];

    try {
      port = Integer.parseInt(args[0]);
    }
    catch (Exception e) {
    }

    try {
      DatagramSocket server = new DatagramSocket(port);
      DatagramPacket packet = new DatagramPacket(buffer, buffer.length);
      while (true) {
        try {
          server.receive(packet);
          String s = new String(packet.getData(), 0, packet.getLength());
          System.out.println(packet.getAddress() + " at port "
            + packet.getPort() + " says " + s);
          // reset the length for the next packet
          packet.setLength(buffer.length);
        }
```

Example 13-4. The UDPDiscardServer (continued)

```
        catch (IOException e) {
          System.err.println(e);
        }
      } // end while
    }  // end try
   catch (SocketException se) {
     System.err.println(se);
   }  // end catch

 }  // end main

}
```

This is a simple class with a single method, `main()`. It reads the port for the server to listen to from the command line. If the port is not specified on the command-line, it is set to 9. It then opens a `DatagramSocket` on that port and creates a `DatagramPacket` with a 65,507-byte buffer—large enough to receive any possible packet. Then the server enters an infinite loop that receives packets and prints the contents and the originating host on the console. A high-performance discard server would skip this step. As each datagram is received, the length of `packet` is set to the length of the data in that datagram. Consequently, as the last step of the loop, the length of the packet is reset to the maximum possible value. Otherwise, the incoming packets would be limited to the minimum size of all previous packets. Try running the discard client on one machine and connecting to the discard server on a second machine to verify that both these programs work.

public void close( )

Calling a `DatagramSocket` object's `close()` method frees the port occupied by that socket. For example:

```
try {
  DatagramSocket theServer = new DatagramSocket();
  theServer.close();
}
catch (SocketException e) {
  System.err.println(e);
}
```

It's never a bad idea to close a `DatagramSocket` when you're through with it; it's particularly important to close an unneeded socket if your program will continue to run for a significant amount of time. For example, the `close()` method was essential in Example 13-2, `UDPPortScanner`: if this program did not close the sockets it opened, it would tie up every UDP port on the system for a significant amount of time. On the other hand, if the program ends as soon as you're through with the DatagramSocket, you don't need to close the socket explicitly; the socket is automatically closed on garbage collection. However, Java won't run the garbage collector just because you've run out of ports or sockets, unless by lucky happenstance you run out of memory at the same time. On the gripping hand, closing unneeded sockets never hurts and is good programming practice.

public int getLocalPort( )

A DatagramSocket's getLocalPort() method returns an int that represents the local port on which the socket is listening. You would use this method if you created a DatagramSocket with an anonymous port and want to find out what port you have been assigned. For example:

```
try {
  DatagramSocket ds = new DatagramSocket();
  System.out.println("The socket is using port " + ds.getLocalPort());
}
catch (SocketException e) {
}
```

Managing Connections

Unlike TCP sockets, datagram sockets aren't very picky about whom they'll talk to. In fact, by default they'll talk to anyone. But this is often not what you want. For instance, applets are only allowed to send datagrams to and receive datagrams from the applet host. An NFS or FSP client should accept packets only from the server it's talking to. A networked game should listen to datagrams only from the people playing the game. In Java 1.1, programs must manually check the source addresses and ports of the hosts sending them data to make sure they're who they should be. However, Java 1.2 adds four methods that let you choose which host you can send datagrams to and receive datagrams from, while rejecting all others' packets.

public void connect(InetAddress host, int port)   // Java 1.2

The connect() method doesn't really establish a connection in the TCP sense. However, it does specify that the DatagramSocket will send packets to and receive packets from only the specified remote host on the specified remote port. Attempts to send packets to a different host or port will throw an IllegalArgumentException. Packets received from a different host or a different port will be discarded without an exception or other notification.

A security check is made when the connect() method is invoked. If the VM is allowed to send data to that host and port, then the check passes silently. Otherwise, a SecurityException is thrown. However, once the connection has been made, send() and receive() on that DatagramSocket no longer make the security checks they'd normally make.

public void disconnect( )   // Java 1.2

The disconnect() method breaks the "connection" of a connected DatagramSocket so that it can once again send packets to and receive packets from any host and port.

public int getPort( )   // Java 1.2

If and only if a DatagramSocket is connected, the getPort() method returns the remote port to which it is connected. Otherwise, it returns –1.

public InetAddress getInetAddress( )   // Java 1.2

If and only if a DatagramSocket is connected, the getInetAddress() method returns the address of the remote host to which it is connected. Otherwise, it returns null.

Socket Options

The only socket option supported for datagram sockets in Java 1.1 is SO_TIME-OUT. Java 1.2 adds SO_SNDBUF and SO_RCVBUF.

SO_TIMEOUT

SO_TIMEOUT is the amount of time, in milliseconds, that receive() waits for an incoming datagram before throwing an InterruptedIOException. Its value must be non-negative. If SO_TIMEOUT is 0, receive() never times out. This value can be changed with the setSoTimeout() method and inspected with the getSoTimeout() method:

```
public synchronized void setSoTimeout(int timeout)
  throws SocketException
public synchronized int getSoTimeout() throws IOException
```

The default is to never time out, and indeed there are few situations in which you would need to set SO_TIMEOUT. You might need it if you were implementing a secure protocol that required responses to occur within a fixed amount of time. You might also decide that the host you're communicating with is dead (unreachable or not responding) if you don't receive a response within a certain amount of time.

The setSoTimeout() method sets the SO_TIMEOUT field for a datagram socket. When the timeout expires, an InterruptedIOException is thrown. You should set this option *before* you call `receive()`. You cannot change it while `receive()` is waiting for a datagram. The `timeout` argument must be greater than or equal to zero; if it is not, `setSoTimeout()` throws a `SocketException`. For example:

```
try {
  buffer = new byte[2056];
  DatagramPacket dp = new DatagramPacket(buffer, buffer.length);
  DatagramSocket ds = new ServerSocket(2048);
  ds.setSoTimeout(30000); // block for no more than 30 seconds
  try {
   ds.receive(dp);
    // process the packet...
  }
  catch (InterruptedIOException e) {
    ss.close();
    System.err.println("No connection within 30 seconds");
  }
}
catch (SocketException e) {
  System.err.println(e);
}
catch (IOException e) {
  System.err.println("Unexpected IOException: " + e);
}
```

The `getSoTimeout()` method returns the current value of this `DatagramSocket` object's SO_TIMEOUT field. For example:

```
public void printSoTimeout(DatagramSocket ds) {

  int timeout = ds.getSoTimeOut();
  if (timeout > 0) {
    System.out.println(ds + " will time out after "
      + timeout + "milliseconds.");
  }
  else if (timeout == 0) {
    System.out.println(ds + " will never time out.");
  }
  else {
    System.out.println("Something is seriously wrong with " + ds);
  }

}
```

SO_RCVBUF

The SO_RCVBUF option of `DatagramSocket` is closely related to the SO_RCVBUF option of `Socket`. It determines the size of the buffer used for network I/O. Larger buffers tend to improve performance for reasonably fast (say, Ethernet-speed) connections because they can store more incoming datagrams before overflowing. Sufficiently large receive buffers are even more important for UDP than for TCP, since a UDP datagram that arrives when the buffer is full will be lost, whereas a TCP datagram that arrives at a full buffer will eventually be retransmitted. Furthermore, SO_RCVBUF sets the maximum size of datagram packets that can be received by the application. Packets that won't fit in the receive buffer are silently discarded.

Starting in Java 1.2, `DatagramSocket` has methods to get and set the suggested receive buffer size used for network input:

```
public void setReceiveBufferSize(int size)
  throws SocketException, IllegalArgumentException
public int getReceiveBufferSize() throws SocketException
```

The `setReceiveBufferSize()` method suggests a number of bytes to use for buffering input from this socket. However, the underlying implementation is free to ignore this suggestion. For instance, many 4.3 BSD–derived systems have a maximum receive buffer size of about 52K and won't let you set a limit higher than this. Other systems raise this to about 240K. The details are highly platform-dependent. Consequently, it's a good idea to check the actual size of the receive buffer with `getReceiveBufferSize()` after setting it. The `getReceiveBufferSize()` method returns the number of bytes in the buffer used for input from this socket.

Both methods throw a `SocketException` if the underlying socket implementation does not recognize the SO_RCVBUF option. This might happen on a non-POSIX operating system. The `setReceiveBufferSize()` method throws an `IllegalArgumentException` if its argument is less than or equal to zero.

SO_SNDBUF

Starting in Java 1.2, `DatagramSocket` has methods to get and set the suggested send buffer size used for network output:

```
public void setSendBufferSize(int size)
  throws SocketException, IllegalArgumentException
public int getSendBufferSize() throws SocketException
```

The `setSendBufferSize()` method suggests a number of bytes to use for buffering output on this socket. Once again, however, the operating system is free to ignore this suggestion. Consequently, you'll want to check the result of `setSendBufferSize()` by immediately following it with a call to `getSendBufferSize()` to find out what the buffer size really is.

Both methods throw a `SocketException` if the underlying native network software doesn't understand the SO_SNDBUF option. The `setSendBufferSize()` method also throws an `IllegalArgumentException` if its argument is less than or equal to zero.

Some Useful Applications

In this section, you'll see several Internet servers and clients that use `DatagramPacket` and `DatagramSocket`. Some of these will be familiar from the last two chapters because many Internet protocols have both TCP and UDP implementations. When an IP packet is received by a host, the host determines whether the packet is a TCP packet or a UDP datagram by inspecting the IP header. As I said earlier, there's no connection between UDP and TCP ports; TCP and UDP servers can share the same port number without problems. By convention, if a service has both TCP and UDP implementations, it uses the same port for both, though there's no technical reason this has to be the case.

Simple UDP Clients

Several Internet services need to know only the client's address and port; they discard any data the client sends in its datagrams. Daytime, quote of the day, time, and chargen are four such protocols. Each of these responds the same way, regardless of the data contained in the datagram, or indeed regardless of whether there actually is any data in the datagram. Clients for these protocols simply send a UDP datagram to the server and read the response that comes back. Therefore, let's begin with a simple client called `UDPPoke`, shown in Example 13-5, that sends an empty UDP packet to a specified host and port and reads a response packet from the same host.

The `UDPPoke` class has three private fields. The `bufferSize` field specifies how large a return packet is expected. An 8,192-byte buffer is large enough for most of the protocols that `UDPPoke` is useful for, but it can be increased by passing a different value to the constructor. The `DatagramSocket` object `ds` will be used to both send and receive datagrams. Finally, the `DatagramPacket` object `outgoing` is the message sent to the individual servers.

The constructors initialize all three fields using an `InetAddress` for the host and `int`s for the port, the buffer length, and the number of milliseconds to wait before timing out. These last three become part of the `DatagramSocket` field `ds`. If the buffer length is not specified, 8,192 bytes is used. If the timeout is not given, 30 seconds (30,000 milliseconds) is used. The host, port, and buffer size are also used to construct the `outgoing` `DatagramPacket`. Although in theory you should be able to send a datagram with no data at all, bugs in some Java implementations require that you add at least one byte of data to the datagram. The simple servers we're currently considering ignore this data.

Once a `UDPPoke` object has been constructed, clients will call its `poke()` method to send an empty `outgoing` datagram to the target and read its response. The response is initially set to null. When the expected datagram appears, its data is copied into the `response` field. This method returns null if the response doesn't come quickly enough or never comes at all.

The `main( )` method merely reads the host and port to connect to from the command-line, constructs a `UDPPoke` object, and pokes it. Most of the simple protocols that this client suits well return ASCII text, so we attempt to convert the response to an ASCII string and print it. Not all VMs support the ASCII character encoding, so we provide the possibility of using the ASCII superset Latin-1 (8859-1) as a backup.

Example 13-5. The UDPPoke Class

```
import java.net.*;
import java.io.*;

public class UDPPoke {

  private int bufferSize; // in bytes
  private DatagramSocket ds;
  private DatagramPacket outgoing;

  public UDPPoke(InetAddress host, int port, int bufferSize,
    int timeout) throws SocketException {

    outgoing = new DatagramPacket(new byte[1], 1, host, port);
    this.bufferSize = bufferSize;
    ds = new DatagramSocket(0);
    ds.connect(host, port); // requires Java 2
    ds.setSoTimeout(timeout);

  }

  public UDPPoke(InetAddress host, int port, int bufferSize)
    throws SocketException {
    this(host, port, bufferSize, 30000);
  }

  public UDPPoke(InetAddress host, int port)
    throws SocketException {
    this(host, port, 8192, 30000);
  }

  public byte[] poke() throws IOException {

    byte[] response = null;
    try {
      ds.send(outgoing);
      DatagramPacket incoming
        = new DatagramPacket(new byte[bufferSize], bufferSize);
```

Example 13-5. The UDPPoke Class (continued)

```
      // next line blocks until the response is received
      ds.receive(incoming);
      int numBytes = incoming.getLength();
      response = new byte[numBytes];
      System.arraycopy(incoming.getData(), 0, response, 0, numBytes);
    }
    catch (IOException e) {
      // response will be null
    }

    // may return null
    return response;
  }

public static void main(String[] args) {

  InetAddress host;
  int port = 0;

  try {
    host = InetAddress.getByName(args[0]);
    port = Integer.parseInt(args[1]);
    if (port < 1 || port > 65535) throw new Exception();
  }
  catch (Exception e) {
    System.out.println("Usage: java UDPPoke host port");
    return;
  }

  try {
    UDPPoke poker = new UDPPoke(host, port);
    byte[] response = poker.poke();
    if (response == null) {
    System.out.println("No response within allotted time");
    return;
    }
    String result = "";
    try {
      result = new String(response, "ASCII");
    }
    catch (UnsupportedEncodingException e) {
    // try a different encoding
    result = new String(response, "8859_1");
    }
    System.out.println(result);
  }
  catch (Exception e) {
    System.err.println(e);
```

Example 13-5. The UDPPoke Class (continued)

```
      e.printStackTrace();
    }

  }  // end main


}
```

For example, this connects to a daytime server over UDP:

```
D:\JAVA\JNP2\examples\12>java UDPPoke vision.poly.edu 13
Sun Oct  3 13:04:22 1999
```

This connects to a chargen server:

```
D:\JAVA\JNP2\examples\12>java UDPPoke vision.poly.edu 19
123456789:;<=>?@ABCDEFGHIJKLMNOPQRSTUVWXYZ[\]^_`abcdefghijklmnopqrstuv
```

Given this class, UDP daytime, time, chargen, and quote of the day clients are almost trivial. Example 13-6 demonstrates a time client. The most complicated part is converting the four raw bytes returned by the server to a `java.util.Date` object. The same algorithm as in Example 10-5 is used here, so I won't repeat that discussion. The other protocols are left as exercises for the reader.

Example 13-6. A UDP Time Client

```
import java.net.*;
import java.util.*;

public class UDPTimeClient {

  public final static int DEFAULT_PORT = 37;
  public final static String DEFAULT_HOST = "tock.usno.navy.mil";

  public static void main(String[] args) {

    InetAddress host;
    int port = DEFAULT_PORT;

    try {
      if (args.length > 0) {
        host = InetAddress.getByName(args[0]);
      }
      else {
        host = InetAddress.getByName(DEFAULT_HOST);
      }
    }
    catch (Exception e) {
      System.out.println("Usage: java UDPTimeClient host port");
      return;
```

Example 13-6. A UDP Time Client (continued)

```
  }

  if (args.length > 1) {
    try {
      port = Integer.parseInt(args[1]);
      if (port <= 0 || port > 65535) port = DEFAULT_PORT;;
    }
    catch (Exception e){
    }
  }

  try {
    UDPPoke poker = new UDPPoke(host, port);
    byte[] response = poker.poke();
      if (response == null) {
      System.out.println("No response within allotted time");
      return;
      }
      else if (response.length != 4) {
      System.out.println("Unrecognized response format");
      return;
      }

    // The time protocol sets the epoch at 1900,
    // the java Date class at 1970. This number
    // converts between them.

    long differenceBetweenEpochs = 2208988800L;

    long secondsSince1900 = 0;
    for (int i = 0; i < 4; i++) {
      secondsSince1900
        = (secondsSince1900 << 8) | (response[i] & 0x000000FF);
    }

    long secondsSince1970
      = secondsSince1900 - differenceBetweenEpochs;
    long msSince1970 = secondsSince1970 * 1000;
    Date time = new Date(msSince1970);

    System.out.println(time);
  }
  catch (Exception e) {
    System.err.println(e);
```

Example 13-6. A UDP Time Client (continued)

```
      e.printStackTrace();
    }

  }

}
```

UDPServer

Clients aren't the only programs that benefit from a reusable implementation. The servers for these protocols are also very similar. They all wait for UDP datagrams on a specified port and reply to each datagram with another datagram. The servers differ only in the content of the datagram that they return. Example 13-7 is a simple UDPServer class that can be subclassed to provide specific servers for different protocols.

The UDPServer class has two fields, the int bufferSize and the Datagram-Socket ds, the latter of which is protected, so it can be used by subclasses. The constructor opens the DatagramSocket ds on a specified local port to receive datagrams of no more than bufferSize bytes.

UDPServer extends Thread so that multiple instances can run in parallel. Its run() method contains an infinite loop that repeatedly receives an incoming datagram, and responds to it by passing it to the abstract respond() method. This method will be overridden by particular subclasses to implement different kinds of servers.

UDPServer is a very flexible class. Subclasses can send zero, one, or many datagrams in response to each incoming datagram. If a lot of processing is required to respond to a packet, the respond() method can spawn a thread to do it. However, UDP servers tend not to have extended interactions with a client. Each incoming packet is treated independently of other packets, so the response can usually be handled directly in the respond() method without spawning a thread.

Example 13-7. The UDPServer Class

```
import java.net.*;
import java.io.*;

public abstract class UDPServer extends Thread {

  private int bufferSize; // in bytes
  protected DatagramSocket ds;

  public UDPServer(int port, int bufferSize)
   throws SocketException {
```

Example 13-7. The UDPServer Class (continued)

```
    this.bufferSize = bufferSize;
    this.ds = new DatagramSocket(port);
  }

  public UDPServer(int port) throws SocketException {
    this(port, 8192);
  }

  public void run() {

    byte[] buffer = new byte[bufferSize];
    while (true) {
      DatagramPacket incoming = new DatagramPacket(buffer, buffer.length);
      try {
        ds.receive(incoming);
        this.respond(incoming);
      }
      catch (IOException e) {
        System.err.println(e);
      }
    } // end while

  }  // end run

  public abstract void respond(DatagramPacket request);


}
```

The easiest protocol to handle is discard. All that needs to be done is to write a main() method that sets the port and start the thread. Example 13-8 is a high-performance UDP discard server that does nothing with incoming packets.

Example 13-8. A High-Performance UDP Discard Server

```
import java.net.*;

public class FastUDPDiscardServer extends UDPServer {

  public final static int DEFAULT_PORT = 9;

  public FastUDPDiscardServer() throws SocketException {
    super(DEFAULT_PORT);
  }

  public void respond(DatagramPacket packet) {}

  public static void main(String[] args) {
```

Example 13-8. A High-Performance UDP Discard Server (continued)

```
  try {
    FastUDPDiscardServer server = new FastUDPDiscardServer();
    server.start();
  }
  catch (SocketException e) {
    System.err.println(e);
  }


  }


}
```

Example 13-9 is a slightly more interesting discard server that prints the incoming
packets on System.out.

Example 13-9. A UDP Discard Server

```
import java.net.*;

public class LoggingUDPDiscardServer extends UDPServer {

  public final static int DEFAULT_PORT = 9999;

  public LoggingUDPDiscardServer() throws SocketException {
    super(DEFAULT_PORT);
  }

  public void respond(DatagramPacket packet) {

    byte[] data = new byte[packet.getLength()];
    System.arraycopy(packet.getData(), 0, data, 0, packet.getLength());
    try {
      String s = new String(data, "ASCII");
      System.out.println(packet.getAddress() + " at port "
        + packet.getPort() + " says " + s);
    }
    catch (java.io.UnsupportedEncodingException e) {
    }

  }

  public static void main(String[] args) {

    try {
      LoggingUDPDiscardServer server = new LoggingUDPDiscardServer();
      server.start();
    }
    catch (SocketException e) {
```

Example 13-9. A UDP Discard Server (continued)

```
      System.err.println(e);
    }


  }


}
```

It isn't much harder to implement an echo server, as Example 13-10 shows:

Example 13-10. A UDP Echo Server

```java
import java.net.*;
import java.io.*;

public class UDPEchoServer extends UDPServer {

  public final static int DEFAULT_PORT = 7;

  public UDPEchoServer() throws SocketException {
    super(DEFAULT_PORT);
  }

  public void respond(DatagramPacket packet) {

    try {
      DatagramPacket outgoing = new DatagramPacket(packet.getData(),
        packet.getLength(), packet.getAddress(), packet.getPort());
      ds.send(outgoing);
    }
    catch (IOException e) {
      System.err.println(e);
    }


  }

  public static void main(String[] args) {

    try {
      UDPEchoServer server = new UDPEchoServer();
      server.start();
    }
    catch (SocketException e) {
      System.err.println(e);
    }


  }

}
```

A daytime server is only mildly more complex. The server listens for incoming UDP datagrams on port 13. When it detects an incoming datagram, it returns the current date and time at the server as a one-line ASCII string. Example 13-11 demonstrates this.

Example 13-11. The UDP Daytime Server

```
import java.net.*;
import java.io.*;
import java.util.*;


public class UDPDaytimeServer extends UDPServer {

  public final static int DEFAULT_PORT = 13;

  public UDPDaytimeServer() throws SocketException {
    super(DEFAULT_PORT);
  }

  public void respond(DatagramPacket packet) {

    try {
      Date now = new Date();
      String response = now.toString() + "\r\n";
      byte[] data = response.getBytes("ASCII");
      DatagramPacket outgoing = new DatagramPacket(data,
        data.length, packet.getAddress(), packet.getPort());
      ds.send(outgoing);
    }
    catch (IOException e) {
      System.err.println(e);
    }

  }

  public static void main(String[] args) {

    try {
      UDPDaytimeServer server = new UDPDaytimeServer();
      server.start();
    }
    catch (SocketException e) {
      System.err.println(e);
    }

  }

}
```

A UDP Echo Client

The UDPPoke class implemented earlier isn't suitable for all protocols. In particular, protocols that require multiple datagrams require a different implementation. The echo protocol has both TCP and UDP implementations. As we saw, implementing the echo protocol with TCP is simple; it's more complex with UDP because you don't have I/O streams or the concept of a connection to work with. A TCP-based echo client can send a message and wait for a response on the same connection. However, a UDP-based echo client has no guarantee that the message it sent was received. Therefore, it cannot simply wait for the response; it needs to be prepared to send and receive data asynchronously.

This behavior is fairly simple to implement using threads, however. One thread can process user input and send it to the echo server, while a second thread accepts input from the server and displays it to the user. The client is divided into three classes: the main UDPEchoClient class, the SenderThread class, and the ReceiverThread class.

The UDPEchoClient class should look familiar. It reads a hostname from the command-line and converts that to an InetAddress object. It uses this and the default echo port to construct a SenderThread object. This constructor can throw a SocketException, so the exception must be caught. Then the SenderThread starts. The same DatagramSocket that the SenderThread uses is used to construct a ReceiverThread, which is then started. It's important to use the same DatagramSocket for both sending and receiving data, because the echo server will send the response back to the port the data was sent from. Example 13-12 shows the code for the UDPEchoClient.

Example 13-12. The UDPEchoClient Class

```
import java.net.*;
import java.io.*;

public class UDPEchoClient {

  public final static int DEFAULT_PORT = 7;

  public static void main(String[] args) {

    String hostname = "localhost";
    int port = DEFAULT_PORT;

    if (args.length > 0) {
      hostname = args[0];
    }
```

Example 13-12. The UDPEchoClient Class (continued)

```
    try {
      InetAddress ia = InetAddress.getByName(hostname);
      SenderThread sender = new SenderThread(ia, DEFAULT_PORT);
      sender.start();
      ReceiverThread receiver = new ReceiverThread(sender.getSocket());
      receiver.start();
    }
    catch (UnknownHostException e) {
      System.err.println(e);
    }
    catch (SocketException se) {
      System.err.println(se);
    }

  } // end main

}
```

The SenderThread class reads input from the console, a line at a time, and sends it to the echo server. It's shown in Example 13-13. The input is provided by System.in, but a different client could include an option to read input from a different stream—perhaps opening a FileInputStream to read from a file. The three fields of this class define the server to which it sends data, the port on that server, and the DatagramSocket that does the sending. SenderThread has a single constructor, which takes an InetAddress and the port as arguments and opens a DatagramSocket.

The run() method processes user input, a line at a time. To do this, the BufferedReader userInput is chained to System.in. An infinite loop reads lines of user input. Each line is stored in theLine. A period on a line by itself signals the end of user input and breaks out of the loop. Otherwise, the bytes of data are stored in the data array, using the getBytes() method from java.lang. String. Next, the data array is placed in the payload part of the DatagramPacket output, along with information about the server, the port, and the data length. This packet is then sent to its destination by socket. This thread then yields to give other threads an opportunity to run.

Example 13-13. The SenderThread Class

```
import java.net.*;
import java.io.*;


public class SenderThread extends Thread {

  private InetAddress server;
```

Example 13-13. The SenderThread Class (continued)

```java
private DatagramSocket socket;
private boolean stopped = false;
private int port;

public SenderThread(InetAddress ia, int port)
 throws SocketException {
   this.server = ia;
   this.socket = new DatagramSocket();
   this.port = port;
}

public void halt() {
   this.stopped = true;
}

public DatagramSocket getSocket() {
   return this.socket;
}

public void run() {

   try {
     BufferedReader userInput
       = new BufferedReader(new InputStreamReader(System.in));
     while (true) {
       if (stopped) return;
       String theLine = userInput.readLine();
       if (theLine.equals(".")) break;
       byte[] data = theLine.getBytes();
       DatagramPacket output
         = new DatagramPacket(data, data.length, server, port);
       socket.send(output);
       Thread.yield();
     }
   } // end try
   catch (IOException e) {
     System.err.println(e);
   }

 } // end run

}
```

The `ReceiverThread` class shown in Example 13-14 waits for datagrams to arrive from the network. When a datagram is received, it is converted to a `String` and printed on `System.out` for display to the user. A more advanced `EchoClient` could include an option to send the output elsewhere; it might also check to make sure that the datagrams were in fact returned by the server to which you're talking. It's rather unlikely that some other server on the Internet is going to bombard this particular port with extraneous data, so this is not a big flaw. However, it's a good habit to make sure that the packets you receive come from the right place, especially if security is a concern.

This class has two fields. The more important is the DatagramSocket, theSocket, which must be the same DatagramSocket used by the EchoInputThread. Data arrives on the port used by that DatagramSocket, and any other DatagramSocket would not be allowed to connect to the same port. The second field, stopped, is a boolean, used to halt this thread without invoking the deprecated stop() method.

The run() method is an infinite loop that uses socket's receive() method to wait for incoming datagrams. When an incoming datagram appears, it is converted into a String with the same length as the incoming data and printed on System.out. As in the input thread, this thread then yields to give other threads an opportunity to execute.

Example 13-14. The ReceiverThread Class

```
import java.net.*;
import java.io.*;

class ReceiverThread extends Thread {

  DatagramSocket socket;
  private boolean stopped = false;

  public ReceiverThread(DatagramSocket ds) throws SocketException {
    this.socket = ds;
  }

  public void halt() {
    this.stopped = true;
  }

  public void run() {

    byte[] buffer = new byte[65507];
    while (true) {
      if (stopped) return;
      DatagramPacket dp = new DatagramPacket(buffer, buffer.length);
      try {
        socket.receive(dp);
        String s = new String(dp.getData(), 0, dp.getLength());
        System.out.println(s);
        Thread.yield();
```

Example 13-14. The ReceiverThread Class (continued)

```
    }
    catch (IOException e) {
      System.err.println(e);
    }


  }


}
```

Try running the echo client on one machine and connecting to the echo server on a second machine to verify that both these programs work.

14

Multicast Sockets

All the sockets you've seen in the previous chapters have been *unicast*: they provided point-to-point communication. That is, unicast sockets create a connection with two well-defined endpoints. There is one sender and one receiver, and, although they may switch roles, at any given time it is easy to tell which is which. However, although point-to-point communications serve many, if not most, needs (people have engaged in one-on-one conversations for millennia), many tasks require a different model. For example, a television station broadcasts data from one location to every point within range of its transmitter. The signal reaches every television set whether or not it's turned on and whether or not it's tuned in to that particular station. Indeed, the signal even reaches homes with cable boxes instead of antennas and homes that don't have a television. This is the classic example of broadcasting. It's quite indiscriminate and quite wasteful of both the electromagnetic spectrum and power.

Videoconferencing, by contrast, sends an audio-video feed to a select group of people. Usenet news is posted at one site and distributed around the world to tens of thousands of people. DNS router updates travel from the site announcing a change to many other routers. However, the sender relies on the intermediate sites to copy and relay the message to downstream sites. The sender does not address its message to every host that will eventually receive it. These are examples of multicasting, though they're implemented with additional application layer protocols on top of TCP or UDP. These protocols require fairly detailed configuration and intervention by human beings. For instance, to join Usenet you have to find a site willing to send news to you and relay your outgoing news to the rest of the world. To add you to the Usenet feed, the news administrator of your news relay has to specifically add your site to their news config files. However, recent developments with the network software in most major operating systems as well as Internet routers have opened up a new possibility, true multicasting in which the

450

WHAT IS A MULTICAST SOCKET?

routers decide how to efficiently move that message to individual hosts. In particular, the initial router sends only one copy of the message to a router near the receiving hosts, which then makes multiple copies for different recipients at or closer to the destinations. Internet multicasting is built on top of UDP. Multicasting in Java uses the `DatagramPacket` class introduced in the previous chapter, along with a new `MulticastSocket` class.

What Is a Multicast Socket?

Multicasting is broader than unicast, point-to-point communication but narrower and more targeted than broadcast communication. Multicasting sends data from one host to many different hosts, but not to everyone; the data goes only to clients that have expressed an interest in the data by joining a particular multicast group. In a way, this is like a public meeting. People can come and go as they please, leaving when the discussion no longer interests them. Before they arrive and after they have left, they don't need to process the information at all: it just doesn't reach them. On the Internet, such "public meetings" are best implemented using a multicast socket that sends a copy of the data to a location (or a group of locations) close to the parties that have declared an interest in the data. In the best case, the data is duplicated only when it reaches the local network serving the interested clients: the data crosses the Internet only once. More realistically, several identical copies of the data traverse the Internet; but, by carefully choosing the points at which the streams are duplicated, the load on the network is minimized. The good news is that programmers and network administrators aren't responsible for choosing the points where the data is duplicated or even for sending multiple copies; the Internet's routers handle all that.

IP supports broadcasting, but the use of broadcasts is strictly limited. Protocols require broadcasts only when there is no alternative, and routers limit broadcasts to the local network or subnet, preventing broadcasts from reaching the Internet at large. Even a few small global broadcasts could bring the Internet to its knees. Broadcasting high-bandwidth data such as audio, video, or even text and still images is out of the question. A single email spam that goes to 6 million addresses is bad enough. Imagine what would happen if a real-time video feed were copied to six million Internet users, whether they wanted to watch it or not.

However, there's a middle ground between point-to-point communications and broadcasts to the whole world. There's no reason to send a video feed to hosts that aren't interested in it; we need a technology that lets us send data to the hosts that want it, without bothering the rest of the world. One way to do this is to use many unicast streams. If 1,000 clients want to listen to a RealAudio broadcast, the data is sent a thousand times. This is inefficient, since it duplicates data needlessly, but it's orders-of-magnitude more efficient than broadcasting the data to every host on the Internet. Still, if the number of interested clients is large enough, you will eventually run out of bandwidth or CPU power—probably sooner rather than later.

Another approach to the problem is to create static *connection trees*. This is the solution used by Usenet news and some conferencing systems (notably CU-SeeMe). Data is fed from the originating site to other servers, which replicate it to still other servers, which eventually replicate it to clients. Each client connects to the nearest server. This is more efficient than sending everything to all interested clients via multiple unicasts, but the scheme is kludgy and beginning to show its age. New sites need to find a place to hook into the tree manually; the tree does not necessarily reflect the best possible topology at any one time; and servers still need to maintain many point-to-point connections to their clients, sending the same data to each one. It would be better to allow the routers in the Internet to dynamically determine the best possible routes for transmitting distributed information and to replicate data only when absolutely necessary. This is where multicasting comes in.

For example, if you're multicasting video in New York, and 20 people attached to one LAN are watching you in Los Angeles, your show will be sent to that LAN only once. If 50 more people are watching in San Francisco, the data stream will be duplicated somewhere (let's say Fresno) and sent to the two cities. If a hundred more people are watching in Houston, another data stream will be sent there (perhaps from St. Louis); see Figure 14-1. Your data has crossed the Internet only three times—not the 170 times required by point-to-point connections, or the millions of times required by a true broadcast. Multicasting is halfway between the point-to-point communication common to the Internet and the broadcast model of television—but it's more efficient than either. When a packet is multicast, it is addressed to a multicast group and sent to each host belonging to the group. It does not go to a single host (as in unicasting), nor does it go to every host (as in broadcasting). Either would be too inefficient.

When people start talking about multicasting, audio and video are the first applications that come to mind; however, they are only the tip of the iceberg. Other possibilities include multiplayer games, distributed filesystems, massively parallel computing, multiperson conferencing, database replication, and more. Usenet news could be sent more efficiently via multicasting. Multicasting can be used to implement name services and directory services that don't require the client to know a server's address in advance; to look up a name, a host could multicast its request to some well-known address, and wait until a response was received from the nearest server.

Multicasting should also make it easier to implement various kinds of caching for the Internet, which will be important if the Net's population continues to grow

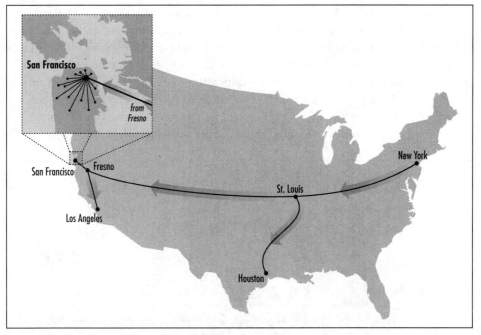

Figure 14-1. Multicast from New York to San Francisco, Los Angeles, and Houston

faster than available bandwidth. Martin Hamilton has proposed using multicasting to build a distributed server system for the World Wide Web.* For example, a high-traffic web server could be split across multiple machines, all of which share a single hostname, mapped to a multicast address. Suppose one machine chunks out HTML files, another handles images, and a third processes CGI requests. When a client makes a request to the multicast address, that request is sent to each of the three servers. When each server receives the request, it looks to see whether the client wants an HTML file, an image, or CGI processing. If the server can handle the request, it responds. Otherwise, the server ignores the request and lets the other servers process it. It is easy to imagine more complex divisions of labor between distributed servers.

Multicasting has been designed to fit into the Internet as seamlessly as possible. Most of the work is done by routers and should be transparent to application programmers. An application simply sends datagram packets to a multicast address, which isn't fundamentally different from any other IP address. The routers make sure that the packet is delivered to all the hosts in the multicast group. The biggest problem is that multicast routers are not yet ubiquitous; therefore, you need

---

* Martin Hamilton, "Evaluating Resource Discovery Applications of IP Multicast", *http://gizmo.lut.ac.uk/ ~martin/eval/eval.html*, 1995.

to know enough about them to find out whether multicasting is supported on your network. As far as the application itself, you need to pay attention to an additional header field in the datagrams called the Time-To-Live (TTL) value. The TTL is the maximum number of routers that the datagram is allowed to cross; when it reaches the maximum, it is discarded. Multicasting uses the TTL as an ad hoc way to limit how far a packet can travel. For example, you don't want packets for a friendly on-campus game of Dogfight reaching routers on the other side of the world. Figure 14-2 shows how TTLs limit a packet's spread.

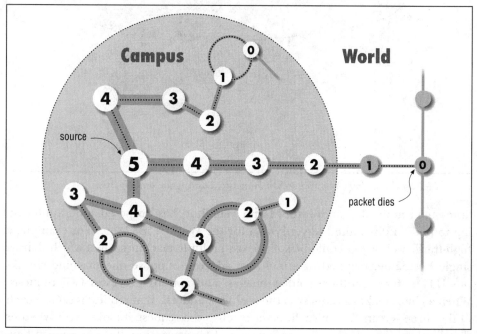

Figure 14-2. Coverage of a packet with a TTL of 5

Multicast Addresses and Groups

A multicast address is the address of a group of hosts called a multicast group. We'll talk about the address first. Multicast addresses are IP addresses in the range 224.0.0.0 to 239.255.255.255. All the addresses in this range have the binary digits 1110 as their first four bits. They are called Class D addresses to distinguish them from the more common Class A, B, and C addresses.* Like any IP address, a multicast address can have a hostname; for example, the multicast address 224.0.1.1 (the address of the Network Time Protocol distributed service) is assigned the name *ntp.mcast.net.*

---

* Addresses starting with 11110 are called Class E addresses; currently, they're unused and reserved for future experimentation.

A multicast group is a set of Internet hosts that share a multicast address. Any data sent to the multicast address is relayed to all the members of the group. Membership in a multicast group is open; hosts can enter or leave the group at any time. Groups can be either permanent or transient. Permanent groups have assigned addresses that remain constant, whether or not there are any members in the group. However, most multicast groups are transient and exist only as long as they have members. All you have to do to create a new multicast group is pick a random address from 225.0.0.0 to 238.255.255.255, construct an `InetAddress` object for that address, and start sending it data.

A number of multicast addresses have been set aside for special purposes. *all-systems.mcast.net*, 224.0.0.1, is a multicast group that includes all systems that support multicasting on the local subnet. This group is commonly used for local testing, as is *experiment.mcast.net*, 224.0.1.20. (There is no multicast address that sends data to all hosts on the Internet.) All addresses beginning with 224.0.0 (i.e., addresses from 224.0.0.0 to 224.0.0.255) are reserved for routing protocols and other low-level activities, such as gateway discovery and group membership reporting. Multicast routers never forward datagrams with destinations in this range.

The IANA is responsible for handing out permanent multicast addresses as needed; so far, about 10,000 have been assigned. Most of these begin with 224.0., 224.1., 224.2., or 239. Table 14-1 lists a few of these permanent addresses. The complete list is available from *ftp://ftp.isi.edu/in-notes/iana/assignments/multicast-addresses*. The remaining 248 million Class D addresses can be used on a temporary basis by anyone who needs them. Multicast routers (*mrouters* for short) are responsible for making sure that two different systems don't try to use the same Class D address at the same time.

Table 14-1. Common Permanent Multicast Addresses

Domain Name	IP Address	Purpose
BASE-ADDRESS.MCAST.NET	224.0.0.0	The reserved base address. This is never assigned to any multicast group.
ALL-SYSTEMS.MCAST.NET	224.0.0.1	All systems on the local subnet.
ALL-ROUTERS.MCAST.NET	224.0.0.2	All routers on the local subnet.
DVMRP.MCAST.NET	224.0.0.4	All Distance Vector Multicast Routing Protocol (DVMRP) routers on this subnet. An early version of the DVMRP protocol is documented in RFC 1075; the current version has changed substantially.
MOBILE-AGENTS.MCAST. NET	224.0.0.11	Mobile agents on the local subnet.

Table 14-1. Common Permanent Multicast Addresses (continued)

Domain Name	IP Address	Purpose
DHCP-AGENTS.MCAST.NET	224.0.0.12	This multicast group allows a client to locate a Dynamic Host Configuration Protocol (DHCP) server or relay agent on the local subnet.
PIM-ROUTERS.MCAST.NET	224.0.0.13	All Protocol Independent Multicasting (PIM) routers on this subnet.
RSVP-ENCAPSULATION. MCAST.NET	224.0.0.14	RSVP encapsulation on this subnet. RSVP stands for Resource reSerVation setup Protocol, an effort to allow people to reserve a guaranteed amount of Internet bandwidth in advance for an event.
NTP.MCAST.NET	224.0.1.1	The Network Time Protocol.
SGI-DOG.MCAST.NET	224.0.1.2	Silicon Graphics Dogfight game.
NSS.MCAST.NET	224.0.1.6	The Name Service Server.
AUDIONEWS.MCAST.NET	224.0.1.7	Audio news multicast.
SUB-NIS.MCAST.NET	224.0.1.8	Sun's NIS+ Information Service.
MTP.MCAST.NET	224.0.1.9	The Multicast Transport Protocol.
IETF-1-LOW-AUDIO.MCAST. NET	224.0.1.10	Channel 1 of low-quality audio from IETF meetings.
IETF-1- AUDIO.MCAST.NET	224.0.1.11	Channel 1 of high-quality audio from IETF meetings.
IETF-1-VIDEO.MCAST.NET	224.0.1.12	Channel 1 of video from IETF meetings.
IETF-2-LOW-AUDIO.MCAST. NET	224.0.1.13	Channel 2 of low-quality audio from IETF meetings.
IETF-2-AUDIO.MCAST.NET	224.0.1.14	Channel 2 of high-quality audio from IETF meetings.
IETF-2-VIDEO.MCAST.NET	224.0.1.15	Channel 2 of video from IETF meetings.
MUSIC-SERVICE.MCAST.NET	224.0.1.16	Music service.
SEANET-TELEMETRY. MCAST.NET	224.0.1.17	Telemetry data for the U.S. Navy's Sea-Net Project to extend the Internet to vessels at sea. See *http://web.nps.navy.mil/*.
SEANET-IMAGE.MCAST.NET	224.0.1.18	SeaNet images.
MLOADD.MCAST.NET	224.0.1.19	MLOADD measures the traffic load through one or more network interfaces over a number of seconds. Multicasting is used to communicate between the different interfaces being measured.
EXPERIMENT.MCAST.NET	224.0.1.20	Experiments that do not go beyond the local subnet.
XINGTV.MCAST.NET	224.0.1.23	XING Technology's Streamworks TV multicast.

Table 14-1. Common Permanent Multicast Addresses (continued)

Domain Name	IP Address	Purpose
MICROSOFT.MCAST.NET	224.0.1.24	Used by Windows Internet Name Service (WINS) servers to locate one another.
MTRACE.MCAST.NET	224.0.1.32	A multicast version of traceroute.
	224.2.0.0-224.2.255.255	The Multicast Backbone on the Internet (MBONE) addresses are reserved for multimedia conference calls, i.e., audio, video, whiteboard, and shared web browsing between many people.
	224.2.2.2	Port 9,875 on this address is used to broadcast the currently available MBONE programming. You can look at this with the X Window utility sdr or the Windows/Unix multikit program.
	239.0.0.0-239.255.255.255	Administrative scope, in contrast to TTL scope, uses different ranges of multicast addresses to constrain multicast traffic to a particular region or group of routers. For example, the IP addresses from 239.178.0 to 239.178.255 might be an administrative scope for the state of New York. Data addressed to one of those addresses would not be forwarded outside of New York. The idea is to allow the possible group membership to be established in advance without relying on less-than-reliable TTL values. The exact divisions of this range into particular scopes remains to be defined.

Although the original IP multicast RFC dates back to 1985, practical IP multicasting is still new and uncommon enough that permanent multicast addresses are assigned manually by the IANA. Manual assignment will certainly break down as IP multicasting becomes more popular. Some automated system for the assignment and allocation of multicast addresses is probably inevitable.

The MBONE (or Multicast Backbone on the Internet) is the range of Class D addresses beginning with 224.2. that are used for audio and video broadcasts over the Internet. The word MBONE is sometimes used less restrictively (and less accurately) to mean the portion of the Internet that understands how to route Class D–addressed packets.

Clients and Servers

When a host wants to send data to a multicast group, it puts that data in multicast datagrams, which are nothing more than UDP datagrams addressed to a multicast group. Most multicast data is either audio or video, or both. These sorts of data tend to be relatively large and relatively robust against data loss. If a few pixels or even a whole frame of video is lost in transit, the signal isn't blurred beyond recognition. Therefore, multicast data is sent via UDP, which, though unreliable, can be as much as three times faster than data sent via connection-oriented TCP.* If you're developing a multicast application that can't tolerate data loss, it's your responsibility to determine whether data was damaged in transit, and how to handle the missing data. For example, if you are building a distributed cache system, you might simply decide to leave any files that don't arrive intact out of the cache.

Earlier, I said that from an application programmer's standpoint, the primary difference between multicasting and using regular UDP sockets is that you have to worry about the TTL value. This is a single byte in the IP header that takes values from 0 to 255; it is interpreted roughly as the number of routers through which a packet can pass before it is discarded. Each time the packet passes through a router, its TTL field is decremented by at least one; some routers may decrement the TTL by two or more. When the TTL reaches zero, the packet is discarded. The TTL field was originally designed to prevent routing loops by guaranteeing that all packets would eventually be discarded; it prevents misconfigured routers from sending packets back and forth to each other indefinitely. In IP multicasting, the TTL is used to limit the multicast geographically. For example, a TTL value of 16 limits the packet to the local area, generally one organization or perhaps an organization and its immediate upstream and downstream neighbors. A TTL of 127, however, sends the packet around the world. Intermediate values are also possible. However, there is no precise way to map TTLs to geographical distance. Generally, the farther away a site is, the more routers a packet has to pass through before reaching it. Therefore, packets with small TTL values won't travel as far as packets with large TTL values. Table 14-2 provides some rough estimates relating TTL values to geographical reach. Packets addressed to a multicast group from 224.0.0.0 to 224.0.0.255 are never forwarded beyond the local subnet, regardless of the TTL values used.

Table 14-2. Estimated TTL Values for Datagrams Originating in the Continental United States

Destinations	TTL Value to Use
The local host	0
The local subnet	1
The local campus—that is, the same side of the nearest Internet router—but on possibly different LANs	16

---

* If you think about it, multicast over TCP would be next to impossible. TCP requires hosts to acknowledge that they have received packets; handling acknowledgements in a multicast situation would be a nightmare.

Table 14-2. Estimated TTL Values for Datagrams Originating in the Continental United States

Destinations	TTL Value to Use
High-bandwidth sites in the United States, generally those fairly close to the backbone	32
The United States	48
North America	64
High-bandwidth sites worldwide	128
All sites worldwide	255

Once the data has been stuffed into one or more datagrams, the sending host launches the datagrams onto the Internet. This is just like sending regular (unicast) UDP data. The sending host begins by transmitting a multicast datagram to the local network. This packet immediately reaches all members of the multicast group in the same subnet. If the Time-To-Live field of the packet is greater than 1, any multicast routers on the local network forward the packet to any other networks that have members of the destination group. When the packet arrives at one of the final destinations, the multicast router on the foreign network transmits the packet to each host it serves that is a member of the multicast group. If necessary, the multicast router also retransmits the packet to the next routers in the paths between the current router and all its eventual destinations.

When data arrives at a host in a multicast group, the host receives it as it receives any other UDP datagram—even though the packet's destination address doesn't match the receiving host. The host recognizes that the datagram is intended for it because it belongs to the multicast group to which the datagram is addressed, much as most of us accept mail addressed to "Occupant", even though none of us are named Mr. or Ms. Occupant. The receiving host must be listening on the proper port and be ready to process the datagram when it arrives.

Routers and Routing

Figure 14-3 shows one of the simplest possible multicast configurations: a single server sending the same data to four clients served by the same router. A multicast socket sends one stream of data over the Internet to the clients' router; the router duplicates the stream and sends it to each of the clients. Without multicast sockets, the server would have to send four separate but identical streams of data to the router, which would route each stream to a client. Using the same stream to send the same data to multiple clients significantly reduces the bandwidth required on the Internet backbone. This moves video and audio on the Internet from something completely impossible to something that is marginally possible, as long as too many people don't try it at the same time. Furthermore, some local network technologies may let the router multicast the data to its clients, reducing the bandwidth required on the LAN.

Of course, real-world routes can be much more complex, involving multiple hierarchies of redundant routers. However, the goal of multicast sockets is simple: no matter how complex the network, the same data should never be sent more than once over any given network segment. Fortunately, you don't need to worry about routing issues. Just create a `MulticastSocket`, have the socket join a multicast group, and stuff the address of the multicast group in the `DatagramPacket` you want to send. The routers and the `MulticastSocket` class take care of the rest.

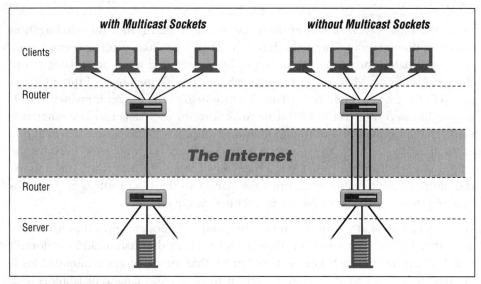

Figure 14-3. With and Without Multicast Sockets

The biggest restriction on multicasting is the availability of special multicast routers (mrouters). Mrouters are reconfigured Internet routers or workstations that support the IP multicast extensions. Many consumer-oriented ISPs quite deliberately do not enable multicasting in their routers. In the year 2000, it is still possible to find hosts between which no multicast route exists (i.e., there is no route between the hosts that travels exclusively over mrouters). This situation is being remedied rapidly, especially in the United States and western Europe. However, it is often the case that a more efficient route would be possible if more multicast routers were available.

Before you can use multicasting, you must be using an operating system, network interface card, and network router that provide multicast support. Most major current Unixes support multicasting. The only notable exceptions are the increasingly obsolete SunOS 4.1 (and earlier), and Digital Ultrix. Both require special patches to the kernel for multicasting. Multicasting is supported in the built-in TCP stack of Microsoft Windows 95, 98, and NT. On Macs, multicasting is supported by OpenTransport but not by MacTCP.

To send and receive multicast data beyond the local subnet, you need a multicast router. Check with your network administrator to see whether your routers support multicasting. You can also try pinging *all-routers.mcast.net*. If any router responds, then your network is hooked up to a multicast router:

```
% ping all-routers.mcast.net
all-routers.mcast.net is alive
```

This still may not allow you to send to or receive from every multicast-capable host on the Internet. For your packets to reach any given host, there must be a path of multicast capable routers between your host and the remote host. Alternately, some sites may be connected by special multicast tunnel software that transmits multicast data over unicast UDP that all routers understand. If you have trouble getting the examples in this chapter to produce the expected results, check with your local network administrator or ISP to see whether multicasting is actually supported by your routers.

Working with Multicast Sockets

Enough theory. In Java, you multicast data using the java.net. MulticastSocket class. This is a subclass of java.net.DatagramSocket:

```
public class MulticastSocket extends DatagramSocket
```

As you would expect, MulticastSocket's behavior is very similar to DatagramSocket's: you put your data in DatagramPacket objects that you send and receive with the MulticastSocket. Therefore, I won't repeat the basics; this discussion assumes that you already know how to work with datagrams. However, if you're jumping around in this book rather than reading it cover to cover, now might be a good time to go back and read the previous chapter on UDP.

To receive data that is being multicast from a remote site, you first create a MulticastSocket with the MulticastSocket() constructor. Next, you join a multicast group using the MulticastSocket's joinGroup() method. This signals the routers in the path between you and the server to start sending data your way and tells the local host that it should pass you IP packets addressed to the multicast group.

Once you've joined the multicast group, you receive UDP data just as you would with a DatagramSocket. That is, you create a DatagramPacket with a byte array that serves as a buffer for data, and enter a loop in which you receive the data by calling the receive() method inherited from the DatagramSocket class. When you no longer want to receive data, you leave the multicast group by invoking the socket's leaveGroup() method. You can then close the socket with the close() method inherited from DatagramSocket.

Sending data to a multicast address is similar to sending UDP data to a unicast address. You do not need to join a multicast group to send data to it. You create a new DatagramPacket, stuff the data and the address of the multicast group into the packet, and pass it to the send() method. The one difference is that you must explicitly specify the packet's TTL value.

There is one caveat to all this: multicast sockets are a security hole big enough to drive a small truck through. Consequently, untrusted applets are not allowed to do anything involving multicast sockets. An untrusted applet is allowed to send datagrams to or receive datagrams from the applet host. However, multicast sockets don't allow this sort of restriction to be placed on the packets they send or receive. Once you send data to a multicast socket, you have very limited and unreliable control over which hosts do and do not receive that data. Consequently, most applet environments take the conservative approach of disallowing all multicasting.

The Constructors

The constructors are simple. Each one calls the equivalent constructor in the DatagramSocket superclass.

public MulticastSocket( ) throws SocketException

This constructor creates a socket that is bound to an anonymous port (i.e., an unused port assigned by the system). It is useful for clients (i.e., programs that initiate a data transfer), because they don't need to use a well-known port: the recipient replies to the port contained in the packet. If you need to know the port number, you can find out with the getLocalPort() method inherited from DatagramSocket. This constructor throws a SocketException if the Socket can't be created. For example:

```
try {
  MulticastSocket ms = new MulticastSocket();
  // send some datagrams...
}
catch (SocketException se) {
  System.err.println(se);
}
```

public MulticastSocket(int port) throws SocketException

This constructor creates a socket that receives datagrams on a well-known port. The port argument specifies the port on which this socket listens for datagrams. As with regular TCP and UDP unicast sockets, on a Unix system a program needs to be run with root privileges to create a MulticastSocket on a port numbered from 1 to 1,023.

This constructor throws a `SocketException` if the `Socket` can't be created. A `Socket` can't be created if you don't have sufficient privileges to bind to the port, or that the port you're trying to connect to is already occupied. Note that since, as far as the operating system is concerned, a multicast socket is a datagram socket, a `MulticastSocket` cannot occupy a port already occupied by a `DatagramSocket`, and vice versa. For example, this code fragment opens a multicast socket on port 4,000:

```
try {
  MulticastSocket ms = new MulticastSocket(4000);
  // receive incoming datagrams...
}
catch (SocketException se) {
  System.err.println(se);
}
```

Communicating with a Multicast Group

Once a `MulticastSocket` has been created, it can perform four key operations. These are:

1. Join a multicast group.
2. Send data to the members of the group.
3. Receive data from the group.
4. Leave the multicast group.

The `MulticastSocket` class has methods for operations 1, 2, and 4. No new method is required to receive data. The `receive()` method of the superclass, `DatagramSocket`, is all that's needed for receiving. You can perform these operations in any order, with the exception that you must join a group before you can receive data from it (or, for that matter, leave it). You do not need to join a group to send data to it, and the sending and receiving of data may be freely interwoven.

public void joinGroup(InetAddress address) throws IOException

To receive data from a `MulticastSocket`, you must first join a multicast group. To join a group, pass an `InetAddress` object for the multicast group to the `joinGroup()` method. If you successfully join the group, you'll receive any datagrams intended for that group. Once you've joined a multicast group, you receive datagrams exactly as you receive unicast datagrams, as shown in the previous chapter. That is, you set up a `DatagramPacket` as a buffer and pass it into this socket's `receive()` method. For example:

```
try {
  MulticastSocket ms = new MulticastSocket(4000);
```

```
    InetAddress ia = InetAddress.getByName("224.2.2.2");
    ms.joinGroup(ia);
    byte[] buffer = new byte[8192];
    while (true) {
      DatagramPacket dp = new DatagramPacket(buffer, buffer.length);
      ms.receive(dp);
      String s = new String(dp.getData(), "8859_1");
      System.out.println(s);
    }
  }
}
catch (IOException ie) {
  System.err.println(ie);
}
```

If the address that you try to join is not a multicast address (that is, it is not from 224.0.0.0 to 239.255.255.255), the `joinGroup()` method throws an `IOException`.

A single `MulticastSocket` can join multiple multicast groups. Information about membership in multicast groups is stored in multicast routers, not in the object. In this case, you'd use the address stored in the incoming datagram to determine which address a packet was intended for.

Multiple multicast sockets on the same machine and even in the same Java program can all join the same group. If so, they'll all receive all data addressed to that group that arrives at the local host.

public void leaveGroup(InetAddress address) throws IOException

The `leaveGroup()` method signals that you no longer want to receive datagrams from the specified multicast group. A signal is sent to the appropriate multicast router telling it to stop sending you datagrams. If the address you try to leave is not a multicast address (that is, it is not from 224.0.0.0 to 239.255.255.255), the method throws an `IOException`. However, no exception occurs if you leave a multicast group you never joined.

public void send(DatagramPacket packet, byte ttl) throws IOException

Sending data with a `MulticastSocket` is similar to sending data with a `DatagramSocket`. Stuff your data into a `DatagramPacket` object and send it off using the `send()` method inherited from `DatagramSocket`:

```
public void send(DatagramPacket p) throws IOException
```

The data is sent to every host that belongs to the multicast group to which your packet is addressed. For example:

```
try {
   InetAddress ia = InetAddress.getByName("experiment.mcast.net");
   byte[] data = "Here's some multicast data\r\n".getBytes();
   int port = 4000;
   DatagramPacket dp = new DatagramPacket(data, data.length, ia, port);
   MulticastSocket ms = new MulticastSocket();
   ms.send(dp);
}
catch (IOException ie) {
   System.err.println(ie);
}
```

However, the `MulticastSocket` class adds an overloaded variant of the `send()` method that lets you provide a value for the Time-To-Live field `ttl`. By default, the `send()` method uses a TTL of 1; that is, packets don't travel outside the local subnet. However, you can change this for an individual packet by passing an integer from 0 to 255 as the second argument to the `send()` method. For   example:

```
DatagramPacket dp = new DatagramPacket(data, data.length, ia, port);
MulticastSocket ms = new MulticastSocket();
ms.send(dp, 64);
```

public void setInterface(InetAddress address) throws SocketException

On a multihomed host, the `setInterface()` method chooses the network interface used for multicast sending and receiving. `setInterface()` throws a `SocketException` if the `InetAddress` you give it is not the address of a network interface on the local machine. It is unclear why the network interface is immutably set in the constructor for unicast `Socket` and `DatagramSocket` objects but is variable and set with a separate method for `MulticastSocket` objects. To be safe, you should set the interface immediately after constructing a `MulticastSocket` and not change it thereafter. Here's how you might use `setInterface()`:

```
MulticastSocket ms;
InetAddress ia;
try {
   ia = new InetAddress("metalab.unc.edu");
   ms = new MulticastSocket(2048);
   ms.setInterface(ia);
   // send and receive data...
}
catch (UnknownHostException ue) {
   System.err.println(ue);
}
```

```
      catch (SocketException se) {
        System.err.println(se);
      }
```

public InetAddress getInterface( ) throws SocketException

If you need to know the address of the interface you're using, you can call getInterface(). It isn't clear why this method would throw an exception; in any case, you must be prepared for it. For example:

```
      try {
        MulticastSocket ms = new MulticastSocket(2048);
        InetAddress ia = ms.getInterface();
      }
      catch (SocketException se) {
        System.err.println(ue);
      }
```

public void setTimeToLive(int ttl) throws IOException   // Java 1.2

The setTimeToLive() method sets the default TTL value used for packets sent from the socket using the send(Datagrampacket dp) method inherited from DatagramSocket (as opposed to the send(Datagrampacket dp, byte ttl) method in MulticastSocket). This method is available only in Java 1.2 and later. In Java 1.1, you have to use the setTTL() method instead:

```
      public void setTTL(byte ttl) throws IOException
```

The setTTL() method is deprecated in Java 2 and later because it allows you only to set TTL values from 1 to 127 rather than the full range from 1 to 255.

public int getTimeToLive( ) throws IOException   // Java 1.2

The getTimeToLive() method returns the default TTL value of the MulticastSocket. It's not needed very much. This method is also available only in Java 1.2 and later. In Java 1.1, you have to use the getTTL() method instead:

```
      public byte getTTL() throws IOException
```

The getTTL() method is deprecated in Java 1.2 and later because it doesn't properly handle TTLs greater than 127. It truncates these to 127. The getTimeToLive() method can handle the full range from 1 to 255 without truncation because it returns an int instead of a byte.

Two Simple Examples

Most multicast servers are indiscriminate about who they will talk to. Therefore, it's easy to join a group—and watch the data that's being sent to it. Example 14-1 is a `MulticastSniffer` class that reads the name of a multicast group from the command-line, constructs an `InetAddress` from that hostname, and then creates a `MulticastSocket`, which attempts to join the multicast group at that hostname. If the attempt succeeds, it receives datagrams from the socket and prints their contents on `System.out`. This program is useful primarily to verify that you are receiving multicast data at a particular host. Most multicast data is binary and won't be intelligible when printed as ASCII.

Example 14-1. Multicast Sniffer

```java
import java.net.*;
import java.io.*;

public class MulticastSniffer {

  public static void main(String[] args) {

    InetAddress group = null;
    int port = 0;

    // read the address from the command line
    try {
      group = InetAddress.getByName(args[0]);
      port = Integer.parseInt(args[1]);
    } // end try
    catch (Exception e) {
      // ArrayIndexOutOfBoundsException, NumberFormatException,
      // or UnknownHostException
      System.err.println(
        "Usage: java MulticastSniffer multicast_address port");
      System.exit(1);
    }

    MulticastSocket ms = null;

    try {
      ms = new MulticastSocket(port);
      ms.joinGroup(group);

      byte[] buffer = new byte[8192];
      while (true) {
        DatagramPacket dp = new DatagramPacket(buffer, buffer.length);
        ms.receive(dp);
        String s = new String(dp.getData());
        System.out.println(s);
      }
    }
    catch (IOException e) {
```

Example 14-1. Multicast Sniffer (continued)

```
      System.err.println(e);
   }
   finally {
     if (ms != null) {
       try {
         ms.leaveGroup(group);
         ms.close();
       }
       catch (IOException e) {}
     }
   }


  }


}
```

The program begins by reading the name and port of the multicast group from the first command-line argument. Next, we create a new `MulticastSocket ms` on the specified port. This socket joins the multicast group at the specified `InetAddress`. Then it enters a loop in which it waits for packets to arrive. As each packet arrives, the program reads its data, converts the data to an ISO Latin-1 `String`, and prints it on `System.out`. Finally, when the user interrupts the program or an exception is thrown, the socket leaves the group and closes itself.

MBONE session announcements are broadcast to the multicast group *sap.mcast.net* on port 9,875. You can use this program to listen to those announcements. Generally, if you're connected to the MBONE (not all sites are), then you should see a site announcement pop through within the first minute or two. In fact, you'll probably see a lot more. I collected about a megabyte and a half of announcements within the first couple of minutes I had this program running. I show only the first two here:

```
% java MulticastSniffer sap.mcast.net 9875
úv=0
o=ellery 3132060082 3138107776 IN IP4 131.182.10.250
s=NASA TV - Broadcast from NASA HQ
i=NASA TV Multicasting from NASA HQ
u=http://www.nasa.gov/ntv
e=Ellery.Coleman@hq.nasa.gov      (Ellery D. Coleman)
p=+202 651 8512
t=3138107776 3153918976
r=15811200 15811200 0
a=recvonly
a=tool:FVC.COM I-Caster V3.1/3101, Windows95/NT
a=cat:Corporate/Events
m=audio 23748 RTP/AVP 0
```

```
c=IN IP4 224.2.203.38/127
m=video 60068 RTP/AVP 31
c=IN IP4 224.2.203.37/127
b=AS:380
a=framerate:9
a=quality:8
a=grayed:0
4 224.2.255.115/15
.77/25
4 RTP wbbesteffort
c=IN IP4 224.2.224.41/25


%Â¡_v=0
o=dax 3137417804 3141052115 IN IP4 horla.enst.fr
s=VREng UDP (Virtual Reality Engine)
i=Virtual Reality Engine: Distributed Interactive 3D Multicast
navigator in Virtual Worlds. For more information and downloading, see
URL: http://www.infres.enst.fr/net/vreng/.
u=http://www.infres.enst.fr/net/vreng/
e=Philippe Dax (ENST) <dax@inf.enst.fr>
p=Philippe Dax (ENST) +33 (0) 145817648
t=0 0
a=tool:sdr v2.9
a=type:test
m=dis 62239 RTP 99
c=IN IP4 224.2.199.133/127
/3
m=mdesk 64538 RTP/AVP mdesk
c=IN IP4 224.2.160.68/3
e please stop your receiving programs and the stream should stop from
coming to you.
u=http://tv.funet.fi/ohjelmat/index.html
e=Harri Salminen <mice-nsc@nic.funet.fi>
p=Harri Salminen +358 400 358 502
t=3085239600 3299658800
a=tool:CDT mAnnouncer 1.1.2
a=type:broadcast
m=audio 4004 RTP/AVP 0
c=IN IP4 239.239.239.239/40
a=ptime:40
m=video 6006 RTP/AVP 31
c=IN IP4 239.239.239.239/40
m=whiteboard 4206 udp wb
c=IN IP4 224.239.239.245/48
```

MBONE session announcements are not pure ASCII text. In particular, they contain a lot of embedded nulls as well as various characters with their high bit set. Consequently, I've had to take a few liberties with the output to print it in this book. To really handle MBONE session announcements, you'd have to parse the relevant ASCII text out of the binary format and display that. Peter Parnes has written a Java program called mSD that does exactly that. If you're interested, you can find it at *http://www.cdt.luth.se/~peppar/progs/mSD/*. However, since this is a book about network programming and not parsing binary file formats, we'll leave our example here and move on to sending multicast data. Example 14-2 is a `MulticastSender` class that sends data read from the command-line to a multicast group. It is fairly simple overall.

Example 14-2. MulticastSender

```
import java.net.*;
import java.io.*;


public class MulticastSender {

  public static void main(String[] args) {

    InetAddress ia = null;
    int port = 0;
    byte ttl = (byte) 1;

    // read the address from the command line
    try {
      ia = InetAddress.getByName(args[0]);
      port = Integer.parseInt(args[1]);
      if (args.length > 2) ttl = (byte) Integer.parseInt(args[2]);
    }
    catch (Exception e)  {
      System.err.println(e);
      System.err.println(
        "Usage: java MulticastSender multicast_address port ttl");
      System.exit(1);
    }

    byte[] data = "Here's some multicast data\r\n".getBytes();
    DatagramPacket dp = new DatagramPacket(data, data.length, ia, port);

    try {
      MulticastSocket ms = new MulticastSocket();
      ms.joinGroup(ia);
      for (int i = 1; i < 10; i++) {
        ms.send(dp, ttl);
      }
      ms.leaveGroup(ia);
      ms.close();
    }
    catch (SocketException se) {
```

Example 14-2. MulticastSender (continued)

```
    System.err.println(se);
  }
  catch (IOException ie) {
    System.err.println(ie);
  }


  }

}
```

Example 14-2 reads the address of a multicast group, a port number, and an optional TTL from the command line. It then stuffs the string `"Here's some multicast data\r\n"` into the byte array `data` using the `getBytes()` method of `java.lang.String`, and places this array in the `DatagramPacket` `dp`. Next, it constructs the `MulticastSocket` `ms`, which joins the group `ia`. Once it has joined the group, `ms` sends the datagram packet `dp` to the group `ia` 10 times. The TTL value is set to one to make sure that this data doesn't go beyond the local subnet. Having sent the data, `ms` leaves the group and closes itself.

Run `MulticastSniffer` on one machine in your local subnet. Listen to the group *all-systems.mcast.net* on port 4,000 like this:

```
% java MulticastSniffer all-systems.mcast.net 4000
```

Then send data to that group by running `MulticastSender` on another machine in your local subnet. You can also run it in a different window on the same machine, though that's not as exciting. However, you must start running the `MulticastSniffer` before you start running the `MulticastSender`. Send to the group *all-systems.mcast.net* on port 4,000 like this:

```
% java MulticastSender all-systems.mcast.net 4000
```

Back on the first machine you should see this output:

```
Here's some multicast data
Here's some multicast data
Here's some multicast data
Here's some multicast data
Here's some multicast data
Here's some multicast data
Here's some multicast data
Here's some multicast data
Here's some multicast data
```

For this to work beyond the local subnet, the two subnets will each have to have multicast routers.

15

The URLConnection Class

URLConnection is an abstract class that represents an active connection to a resource specified by a URL. The URLConnection class has two different but related purposes. First, it provides more control over the interaction with a server than the URL class. With a URLConnection, you can inspect the MIME headers sent by an HTTP server and respond accordingly. You can adjust the MIME header fields used in the client request. You can use a URLConnection to download binary files. Finally, a URLConnection lets you send data back to a web server with POST or PUT and use other HTTP request methods. We will explore all of these techniques in this chapter.

Second, the URLConnection class is part of Java's *protocol handler* mechanism, which also includes the URLStreamHandler class. The idea behind protocol handlers is simple: they separate the details of processing a protocol from processing particular data types, providing user interfaces, and doing the other work that a monolithic web browser performs. The base java.net.URLConnection class is abstract; to implement a specific protocol, you write a subclass. These subclasses can be loaded at runtime by your own applications or by the HotJava browser; in the future, it may be possible for Java applications to download protocol handlers over the Net as needed, making them automatically extensible. For example, if your browser runs across a URL with a strange prefix, such as *compress:*, rather than throwing up its hands and issuing an error message, it could download a protocol handler for this unknown protocol and use it to communicate with the server. Writing protocol handlers is the subject of the next chapter.

Only abstract `URLConnection` classes are present in the `java.net` package. The concrete subclasses are hidden inside the `sun.net` package hierarchy. Many of the methods and fields as well as the single constructor in the `URLConnection` class are *protected*. In other words, they can be accessed only by instances of the `URLConnection` class or its subclasses. It is rare to instantiate `URLConnection` objects directly in your source code; instead, the runtime environment creates these objects as needed, depending on the protocol in use. The class (which is unknown at compile time) is then instantiated using the `forName()` and `newInstance()` methods of the `java.lang.Class` class.

NOTE   `URLConnection` does not have the best designed API in the Java class library. It's been cleaned up somewhat in Java 1.1 and 1.2, but it's still a lot more confusing than it should be. Since the `URLConnection` class itself relies on the `Socket` class for network connectivity, there's little you can do with `URLConnection` that can't also be done with `Socket`. The `URLConnection` class is supposed to provide an easier-to-use, higher-level abstraction for network connections than `Socket` does. In practice, however, it's so poorly designed that most programmers have chosen to ignore it and simply use the `Socket` class instead. One of several problems is that the `URLConnection` class is too closely tied to the HTTP protocol. For instance, it assumes that each file transferred is preceded by a MIME header or something very much like one. However, most classic protocols such as FTP and SMTP don't use MIME headers. Another problem, one I hope to alleviate in this chapter, is that the `URLConnection` class is extremely poorly documented, so very few programmers understand how it's really supposed to work.

Opening URLConnections

A program that uses the `URLConnection` class directly follows this basic sequence of steps:

1. Construct a `URL` object.

2. Invoke the `URL` object's `openConnection()` method to retrieve a `URLConnection` object for that URL.

3. Configure the `URLConnection`.

4. Read the header fields.

5. Get an input stream and read data.

6. Get an output stream and write data.

7. Close the connection.

You don't always perform all these steps. For instance, if the default setup for a particular kind of URL is acceptable, then you're likely to skip step 3. If you want only the data from the server and don't care about any meta-information, or if the protocol doesn't provide any meta-information, you'll skip step 4. If you want only to receive data from the server but not send data to the server, you'll skip step 6. Depending on the protocol, steps 5 and 6 may be reversed or interlaced.

The single constructor for the URLConnection class is protected:

```
protected URLConnection(URL url)
```

Consequently, unless you're subclassing URLConnection to handle a new kind of URL (that is, writing a protocol handler), you can get a reference to one of these objects only through the openConnection() methods of the URL and URLStreamHandler classes. For example:

```
try {
  URL u = new URL("http://www.greenpeace.org/");
  URLConnection uc = u.openConnection();
}
catch (MalformedURLException e) {
  System.err.println(e);
}
catch (IOException e) {
  System.err.println(e);
}
```

NOTE   In practice, the openConnection() method of java.net.URL is the same as the openConnection() method of java.net. URLStreamHandler. All a URL object's openConnection() method does is call its URLStreamHandler's openConnection() method.

The URLConnection class is declared abstract. However, all but one of its methods are implemented. The single method that subclasses are forced to implement is connect(), which makes a connection to a server and thus depends on the type of service you're implementing (HTTP, FTP, etc.). For example, a sun.net.www. protocol.file.FileURLConnection's connect() method converts the URL to a filename in the appropriate directory, creates MIME information for the file, and then opens a buffered FileInputStream to the file. The connect() method of sun.net.www.protocol.http.HttpURLConnection creates an HttpClient object (from sun.net.www.http.HttpClient), which is responsible for connecting to the server. Of course, you may find it convenient or necessary to override other methods in the class.

```
public abstract void connect() throws IOException
```

When a URLConnection is first constructed, it is unconnected; that is, the local and remote host cannot send and receive data. There is no socket connecting the two hosts. The connect() method establishes a connection—normally using TCP sockets but possibly through some other mechanism—between the local and remote host so that you can send and receive data. However, the getInputStream(), getContent(), getHeaderField(), and other methods that require an open connection will themselves call connect() if the connection isn't yet open. Therefore, you rarely need to call connect() directly.

Reading Data from a Server

The minimal set of steps needed to retrieve data from a URL using a URLConnection object are these:

1. Construct a URL object.
2. Invoke the URL object's openConnection() method to retrieve a URLConnection object for that URL.
3. Invoke the URLConnection's getInputStream() method.
4. Read from the input stream using the usual stream API.

The getInputStream() method returns a generic InputStream, which lets you read and parse the data that the server sends yourself.

```
public InputStream getInputStream()
```

Example 15-1 uses the getInputStream() method to download a web page.

Example 15-1. Download a Web Page with a URLConnection

```
import java.net.*;
import java.io.*;

public class SourceViewer2 {

  public static void main (String[] args) {

    if   (args.length > 0) {
      try {
        //Open the URLConnection for reading
        URL u = new URL(args[0]);
        URLConnection uc = u.openConnection();
        InputStream raw = uc.getInputStream();
        InputStream buffer = new BufferedInputStream(raw);
        // chain the InputStream to a Reader
        Reader r = new InputStreamReader(buffer);
        int c;
        while ((c = r.read()) != -1) {
```

Example 15-1. Download a Web Page with a URLConnection (continued)

```
        System.out.print((char) c);
      }
    }
    catch (MalformedURLException e) {
      System.err.println(args[0] + " is not a parseable URL");
    }
    catch (IOException e) {
      System.err.println(e);
    }

  } // end if

 } // end main

} // end SourceViewer2
```

It is no accident that this program is almost the same as Example 15-5. The openStream() method of the URL class just returns an InputStream from its own URLConnection object. The output is identical as well, so I won't repeat it here.

The differences between URL and URLConnection aren't apparent with just a simple input stream as in this example. The biggest differences between the two classes are:

- URLConnection provides access to the MIME header associated with an HTTP 1.0 response.

- URLConnection lets you configure the request parameters sent to the server.

- URLConnection lets you write data to the server as well as read data from the server.

Reading the Header

HTTP servers provide a substantial amount of information in the MIME headers that precede each response. For example, here's a typical MIME header returned by an Apache web server running on Solaris:

```
HTTP/1.1 200 OK
Date: Mon, 18 Oct 1999 20:06:48 GMT
Server: Apache/1.3.4 (Unix) PHP/3.0.6 mod_perl/1.17
Last-Modified: Mon, 18 Oct 1999 12:58:21 GMT
ETag: "1e05f2-89bb-380b196d"
Accept-Ranges: bytes
Content-Length: 35259
Connection: close
Content-Type: text/html
```

There's a lot of information there. In general, an HTTP MIME header may include the content type of the requested document, the length of the document in bytes, the character set in which the content is encoded, the date and time, the date the content expires, and the date the content was last modified. However, the information sent depends on the server; some servers send all this information for each request, others send some information, and a few don't send anything. The methods of this section allow you to query a URLConnection to find out what MIME information the server has provided.

Aside from HTTP, very few protocols use MIME headers. When writing your own subclass of URLConnection, it is often necessary to override these methods so that they return sensible values. The most important piece of information you may be lacking is the MIME content type. URLConnection provides some utility methods that help you guess the data's content type, based on its filename or (in the worst case) the first few bytes of the data itself.

Retrieving Specific MIME Header Fields

The first six methods request specific, particularly common fields from the MIME header. These are:

- Content-type
- Content-length
- Content-encoding
- Date
- Last-modified
- Expires

public String getContentType( )

This method returns the MIME content type of the data. It relies on the web server to send a proper MIME header, including a valid content type. (In a later section, we'll see how recalcitrant servers are handled.) It throws no exceptions and returns null if the content type isn't available. text/html will be by far the most common content type you'll encounter when connecting to web servers. Other commonly used types include text/plain, image/gif, and image/jpeg.

public int getContentLength( )

This method tells you how many bytes there are in the content. Many servers send Content-length headers only when they're transferring a binary file, not when transferring a text file. If there is no Content-length header, getContentLength( ) returns –1. The method throws no exceptions. It is used when you need to know exactly how many bytes to read or when you need to create a buffer large enough to hold the data in advance.

In Chapter 7, *Retrieving Data with URLs*, you saw how to use the openStream() method of the URL class to download text files from an HTTP server. Although in theory you should be able to use the same method to download a binary file, such as a GIF image or a *.class* byte code file, in practice this procedure presents a problem. HTTP servers don't always close the connection and give you an EOF character exactly where you need it; therefore, you don't know when to stop reading. To download a binary file, it is more reliable to use a URLConnection's getContentLength() method to find the file's length, then read exactly the number of bytes indicated. Example 15-2 is a program that uses this technique to save a binary file on a disk.

Example 15-2. This Program Downloads a Binary File from a Web Site and Saves It to Disk

```
import java.net.*;
import java.io.*;

public class BinarySaver {

  public static void main (String args[]) {

    for (int i = 0; i < args.length; i++) {

      try {
        URL root = new URL(args[i]);
        saveBinaryFile(root);
      }
      catch (MalformedURLException e) {
        System.err.println(args[i] + " is not URL I understand.");
      }
      catch (IOException e) {
        System.err.println(e);
      }
    } // end for

  } // end main


  public static void saveBinaryFile(URL u) throws IOException {

    URLConnection uc = u.openConnection();
    String contentType = uc.getContentType();
    int contentLength = uc.getContentLength();
    if (contentType.startsWith("text/") || contentLength == -1 ) {
      throw new IOException("This is not a binary file.");
    }
```

Example 15-2. This Program Downloads a Binary File from a Web Site and Saves It to Disk (continued)

```
    InputStream raw = uc.getInputStream();
    InputStream in  = new BufferedInputStream(raw);
    byte[] data = new byte[contentLength];
    int bytesRead = 0;
    int offset = 0;
    while (offset < contentLength) {
       bytesRead = in.read(data, offset, data.length-offset);
       if (bytesRead == -1) break;
       offset += bytesRead;
    }
    in.close();

    if (offset != contentLength) {
      throw new IOException("Only read " + offset
       + " bytes; Expected " + contentLength + " bytes");
    }

    String filename = u.getFile();
    filename = filename.substring(filename.lastIndexOf('/') + 1);
    FileOutputStream fout = new FileOutputStream(filename);
    fout.write(data);
    fout.flush();
    fout.close();


  }

} // end BinarySaver
```

As usual, the `main()` method loops over the URLs entered on the command-line, passing each URL to the `saveBinaryFile()` method. `saveBinaryFile()` opens a URLConnection uc to the URL. It puts the type into the variable `contentType` and the content length into the variable `contentLength`. Next, an `if` statement checks whether the MIME type is `text`, or the content-length field is missing or invalid (`contentLength == -1`). If either of these is true, an IOException is thrown. If these assertions are both false, we have a binary file of known length: that's what we want.

Now that we have a genuine binary file on our hands, we prepare to read it into an array of bytes called `data`. `data` is initialized to the number of bytes required to hold the binary object, `contentLength`. Ideally, you would like to fill `data` with a single call to `read()`, but you probably won't get all the bytes at once so the read is placed in a loop. The number of bytes read up to this point is accumulated into the `offset` variable, which also keeps track of the location in the `data` array at which to start placing the data retrieved by the next call to `read()`. The loop continues until `offset` equals or exceeds `contentLength`; that is, the array has been filled with the expected number of bytes. We also break out of the while loop if read() returns –1, indicating an unexpected end of stream. The offset variable now contains the total number of bytes read, which should be equal to the content length. If they are not equal, an error has occurred, so saveBinaryFile() throws an IOException. This is the general procedure for reading binary files from HTTP connections.

Now we are ready to save the data in a file. saveBinaryFile() gets the filename from the URL using the getFile() method and strips any path information by calling filename.substring(theFile.lastIndexOf('/') + 1). A new FileOutputStream fout is opened into this file, and the data is written in one large burst with fout.write(b).

public String getContentEncoding( )

This method returns a String that tells you how the content is encoded. If the content is sent unencoded (as is commonly the case with HTTP servers), then this method returns null. It throws no exceptions. The most commonly used content encoding on the Web is probably x-gzip, which can be straightforwardly decoded using a java.util.zip.GZipInputStream.

When writing your own URLConnection subclass, you need to override this method if you expect to be dealing with encoded data. This might be the case for an NNTP or SMTP protocol handler; in these applications, many different encoding schemes, such as BinHex and uuencode, are used to pass 8-bit binary data through a 7-bit ASCII connection.

public long getDate( )

The getDate() method returns a long that tells you when the document was sent, in milliseconds since midnight, GMT, January 1, 1970. You can convert it to a java.util.Date. For example:

```
Date documentSent = new Date(uc.getDate());
```

This is the time the document was sent as seen from the server; it may not agree with the time on your local machine. If the MIME header does not include a Date header, getDate() returns 0.

public long getExpiration( )

Some documents have server-based expiration dates that indicate when the document should be deleted from the cache and reloaded from the server. getExpiration() is very similar to getDate(), differing only in how the return value is interpreted. It returns a long indicating the number of milliseconds after 12:00 A.M., GMT, January 1, 1970, at which point the document expires. In practice, few servers send expiration dates. If the MIME header does not include an Expiration header, getExpiration() returns 0, which means 12:00 A.M., GMT, January 1, 1970. The only reasonable interpretation of this date is that the document does not need to be expired, and can remain in the cache indefinitely.

public long getLastModified( )

The final date method, getLastModified(), returns the date on which the document was last modified. Again, the date is given as the number of milliseconds since midnight, GMT, January 1, 1970. If the MIME header does not include a Last-modified header (and many don't), this method returns 0.

Example 15-3 reads URLs from the command-line and uses these six methods to print their content type, content length, content encoding, date of last modification, expiration date, and current date.

Example 15-3. Return the MIME Header

```
import java.net.*;
import java.io.*;
import java.util.*;

public class MIMEHeadersViewer {

  public static void main(String args[]) {

    for (int i=0; i < args.length; i++) {
      try {
        URL u = new URL(args[0]);
        URLConnection uc = u.openConnection();
        System.out.println("Content-type: " + uc.getContentType());
        System.out.println("Content-encoding: "
         + uc.getContentEncoding());
        System.out.println("Date: " + new Date(uc.getDate()));
        System.out.println("Last modified: "
         + new Date(uc.getLastModified()));
        System.out.println("Expiration date: "
         + new Date(uc.getExpiration()));
        System.out.println("Content-length: " + uc.getContentLength());
      } // end try
      catch (MalformedURLException e) {
        System.err.println(args[i] + " is not a URL I understand");
      }
      catch (IOException e) {
        System.err.println(e);
      }
      System.out.println();
    } // end for
```

Example 15-3. Return the MIME Header (continued)

```
}   // end main
```

```
}   // end MIMEHeadersViewer
```

Here's the result when used to look at *http://www.oreilly.com*:

```
% java MIMEHeadersViewer http://www.oreilly.com
Content-type: text/html
Content-encoding: null
Date: Mon Oct 18 13:54:52 PDT 1999
Last modified: Sat Oct 16 07:54:02 PDT 1999
Expiration date: Wed Dec 31 16:00:00 PST 1969
Content-length: -1
```

The MIME type of the file at *http://www.oreilly.com* is text/html. No content encoding was used. The file was sent on Monday, October 18, 1999 at 1:54 P.M., Pacific Daylight Time. It was last modified on Saturday, October 16, 1999 at 7:54 A.M. Pacific Daylight Time; and it expires on Wednesday, December 31, 1969 at 4:00 P. M, Pacific Standard Time. Did this document really expire 31 years ago? No. Remember that what's being checked here is whether the copy in your cache is more recent than 4:00 P.M. PST, December 31, 1969. If it is, you don't need to reload it. More to the point, after adjusting for time zone differences, this date looks suspiciously like 12:00 A.M., Greenwich Mean Time, January 1, 1970, which happens to be the default if the server doesn't send an expiration date. (Most don't.)

Finally the content length of –1 means that there was no Content-length header. Many servers don't bother to provide a Content-length header for text files. However, a Content-length header should always be sent for a binary file. Here's the MIME header you get when you request the GIF image *http://www.oreilly.com/ graphics/space.gif*. Now the server sends a Content-length header with a value of 57.

```
% java MIMEHeadersViewer http://www.oreilly.com/graphics/space.gif
Content-type: image/gif
Content-encoding: null
Date: Mon Oct 18 14:00:07 PDT 1999
Last modified: Thu Jan 09 12:05:11 PST 1997
Expiration date: Wed Dec 31 16:00:00 PST 1969
Content-length: 57
```

Retrieving Arbitrary MIME Header Fields

The last six methods requested specific fields from a MIME header, but there's no theoretical limit to the number of header fields a MIME message can contain. The

next five methods inspect arbitrary fields in a MIME header. Indeed, the methods
of the last section are just thin wrappers over the methods discussed here; you can
use these methods to get MIME headers that Java's designers did not plan for. If
the requested header is found, it is returned. Otherwise, the method returns null.

public String getHeaderField(String name)

The getHeaderField() method returns the value of a named MIME header
field. The name of the header is not case-sensitive and does not include a closing
colon. For example, to get the value of the Content-type and Content-encoding
header fields of a URLConnection object uc, you would write:

```
String contentType = uc.getHeaderField("content-type");
String contentEncoding = uc.getHeaderField("content-encoding"));
```

To get the Date, Content-length, or Expires headers, you'd do the same:

```
String data = uc.getHeaderField("date");
String expires = uc.getHeaderField("expires");
String contentLength = uc.getHeaderField("Content-length");
```

These methods all return String, not int or long as the getContentLength(),
getExpirationDate(), getLastModified(), and getDate() methods of the
last section did. If you are interested in a numeric value, you must convert the
String to a long or an int.

Do not assume the value returned by getHeaderField() is valid. You must check
to make sure it is non-null.

public String getHeaderFieldKey(int n)

This method returns the key (that is, the field name: for example, Content-
length or Server) of the nth MIME header field. The request method is header
zero and has a null key. The first header is one. For example, to get the sixth key
of the MIME header of the URLConnection uc, you would write:

```
String header6 = uc.getHeaderFieldKey(6);
```

public String getHeaderField(int n)

This method returns the value of the nth MIME header field. The request method
is header field zero, and the first actual header is one. Example 15-4 uses this
method in conjunction with getHeaderFieldKey() to print the entire MIME
header.

Example 15-4. Print the Entire MIME Header

```
import java.net.*;
import java.io.*;

public class AllMIMEHeaders {

  public static void main(String args[]) {

    for (int i=0; i < args.length; i++) {
      try {
        URL u = new URL(args[i]);
        URLConnection uc = u.openConnection();
        for (int j = 1; ; j++) {
          String header = uc.getHeaderField(j);
          if (header == null) break;
          System.out.println(uc.getHeaderFieldKey(j) + ": " + header);
        }  // end for
      }  // end try
      catch (MalformedURLException e) {
        System.err.println(args[i] + " is not a URL I understand.");
      }
      catch (IOException e) {
        System.err.println(e);
      }
      System.out.println();
    }  // end for

  }  // end main

}  // end AllMIMEHeaders
```

For example, here's the output when this program is run against *http://www.oreilly. com*:

```
% java AllMIMEHeaders http://www.oreilly.com
Server: WN/1.15.1
Date: Mon, 18 Oct 1999 21:20:26 GMT
Last-modified: Sat, 16 Oct 1999 14:54:02 GMT
Content-type: text/html
Title: www.oreilly.com -- Welcome to O'Reilly &amp; Associates!
-- computer  books, software, online publishing
Link: <mailto:webmaster@oreilly.com>; rev="Made"
```

You can see that besides Date, Last-modified, and Content-type headers, this server also provides Server, Title, and Link headers. Other servers may have different sets of headers.

public long getHeaderFieldDate(String name, long default)

This method first retrieves the header field specified by the name argument and tries to convert the string to a long that specifies the milliseconds since midnight, January 1, 1970, GMT. getHeaderFieldDate() can be used to retrieve a MIME header that represents a date: for example, the Expires, Date, or Last-modified headers. To convert the string to an integer, getHeaderFieldDate() uses the parseDate() method of java.util.Date. The parseDate() method does a decent job of understanding and converting most common date formats, but it can be stumped; for instance, if you ask for a header field that contains something other than a date. If parseDate() doesn't understand the date, or if getHeaderFieldDate() is unable to find the requested header field, then getHeaderFieldDate() returns the default argument. For example:

```
Date expires = new Date(uc.getHeaderFieldDate("expires", 0));
long lastModified = uc.getHeaderFieldDate("last-modification", 0);
Date now = new Date(uc.getHeaderFieldDate("date", 0));
```

You can use the methods of the Date class to convert the long to a String.

public int getHeaderFieldInt(String name, int default)

This method retrieves the value of the MIME header field name and tries to convert it to an int. If it fails, either because it can't find the requested header field or because that field does not contain a recognizable integer, then getHeaderFieldInt() returns the default argument. This method is often used to retrieve the Content-length field. For example, to get the content length from a URLConnection uc, you would write:

```
int contentLength = uc.getHeaderFieldInt("content-length", -1);
```

In this code fragment, getHeaderFieldInt() returns –1 if the Content-length header doesn't exist or is garbled.

Configuring the Connection

The URLConnection class has seven protected instance fields that define exactly how the client will make the request to the server. These are:

```
protected URL      url;
protected boolean doInput = true;
protected boolean doOutput = false;
protected boolean allowUserInteraction = defaultAllowUserInteraction;
protected boolean useCaches = defaultUseCaches;
protected long     ifModifiedSince = 0;
protected boolean connected = false;
```

For instance, if doOutput is true, then you'll be able to write data to the server over this URLConnection as well as read data from it. If useCaches is false, the connection will bypass any local caching and download the file from the server afresh.

Since these fields are all protected, their values are accessed and modified via obviously named setter and getter methods:

```
public URL      getURL()
public void     setDoInput(boolean doInput)
public boolean  getDoInput()
public void     setDoOutput(boolean doOutput)
public boolean  getDoOutput()
public void     setAllowUserInteraction(boolean allowUserInteraction)
public boolean  getAllowUserInteraction()
public void     setUseCaches(boolean useCaches)
public boolean  getUseCaches()
public void     setIfModifiedSince(long ifModifiedSince)
public long     getIfModifiedSince()
```

You can modify these fields only before the URLConnection is connected (that is, before you try to read content or headers from the connection). Most of the methods that set fields throw an IllegalAccessError if they are called while the connection is open. In general, you can set the properties of a URLConnection object only before the connection is opened.

NOTE   Throwing an *error* instead of an *exception* here is very unusual. An error generally indicates an unpredictable, generally unhandleable fault in the VM, whereas an exception indicates a predictable, manageable problem. More specifically, a java.lang.IllegalAccess-Error is supposed to indicate that an application is trying to access a nonpublic field it doesn't have access to. According to the class library documentation, "Normally, this error is caught by the compiler; this error can only occur at run time if the definition of a class has incompatibly changed." Clearly, that's not what's going on here. This is simply a mistake on the part of the programmer who wrote this class.

A better solution here would be to throw an IllegalState-Exception or some other runtime exception. Sun has acknowledged the problem—it's bug #4082758 in the Bug Parade on the Java Developer Connection at *http://developer.java.sun.com/developer/ bugParade/index.html*—however, they have not yet fixed it, nor apparently do they have any plans to fix it in future releases.

There are also some private static fields that define the default behavior for all instances of URLConnection. These are:

```
private static boolean      defaultAllowUserInteraction = false;
private static boolean      defaultUseCaches = true;
private static FileNameMap fileNameMap;
```

These fields are also accessed and modified via obviously named setter and getter methods:

```
public boolean              getDefaultUseCaches()
public void                 setDefaultUseCaches(boolean defaultUseCaches)
public static void          setDefaultAllowUserInteraction(
  boolean defaultAllowUserInteraction)
public static boolean       getDefaultAllowUserInteraction()
public static FileNameMap getFileNameMap()
public static void          setFileNameMap(FileNameMap map)
```

Unlike the instance fields, these fields can be changed at any time. The new defaults will apply only to URLConnection objects constructed after the new default values are set.

protected URL url

The url field specifies the URL that this URLConnection connects to. It is set by the constructor when the URLConnection is created and should not change. You can retrieve the value by calling the getURL() method. Example 15-5 opens a URLConnection to *http://www.oreilly.com/*, gets the URL of that connection, and prints it.

Example 15-5. Print the URL of a URLConnection to http://www.oreilly.com/

```
import java.net.*;
import java.io.*;


public class URLPrinter {

  public static void main(String args[]) {

    try {
      URL u = new URL("http://www.oreilly.com/");
      URLConnection uc = u.openConnection();
      System.out.println(uc.getURL());
    }
    catch (IOException e) {
      System.err.println(e);
    }


  }


}
```

Here's the result, which should be no great surprise. The URL that is printed is the one used to create the URLConnection.

```
% java URLPrinter
http://www.oreilly.com/
```

connected

The boolean field connected is true if the connection is open and false if it's closed. Since the connection has not yet been opened when a new URLConnection object is created, its initial value is false. This variable can be accessed only by instances of java.net.URLConnection and its subclasses.

There are no methods that directly read or change the value of connected. However, any method that causes the URLConnection to connect should set this variable to true. This includes connect(), getInputStream(), and getOutputStream(). Any method that causes the URLConnection to disconnect should set this field to false. There are no such methods in java.net. URLConnection, but some of its subclasses, such as java.net.HttpURL-Connection, have disconnect() methods.

If you subclass URLConnection to write a protocol handler, you are responsible for setting connected to true when you are connected and resetting it to false when the connection closes. Many methods in java.net.URLConnection read this variable to determine what they can do. If it's set incorrectly, your program will have severe bugs that are not easy to diagnose.

allowUserInteraction

Some URLConnections need to interact with a user. For example, a web browser may need to ask for a username and password. However, many applications cannot assume that a user is present to interact with it. For instance, a search engine robot is probably running in the background without any user to provide a username and password. As its name suggests, the allowUserInteraction field specifies whether user interaction is allowed. It is false by default.

Since this variable is protected, you use the public getAllowUserInteraction() method to read its value, and the public setAllowUserInteraction() method to set it:

```
public void setAllowUserInteraction(boolean allowUserInteraction)
  throws IllegalAccessError
public boolean getAllowUserInteraction()
```

The value true indicates that user interaction is allowed; false indicates that there is no user interaction. The value may be read at any time but may be set only when the connection is closed. Calling `setAllowUserInteraction()` when the URLConnection is connected throws an `IllegalAccessError`. Programs usually don't catch errors (unlike exceptions); an uncaught error usually forces the program to terminate.

Example 15-6 creates a new `HttpURLConnection`, uses `getAllowUserInteraction()` to see whether user interaction is allowed, and, if it isn't, uses `setAllowUserInteraction()` to allow user interaction. Of the major standalone VMs, only Apple's Macintosh Runtime for Java will pop up an authentication dialog box in a standalone application like Example 15-6, even when `allowUserInteraction` is true. Specifically, Sun's JDK on Windows and Unix will not ask the user for authentication unless you've installed an Authenticator as was discussed in Chapter 7. Unfortunately, this class is available only in Java 1.2 and later. However, most web browsers will ask if `allowUserInteraction` is true and the request is made from inside an applet.

NOTE   You actually can get Sun's JDK to pop up an authentication dialog in
              Java 1.1, but you have to use undocumented methods in sun.net.
              `www.protocol.http.HttpURLConnection` and sun.net.www.
              `protocol.http.HttpAuthenticator` classes to do so.

Example 15-6. A URLConnection That's Allowed to Interact with the User If Necessary

```java
import java.net.*;
import java.io.*;
import java.awt.*;


public class PasswordedPageViewer {

  public static void main(String[] args) {

    for (int i = 0; i < args.length; i++) {
      try {
        URL u = new URL(args[i]);
        URLConnection uc = u.openConnection();
        uc.setAllowUserInteraction(true);
        InputStream in = uc.getInputStream();
        Reader r = new InputStreamReader(in);
        int c;
        while ((c = r.read()) != -1) {
          System.out.print((char) c);
        }
        System.out.println();
      }
      catch (IOException e) {
```

Example 15-6. A URLConnection That's Allowed to Interact with the User If Necessary (continued)

```
        System.err.println(e);
      }


    }

  }

}
```

Figure 15-1 shows the dialog box that pops up when you try to access a password-sprotected page. If you cancel this dialog, you'll get 401 Authorization Required error and whatever text the server sends to unauthorized users. However, if you refuse to send authorization at all, which you can do by pressing OK, then answering No when asked if you want to retry authorization, getInputStream() will throw a ProtocolException.

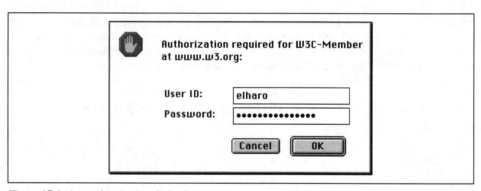

Figure 15-1. An authentication dialog box

defaultAllowUserInteraction

The static defaultAllowUserInteraction field determines whether URLConnection objects whose setAllowUserInteraction() method is not explicitly invoked are allowed to pop up dialogs or otherwise interact with the user. It may be read by calling the public method getDefaultAllowUserInteraction() and set by calling the public method setDefaultAllowUserInteraction(). Since this field is static (i.e., a class variable instead of an instance variable), setting it changes the default behavior for all instances of the URLConnection class that are created after setDefaultAllowUserInteraction() is called.

For instance, the following code fragment checks to see whether user interaction is allowed by default with getDefaultAllowUserInteraction(). If user interaction is not allowed by default, the code uses setDefaultAllowUser-Interaction() to make allowing user interaction the default behavior.

```
if (!URLConnection.getDefaultAllowUserInteraction()) {
  URLConnection.setDefaultAllowUserInteraction(true);
}
```

doInput

Most URLConnection objects provide input to a client program. For example, a connection to a web server with the GET method would produce input for the client. However, a connection to a web server with the POST method might not. A URLConnection can be used for input to the program, output from the program, or both. The protected boolean field doInput is true if the URLConnection can be used for input, false if it cannot be. The default is true. To access this protected variable, use the public getDoInput() and setDoInput() methods:

```
public void     setDoInput(boolean doInput)
public boolean getDoInput()
```

For example:

```
try {
  URL u = new URL("http://www.oreilly.com");
  URLConnection uc = u.openConnection();
  if (!uc.getDoInput()) {
    uc.setDoInput(true);
  }
  // read from the connection...
catch (IOException e) {
  System.err.println(e);
}
```

doOutput

Programs can use a URLConnection to send output back to the server. For example, a program that needs to send data to the server using the POST method could do so by getting an output stream from a URLConnection. The protected boolean field doOutput is true if the URLConnection can be used for output, false if it cannot be; it is false by default. To access this protected variable, use the getDoOutput() and setDoOutput() methods:

```
public void     setDoOutput(boolean dooutput)
public boolean getDoOutput()
```

For example:

```
try {
  URL u = new URL("http://www.oreilly.com");
  URLConnection uc = u.openConnection();
  if (!uc.getDoOutput()) {
    uc.setDoOutput(true);
  }
  // write to the connection...
catch (IOException e) {
  System.err.println(e);
}
```

When you set doOutput to true for an *http* URL, the request method is changed from GET to POST. In Chapter 7, you saw how to send data to CGI programs with GET. GET is straightforward to work with, but it does limit the amount of data you can send. Some web servers have maximum numbers of characters they'll accept as part of a GET request, typically 255 or 1,024. This is generally enough for a simple search request or page navigation, but not enough for a form that allows journalists to submit articles, for example. Forms that allow larger blocks of text should use POST instead. We'll explore this more below when we talk about writing data to a server.

ifModifiedSince

Many clients, especially web clients, keep caches of previously retrieved documents. If the user asks for the same document again, it can be retrieved from the cache. However, it may have changed on the server since it was last retrieved. The only way to tell is to ask the server. Clients can include an If-modified-since in the client request MIME header. This header includes a date and time. If the document has changed since that time, the server should send it. Otherwise, it should not. Typically, this time is the last time the client fetched the document. For example, this client request says the document should be returned only if it has changed since 7:22:07 A.M., October 31, 1999, Greenwich Mean Time:

```
GET / HTTP/1.1
User-Agent: Java1.3beta
Host: login.metalab.unc.edu:56452
Accept: text/html, image/gif, image/jpeg, *; q=.2, */*; q=.2
Connection: close
If-Modified-Since: Sun, 31 Oct 1999 19:22:07 GMT
```

If the document has changed since that time, the server will send it as usual. Otherwise, it will reply with a 304 Not Modified message like this:

```
HTTP 1.0 304 Not Modified
Server: WN/1.15.1
Date: Mon, 01 Nov 1999 16:26:16 GMT
Last-modified: Fri, 29 Oct 1999 23:40:06 GMT
```

The client will then load the document from its cache. Not all web servers respect the If-modified-since field. Some will send the document whether it's changed or not.

The ifModifiedSince field in the URLConnection class specifies the date (in milliseconds since midnight, Greenwich Mean Time, January 1, 1970), which will be placed in the If-modified-since MIME header field. Because ifModifiedSince is protected, programs should call the getIfModifiedSince() and setIfModifiedSince() methods to read or modify it:

```
public long getIfModifiedSince()
public void setIfModifiedSince(long ifModifiedSince)
```

Example 15-7 prints the default value of ifModifiedSince, sets its value to 24 hours ago, and prints the new value. It then downloads and displays the document but only if it's been modified in the last 24 hours.

Example 15-7. Set ifModifiedSince to 24 Hours Prior to Now

```
import java.net.*;
import java.io.*;
import java.util.*;

public class Last24 {

  public static void main (String[] args) {

    // Initialize a Date object with the current date and time
    Date today = new Date();
    long millisecondsPerDay = 24 * 60 * 60 * 1000;

    for (int i = 0; i < args.length; i++) {
      try {
        URL u = new URL(args[i]);
        URLConnection uc = u.openConnection();
        System.out.println("Will retrieve file if it's modified since "
          + new Date(uc.getIfModifiedSince()));
        uc.setIfModifiedSince((new Date(today.getTime()
          - millisecondsPerDay)).getTime());
        System.out.println("Will retrieve file if it's modified since "
          + new Date(uc.getIfModifiedSince()));
        InputStream in = new BufferedInputStream(uc.getInputStream());
        Reader r = new InputStreamReader(in);
        int c;
        while ((c = r.read()) != -1) {
          System.out.print((char) c);
        }
        System.out.println();
```

Example 15-7. Set ifModifiedSince to 24 Hours Prior to Now (continued)

```
    }
    catch (Exception e) {
      System.err.println(e);
    }

  }

}
```

Here's the result. First, we see the default value: midnight, January 1, 1970, GMT, converted to Pacific Standard Time. Next, we see the new time, which we set to 24 hours prior to the current time:

```
% java Last24 http://www.oreilly.com
Will retrieve file if it's been modified since Wed Dec 31 16:00:00 PST 1969
Will retrieve file if it's been modified since Sun Oct 31 11:17:04 PST 1999
```

Since this document hasn't changed in the last 24 hours, it is not reprinted.

useCaches

Some clients, notably web browsers, can retrieve a document from a local cache, rather than retrieving it from a server. The useCaches variable determines whether a cache will be used if it's available. The default value is true, meaning that the cache will be used; false means the cache won't be used. Because useCaches is protected, programs access it using the getUseCaches() and setUseCaches() methods:

```
public void    setUseCaches(boolean useCaches)
public boolean getUseCaches()
```

This code fragment disables caching to ensure that the most recent version of the document is retrieved:

```
try {
  URL u = new URL("http://www.sourcebot.com/sourcebot/");
  URLConnection uc = u.openConnection();
  if (uc.getUseCaches()) {
    uc.setUseCaches(false);
  }
}
catch (IOException e) {
  System.err.println(e);
}
```

defaultUseCaches

`defaultUseCaches` defines the initial value of the `useCaches` field. `defaultUseCaches` can be read and modified by the public `getDefaultUseCaches()` and `setDefaultUseCaches()` methods:

```
public void     setDefaultUseCaches(boolean useCaches)
public boolean getDefaultUseCaches()
```

Since this variable is `static` (i.e., a class variable instead of an instance variable), setting it changes the default behavior for all instances of the `URLConnection` class created after the change. The next code fragment disables caching by default; after this code runs, `URLConnections` that want caching must enable it explicitly using `setUseCaches(true)`.

```
if (uc.getDefaultUseCaches()) {
  uc.setDefaultUseCaches(false);
}
```

Configuring the Client Request MIME Header

In HTTP 1.0 and later, the client sends the server not only a request line, but also a MIME header. For example, here's the MIME header that Netscape Navigator 4.6 for Windows uses:

```
Connection: Keep-Alive
User-Agent: Mozilla/4.6 [en] (WinNT; I)
Host: login.metalab.unc.edu:38309
Accept: image/gif, image/x-xbitmap, image/jpeg, image/pjpeg, image/png, */*
Accept-Encoding: gzip
Accept-Language: en
Accept-Charset: iso-8859-1,*,utf-8
```

A simple web server can ignore this. A more sophisticated web server can use this information to serve different pages to different clients, to get and set cookies, to authenticate users through passwords, and more. All of this is done by placing different fields in the MIME headers that the client sends and the server responds with.

NOTE   It's important to understand that this is *not the MIME header that the server sends to the client*, and that is read by the various `getHeaderField()` and `getHeaderFieldKey()` methods discussed previously. This is the *MIME header that the client sends to the server.*

Each concrete subclass of URLConnection sets a number of different name-value pairs in its MIME header by default. (Really, only HttpURLConnection does this, since HTTP is the only major protocol that uses MIME headers in this way.) For instance, here's the MIME header that a connection from the SourceViewer2 program of Example 15-1 sends:

```
User-Agent: Java1.3beta
Host: login.metalab.unc.edu:38358
Accept: text/html, image/gif, image/jpeg, *; q=.2, */*; q=.2
Connection: close
```

As you can see, it's a little simpler than the one Netscape Navigator sends, and it has a different user agent and accepts different kinds of files. However, you can modify these and add new fields before connecting. In Java 1.3 and earlier, you do this with the static URLConnection.setDefaultRequestProperty() and URL-Connection.getDefaultRequestProperty() methods:

```
public String getDefaultRequestProperty(String name)
public static void setDefaultRequestProperty(String name, String value)
```

The setDefaultRequestProperty() method adds a field with a specified name and value to the MIME header of all subsequently created URLConnection objects. The getDefaultRequestProperty() method returns the value of the named field of MIME header used by all URLConnection objects. For example, if you wanted to add Accept-language and Accept-charset headers to all your outgoing connections, you'd use this code before you opened the connection:

```
URLConnection.setDefaultRequestProperty("Accept-Language", "en");
URLConnection.setDefaultRequestProperty("Accept-Charset",
  "iso-8859-1,utf-8");
```

This is frankly a rather strange approach. For instance, you normally wouldn't use an Accept-language header when requesting a binary file such as a JPEG image. However, you'll get one anyway because this is pretty much an all-or-nothing approach. It would make more sense to set custom MIME headers on a connection-by-connection basis. Indeed, Sun has realized this, and both of these methods are deprecated in Java 1.3. Instead, their functionality is provided by the setRequestProperty() and getRequestProperty() instance methods:

```
public void    setRequestProperty(String name, String value)  // Java 1.3
public String getRequestProperty(String name)  // Java 1.3
```

Both the instance and static methods really have meaning only when the URL being connected to is an *http* URL, since only the HTTP protocol makes use of MIME headers. While they could possibly have other meanings in other protocols, such as NNTP, this is really just an example of poor API design. These methods should be part of the more specific HttpURLConnection class and not the generic URLConnection class.

The setRequestProperty() method adds a field to the MIME header of this URLConnection with a specified name and value. This method can be used only before the connection is opened. It throws an IllegalAccessError if the connection is already open. The getRequestProperty() method returns the value of the named field of the MIME header used by this URLConnection.

For example, web servers and clients store some limited persistent information by using cookies. A cookie is simply a name-value pair. The server sends a cookie to a client using the response MIME header. From that point forward, whenever the client requests a URL from that server, it includes a Cookie field in the MIME request header. That field looks like this:

```
Cookie: username=elharo; password=ACD0X9F23JJJn6G; session=100678945
```

This particular Cookie field would send three name-value pairs to the server. There's no limit to the number of name-value pairs that can be included in any one cookie. Given a URLConnection object uc, you could add this cookie to the connection like this:

```
uc.setRequestProperty("Cookie",
  "username=elharo; password=ACD0X9F23JJJn6G; session=100678945");
```

Writing Data to a Server

Sometimes you need to write data to a URLConnection—for example, when you submit a form to a web server using POST or upload a file using PUT. The getOutputStream() method returns an OutputStream on which you can write data for transmission to a server:

```
public OutputStream getOutputStream()
```

Since a URLConnection doesn't allow output by default, you have to call setDoOutput(true) before asking for an output stream. When you set doOutput to true for an *http* URL, the request method is changed from GET to POST. In Chapter 7, you saw how to send data to CGI programs with GET. GET is straightforward to work with, but it does limit the amount of data you can send. Some web servers have maximum lengths of lines they'll accept as part of a GET request, typically 255 or 1,024. This is generally enough for a simple search request or page

navigation, but not enough for a form that allows users to contribute to a bulletin
board, for example. Forms that allow larger blocks of text should use POST
instead. We'll explore this more shortly.

Once you've got the OutputStream, you should buffer it by chaining it to a
BufferedOutputStream or a BufferedWriter. You generally also chain it to a
DataOutputStream, an OutputStreamWriter, or some other class that's more
convenient to use than a raw OutputStream. For example:

```
try {

  URL u = new URL("http://www.somehost.com/cgi-bin/acgi");
  // open the connection and prepare it to POST
  URLConnection uc = u.openConnection();
  uc.setDoOutput(true);

  OutputStream raw = uc.getOutputStream();
  OutputStream buffered = new BufferedOutputStream(raw);
  OutputStreamWriter out = new OutputStreamWriter(buffered, "8859_1");
  out.write("first=Julie&middle=&last=Harting&work=String+Quartet\r\n");
  out.flush();
  out.close();

}
catch (IOException e) {
  System.err.println(e);
}
```

Sending data with POST is almost as easy as with GET. You invoke
setDoOutput(true), then use the URLConnection's getOutputStream()
method to write the query string rather than attaching it to the URL. Java buffers
all the data written onto the output stream until the stream is closed. This is necessary so that it can determine the necessary Content-length header. The request it
sends, including request line and MIME header, looks something like this:

```
POST /cgi-bin/register.pl HTTP/1.0
Content-type: application/x-www-form-urlencoded
Content-length: 66

username=Elliotte+Rusty+Harold&email=elharo%40metalab%2eunc%2eedu
```

The query string contains two name-value pairs, separated by ampersands. When
using POST, you can also put each name-value pair on a line by itself; this avoids
problems if the server doesn't like lines greater than some maximum length. For
example:

```
% telnet hoohoo.ncsa.uiuc.edu 80
Trying 141.142.103.54...
Connected to hoohoo.ncsa.uiuc.edu.
```

```
Escape character is '^]'.
POST /cgi-bin/post-query HTTP/1.0
ACCEPT: text/plain
Content-type: application/x-www-form-urlencoded
Content-length: 66

username=Elliotte+Rusty+Harold
email=elharo%40metalab%2eunc%2eedu
HTTP 1.0 200 Document follows
Date: Tue, 30 Jul 1996 15:10:41 GMT
Server: NCSA/1.5.2
Content-type: text/html

<H1>Query Results</H1>You submitted the following name/value pairs:<p>
<ul>
<li> <code>name = Elliotte Rusty Harold</code>
<li> <code>email = elharo@metalab.unc.edu</code>
</ul>
Connection closed by foreign host.
```

For that matter, as long as you control both the client and the server, you can use any other sort of data encoding you like. However, if you deviate from the standard, you'll find that your nonconforming client can't talk to most CGI programs or that your nonconforming CGI program can't process requests from most clients. The query string format used here, in which either an & or a \r\n separates name-value pairs, is used by all web browsers and is expected by most CGI programs.

Example 15-8 is a program called FormPoster that uses the URLConnection class and the QueryString class from Chapter 7 to post form data. The constructor sets the URL. The query string is built using the add() method. The post() method actually sends the data to the server by opening a URLConnection to the specified URL, setting its doOutput field to true, then writing the query string on the output stream. It then returns the input stream containing the server's response.

The main() method is a simple test for this program that sends the name "Elliotte Rusty Harold" and the email address *elharo@metalab.unc.edu* to the CGI program *http://hoohoo.ncsa.uiuc.edu/cgi-bin/post-query*. This CGI program is a simple form tester that accepts any input using the POST method and returns an HTML page showing the names and values that were submitted. The data returned is HTML; this example simply displays the HTML rather than attempting to parse it. It would be easy to extend this program by adding a user interface that lets you enter the name and email address to be posted, but since that triples the size of the program while showing nothing more of network programming, it is left as an exercise for the reader. Once you understand this example, it should be easy to write Java programs that communicate with other CGI scripts.

Example 15-8. Posting a Form

```java
import java.net.*;
import java.io.*;
import com.macfaq.net.*;


public class FormPoster {

  private URL url;
  // from Chapter 7, Example 7-9
  private QueryString query = new QueryString();

  public FormPoster (URL url) throws IllegalArgumentException {
    if (!url.getProtocol().toLowerCase().startsWith("http")) {
      throw new IllegalArgumentException(
        "Posting only works for http URLs");
    }
    this.url = url;
  }

  public void add(String name, String value) {
    query.add(name, value);
  }

  public URL getURL() {
    return this.url;
  }

  public InputStream post() throws IOException {

    // open the connection and prepare it to POST
    URLConnection uc = url.openConnection();
    uc.setDoOutput(true);
    OutputStreamWriter out
      = new OutputStreamWriter(uc.getOutputStream(), "ASCII");

    // The POST line, the Content-type header,
    // and the Content-length headers are sent by the URLConnection.
    // We just need to send the data
    out.write(query.toString());
    out.write("\r\n");
    out.flush();
    out.close();


    // Return the response
    return uc.getInputStream();
```

Example 15-8. Posting a Form (continued)

```java
  }

  public static void main(String args[]) {

    URL url;

    if (args.length > 0) {
      try {
        url = new URL(args[0]);
      }
      catch (MalformedURLException e) {
        System.err.println("Usage: java FormPoster url");
        return;
      }
    }
    else {
      try {
        url = new URL("http://hoohoo.ncsa.uiuc.edu/cgi-bin/post-query");
      }
      catch (MalformedURLException e) { // shouldn't happen
        System.err.println(e);
        return;
      }
    }

    FormPoster poster = new FormPoster(url);
    poster.add("name", "Elliotte Rusty Harold");
    poster.add("email", "elharo@metalab.unc.edu");

    try {
      InputStream in = poster.post();

      // Read the response
      InputStreamReader r = new InputStreamReader(in);
      int c;
      while((c = r.read()) != -1) {
        System.out.print((char) c);
      }
      System.out.println();
      in.close();
    }
    catch (IOException e) {
      System.err.println(e);
    }

  }

}
```

Here's the response from the CGI program:

```
% java FormPoster
<H1>Query Results</H1>You submitted the following name/value pairs:<p>
<ul>
<li> <code>name = Elliotte Rusty Harold</code>
<li> <code>email = elharo@metalab.unc.edu</code>
</ul>
```

The `main()` method tries to read the first command-line argument from `args[0]`. The argument is optional; if there is an argument, it is assumed to be the URL of a CGI script. If there are no arguments, `main()` initializes `url` with a default URL, *http://hoohoo.ncsa.uiuc.edu/cgi-bin/post-query*. `main()` then constructs a `FormPoster` object. Two name-value pairs are added to this `FormPoster` object. Next, the `post()` method is invoked and its response read and printed on `System.out`.

The `post()` method is the heart of the class. It first opens a connection to the URL stored in the `url` field. It sets the `doOutput` field of this connection to `true` since this `URLConnection` needs to send output. Then it chains the `OutputStream` for this URL to an ASCII `OutputStreamWriter` that sends the data; then flushes and closes the stream. *Do not forget to close the stream!* If the stream isn't closed, no data will be sent. Finally, the `URLConnection`'s `InputStream` is returned.

To summarize, posting data to a form requires these steps:

1. Decide what name-value pairs you'll use send data to the CGI program.

2. Write the CGI! If it doesn't use any custom data encoding, you can test the CGI program using a regular HTML form and your web browser.

3. Create a query string in your Java program. The string should look like this:

   ```
   name1=value1&name2=value2&name3=value3
   ```

   Pass each name and value in the query string to `URLEncoder.encode()` before adding it to the query string.

4. Open a `URLConnection` to the CGI program.

5. Set `doOutput` to `true` by invoking `setDoOutput(true)`.

6. Write the query string onto the `URLConnection`'s `OutputStream`.

7. Close the `URLConnection`'s `OutputStream`.

8. Read the server response from the `URLConnection`'s `InputStream`.

Posting forms is considerably more complex than using the GET method described in Chapter 7. However, with POST you get more control over the connection. More important, GET has an annoying habit of failing once the query string grows past 200 characters. (The exact point where GET fails varies from operating system to operating system and from web server to web server.) POST lets you send long strings of data reliably.

The getOutputStream() method is also used for the PUT request method, a means of storing files on a web server. The data to be stored is written onto the OutputStream that getOutputStream() returns. However, this can be done only from within the HttpURLConnection subclass of URLConnection, so discussion of PUT will have to wait a little while.

Content Handlers

The URLConnection class is intimately tied to Java's protocol and content handler mechanism. The protocol handler is responsible for making connections, exchanging headers, requesting particular documents, and so forth. It handles all the overhead of the protocol for requesting files. The content handler deals only with the actual data. It takes the raw input after all headers and so forth are stripped and converts it to the right kind of object for Java to deal with; for instance, an InputStream or an ImageProducer.

Getting Content

The getContent() methods of URLConnection use a content handler to turn the raw data of a connection into a Java object.

public Object getContent( ) throws IOException

This method is virtually identical to the getContent() method of the URL class. In fact, that method just calls this method. getContent() downloads the object selected by the URL of this URLConnection. For getContent() to work, the environment needs to recognize and understand the content type. The only content types that are supported in the JDK are text/plain, image/gif, and image/jpeg. Other VMs and applications may support additional types. For instance, HotJava 3.0 includes a PDF content handler. Furthermore, you can install additional content handlers that understand other content types.

getContent() works only for protocols like HTTP that have a clear understanding of MIME content types. If the content type is unknown, or the protocol doesn't understand content types, getContent() throws an UnknownServiceException.

public Object getContent(Class[ ] classes) throws IOException   //
Java 1.3

Java 1.3 lets a content handler provide different object representations of data.
This overloaded variant of the getContent() method lets you choose what class
you'd like the content returned as. The method will attempt to return the content
in the form of one of the classes in the classes array. The order of preference is
the order of the array. For instance, if you'd prefer an HTML file to be returned as
a String, but your second choice is a Reader and your third choice is an
InputStream, you would write:

```
URL u = new URL("http://www.thehungersite.com/");
URLConnection uc = u.openConnection()
Class[] types = {String.class, Reader.class, InputStream.class};
Object o = uc.getContent(types);
```

You would then have to test for the type of the returned object using instanceof.
For example:

```
if (o instanceof String) {
  System.out.println(o);
}
else if (o instanceof Reader) {
  int c;
  Reader r = (Reader) o;
  while ((c = r.read()) != -1) System.out.print((char) c);
}
else if (o instanceof InputStream) {
  int c;
  InputStream in = (InputStream) o;
  while ((c = in.read()) != -1) System.out.write(c);
}
else if (o == null) {
  System.out.println("None of the requested types were available.");
}
else {
  System.out.println("Error: unexpected type " + o.getClass());
}
```

That last else clause isn't supposed to be reached. If none of the requested types
are available, this method is supposed to return null rather than returning an
unexpected type.

ContentHandlerFactory

The URLConnection class contains a static Hashtable of ContentHandler
objects. Whenever the getContent() method of URLConnection is invoked, Java
looks in this Hashtable to find the right content handler for the current URL, as

indicated by the URL's Content-type. If it doesn't find a `ContentHandler` object for the MIME type, then it tries to create one using a `ContentHandlerFactory`, which you'll learn more about in Chapter 17, *Content Handlers*. That is, a content handler factory tells the program where it can find a content handler for a `text/html` file, an `image/gif` file, or some other kind of file. You can set the `ContentHandlerFactory` by passing an instance of the `java.net.Content-HandlerFactory` interface to the `setContentHandlerFactory()` method:

```
public static synchronized void setContentHandlerFactory(
  ContentHandlerFactory factory) throws SecurityException, Error
```

You may set the `ContentHandlerFactory` only once per application; this method throws a generic `Error` if it is called a second time. As with most other `setFactory()` methods, untrusted applets will generally not be allowed to set the content handler factory whether one has already been set or not. Attempting to do so will throw a `SecurityException`.

The Object Methods

The `URLConnection` class overrides only one method from `java.lang.Object`, `toString()`:

```
public String toString()
```

Even so, there is little reason to print a `URLConnection` object or to convert one to a `String`, except perhaps for debugging. `toString()` is called the same way as every other `toString()` method.

Security Considerations for URLConnections

`URLConnection` objects are subject to all the usual security restrictions about making network connections, reading or writing files, and so forth. For instance, a `URLConnection` can be created by an untrusted applet only if the `URLConnection` is pointing to the host that the applet came from. However, the details can be a little tricky because different URL schemes and their corresponding connections can have different security implications. For example, a jar URL that points into the applet's own jar file should be fine. However, a file URL that points to a local hard drive should not be.

Before attempting to connect a URL, you may want to know whether that connection will be allowed. Starting in Java 1.2, the `URLConnection` class has a `getPermission()` method:

```
public Permission getPermission() throws IOException  // Java 1.2
```

This returns a `java.security.Permission` object that specifies what permission is needed to connect to the URL. It returns `null` if no permission is needed (e.g., there's no security manager in place). Subclasses of `URLConnection` will return different subclasses of `java.io.Permission`. For instance, if the underlying URL pointed to *www.gwbush.org*, then `getPermission()` would return a `java.net.SocketPermission` for the host *www.gwbush.org* with the connect and resolve actions.

Guessing MIME Types

If this were the best of all possible worlds, every protocol and every server would use the MIME typing method to specify what kind of file it was transferring. Unfortunately, that's not the case. Not only do we have to deal with older protocols, such as FTP, that predate MIME, but also many HTTP servers that should use MIME either don't provide MIME headers at all, or they lie and provide headers that are incorrect (usually because the server has been misconfigured). The `URLConnection` class provides two static methods to help programs figure out the MIME type of some data; you can use these if the content type just isn't available, or if you have reason to believe that the content type you're given isn't correct. The first of these is `URLConnection.guessContentTypeFromName()`:

```
protected static String guessContentTypeFromName(String name)
```

This method tries to guess the content type of an object based upon the extension in the filename portion of the object's URL. It returns its best guess about the content type as a `String`. This guess is likely to be correct; people follow some fairly regular conventions when thinking up filenames. It's unfortunate that `guessContentTypeFromName()` is protected. It's useful for any class that needs to deal with MIME types (for example, mail clients and HTTP servers), not just for `URLConnection`.

The guesses are determined by the *content-types.properties* file, probably found in your *jre/lib* directory. On Unix, Java may also look at the *mailcap* file to help it guess. Table 15-1 shows the guesses the JDK 1.3 makes.

Table 15-1. Java Extension-Content-Type Mappings

Extension	MIME Content Type
No extension	content/unknown
.saveme, .dump, .hqx, .arc, .obj, .lib, .bin, .exe, .zip, .gz	application/octet-stream
.oda	application/oda
.pdf	application/pdf
.eps, .ai, .ps	application/postscript
.rtf	application/rtf

Table 15-1. Java Extension-Content-Type Mappings (continued)

Extension	MIME Content Type
.dvi	application/x-dvi
.hdf	application/x-hdf
.latex	application/x-latex
.nc, .cdf	application/x-netcdf
.tex	application/x-tex:
.texinfo, .texi	application/x-texinfo
.t, .tr, .roff	application/x-troff
.man	application/x-troff-man
.me	application/x-troff-me
.ms	application/x-troff-ms
.src, .wsrc	application/x-wais-source
.zip	application/zip
.bcpio	application/x-bcpio
.cpio	application/x-cpio
.gtar	application/x-gtar
.sh, .shar	application/x-shar
.sv4cpio	application/x-sv4cpio:
.sv4crc	application/x-sv4crc
.tar	application/x-tar
.ustar	application/x-ustar
.snd, .au	audio/basic
.aifc, .aif, .aiff	audio/x-aiff
.wav	audio/x-wav
.gif	image/gif
.ief	image/ief
.jfif, .jfif-tbnl, .jpe, .jpg, .jpeg	image/jpeg
.tif, .tiff	image/tiff
.fpx, .fpix	image/vnd.fpx
.ras	image/x-cmu-rast
.pnm	image/x-portable-anymap
.pbm	image/x-portable-bitmap
.pgm	image/x-portable-graymap
.ppm	image/x-portable-pixmap
.rgb	image/x-rgb
.xbm, .xpm	image/x-xbitmap
.xwd	image/x-xwindowdump

Table 15-1. Java Extension-Content-Type Mappings (continued)

Extension	MIME Content Type
.png	image/png
.htm, .html	text/html
.text, .c, .cc, .c++, .h, .pl, .txt, .java, .el	text/plain
.tsv	text/tab-separated-values
.etx	text/x-setext
.mpg, .mpe, .mpeg	video/mpeg
.mov, .qt	video/quicktime
.avi	application/x-troff-msvideo
.movie, .mv	video/x-sgi-movie
.mime	message/rfc822
.xml	application/xml

This list is not complete by any means. For instance, it omits various XML applications such as RDF (*.rdf*), XSL (*.xsl*), and so on that should have the MIME-type application/xml. It also doesn't provide a MIME type for CSS stylesheets (*.css*). However, it's a good start.

The second MIME type guesser method is URLConnection.guessContentType-FromStream():

```
protected static String guessContentTypeFromStream(InputStream in)
```

This tries to guess the content type by looking at the first few bytes of data in the stream. For this method to work, the InputStream must support marking so that you can return to the beginning of the stream after the first bytes have been read. Java 1.2 inspects the first eight bytes of the InputStream, though sometimes fewer than eight bytes are needed to make an identification. Table 15-2 shows how Java 1.3 guesses. Note that these guesses are nowhere near as reliable as the guesses made by the previous method. For example, a file that begins with the Unicode byte order mark 0xFEFF or 0xFFFE may merely be a plain Unicode text file rather than an XML file, and it won't recognize a document that begins "<!DOCTYPE html" as an HTML file. Therefore, this method should be used only as a last resort.

Table 15-2. Java First Bytes-Content-Type Mappings

First Bytes in Hexadecimal	First Bytes in ASCII	MIME Content Type
0xACED		application/x-java-serialized-object
0xCAFEBABE		application/java-vm
	GIF8	image/gif
	#def	image/x-bitmap

Table 15-2. Java First Bytes-Content-Type Mappings (continued)

First Bytes in Hexadecimal	First Bytes in ASCII	MIME Content Type
! XPM2		image/x-pixmap
0x89504E 470D0A1A0A		image/png
0x2E736E64		audio/basic
0x646E732E		audio/basic
	<?xml	application/xml
0xFEFF		application/xml
0xFFFE		application/xml
	<html	text/html
	<body	text/html
	<head	text/html
	<HTML	text/html
	<BODY	text/html
	<HEAD	text/html
0xFFD8FFE0		image/jpeg
0xFFD8FFEE		image/jpeg
	RIFF	audio/x-wav
0xD0CF11E0A1B11AE1a		image/vnd.fpx

a This actually just checks for a Microsoft structured storage document. Several other more complicated checks have to be made before deciding whether this is indeed an image/vnd.fpx document.

ASCII mappings, where they exist, are case-sensitive. For example, guessContentTypeFromStream() does not recognize <Html> as the beginning of a text/html file.

HttpURLConnection

The java.net.HttpURLConnection class is an abstract subclass of URLConnection that provides some additional methods that are helpful when working specifically with *http* URLs.

```
public abstract class HttpURLConnection extends URLConnection
```

In particular, it contains methods to get and set the request method, to decide whether to follow redirects, to get the response code and message, and to figure out whether a proxy server is being used. It also includes several dozen mnemonic constants matching the various HTTP response codes. Finally, it overrides the getPermission() method from the URLConnection superclass, though it doesn't change the semantics of this method at all.

Since this class is abstract and since its only constructor is protected, you can't directly create instances of HttpURLConnection. However, if you construct a URL object using an *http* URL, and then invoke its openConnection() method, the URLConnection object returned will be an instance of HttpURLConnection. You can cast that URLConnection to HttpURLConnection like this:

```
URL u = new URL("http://www.amnesty.org/");
URLConnection uc = u.openConnection();
HttpURLConnection http = (HttpURLConnection) uc;
```

Or, skipping a step, like this:

```
URL u = new URL("http://www.amnesty.org/");
HttpURLConnection http = (HttpURLConnection) u.openConnection();
```

NOTE   There's another HttpURLConnection class in the undocumented sun.net.www.protocol.http package. This is a concrete subclass of java.net.HttpURLConnection that actually implements the abstract connect() method.

```
public class HttpURLConnection extends java.net.
HttpURLConnection
```

There's little reason to access this class directly. It doesn't add any important methods that aren't already declared in java.net. HttpURLConnection or java.net.URLConnection. However, any URLConnection you open to an *http* URL will be an instance of this class.

The Request Method

When a web client contacts a web server, the first thing it sends is a request line. Typically, this line begins with GET and is followed by the name of the file that the client wants to retrieve and the version of the HTTP protocol that the client understands. For example:

```
GET /catalog/jfcnut/index.html HTTP/1.0
```

As you saw just previously, this is generally followed by a MIME header. However, modern web clients can do more than simply GET files from web servers. They can POST responses to forms. They can PUT a file on a web server or DELETE a file from a server. And they can ask for just the MIME HEAD of a document. They can ask the web server for a list of the OPTIONS supported at a given URL. They can even TRACE the request itself. All of these are accomplished by changing the request method from GET to a different keyword. For example, here's how a browser asks for just the MIME header of a document using HEAD:

```
HEAD /catalog/jfcnut/index.html HTTP/1.1
User-Agent: Java1.3beta
Host: www.oreilly.com
Accept: text/html, image/gif, image/jpeg, *; q=.2, */*; q=.2
```

```
Connection: close
```

By default, `HttpURLConnection` uses the GET method. However, you can change this with the `setRequestMethod()` method:

```
public void setRequestMethod(String method) throws ProtocolException
```

The method argument should be one of these seven case-sensitive strings:

- GET
- POST
- HEAD
- PUT
- OPTIONS
- DELETE
- TRACE

If it's some other method, then a `java.net.ProtocolException`, a subclass of `IOException`, is thrown. However, it's generally not enough to simply set the request method. Depending on what you're trying to do, you may need to adjust the MIME header and provide a message body as well. For instance, POSTing a form requires you to provide a Content-length header. We've already explored the GET and POST methods. Let's look at the other five possibilities.

NOTE   Some web servers support additional request methods. For instance, Apache 1.3 also supports CONNECT, OPTIONS, PROPFIND, PROPPATCH, MKCOL, COPY, MOVE, LOCK, and UNLOCK. However, Java doesn't support any of these, at least as of Java 1.3.

HEAD

The HEAD function is possibly the simplest of all the request methods. It behaves much like GET. However, it tells the server only to return the MIME header, not to actually send the file. The most common use of this method is to check whether a file has been modified since the last time it was cached. Example 15-9 is a simple program that uses the HEAD request method and prints the last time a file on a server was modified.

Example 15-9. Get the Time When a URL Was Last Changed

```
import java.net.*;
import java.io.*;
import java.util.*;

public class LastModified {
```

Example 15-9. Get the Time When a URL Was Last Changed (continued)

```
public static void main(String args[]) {

  for (int i=0; i < args.length; i++) {
    try {
      URL u = new URL(args[i]);
      HttpURLConnection http = (HttpURLConnection) u.openConnection();
      http.setRequestMethod("HEAD");
      System.out.println(u + "was last modified at "
        + new Date(http.getLastModified()));
    }  // end try
    catch (MalformedURLException e) {
      System.err.println(args[i] + " is not a URL I understand");
    }
    catch (IOException e) {
      System.err.println(e);
    }
    System.out.println();
  }  // end for

  }  // end main

}  // end LastModified
```

Here's the output from one run:

```
D:\JAVA\JNP2\examples\14>java LastModified http://metalab.unc.edu/xml/
http://metalab.unc.edu/xml/was last modified at Thu Oct 21 06:06:57 PDT 1999
```

It was not absolutely necessary to use the HEAD method here. We'd have got the same results using GET. However, by using GET, the entire file at *http://metalab.unc.edu/xml/* would have been sent across the network, whereas all we cared about was one line in the MIME header. When you can use HEAD, it's much more efficient to do so.

OPTIONS

The OPTIONS request method asks what options are supported for a particular URL. If the request URL is an asterisk (*), that indicates that the request applies to the server as a whole rather than to one particular URL on the server. For example:

```
OPTIONS /xml/ HTTP/1.1
User-Agent: Java1.3beta
Host: metalab.unc.edu
Accept: text/html, image/gif, image/jpeg, *; q=.2, */*; q=.2
Connection: close
```

The server responds to an OPTIONS request by sending back a MIME header containing a list of the commands it allows on that URL. For example, when the previous command was sent, here's what Apache responded with:

```
Date: Thu, 21 Oct 1999 18:06:10 GMT
Server: Apache/1.3.4 (Unix) PHP/3.0.6 mod_perl/1.17
Content-Length: 0
Allow: GET, HEAD, POST, PUT, DELETE, CONNECT, OPTIONS, PATCH, PROPFIND, PROPPATCH,
MKCOL, COPY, MOVE, LOCK, UNLOCK, TRACE
Connection: close
```

The list of legal commands is found in the Allow field. However, in practice, these are just the commands the server understands, not necessarily the ones it will actually perform on that URL. For instance, let's look at what happens when you try the DELETE request method.

DELETE

The DELETE method removes a file at a specified URL from a web server. Since this is an obvious security risk, not all servers will be configured to support this, and those that are will generally demand some sort of authentication. A typical DELETE request looks like this:

```
DELETE /javafaq/1999march.html HTTP/1.1
User-Agent: Java1.3beta
Host: metalab.unc.edu
Accept: text/html, image/gif, image/jpeg, *; q=.2, */*; q=.2
Connection: close
```

The server is free to refuse this request or ask for identification For example:

```
Date: Fri, 22 Oct 1999 14:32:15 GMT
Server: Apache/1.3.4 (Unix) PHP/3.0.6 mod_perl/1.17
Allow: GET, HEAD, POST, PUT, DELETE, CONNECT, OPTIONS, PATCH, PROPFIND,
PROPPATCH, MKCOL, COPY, MOVE, LOCK, UNLOCK, TRACE
Connection: close
Transfer-Encoding: chunked
Content-Type: text/html
content-length: 313


<!DOCTYPE HTML PUBLIC "-//IETF//DTD HTML 2.0//EN">
<HTML><HEAD>
<TITLE>405 Method Not Allowed</TITLE>
</HEAD><BODY>
<H1>Method Not Allowed</H1>
The requested method DELETE is not allowed for the
URL /javafaq/1999march.html.<P>
<HR>
<ADDRESS>Apache/1.3.4 Server at metalab.unc.edu Port 80</ADDRESS>
```

```
</BODY></HTML>
```

Even if the server accepts this request, how it responds is implementation-dependent. Some servers may delete the file. Others may simply move it to a trash directory. Others may simply mark it as not readable. Details are left up to the server vendor.

PUT

The PUT method is used by many HTML editors and other programs that want to store files on a web server. It allows clients to place documents in the abstract hierarchy of the site without necessarily knowing how the site maps to the actual local filesystem. This contrasts with FTP, where the user has to know the actual directory structure as opposed to the server's virtual directory structure.

Here's a how a browser might PUT a file on a web server:

```
PUT /hello.html HTTP/1.0
Connection: Keep-Alive
User-Agent: Mozilla/4.6 [en] (WinNT; I)
Pragma: no-cache
Host: metalab.unc.edu
Accept: image/gif, image/x-xbitmap, image/jpeg, image/pjpeg, image/png, */*
Accept-Encoding: gzip
Accept-Language: en
Accept-Charset: iso-8859-1,*,utf-8
Content-Length: 364

<!doctype html public "-//w3c//dtd html 4.0 transitional//en">
<html>
<head>
    <meta http-equiv="Content-Type" content="text/html; charset=iso-8859-1">
    <meta name="Author" content="Elliotte Rusty Harold">
    <meta name="GENERATOR" content="Mozilla/4.6 [en] (WinNT; I) [Netscape]">
    <title>Mine</title>
</head>
<body>
<b>Hello</b>
</body>
</html>
```

As with deleting files, allowing arbitrary users to PUT files on your web server is a clear security risk. Generally, some sort of authentication will be required, and the server will have to be specially configured to support PUT. The details are likely to vary from server to server. Most web servers do not include full support for PUT out of the box. For instance, Apache requires you to install either an additional CGI script or module just to handle PUT requests.

TRACE

The TRACE request method sends back the MIME header that the server received from the client. The main reason for this is to see what any proxy servers between the server and client might be changing. For example, suppose this TRACE request is sent:

```
TRACE /xml/ HTTP/1.1
Hello: Push me
User-Agent: Java1.3beta
Host: metalab.unc.edu
Accept: text/html, image/gif, image/jpeg, *; q=.2, */*; q=.2
Connection: close
```

The server should respond like this:

```
Date: Thu, 21 Oct 1999 17:50:02 GMT
Server: Apache/1.3.4 (Unix) PHP/3.0.6 mod_perl/1.17
Connection: close
Transfer-Encoding: chunked
Content-Type: message/http
content-length: 169

TRACE /xml/ HTTP 1.1
Accept: text/html, image/gif, image/jpeg, *; q=.2, */*; q=.2
Connection: close
Hello: Push me
Host: metalab.unc.edu
User-Agent: Java1.3beta
```

The first six lines are the server's normal response MIME header. The lines from TRACE /xml/ HTTP/1.1 on are the echo of the original client request. In this case, the echo is faithful, though out of order. However, if there were a proxy server between the client and server, it might not be.

NOTE   Apache 1.3.4 (and possibly other versions) actually has a bug in responding to this request. It omits the blank line separating the header from the body, so some browsers (and Java) think that all it sends back is a MIME header.

Disconnecting from the Server

Recent versions of HTTP support what's known as *Keep-Alive*. Keep-Alive enhances the performance of some web connections by allowing multiple requests and responses to be sent in series over a single TCP connection. A client indicates that it's willing to use HTTP Keep-Alive by including a Connection field in the MIME request header with the value Keep-Alive.

```
Connection: Keep-Alive
```

However, when Keep-Alive is being used, the server can no longer close the connection simply because it has sent the last byte of data to the client. The client may, after all, send another request. Consequently, it is now up to the client to decide when to close the connection when it's done.

Java marginally supports HTTP Keep-Alive, mostly by piggybacking on top of browser support. It doesn't provide any convenient API for making multiple requests over the same connection. However, in anticipation of a day when Java better supports Keep-Alive, the `HttpURLConnection` class adds a `disconnect()` method that allows the client to break the connection:

```
public abstract void disconnect()
```

In practice, you rarely if ever need to call this.

Handling Server Responses

Beginning with HTTP 1.0, the first line of an HTTP server's response includes a numeric code and a message indicating what sort of response is made. For instance, the most common response is 200 OK, indicating that the requested document was found, and follows the response MIME header. For example:

```
HTTP/1.1 200 OK
Date: Fri, 22 Oct 1999 15:33:40 GMT
Server: Apache/1.3.4 (Unix) PHP/3.0.6 mod_perl/1.17
Last-Modified: Sun, 06 Jun 1999 16:30:33 GMT
ETag: "28d907-657-375aa229"
Accept-Ranges: bytes
Content-Length: 1623
Connection: close
Content-Type: text/html

<HTML>
<HEAD>
rest of document follows...
```

Another response that you're undoubtedly all too familiar with is 404 Not Found, indicating that the URL you requested no longer points to a document. For example:

```
HTTP/1.1 404 Not Found
Date: Fri, 22 Oct 1999 15:39:16 GMT
Server: Apache/1.3.4 (Unix) PHP/3.0.6 mod_perl/1.17
Last-Modified: Mon, 20 Sep 1999 19:25:05 GMT
ETag: "5-14ab-37e68a11"
Accept-Ranges: bytes
Content-Length: 5291
```

```
Connection: close
Content-Type: text/html

<html>
<head>
<title>Lost ... and lost</title>
<meta http-equiv="Content-Type" content="text/html; charset=iso-8859-1">
</head>

<body bgcolor="#FFFFFF">
<div align="left">
  <h1>404 FILE NOT FOUND</h1>
Rest of error message follows...
```

There are many other, less common responses. For instance, code 301 indicates that the resource has permanently moved to a new location. The browser should redirect itself to the new location and update any bookmarks that point to the old location. For example:

```
HTTP/1.1 301 Moved Permanently
Date: Fri, 22 Oct 1999 15:36:44 GMT
Server: Apache/1.3.4 (Unix) PHP/3.0.6 mod_perl/1.17
Location: http://metalab.unc.edu/javafaq/books/beans/index.html
Connection: close
Content-Type: text/html

<!DOCTYPE HTML PUBLIC "-//IETF//DTD HTML 2.0//EN">
<HTML><HEAD>
<TITLE>301 Moved Permanently</TITLE>
</HEAD><BODY>
<H1>Moved Permanently</H1>
The document has moved <A HREF="http://metalab.unc.edu/javafaq/books/beans/index
.html">here</A>.<P>
<HR>
<ADDRESS>Apache/1.3.4 Server at metalab.unc.edu Port 80</ADDRESS>
</BODY></HTML>
```

The first line of this response is called the response message. It is not part of the MIME header and it will not be returned by the various `getHeaderField()` methods in `URLConnection`. However, `HttpURLConnection` has a method to read and return just the response message. This is the aptly named `getResponseMessage()`:

```
public String getResponseMessage() throws IOException
```

Often all you need from the response message is the numeric response code. `HttpURLConnection` also has a `getResponseCode()` method to return this as an `int`:

```
public int getResponseCode() throws IOException
```

CHAPTER 15: THE URLCONNECTION CLASS

HTTP 1.0 defines 16 response codes. HTTP 1.1 expands this to 40 different codes. While some numbers, notably 404, have become slang almost synonymous with their semantic meaning, most of them are less familiar. The `HttpURLConnection` class includes 36 named constants representing the most common response codes. These are summarized in Table 15-3.

Table 15-3. The HTTP 1.1 Response Codes

Code	Meaning	Java Constant
1XX	Informational	
100	The server is prepared to accept the request body and the client should send it; a new feature in HTTP 1.1 that allows clients to ask whether the server will accept a request before they send a large amount of data as part of the request.	N/A
101	The server accepts the client's request in the Upgrade header field to change the application protocol; e.g., from HTTP 1.0 to HTTP 1.1.	N/A
2XX	Request succeeded.	
200	The most common response code. If the request method was GET or POST, then the requested data is contained in the response along with the usual headers. If the request method was HEAD, then only the header information is included.	HttpURLConnection. HTTP_OK
201	The server has created a data file at the URL specified in the body of the response. The web browser should now attempt to load that URL. This code is sent only in response to POST requests.	HttpURLConnection. HTTP_CREATED
202	This rather uncommon response indicates that a request (generally from POST) is being processed, but the processing is not yet complete, so no response can be returned. However, the server should return an HTML page that explains the situation to the user, and provide an estimate of when the request is likely to be completed, and, ideally, a link to a status monitor of some kind.	HttpURLConnection. HTTP_ACCEPTED
203	The information was returned from a caching proxy or other local source, and is not guaranteed to be up to date.	HttpURLConnection. HTTP_NOT_ AUTHORITATIVE

Table 15-3. The HTTP 1.1 Response Codes (continued)

Code	Meaning	Java Constant
204	The server has successfully processed the request but has no information to send back to the client. This is normally the result of a poorly written form-processing CGI that accepts data but does not return a response to the user.	HttpURLConnection. HTTP_NO_CONTENT
205	The server has successfully processed the request but has no information to send back to the client. Furthermore the client should clear the form to which the request is sent.	HttpURLConnection. HTTP_RESET
206	The server has returned the part of the document the client requested using the byte range extension to HTTP, rather than the whole document.	HttpURLConnection. HTTP_PARTIAL
3XX	Relocation and redirection.	
300	The server is providing a list of different representations (e.g., PostScript and PDF) for the requested document.	HttpURLConnection. HTTP_MULT_CHOICE
301	The page has moved to a new URL. The web browser should automatically load the page at this URL, and update any bookmarks that point to the old URL.	HttpURLConnection. HTTP_MOVED_PERM
302	This unusual response code indicates that a page is at a new URL temporarily, but its location will change again in the foreseeable future, and therefore bookmarks should not be updated.	HttpURLConnection. HTTP_MOVED_TEMP
303	Generally used in response to a POST form request, this code indicates that the user should retrieve a document other than the one requested (as opposed to a different location for the requested document).	HttpURLConnection. HTTP_SEE_OTHER
304	The If-modified-since header indicates that the client wants the document only if it has been recently updated. This status code is returned if the document has not been updated. In this case, the web browser should load the document from its cache.	HttpURLConnection. HTTP_NOT_MODIFIED
305	The Location MIME header field contains the address of a proxy that will serve the response.	HttpURLConnection. HTTP_USE_PROXY

Table 15-3. The HTTP 1.1 Response Codes (continued)

Code	Meaning	Java Constant
307	Almost the same as code 303, a 307 response indicates that the page has moved to a new URL, though it may move again to a different URL in the future. The web browser should automatically load the page at this URL.	N/A
4XX	Client error.	
400	The client request to the server used improper syntax. This is rather unusual, but may become more common as more programmers start writing custom clients and servers.	HttpURLConnection. HTTP_BAD_REQUEST
401	Authorization, generally username, and password controlled, is required to access this page. Either a username and password have not yet been presented or the username and password are invalid.	HttpURLConnection. HTTP_UNAUTHORIZED
402	Not used today, but may be used in the future to indicate that some sort of digital cash transaction is required to access the resource.	HttpURLConnection. HTTP_PAYMENT_ REQUIRED
403	The server understood the request, but is deliberately refusing to process it. Authorization will not help. This might be used when access to a certain page is denied to a certain range of IP addresses.	HttpURLConnection. HTTP_FORBIDDEN
404	This most common error response indicates that the server cannot find the requested page. It may indicate a bad link, a page that has moved with no forwarding address, a mistyped URL, or something similar.	HttpURLConnection. HTTP_NOT_FOUND
405	The request method is not allowed for the specified resource; for instance, you tried to PUT a file on a web server that doesn't support PUT or tried to POST a URI that doesn't refer to a CGI script.	HttpURLConnection. HTTP_BAD_METHOD
406	The requested resource cannot be provided in a format the client is willing to accept, as indicated by the Allow field of the request MIME header.	HttpURLConnection. HTTP_NOT_ ACCEPTABLE
407	An intermediate proxy server requires authentication from the client, again probably in the form of a username and password, before it will retrieve the requested resource.	HttpURLConnection. HTTP_PROXY_AUTH

Table 15-3. The HTTP 1.1 Response Codes (continued)

Code	Meaning	Java Constant
408	The client took too long to send the request, perhaps because of network congestion.	HttpURLConnection. HTTP_CLIENT_ TIMEOUT
409	A temporary conflict prevents the request from being fulfilled; for instance, two clients are trying to PUT the same file at the same time.	HttpURLConnection. HTTP_CONFLICT
410	Like a 404, but makes a stronger assertion about the existence of the resource. The resource has been deliberately deleted (not moved) and will not be restored. Links to it should be removed.	HttpURLConnection. HTTP_GONE
411	The client must but did not send a Content-length field in the client request MIME header.	HttpURLConnection. HTTP_LENGTH_ REQUIRED
412	A condition for the request that the client specified in the request MIME header is not satisfied.	HttpURLConnection. HTTP_PRECON_FAILED
413	The body of the client request is larger than the server is able to process at this time.	HttpURLConnection. HTTP_ENTITY_TOO_ LARGE
414	The URI of the request is too long. This is important to prevent certain buffer overflow attacks.	HttpURLConnection. HTTP_REQ_TOO_LONG
415	The server does not understand or accept the MIME type of the request body.	HttpURLConnection. HTTP_UNSUPPORTED_ TYPE
416	The server cannot send the byte range the client requested.	N/A
417	The server cannot meet the client's expectation given in an Expect-request header field.	N/A
5XX	Server error.	
500	An unexpected condition occurred that the server does not know how to handle.	HttpURLConnection. HTTP_SERVER_ERROR HttpURLConnection. HTTP_INTERNAL_ ERROR
501	The server does not have a feature that is needed to fulfill this request. A server that cannot handle POST requests might send this response to a client that tried to POST form data to it.	HTTP_NOT_ IMPLEMENTED

Table 15-3. The HTTP 1.1 Response Codes (continued)

Code	Meaning	Java Constant
502	This code is applicable only to servers that act as proxies or gateways. It indicates that the proxy received an invalid response from a server it was connecting to in an effort to fulfill the request.	HttpURLConnection. HTTP_BAD_GATEWAY
503	The server is temporarily unable to handle the request, perhaps overloading or maintenance.	HttpURLConnection. HTTP_UNAVAILABLE
504	The proxy server did not receive a response from the upstream server within a reasonable amount of time, so it can't send the desired response to the client.	HttpURLConnection. HTTP_GATEWAY_ TIMEOUT
505	The server does not support the version of HTTP the client is using (e.g., the as-yet-non-existent HTTP 2.0).	HttpURLConnection. HTTP_VERSION

Example 15-10 is a revised source viewer program that now includes the response message. The lines added since `SourceViewer2` are in bold.

Example 15-10. A SourceViewer That Includes the Response Code and Message

```
import java.net.*;
import java.io.*;
import javax.swing.*;
import java.awt.*;

public class SourceViewer3 {

  public static void main (String[] args) {

    for (int i = 0; i < args.length; i++) {
      try {

        //Open the URLConnection for reading
        URL u = new URL(args[i]);
        HttpURLConnection uc = (HttpURLConnection) u.openConnection();
        int code = uc.getResponseCode();
        String response = uc.getResponseMessage();
        System.out.println("HTTP/1.x " + code + " " + response);
        for (int j = 1; ; j++) {
          String header = uc.getHeaderField(j);
          String key = uc.getHeaderFieldKey(j);
          if (header == null || key == null) break;
          System.out.println(uc.getHeaderFieldKey(j) + ": " + header);
        }  // end for
        InputStream in = new BufferedInputStream(uc.getInputStream());
        // chain the InputStream to a Reader
```

Example 15-10. A SourceViewer That Includes the Response Code and Message (continued)

```
        Reader r = new InputStreamReader(in);
        int c;
        while ((c = r.read()) != -1) {
          System.out.print((char) c);
        }
      }
      catch (MalformedURLException e) {
        System.err.println(args[0] + " is not a parseable URL");
      }
      catch (IOException e) {
        e.printStackTrace();
        System.err.println(e);
      }

    } //  end if

  } // end main

} // end SourceViewer3
```

The only thing this program doesn't read that the server sends is the version of HTTP the server is using. There's currently no method to return that. If you need it, you'll just have to use a raw socket instead. Consequently, in this example, we just fake it as "HTTP 1.x" like this:

```
% java SourceViewer3 http://www.oreilly.com
HTTP/1.x 200 OK
Server: WN/1.15.1
Date: Mon, 01 Nov 1999 23:39:19 GMT
Last-modified: Fri, 29 Oct 1999 23:40:06 GMT
Content-type: text/html
Title: www.oreilly.com -- Welcome to O'Reilly &amp; Associates! --
computer  books, software, online publishing
Link: <mailto:webmaster@ora.com>; rev="Made"
<HTML>
<HEAD>
...
```

Error conditions

On occasion, the server will encounter an error but return useful information in the message body nonetheless. For example, when a client requests a non-existent page from the *metalab.unc.edu* web site, rather than simply returning a 404 error code, the server sends the search page shown in Figure 15-2 to help the user figure out where the missing page might have gone.

Figure 15-2. Metalab's 404 page

The getErrorStream() method returns an InputStream containing this data or
null if no error was encountered or no data returned:

```
public InputStream getErrorStream()
```

In practice, this isn't necessary. Most implementations will return this data from
getInputStream() as well.

Redirects

The 300-level response codes all indicate some sort of redirect; that is, that the
requested resource is no longer available at the expected location but that it may
be found at some other location. When encountering such a response, most
browsers will automatically load the document from its new location. However, this

can be a security risk, because it has the potential to move the user from a trusted site to an untrusted one, perhaps without his even noticing.

By default, an `HttpURLConnection` will follow redirects. However, the `HttpURLConnection` class has two static methods that let you decide whether to follow redirects:

```
public static boolean getFollowRedirects()
public static void    setFollowRedirects(boolean follow)
```

The `getFollowRedirects()` method returns true if redirects are being followed, false if they aren't. With an argument of true, the `setFollowRedirects()` method makes `HttpURLConnection` objects follow redirects. With an argument of false, it makes them not follow redirects. Since these are static methods, they change the behavior of all `HttpURLConnection` objects constructed after the method is invoked. The `setFollowRedirects()` method may throw a `SecurityException` if the security manager disallows the change. Applets especially are not allowed to change this value.

Java 1.3 adds methods to configure redirection on an instance-by-instance basis. These are:

```
public boolean getInstanceFollowRedirects()
public void    setInstanceFollowRedirects(boolean followRedirects)
```

If `setInstanceFollowRedirects()` is not invoked on a given `HttpURL-Connection`, then that `HttpURLConnection` simply follows the default behavior as set by the class method `HttpURLConnection.setFollowRedirects()`.

Proxies

Many users behind firewalls or simply using AOL or other high-volume ISPs access the web through proxy servers. Starting in Java 1.3, the `usingProxy()` method tells you whether the particular `HttpURLConnection` is going through a proxy server:

```
public abstract boolean usingProxy()
```

It returns true if a proxy is being used, false if it isn't. In some contexts, the existence or use of a proxy server may have security implications.

JarURLConnection

Applets often store their *.class* files in a JAR archive. This bundles all the classes in one package that still maintains the directory hierarchy needed to resolve fully qualified class names like `com.macfaq.net.QueryString`. Furthermore, since the entire archive is compressed and can be downloaded in a single HTTP connection, it requires much less time to download the *.jar* file than to download its contents one file at a time. Some programs store needed resources such as sounds, images, and even text files inside these JAR archives. Java provides several mechanisms for getting the resources out of the JAR archive, but the one that we'll address here is the *jar* URL. Java 1.2 introduces a new class that allows you to use URLs that point inside JAR archives, `JarURLConnection`:

```
public abstract class JarURLConnection extends URLConnection  // Java 1.2
```

A *jar* URL starts with a normal URL that points to a JAR archive like *http://metalab. unc.edu/javafaq/network.jar* or *file:///D%7C/javafaq/network.jar*. Then the protocol *jar:* is prefixed to this URL. Finally, *!/* and the path to the desired file inside the JAR archive are suffixed to the original URL. For example, to find the file *com/ macfaq/net/QueryString.class* inside the previous *.jar* files, you'd use the URLs *jar: http://metalab.unc.edu/javafaq/network.jar!/com/macfaq/net/QueryString.class* or *jar: file:///D%7C/javafaq/network.jar!/com/macfaq/net/QueryString.class*. Of course, this isn't limited simply to Java *.class* files. You can use *jar* URLs to point to any kind of file that happens to be stored inside a JAR archive, including images, sounds, text, HTML files, and more. If the path is left off, then the URL refers to the entire JAR archive; e.g., *jar:http://metalab.unc.edu/javafaq/network.jar!/* or *jar:file:///D%7C/ javafaq/network.jar!/*.

Web browsers don't understand *jar* URLs though. They're used only inside Java programs. To get a `JarURLConnection`, you construct a URL object using a *jar* URL, then cast the return value of its `openConnection()` method to `JarURLConnection`. Java downloads the entire JAR archive to a temporary file, opens it, and positions the file pointer at the beginning of the particular entry you requested. You can then read the contents of the particular file inside the JAR archive using the `InputStream` returned by `getInputStream()`. For example:

```
try {
  //Open the URLConnection for reading
  URL u = new URL(
    "jar:http://metalab.unc.edu/javafaq/course/week1.jar!/week1/05.html");
  URLConnection uc = u.openConnection();

  InputStream in = uc.getInputStream();
  // chain the InputStream to a Reader
  Reader r = new InputStreamReader(in);
  int c;
  while ((c = r.read()) != -1) {
    System.out.print((char) c);
  }
}
catch (IOException e) {
  System.err.println(e);
}
```

Besides the usual methods of the `URLConnection` class that `JarURLConnection` inherits, this class adds eight new methods, mostly to return information about the JAR archive itself. These are:

```
public URL            getJarFileURL()                            // Java 1.2
public String         getEntryName()                             // Java 1.2
public JarEntry       getJarEntry() throws IOException           // Java 1.2
public Manifest       getManifest() throws IOException           // Java 1.2
public Attributes     getAttributes() throws IOException         // Java 1.2
public Attributes     getMainAttributes() throws IOException     // Java 1.2
public Certificate[]  getCertificates() throws IOException       // Java 1.2
public abstract JarFile getJarFile() throws IOException          // Java 1.2
```

The `getJarFileURL()` method is the simplest. It merely returns the URL of the *jar* file being used by this connection. This generally differs from the URL of the file in the archive being used for this connection. For instance, the *jar* file URL of *jar:http://metalab.unc.edu/javafaq/network.jar!/com/macfaq/net/QueryString.class* is *http://metalab.unc.edu/javafaq/network.jar.* The `getEntryName()` returns the other part of the *jar* URL; that is, the path to the file inside the archive. The entry name of *jar: http://metalab.unc.edu/javafaq/network.jar!/com/macfaq/net/QueryString.class* is *com/macfaq/net/QueryString.class.*

The `getJarFile()` method returns a `java.util.jar.JarFile` object that you can use to inspect and manipulate the archive contents. The `getJarEntry()` method returns a `java.util.jar.JarEntry` object for the particular file in the archive that this `URLConnection` is connected to. It returns null if the URL points to a whole JAR archive rather than a particular entry in the archive.

Much of the functionality of both `JarFile` and `JarEntry` is duplicated by other methods in the `JarURLConnection` class. Which to use is mostly a matter of personal preference. For instance, the `getManifest()` method returns a `java.util.jar.Manifest` object representing the contents of this JAR archive's manifest file. A manifest file is included in the archive to supply meta-information about the contents of the archive, such as which file contains the `main()` method and which classes are Java beans. It's called *MANIFEST.MF*, placed in the *META-INF* directory, and its contents typically look something like this:

```
Manifest-Version: 1.0
Required-Version: 1.0


Name: com/macfaq/net/FormPoster.class
Java-Bean: true
Last-modified: 10-21-1999
Depends-On: com/macfaq/net/QueryString.class
Digest-Algorithms: MD5
MD5-Digest: XD4578YEEIK9MGX54RFGT7UJUI9810
```

```
Name: com/macfaq/net/QueryString.class
Java-Bean: false
Last-modified: 9-11-1999
Digest-Algorithms: MD5
MD5-Digest: YP7659YEEIK0MGJ53RYHG787YI8900
```

The name-value pairs associated with each entry are called the *attributes* of that entry. The name-value pairs not associated with any entry are called the *main attributes* of the archive. The getAttributes() method returns a java.util.jar.Attributes object representing the attributes that the manifest file specifies for this jar entry, or null if the URL points to a whole JAR archive. The getMainAttributes() method returns a java.util.jar.Attributes object representing the attributes that the manifest file specifies for the entire JAR archive as a whole.

Finally, the getCertificates() method returns an array of digital signatures (each represented as a java.security.cert.Certificate object) that apply to this *jar* entry, or null if the URL points to a JAR archive instead of a particular entry. These are actually read from separate signature files for each *jar* entry, and not from the manifest file. Unlike the other methods of JarURLConnection, getCertificates() can be called only after the entire input stream for the *jar* URL has been read. This is because the current hash of the data needs to be calculated, and that can be done only when the entire entry is available.

NOTE   More details about the java.util.jar package, JAR archives, manifest files, entries, attributes, digital signatures, how this all relates to zip files and zip and *jar* streams, and so forth can be found on Sun's web site at *http://java.sun.com/products/jdk/1.2/docs/guide/jar/index.html* or in Chapter 9 of my previous book, *Java I/O* (O'Reilly & Associates, Inc., 1999).

In this chapter:

Protocol Handlers

When designing an architecture that would allow them to build a self-extensible browser, the engineers at Sun divided the problem into two parts: handling protocols and handling content. Handling a protocol means taking care of the interaction between a client and a server: generating requests in the correct format, interpreting the headers that come back with the data, acknowledging that the data has been received, etc. Handling the content means converting the raw data into a format Java understands, for example, an `InputStream` or an `AudioClip`. These two problems, handling protocols and handling content, are distinct. The software that displays a GIF image doesn't care whether the image was retrieved via FTP, HTTP, gopher, or some new protocol. Likewise, the protocol handler, which manages the connection and interacts with the server, doesn't care if it's receiving an HTML file or an MPEG movie file; at most, it will extract a content type from the headers to pass along to the content handler.

Java divides the task of handling protocols into a number of pieces. As a result, there is no single class called `ProtocolHandler`. Instead, pieces of the protocol handler mechanism are implemented by four different classes in the `java.net` package: `URL`, `URLStreamHandler`, `URLConnection`, and `URLStreamHandlerFactory`. `URL` is the only concrete class in this group; `URLStreamHandler` and `URLConnection` are both abstract classes, and `URLStreamHandlerFactory` is an interface. Therefore, if you are going to implement a new protocol handler, you have to write concrete subclasses for the `URLStreamHandler` and the `URLConnection`. To use these classes, you may also have to write a class that implements the `URLStreamHandlerFactory` interface.

What Is a Protocol Handler?

The way the URL, URLStreamHandler, URLConnection, and URLStreamHandler-Factory classes work together can be confusing. Everything starts with a URL, which represents a pointer to a particular Internet resource. Each URL specifies the protocol used to access the resource; typical values for the protocol include mailto, http, and ftp. When you construct a URL object from the URL's string representation, the constructor strips the protocol field and passes it to the URLStreamHandlerFactory. The factory's job is to take the protocol, locate the right subclass of URLStreamHandler for the protocol, and create a new instance of that stream handler, which is stored as a field within the URL object. Each application has at most one URLStreamHandlerFactory; once the factory has been installed, attempting to install another will throw an Error.

Now that the URL object has a stream handler, it asks the stream handler to finish parsing the URL string and create a subclass of URLConnection that knows how to talk to servers using this protocol. URLStreamHandler subclasses and URLConnection subclasses always come in pairs; the stream handler for a protocol always knows how to find an appropriate URLConnection for its protocol. It is worth noting that the stream handler does most of the work of parsing the URL. The format of the URL, although it is standard, depends on the protocol; therefore, it must be parsed by a URLStreamHandler, which knows about a particular protocol, and not by the URL object, which is generic and thus should have no knowledge of specific protocols. This also means that if you are writing a new stream handler, you can define a new URL format that's appropriate to your task.

The URLConnection class, which you learned about in the previous chapter, represents an active connection to the Internet resource. It is responsible for interacting with the server. A URLConnection knows how to generate requests and interpret the headers that the server returns. The output from a URLConnection is the raw data requested with all traces of the protocol (headers, etc.) stripped, ready for processing by a content handler.

In most applications, you don't need to worry about URLConnection objects and stream handlers; they are hidden by the URL class, which provides a simple interface to the methods you need. When you call the getInputStream(), getOutputStream(), and getContent() methods of the URL class, you are really calling similarly named methods in the URLConnection class. We have seen that interacting directly with a URLConnection can be convenient when you need a little more control over communication with a server, most commonly when downloading binary files.

However, the URLConnection and URLStreamHandler classes are even more important when you need to add new protocols. By writing subclasses of these classes, you can add support for standard protocols such as finger, whois, or NTP that Java doesn't support out of the box. Furthermore, you're not limited to established protocols with well-known services. You can create new protocols that perform database queries, search across multiple Internet search engines, view pictures from binary newsgroups, and more. You can add new kinds of URLs as needed to represent the new types of resources. Furthermore, Java applications can be built so that they can load new protocol handlers at runtime. Unlike current browsers such as Mozilla and Internet Explorer, which contain explicit knowledge of all the protocols and content types they can handle, a Java browser can be a relatively lightweight skeleton that loads new handlers as needed. Supporting a new protocol just means adding some new classes in predefined locations, not writing an entirely new release of the browser.

What's involved in adding support for a new protocol? As I said earlier, you need to write two new classes: a subclass of `URLConnection` and a subclass of `URLStreamHandler`. You may also need to write a class that implements the `URLStreamHandlerFactory` interface. Your `URLConnection` subclass handles the interaction with the server, converts anything the server sends into an `InputStream`, and converts anything the client sends into an `OutputStream`. This subclass must implement the abstract method `connect()`; it may also override the concrete methods `getInputStream()`, `getOutputStream()`, and `getContent Type()`.

The `URLStreamHandler` subclass parses the string representation of the URL into its separate parts and creates a new `URLConnection` object that understands that URL's protocol. This subclass must implement the abstract `openConnection()` method, which returns the new `URLConnection` to its caller. If the `String` representation of the URL doesn't look like a standard *http* URL, then you should also override the `parseURL()` and `toExternalForm()` methods.

Finally, you may need to create a class that implements the `URLStreamHandlerFactory` interface. The `URLStreamHandlerFactory` helps the application find the right protocol handler for each type of URL. The `URLStreamHandlerFactory` interface has a single method, `create URLStreamHandler()`, which returns a `URLStreamHandler` object. This method must find the appropriate subclass of `URLStreamHandler` given only the protocol (e.g., *ftp*); that is, it must understand whatever package and class naming conventions you use for your stream handlers. Since `URLStreamHandlerFactory` is an interface, you can place your `createURLStreamHandler()` method in any convenient class, perhaps the main class of your application.

When it first encounters a protocol, Java looks for `URLStreamHandler` classes in this order:

1. First, Java checks to see whether a `URLStreamHandlerFactory` is installed. If it is, the factory is asked for a `URLStreamHandler` for the protocol.

2. If a `URLStreamHandlerFactory` isn't installed or if Java can't find a `URLStreamHandler` for the protocol, then Java looks in the packages named in the `java.protocol.handler.pkgs` system property for a sub-package that shares the protocol name and a class called `Handler`. The value of this property is a list of package names separated by a vertical bar (|). Thus, to indicate that Java should seek protocol handlers in the `com.macfaq.net.www` and `org.cafeaulait.protocols` packages, you would add this line to your properties file:

   ```
   java.protocol.handler.pkgs=com.macfaq.net.www|org.cafeaulait.protocols
   ```

   Then to find an FTP protocol handler (for example), Java would look first for the class `com.macfaq.net.www.ftp.Handler`. If that weren't found, Java would next try to instantiate `org.cafeaulait.protocols.ftp.Handler`.

3. Finally, if all else fails, Java looks for a `URLStreamHandler` named `sun.net.www.protocol.name.Handler`, where *name* is replaced by the name of the protocol; for example, `sun.net.www.protocol.ftp.Handler`.

NOTE   In the early days of Java (circa 1995) Sun was promising that protocols could be installed at runtime from the server that used them. For instance, in 1996, James Gosling and Henry McGilton wrote: "The HotJava Browser is given a reference to an object (a URL). If the handler for that protocol is already loaded, it will be used. If not, the HotJava Browser will search first the local system and then the system that is the target of the URL."* However, the loading of protocol handlers from web sites was never implemented; and Sun doesn't much talk about it anymore.

Most of the time, an end user who wants to permanently install an extra protocol handler in a program such as HotJava will place the necessary classes in the program's class path and add the package prefix to the `java.protocol.handler.pkgs` property. However, a programmer who just wants to add a custom protocol handler to her program at compile time will write and install a `URLStreamHandlerFactory` that knows how to find her custom protocol handlers. The factory can tell an application to look for `URLStreamHandler` classes in any place that's convenient: on a web site, in the same directory as the application, or somewhere in the user's class path.

---

* James Gosling and Henry McGilton, *The Java Language Environment, A White Paper*, May 1996, *http://java.sun.com/docs/white/langenv/HotJava.doc1.html.*

When each of these classes has been written and compiled, you're ready to write an application that uses your new protocol handler. Assuming that you're using a URLStreamHandlerFactory, pass the factory object to the static URL.setURL StreamHandlerFactory() method like this:

```
URL.setURLStreamHandlerFactory(new MyURLStreamHandlerFactory());
```

This method can be called only once in the lifetime of an application. If it is called a second time, it will throw an Error. Untrusted applets will generally not be allowed to install factories or change the java.protocol.handler.pkgs property. Consequently, protocol handlers are primarily of use to standalone applications such as HotJava; Netscape and Internet Explorer use their own native C code instead of Java to handle protocols, so they're limited to a fixed set of protocols.

To summarize, here's the sequence of events:

1. The program constructs a URL object.

2. The constructor uses the arguments it's passed to determine the protocol part of the URL, e.g., *http*.

3. The URL() constructor tries to find a URLStreamHandler for the given protocol like this:

   a. If the protocol has been used before, then the URLStreamHandler object is retrieved from a cache.

   b. Otherwise, if a URLStreamHandlerFactory has been set, then the protocol string is passed to the factory's createURLStreamHandler() method.

   c. If the protocol hasn't been seen before and there's no URlStream HandlerFactory, then the constructor attempts to instantiate a URL–StreamHandler object named *protocol*.Handler in one of the packages listed in the java.protocol.handler.pkgs property.

   d. Failing that, the constructor attempts to instantiate a URLStreamHandler object named *protocol*.Handler in the sun.net.www.protocol package.

   e. If any of these attempts succeed in retrieving a URLStreamHandler object, the URL constructor sets the URL object's handler field. If none of the attempts succeed, the constructor throws a MalformedURLException.

4. The program calls the URL object's openConnection() method.

5. The URL object asks the URLStreamHandler to return a URLConnection object appropriate for this URL. If there's any problem, an IOException is thrown. Otherwise, a URLConnection object is returned.

6. The program uses the methods of the URLConnection class to interact with the remote resource.

Instead of calling openConnection() in step 4, the program can call
getContent() or getInputStream(). In this case, the URLStreamHandler still
instantiates a URLConnection object of the appropriate class. However, instead of
returning the URLConnection object itself, the URLStreamHandler returns the
result of URLConnection's getContent() or getInputStream() method.

The URLStreamHandler Class

The abstract URLStreamHandler class is a superclass for classes that handle specific protocols—for example, HTTP. You rarely call the methods of the
URLStreamHandler class directly; they are called by other methods in the URL and
URLConnection classes. By overriding the URLStreamHandler methods in your
own subclass, you teach the URL class how to handle new protocols. Therefore,
we'll focus on overriding the methods of URLStreamHandler rather than on calling the methods.

The Constructor

You do not create URLStreamHandler objects directly. Instead, when a URL is constructed with a protocol that hasn't been seen before, Java asks the application's
URLStreamHandlerFactory to create the appropriate URLStreamHandler subclass for the protocol. If that fails, Java guesses at the fully package-qualified name of
the URLStreamHandler class and uses Class.forName() to attempt to construct
such an object. This means concrete subclasses should have a noargs constructor.
The single constructor for URLStreamHandler doesn't take any arguments:

```
public URLStreamHandler()
```

Because URLStreamHandler is an abstract class, this constructor is never called
directly; it is only called from the constructors of subclasses.

Methods for Parsing URLs

The first responsibility of a URLStreamHandler is to split a string representation
of a URL into its component parts and use those parts to set the various fields of
the URL object. The parseURL() method splits the URL into parts, possibly using
setURL() to assign values to the URL's fields. It is very difficult to imagine a situation in which you would call parseURL() directly; instead, you override it to
change the behavior of the URL class.

Protected void parseURL(URL u, String spec, int start, int limit)

This method parses a string spec into a URL u. All characters in the spec string
before start should already have been parsed into the URL u. Characters after
limit are ignored. Generally, the protocol will have already been parsed and

stored in u before this method is invoked, and start will be adjusted so that it starts with the character after the colon that delimits the protocol.

The task of parseURL() is to set the URL u's protocol, host, port, file, and ref fields. It can assume that any parts of the String that are before start and after limit have already been parsed or can be ignored.

The parseURL() method that Java supplies assumes that the URL looks more or less like an *http* URL:

```
protocol://www.host.com:port/directory/another_directory/file#ref
```

This works for *ftp* and *gopher* URLs. It does not work for *mailto* or *news* URLs and may not be appropriate for any new URL types you define. If your protocol handler uses URLs that fit this form, you don't have to override parseURL() at all; the method inherited from URLStreamHandler will work just fine. If your URLs are completely different, you must supply a parseURL() method that parses the URL completely. However, there's often a middle ground that can make your task easier. If your URL looks somewhat like a standard URL, you can implement a parseURL() method that handles the nonstandard portion of your URL and then calls super.parseURL() to do the rest of the work, setting the offset and limit arguments to indicate the portion of the URL that you didn't parse.

For example, a *mailto* URL looks like *mailto:elharo@metalab.unc.edu*. First, you need to figure out how to map this into the URL class's protocol, host, port, file, and ref fields. The protocol is clearly mailto. Everything after the @ can be the host. The hard question is what to do with the username. Since a *mailto* URL really doesn't have a file portion, we will use the URL class's file field to hold the username. The ref can be set to the empty string or null. The parseURL() method that follows implements this scheme:

```
public void parseURL(URL u, String spec, int start, int limit) {

    String protocol = u.getProtocol();
    String host = "";
    int port = u.getPort();
    String file = ""; // really username
    String ref = null;

    if( start < limit) {
      String address = spec.substring(start, limit);
      int atSign = address.indexOf('@');
      if (atSign >= 0) {
        host = address.substring(atSign+1);
        file = address.substring(0, atSign);
      }
    }
    this.setURL(u, protocol, host, port, file, ref);
  }
```

Rather than borrowing an unused field from the URL object, it's possibly a better idea to store protocol-specific parts of the URL, such as the username, in fields of the URLStreamHandler subclass. The disadvantage of this approach is that such fields can be seen only by your own code; in this example, you couldn't use the getFile() method in the URL class to retrieve the username. Here's a version of parseURL() that stores the username in a field of the Handler subclass. When the connection is opened, the username can be copied into the Mailto URLConnection object that results. That class would provide some sort of getUserName() method:

```
String username = "";

public void parseURL(URL u, String spec, int start, int limit) {

    String protocol = u.getProtocol();
    String host = "";
    int port = u.getPort();
    String file = "";
    String ref = null;

    if( start < limit) {
      String address = spec.substring(start, limit);
      int atSign = address.indexOf('@');
      if (atSign >= 0) {
        host = address.substring(atSign+1);
        this.username = address.substring(0, atSign);
      }
    }
    this.setURL(u, protocol, host, port, file, ref);

  }
```

Protected String toExternalForm(URL u)

This method puts the pieces of the URL u—that is, its protocol, host, port, file, and ref fields—back together in a String. If you override parseURL(), you should also override toExternalForm(). Here's a toExternalForm() method for a *mailto* URL; it assumes that the username has been stored in the URL's host field:

```
protected String toExternalForm(URL u) {

    return "mailto:" + u.getFile() + "@" + u.getHost();

  }
```

Since toExternalForm() is protected, you probably won't call this method directly. However, it is called by the public toExternalForm() and toString() methods of the URL class, so any change you make here is reflected when you convert URL objects to strings.

Protected void setURL(URL u, String protocol, String host, int port, String file, String ref)

This method sets the host, port, file, and ref fields of the URL u to the given values. It sets the protocol field to the protocol argument in Java 1.1.x and earlier only. (In Java 1.2 and later, this field is set before this method is called and cannot be changed. The protocol argument is ignored.) This method is used by parseURL() to set these fields to the values it has found by parsing the URL. You need to call this method at the end of the parseURL() method when you subclass URLStreamHandler.

This method is deprecated in Java 1.3 (though not in Java 1.2). The reason is that Java 1.3 also allows you to add a query string, user info, and an authority to the URL. Thus, Java 1.3 prefers this alternative setURL() method, which supports those features:

```
protected void setURL(URL u, String protocol, String host, int port, // Java 1.3
    String authority, String userInfo, String path, String query,
    String ref)
```

In Java 1.2 and earlier, user info and authority can be included as part of the host argument. The query string can be included at the end of the file. Even in Java 1.3, this method is a little flaky, since the host, port, and user info together make up the authority. In the event of a conflict between them, they're all stored separately, but the host, port, and user info are used in preference to the authority when deciding which site to connect to.

This is actually quite relevant to the *mailto* example, since *mailto* URLs often have query strings that indicate the subject or other header; for example, *mailto: elharo@metalab.unc.edu?subject=JavaReading*. Here the query string is *subject=JavaReading*. If we were to rewrite the above parseURL() method to support *mailto* URLs in this format, the result would look like this:

```
public void parseURL(URL u, String spec, int start, int limit) {

    String protocol = u.getProtocol();
    String host     = "";
    int port        = u.getPort();
    String file     = "";
    String userInfo = null;
```

```
    String query    = null;
    String ref      = null;

    if (start < limit) {
      String address = spec.substring(start, limit);
      int atSign = address.indexOf('@');
      int questionMark = address.indexOf('?');
      int hostEnd = questionMark >= 0 ? questionMark : address.length();
      if (atSign >= 0) {
        host = address.substring(atSign+1, hostEnd);
        userInfo = address.substring(0, atSign);
      }
      if (questionMark >= 0 && questionMark > atSign) {
        query = address.substring(questionMark + 1);
      }
    }
    String authority = "";
    if (userInfo != null) authority += userInfo + '@';
    authority += host;
    if (port >= 0) authority += ":" + port;

    this.setURL(u, protocol, host, port, authority, userInfo, file,
      query, ref);


  }
```

Note that this works only in Java 1.3 and later. It will not work in Java 1.1 or 1.2.

Protected int getDefaultPort( )   // Java 1.3

Java 1.3 adds a `getDefaultPort()` method to the `URLStreamHandler` class whose responsibility is to return the default port for the protocol; e.g., 80 for HTTP. The default implementation of this method simply returns –1, but each subclass should override that with the appropriate default port for the protocol it handles. For example, here's a `getDefaultPort()` method for the finger protocol that normally operates on port 79:

```
public int getDefaultPort() {
  return 79;
}
```

As well as providing the right port for finger, this overriding method also makes `getDefaultPort()` public. Although there's only a default implementation of this method in Java 1.3, there's no reason you can't provide it in your own subclasses in any version of Java. You simply won't be able to invoke it polymorphically from a reference typed as the superclass.

Protected InetAddress getHostAddress(URL u)   *// Java 1.3*

Java 1.3 also adds a `getHostAddress()` method to the `URLStreamHandler` class whose responsibility is to return an `InetAddress` object pointing to the server in the URL. This requires a DNS lookup, and the method does block while the lookup is made. However, it does not throw any exceptions. If the host can't be located, whether because the URL does not contain a host part or there is a DNS failure or a `SecurityException`, then it simply returns null. The default implementation of this method is sufficient for any reasonable case. It shouldn't be necessary to override it.

Protected boolean hostsEqual(URL u1, URL u2)   *// Java 1.3*

Java 1.3's `hostsEqual()` determines whether the two URLs refer to the same server. This method attempts to use DNS to actually look up the hosts. If that succeeds for both hosts, then it can tell that, for example, *http://metalab.unc.edu/Dave/Dr-Fun/latest.jpg* and *ftp://sunsite.unc.edu/pub/linux/distributions/redhat/current/* are the same host. However, if the DNS lookup fails for any reason, then `hostsEqual()` falls back to a simple case-insensitive string comparison, in which case it would think those were two different hosts.

The default implementation of this method is sufficient for most cases. You probably won't need to override it. The only case I can imagine where you might want to is if you were trying to make mirror sites on different servers appear equal.

Protected boolean sameFile(URL u1, URL u2)   *// Java 1.3*

Java 1.3's `sameFile()` determines whether two URLs point to the same file. It does this by comparing the protocol, host, port, and path. The files are considered to be the same only if each of those four pieces is the same. However, it does not consider the query string or the ref. Furthermore, the hosts are compared by the `hostsEqual()` method so that *metalab.unc.edu* and *sunsite.unc.edu* can be recognized as the same if DNS can resolve them. This is similar to the `sameFile()` method of the URL class. Indeed, in Java 1.3, that `sameFile()` method just calls this `sameFile()` method.

The default implementation of this method is sufficient for most cases. You probably won't need to override it. You might perhaps want to do so though if you needed a more sophisticated test that converted paths to canonical paths or followed redirects before determining whether two URLs had the same file part.

Protected boolean equals(URL u1, URL u2)   *// Java 1.3*

The final equality method added by Java 1.3 tests almost the entire URL, including protocol, host, file, path, and ref. Only the query string is ignored. All five of these must be equal for the two URLs to be considered equal. Everything except the ref is compared by the sameFile() method, so overriding that method changes the behavior of this one. The refs are compared by simple string equality. Since the sameFile() method uses hostsEqual() to compare hosts, this method does too. Thus it performs a DNS lookup if possible and may block. In Java 1.3, the equals() method of the URL class calls this method to compare two URL objects for equality. Again, you probably won't need to override this method. The default implementation should suffice for most purposes.

Protected int hashCode(URL u)   // Java 1.3

Java 1.3 also gives URLStreamHandlers the opportunity to change the default hash code calculation by overriding this method. You should do this if you override equals(), sameFile(), or hostsEqual() to make sure that two equal URL objects will have the same hash code, and two unequal URL objects will not have the same hash code, at least to a very high degree of probability.

A Method for Connecting

The second responsibility of a URLStreamHandler is to create a URLConnection object appropriate to the URL. This is done by the abstract openConnection() method.

Protected abstract URLConnection openConnection(URL u) throws IOException

This method must be overridden in each subclass of URLConnection. It takes a single argument u, which is the URL to connect to. It returns an unopened URLConnection, directed at the resource u points to. Each subclass of URL-StreamHandler should know how to find the right subclass of URLConnection for the protocol it handles.

The openConnection() method is protected, so you usually do not call it directly; it is called by the openConnection() method of a URL class. The URL u that is passed as an argument is the URL that needs a connection. You override this method in your subclasses to handle a specific protocol. Your subclass's openConnection() method is usually extremely simple; in most cases, it just calls the constructor for the appropriate subclass of URLConnection. For example, URLStreamHandler for the *mailto* protocol might have an openConnection() method that looks like this:

```
protected URLConnection openConnection(URL u) throws IOException {
    return new com.macfaq.net.www.protocol.MailtoURLConnection(u);
}
```

Example 16-1 demonstrates a complete URLStreamHandler for *mailto* URLs. The name of the class is Handler, following Sun's naming conventions. It assumes the existence of a MailtoURLConnection class.

Example 16-1. A mailto URLStreamHandler

```
package com.macfaq.net.www.protocol.mailto;

import java.net.*;
import java.io.*;
import java.util.*;

public class Handler extends URLStreamHandler {

  protected URLConnection openConnection(URL u) throws IOException {
    return new MailtoURLConnection(u);
  }

  public void parseURL(URL u, String spec, int start, int limit) {

    String protocol  = u.getProtocol();
    String host      = "";
    int    port      = u.getPort();
    String file      = ""; // really username
    String userInfo  = null;
    String authority = null;
    String query     = null;
    String ref       = null;

    if( start < limit) {
      String address = spec.substring(start, limit);
      int atSign = address.indexOf('@');
      if (atSign >= 0) {
        host = address.substring(atSign+1);
        file = address.substring(0, atSign);
      }
    }

    // For Java 1.2 comment out this next line
    this.setURL(u, protocol, host, port, authority,
                userInfo, file, query, ref);

    // In Java 1.2 and earlier uncomment the following line:
    // this.setURL(u, protocol, host, port, file, ref);

  }
```

Example 16-1. A mailto URLStreamHandler (continued)

```
protected String toExternalForm(URL u) {

  return "mailto:" + u.getFile() + "@" + u.getHost();;

 }
}
```

Writing a Protocol Handler

To demonstrate a complete protocol handler, let's write one for the finger protocol, which is defined in RFC 1288 and was introduced in Chapter 10, *Sockets for Clients*. Finger is a relatively simple protocol compared to JDK-supported protocols such as HTTP and FTP. The client connects to port 79 on the server and sends a list of usernames followed by a carriage return/linefeed pair. The server responds with ASCII text containing information about each of the named users or, if no names were listed, a list of the currently logged in users. For example:

```
% telnet rama.poly.edu 79
Trying 128.238.10.212...
Connected to rama.poly.edu.
Escape character is '^]'.

Login       Name          TTY     Idle   When     Where
jacola    Jane Colaginae  *pts/7         Tue 08:01 208.34.37.104
marcus    Marcus Tullius   pts/15  13d Tue 17:33  farm-dialup11.poly.e
matewan   Sepin Matewan   *pts/17  17: Thu 15:32  128.238.10.177
hengpi    Heng Pin        *pts/10        Tue 10:36 128.238.18.119
nadats    Nabeel Datsun    pts/12   56 Mon 10:38  128.238.213.227
matewan   Sepin Matewan   *pts/8     4 Sun 18:39  128.238.10.177
Connection closed by foreign host.
```

Or, requesting information about a specific user:

```
% telnet rama.poly.edu 79
Trying 128.238.10.212...
Connected to rama.poly.edu.
Escape character is '^]'.
marcus
Login       Name          TTY     Idle   When     Where
marcus    Marcus Tullius   pts/15  13d Tue 17:33  farm-dialup11.poly.e
```

Since there's no standard for the format of a finger URL, we will start by creating one. Ideally, this should look as much like an *http* URL as possible. Therefore, we will implement a finger URL like this:

```
finger://hostname:port/username
```

Second, we need to determine the content type returned by the finger protocol's `getContentType()` method. New protocols such as HTTP use MIME headers to indicate the content type; in these cases, you do not need to override the default `getContentType()` method provided by the `URLConnection` class. However, since most protocols precede MIME, you often need to specify the MIME type explicitly or use the static methods `URLConnection.guess Content TypeFromName(String name)` and `URLConnection.guessContent TypeFromStream(InputStream in)` to make an educated guess. This example doesn't need anything so complicated, however. A finger server returns ASCII text, so the `getContentType()` method should return the string `text/plain`. The `text/plain` MIME type has the advantage that Java already understands it. In the next chapter, you'll learn how to write content handlers that let Java understand additional MIME types.

Example 16-2 is a `FingerURLConnection` class that subclasses `URLConnection`. This class overrides the `getContentType()` and `getInputStream()` methods of `URLConnection` and implements `connect()`. It also has a constructor that builds a new `URLConnection` from a URL.

Example 16-2. The FingerURLConnection Class

```
package com.macfaq.net.www.protocol.finger;

import java.net.*;
import java.io.*;

public class FingerURLConnection extends URLConnection {

  private Socket connection = null;

  public final static int DEFAULT_PORT = 79;

  public FingerURLConnection(URL u) {
    super(u);
  }

  public synchronized InputStream getInputStream() throws IOException {

    if (!connected) this.connect();
    InputStream in = this.connection.getInputStream();
    return in;

  }

  public String getContentType() {
    return "text/plain";
  }
```

Example 16-2. The FingerURLConnection Class (continued)

```
  public synchronized void connect() throws IOException {

    if (!connected) {
      int port = url.getPort();
      if ( port < 1 || port > 65535) {
        port = DEFAULT_PORT;
      }
      this.connection = new Socket(url.getHost(), port);
      OutputStream out = this.connection.getOutputStream();
      String names = url.getFile();
      if (names != null && !names.equals("")) {
        // delete initial /
        names = names.substring(1);
        names = URLDecoder.decode(names);
        byte[] result;
        try {
          result = names.getBytes("ASCII");
        }
        catch (UnsupportedEncodingException e) {
          result = names.getBytes();
        }
        out.write(result);
      }
      out.write('\r');
      out.write('\n');
      out.flush();
      this.connected = true;
    }
  }
}
```

This class has two fields. `connection` is a `Socket` between the client and the server. Both the `getInputStream()` method and the `connect()` method need access to this field, so it can't be a local variable. The second field is `DEFAULT_PORT`, a `final static int`, that contains the finger protocol's default port; this port is used if the URL does not specify the port explicitly.

The class's constructor holds no surprises. It just calls the superclass's constructor with the same argument, the `URL` `u`. The `connect()` method opens a connection to the specified server on the specified port or, if no port is specified, then to the default finger port, 79. It sends the necessary request to the finger server. If any usernames were specified in the file part of the URL, they're sent. Otherwise, a blank line is sent. Assuming the connection is successfully opened (no exception is thrown), it sets the `boolean` field `connected` to `true`. Recall from the previous chapter that `connected` is a protected field in `java.net.URLConnection`, which is inherited by this subclass. The `Socket` that `connect()` opens is stored in the field connection for later use by getInputStream(). The connect() and getInputStream() methods are synchronized to avoid a possible race condition on the connected variable.

The getContentType() method returns a String containing a MIME type for the data. This is used by the getContent() method of java.net. URLConnection to select the appropriate content handler. The data returned by a finger server is almost always ASCII text or some reasonable approximation thereof, so this getContentType() method always returns text/plain. The getInputStream() method returns an InputStream, which it gets from the Socket that connect created. If the connection has not already been established when getInputStream() is called, the method calls connect() itself.

Once you have a URLConnection, you need a subclass of URLStreamHandler that knows how to handle a finger server. This class needs an openConnection() method that builds a new FingerURLConnection from a URL. Since we defined the *finger* URL so that it is similar to an *http* URL, we don't need to implement a parseURL() method. Example 16-3 is a stream handler for the finger protocol. For the moment, we're going to use Sun's convention for naming protocol handlers, so we call this class Handler and place it in the package com.macfaq.net. www.protocol.finger.

Example 16-3. The Finger Handler Class

```
package com.macfaq.net.www.protocol.finger;

import java.net.*;
import java.io.*;

public class Handler extends URLStreamHandler {

  public int getDefaultPort() {
    return 79;
  }

  protected URLConnection openConnection(URL u) throws IOException {
    return new FingerURLConnection(u);
  }

}
```

You can use HotJava to test this protocol handler. Add the following line to your *.hotjava/properties* file or some other place from which HotJava will load it:

```
java.protocol.handler.pkgs=com.macfaq.net.www.protocol
```

Some (but not all) versions of HotJava may also allow you to set the property from the command line:

```
% hotjava -Djava.protocol.handler.pkgs=com.macfaq.net.www.protocol
```

You also need to make sure that your classes are somewhere in HotJava's class path. Note that HotJava does not normally use the CLASSPATH environment variable to look for classes, so just putting them someplace where the JDK or JRE can find them may not be sufficient. Using HotJava 3.0 on Windows with the JDK 1.3b1, I was able to put my classes in the *jdk1.3/jre/lib/classes* folder. Your mileage may vary depending on what version of HotJava you're using with which version of the JDK on which platform.

Run it, and ask for a URL of a site running finger, such as *utopia.poly.edu.* Figure 16-1 shows the result.

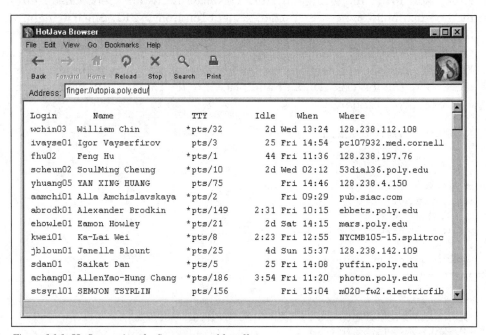

Figure 16-1. HotJava using the finger protocol handler

More Protocol Handler Examples and Techniques

Now that you've seen how to write one protocol handler, it's not at all difficult to write more. Remember the five basic steps of creating a new protocol handler:

1. Design a URL for the protocol, if a standard URL for that protocol doesn't already exist. As of July 2000, the official list of URL schemes at the IANA

(*http://www.isi.edu/in-notes/iana/assignments/url-schemes*) includes only 29 different schemes and reserves three more. For anything else, you need to define your own. Make your new URL as similar to an *http* URL as possible.

2. Decide what MIME type should be returned by the protocol handler's `getContentType()` method. The text/plain content type is often appropriate for legacy protocols. Another option is to convert the incoming data to HTML inside `getInputStream()` and return text/html. Binary data often uses one of the many application types. In some cases, you may be able to use the `URLConnection.guessContentTypeFromName()` or `URLConnection.guessContentTypeFromStream()` methods to determine the right MIME type.

3. Write a subclass of `URLConnection` that understands this protocol. It should implement the `connect()` method and may override the `getContent Type()`, `getOutputStream()`, and `getInputStream()` methods of `URL Connection`. It also needs a constructor that builds a new `URLConnection` from a URL.

4. Write a subclass of `URLStreamHandler` with an `openConnection()` method that knows how to return a new instance of your subclass of `URLConnection`. Also provide a `getDefaultPort()` method that returns the well-known port for the protocol. If your URL does not look like an *http* URL, override `parseURL()` and `toExternalForm()` as well.

5. Implement the `URLStreamHandlerFactory` interface and the `createStream Handler()` method in a convenient class.

Let's look at handlers for two more protocols, daytime and chargen, that will bring up different challenges.

A daytime Protocol Handler

For a daytime protocol handler, let's say that the URL should look like *daytime:// metalab.unc.edu*. We'll allow for nonstandard port assignments in the same way as with HTTP: follow the hostname with a colon and the port (*daytime://metalab.unc. edu:2082*). Finally, allow a terminating slash, and ignore everything following the slash. For example, *daytime://metalab.unc.edu/index.html* is equivalent to *daytime:// metalab.unc.edu*. This is similar enough to an *http* URL that you'll be able to use the default `toExternalForm()` and `parseURL()` methods.

Although the content returned by the daytime protocol is really text/plain, this protocol handler is going to reformat the data into an HTML page. Then it can return a content type of text/html and let the web browser display it more dramatically. The resulting HTML will look like this:

```
<html><head><title>The Time at metalab.unc.edu</title></head><body>
<h1>Fri Oct 29 14:32:07 1999</h1>
</body></html>
```

The trick is that the page can be broken up into three different strings:

- Everything before the time
- The time
- Everything after the time

The first and the third strings can be calculated before the connection is even opened. We'll formulate these as byte arrays of ASCII text and use them to create two `ByteArrayInputStreams`. Then we'll use a `SequenceInputStream` to combine those two streams with the data actually returned from the server. Example 16-4 demonstrates. This is a neat trick for protocols such as daytime that return a very limited amount of data; it can be inserted in a single place in an HTML document. Protocols such as finger that return more complex and less predictable text might need to use a `FilterInputStream` that inserts the HTML on the fly instead. And of course a third possibility is simply to return a custom content type and use a custom content handler to display it. This third option will be explored in the next chapter.

Example 16-4. The DaytimeURLConnection Class

```
package com.macfaq.net.www.protocol.daytime;

import java.net.*;
import java.io.*;

public class DaytimeURLConnection extends URLConnection {

  private Socket connection = null;
  public final static int DEFAULT_PORT = 13;

  public DaytimeURLConnection (URL u) {
    super(u);
  }

  public synchronized InputStream getInputStream() throws IOException {

    if (!connected)  connect();

    String header = "<html><head><title>The Time at "
      + url.getHost() + "</title></head><body><h1>";
    String footer = "</h1></body></html>";
```

Example 16-4. The DaytimeURLConnection Class (continued)

```
    InputStream in1 = new ByteArrayInputStream(header.getBytes("8859_1"));
    InputStream in2 = this.connection.getInputStream();
    InputStream in3 = new ByteArrayInputStream(footer.getBytes("8859_1"));

    SequenceInputStream result = new SequenceInputStream(in1, in2);
    result = new SequenceInputStream(result, in3);
    return result;

  }

  public String getContentType() {
    return "text/html";
  }

  public synchronized void connect() throws IOException {

    if (!connected) {
      int port = url.getPort();
      if ( port <= 0 || port > 65535) {
        port = DEFAULT_PORT;
      }
      this.connection = new Socket(url.getHost(), port);
      this.connected = true;
    }
  }
}
```

This class declares two fields. The first is connection, which is a Socket between the client and the server. The second field is DEFAULT_PORT, a final static int variable, that holds the default port for the daytime protocol (port 13) and is used if the URL doesn't specify the port explicitly.

The constructor has no surprises. It just calls the superclass's constructor with the same argument, the URL u. The connect() method opens a connection to the specified server on the specified port (or, if no port is specified, to the default port); if the connection is opened successfully, connect() sets the boolean variable connected to true. Recall from the previous chapter that connected is a protected field in URLConnection that is inherited by this subclass. The Socket that's opened by this method is stored in the connection field for later use by getInputStream().

The getContentType() method returns a String containing a MIME type for the data. This method is called by the getContent() method of URLConnection to select the appropriate content handler. The getInputStream() method reformats the text into HTML, so the getContentType() method returns text/html.

The getInputStream() method builds a SequenceInputStream out of several string literals, the host property of url, and the actual stream provided by the Socket connecting the client to the server. If the socket is not connected when this method is called, then the method calls connect() to establish the connection.

Next, you need a subclass of URLStreamHandler that knows how to handle a daytime server. This class needs an openConnection() method that builds a new DaytimeURLConnection from a URL and a getDefaultPort() method that returns the well-known daytime port 13. Since the daytime URL has been made similar to an *http* URL, we don't need to override parseURL(); once we have written openConnection(), we're done. Example 16-5 shows the daytime protocol's URLStreamHandler.

Example 16-5. The DaytimeURLStreamHandler Class

```
package com.macfaq.net.www.protocol.daytime;

import java.net.*;
import java.io.*;

public class Handler extends URLStreamHandler {

  public int getDefaultPort() {
    return 13;
  }

  protected URLConnection openConnection(URL u) throws IOException {
    return new DaytimeURLConnection(u);
  }
}
```

Since we've used the same package-naming convention here as for the previous finger protocol handler, no further changes to HotJava's properties need to be made to let HotJava find this. Just compile the files, put the classes somewhere in HotJava's class path, and load a URL that points to an active daytime server. Figure 16-2 demonstrates.

A chargen Protocol Handler

The chargen protocol, which is defined in RFC 864, is a very simple protocol designed for testing clients. The server listens for connections on port 19. When a client connects, the server sends an endless stream of characters until the client disconnects. Any input from the client is ignored. The RFC does not specify which character sequence to send, but recommends that the server use a recognizable

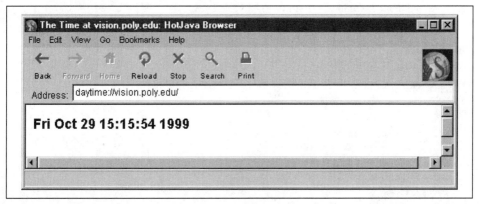

Figure 16-2. HotJava using our daytime protocol handler

pattern. One common pattern is rotating, 72-character carriage return/linefeed delimited lines of the 95 ASCII printing characters like this:

```
!"#$%&'()*+,-./0123456789:;<=>?@ABCDEFGHIJKLMNOPQRSTUVWXYZ[\]^_`abcdefgh
"#$%&'()*+,-./0123456789:;<=>?@ABCDEFGHIJKLMNOPQRSTUVWXYZ[\]^_`abcdefghi
#$%&'()*+,-./0123456789:;<=>?@ABCDEFGHIJKLMNOPQRSTUVWXYZ[\]^_`abcdefghij
$%&'()*+,-./0123456789:;<=>?@ABCDEFGHIJKLMNOPQRSTUVWXYZ[\]^_`abcdefghijk
%&'()*+,-./0123456789:;<=>?@ABCDEFGHIJKLMNOPQRSTUVWXYZ[\]^_`abcdefghijkl
&'()*+,-./0123456789:;<=>?@ABCDEFGHIJKLMNOPQRSTUVWXYZ[\]^_`abcdefghijklm
'()*+,-./0123456789:;<=>?@ABCDEFGHIJKLMNOPQRSTUVWXYZ[\]^_`abcdefghijklmn
()*+,-./0123456789:;<=>?@ABCDEFGHIJKLMNOPQRSTUVWXYZ[\]^_`abcdefghijklmno
```

The big trick with this protocol is deciding when to stop. A TCP chargen server sends an unlimited amount of data. Most web browsers don't deal well with this. HotJava won't even attempt to display a file until the end of stream is seen. Consequently, the first thing we'll need is a `FilterInputStream` subclass that cuts off the server (or at least starts ignoring it) after a certain amount of data has been sent. Example 16-6 is such a class.

Example 16-6. FiniteInputStream

```java
package com.macfaq.io;

import java.io.*;

public class FiniteInputStream extends FilterInputStream {

  private int limit = 8192;
  private int bytesRead = 0;

  public FiniteInputStream(InputStream in) {
    this(in, 8192);
```

Example 16-6. FiniteInputStream (continued)

```
  }

  public FiniteInputStream(InputStream in, int limit) {
    super(in);
    this.limit = limit;
  }

  public int read() throws IOException {

    if (bytesRead >= limit) return -1;
    int c = in.read();
    bytesRead++;
    return c;

  }

  public int read(byte[] data) throws IOException {
    return this.read(data, 0, data.length);
  }

  public int read(byte[] data, int offset, int length)
   throws IOException {

    if (data == null) throw new NullPointerException();
    else if ((offset < 0) || (offset > data.length) || (length < 0) ||
      ((offset + length) > data.length) || ((offset + length) < 0)) {
      throw new IndexOutOfBoundsException();
    }
    else if (length == 0) {
      return 0;
    }

    if (bytesRead >= limit) return -1;
    else if (bytesRead + length > limit) {
      int numToRead = bytesRead + length - limit;
      int numRead = in.read(data, offset, numToRead);
      if (numRead == -1) return -1;
      bytesRead += numRead;
      return numRead;
    }
    else { // will not exceed limit
      int numRead = in.read(data, offset, length);
      if (numRead == -1) return -1;
      bytesRead += numRead;
      return numRead;
```

Example 16-6. FiniteInputStream (continued)

```
    }
  }

  public int available() throws IOException {
    if (bytesRead >= limit) return 1;
    else return in.available();
  }
}
```

Next, since there's no standard for the format of a chargen URL, we have to create one. Ideally, this should look as much like an *http* URL as possible. Therefore, we will implement a chargen URL like this:

```
chargen://hostname:port
```

Second, we need to choose the content type to be returned by the chargen protocol's getContentType() method. A chargen server returns ASCII text, so the getContentType() method should return the string text/plain. The text/plain MIME type has the advantage that Java already understands it.

Example 16-7 is a ChargenURLConnection class that subclasses URLConnection. This class overrides the getContentType() and getInputStream() methods of URLConnection and implements connect(). It also has a constructor that builds a new URLConnection from a URL.

Example 16-7. The ChargenURLConnection Class

```
package com.macfaq.net.www.protocol.chargen;

import java.net.*;
import java.io.*;
import com.macfaq.io.*;

public class ChargenURLConnection extends URLConnection {

  private Socket connection = null;

  public final static int DEFAULT_PORT = 19;

  public ChargenURLConnection(URL u) {
    super(u);
  }

  public synchronized InputStream getInputStream() throws IOException {

    if (!connected) this.connect();
    return new FiniteInputStream(this.connection.getInputStream());
```

Example 16-7. The ChargenURLConnection Class (continued)

```
  }

  public String getContentType() {
    return "text/plain";
  }

  public synchronized void connect() throws IOException {

    if (!connected) {
      int port = url.getPort();
      if ( port < 1 || port > 65535) {
        port = DEFAULT_PORT;
      }
      this.connection = new Socket(url.getHost(), port);
      this.connected = true;
    }
  }
}
```

This class has two fields. `connection` is a `Socket` between the client and the server. The second field is `DEFAULT_PORT`, a `final static int` that contains the chargen protocol's default port; this port is used if the URL does not specify the port explicitly.

The class's constructor just passes the URL u to the superclass's constructor. The `connect()` method opens a connection to the specified server on the specified port (or, if no port is specified, then to the default chargen port, 19) and, assuming the connection is successfully opened, sets the `boolean` field `connected` to true. The `Socket` that `connect()` opens is stored in the field `connection` for later use by `getInputStream()`. The `connect()` method is synchronized to avoid a possible race condition on the `connected` variable.

The `getContentType()` method returns a `String` containing a MIME type for the data. The data returned by a chargen server is always ASCII text, so this `getContentType()` method always returns `text/plain`.

The `getInputStream()` connects if necessary, then gets the `InputStream` from `this.connection`. Rather than returning it immediately, `getInputStream()` first chains it to a `FiniteInputStream`.

Now that we have a `URLConnection`, we need a subclass of `URLStreamHandler` that knows how to handle a chargen server. This class needs an `openConnection()` method that builds a new `ChargenURLConnection` from a URL and a `getDefaultPort()` method that returns the well-known chargen port. Since we defined the *chargen* URL so that it is similar to an *http* URL, we don't need to implement a `parseURL()` method. Example 16-8 is a stream handler for the chargen protocol.

Example 16-8. The chargen Handler Class

```
package com.macfaq.net.www.protocol.chargen;

import java.net.*;
import java.io.*;

public class Handler extends URLStreamHandler {

  public int getDefaultPort() {
    return 19;
  }

  protected URLConnection openConnection(URL u) throws IOException {
    return new ChargenURLConnection(u);
  }
}
```

You can use HotJava to test this protocol handler. Run it, and ask for a URL of a site running a chargen server, such as *vision.poly.edu.* Figure 16-3 shows the result.

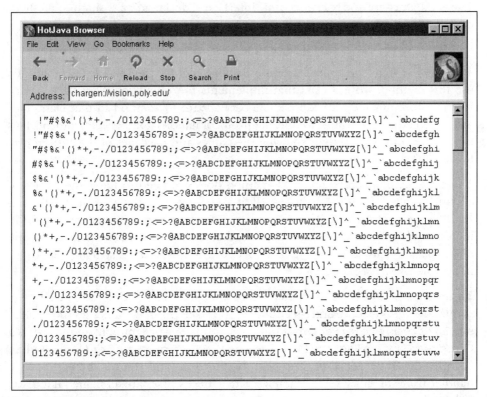

Figure 16-3. HotJava using the chargen protocol handler

The URLStreamHandlerFactory Interface

The last section showed you how to install new protocol handlers that you wrote into HotJava, an application that someone else wrote. However, if you write your own application, you can implement your own scheme for finding and loading protocol handlers. The easiest way to do this is to install a `URLStreamHandlerFactory` in your application:

```
public abstract interface URLStreamHandlerFactory
```

NOTE   Only applications are allowed to install a new URL
              StreamHandlerFactory. Applets that run in the applet viewer or a
              web browser must use the `URLStreamHandlerFactory` that is pro-
              vided. An attempt to set a different one will fail, either because
              another factory is already installed or because of a `Security`
              `Exception`.

The `URLStreamHandlerFactory` interface declares a single method, `createURLStreamHandler()`:

```
public abstract URLStreamHandler createURLStreamHandler(String protocol)
```

This method loads the appropriate protocol handler for the specified protocol. To use this method, write a class that implements the `URLStreamHandlerFactory` interface and include a `createURLStreamHandler()` method in that class. This method needs to know how to find the protocol handler for a given protocol. This is no more complicated than knowing the names and packages of the custom protocols you've implemented.

The `createURLStreamHandler()` method does not need to know the names of all the installed protocol handlers. If it doesn't recognize a protocol, then it should simply return null. This tells Java to follow the default procedure for locating stream handlers; that is, to look for a class named *protocol*.`Handler` in one of the packages listed in the `java.protocol.handler.pkgs` system property or in `sun.net.www.protocol`.

To install the stream handler factory, pass an instance of the class that implements the `URLStreamHandlerFactory` interface to the static method `URL.setURLStreamHandlerFactory()` at the start of your program. Example 16-9 is a `URLStreamHandlerFactory()` whose `createURLStreamHandler()` method recognizes the finger, daytime, and chargen protocols and returns the appropriate handler from the last several examples. Since these classes are all named `Handler`, fully package-qualified names are used.

Example 16-9. A URLStreamHandlerFactory for finger, daytime, and chargen

```
package com.macfaq.net.www.protocol;

import java.net.*;

public class NewFactory implements URLStreamHandlerFactory {

  public URLStreamHandler createURLStreamHandler(String protocol) {

    if (protocol.equalsIgnoreCase("finger")) {
      return new com.macfaq.net.www.protocol.finger.Handler();
    }
    else if (protocol.equalsIgnoreCase("chargen")) {
      return new com.macfaq.net.www.protocol.chargen.Handler();
    }
    else if (protocol.equalsIgnoreCase("daytime")) {
      return new com.macfaq.net.www.protocol.daytime.Handler();
    }
    else {
      return null;
    }
  }
}
```

We use the `equalsIgnoreCase()` method from `java.lang.String` to test the
identity of the protocol because it shouldn't make a difference whether you ask for
finger://rama.poly.edu or *FINGER://RAMA.POLY.EDU*. If the protocol is recognized, then `createURLStreamHandler()` creates an instance of the proper
`Handler` class and returns it; otherwise, the method returns `null`, which tells the
`URL` class to look for a `URLStreamHandler` in the standard locations.

Since browsers, HotJava included, generally don't allow you to install your own
`URLStreamHandlerFactory`, this will be of use only in applications.
Example 16-10 is a simple character mode program that uses this factory and its
associated protocol handlers to print server data on `System.out`. Notice that it
does not import `com.macfaq.net.www.protocol.chargen`, `com.macfaq.net.`
`www.protocol.finger`, or `com.macfaq.net.www.protocol.daytime`. All this
program knows is that it has a URL. It does not need to know how that protocol is
handled or even how the right `URLConnection` object is instantiated.

Example 16-10. A SourceViewer Program That Sets a URLStreamHandlerFactory

```
import java.net.*;
import java.io.*;
import com.macfaq.net.www.protocol.*;

public class SourceViewer3 {
```

Example 16-10. A SourceViewer Program That Sets a URLStreamHandlerFactory (continued)

```
public static void main (String[] args) {

  URL.setURLStreamHandlerFactory(new NewFactory());

  if  (args.length > 0) {
    try {
      //Open the URL for reading
      URL u = new URL(args[0]);
      InputStream in = new BufferedInputStream(u.openStream());
      // chain the InputStream to a Reader
      Reader r = new InputStreamReader(in);
      int c;
      while ((c = r.read()) != -1) {
        System.out.print((char) c);
      }
    }
    catch (MalformedURLException e) {
      System.err.println(args[0] + " is not a parseable URL");
    }
    catch (IOException e) {
      System.err.println(e);
    }
  } //  end if
} // end main
}  // end SourceViewer3
```

Aside from the one line where the `URLStreamHandlerFactory` is set, this is almost exactly like the earlier `SourceViewer` program of Example 7-5 in Chapter 7, *Retrieving Data with URLs*. For instance, here the program reads from a *finger* URL:

```
D:\JAVA\JNP2\examples\15>java SourceViewer3 finger://rama.poly.edu/
Login      Name              TTY        Idle   When     Where
nadats     Nabeel Datsun     pts/0        55 Fri 16:54  128.238.213.227
marcus     Marcus Tullius    *pts/1       20 Thu 12:12  128.238.10.177
marcus     Marcus Tullius    *pts/5     2:24 Thu 16:42  128.238.10.177
wri        Weber Research Insti  pts/10   55 Fri 13:26  rama.poly.edu
jbjovi     John B. Jovien    pts/9      25d Mon 14:54  128.238.213.229
```

Here it reads from a *daytime* URL:

```
% java SourceViewer3 daytime://tock.usno.navy.mil/
<html><head><title>The Time at tock.usno.navy.mil</title></head><body><h1>Fri Oc
t 29 21:22:49 1999
</h1></body></html>
```

However, it still works with all the usual protocol handlers that come bundled with the JDK. For instance here are the first few lines of output when it reads from an *http* URL:

```
% java SourceViewer3 http://www.oreilly.com/oreilly/about.html
<HTML>
<HEAD>
<TITLE>About O'Reilly &amp; Associates</TITLE>
</HEAD>
<BODY LINK="#770000" VLINK="#0000AA" BGCOLOR="#ffffff">

<table border=0 cellspacing=0 cellpadding=0 width=515>
<tr>
<td>
<img src="http://www.oreilly.com/graphics_new/generic_ora_header_wide.gif"
width="515" height="37" ALT="O'Reilly and Associates">
```

17

Content Handlers

Content handlers are one of the ideas that got developers excited about Java in the first place. At the time that HotJava was created, Netscape, NCSA, Spyglass, and a few other combatants were fighting a battle over who would control the standards for web browsing. One of the battlegrounds was the ability of different browsers to handle various kinds of files. The first browsers understood only HTML. The next generation understood HTML and GIF. JPEG support was soon added. The intensity of this battle meant that new versions of browsers were released every couple of weeks. Netscape made the first attempt to break this infinite loop by introducing plug-ins in Navigator 2.0. Plug-ins are platform-dependent browser extenders written in C that add the ability to view new content types such as Adobe PDF and VRML. However, plug-ins have their drawbacks. Each new content type requires the user to download and install a new plug-in, if indeed the right plug-in is even available for the user's platform. To keep up, users had to use huge amounts of bandwidth just to download new browsers and plug-ins, each of which would fix a few bugs and add a few new features.

The Java team saw a way around this. Their idea was to use Java to download only the parts of the program that had to be updated rather than the entire browser. Furthermore, when the user encountered a web page that used a new content type, the browser could automatically download the code that was needed to view that content type. The user wouldn't have to stop, ftp a plug-in, quit the browser, install the plug-in, restart the browser, and reload the page. The mechanism that the Java team envisioned was the content handler. Each new data type that a web site wanted to serve would be associated with one content handler written in Java. The content handler would be responsible for parsing the content and displaying it to the user in the web browser window. The abstract class that content handlers for specific data types such as PNG or RTF would extend was `java.net.ContentHandler`. James Gosling and Henry McGilton described this scenario in 1996:

> HotJava's dynamic behavior is also used for understanding different types of objects. For example, most Web browsers can understand a small set of image formats (typically GIF, X11 pixmap, and X11 bitmap). If they see some other type, they have no way to deal with it. HotJava, on the other hand, can dynamically link the code from the host that has the image allowing it to display the new format. So, if someone invents a new compression algorithm, the inventor just has to make sure that a copy of its Java code is installed on the server that contains the images they want to publish; they don't have to upgrade all the browsers in the world. HotJava essentially upgrades itself on the fly when it sees this new type.[*]

Unfortunately, content handlers never really made it out of Sun's white papers into shipping software. The `ContentHandler` class still exists in the standard library, and it has some uses in custom applications. However, neither HotJava nor any other web browser actually uses it to display content. When HotJava downloads an HTML page or a bitmapped image, it handles it with hardcoded routines that process that particular kind of data. When HotJava encounters an unknown content type, it simply asks the user to locate a helper application that can display the file, almost exactly as a traditional web browser such as Netscape Navigator or Internet Explorer would do. (Figure 17-1 demonstrates.) The promise of dynamically extensible web browsers automatically downloading content handlers for new data types as they encounter them was never realized. Perhaps the biggest problem was that the `ContentHandler` class was too generic, providing too little information about what kind of object was being downloaded and how it should be displayed.

NOTE   A much more robust and better thought-out content handler mechanism is now available under the name JavaBeans Activation Framework. This is a standard extension to Java 1.1 and later that provides the necessary API for deciding what to do with arbitrary datatypes at runtime. However, JAF has not yet been used inside web browsers or even widely adopted, though certainly that shouldn't stop you from using it inside your own applications if you find it useful. See *http://java.sun.com/beans/glasgow/jaf.html* for more details.

---

[*] James Gosling and Henry McGilton, *The Java Language Environment, A White Paper*, May 1996, *http://java.sun.com/docs/white/langenv/HotJava.doc1.html*.

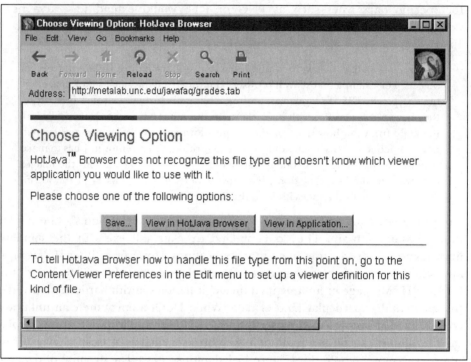

Figure 17-1. HotJava's reaction to an unexpected content type, even though a content handler for this type is installed

What Is a Content Handler?

A content handler is an instance of a subclass of `java.net.ContentHandler`:

```
public abstract class ContentHandler extends Object
```

NOTE   The SAX2 interface for XML parsing defines a completely separate
           interface named ContentHandler. This has nothing to do with the
           content handlers we're discussing in this chapter.

This class knows how to take a `URLConnection` and a MIME type and turn the
data coming from the `URLConnection` into a Java object of an appropriate type.
Thus, a content handler allows an applet to understand new kinds of data. Since
Java lowers the bar for writing code below what's needed to write a browser or a
Netscape plug-in, the theory is that many different web sites can write custom handlers, rather than having to rely on the overworked browser manufacturers.

Java can already download classes from the Internet. Thus, there isn't much magic
to getting it to download a class that can understand a new content type. A content

handler is just a *.class* file like any other. The magic is all inside the web browser, which knows when and where to request a *.class* file to view a new content type. Of course, some browsers are more magical than others. Currently, the only way to make this work in a browser is in conjunction with an applet that knows how to request the content handler explicitly. It can also be used—in fact, it can be used considerably more easily—in a standalone application that ignores browsers completely.

Specifically, a content handler reads data from a URLConnection and constructs an object appropriate for the content type from the data. Each subclass of ContentHandler handles a specific MIME type and subtype, such as text/plain or image/gif. Thus, an image/gif content handler returns a URLImageSource object (a class that implements the ImageProducer interface), while a text/ plain content handler returns a String. A database content handler might return a java.sql.ResultSet object. An application/x-macbinhex40 content handler might return a BinhexDecoder object written by the same programmer who wrote the application/x-macbinhex40 content handler.

Content handlers are intimately tied to protocol handlers. In the previous chapter, the getContent() method of the URLConnection class returned an InputStream that fed the data from the server to the client. This works for simple protocols that return only ASCII text, such as finger, whois, and daytime. However, returning an input stream doesn't work well for protocols such as FTP, gopher, and HTTP that can return many different content types, many of which can't be understood as a stream of ASCII text. For protocols like these, getContent() needs to check the MIME type, and then use the createContentHandler() method of the application's ContentHandlerFactory to produce a matching content handler. Once a ContentHandler exists, the URLConnection's getContent() method calls the ContentHandler's getContent() method, which creates the Java object to be returned. Outside of the getContent() method of a URLConnection, you rarely, if ever, call any ContentHandler method. Applications should never call the methods of a ContentHandler directly. Instead, they should use the getContent() method of URL or URLConnection.

An object that implements the ContentHandlerFactory interface is responsible for choosing the right ContentHandler to go with a MIME type. A ContentHandlerFactory is installed in a program by the static URLConnection. setContentHandlerFactory() method. Only one ContentHandlerFactory may be chosen during the lifetime of an application. When a program starts running, there is no ContentHandlerFactory; that is, the ContentHandlerFactory is null.

When there is no factory, Java looks for content handler classes with the name type.subtype, where type is the MIME type of the content and subtype is the MIME subtype. It looks for these classes first in any packages named by the java.content.handler.pkgs property, then in the sun.net.www.content package. The java.content.handler.pkgs property should contain a list of package prefixes separated from each other by a vertical bar (|). This is similar to how Java finds protocol handlers. For example, if the java.content.handler.pkgs property has the value com.macfaq.net.www.content|org.cafeaulait.content and your program is looking for a content handler for text/xml files, then it would first try to instantiate com.macfaq.net.www.content.text.xml. If that fails, it would next try to instantiate, org.cafeaulait.content.text.xml. If that fails, as a last resort, it would try to instantiate sun.net.www.content.text.xml. These conventions are also used to search for a content handler if a ContentHandlerFactory is installed but the createContentHandler() method returns null.

To summarize, here's the sequence of events:

1. A URL object is created that points at some Internet resource.

2. The URL's getContent() method is called to return an object representing the contents of the resource.

3. The getContent() method of the URL calls the getContent() method of its underlying URLConnection.

4. The URLConnectiongetContent() method calls the nonpublic method getContentHandler() to find a content handler for the MIME type and subtype.

5. getContentHandler() checks to see whether it already has a handler for this type in its cache. If it does, that handler is returned to getContent(). Thus, browsers won't download content handlers for common types, such as text/html, every time the user goes to a new web page.

6. If there wasn't an appropriate ContentHandler in the cache and the ContentHandlerFactory isn't null, getContentHandler() calls the ContentHandlerFactory's createContentHandler() method to instantiate a new ContentHandler. If this is successful, the ContentHandler object is returned to getContent().

7. If the ContentHandlerFactory is null or createContentHandler() fails to instantiate a new ContentHandler, then Java looks for a content handler class named type.subtype, where type is the MIME type of the content and subtype is the MIME subtype in one of the packages named in the java.content.handler.pkgs system property. If a content handler is found, it is returned. Otherwise. . .

8. Java looks for a content handler class named sun.net.www.content.*type*. *subtype*. If it's found, it's returned. Otherwise, createContentHandler() returns null.

9. If the ContentHandler object is not null, then this ContentHandler's getContent() method is called. This method returns an object appropriate for the content type. If the ContentHandler is null, an IOException is thrown.

10. Either the returned object or the exception is passed up the call chain, eventually reaching the method that invoked getContent().

You can affect this chain of events in three ways: first, by constructing a URL and calling its getContent() method; second, by creating a new ContentHandler subclass that getContent() can use; third, by installing a ContentHandlerFactory with URLConnection.setContentHandlerFactory(), changing the way the application looks for content handlers.

The ContentHandler Class

A subclass of ContentHandler overrides the getContent() method to return an object that's the Java equivalent of the content. This method can be quite simple or quite complex, depending almost entirely on the complexity of the content type you're trying to parse. A text/plain content handler is quite simple; a text/rtf content handler would be very complex.

The ContentHandler class has only a simple noargs constructor:

```
public ContentHandler()
```

Since ContentHandler is an abstract class, you never call its constructor directly, only from inside the constructors of subclasses.

The primary method of the class, albeit an abstract one, is getContent():

```
public abstract Object getContent(URLConnection uc) throws IOException
```

This method is normally called only from inside the getContent() method of a URLConnection object. It is overridden in a subclass that is specific to the type of content being handled. getContent() should use the URLConnection's InputStream to create an object. There are no rules about what type of object a content handler should return. In general, this depends on what the application requesting the content expects. Content handlers for text-like content bundled with the JDK return some subclass of InputStream. Content handlers for images return ImageProducer objects.

The getContent() method of a content handler does not get the full InputStream that the URLConnection has access to. The InputStream that a content handler sees should include only the content's raw data. Any MIME headers or other protocol-specific information that come from the server should be stripped by the URLConnection before it passes the stream to the ContentHandler. A ContentHandler is responsible only for content, not for any protocol overhead that may be present. The URLConnection should have already performed any necessary handshaking with the server and interpreted any headers it sends.

A Content Handler for Tab-Separated Values

To see how content handlers work, let's create a ContentHandler that handles the text/tab-separated-values content type. We aren't concerned with how the tab-separated values get to us. That's for a protocol handler to deal with. All a ContentHandler needs to know is the MIME type and format of the data.

Tab-separated values are produced by many database and spreadsheet programs. A tab-separated file may look something like this. Tabs are indicated by arrows:

> JPE Associates   →341 Lafayette Street, Suite 1025 →New York ÆNY ÆE10012
> O'Reilly & Associates →103 Morris Street, Suite A   →Sebastopol ÆCA ÆE95472

In database parlance, each line is a *record*, and the data before each tab is a *field*. It is usually (though not necessarily) true that each field has the same meaning in each record. In the previous example, the first field is the company name.

The first question to ask is: what kind of Java object should we convert the tab-separated values to? The simplest and most general way to store each record is as an array of Strings. Successive records can be collected in a Vector. In many applications, however, you have a great deal more knowledge about the exact format and meaning of the data than we do here. The more you know about the data you're dealing with, the better a ContentHandler you can write. For example, if you know that the data you're downloading represents U.S. addresses, then you could define a class like this:

```
public class Address {

    private String name;
    private String street;
    private String city;
    private String state;
    private String zip;


}
```

This class would also have appropriate constructors and other methods to represent each record. In this example, we don't know anything about the data in advance, or how many records we'll have to store. Therefore, we will take the most general approach and convert each record into an array of strings, using a Vector to store each array until there are no more records. The getContent() method can return the Vector of String arrays.

Example 17-1 shows the code for such a ContentHandler. The full package-qualified name is com.macfaq.net.www.content.text.tab_separated_ values. This unusual class name follows the naming convention for a content handler for the MIME type text/tab-separated-values. Since MIME types often contain hyphens, as in this example, a convention exists to replace these with the underscore (_). Thus text/tab-separated-values becomes text.tab_ separated_values. To install this content handler, all that's needed is to put the compiled *.class* file somewhere the class loader can find it and set the java. content.handler.pkgs property to com.macfaq.net.www.content.

Example 17-1. A ContentHandler for text/tab-separated-values

```java
package com.macfaq.net.www.content.text;

import java.net.*;
import java.io.*;
import java.util.*;
import com.macfaq.io.SafeBufferedReader  // From Chapter 4


public class tab_separated_values extends ContentHandler {

  public Object getContent(URLConnection uc) throws IOException {

    String theLine;
    Vector v = new Vector();

    InputStreamReader isr = new InputStreamReader(uc.getInputStream());
    SafeBufferedReader in = new SafeBufferedReader(isr);
    while ((theLine = in.readLine()) != null) {
      String[] linearray = lineToArray(theLine);
      v.addElement(linearray);
    }

    return v;

  }

  private String[] lineToArray(String line)  {

    int numFields = 1;
    for (int i = 0; i < line.length(); i++) {
      if (line.charAt(i) == '\t') numFields++;
```

Example 17-1. A ContentHandler for text/tab-separated-values (continued)

```
  }
  String[] fields = new String[numFields];
  int position = 0;
  for (int i = 0; i < numFields; i++) {
    StringBuffer buffer = new StringBuffer();
    while (position < line.length() && line.charAt(position) != '\t') {
      buffer.append(line.charAt(position));
      position++;
    }
    fields[i] = buffer.toString();
    position++;
  }

  return fields;

 }
}
```

Example 17-1 has two methods. The private utility method `lineToArray()` converts a tab-separated string into an array of strings. This method is for the private use of this subclass and is not required by the `ContentHandler` interface. The more complicated the content you're trying to parse, the more such methods your class will need. The `lineToArray()` method begins by counting the number of tabs in the string. This sets the `numFields` variable to one more than the number of tabs. An array is created for the fields with the length `numFields`. Then a `for` loop fills the array with the strings between the tabs. Then this array is returned.

NOTE   You may have expected a `StringTokenizer` to split the line into parts. However, that class has unusual ideas about what makes up a token. In particular, it would interpret multiple tabs in a row as a single delimiter. That is, it never returns an empty string as a token.

The `getContent()` method starts by instantiating a `Vector`. Then it gets the `InputStream` from the `URLConnection` `uc` and chains this to an `InputStreamReader`, which is in turn chained to the `SafeBufferedReader` introduced in Chapter 4, *Java I/O*, so it can read it one line at a time in a while loop. Each line is fed to the `lineToArray()` method, which splits it into a `String` array. This array is then added to the `Vector`. When no more lines are left, the loop exits and the `Vector` is returned.

Using Content Handlers

Now that you've written your first `ContentHandler`, let's see how to use it in a program. Files of MIME type `text/tab-separated-values` can be served by gopher servers, HTTP servers, FTP servers, and more. Let's assume you're retrieving a tab-separated-values file from an HTTP server. The filename should end with the *.tsv* or *.tab* extension so that the server knows it's a text/tab-separated-values file.

NOTE   Not all servers are configured to support this type out of the box. Consult your server documentation to see how to set up a MIME-type mapping for your server. For instance, to configure my Apache server, I added these lines to my *.htaccess* file:

```
AddType text/tab-separated-values tab
AddType text/tab-separated-values tsv
```

You can test the web server configuration by connecting to port 80 of the web server with Telnet and requesting the file manually:

```
% telnet metalab.unc.edu 80
Trying 127.0.0.1...
Connected to metalab.unc.edu.
Escape character is '^]'.
GET /javafaq/addresses.tab HTTP 1.0

HTTP 1.0 200 OK
Date: Mon, 15 Nov 1999 18:36:51 GMT
Server: Apache/1.3.4 (Unix) PHP/3.0.6 mod_perl/1.17
Last-Modified: Thu, 04 Nov 1999 18:22:51 GMT
Content-type: text/tab-separated-values
Content-length: 163

JPE Associates 341 Lafayette Street, Suite 1025 New York NY
10012
O'Reilly & Associates 103 Morris Street, Suite A Sebastopol
CA 95472
Connection closed by foreign host.
```

You're looking for a line that says Content-type: text/tab-separated-values. If you see a Content-type of text/plain, application/octet-stream, or some other value, or you don't see any Content-type at all, the server is misconfigured and must be fixed before you continue.

The application that uses the tab-separated-values content handler does not need to know about it explicitly. It simply has to call the getContent() method of URL or URLConnection on a URL with a matching MIME type. Furthermore, the package where the content handler can be found has to be listed in the java.content.handlers.pkg property.

Example 17-2 is a class that downloads and prints a text/tab-separated-values file using the ContentHandler of Example 17-1. However, note that it

does not import com.macfaq.net.www.content.text and that it never references the tab_separated_values class. It does explicitly add com.macfaq.net.
www.content to the java.content.handlers.pkgs property because that's the
simplest way to make sure this standalone program works. However, the lines that
do that could be deleted if the property were set in a property file or from the
command line, and indeed this is required in Java 1.1.

Example 17-2. The tab-separated-values ContentTester Class

```
import java.io.*;
import java.net.*;
import java.util.*;

public class TSVContentTester {

  private static void test(URL u) throws IOException {

    Object content = u.getContent();
    Vector v = (Vector) content;
    for (Enumeration e = v.elements() ; e.hasMoreElements() ;) {
      String[] sa = (String[]) e.nextElement();
      for (int i = 0; i < sa.length; i++) {
        System.out.print(sa[i] + "\t");
      }
      System.out.println();
    }


  }

  public static void main (String[] args) {

    // If you uncomment these lines in Java 1.2, then you don't
    // have to set the java.content.handler.pkgs property from the
    // command line or your properties files.

/*    String pkgs = System.getProperty("java.content.handler.pkgs", "");
    if (!pkgs.equals("")) {
      pkgs = pkgs + "|";
    }
    pkgs += "com.macfaq.net.www.content";
    System.setProperty("java.content.handler.pkgs", pkgs);  */

    for (int i = 0; i < args.length; i++) {
      try {
        URL u = new URL(args[i]);
        test(u);
      }
      catch (MalformedURLException e) {
        System.err.println(args[i] + " is not a good URL");
```

Example 17-2. The tab-separated-values ContentTester Class (continued)

```
      }
      catch (Exception e) {
        e.printStackTrace();
      }
    }
  }
}
```

Here's how you run this program in Java 1.1 and 1.3. The arrows indicate tabs:

```
% java -Djava.content.handler.pkgs=com.macfaq.net.www.content\
 TSVContentTester http://metalab.unc.edu/javafaq/addresses.tab
JPE Associates→341 Lafayette Street, Suite 1025→New York→NY→10012
O'Reilly & Associates→103 Morris Street, Suite A→Sebastopol→CA→95472
```

Java 1.2 is trickier because the new class-loading policy used in Java 1.2 prevents content handlers from being loaded from the local class path. This bug is fixed in Java 1.3. However, in Java 1.2, simply running Example 17-2 will result in a ClassCastException. Since the custom content handler isn't found, getContent() returns an InputStream (specifically a sun.net.www.MeteredStream) instead:

```
% java TSVContentTester http://metalab.unc.edu/javafaq/addresses.tab
java.lang.ClassCastException: sun.net.www.MeteredStream
        at TSVContentTester.test(TSVContentTester.java:10)
        at TSVContentTester.main(TSVContentTester.java:35)
```

There are a couple of ways around this. You can use the oldjava interpreter instead. This does load content handlers from the local class path. For example:

```
% oldjava TSVContentTester http://metalab.unc.edu/javafaq/addresses.tab
JPE Associates→341 Lafayette Street, Suite 1025→New York→NY→10012
O'Reilly & Associates→103 Morris Street, Suite A→Sebastopol→CA→95472
```

Alternatively, you can use the nonstandard -Xbootclasspath command-line switch to tell Java where to find the content handlers. For example, this line tells Java to look in the current directory for content handlers and other files before looking in the *rt.jar* file (the exact location of the *rt.jar* file will have to be adjusted to match your system):

```
% java -Xbootclasspath:.;/usr/local/jdk1.3/jre/lib/rt.jar\
TSVContentTester http://metalab.unc.edu/javafaq/addresses.tab
JPE Associates→341 Lafayette Street, Suite 1025→New York→NY→10012
O'Reilly & Associates→103 Morris Street, Suite A→Sebastopol→CA→95472
```

The bug that requires these workarounds is present in all versions of Java 1.2, though it doesn't manifest itself in applets because of the different nature of the ClassLoader that a web browser uses. Of course, the ultimate solution is to use a ContentHandlerFactory, an option I'll discuss later.

Choosing Return Types

Java 1.3 adds one overloaded variant of the getContent() method to the ContentHandler class:

```
public Object getContent(URLConnection uc, Class[] classes) // Java 1.3
  throws IOException
```

The difference is the array of java.lang.Class objects passed as the second argument. This allows the caller to request that the content be returned as one of the types in the array and enables content handlers to support multiple types. For example, the text/tab-separated-values content handler could return data as a Vector, an array, a string, or an InputStream. One would be the default used by the single argument getContent() method, while the others would be options that a client could request. If the client doesn't request any of the classes this ContentHandler knows how to provide, then it returns null.

To call this method, the client invokes the method with the same arguments in a URL or URLConnection object. It passes an array of Class objects in the order it wishes to receive the data. Thus, if it prefers to receive a String but is willing to accept an InputStream and will take a Vector as a last resort, then it would put String.class in the zeroth component of the array, InputStream.class in the first component of the array, and Vector.class in the last component of the array. Then it would use instanceof to test what was actually returned and either process it or convert it into the preferred type. For example:

```
Class[] requestedTypes = {String.class, InputStream.class,
  Vector.class};
Object content = url.getContent(requestedTypes);
if (content instanceof String) {
  String s = (String) content;
  System.out.println(s);
}
else if (content instanceof InputStream) {
  InputStream in = (InputStream) content;
  int c;
  while ((c = in.read()) != -1) System.out.write(c);
}
else if (content instanceof Vector) {
  Vector v = (Vector) content;
  for (Enumeration e = v.elements() ; e.hasMoreElements() ;) {
    String[] sa = (String[]) e.nextElement();
    for (int i = 0; i < sa.length; i++) {
      System.out.print(sa[i] + "\t");
    }
    System.out.println();
  }
}
```

```
else {
  System.out.println("Unrecognized content type " + content.getClass());
}
```

To demonstrate this, let's write a content handler that can be used in association with the time protocol. Recall that the time protocol returns the current time at the server as a 4-byte, big-endian unsigned integer giving the number of seconds since midnight, January 1, 1900, Greenwich Mean Time. There are several obvious candidates for storing this data in a Java content handler, including `java.lang.Long` (`java.lang.Integer` won't work since the unsigned value may overflow the bounds of an `int`), `java.util.Date`, `java.util.Calendar`, `java.lang.String`, and `java.io.InputStream`, which often works as a last resort. Example 17-3 provides all five options. Since there's no standard MIME type for the time format, we'll use `application` for the type to indicate that this is binary data, and `x-time` for the subtype to indicate that this is a nonstandard extension type. It will be up to the time protocol handler to return the right content type.

Example 17-3. A Time Content Handler

```
package com.macfaq.net.www.content.application;

import java.net.*;
import java.io.*;
import java.util.*;


public class x_time extends ContentHandler {

  public Object getContent(URLConnection uc) throws IOException {

    Class[] classes = new Class[1];
    classes[0] = Date.class;
    return this.getContent(uc, classes);

  }

  public Object getContent(URLConnection uc, Class[] classes)
    throws IOException {

    InputStream in = uc.getInputStream();
    for (int i = 0; i < classes.length; i++) {
      if (classes[i] == InputStream.class) {
        return in;
      }
      else if (classes[i] == Long.class) {
        long secondsSince1900 = readSecondsSince1900(in);
        return new Long(secondsSince1900);
      }
```

Example 17-3. A Time Content Handler (continued)

```
      else if (classes[i] == Date.class) {
        long secondsSince1900 = readSecondsSince1900(in);
        Date time = shiftEpochs(secondsSince1900);
        return time;
      }
      else if (classes[i] == Calendar.class) {
        long secondsSince1900 = readSecondsSince1900(in);
        Date time = shiftEpochs(secondsSince1900);
        Calendar c = Calendar.getInstance();
        c.setTime(time);
        return c;
      }
      else if (classes[i] == String.class) {
        long secondsSince1900 = readSecondsSince1900(in);
        Date time = shiftEpochs(secondsSince1900);
        return time.toString();
      }
    }

    return null; // no requested type available

  }

  private long readSecondsSince1900(InputStream in)
    throws IOException {

    long secondsSince1900 = 0;
    for (int j = 0; j < 4; j++) {
      secondsSince1900 = (secondsSince1900 << 8) | in.read();
    }
    return secondsSince1900;

  }

  private Date shiftEpochs(long secondsSince1900) {

    // The time protocol sets the epoch at 1900, the Java Date class
    //   at 1970. This number converts between them.
    long differenceBetweenEpochs = 2208988800L;

    long secondsSince1970 = secondsSince1900 - differenceBetweenEpochs;
    long msSince1970 = secondsSince1970 * 1000;
    Date time = new Date(msSince1970);
    return time;

  }
}
```

Most of the work is performed by the second getContent() method. This checks to see whether it recognizes any of the classes in the classes array. If so, it attempts to convert the content into an object of that type. The for loop is arranged so that classes earlier in the array take precedence; that is, first we try to match the first class in the array; next we try to match the second class in the array; then the third class in the array; and so on. As soon as one class is matched, the method returns so later classes won't be matched even if they're an allowed choice.

Once a type is matched, a simple algorithm converts the four bytes that the time server sends into the right kind of object, either an InputStream, a Long, a Date, a Calendar, or a String. The InputStream conversion is trivial. The Long conversion is one of those rare times when it seems a little inconvenient that primitive data types aren't objects. Although you can convert to and return any object type, you can't convert to and return a primitive data type like long, so we return the type wrapper class Long instead. The Date and Calendar conversions require shifting the origin of the time from January 1, 1900 to January 1, 1970 and changing the units from seconds to milliseconds as discussed in Chapter 10, *Sockets for Clients*. Finally, the conversion to a String simply converts to a Date first, then invokes the Date object's toString() method.

While it would be possible to configure a web server to send data of MIME type application/x-time, this class is really designed to be used by a custom protocol handler. This handler would know not only how to speak the time protocol, but also how to return application/x-time from the getContentType() method. Example 17-4 and Example 17-5 demonstrate such a protocol handler. It assumes that time URLs look like *time://vision.poly.edu:3737/*.

Example 17-4. The URLConnection for the Time Protocol Handler

```
package com.macfaq.net.www.protocol.time;

import java.net.*;
import java.io.*;
import com.macfaq.net.www.content.application.*;

public class TimeURLConnection extends URLConnection {

  private Socket connection = null;
  public final static int DEFAULT_PORT = 37;

  public TimeURLConnection (URL u) {
    super(u);
  }

  public String getContentType() {
```

Example 17-4. The URLConnection for the Time Protocol Handler (continued)

```
    return "application/x-time";
  }

  public Object getContent() throws IOException {
    ContentHandler ch = new x_time();
    return ch.getContent(this);
  }

  public Object getContent(Class[] classes) throws IOException {
    ContentHandler ch = new x_time();
    return ch.getContent(this, classes);
  }

  public InputStream getInputStream() throws IOException {
    if (!connected) this.connect();
      return this.connection.getInputStream();
  }

  public synchronized void connect() throws IOException {

    if (!connected) {
      int port = url.getPort();
      if ( port < 0) {
        port = DEFAULT_PORT;
      }
      this.connection = new Socket(url.getHost(), port);
      this.connected = true;
    }
  }
}
```

In general, it should be enough for the protocol handler to simply know or be able to deduce the correct MIME content type. However, in a case like this where both content and protocol handlers must be provided, you can tie them a little more closely together by overriding getContent() as well. This allows you to avoid messing with the java.content.handler.pkgs property or installing a ContentHandlerFactory. You will still need to set the java.protocol-handler.pkgs property to point to your package or install a URLS StreamHandlerFactory, however. Example 17-5 is a simple URLStream-Handler for the time protocol handler.

Example 17-5. The URLStreamHandler for the Time Protocol Handler

```
package com.macfaq.net.www.protocol.time;

import java.net.*;
import java.io.*;
```

Example 17-5. The URLStreamHandler for the Time Protocol Handler (continued)

```
public class Handler extends URLStreamHandler {

  protected URLConnection openConnection(URL u) throws IOException {
    return new TimeURLConnection(u);
  }
}
```

We could install the time protocol handler into HotJava, as in the previous chapter. However, even if we place the time content handler in HotJava's class path, HotJava won't use it. Consequently, I've written a simple standalone application, shown in Example 17-6, that uses these protocol and content handlers to tell the time. Notice that it does not need to import or directly refer to any of the classes involved. It simply lets the URL find the right content handler.

Example 17-6. URLTimeClient

```
import java.net.*;
import java.util.*;
import java.io.*;

public class URLTimeClient {

  public static void main(String[] args) {

    System.setProperty("java.protocol.handler.pkgs",
      "com.macfaq.net.www.protocol");

    try {
      // You can replace this with your own time server
      URL u = new URL("time://tock.usno.navy.mil/");
      Class[] types = {String.class, Date.class,
        Calendar.class, Long.class};
      Object o = u.getContent(types);
      System.out.println(o);
    }
    catch (IOException e) {
      // Let's see what went wrong
      e.printStackTrace();
    }
  }
}
```

Here's a sample run:

```
D:\JAVA\JNP2\examples\16>java URLTimeClient
Thu Nov 18 08:27:31 PST 1999
```

In this case, a `String` object was returned. This was the first choice of
`URLTimeClient` but the last choice of the content handler. The client choice
always takes precedence.

The ContentHandlerFactory Interface

A `ContentHandlerFactory` defines the rules for where `ContentHandler` classes
are stored. Create a class that implements `ContentHandlerFactory`, and give this
class a `createContentHandler()` method that knows how to instantiate your
`ContentHandler`. The `createContentHandler()` method should return `null` if
it can't find a `ContentHandler` appropriate for a MIME type; `null` signals Java to
look for `ContentHandler` classes in the default locations. When your application
starts, call the `URLConnection`'s `setContentHandlerFactory()` method to set
the `ContentHandlerFactory`. This method may be called only once in the lifetime of an application.

The createContentHandler() Method

Just as the `createURLStreamHandler()` method of the `URLStreamHandler-`
`Factory` interface was responsible for finding and loading the appropriate protocol handler, so too the `createContentHandler()` method of the
`ContentHandlerFactory` interface is responsible for finding and loading the
appropriate `ContentHandler` given a MIME type:

```
public abstract ContentHandler createContentHandler(String mimeType)
```

This method should be called only by the `getContent()` method of a
`URLConnection` object. For instance, Example 17-7 is a `ContentHandlerFactory`
that knows how to find the right handler for the `text/tab-separated-`
`values` content handler of Example 17-1:

Example 17-7. TabFactory

```
package com.macfaq.net.www.content;

import java.net.*;

public class TabFactory implements ContentHandlerFactory {

  public ContentHandler createContentHandler(String mimeType)) {

    if (mimeType.equals("text/tab-separated-values") {
      return new com.macfaq.net.www.content.text.tab_separated_values();
    }
    else {
```

Example 17-7. TabFactory (continued)

```
        return null; // look for the handler in the default locations
    }
  }
}
```

This factory knows how to find only one kind of content handler, but there's no limit to how many a factory can know about. For example, this `createContentHandler()` method also suggests handlers for `application/x-time`, `text/plain`, `video/mpeg`, and `model/vrml`. Notice that when you're using a `ContentHandlerFactory`, you don't necessarily have to stick to standard naming conventions for `ContentHandler` subclasses:

```
public ContentHandler createContentHandler(String mimeType)) {

    if (mimeType.equals("text/tab-separated-values") {
        return new com.macfaq.net.www.content.text.tab_separated_values();
    }
    else if (mimeType.equals("application/x-time") {
        return new com.macfaq.net.www.content.application.x_time();
    }
    else if (mimeType.equals("text/plain") {
        return new sun.net.www.content.text.plain();
    }
    if (mimeType.equals("video/mpeg") {
        return new com.macfaq.video.MPEGHandler();
    }
    if (mimeType.equals("model/vrml") {
        return new com.macfaq.threed.VRMLModel();
    }
    else {
        return null; // look for the handler in the default locations
    }
}
```

Installing Content Handler Factories

A `ContentHandlerFactory` is installed in an application using the static `URLConnection.setContentHandlerFactory()` method:

```
public static void setContentHandlerFactory(ContentHandlerFactory fac)
    throws SecurityException, Error
```

Note that this method is in the `URLConnection` class, not the `ContentHandler` class. It may be invoked at most once during any run of an application. It throws an `Error` if it is called a second time.

Using a `ContentHandlerFactory` such as the `TabFactory` in Example 17-5, it's possible to write a standalone application that can automatically load our tab-separated-values content handler and that runs in Java 1.1 through 1.3 without any major hassles with the class path. Example 17-8 is such a program. However, as with most other `setFactory()` methods, untrusted applets will generally not be allowed to set the content handler factory. Attempting to do so will throw a `SecurityException`. Consequently, installing new content handlers in applets pretty much requires directly accessing the `getContent()` method of the `ContentHandler` subclass itself. Ideally, this shouldn't be necessary, but until Sun provides better support for downloadable content handlers in browsers, this is what we're stuck with.

Example 17-8. TabLoader That Uses a ContentHandlerFactory

```java
import java.io.*;
import java.net.*;
import java.util.*;
import com.macfaq.net.www.content.*;

public class TabLoader {

  public static void main (String[] args) {

    URLConnection.setContentHandlerFactory(new TabFactory());

    for (int i = 0; i < args.length; i++) {
      try {
        URL u = new URL(args[i]);
        Object content = u.getContent();
        Vector v = (Vector) content;
        for (Enumeration e = v.elements() ; e.hasMoreElements() ;) {
          String[] sa = (String[]) e.nextElement();
          for (int j = 0; j < sa.length; j++) {
            System.out.print(sa[j] + "\t");
          }
          System.out.println();
        }
      }
      catch (MalformedURLException e) {
        System.err.println(args[i] + " is not a good URL");
      }
      catch (Exception e) {
        e.printStackTrace();
      }
    }
  }
}
```

Here's a typical run. As usual, tabs are indicated by arrows:

```
% java TabLoader http://metalab.unc.edu/javafaq/addresses.tab
JPE Associates                →341 Lafayette St, Suite 1025  →New York  →NY →10012
O'Reilly & Associates →103 Morris St, Suite A              →Sebastopol  →CA →95472
```

A Content Handler for an Image Format: image/x-fits

That's really all there is to content handlers. As one final example, I'll show you how to write a content handler for image files. These differ from the text-based content handlers you've already seen in that they generally produce an object that implements the java.awt.ImageProducer interface rather than an Input Stream object. The specific example we'll choose is the Flexible Image Transport System (FITS) format in common use among astronomers. FITS files are grayscale, bitmapped images with headers that determine the bit depth of the picture, the width and the height of the picture, and the number of pictures in the file. Although FITS files commonly contain several images (typically pictures of the same thing taken at different times), in this example we look at only the first image in a file.[*]

There are a few key things you need to know to process FITS files. First, FITS files are broken up into blocks of exactly 2,880 bytes. If there isn't enough data to fill a block, it is padded with spaces at the end. Each FITS file has two parts, the header and the primary data unit. The header occupies an integral number of blocks, as does the primary data unit. If the FITS file contains extensions, there may be additional data after the primary data unit, but we ignore that here. Any extensions that are present will not change the image contained in the primary data unit.

The header begins in the first block of the FITS file. It may occupy one or more blocks; the last block may be padded with spaces at the end. The header is ASCII text. Each line of the header is exactly 80 bytes wide. The first eight characters of each header line contain a keyword, which is followed by an equals sign (character 9), followed by a space (10). The keyword is padded on the right with spaces to make it eight characters long. Columns 11 through 30 contain a value; the value may be right-justified and padded on the left with spaces if necessary. The value may be an integer, a floating point number, a T or an F signifying the boolean values true and false, or a string delimited with single quotes. A comment may appear in columns 31 through 80; comments are separated from the value of a field by a slash (/). Here's a simple header taken from a FITS image produced by K. S.

---

[*] For more details about the FITS format and how to handle FITS files, see *The Encyclopedia of Graphics File Formats*, 2nd ed., by James D. Murray and William vanRyper, pp. 392–400 (O'Reilly & Associates, Inc.)

Balasubramaniam at the Vacuum Tower Telescope at the National Solar Observatory in Sunspot, New Mexico (*http://www.sunspot.noao.edu/*):

```
SIMPLE  =                     T /
BITPIX  =                    16 /
NAXIS   =                     2 /
NAXIS1  =                   242 /
NAXIS2  =                   252 /
DATE    = '19 Aug 1996'        /
TELESC  = 'NSO/SP - VTT'       /
IMAGE   = 'Continuum'          /
COORDS  = 'N29.1W34.2'         /
OBSTIME = '13:59:00 UT'        /
END
```

Every FITS file begins with the keyword SIMPLE. This keyword always has the value T. If this isn't the case, the file is not valid. The second line of a FITS file always has the keyword BITPIX, which tells you how the data is stored. There are five possible values for BITPIX, four of which correspond exactly to Java primitive data types. The most common value of BITPIX is 16, meaning that there are 16 bits per pixel, which is equivalent to a Java short. A BITPIX of 32 is a Java int. A BITPIX of –32 means that each pixel is represented by a 32-bit floating point number (equivalent to a Java float); a BITPIX of –64 is equivalent to a Java double. A BITPIX of 8 means that 8 bits are used to represent each pixel; this is similar to a Java byte, except that FITS uses unsigned bytes ranging from 0 to 255; Java's byte data type is signed, taking values that range from –128 to 127.

The remaining keywords in a FITS file may appear in any order. They are *not* necessarily in the order shown here. In our FITS content handler, we first read all the keywords into a Hashtable and then extract the ones we want by name.

The NAXIS header specifies the number of axes (that is, the dimension) of the primary data array. A NAXIS value of one identifies a one-dimensional image. A NAXIS value of two indicates a normal two-dimensional rectangular image. A NAXIS value of three is called a *data cube* and generally means the file contains a series of pictures of the same object taken at different moments in time. In other words, time is the third dimension. On rare occasions, the third dimension can represent depth: i.e., the file contains a true three-dimensional image. A NAXIS of four means the file contains a sequence of three-dimensional pictures taken at different moments in time. Higher values of NAXIS, while theoretically possible, are rarely seen in practice. Our example is going to look at only the first two-dimensional image in a file.

The NAXIS*n* headers (where *n* is an integer ranging from 1 to NAXIS) give the length of the image in pixels along that dimension. In this example, NAXIS1 is 242, so the image is 242 pixels wide. NAXIS2 is 252, so this image is 252 pixels high. Since FITS images are normally pictures of astronomical bodies like the sun, it doesn't really matter if you reverse width and height. All FITS images contain the SIMPLE, BITPIX, END, and NAXIS keywords, plus a series of NAXISn keywords. These keywords all provide information that is essential for displaying the image.

The next five keywords are specific to this file and may not be present in other FITS files. They give meaning to the image, though they are not needed to display it. The DATE keyword says this image was taken on August 19, 1996. The TELESC keyword says this image was taken by the Vacuum Tower Telescope (VTT) at the National Solar Observatory (NSO) on Sacramento Peak (SP). The IMAGE keyword says that this is a picture of the white light continuum; images taken through spectrographs might look at only a particular wavelength in the spectrum. The COORDS keyword gives the latitude and longitude of the telescope. Finally, the OBSTIME keyword says this image was taken at 1:59 P.M. Universal Time (essentially, Greenwich Mean Time). There are many more optional headers that don't appear in this example. Like the five discussed here, the remaining keywords may help someone interpret an image, but they don't provide the information needed to display it.

The keyword END terminates the header. Following the END keyword, the header is padded with spaces so that it fills a 2,880-byte block. A header may take up more than one 2,880-byte block, but it must always be padded to an integral number of blocks.

The image data follows the header. How the image is stored depends on the value of BITPIX, as explained earlier. Fortunately, these data types are stored in formats (big-endian, two's complement) that can be read directly with a `DataInput-Stream`. The exact meaning of each number in the image data is completely file-dependent. More often than not, it's the number of electrons that were collected in a specific time interval by a particular pixel in a charge coupled device (CCD); in older FITS files, the numbers could represent the value read from photographic film by a densitometer. However, the unifying theme is that larger numbers represent brighter light. To interpret these numbers as a grayscale image, you map the smallest value in the data to pure black, the largest value in the data to pure white, and scale all intermediate values appropriately. A general-purpose FITS reader cannot interpret the numbers as anything except abstract brightness levels. Without scaling, differences tend to get washed out. For example, a dark spot on the Sun tends to be about 4,000K. That is dark compared to the normal solar surface temperature of 6,000K, but considerably brighter than anything you're likely to see on the surface of the Earth.

Example 17-9 is a FITS content hander. FITS files should be served with the MIME type `image/x-fits`. This is almost certainly not included in your server's default

MIME-type mappings, so make sure to add a mapping between files that end in *.fit*, *.fts*, or *.fits* and the MIME type `image/x-fits`.

Example 17-9. An x-fits Content Handler

```
package com.macfaq.net.www.content.image;

import java.net.*;
import java.io.*;
import java.awt.image.*;
import java.util.*;


public class x_fits extends ContentHandler {

  public Object getContent(URLConnection uc) throws IOException {

    int width = -1;
    int height = -1;
    int bitpix = 16;
    int[] data = null;
    int naxis = 2;
    Hashtable header = null;

    DataInputStream dis = new DataInputStream(uc.getInputStream());
    header = readHeader(dis);

    bitpix = getIntFromHeader("BITPIX  ", -1, header);
    if (bitpix <= 0) return null;
    naxis = getIntFromHeader("NAXIS   ", -1, header);
    if (naxis < 1) return null;
    width = getIntFromHeader("NAXIS1  ", -1, header);
    if (width <= 0) return null;
    if (naxis == 1) height = 1;
    else height = getIntFromHeader("NAXIS2  ", -1, header);
    if (height <= 0) return null;

    if (bitpix == 16) {
      short[] theInput = new short[height * width];
      for (int i = 0; i < theInput.length; i++) {
        theInput[i] = dis.readShort();
      }
      data = scaleArray(theInput);
    }
    else if (bitpix == 32) {
      int[] theInput = new int[height * width];
      for (int i = 0; i < theInput.length; i++) {
        theInput[i] = dis.readInt();
      }
```

Example 17-9. An x-fits Content Handler (continued)

```
      data = scaleArray(theInput);
  }
  else if (bitpix == 64) {
    long[] theInput = new long[height * width];
    for (int i = 0; i < theInput.length; i++) {
      theInput[i] = dis.readLong();
    }
    data = scaleArray(theInput);
  }
  else if (bitpix == -32) {
    float[] theInput = new float[height * width];
    for (int i = 0; i < theInput.length; i++) {
      theInput[i] = dis.readFloat();
    }
    data = scaleArray(theInput);
  }
  else if (bitpix == -64) {
    double[] theInput = new double[height * width];
    for (int i = 0; i < theInput.length; i++) {
      theInput[i] = dis.readDouble();
    }
    data = scaleArray(theInput);
  }
  else {
    System.err.println("Invalid BITPIX");
    return null;
  } // end if-else-if

  return new MemoryImageSource(width, height, data, 0, width);

} // end getContent

private Hashtable readHeader(DataInputStream dis)
 throws IOException {

  int blocksize = 2880;
  int fieldsize = 80;
  String key, value;
  int linesRead = 0;

  byte[] buffer = new byte[fieldsize];

  Hashtable header = new Hashtable();
  while (true) {
    dis.readFully(buffer);
    key = new String(buffer, 0, 8, "ASCII");
    linesRead++;
    if (key.substring(0, 3).equals("END")) break;
```

Example 17-9. An x-fits Content Handler (continued)

```
      if (buffer[8] != '=' || buffer[9] != ' ') continue;
      value = new String(buffer, 10, 20, "ASCII");
      header.put(key, value);
    }
    int linesLeftToRead
     = (blocksize - ((linesRead * fieldsize) % blocksize))/fieldsize;
    for (int i = 0; i < linesLeftToRead; i++) dis.readFully(buffer);

    return header;

  }

  private int getIntFromHeader(String name, int defaultValue,
   Hashtable header) {

    String s = "";
    int result = defaultValue;

    try {
      s = (String) header.get(name);
    }
    catch (NullPointerException e) {
      return defaultValue;
    }
    try {
      result = Integer.parseInt(s.trim());
    }
    catch (NumberFormatException e) {
      System.err.println(e);
      System.err.println(s);
      return defaultValue;
    }

    return result;

  }

  // parameterized types (templates) would help a lot here
  private int[] scaleArray(short[] theInput) {

    int data[] = new int[theInput.length];
    int max = 0;
    int min = 0;
    for (int i = 0; i < theInput.length; i++) {
      if (theInput[i] > max) max = theInput[i];
      if (theInput[i] < min) min = theInput[i];
    }
```

Example 17-9. An x-fits Content Handler (continued)

```
    long r = max - min;
    double a = 255.0/r;
    double b = -a * min;
    int opaque = 255;
    for (int i = 0; i < data.length; i++) {
      int temp = (int) (theInput[i] * a + b);
      data[i] =  (opaque << 24)  | (temp << 16)  | (temp << 8) | temp;
    }
    return data;

  }


  private int[] scaleArray(int[] theInput) {

    int data[] = new int[theInput.length];
    int max = 0;
    int min = 0;
    for (int i = 0; i < theInput.length; i++) {
      if (theInput[i] > max) max = theInput[i];
      if (theInput[i] < min) min = theInput[i];
    }
    long r = max - min;
    double a = 255.0/r;
    double b = -a * min;
    int opaque = 255;
    for (int i = 0; i < data.length; i++) {
      int temp = (int) (theInput[i] * a + b);
      data[i] =  (opaque << 24)  | (temp << 16)  | (temp << 8) | temp;
    }
    return data;

  }


  private int[] scaleArray(long[] theInput) {

    int data[] = new int[theInput.length];
    long max = 0;
    long min = 0;
    for (int i = 0; i < theInput.length; i++) {
      if (theInput[i] > max) max = theInput[i];
      if (theInput[i] < min) min = theInput[i];
    }
    long r = max - min;
    double a = 255.0/r;
    double b = -a * min;
    int opaque = 255;
    for (int i = 0; i < data.length; i++) {
      int temp = (int) (theInput[i] * a + b);
```

Example 17-9. An x-fits Content Handler (continued)

```
      data[i] =  (opaque << 24)  | (temp << 16)  | (temp << 8) | temp;
    }
    return data;

  }

  private int[] scaleArray(double[] theInput) {

    int data[] = new int[theInput.length];
    double max = 0;
    double min = 0;
    for (int i = 0; i < theInput.length; i++) {
      if (theInput[i] > max) max = theInput[i];
      if (theInput[i] < min) min = theInput[i];
    }
    double r = max - min;
    double a = 255.0/r;
    double b = -a * min;
    int opaque = 255;
    for (int i = 0; i < data.length; i++) {
      int temp = (int) (theInput[i] * a + b);
      data[i] =  (opaque << 24)  | (temp << 16)  | (temp << 8) | temp;
    }
    return data;

  }

  private int[] scaleArray(float[] theInput) {

    int data[] = new int[theInput.length];
    float max = 0;
    float min = 0;
    for (int i = 0; i < theInput.length; i++) {
      if (theInput[i] > max) max = theInput[i];
      if (theInput[i] < min) min = theInput[i];
    }
    double r = max - min;
    double a = 255.0/r;
    double b = -a * min;
    int opaque = 255;
    for (int i = 0; i < data.length; i++) {
      int temp = (int) (theInput[i] * a + b);
      data[i] =  (opaque << 24)  | (temp << 16)  | (temp << 8) | temp;
    }
    return data;
  }
}
```

The key method of the x_fits class is getContent(); it is the one method that the ContentHandler class requires subclasses to implement. The other methods in this class are all simply utility methods that help to break up the program into easier-to-digest chunks. getContent() is called by a URLConnection, which passes a reference to itself in the argument uc. The getContent() method reads data from that URLConnection and uses it to construct an object that implements the ImageProducer interface. To simplify the task of creating an ImageProducer, we create an array of image data and use a MemoryImageSource object, which implements the ImageProducer interface, to convert that array into an image. getContent() returns this MemoryImageSource.

MemoryImageSource has several constructors. The one we use here requires us to provide the width and height of the image, an array of integer values containing the RGB data for each pixel, the offset of the start of that data in the array, and the number of pixels per line in the array:

```
public MemoryImageSource(int width, int height, int[] pixels,
   int offset, int scanlines);
```

The width, height, and pixel data can be read from the header of the FITS image. Since we are creating a new array to hold the pixel data, the offset is zero and the scanlines are the width of the image.

Our content handler has a utility method called readHeader() that reads the image header from uc's InputStream. This method returns a Hashtable containing the keywords and their values as String objects. Comments are thrown away. readHeader() reads 80 bytes at a time, since that's the length of each field. The first eight bytes are transformed into the String key. If there is no key, the line is a comment and is ignored. If there is a key, then the eleventh through thirtieth bytes are stored in a String called value. The key-value pair is stored in the Hashtable. This continues until the END keyword is spotted. At this point, we break out of the loop and read as many lines as necessary to finish the block. (Recall that the header is padded with spaces to make an integral multiple of 2,880). Finally, readHeader() returns the Hashtable header.

After the header has been read into the Hashtable header, the InputStream is now pointing at the first byte of data. However, before we're ready to read the data, we must extract the height, width, and bits per pixel of the primary data unit from the header. These are all integer values, so to simplify the code, we use the getIntFromHeader(String name, int defaultValue, Hashtable header) method. This method takes as arguments the name of the header whose value we want (e.g., BITPIX), a default value for that header, and the Hashtable that contains the header. This method retrieves the value associated with the string name from the Hashtable and casts the result to a String object—we know this cast is safe because we put only String data into the Hashtable. This String is then converted to an int using `Integer.parseInt(s.trim())`; we then return the resulting `int`. If an exception is thrown, `getIntFromHeader()` returns the `defaultValue` argument instead. In this content handler, we use an impossible flag value (–1) as the default to indicate that `getIntFromHeader()` failed.

`getContent()` uses `getIntFromHeader()` to retrieve four crucial values from the header: NAXIS, NAXIS1, NAXIS2, and BITPIX. NAXIS is the number of dimensions in the primary data array; if it is greater than or equal to two, we read the width and height from NAXIS1 and NAXIS2. If there are more than two dimensions, we still read a single two-dimensional frame from the data. A more advanced FITS content handler might read subsequent frames and include them below the original image, or display the sequence of images as an animation. If NAXIS is one, the width is read from NAXIS1, and the height is set to one.* If NAXIS is less than one, there's no image data at all, so we return `null`.

Now we are ready to read the image data. The data can be stored in one of five formats, depending on the value of BITPIX: unsigned bytes, `shorts`, `ints`, `floats`, or `doubles`. This is where the lack of parameterized types and templates in Java makes coding painful: we need to repeat the algorithm for reading data five times, once for each of the five possible data types. In each case, the data is first read from the stream into an array of the appropriate type called `theInput`. Then this array is passed to the `scaleArray()` method, which returns a scaled array. `scaleArray()` is an overloaded method that reads the data in `theInput` and copies the data into the `int` array `theData`, while scaling the data to fall from 0 to 255; there is a different version of `scaleArray()` for each of the five data types we might need to handle. Thus, no matter what format the data starts in, it becomes an `int` array with values from 0 to 255. This data now needs to be converted into grayscale RGB values. The standard 32-bit RGB color model allows 256 different shades of gray ranging from pure black to pure white; 8 bits are used to represent opacity, usually called "alpha". To get a particular shade of gray, the red, green, and blue bytes of an RGB triple should all be set to the same value, and the alpha value should be 255 (fully opaque). Thinking of these as four byte values, you need colors like 255.127.127.127 (medium gray) or 255.255.255.255 (pure white). This is produced by the lines:

```
int temp = (int) (theInput[i] * a + b);
theData[i] = (opaque << 24) | (temp << 16) | (temp << 8) | temp;
```

Once it has converted every pixel in `theInput[]` into a 32-bit color value and stored the result in `theData[]`, `scaleArray()` returns `theData`. The only thing

---

* A FITS file with NAXIS as one would typically be produced from observations that used a one-dimensional CCD.

left for getContent() to do is feed this array, along with the header values previously retrieved, into the MemoryImageSource constructor and return the result.

This FITS content handler has one glaring problem. The image has to be completely loaded before the method returns. Since FITS images are quite literally astronomical in size, loading the image can take a significant amount of time. It would be better to create a new class for FITS images that implements the ImageProducer interface and into which the data can be streamed asynchronously. The ImageConsumer that eventually displays the image can use the methods of ImageProducer to determine when the height and width are available, when a new scanline has been read, when the image is completely loaded or errored out, and so on. getContent() would spawn a separate thread to feed the data into the ImageProducer and would return almost immediately. However, a FITS ImageProducer would not be able to take significant advantage of progressive loading, because the file format doesn't define unambiguously what each data value means; before you can generate RGB pixels, you must read all of the data and find the minimum and maximum values.

Example 17-10 is a simple ContentHandlerFactory that recognizes FITS images. For all types other than image/x-fits, it returns null so that the default locations will be searched for content handlers.

Example 17-10. The FITS ContentHandlerFactory

```
import java.net.*;

public class FitsFactory implements ContentHandlerFactory {

  public ContentHandler createContentHandler(String mimeType) {

    if (mimeType.equalsIgnoreCase("image/x-fits")) {
      return new com.macfaq.net.www.content.image.x_fits();
    }
    return null;

  }
}
```

Example 17-11 is a simple program that tests this content handler by loading and displaying a FITS image from a URL. In fact, it can display any image type for which a content handler is installed. However, it does use the FitsFactory to recognize FITS images.

Example 17-11. The FITS Viewer

```
import java.awt.*;
import javax.swing.*;
import java.awt.image.*;
import java.net.*;
import java.io.*;

public class FitsViewer extends JFrame {

  private URL url;
  private Image theImage;

  public FitsViewer(URL u) {
    super(u.getFile());
    this.url = u;
  }

  public void loadImage() throws IOException {

    Object content = this.url.getContent();
    ImageProducer producer;
    try {
      producer = (ImageProducer) content;
    }
    catch (ClassCastException e) {
      throw new IOException("Unexpected type " + content.getClass());
    }
    if (producer == null) theImage = null;
    else {
      theImage = this.createImage(producer);
      int width = theImage.getWidth(this);
      int height = theImage.getHeight(this);
      if (width > 0 && height > 0) this.setSize(width, height);
    }

  }

  public void paint(Graphics g) {
    if (theImage != null) g.drawImage(theImage, 0, 0, this);
  }

  public static void main(String[] args) {

    URLConnection.setContentHandlerFactory(new FitsFactory());
    for (int i = 0; i < args.length; i++) {
      try {
        FitsViewer f = new FitsViewer(new URL(args[i]));
        f.setSize(252, 252);
```

Example 17-11. The FITS Viewer (continued)

```
        f.loadImage();
        f.show();
      }
      catch (MalformedURLException e) {
        System.err.println(args[i] + " is not a URL I recognize.");
      }
      catch (IOException e) {
        e.printStackTrace();
      }
    }
  }
}
```

The `FitsViewer` program extends `JFrame`. The `main()` method loops through all the command-line arguments creating a new window for each one. Then it loads the image into the window and shows it. The `loadImage()` method actually downloads the requested picture by implicitly using the content handler of Example 17-9 to convert the FITS data into a `java.awt.Image` object stored in the field `theImage`. If the width and the height of the image are available (as they will be for a FITS image using our content handler but maybe not for some other image types that load the image in a separate thread), then the window is resized to the exact size of the image. The `paint()` method simply draws this image on the screen. Most of the work is done inside the content handler. In fact, this program can actually display images of any type for which a content handler is installed and available. For instance, it works equally well for GIF and JPEG images. Figure 17-2 shows this program displaying a picture of part of solar granulation.

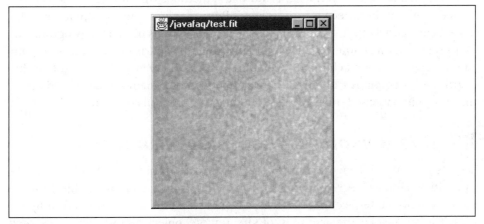

Figure 17-2. The FitsViewer application displaying a FITS image of solar granulation

18

In this chapter:
- *What Is Remote Method Invocation?*
- *Implementation*
- *Loading Classes at Runtime*
- *The java.rmi Package*
- *The java.rmi.registry Package*
- *The java.rmi.server Package*

Remote Method Invocation

Historically, networking has been concerned with two fundamental applications. The first application is moving files and data between hosts, which is handled by FTP, SMTP (email), HTTP, NFS, and many other protocols. The second application is allowing one host to run programs on another host. This is the traditional province of Telnet, rlogin, Remote Procedure Call (RPC), and a lot of database middleware; you can also think of CGI as a means to get a server to run a program for a client. Except for the sections on CGI, most of this book has implicitly concerned itself with file and data transfer. Remote Method Invocation (RMI), however, is an example of the second application for networking: running a program on a remote host from a local machine.

RMI is a core Java API and class library that allows Java programs to call certain methods on a remote server. Furthermore, the methods running on the server can invoke methods in objects on the client. Return values and arguments can be passed back and forth in both directions. In essence, parts of a single program run in a Java virtual machine on a local client while other parts of the same program run on a Java virtual machine on a remote server. RMI creates the illusion that this distributed program is running on one system with one memory space holding all the code and data used on either side of the actual physical connection.

What Is Remote Method Invocation?

The Remote Method Invocation API lets Java objects on different hosts communicate with each other. A remote object lives on a server. Each remote object implements a remote interface that specifies which of its methods can be invoked by clients. Clients invoke the methods of the remote object almost exactly as they invoke local methods. For example, an object running on a local client can pass a database query as a `String` argument to a method in a database object running

594

on a remote server to ask it to sum up a series of records. The server can return the result to the client as a `double`. This is more efficient than downloading all the records and summing them up locally. Java-compatible web servers can implement remote methods that allow clients to ask for a complete index of the public files on the site. This could dramatically reduce the time a server spends filling requests from web spiders such as Lycos and AltaVista. Indeed, Excite already uses a non-Java-based version of this idea.

From the programmer's perspective, remote objects and methods work just like the local objects and methods you're accustomed to. All the implementation details are hidden. You just import one package, look up the remote object in a registry (which takes one line of code), and make sure that you catch `RemoteException` when you call the object's methods. From that point on, you can use the remote object almost as freely and easily as you use an object running on your own system.

More formally, a *remote object* is an object whose methods may be invoked from a different Java virtual machine than the one in which the object itself lives, generally one running on a different computer. Each remote object implements one or more *remote interfaces* that declare which methods of the remote object can be invoked by the foreign system. RMI is the facility by which a Java program running on one machine, say *java.oreilly.com*, can invoke a method in an object on a completely different machine, say *metalab.unc.edu*.

For example, suppose an object on *metalab.unc.edu* has a query method that looks up information in a local database. The query method would be exported in a remote interface. The client on *java.oreilly.com* would look up the object in Meta-Lab's registry, then call the query method, just as it would call a query method in an object on *java.oreilly.com*. The object that queries the database runs on the server, but it accepts arguments from and returns results to the client on *java.oreilly.com*. This is simpler than designing and implementing a new socket-based protocol for communication between the database server and its client. The details of making the connections between the hosts and transferring the data are hidden in the RMI classes.

Security

The prospect of remote hosts invoking methods in the local host's objects raises many security issues. *Super.secret.cia.gov* probably doesn't want *kgb.kremlin.ru* to be able to call `readFile()` methods on its machine. Java is uniquely suited to solving these problems. Just as an applet host can limit the activities of an applet, so too can a host that allows Remote Method Invocation to limit what the remote hosts can do.

RPC

Remote Procedure Call (RPC), an older technology that Sun developed, does much the same thing as RMI. RPC is language- and processor-independent; RMI is processor-independent by nature but limited to programs written in Java. To get the cross-platform portability that Java provides, RPC requires a lot more overhead than RMI. RPC has to convert arguments between architectures so that each computer can use its native datatypes. For example, integers have to be converted between big-endian and little-endian implementations. Further-more, RPC can send only primitive datatypes, while RMI can send objects. Sun doesn't support RPC in Java, though there are some third-party implementa-tions. See, for example, Netbula JavaRPC (*http://netbula.com/javarpc/*). In short, RMI is the simplest solution for communication between Java programs on dif-ferent hosts. If you need to connect with programs written in other languages, however, you should investigate RPC or look into CORBA or SOAP.

The activities that a remote object can perform are limited in much the same way an applet's activity is limited. A `SecurityManager` object checks all operations to make sure they're allowed. Custom security managers can be defined for specific applications. Public key authentication can be used to verify a user's identity and allow different users different levels of access to a remote object. For example, the general public may be allowed to query a database but not update it, while users from inside a company might be allowed to both query and update the database.

Object Serialization

When an object is passed to or returned from a Java method, what's really trans-ferred is a reference to the object. In most current implementations of Java, refer-ences are handles (doubly indirected pointers) to the location of the object in the memory of the virtual machine. Passing objects between two machines thus raises some problems. The remote machine can't read what's in the memory of the local machine. A reference that's valid on one machine isn't meaningful on the other.

There are two ways around this problem. A special remote reference to the object (a reference that points to the memory in the remote machine) can be passed, or a copy of the object can be passed. When the local machine passes a remote object to the remote machine, it passes a remote reference. The object has never really left the remote machine. However, when the local machine passes one of its own objects to the remote machine, it makes a copy of the object and sends the copy. The copy moves from the local machine to the remote machine.

To copy an object, you need a way to convert the object into a stream of bytes. This is more difficult than it appears at first glance because objects can include other objects as fields; these fields also need to be copied when the object is copied. Object serialization is a scheme by which objects can be converted into a byte stream and then passed around to other machines, which rebuild the original objects from the bytes. These bytes can also be written to disk and read back from disk at a later time, allowing you to save the state of a program (or even an individual object).

For security reasons, Java places some limitations on which objects can be serialized. All Java primitive types can be serialized, but nonremote Java objects can be serialized only if they implement the `java.io.Serializable` interface. Basic Java types that implement `Serializable` include `String` and `Component`. Container classes such as `Vector` are serializable if all the objects they contain are serializable. Furthermore, subclasses of a serializable class are also serializable. For example, `java.lang.Integer` and `java.lang.Float` are serializable because the class they extend, `java.lang.Number`, is serializable. Exceptions, errors, and other throwable objects are always serializable. Most AWT and Swing components, containers, and events are serializable. However, event adapters, image filters, and peer classes are not. Streams, readers and writers, and most other I/O classes are not serializable. Type wrapper classes are serializable except for `Void`. Classes in `java.math` are serializable. Classes in `java.lang.reflect` are not serializable. The `URL` class is serializable. However, `Socket`, `URLConnection`, and most other classes in `java.net` are not. If in doubt, the class library documentation will tell you whether a given class is serializable.

NOTE   Object serialization is discussed in much greater detail in Chapter 11
             of my previous book, *Java I/O* (O'Reilly & Associates, Inc., 1999).

Under the Hood

The last two sections skimmed over a lot of details. Fortunately, Java hides most of the details from you. However, it never hurts to understand how things really work.

The fundamental difference between remote objects and local objects is that remote objects reside in a different virtual machine. Normally, object arguments are passed to methods and object values are returned from methods by referring to something in a particular virtual machine. This is called *passing a reference*. However, this method doesn't work when the invoking method and the invoked method aren't in the same virtual machine; for example, object 243 in one virtual machine has nothing to do with object 243 in a different virtual machine. In fact, different virtual machines may implement references in completely different and incompatible ways.

CORBA and Friends

RMI isn't the final word in distributed object systems. Its biggest limitation is that you can call only methods written in Java. What if you already have an application written in some other language, such as C++, and you want to communicate with it? You could use RPC, which I mentioned earlier—but RPC isn't well adapted for object-oriented programming. The most general solution for distributed objects is CORBA, the Common Object Request Broker Architecture. CORBA lets objects written in different languages communicate with each other. Java hooks into CORBA through the Java-IDL. This goes beyond the scope of this book; to find out about these topics, see:

Java-IDL
    http://java.sun.com/products/jdk/idl/index.html

CORBA for Beginners
    http://www.omg.org/corba/beginners.html

The CORBA FAQ list
    http://www.cerfnet.com/~mpcline/Corba-FAQ/

Client/Server Programming with Java and CORBA
    By Dan Harkey and Robert Orfali (John Wiley & Sons, 1998, ISBN 0-471-24578-X)

Therefore, three different mechanisms are used to pass arguments to and return results from remote methods, depending on the type of the data being passed. Primitive types (int, boolean, double, etc.) are passed by value, just as in local Java method invocation. References to remote objects (that is, objects that implement the Remote interface) are passed as a *remote reference* that allows the recipient to invoke methods on the remote object. This is similar to the way local object references are passed to local Java methods. Objects that do not implement the Remote interface are passed by value; that is, complete copies are passed, using object serialization. Objects that do not allow themselves to be serialized cannot be passed to remote methods. Remote objects run on the server but can be called by objects running on the client. Nonremote, serializable objects run on the client system.

To ensure compatibility with existing Java programs and implementations, and to make the process as transparent to the programmer as possible, communication between a remote object client and a server is implemented in a series of layers as shown in Figure 18-1.

To the programmer, the client appears to talk directly to the server. In reality, the client program talks only to a stub. The stub passes that conversation along to the

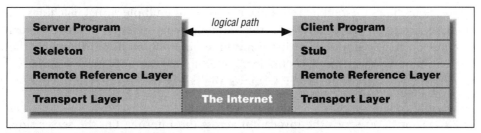

Server Program	logical path	Client Program
Skeleton		Stub
Remote Reference Layer		Remote Reference Layer
Transport Layer	The Internet	Transport Layer

Figure 18-1. The RMI Layer Model

remote reference layer, which talks to the transport layer. The transport layer on the client passes the data across the Internet to the transport layer on the server. The server's transport layer then communicates with the server's remote reference layer, which talks to a piece of server software called the skeleton. The skeleton communicates with the server itself. (Servers written in Java 1.2 and later omit the skeleton layer.) In the other direction (server-to-client), this flow is simply reversed. Logically, data flows horizontally (client-to-server and back), but the actual flow of data is vertical.

This approach may seem overly complex, but remember that most of the time you don't need to think about it, any more than you need to think about how a telephone translates your voice into a series of electrical impulses that get translated back to sound at the other end of the phone call. You just call methods and return values.

Before you can call a method in an object, you need a reference to that object. To get this reference, you'll ask a registry for it by name. The registry is a program that runs on the server. It contains a list of all the remote objects that server is prepared to export and their names. A client connects to the registry and gives it the name of the remote object that it wants. Then the registry sends the client a reference to the object that it can use to invoke methods on the server.

In reality, the client is only invoking local methods in a *stub*. The stub is a local object that implements the remote interfaces of the remote object; this means that the stub has methods matching the signatures of all the methods the remote object exports. In effect, the client thinks it is calling a method in the remote object, but it is really calling an equivalent method in the stub. Stubs are used in the client's virtual machine in place of the real objects and methods that live on the server; you may find it helpful to think of the stub as the remote object's surrogate on the client. When the client invokes a method, the stub passes the invocation to the remote reference layer.

The remote reference layer carries out a specific remote reference protocol, which is independent of the specific client stubs and server skeletons. The remote reference layer is responsible for understanding what a particular remote reference means. Sometimes the remote reference may refer to multiple virtual machines on multiple hosts. In other situations, the reference may refer to a single virtual machine on the local host or a virtual machine on a remote host. In essence, the remote reference layer translates the local reference to the stub into a remote reference to the object on the server, whatever the syntax or semantics of the remote reference may be. Then it passes the invocation to the transport layer.

The transport layer sends the invocation across the Internet. On the server side, the transport layer listens for incoming connections. Upon receiving an invocation, the transport layer forwards it to the remote reference layer on the server. The remote reference layer converts the remote references sent by the client into references for the local virtual machine. Then it passes the request to the skeleton. The skeleton reads the arguments and passes the data to the server program, which makes the actual method call. If the method call returns a value, that value is sent down through the skeleton, remote reference, and transport layers on the server side, across the Internet and then up through the transport, remote reference, and stub layers on the client side. In Java 1.2 and later, the skeleton layer is omitted and the server talks directly to the remote reference layer. Otherwise, the protocol is the same.

Implementation

Most of the methods you need for working with remote objects are in three packages: `java.rmi`, `java.rmi.server`, and `java.rmi.registry`. The `java.rmi` package defines the classes, interfaces, and exceptions that will be seen on the client side. You need these when you're writing programs that access remote objects but are not themselves remote objects. The `java.rmi.server` package defines the classes, interfaces, and exceptions that will be visible on the server side. You use these classes when you are writing a remote object that will be called by clients. The `java.rmi.registry` package defines the classes, interfaces, and exceptions that are used to locate and name remote objects. These packages are part of the core API starting in Java 1.1.

NOTE   In this chapter and in Sun's documentation, the server side is always considered to be "remote" and the client is always considered "local". This can be confusing, particularly when you're writing a remote object. When writing a remote object, you're probably thinking from the viewpoint of the server, so that the client appears to be remote.

The Server Side

To create a new remote object, you first define an interface that extends the `java.rmi.Remote` interface. The `Remote` interface does not have any methods of its own; its sole purpose is to tag remote objects so that they can be identified as such. One definition of a remote object is an instance of a class that implements the `Remote` interface, or any interface that extends `Remote`.

Your subinterface of `Remote` determines which methods of the remote object may be called by clients. A remote object may have many public methods, but only those declared in a remote interface can be invoked remotely. The other public methods may be invoked only from within the virtual machine where the object lives.

Each method in your subinterface must declare that it throws `RemoteException`. `RemoteException` is the superclass for most of the exceptions that can be thrown when RMI is used. Many of these are related to the behavior of external systems and networks and are thus beyond your control.

Example 18-1 is a simple interface for a remote object that calculates Fibonacci numbers of arbitrary size. (Fibonacci numbers are the sequence that begins 0, 1, 1, 2, 3, 5, 8, 13 . . . in which each number is the sum of the previous two.) This remote object can run on a high-powered server to calculate results for low-powered clients. The interface declares two overloaded `getFibonacci()` methods, one of which takes an `int` as an argument and the other of which takes a `BigInteger`. Both methods return `BigInteger` because Fibonacci numbers grow very large very quickly. A more complex remote object could have many more methods.

Example 18-1. The Hello Interface

```
import java.rmi.*;
import java.math.BigInteger;

public interface Fibonacci extends Remote {

  public BigInteger getFibonacci(int n) throws RemoteException;
  public BigInteger getFibonacci(BigInteger n) throws RemoteException;

}
```

Nothing in this interface says anything about how the calculation is implemented. For instance, it could be calculated directly, using the methods of the `java.math.BigInteger` class. It could be done equally easily with the more efficient methods of the `com.ibm.BigInteger` class from IBM's alphaWorks (*http://www.alphaworks.ibm.com/tech/bigdecimal*). It could be calculated with `int`s for small values of n and

BigInteger for large values of n. Every calculation could be performed immediately, or a fixed number of threads could be used to limit the load that this remote
object places on the server. Calculated values could be cached for faster retrieval
on future requests, either internally or in a file or database. Any or all of these are
possible. The client neither knows nor cares how the server gets the result as long
as it produces the correct one.

The next step is to define a class that implements this remote interface. This class
should extend java.rmi.server.UnicastRemoteObject, either directly or indirectly (i.e., by extending another class that extends UnicastRemoteObject):

```
public class UnicastRemoteObject extends RemoteServer
```

Without going into much detail, the UnicastRemoteObject provides a number
of methods that make Remote Method Invocation work. In particular, it marshals
and unmarshals remote references to the object. (Marshaling is the process by
which arguments and return values are converted into a stream of bytes that can
be sent over the network. Unmarshaling is the reverse: the conversion of a stream
of bytes into a group of arguments or a return value.)

If extending UnicastRemoteObject isn't convenient—for instance, because
you'd like to extend some other class—then you can instead export your object as
a remote object by passing it to one of the static UnicastRemoteObject.
exportObject() methods:

```
public static RemoteStub exportObject(Remote obj)
  throws RemoteException
public static Remote exportObject(Remote obj, int port)   // Java 1.2
  throws RemoteException
public static Remote exportObject(Remote obj, int port,   // Java 1.2
  RMIClientSocketFactory csf, RMIServerSocketFactory ssf)
  throws RemoteException
```

These create a remote object that uses your object to do the work. It's similar to
how a Runnable object can be used to give a thread something to do when it's
inconvenient to subclass Thread. In Java 1.2, you can pick the port your server
runs on and even the socket factories used to make the connections. In Java 1.1,
you can use only a randomly selected port. However, the registry will be able to tell
clients which port the server is running on. The registry generally runs on a well-
known port.

Java 1.2 adds another kind of RemoteServer, the java.rmi.activation.
Activatable class:

```
public abstract class Activatable extends RemoteServer // Java 1.2
```

A UnicastRemoteObject exists only as long as the server that created it still runs.
When the server dies, the object is gone forever. Activatable objects allow cli-

ents to reconnect to servers at different times across server shutdowns and restarts and still get access to the same remote objects. It also has static `Activatable.exportObject()` methods to invoke if you don't want to subclass `Activatable`.

Example 18-2, the `FibonacciImpl` class, implements the remote interface `Fibonacci`. This class has a constructor and two `getFibonacci()` methods. Only the `getFibonacci()` methods will be available to the client, because they're the only ones defined by the `Fibonacci` interface. The constructor is used on the server side but is not available to the client.

Example 18-2. The FibonacciImpl Class

```
import java.rmi.*;
import java.rmi.server.UnicastRemoteObject;
import java.math.BigInteger;


public class FibonacciImpl implements Fibonacci {

  public FibonacciImpl() throws RemoteException {
    UnicastRemoteObject.exportObject(this);
  }

  public BigInteger getFibonacci(int n) throws RemoteException {

    return this.getFibonacci(new BigInteger(Long.toString(n)));

  }

  public BigInteger getFibonacci(BigInteger n) throws RemoteException {

    System.out.println("Calculating the " + n + "th Fibonacci number");
    BigInteger zero = new BigInteger("0");
    BigInteger one  = new BigInteger("1");

    if (n.equals(zero)) return zero;
    if (n.equals(one)) return one;

    BigInteger i  = one;
    BigInteger a  = zero;
    BigInteger b  = one;

    while (i.compareTo(n) == -1) {
      BigInteger temp = b;
      b = b.add(a);
      a = temp;
      i = i.add(one);
    }
```

Example 18-2. The FibonacciImpl Class (continued)

```
    return b;

  }
}
```

The `FibonacciImpl()` constructor exports the object; that is, it creates a `UnicastRemoteObject` on some port and starts it listening for connections. The constructor is declared to throw `RemoteException` because `UnicastRemote-Object.exportObject()` can throw that exception.

The `getFibonacci(int n)` method is trivial. It simply returns the result of converting its argument to a `BigInteger` and calling the second `getFibonacci()` method. The second method actually performs the calculation. It uses `BigInteger` throughout the calculation to allow for arbitrarily large Fibonacci numbers of an arbitrarily large index to be calculated. This can use a lot of CPU power and huge amounts of memory. That's why you might want to move it to a special-purpose calculation server rather than performing the calculation locally.

Although `getFibonacci()` is a remote method, there's nothing different about the method itself. This is a simple case, but even vastly more complex remote methods are not algorithmically different than their local counterparts. The only difference—that a remote method is declared in a remote interface and a local method is not—is completely external to the method itself.

Next we need to write a server that makes the `Fibonacci` remote object available to the world. Example 18-3 is such a server. All it has is a `main()` method. It begins by entering a `try` block that catches `RemoteException`. Then it constructs a new `FibonacciImpl` object and binds that object to the name "fibonacci" using the `Naming` class to talk to the local registry. A registry keeps track of the available objects on an RMI server and the names by which they can be requested. When a new remote object is created, the object adds itself and its name to the registry with the `Naming.bind()` or `Naming.rebind()` method. Clients can then ask for that object by name or get a list of all the remote objects that are available. Note that there's no rule that says the name the object has in the registry has to have any necessary relation to the class name. For instance, we could have called this object "Fred". Indeed, there might be multiple instances of the same class all bound in a registry, each with a different name. After registering itself, the server prints a message on `System.out` signaling that it is ready to begin accepting remote invocations. If something goes wrong, then the `catch` block prints a simple error message.

Example 18-3. The FibonacciServer Class

```
import java.net.*;
import java.rmi.*;

public class FibonacciServer {

  public static void main(String[] args) {

    try {
      FibonacciImpl f = new FibonacciImpl();
      Naming.rebind("fibonacci", f);
      System.out.println("Fibonacci Server ready.");
    }
     catch (RemoteException re) {
      System.out.println("Exception in FibonacciImpl.main: " + re);
    }
    catch (MalformedURLException e) {
      System.out.println("MalformedURLException " + e);
    }

  }

}
```

Although the main() method finishes fairly quickly here, the server will continue to run because a nondaemon thread is spawned when the FibonacciImpl() exports the FibonacciImpl object. This completes the server code you need to write.

The Client Side

Before a client can call a remote method, it needs to retrieve a remote reference to the remote object. A program retrieves a remote reference by asking a registry on the server for a remote object. It asks by calling the registry's lookup() method. The exact naming scheme depends on the registry you use; the java.rmi.Naming class provides a URL-based scheme for locating objects. As you can see in the following code, these URLs have been designed so that they are similar to *http* URLs. The protocol is *rmi*. The URL's file field specifies the remote object's name. The fields for the hostname and the port number are unchanged:

```
Object o1 = Naming.lookup("rmi://metalab.unc.edu/fibonacci");
Object o2 = Naming.lookup("rmi://metalab.unc.edu:2048/fibonacci");
```

Like objects stored in Hashtables, Vectors, and other data structures that store objects of different classes, the object that is retrieved from a registry loses its type information. Therefore, before using the object, you must cast it to the remote interface that the remote object implements (not to the actual class, which is hidden from clients):

```
Fibonacci calculator = (Fibonacci) Naming.lookup("fibonacci");
```

Once a reference to the object has been retrieved and its type restored, the client can call the object's remote methods pretty much as it would call methods in a local object. The only difference is that you'll need to catch `RemoteException` for each remote invocation:

```
try {
   BigInteger f56 = calculator.getFibonacci(56);
   System.out.println("The 56th Fibonacci number is " + f56);
   BigInteger f156 = calculator.getFibonacci(new BigInteger(156));
   System.out.println("The 156th Fibonacci number is " + f156);
}
catch (RemoteException e) {
   System.err.println(e)
}
```

Example 18-4 is a simple client for the `Fibonacci` interface of the last section.

Example 18-4. The FibonacciClient

```
import java.rmi.*;
import java.net.*;
import java.math.BigInteger;


public class FibonacciClient {

  public static void main(String args[]) {

    if (args.length == 0 || !args[0].startsWith("rmi:")) {
      System.err.println(
          "Usage: java Fibonacci client rmi://host.domain:port/fibonacci number");
      return;
    }

    try {
      Object o = Naming.lookup(args[0]);
      Fibonacci calculator = (Fibonacci) o;
      for (int i = 1; i < args.length; i++) {
        try {
          BigInteger index = new BigInteger(args[i]);
          BigInteger f = calculator.getFibonacci(index);
          System.out.println("The " + args[i] + "th Fibonacci number is "
            + f);
        }
        catch (NumberFormatException e) {
```

Example 18-4. The FibonacciClient (continued)

```
        System.err.println(args[i] + "is not an integer.");
      }
    }
  }
  catch (MalformedURLException e) {
    System.err.println(args[0] + " is not a valid RMI URL");
  }
  catch (RemoteException e) {
    System.err.println("Remote object threw exception " + e);
  }
  catch (NotBoundException e) {
    System.err.println(
      "Could not find the requested remote object on the server");
  }
  }
}
```

Compile the class as usual. Notice that because the object that Naming.lookup() returns is cast to a Fibonacci, either the *Fibonacci.java* or *Fibonacci.class* file needs to be available on the local host. A general requirement for compiling a client is to have either the byte or source code for the remote object you're connecting to. To some extent, you can relax this a little bit by using the reflection API, but you'll still need to know at least something about the remote interface's API. Most of the time, this isn't an issue, since the server and client are written by the same programmer or team. The point of RMI is to allow a VM to invoke methods on remote objects, not to compile against remote objects.

Compiling the Stubs

Before your server can begin accepting invocations, you must generate the stubs and skeletons that the program requires. We have already discussed what the stubs and skeletons do: the stub contains the information in the Remote interface (in this example, an object with two getFibonacci() methods), and a skeleton is similar but on the server side. Fortunately, we don't have to write them ourselves: they can be generated automatically from the remote object's Java source code, using a utility called *rmic* included with the JDK. To generate the stubs and skeletons for the FibonacciImpl remote object, run *rmic* on the remote object's class. For example:

```
% rmic FibonacciImpl
% ls Fibonacci*
Fibonacci.class          FibonacciImpl.class        FibonacciServer.class
Fibonacci.java           FibonacciImpl.java         FibonacciServer.java
FibonacciClient.class    FibonacciImpl_Skel.class
FibonacciClient.java     FibonacciImpl_Stub.class
```

rmic reads the *.class* file of a remote object and produces *.class* files for the stubs and skeletons needed for the remote object. The command-line argument to *rmic* is the fully package-qualified class name (e.g., `com.macfaq.rmi.examples.Chat`, not just `Chat`) of the remote object class.

rmic supports the same command-line options as the *javac* compiler for example, **-classpath** and **-d**. For instance, if the class doesn't fall in the class path, then you can specify the location with the **-classpath** command-line argument. For example, the following command searches for *FibonacciImpl.class* in the directory *test/classes*:

```
% rmic -classpath test/classes FibonacciImpl
```

For the moment, copy the *Fibonacci.class* and *FibonacciImpl_Stub.class* files to both the directory on the remote server from which the `Fibonacci` object will be run and the directory on the local client where the `Fibonacci` object will be invoked.

Starting the Server

Now you're ready to start the server. There are actually two servers you need to run, the remote object server itself (`FibonacciServer` in this example) and the registry that allows local clients to connect to the remote server. Since the server expects to talk to the `Naming` registry, you must start the registry first. Make sure all the stub, skeleton, and server classes are in the server's class path and type:

```
% rmiregistry &
```

On Windows, you start it from a DOS prompt like this:

```
C:> start rmiregistry
```

In both examples here, the registry runs in the background. The registry tries to listen to port 1,099 by default. If it fails, especially with a message like "java.net. SocketException: Address already in use", then some other program is using port 1099, possibly (though not necessarily) another registry service. You can run the registry on a different port by appending a port number like this:

```
% rmiregistry 2048 &
```

If you use a different port, you'll need to include that port in URLs that refer to this registry service.

Finally, you're ready to start your server. Run the server program just as you'd run any Java class with a `main()` method:

```
% java FibonacciServer
Fibonacci Server ready.
```

Now your server and registry are ready to accept remote method calls.

Running the Client

Go back to the client system. Make sure that the client system has *FibonacciClient. class, Fibonacci.class,* and *FibonacciImpl_Stub.class* in its class path. On the client system, type:

```
C:\>java FibonacciClient rmi://host.com/fibonacci 0 1 2 3 4 5 56 156
The 0th Fibonacci number is 0
The 1th Fibonacci number is 1
The 2th Fibonacci number is 1
The 3th Fibonacci number is 2
The 4th Fibonacci number is 3
The 5th Fibonacci number is 5
The 56th Fibonacci number is 225851433717
The 156th Fibonacci number is 178890334785183168257455287891792
```

The client converts the command-line arguments to `BigInteger` objects. It sends those objects over the wire to the remote server. The server receives each of those objects, calculates the Fibonacci number for that index, and sends a `BigInteger` object back over the Internet to the client. Here, I'm using a PC for the client and a remote Unix box for the server. You can actually run both server and client on the same machine, though that's not as interesting.

Loading Classes at Runtime

All the client really has to know about the remote object is its remote interface. Everything else it needs—for instance, the stub classes—can be loaded from a web server (though not an RMI server) at runtime using a class loader. Indeed, this ability to load classes from the network is one of the unique features of Java. This is especially useful in applets. The web server can send the browser an applet that communicates back with the server for instance, to allow the client to read and write files on the server. As with any time that classes are loaded from a potentially untrusted host, they must be checked by a `SecurityManager`.

Unfortunately, while remote objects are actually quite easy to work with when you can install the necessary stubs and classes in the local client class path, doing so when you have to dynamically load the stubs and other classes is fiendishly difficult. While Sun is good at application programming interface design, it is poor at user interface design. The class path, the security architecture, and the reliance on poorly documented environment variables are all bugbears that torment Java programmers. Getting a local client object to download remote objects from a server requires manipulating all of these in precise detail. Making even a small mistake will prevent programs from running, with only the most generic of exceptions being provided to tell the poor programmer what he or she did wrong. Exactly how difficult it is to make the programs work depends on the context in which the remote objects are running. In general, applet clients that use RMI are somewhat easier to manage than standalone application clients. Standalone applications are feasible if the client can be relied on to have access to the same *.class* files as the server has. Standalone applications that need to load classes from the server border on impossible.

An Applet Client for a Remote Object

Example 18-5 is an applet client for the `Fibonacci` remote object. It has the same basic structure as the `FibonacciClient` in Example 18-4. However, it uses a `TextArea` to display the message from the server instead of using `System.out`.

Example 18-5. An Applet Client for the Fibonacci Object

```
import java.applet.Applet;
import java.awt.*;
import java.awt.event.*;
import java.rmi.*;
import java.math.BigInteger;

public class FibonacciApplet extends Applet {

  private TextArea  resultArea
   = new TextArea("", 20, 72, TextArea.SCROLLBARS_BOTH);
  private TextField inputArea  = new TextField(24);
  private Button calculate = new Button("Calculate");
  private String server;

  public void init() {

    this.setLayout(new BorderLayout());

    Panel north = new Panel();
    north.add(new Label("Type a non-negative integer"));
    north.add(inputArea);
    north.add(calculate);
    this.add(resultArea, BorderLayout.CENTER);
    this.add(north, BorderLayout.NORTH);
    Calculator c = new Calculator();
    inputArea.addActionListener(c);
    calculate.addActionListener(c);
    resultArea.setEditable(false);

    server = "rmi://" + this.getCodeBase().getHost() + "/fibonacci";

  }

  class Calculator implements ActionListener {
```

Example 18-5. An Applet Client for the Fibonacci Object (continued)

```
public void actionPerformed(ActionEvent e) {

  try {
    String input = inputArea.getText();
    if (input != null) {
      BigInteger index = new BigInteger(input);
      Fibonacci f = (Fibonacci) Naming.lookup(server);
      BigInteger result =  f.getFibonacci(index);
      resultArea.setText(result.toString());
    }
  }
  catch (Exception ex) {
    resultArea.setText(ex.getMessage());
  }
}
}
```

You'll notice that the *rmi* URL is built from the applet's own codebase. This helps avoid nasty security problems that arise when an applet tries to open a network connection to a host other than the one it came from. RMI-based applets are certainly not exempt from the usual restrictions on network connections.

Example 18-6 is a simple HTML file that can be used to load the applet from the web browser.

Example 18-6. FibonacciApplet.html

```
<html>
<head>
<title>RMI Applet</title>
</head>
<body>
<h1>RMI Applet</h1>

<P>
<applet align="center" code=FibonacciApplet width=300 height=100>
</applet>
<hr>
</P>
</body>
</html>
```

Place *FibonacciImpl_Stub.class, Fibonacci.class, FibonacciApplet.html,* and *FibonacciServer. class* in the same directory on your web server. Add this directory to the server's class path, and start *rmiregistry* on the server. Then start `FibonacciServer` on the server. For example:

```
% rmiregistry &
% java FibonacciServer &
```

Make sure that both of these are running on the actual web server machine. Many web server farms use different machines for site maintenance and web serving, even though both mount the same filesystems. To get past the applet security restriction, both *rmiregistry* and `FibonacciServer` have to be running on the machine that serves the *FibonacciApplet.class* file to web clients.

Now load *FibonacciApplet.html* into a web browser from the client. Figure 18-2 shows the result.

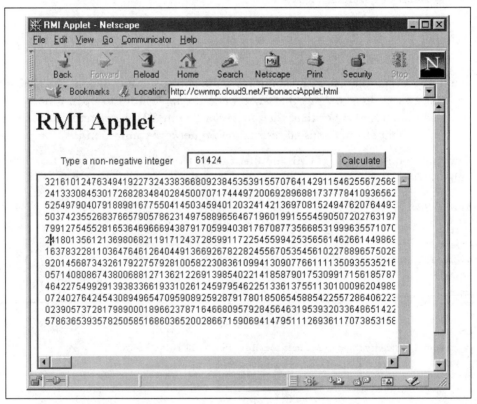

Figure 18-2. The Fibonacci applet

An Application Client for a Remote Object

RMI is one of the few areas of Java where it's actually easier to write an applet than a standalone application. Writing standalone applications that can talk to remote objects without already having the necessary *.class* files installed in the local class path is a black art that has driven more than one humble programmer to madness. When you're writing an applet, you rely on the web browser to handle security and class loading for you. When you're writing a standalone application, you have to do all this yourself. Most standalone applications ignore security and don't load classes from the network. However, these are fundamental features of any program that uses RMI, whether an applet or an application. Consequently, you have to deal with these issues, painful as they are.

Java loads stubs from a remote host only if several conditions are met. These include:

- The application must be running under the control of a `SecurityManager`.

- The registry's `java.rmi.server.codebase` property must specify a URL from which classes can be loaded.

- The stub and implementation classes must *not* be in the registry's class path.

The first thing to provide is a `SecurityManager`. The `java.rmi` package includes an `RMISecurityManager` class. In Java 1.1, this class does permit access to the methods needed to load classes from the network. Unfortunately, in Java 1.2, this class relies on the default security policy, which is far too restrictive to allow classes to be loaded from the network. This policy can be edited with the *policytool*, but only on a host-by-host basis. Consequently, the only thing that really works is to write and install your own subclass of `SecurityManager` that implements a looser policy. Example 18-7 is a `SecurityManager` that permits everything in Java 1.2 but only what is required for RMI in Java 1.1.

Example 18-7. A Very Lax SecurityManager

```
import java.rmi.*;
import java.security.*;

public class LaxSecurityManager extends RMISecurityManager {

  public void checkPermission(Permission p) {
    // do nothing
  }

}
```

You'll need to use Java 1.2 or later to compile this because Java 1.1 doesn't have a `Permission` class. However, it can run in Java 1.1 provided you set Java 1.1 as your target (the default target used by *javac*) and no code running in a 1.1 VM actually invokes the `checkPermission()` method. This will work because Java 1.1 ignores the `checkPermission()` method. Security checks are made by invoking methods such as checkConnect() and checkRead() directly. These invocations will fall back to the same methods in the RMISecurityManager superclass. In Java 1.2 and later, however, all security checks go through the checkPermission() method. If this method doesn't throw a SecurityException, then the action is allowed. A better implementation would allow only those actions (like resolving hosts and connecting to the codebase) that were really needed to implement class loading for RMI, but I'd like to keep this example as simple as possible.

Next, this SecurityManager has to be installed in the client application. Example 18-8 is a very slight modification of the FibonacciClient of Example 18-4. All it adds is three lines (shown in bold) to install the LaxSecurityManager. Otherwise, it's the same.

Example 18-8. A FibonacciClient That Can Load Stubs from the Network

```
import java.rmi.*;
import java.net.*;
import java.math.BigInteger;


public class FibonacciClient {

  public static void main(String args[]) {

    if (args.length == 0 || !args[0].startsWith("rmi://")) {
      System.err.println(
          "Usage: java Fibonacci client rmi://host.domain:port/fibonacci number");
      return;
    }

    if (System.getSecurityManager() == null) {
      System.setSecurityManager(new LaxSecurityManager());
    }

    try {
      Object o = Naming.lookup(args[0]);
      Fibonacci calculator = (Fibonacci) o;
      for (int i = 1; i < args.length; i++) {
        try {
          BigInteger index = new BigInteger(args[i]);
          BigInteger f = calculator.getFibonacci(index);
          System.out.println("The " + args[i] + "th Fibonacci number is "
            + f);
        }
        catch (NumberFormatException e) {
          System.err.println(args[i] + "is not an integer.");
        }
```

Example 18-8. A FibonacciClient That Can Load Stubs from the Network (continued)

```
      }
    }
    catch (MalformedURLException e) {
      System.err.println(args[0] + " is not a valid RMI URL");
    }
    catch (RemoteException e) {
      System.err.println("Remote object threw exception " + e);
    }
    catch (NotBoundException e) {
      System.err.println(
        "Could not find the requested remote object on the server");
    }
  }
}
```

Now comes the tricky part. You'll need three machines: a client, an RMI server, and a web server. (An anonymous FTP server can be used instead of the web server in a pinch. Furthermore, all three can run on the same machine, though it's more interesting if they run on different machines.) Compile all the files and generate the necessary stubs. Make sure that any stubs and classes from previous examples are safely out of the way and outside the class path. On the client, put the three files *FibonacciClient.class, Fibonacci.class, LaxSecurityManager.class*—and *nothing else.* On the web server, put the files that the client will need to load in a publicly accessible directory: the stub and skeleton files as well the remote interface file *Fibonacci.class.* And on the RMI server, put *FibonacciServer.class, FibonacciImpl.class, Fibonacci.class,* and all the stub and skeleton files. However, make sure that the directory containing these files is *not* in the class path of the RMI server.

Check that the *.class* files on the web server are accessible. The easiest way to do this is just to try to load one from your web browser, then cancel out of the dialog box that asks you what to do with the *.class* file. Take note of the URL of the directory where the *.class* files are.

On the RMI server, change to a directory that does *not* contain *FibonacciServer.class, FibonacciImpl.class, Fibonacci.class,* and the stub and skeleton files. (Remember, you need to keep these out of your class path. Otherwise, they'll be loaded from there instead of from the network as you want.) Start *rmiregistry* in the background in the usual fashion, that is:

```
% rmiregistry &
```

Or on Windows from a DOS prompt like this:

```
C:> start rmiregistry
```

If *rmiregistry* is already running, you can load new remote objects without shutting it down. However, loading changed versions of old classes requires you to shut it down and restart it.

Now, still on the RMI server, change into the directory that contains all your *.class* files and stubs and skeletons. From here, start the FibonacciServer program while setting the java.rmi.server.codebase property to the URL where the *.class* files are stored on the network. For example, to specify that the classes can be found at *http://metalab.unc.edu/javafaq/rmi2/*, you would type:

```
% java -Djava.rmi.server.codebase=http://metalab.unc.edu/javafaq/rmi2/
FibonacciServer &
Fibonacci Server ready.
```

If the classes are in packages, then the java.rmi.server.codebase property would point to the directory containing the top-level *com* or *org* directory rather than the directory containing the *.class* files themselves. Both servers and clients will load the *.class* files from this location if the files are not found in the local class path first.

Now the server's started and you're ready to connect to it from the client on the third machine. The client will need to have the *FibonacciClient.class* file as well as the *LaxSecurityManager.class* file. However, the client does not need to have the stub nor any *.class* files for classes that the server uses. Run the FibonacciClient from the command line as normal, and this is what you should see:

```
% java FibonacciClient rmi://login.metalab.unc.edu/fibonacci 0 1 56 156
The 0th Fibonacci number is 0
The 1th Fibonacci number is 1
The 56th Fibonacci number is 225851433717
The 156th Fibonacci number is 17889033478518316825745528789179
```

However, there are a lot of things that can go wrong, resulting in a variety of not particularly helpful exceptions. If the java.rmi.server.codebase property is not set on the server, or if the value of that property does not end in a / or the name of a JAR archive, or if the directory structure doesn't match the package structure, then you'll get some sort of MarshalException. If *rmiregistry* is using an older version of the classes than some other part of the system, then the client will get a RemoteException wrapping an UnmarshalException. If the *.class* files on the server are in the *rmiregistry*'s class path, then the client won't be able to load the stubs from the web server, and you'll get a Class NotFoundException even though the classes are right where they're supposed to be on the web server and even though the java.rmi.server.codebase property is set to point to them. Getting all the details right is challenging; so challenging, in fact, that I recommend you simply don't try to load RMI classes from the network in standalone applications until Sun makes some much needed simplifications in the setup required.

This still hasn't gone quite as far as it's possible to go. It loaded only the stubs from the remote server. The client still needed to have the `Fibonacci.class` file on the local system. An alternate approach is to load everything, including the main client class itself from the server. Only a small bootstrap program is needed on the client. This bootstrap program knows either the name of the client class it needs or how to calculate it from the names in the registry. (For example, you might adopt a convention that for every name `Foo` in the registry, there's a `FooClient` class that accesses that service.) However, instead of casting the object returned by `Naming.lookup("Foo")` to `FooClient`, which would require the local system to already have the *.class* file for `FooClient`, you cast it to a well-known interface or superclass. (For instance, you can adopt the convention that all your clients implement `java.lang.Runnable` and that they are started by invoking their `run()` method. Or perhaps you decided that all clients are applets that are started by invoking their `init()` and `start()` methods.) The exact convention for naming and classes is up to you, as long as a client can start simply by using well-known classes in the Java core API.

The java.rmi Package

The `java.rmi` package contains the classes that are seen by clients (objects that invoke remote methods). Both clients and servers should import `java.rmi`. While servers need a lot more infrastructure than what's present in this package, `java.rmi` is all that's needed by clients. This package contains one interface, three classes, and a handful of exceptions.

The Remote Interface

The `Remote` interface tags objects as being remote objects. It doesn't declare any methods; remote objects usually implement a subclass of `Remote` that does declare some methods. The methods that are declared in the interface are the methods that can be invoked remotely.

Example 18-9 is a database interface that declares a single method, `SQLQuery()`, which accepts a `String` and returns a `String` array. A class that implements this interface would include the code to send an SQL query to a database and return the result as a `String` array.

Example 18-9. A Database Interface

```
import java.rmi.*;

public interface SQL extends Remote {

  public String[] SQLQuery(String query) throws RemoteException;

}
```

An `SQLImpl` class that implemented the `SQL` interface would probably have more methods, some of which might be public. However, only the `SQLQuery()` method can be invoked by a client. Because the `Remote` interface is not a class, a single object can implement multiple `Remote` subinterfaces. In this case, any method declared in any `Remote` interface can be invoked by a client.

The Naming Class

The `java.rmi.Naming` class talks to a registry running on the server in order to map URLs like *rmi://metalab.unc.edu/myRemoteObject* to particular remote objects on particular hosts. You can think of a registry as a DNS for remote objects. Each entry in the registry has a name and an object reference. Clients give the name (via a URL) and get back a reference to the remote object.

`Naming` is the only means of communicating with the registry included with RMI at this time; others may be included in the future or may be provided by other vendors. The biggest deficiency of `Naming` is that it requires the client to know the server on which the remote object lives; you might also complain that `Naming` implements a flat (i.e., nonhierarchical) namespace. As you've seen, an *rmi* URL looks exactly like an *http* URL except that the protocol field is `rmi` instead of `http`. Furthermore, the file part of the URL is an arbitrary name that the server has bound to a particular remote object, not a filename.

The `Naming` class has five public methods: `list()`, to list all the names bound in the registry; `lookup()`, to find a specific remote object given its URL; `bind()`, to bind a name to a specific remote object; `rebind()`, to bind a name to a different remote object; and `unbind()`, to remove a name from the registry. Let's look at these methods in turn.

public static String[ ] list(String url) throws RemoteException, MalformedURLException

The `list()` method returns all the URLs that are currently bound as an array of strings. The `url` argument is the URL of the `Naming` registry to query. Only the protocol, host, and port are used. The file part of the URL is ignored. `list()` throws a `MalformedURLException` if `url` is not a valid *rmi* URL. A

`RemoteException` is thrown if anything else goes wrong, such as the registry's not being reachable or refusing to supply the requested information.

Example 18-10 is a simple program to list all the names currently bound in a particular registry. It's sometimes useful when debugging RMI programs. It allows you to determine whether the names you're using are the names the server expects.

Example 18-10. RegistryLister

```
import java.rmi.*;

public class RegistryLister {

  public static void main(String[] args) {

    int port = 1099;

    if (args.length == 0) {
      System.err.println("Usage: java RegistryLister host port");
      return;
    }

    String host = args[0];

    if (args.length > 1) {
      try {
        port = Integer.parseInt(args[1]);
        if (port <1 || port > 65535) port = 1099;
      }
      catch (NumberFormatException e) {}
    }

    String url = "rmi://" + host + ":" + port + "/";
    try {
      String[] remoteObjects = Naming.list(url);
      for (int i = 0; i < remoteObjects.length; i++) {
        System.out.println(remoteObjects[i]);
      }
    }
    catch (RemoteException e) {
      System.err.println(e);
    }
    catch (java.net.MalformedURLException e) {
      System.err.println(e);
    }
  }
}
```

Here's a result from a run against the RMI server I was using to test the examples in this chapter:

```
% java RegistryLister login.metalab.unc.edu
rmi://login.metalab.unc.edu:1099/fibonacci
rmi://login.metalab.unc.edu:1099/hello
```

You can see that the format for the strings is full *rmi* URLs rather than just names.

public static Remote lookup(String url) throws RemoteException, NotBoundException, AccessException, MalformedURLException

A client uses the `lookup()` method to retrieve the remote object associated with the file portion of the name; so, given the URL *rmi://metalab.unc.edu:2001/ myRemoteObject*, it would return the object bound to `myRemoteObject` from *metalab.unc.edu* on port 2,001.

This method throws a `NotBoundException` if the name is not recognized by the remote server. A `RemoteException` is thrown if the remote registry can't be reached; for instance, because the network is down or because no registry service is running on the specified port. An `AccessException` is thrown if the server refuses to look up the name for the particular host. Finally, if the URL is not a proper *rmi* URL, a `MalformedURLException` is thrown.

public static void bind(String url, Remote object) throws RemoteException, AlreadyBoundException, MalformedURLException, AccessException

A server uses the `bind()` method to link a name like `myRemoteObject` to a remote object. If the binding is successful, then clients will be able to retrieve the remote object stub from the registry using a URL like *rmi://metalab.unc.edu:2001/ myRemoteObject*.

Many things can go wrong with the binding process. `bind()` throws a `MalformedURLException` if url is not a valid *rmi* URL. A `RemoteException` is thrown if the registry cannot be reached. An `AccessException`, a subclass of `RemoteException`, is thrown if the client is not allowed to bind objects in this registry. If the URL is already bound to a local object, `bind()` throws an `AlreadyBoundException`.

public static void unbind(String url) throws RemoteException, NotBoundException, AlreadyBoundException, MalformedURLException, AccessException   // Java 1.2

The `unbind()` method removes the object with the given URL from the registry. It is the opposite of the `bind()` method. What `bind()` has bound, `unbind()`

releases. unbind() throws a NotBoundException if url was not bound to an object in the first place. Otherwise, this method can throw the same exceptions for the same reasons as bind().

public static void rebind(String url, Remote object)
throws RemoteException, AccessException,
MalformedURLException

The rebind() method is just like the bind() method, except that it binds the URL to the object, even if the URL is already bound. If the URL is already bound to an object, the old binding is lost. Thus, this method does not throw an AlreadyBoundException. It can still throw RemoteException, Access-Exception, or MalformedURLException, which have the exact same meanings as they do when thrown by bind().

The RMISecurityManager Class

A client loads stubs from a potentially untrustworthy server; in this sense, the relationship between a client and a stub is somewhat like the relationship between a browser and an applet. Although a stub is only supposed to marshal arguments and unmarshal return values and send them across the network, from the standpoint of the virtual machine, a stub is just another class with methods that can do just about anything. Stubs produced by *rmic* shouldn't misbehave, but there's no reason someone couldn't handcraft a stub that would do all sorts of nasty things, such as reading files or erasing data. The Java virtual machine does not allow stub classes to be loaded across the network unless there's some SecurityManager object in place. (Like other classes, stub classes can always be loaded from the local class path.) For applets, the standard AppletSecurityManager fills this need. Applications can use the RMISecurityManager class to protect themselves from miscreant stubs:

```
public class RMISecurityManager extends SecurityManager
```

In Java 1.1, this class implements a policy that allows classes to be loaded from the server's codebase (which is not necessarily the same as the server) and allows the necessary network communications between the client, the server, and the codebase. In Java 1.2 and later, the RMISecruity Manager doesn't allow even that, and this class is so restrictive, it's essentially useless.

public RMISecurityManager( )

RMISecurityManager has a single constructor that takes no arguments. To set the security manager, use the static System.setSecurityManager() method.

Most often, you create a new `SecurityManager` directly inside this method. For example:

```
System.setSecurityManager(new RMISecurityManager());
```

public Object getSecurityContext( )

The `getSecurityContext()` method determines the environment for certain operations. An `RMISecurityManager` allows more operations by a class loaded from a local host than from a network host. Eventually (though not as of this writing), public key signatures will be used to grant different classes different trust levels.

Checking operations

There are 23 methods that check various operations to see whether they're allowed. All are `public synchronized`, and `void`, except for `checkTopLevelWindow()`, which returns a `boolean`. Each one throws a `StubSecurityException` if the action is forbidden; if the action is allowed, the method just returns. These methods check only actions perfomed by stubs, not by other classes in the application. Since only one `SecurityManager` can be installed in an application, you may have to replace this class with a class of your own if you want to check both actions performed by stubs and actions performed by other classes such as applets.

Table 18-1 lists the methods of the `RMISecurityManager`, what they check for, and the circumstances under which the operation will be allowed for Java 1.1. (Java 1.2 and later uses a completely different setup that doesn't allow remote stubs to do anything interesting.) It is unlikely that you will need to call these methods yourself. However, knowledge of these methods is required to understand what a stub can and cannot do.

Table 18-1. RMISecurityManager Permissions in Java 1.1

Method	Checks For	If Stub is Local	If Stub is Remote
checkCreateClass Loader()	Can a stub create a ClassLoader?	No	No
checkAwtEventQueue Access()	Can a stub retrieve events from or post events to the AWT event queue?	No	No
checkMemberAccess (Class c, int which)	Can a stub use the Reflection API to access members of other classes?	Only of classes loaded by the same class loader.	Only of classes loaded by the same class loader.

Table 18-1. RMISecurityManager Permissions in Java 1.1 (continued)

Method	Checks For	If Stub is Local	If Stub is Remote
checkAccess (Thread t) checkAccess (ThreadGroup g)	Can a stub manipulate threads outside its own thread group?	No	No
checkExit(int status)	Can a stub force the virtual machine to exit? i.e., can it call System.exit()?	No	No
checkExec(String cmd)	Can a stub execute system processes? i. e., can it call System.exec()?	No	No
checkLink(String lib)	Can a stub link to dynamic libraries?	No	No
checkProperties Access()	Can a stub read the properties of the local machine?	No	No
checkProperty Access(String key)	Can a stub check a specific property?	No	No
checkRead(String file) checkRead(String file, Object context) checkRead(File Descriptor fd)	Can a stub read a file?	No	No
checkWrite (String file) checkWrite(File Descriptor fd)	Can a stub write to a file?	No	No
checkListen(int port)	Can a stub listen for connections on a port?	No	No
checkAccept (String host, int port)	Can a stub accept connections on a port?	No	No
checkConnect (String host, int port) checkConnect (String host, int port, Object context)	Can a stub open a connection to this host on this port?	Yes	Yes, if the host is the one from which the stub was downloaded; otherwise, no.

Table 18-1. RMISecurityManager Permissions in Java 1.1 (continued)

Method	Checks For	If Stub is Local	If Stub is Remote
checkMulticast (InetAddress address) checkMulticast (InetAddress address, byte ttl)	Can a stub send a datagram to the specified address with the specified TTL?	Yes	No
checkTopLevelWind ow(Object window)	Can the stub create a new window?	No	No
checkPackage Access(String pkg)	Can a stub access the specified package?	Varies depending on package.	Varies depending on package.
checkPackageDefin ition(String pkg)	Can a stub define classes in the specified package?	Yes, except in the java and sun packages.	Yes, except in the java and sun packages.
checkSetFactory()	Can a stub set a network factory?	No.	No.

Except for checkPackageAccess(), these methods have all been removed from the RMISecurityManager class in Java 1.2 This doesn't break any existing code, however, because RMISecurityManager still inherits them from its Security-Manager superclass.

Remote Exceptions

The java.rmi package defines 16 exceptions, listed in Table 18-2. All except RemoteException extend java.rmi.RemoteException; java.rmi.Remote Exception extends java.lang.Exception. Thus, all are checked exceptions that must be enclosed in a try block or declared in a throws clause.

Remote methods depend on many things that are not under your control: for example, the state of the network and other necessary services such as DNS. Therefore, any remote method can fail: there's no guarantee that the network won't be down when the method is called. Consequently, all remote methods must be declared to throw the generic RemoteException and all calls to remote methods should be wrapped in a try block. When you just want to get a program working, it's simplest to catch RemoteException:

```
try {
  // call remote methods...
}
catch (RemoteException e) {
  System.err.println(e);
}
```

More robust programs should try to catch more specific exceptions and respond accordingly.

Table 18-2. Remote Exceptions

Exception	Meaning
AccessException	A client tried to do something that only local objects are allowed to do.
AlreadyBoundException	The URL is already bound to another object.
ConnectException	The server refused the connection.
ConnectIOException	An I/O error occurred while trying to make the connection between the local and the remote host.
MarshalException	An I/O error occurred while attempting to marshal (serialize) arguments to a remote method. This exception could be caused by a corrupted I/O stream, and making the remote method call again may be successful.
UnmarshalException	An I/O error occurred while attempting to unmarshal (deserialize) the value returned by a remote method. This exception could be caused by a corrupted I/O stream, and making the remote method call again may be successful.
NoSuchObjectException	The object reference is invalid or obsolete. This might occur if the remote host becomes unreachable while the program is running, perhaps because of network congestion, system crash, or some other malfunction.
NotBoundException	The URL is not bound to an object. This might be thrown when you try to reference an object whose URL was rebound out from under it.
RemoteException	The generic superclass for all exceptions having to do with remote methods.
ServerError	An error (that is, an instance of a subclass of `java.lang.Error`) was thrown while the remote method was executing.
ServerException	A `RemoteException` was thrown while the remote method was executing.
StubNotFoundException	The stub for a class could not be found. The stub file may be in the wrong directory on the server. There could be a namespace collision between the class that the stub substitutes for and some other class. The client could have requested the wrong URL.
UnexpectedException	Something unforeseen happened. This is a catchall that should occur only in bizarre situations.
UnknownHostException	The host cannot be found. This is very similar to `java.net.UnknownHostException`.
RMISecurityException	An object tried to do something that is prohibited by the stub's `SecurityManager`. This class is deprecated and no longer used starting in Java 1.2.

Table 18-2. Remote Exceptions (continued)

Exception	Meaning
ServerRuntimeException	An unchecked, uncaught runtime exception occurred on the server, such as ArrayIndexOutOfBoundsException This class is deprecated and no longer used starting in Java 1.2.

The RemoteException class contains a single public field called detail:

```
public Throwable detail
```

This field may contain the actual exception thrown on the server side, so it may give you further information about what went wrong. For example:

```
try {
  // call remote methods...
}
catch (RemoteException e) {
  System.err.println(e.detail);
  e.detail.printStackTrace();
}
```

The java.rmi.registry Package

How does a client that needs a remote object locate that object on a distant server? More precisely, how does it get a remote reference to the object? Clients find out what remote objects are available by querying the server's *registry*. A registry advertises the availability of the server's remote objects. Clients query the registry to find out what remote objects are available and to get remote references to those objects. You've already seen one: the java.rmi.Naming class for interfacing with registries.

The Registry interface and the LocateRegistry class allow clients to retrieve remote objects on a server by name. A RegistryImpl is a subclass of RemoteObject, which links names to particular RemoteObject objects. The methods of the LocateRegistry class are used by clients to retrieve the RegistryImpl for a specific host and port.

The Registry Interface

The java.rmi.registry.Registry interface has five public methods: bind(), to bind a name to a specific remote object; list(), to list all the names bound in the registry; lookup(), to find a specific remote object given its URL; rebind(), to bind a name to a different remote object; and unbind(), to remove a name from the registry. All of these behave exactly as previously described in the java.rmi.Naming class, which implements this interface. Other classes that implement this interface may use a different scheme for mapping names to particular objects, but the methods still have the same meaning and signatures.

Besides these five methods, the `Registry` interface also has one field, `Registry.REGISTRY_PORT`, the default port on which the registry listens. Its value is 1,099.

The LocateRegistry Class

The `java.rmi.registry.LocateRegistry` class lets the client find the registry in the first place. This is achieved with five overloaded versions of the `static` `LocateRegistry.getRegistry()` method:

```
public static Registry getRegistry() throws RemoteException
public static Registry getRegistry(int port) throws RemoteException
public static Registry getRegistry(String host) throws RemoteException
public static Registry getRegistry(String host, int port)
  throws RemoteException
public static Registry getRegistry(String host, int port,  // Java 1.2
  RMIClientSocketFactory factory) throws RemoteException
```

Each of these methods returns a `Registry` object that can be used to get remote objects by name. `LocateRegistry.getRegistry()` returns a stub for the `Registry` running on the local host on the default port, 1,099. `LocateRegistry.getRegistry(int port)` returns a stub for the `Registry` running on the local host on the specified port. `LocateRegistry.getRegistry(String host)` returns a stub for the `Registry` for the specified host on the default port, 1,099. `LocateRegistry.getRegistry(String host, int port)` returns a stub for the `Registry` on the specified host on the specified port. Finally, `LocateRegistry.getRegistry(String host, int port, RMIClientSocketFactory factory)` returns a stub to the registry running on the specified host and port, which will be contacted using sockets created by the provided `java.rmi.server.RMIClientSocketFactory` object. If the host `String` is `null`, `getRegistry()` uses the local host; if the `port` argument is negative, it uses the default port. Each of these methods can throw an arbitrary `RemoteException`.

For example, a remote object that wanted to make itself available to clients might do this:

```
Registry r = LocateRegistry.getRegistry();
r.bind("My Name", this);
```

A remote client that wished to invoke this remote object might then say:

```
Registry r = LocateRegistry.getRegistry("thehost.site.com");
RemoteObjectInterface tro = (RemoteObjectInterface) r.lookup("MyName");
tro.invokeRemoteMethod();
```

The final two methods in the `LocateRegistry` class are the overloaded `LocateRegistry.createRegistry()` methods. These create a registry and start it listening on the specified port. As usual, each can throw a `RemoteException`. Their signatures are:

```
public static Registry createRegistry(int port) throws RemoteException
public static Registry createRegistry(int port,
  RMIClientSocketFactory csf, RMIServerSocketFactory ssf) // Java 1.2
  throws RemoteException
```

The java.rmi.server Package

The `java.rmi.server` package is the most complex of all the RMI packages; it contains the scaffolding for building remote objects and thus is used by objects whose methods will be invoked by clients. The package defines 6 exceptions, 9 interfaces, and 10 classes. Fortunately, you need to be familiar with only a few of these to write remote objects. The important classes are the `RemoteObject` class, which is the basis for all remote objects; the `RemoteServer` class, which extends `RemoteObject`; and the `UnicastRemoteObject` class, which extends `Remote Server`. Any remote objects you write will likely either extend or use `UnicastRemoteObject`. Clients that call remote methods but are not themselves remote objects don't use these classes, and therefore don't need to import `java.rmi.server`.

The RemoteObject Class

Technically, a remote object is not an instance of the `RemoteObject` class but an instance of any class that implements a `Remote` interface. In practice, most remote objects will be instances of a subclass of `java.rmi.server.RemoteObject`:

```
public abstract class RemoteObject extends Object
  implements Remote, Serializable
```

You can think of this class as a special version of `java.lang.Object` for remote objects. It provides `toString()`, `hashCode()`, `clone()`, and `equals()` methods that make sense for remote objects. If you create a remote object that does not extend `RemoteObject`, you need to override these methods yourself.

The `equals()` method compares the remote object references of two `RemoteObject`s and returns true if they point to the same remote object. As with the `equals()` method in the `Object` class, you may want to override this method to provide a more meaningful definition of equality.

The `toString()` method returns a `String` that describes the remote object. Most of the time, `toString()` returns the hostname and port from which the remote object came as well as a reference number for the object. You can override this method in your own subclasses to provide more meaningful string representations.

The hashCode() method maps a presumably unique int to each unique object; this integer may be used as a key in a Hashtable. It returns the same value for all remote references that refer to the same remote object. Thus, if a client has several remote references to the same object on the server, or multiple clients have references to that object, they should all have the same hash code.

Starting in Java 1.2, there's one other instance method in this class, getRef():

```
public RemoteRef getRef() // Java 1.2
```

This returns a remote reference to the class:

```
public abstract interface RemoteRef extends Externalizable
```

Java 1.2 also adds one static method, RemoteObject.toStub():

```
public static Remote toStub(Remote ro) // Java 1.2
  throws NoSuchObjectException
```

RemoteObject.toStub() converts a given remote object into the equivalent stub object for use in the client virtual machine. This can help you dynamically generate stubs from within your server without using *rmic*.

The RemoteServer Class

The RemoteServer class extends RemoteObject; it is an abstract superclass for server implementations such as UnicastRemoteObject. It provides a few simple utility methods needed by most server objects:

```
public abstract class RemoteServer extends RemoteObject
```

In Java 1.1, UnicastRemoteObject is the only subclass of RemoteServer included in the core library. Java 1.2 adds the java.rmi.activation.Activatable and java.rmi.activation.ActivationGroup classes. You can add others (for example, a UDP or multicast remote server) by writing your own subclass of RemoteServer.

Constructors

There are two constructors for this class:

```
protected RemoteServer()
protected RemoteServer(RemoteRef r)
```

However, you won't instantiate this class yourself. Instead, you will instantiate a subclass like UnicastRemoteObject. That class's constructor will call one of these protected constructors from the first line of its constructor.

Getting information about the client

The RemoteServer class has one method to locate the client with which you're communicating:

```
public static String getClientHost() throws ServerNotActiveException
```

RemoteServer.getClientHost() returns a String that contains the hostname of the client that invoked the currently running method. This method throws a ServerNotActiveException if the current thread is not running a remote method.

Logging

For debugging purposes, it is sometimes useful to see the calls that are being made to your remote object and the object's responses. You can get a log for your RemoteServer by passing an OutputStream object to the setLog() method:

```
public static void setLog(OutputStream out)
```

Passing null turns off logging. For example, to see all the calls on System.err (which sends the log to the Java console), you would write:

```
myRemoteServer.setLog(System.err);
```

For example, here's some log output I collected while debugging the Fibonacci programs in this chapter:

```
Sat Apr 29 12:20:36 EDT 2000:RMI:TCP Accept-1:[titan.oit.unc.edu:
sun.rmi.transport.DGCImpl[0:0:0, 2]: java.rmi.dgc.Lease
dirty(java.rmi.server.ObjID[], long, java.rmi.dgc.Lease)]
Fibonacci Server ready.
Sat Apr 29 12:21:27 EDT 2000:RMI:TCP Accept-2:[macfaq.dialup.cloud9.net:
sun.rmi.transport.DGCImpl[0:0:0, 2]: java.rmi.dgc.Lease
dirty(java.rmi.server.ObjID[], long, java.rmi.dgc.Lease)]
Sat Apr 29 12:22:36 EDT 2000:RMI:TCP Accept-3:[macfaq.dialup.cloud9.net: sun.rmi.
transport.DGCImpl[0:0:0, 2]: java.rmi.dgc.Lease
dirty(java.rmi.server.ObjID[], long, java.rmi.dgc.Lease)]
Sat Apr 29 12:22:39 EDT 2000:RMI:TCP Accept-3:[macfaq.dialup.cloud9.net:
FibonacciImpl[0]: java.math.BigInteger getFibonacci(java.math.BigInteger)]
Sat Apr 29 12:22:39 EDT 2000:RMI:TCP Accept-3:[macfaq.dialup.cloud9.net:
FibonacciImpl[0]: java.math.BigInteger getFibonacci(java.math.BigInteger)]
```

If you want to add extra information to the log, in addition to what's provided by the RemoteServer class, you can retrieve the log's PrintStream with the getLog() method:

```
public static PrintStream getLog()
```

Once you have the print stream, you can write on it to add your own comments to the log. For example:

```
PrintStream p = RemoteServer.getLog();
p.println("There were " + n + " total calls to the remote object.");
```

The UnicastRemoteObject Class

The UnicastRemoteObject class is a concrete subclass of RemoteServer. To create a remote object, you can extend UnicastRemoteObject in your own subclass and declare that your subclass implements some subclass of the java.rmi.Remote interface. The methods of the interface provide functionality specific to the class, while the methods of UnicastRemoteObject handle general remote object tasks like marshaling and unmarshaling arguments and return values. All of this happens behind the scenes. As an application programmer, you don't need to worry about it.

A UnicastRemoteObject runs on a single host, uses TCP sockets to communicate, and has remote references that do not remain valid across server restarts. While this is a good general-purpose framework for remote objects, it is worth noting that you can implement other kinds of remote objects. For example, you may want a remote object that uses UDP, or one that remains valid if the server is restarted, or even one that distributes the load across multiple servers. To create remote objects with these properties, you would extend RemoteServer directly and implement the abstract methods of that class. However, if you don't need anything so esoteric, you will find it much easier to subclass UnicastRemoteObject.

The UnicastRemoteObject class has three protected constructors:

```
protected UnicastRemoteObject() throws RemoteException
protected UnicastRemoteObject(int port)                    // Java 1.2
   throws RemoteException
protected UnicastRemoteObject(int port, RMIClientSocketFactory csf,
RMIServerSocketFactory ssf) throws RemoteException  // Java 1.2
```

The noargs constructor creates a UnicastRemoteObject that listens on an anonymous port chosen at runtime.* Java 1.2 adds two more constructors that listen on the specified port. The third constructor also allows you to specify the socket factories used by this UnicastRemoteObject. When you write a subclass of UnicastRemoteObject, you call one of these constructors, either explicitly or

---

* By the way, this is an example of an obscure situation I mentioned in Chapter 10, *Sockets for Clients*, and Chapter 11, *Sockets for Servers*. The server is listening on an anonymous port. Normally, this would be next to useless because it would be impossible for clients to locate the server. In this case, clients locate servers by using a registry, which keeps track of what servers are available and what ports they are listening to.

implicitly, in the first line of each constructor of your subclass. All three constructors can throw a `RemoteException` if the remote object cannot be created.

The `UnicastRemoteObject` class has several public methods:

```
public Object clone() throws CloneNotSupportedException
public static RemoteStub exportObject(Remote r) throws RemoteException
public static Remote exportObject(Remote r, int port)
  throws RemoteException        // Java 1.2
public static Remote exportObject(Remote r, int port,
  RMIClientSocketFactory csf, RMIServerSocketFactory ssf)
  throws RemoteException        // Java 1.2
public static boolean unexportObject(Remote r, boolean force)
  throws NoSuchObjectException // Java 1.2
```

The `clone()` method simply creates a clone of the remote object. You call the
`UnicastRemoteObject.exportObject()` to use the infrastructure that
`Unicast RemoteObject` provides for an object that can't subclass `Unicast
RemoteObject` Similarly, you pass an object `UnicastRemoteObject.
unexportObject()` to stop a particular remote object from listening for invoca-
tions.

Exceptions

The `java.rmi.server` package defines six new exceptions. The exceptions and
their meanings are listed in Table 18-3. All except `java.rmi.server.
ServerNotActiveException` extend, directly or indirectly, `java.rmi.Remote-
Exception`. All are checked exceptions that must be caught or declared in a
`throws` clause.

Table 18-3. java.rmi.server Exceptions

Exception	Meaning
ExportException	You're trying to export a remote object on a port that's already in use.
ServerNotActiveException	An attempt was made to invoke a method in a remote object that wasn't running.
ServerCloneException	An attempt to clone a remote object on the server failed.
SocketSecurityException	This subclass of `ExportException` is thrown when the `SecurityManager` prevents a remote object from being exported on the requested port.

Table 18-3. java.rmi.server Exceptions (continued)

Exception	Meaning
SkeletonNotFoundException	The server is unable to load the skeleton it needs to respond to a remote method invocation. This can mean several things: the skeleton class file may not be anywhere in the codebase; the skeleton is in the codebase but has a name conflict with another class; the URL given may be incorrect; or the skeleton may be of the wrong class. This is deprecated starting in Java 1.2 because skeletons are no longer used.
SkeletonMismatchException	The skeleton and the stub for a class don't match. This is unusual but may happen if different versions of the source code are used to make the stub and the skeleton. This is deprecated starting in Java 1.2 because skeletons are no longer used.

This chapter has been a fairly quick look at Remote Method Invocation. For a more detailed treatment, see *Java Distributed Computing*, by Jim Farley (O'Reilly & Associates, Inc., 1998).

19

The JavaMail API

Email was the Internet's first killer app, and still generates more Internet traffic than any protocol except HTTP. One of the most frequently asked questions about Java is how to send email from a Java applet or application. While it's certainly possible to write a Java program that uses sockets to communicate with mail servers, doing this for more than the most trivial of applications requires detailed knowledge of some fairly complicated protocols, such as SMTP, POP, and IMAP. Just as the URL class makes interacting with HTTP servers a lot simpler than it would be with raw sockets, so too can a class library dedicated to handling email make writing email clients a lot simpler.

The JavaMail API is a standard extension to Java 1.1 and later that provides a class library for fairly sophisticated email clients. It's a required component of the Java 2 Platform, Enterprise Edition (J2EE). The JavaMail API can be implemented in 100% Pure Java™ using sockets and streams, and indeed Sun's reference implementation is so implemented. Programs use the JavaMail API to communicate with SMTP and IMAP servers to send and receive email. By taking advantage of this API, you can avoid focusing on the low-level protocol details and focus instead on what you want to say with the message. Additional providers can add support for other mail systems such as POP3, Lotus Notes, or MH. You can even get providers that add support for NNTP, the protocol used to transport Usenet news.

There's no limit to the uses Java programs have for the JavaMail API. Most obviously, you can write standard email clients such as Eudora. Or it can be used for email-intensive applications such as mailing list managers, like majordomo. But the JavaMail API is also useful as one part of larger applications that simply need to send or receive a little email. For instance, a server monitoring application such as Whistle Blower can periodically load pages from a web server running on a different host and email the webmaster if the web server has crashed. An applet can use email to send data to any process or person on the Internet that has an email address, in essence using the web server's SMTP server as a simple proxy to bypass the usual security restrictions about whom an applet is allowed to talk to. In reverse, an applet can talk to an IMAP server on the applet host to receive data from many hosts around the Net. A newsreader could be implemented as a custom service provider that treats NNTP as just one more means of exchanging messages. And that's just the beginning of the sort of programs the JavaMail API makes it very straightforward to write.

What Is the JavaMail API?

The JavaMail API is a fairly high-level representation of the basic components of any email system. The components are represented by abstract classes in the `javax.mail` package. For instance, the abstract class `javax.mail.Message` represents an email message. It declares abstract methods to get and set various envelope information for the message, such as the sender and addressee, the date sent, and the subject of the message. The abstract class `javax.mail.Folder` represents a message container. It declares abstract methods to get messages from a folder, to move messages between folders, and to delete messages from a folder.

These classes are all abstract because they don't make many assumptions about how the email is stored or transferred between machines. For instance, they do not assume that messages are sent using SMTP or that they're structured as specified in RFC 822. Concrete subclasses of these classes specialize the abstract classes to particular protocols and mail formats. If you want to work with standard Internet email, you might use `javax.mail.MimeMessage` instead of `javax.mail.Message`, `javax.mail.InternetAddress` instead of `javax.mail.Address`, and `com.sun.mail.imap.IMAPStore` instead of `javax.mail.Store`. If you were writing code for a Lotus Notes–based system, you'd use different concrete implementation classes but the same abstract base classes.

The JavaMail API roughly follows the abstract factory design pattern. This pattern allows you to write your code based on the abstract superclasses without worrying too much about the lower-level details. The protocols and formats used and the associated concrete implementation classes are determined mostly by one line of code early in your program that names the protocol. Changing the protocol name goes 90% of the way to porting your program from one protocol (say, POP) to another (say, IMAP).

Service providers implement particular protocols. A service provider is a group of concrete subclasses of the abstract JavaMail API classes that specialize the general API to a particular protocol and mail format. These subclasses are probably (though not necessarily) organized into one package. Some of these (IMAP, SMTP) are provided by Sun with its reference implementation in the undocumented com.sun.mail package. Others (NNTP, MH) are available from third parties. And some (POP) are available from both Sun and third parties. The purpose of the abstract JavaMail API is to shield you from low-level details like this. You don't write code to access an IMAP server or a POP server. You write your programs to speak to the JavaMail API. Then, the JavaMail API uses the service provider to speak to the server using its native protocol. This is middleware for email. All you need to do to add support for a new protocol is install the service provider's JAR file. Simple, carefully designed programs that use only the core features of the JavaMail API may be able to use the new provider without even being recompiled. Of course, programs that make use of special features of individual protocols may need to be rewritten.

Since mail arrives from the network at unpredictable times, the JavaMail API relies on an event-based callback mechanism to handle incoming mail. This is exactly the same pattern (even using some of the same classes) used by the AWT and Java-Beans starting in Java 1.1. The javax.mail.event package defines about a half dozen different kinds of mail events as well as the associated listener interfaces and adapter classes for these events.

While many people still fondly recall the early days of ASCII email and even ASCII pictures like the one shown in Figure 19-1, modern email messages contain a bewildering array of multilingual text and multimedia data encoded in formats such as Base64, quoted-printable, BinHex, and uuencode. To handle this, the Java-Mail API uses the JavaBeans Activation Framework (JAF) to describe and display this content.

This chapter covers Version 1.1.3 of the JavaMail API, which is compatible with Java 1.1 and higher. Version 1.2 of the Java Mail API is currently making its way through the Java Community Process. This seems likely to add a few convenience methods and classes, but will not significantly change anything described here. The JavaMail API is a standard extension to Java, not part of the core JDK or JRE class library, even in Java 1.3. Consequently, you'll need to download it separately from Sun and install it on your system. At the time of this writing, it's freely available from *http://java.sun.com/products/javamail/*, though of course this URL is subject to change. It comes as a zip archive containing documentation, sample code, and the all-important *mail.jar* file. This file contains the actual *.class* files that implement the JavaMail API. To compile or run the examples in this chapter, you'll need to add this file to your class path, either by adding its path to the

CLASSPATH environment variable or, in Java 1.2 and later, by placing *mail.jar* in your *jre/lib/ext* directory.

The JavaBeans Activation Framework is also a standard extension to Java, not part of the core API. You can download it from *http://java.sun.com/beans/glasgow/jaf. html*, though as always the URL is subject to change. This download contains the *activation.jar* archive, which you'll also need to place in your class path.

Finally, you may want to add some additional providers. Sun's implementation includes SMTP and IMAP providers. However, both Sun and third parties have written providers for other protocols such as POP3, NNTP, MH, and more. Table 19-1 lists some of these.

Table 19-1. Mail Providers

Product (Company)	URL	Protocols	License
JavaMail (Sun)	*http://java.sun.com/ products/javamail/*	SMTP, IMAP	Free
POP3 Provider (Sun)	*http://java.sun.com/ products/javamail/*	POP3	Free
POP3 Provider for JavaMail (Jason Diamond)	*http://injektilo.org/ pop3mail.html*	POP3	Free
ICE MH JavaMail Provider (ICE Engineering, Inc.)	*http://www.trustice. com/java/icemh*	MH	Public domain
POP3 Provider for JavaMail 1.1 (Linkable Software)	*http://www.linkable. com/products/pop3/*	POP3, mbox	Evaluation only
POPpers (Y. Miyadate)	*http://www2s.biglobe. ne.jp/~dat/java/project/ poppers/index_en.html*	POP3	GPL
dog.mail (Christopher Burdess)	*http://www.dog.net.uk/ knife/*	POP3, NNTP, mbox	Mozilla Public License

Sending Email

The most basic email need of a Java program is to send messages. While email clients like Eudora and mailing list managers like listproc are the only common programs that receive messages, all sorts of programs send messages. For instance, web browsers can submit HTML forms via email. Security scanning tools like Satan can run in the background and email their results to the administrator when they're done. When the Unix cron program detects a misconfigured *crontab* file, it emails the error to the owner. Books & Writers runs a service that's very popular with authors to track the sales rank of their books on Amazon.com and notify them periodically via email. (See *http://www.booksandwriters.com/rank.html*.) A massively parallel computation like the SETI@home project can submit individual results via email. Some multiplayer games like chess can be played across the network by emailing the moves back and forth (though this scheme wouldn't work for faster-moving games like Quake or even for speed chess). And these are just a few of the different kinds of programs that send email. In today's wired world, by far the simplest way to notify a user of an event when he's not currently sitting in front of the computer that the program is running on is to send him email.

The JavaMail API provides everything your programs need to send email. To send a message, a program just follows these eight steps:

1. Set the `mail.host` property to point to the local mail server.

2. Start a mail session with the `Session.getInstance()` method.

3. Create a new `Message` object, probably by instantiating one of its concrete subclasses.

4. Set the message's From: address.

5. Set the message's To: address.

6. Set the message's Subject:.

7. Set the content of the message.

8. Send the message with the `Transport.send()` method.

The order of these steps is not especially rigid. For instance, steps 4 through 7 can be performed in any order. Furthermore, each of these steps is individually quite simple.

The first step is to set up the properties for the mail session. The only property you have to set in order to send mail is `mail.host`. This is configured as a `java.util.Properties` object rather than an environment variable. For example, this code fragment sets the `mail.host` property to *mail.cloud9.net*:

```
Properties props = new Properties();
props.put("mail.host", "mail.cloud9.net");
```

Your programs will of course have to set this property to the name of your own mail server. These properties are used to retrieve a `Session` object from the `Session.getInstance()` factory method like this:

```
Session mailConnection = Session.getInstance(props, null);
```

The `Session` object represents an ongoing communication between a program and one mail server. The second argument to the `getInstance()` method, `null` here, is a `javax.mail.Authenticator` that will ask the user for a password if one is requested by the server. We'll discuss this more later in the section on password authentication. Most of the time, you do not need to provide a username and password to send email, only to receive it.

The `Session` object is used to construct a new `Message` object:

```
Message msg = new MimeMessage(mailConnection);
```

I specify the `MimeMessage` class in particular since I know I'm sending Internet email. However, this is the one place where I do explicitly choose a format for the email message. In some cases, this may not be necessary if I can copy the incoming message format instead.

Now that I have a `Message` object, I need to set up its fields and contents. The From: address and To: address will each be `javax.mail.internet.InternetAddress` objects. You can provide either an email address alone or an email address and a real name. For example:

```
Address bill = new InternetAddress("god@microsoft.com", "Bill Gates");
Address elliotte = new InternetAddress("elharo@metalab.unc.edu");
```

The `setFrom()` message allows us to say who's sending the message by setting the From: header. There's no protection against forgery here. It's quite easy for me to masquerade as Bill Gates at a (presumably) fictitious email address:

```
msg.setFrom(bill);
```

The `setRecipient()` method is slightly more complex. You not only have to specify the address that the message will be sent to, but how that address is used; that is, as a To: field, a Cc: field, or a Bcc: field. These are indicated by three mnemonic constants of the `Message.RecipientType` class:

```
Message.RecipientType.TO
Message.RecipientType.CC
Message.RecipientType.BCC
```

For example:

```
msg.setRecipient(Message.RecipientType.TO, elliotte);
```

The subject is set as a simple string of text. For example:

```
msg.setSubject("You must comply.");
```

The body is also set as a single string of text. However, as well as that text you need to provide the MIME type of the text. The most common type is text/plain. For example:

```
msg.setContent("Resistance is futile. You will be assimilated!",
    "text/plain");
```

Finally, the static `Transport.send()` method connects to the mail server specified by the `mail.host` property and sends the message on its way:

```
Transport.send(msg);
```

Example 19-1 puts all these steps together into a standalone program that sends
the following message:

```
Date: Mon, 29 Nov 1999 15:55:42 -0500 (EST)
From: Bill Gates <god@microsoft.com>
To: elharo@metalab.unc.edu
Subject: You must comply.

Resistance is futile. You will be assimilated!
```

I've shown this message here in standard RFC 822 format used for Internet email.
However, that isn't necessary. The main point is that you need to know the
addressee (*elharo@metalab.unc.edu*), the sender (*god@microsoft.com*), and the subject
and body of the message.

Example 19-1. Sending a Very Simple Mail Message

```java
import javax.mail.*;
import javax.mail.internet.*;
import java.util.*;

public class Assimilator {

  public static void main(String[] args) {

    try {
      Properties props = new Properties();
      props.put("mail.host", "mail.cloud9.net");

      Session mailConnection = Session.getInstance(props, null);
      Message msg = new MimeMessage(mailConnection);

      Address bill = new InternetAddress("god@microsoft.com",
        "Bill Gates");
      Address elliotte = new InternetAddress("elharo@metalab.unc.edu");

      msg.setContent("Resistance is futile. You will be assimilated!",
        "text/plain");
      msg.setFrom(bill);
      msg.setRecipient(Message.RecipientType.TO, elliotte);
      msg.setSubject("You must comply.");

      Transport.send(msg);

    }
    catch (Exception e) {
      e.printStackTrace();
    }

  }
}
```

Sending Email from an Application

Example 19-1 is a simple application that sends a fixed message to a known address with a specified subject. Once you see how to do this, it's straightforward to replace the strings that give the message address, subject, and body with data read from the command line, a GUI, a database, or some other source. For instance, Example 19-2 is a very simple GUI for sending email. Figure 19-1 shows the program running. The mail code is all tied up in the `actionPerformed()` method and looks very similar to the `main()` method of Example 19-1. The big difference is that now the host, subject, from: address, to: address, and text of the message are all read from the GUI components at runtime rather than being hard-coded as string literals in the source code. The rest of code is related to setting up the GUI and has little to do with the JavaMail API.

Example 19-2. A Graphical SMTP Client

```java
import javax.mail.*;
import javax.mail.internet.*;
import java.util.*;
import javax.swing.*;
import java.awt.event.*;
import java.awt.*;


public class SMTPClient extends JFrame {

    private JButton     sendButton   = new JButton("Send Message");
    private JLabel      fromLabel    = new JLabel("From: ");
    private JLabel      toLabel      = new JLabel("To: ");
    private JLabel      hostLabel    = new JLabel("SMTP Server: ");
    private JLabel      subjectLabel = new JLabel("Subject: ");
    private JTextField  fromField    = new JTextField(40);
    private JTextField  toField      = new JTextField(40);
    private JTextField  hostField    = new JTextField(40);
    private JTextField  subjectField = new JTextField(40);
    private JTextArea   message      = new JTextArea(40, 72);
    private JScrollPane jsp          = new JScrollPane(message);

    public SMTPClient() {

      super("SMTP Client");
      Container contentPane = this.getContentPane();
      contentPane.setLayout(new BorderLayout());

      JPanel labels = new JPanel();
      labels.setLayout(new GridLayout(4, 1));
      labels.add(hostLabel);
```

Example 19-2. A Graphical SMTP Client (continued)

```java
    JPanel fields = new JPanel();
    fields.setLayout(new GridLayout(4, 1));
    String host = System.getProperty("mail.host", "");
    hostField.setText(host);
    fields.add(hostField);

    labels.add(toLabel);
    fields.add(toField);

    String from = System.getProperty("mail.from", "");
    fromField.setText(from);
    labels.add(fromLabel);
    fields.add(fromField);

    labels.add(subjectLabel);
    fields.add(subjectField);

    Box north = Box.createHorizontalBox();
    north.add(labels);
    north.add(fields);

    contentPane.add(north, BorderLayout.NORTH);

    message.setFont(new Font("Monospaced", Font.PLAIN, 12));
    contentPane.add(jsp, BorderLayout.CENTER);

    JPanel south = new JPanel();
    south.setLayout(new FlowLayout(FlowLayout.CENTER));
    south.add(sendButton);
    sendButton.addActionListener(new SendAction());
    contentPane.add(south, BorderLayout.SOUTH);

    this.pack();

}

class SendAction implements ActionListener {

  public void actionPerformed(ActionEvent evt) {

    try {
      Properties props = new Properties();
      props.put("mail.host", hostField.getText());

      Session mailConnection = Session.getInstance(props, null);
      final Message msg = new MimeMessage(mailConnection);
```

Example 19-2. A Graphical SMTP Client (continued)

```
      Address to = new InternetAddress(toField.getText());
      Address from = new InternetAddress(fromField.getText());

      msg.setContent(message.getText(), "text/plain");
      msg.setFrom(from);
      msg.setRecipient(Message.RecipientType.TO, to);
      msg.setSubject(subjectField.getText());

      // This can take a non-trivial amount of time so
      // spawn a thread to handle it.
      Runnable r = new Runnable() {
        public void run() {
          try {
            Transport.send(msg);
          }
          catch (Exception e) {
            e.printStackTrace();
          }
        }
      };
      Thread t = new Thread(r);
      t.start();

      message.setText("");
    }
    catch (Exception e) {
      // We should really bring up a more specific error dialog here.
      e.printStackTrace();
    }

  }

}

public static void main(String[] args) {

  SMTPClient client = new SMTPClient();
  // Next line requires Java 1.3. We want to set up the
  // exit behavior here rather than in the constructor since
  // other programs that use this class may not want to exit
  // the application when the SMTPClient window closes.
  client.setDefaultCloseOperation(JFrame.EXIT_ON_CLOSE);
  client.show();

}
}
```

This is far from an ideal program. The GUI could be more cleanly separated from the mailing code. And it would be better to bring up an error dialog if something went wrong rather than just printing a stack trace of the exception on System. err. However, since none of that would teach us anything about the JavaMail API, I leave all that as an exercise for the interested reader.

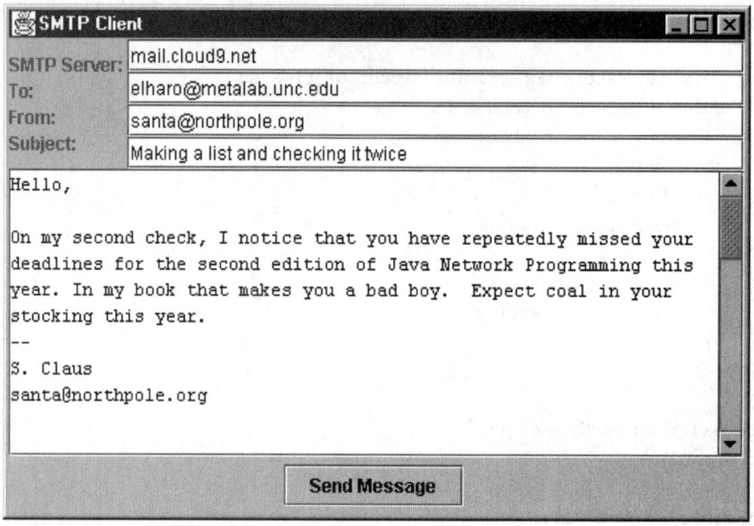

Figure 19-1. A simple GUI mail program

Sending Email from an Applet

In terms of GUIs and the JavaMail API, there's no difference between sending email from an applet and an application. However, the browser's security manager can get in your way. Like everything else in this book, the JavaMail API can't get around the normal restrictions on network connections from applets. An applet that wants to send email can still talk only to the host the applet itself came from.

Fortunately, however, most hosts that run web servers also run SMTP servers.* If this is the case, then it's quite straightforward to make an applet that sends email. The JavaMail API and the Java Activation Framework on which it depends aren't included with most browsers, but since they're implemented in pure Java in the javax package, browsers can download the necessary classes from the server. For example, this APPLET element references not only the applet's own code but also

---

* This is perhaps a little more likely to be true of a Unix web server than a Mac or Windows web server, since most Mac and Windows servers don't ship with SMTP servers by default.

the *mail.jar* and *activation.jar* files for the JavaMail API and the Java Activation Framework, respectively:

```
<APPLET CODE=SMTPApplet ARCHIVE="activation.jar,mail.jar"
       WIDTH=600 HEIGHT=400>
  <PARAM NAME="to" VALUE="hamp@sideview.mtsterling.ky.us">
  <PARAM NAME="subject" VALUE="Hay Orders">
  <PARAM NAME="from" VALUE="noone">
</APPLET>
```

NOTE In practice, the JavaMail API works only in HotJava and Internet Explorer. Netscape Navigator 4.x and earlier place additional restrictions on what resources an untrusted applet is allowed to load. These restrictions break the JavaMail API in applets.

Example 19-3 is a simple applet that sends email. The address to send email to and the subject are read from PARAM tags. The address to send email from is also read from a PARAM tag, but the user has the option to change it. The text to send is typed into a text area by the user. Finally, the server is determined by looking at the applet's codebase.

Example 19-3. An Applet That Sends Email

```
import java.applet.*;
import javax.mail.*;
import javax.mail.internet.*;
import java.util.Properties;
import java.awt.event.*;
import java.awt.*;


public class SMTPApplet extends Applet {

   private Button     sendButton   = new Button("Send Message");
   private Label      fromLabel    = new Label("From: ");
   private Label      subjectLabel = new Label("Subject: ");
   private TextField  fromField    = new TextField(40);
   private TextField  subjectField = new TextField(40);
   private TextArea   message      = new TextArea(30, 60);

   private String toAddress = "";

   public SMTPApplet() {

     this.setLayout(new BorderLayout());

     Panel north = new Panel();
     north.setLayout(new GridLayout(3, 1));
```

Example 19-3. An Applet That Sends Email (continued)

```
        Panel n1 = new Panel();
        n1.add(fromLabel);
        n1.add(fromField);
        north.add(n1);

        Panel n2 = new Panel();
        n2.add(subjectLabel);
        n2.add(subjectField);
        north.add(n2);

        this.add(north, BorderLayout.NORTH);

        message.setFont(new Font("Monospaced", Font.PLAIN, 12));
        this.add(message, BorderLayout.CENTER);

        Panel south = new Panel();
        south.setLayout(new FlowLayout(FlowLayout.CENTER));
        south.add(sendButton);
        sendButton.addActionListener(new SendAction());
        this.add(south, BorderLayout.SOUTH);

    }

    public void init() {

        String subject = this.getParameter("subject");
        if (subject == null) subject = "";
        subjectField.setText(subject);

        toAddress = this.getParameter("to");
        if (toAddress == null) toAddress = "";

        String fromAddress = this.getParameter("from");
        if (fromAddress == null) fromAddress = "";
        fromField.setText(fromAddress);

    }

    class SendAction implements ActionListener {

        public void actionPerformed(ActionEvent evt) {

            try {
                Properties props = new Properties();
                props.put("mail.host", getCodeBase().getHost());

                Session mailConnection = Session.getInstance(props, null);
                final Message msg = new MimeMessage(mailConnection);
```

Example 19-3. An Applet That Sends Email (continued)

```
        Address to = new InternetAddress(toAddress);
        Address from = new InternetAddress(fromField.getText());

        msg.setContent(message.getText(), "text/plain");
        msg.setFrom(from);
        msg.setRecipient(Message.RecipientType.TO, to);
        msg.setSubject(subjectField.getText());

        // This can take a non-trivial amount of time so
        // spawn a thread to handle it.
        Runnable r = new Runnable() {
          public void run() {
            try {
              Transport.send(msg);
            }
            catch (Exception e) {
              e.printStackTrace();
            }
          }
        };
        Thread t = new Thread(r);
        t.start();

        message.setText("");
      }
      catch (Exception e) {
        // We should really bring up a more specific error dialog here.
        e.printStackTrace();
      }
    }
  }
}
```

Figure 19-2 shows this applet running in Internet Explorer 4.0.1 on the Macintosh. I've been careful to only use methods and classes available in Java 1.1 so that this applet will run across the most web browsers possible. I also avoided using Swing so that there'd be one less large JAR file to download. As it is, the *mail.jar* and *activation.jar* files that this applet requires take up almost 300K, more than I'm comfortable with but manageable on a fast connection.

Proper behavior of this applet depends on several external factors:

• The browser must support at least Java 1.1 with a security model no stricter than the default.

• The *mail.jar* and *activation.jar* files must be available in the applet's codebase.

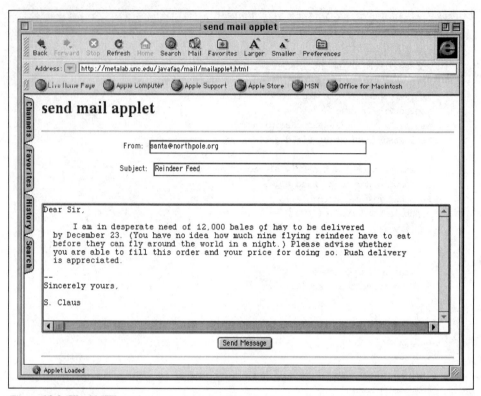

Figure 19-2. The SMTP applet

- The web server that serves the applet must also be an SMTP server willing to relay mail from the client system to the receiver system. Nowadays, most open SMTP relays have been shut down to avoid abuse by spammers, so this can be a sticking point. If it is, you'll get an exception like this:

```
javax.mail.SendFailedException: 550 <hamp@sideview.mtsterling.ky.us>... Relaying
denied
```

However, you should at least be able to send email to addresses in the web server's domain.

Receiving Mail

Receiving mail is considerably more complex than sending it. For instance, where a simple HELLO command is sufficient to access most SMTP servers (a fact that is the source of much forged email and spam), retrieving email generally requires providing both a username and a password. SMTP uses only 14 different commands, and a simple email client can be implemented with just five of them. POP3, however, has 12 commands, almost all of which a client must be able to handle, and IMAP4 has 24 different commands.

The JavaMail API is designed around the idea that you're retrieving messages from an IMAP or perhaps an NNTP server. That is, it assumes that the server can return headers separate from the messages they belong to, that it can search through mailboxes, that it provides the storage for the messages rather than the client, and so forth. The JavaMail API provides less of what you need for client-oriented mail access protocols, such as POP3, that assume the client stores and manage the mail archive, but it still gives you the tools to download the mail from the server. You just have to implement your own storage system on the client.

More clients today use POP rather than IMAP to access their mail (especially at ISPs that don't want to spend disk space on storing users' mailboxes), so we'll begin with the simpler POP protocol, then move on to IMAP. From the perspective of JavaMail, IMAP can be viewed largely as POP plus some commands for manipulating folders. For simple programs that operate only on the INBOX folder, POP and IMAP clients are more or less the same. Sun's implementation of JavaMail does not include a POP3 service provider, so to connect to a POP server, you'll have to install one. Several POP providers are listed in Table 19-1. For the examples in this chapter, Sun's POP3 provider will be sufficient, though Linkable Software's POP3 Provider for JavaMail 1.1 is more feature complete. Both of these include a *.jar* file you add to your CLASSPATH environment variable or place in your *ext* directory.

There are about 12 steps to reading a remote mailbox. (The exact number can vary a little, since some steps are optional or can be combined with or replaced by others.)

1. Set up the properties you'll use for the connection.

2. Construct the `Authenticator` you'll use for the connection.

3. Get a `Session` object with `Session.getDefaultInstance()`.

4. Use the session's `getStore()` method to return a `Store`.

5. Connect to the store.

6. Get the INBOX folder from the store with the `getFolder()` method.

7. Open the INBOX folder.

8. Open the folder you want inside the INBOX folder. Repeat as many times as necessary to reach the folder you're seeking.

9. Get the messages from the folder as an array of `Message` objects.

10. Iterate through the array of messages, processing each one in turn using the methods of the `Message` class. For instance, you might print out each message or simply display the sender, subject, and other vital information in a GUI for the user to select from, as in Figure 19-3.

11. Close the folder.

12. Close the store.

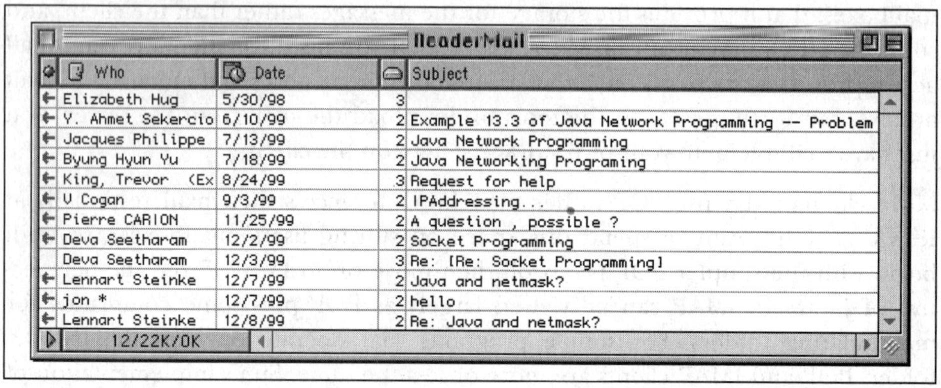

☑	🗒 Who	🕓 Date	🗂	Subject
←	Elizabeth Hug	5/30/98	3	
←	Y. Ahmet Sekercio	6/10/99	2	Example 13.3 of Java Network Programming -- Problem
←	Jacques Philippe	7/13/99	2	Java Network Programming
←	Byung Hyun Yu	7/18/99	2	Java Networking Programing
←	King, Trevor (Ex	8/24/99	3	Request for help
←	U Cogan	9/3/99	2	IPAddressing...
←	Pierre CARION	11/25/99	2	A question , possible ?
←	Deva Seetharam	12/2/99	2	Socket Programming
	Deva Seetharam	12/3/99	3	Re: [Re: Socket Programming]
←	Lennart Steinke	12/7/99	2	Java and netmask?
←	jon *	12/7/99	2	hello
←	Lennart Steinke	12/8/99	2	Re: Java and netmask?

Figure 19-3. A GUI for selecting mail messages

Each of these steps is individually quite simple. The first is to set up the properties for the mail session. Properties you might want to set include `mail.host`, `mail.store.protocol`, `mail.user`, `mail.pop3.user`, and `mail.pop3.host`. However, you don't absolutely need to set any of these. If the `Session` will be used only to retrieve mail, then an empty `Properties` object will be enough. For example:

```
Properties props = new Properties();
```

Next, you'll want to create an instance of the `javax.mail.Authenticator` class (more properly, an instance of a concrete subclass of the abstract `Authenticator` class) that can ask the user for her password. For now, we'll simply hardcode those values and pass null instead of an actual `Authenticator`. However, we'll fix this later when we discuss authentication:

```
Authenticator a = null;
```

Then, use your `Properties` and `Authenticator` objects to get a `Session` instance like this:

```
Session session = Session.getDefaultInstance(props, a);
```

Next ask the session for a store for the provider. Here, we want a provider for POP3:

```
Store store = session.getStore("POP3");
```

Finally, you're ready to actually connect to the store using the `connect()` method. You'll need to provide the host to connect to and the username and password to use:

```
store.connect("mail.cloud9.net", "elharo", "my_password");
```

You can pass null for the password to indicate that the previously specified `Authenticator` should be queried for the password.

Now that the store is connected, you're ready to open a folder in the store. This step is really more oriented to IMAP than POP, since POP servers don't keep track of different folders. They simply provide all of a user's incoming mail as one undifferentiated amalgam. For purposes of the JavaMail API, POP3 providers use the folder name INBOX:

```
Folder inbox = store.getFolder("INBOX");
```

The folder is closed when you get it. You can perform some operations on a closed folder including deleting or renaming it, but you can't get the messages out of a closed folder. First you have to open it. You can open a folder for read access by passing the mnemonic constant `Folder.READ_ONLY` to the `open()` method for read access, or `Folder.READ_WRITE` for read/write access:

```
inbox.open(Folder.READ_ONLY);
```

Now you're ready to download the messages. Do this with the `getMessages()` method, which returns an array containing all the messages in the folder:

```
Message[] messages = inbox.getMessages();
```

(If you were using IMAP instead of POP, this step would not actually download the messages. Each one would stay on the server until you accessed it specifically. You'd just get a pointer to the actual message.)

The `Message` class provides many methods for working with individual messages. It has methods to get the various header fields of the message, to get the content of the message, to reply to the message, and more. We'll discuss these soon, when we talk about the `Message` and `MimeMessage` classes. For now, we'll do just about the simplest thing imaginable, print each message on `System.out` using the message's `writeTo()` method:

```
for (int i = 0; i < messages.length; i++) {
  System.out.println("------------ Message " + (i+1)
    + " ------------");
  messages[i].writeTo(System.out);
}
```

Once you're done with the messages, you should close the folder, then close the message store with the aptly named `close()` methods:

```
inbox.close(false);
store.close();
```

The `false` argument to the folder's `close()` method indicates that we do not want the server to actually expunge any deleted messages in the folder. We simply want to break our connection to this folder.

Example 19-4 puts this all together with a simple program that downloads and prints out the contents of a specified POP mailbox. Messages are simply dumped on System.out in the default encoding. The servers, usernames, and so forth are all hardcoded. However, this quickly demonstrates most of the key points of receiving mail with the JavaMail API. A more advanced program would include an appropriate GUI.

Example 19-4. POP3Client

```java
import javax.mail.*;
import javax.mail.internet.*;
import java.util.*;
import java.io.*;

public class POP3Client {

  public static void main(String[] args) {

    Properties props = new Properties();

    String host = "utopia.poly.edu";
    String username = "eharold";
    String password = "mypassword";
    String provider = "pop3";

    try {

      // Connect to the POP3 server
      Session session = Session.getDefaultInstance(props, null);
      Store store = session.getStore(provider);
      store.connect(host, username, password);

      // Open the folder
      Folder inbox = store.getFolder("INBOX");
      if (inbox == null) {
        System.out.println("No INBOX");
        System.exit(1);
      }
      inbox.open(Folder.READ_ONLY);

      // Get the messages from the server
      Message[] messages = inbox.getMessages();
      for (int i = 0; i < messages.length; i++) {
        System.out.println("------------ Message " + (i+1)
          + " ------------");
        messages[i].writeTo(System.out);
      }

      // Close the connection
```

Example 19-4. POP3Client (continued)

```
      // but don't remove the messages from the server
      inbox.close(false);
      store.close();

    }
    catch (Exception e) {
      e.printStackTrace();
    }
  }
}
```

Here's some sample output I got when I pointed it at an account I don't use much:

```
D:\JAVA\JNP2\examples\18>java POP3Client
------------ Message 1 ------------
Received: (from eharold@localhost)
        by utopia.poly.edu (8.8.8/8.8.8) id QAA05728
        for eharold; Tue, 30 Nov 1999 16:14:29 -0500 (EST)
Date: Tue, 30 Nov 1999 16:14:29 -0500 (EST)
From: Elliotte Harold <eharold@utopia.poly.edu>
Message-Id: <199911302114.QAA05728@utopia.poly.edu>
To: eharold@utopia.poly.edu
Subject: test
Content-Type: text
X-UIDL: 87e3f1ba71738c8f772b15e3933241f0
Status: RO

hello you

------------ Message 2 ------------
Received: from russian.cloud9.net (russian.cloud9.net [
.4])
        by utopia.poly.edu (8.8.8/8.8.8) with ESMTP id OAA28428
        for <eharold@utopia.poly.edu>; Wed, 1 Dec 1999 14:05:06 -0500 (
Received: from [168.100.203.234] (macfaq.dialup.cloud9.net [168.100.203
        by russian.cloud9.net (Postfix) with ESMTP id 24B93764F
        for <eharold@utopia.poly.edu>; Wed,  1 Dec 1999 14:02:50 -0500
Mime-Version: 1.0
X-Sender: macfaq@mail.cloud9.net
Message-Id: <v04210100b46b1f97969d@[168.100.203.234]>
Date: Wed, 1 Dec 1999 13:55:40 -0500
To: eharold@utopia.poly.edu
From: Elliotte Rusty Harold <elharo@macfaq.com>
Subject: New system
Content-Type: text/plain; charset="us-ascii" ; format="flowed"
X-UIDL: 01fd5cbcf1768fc6c28f9c8f934534b5
```

```
Just thought you'd be happy to know that now that I've got my desk
moved over from my old apartment, I've finally ordered the Windows NT
system I've been promising for months.
--
David
```

About the only change you'd need to make to port this program to IMAP would be setting the provider variable to imap instead of pop3.

Password Authentication

Hardcoding passwords in source code as Example 19-4 does is, to say the least, a very bad idea. If a password is required, you should ask the user for it at runtime. Furthermore, when the user types the password, it should not be displayed on the screen. Ideally, it should not even be transmitted in clear text across the network, though in fact many current POP clients and servers do exactly that. (IMAP tends to be a little more secure.)

When you open a connection to a message store, the JavaMail API allows you to provide a javax.mail.Authenticator object that it can use to get the username and password. Authenticator is an abstract class:

```
public abstract class Authenticator extends Object
```

When the provider needs to know a username or password, it calls back to the getPasswordAuthentication() method in a user-defined subclass of Authenticator. This returns a PasswordAuthentication object containing this information:

```
protected PasswordAuthentication getPasswordAuthentication()
```

NOTE   These two classes are almost exactly the same as the java.net.
Authenticator and java.net.PasswordAuthentication classes discussed in Chapter 7, *Retrieving Data with URLs*. However, those classes are available only in Java 1.2 and later. To make the JavaMail API work in Java 1.1, Sun had to duplicate their functionality in the javax.mail package. Sun could have included java.net. Authenticator and java.net.PasswordAuthentication in *mail. jar*, but that would have meant that the JavaMail API could not be certified as 100% Pure Java. However, everything you learned about java.net.Authenticator and java.netPasswordAuthentication in Chapter 7 is true of javax.mail.Authenticator and javax.mailPasswordAuthentication in this chapter. The only thing you have to watch out for is that if you import both java. net.* and javax.mail.* in a class, then your source code will have to use fully qualified names like java.net.Authenticator instead of short names like Authenticator.

To add runtime password authentication to your programs, you subclass
`Authenticator` and override `getPasswordAuthentication()` with a method
that knows how to securely ask the user for a password. One useful tool for this
process is the `JPasswordField` component from Swing. Example 19-5 demonstrates a Swing-based `Authenticator` subclass that brings up a dialog to ask the
user for his username and password.

Example 19-5. A GUI Authenticator

```
import javax.mail.*;
import javax.swing.*;
import java.awt.*;
import java.awt.event.*;


public class MailAuthenticator extends Authenticator {

  private JDialog passwordDialog = new JDialog(new JFrame(), true);
  private JLabel mainLabel = new JLabel(
   "Please enter your user name and password: ");
  private JLabel userLabel = new JLabel("User name: ");
  private JLabel passwordLabel = new JLabel("Password: ");
  private JTextField usernameField = new JTextField(20);
  private JPasswordField passwordField = new JPasswordField(20);
  private JButton okButton = new JButton("OK");

  public MailAuthenticator() {
    this("");
  }

  public MailAuthenticator(String username) {

    Container pane = passwordDialog.getContentPane();
    pane.setLayout(new GridLayout(4, 1));
    pane.add(mainLabel);
    JPanel p2 = new JPanel();
    p2.add(userLabel);
    p2.add(usernameField);
    usernameField.setText(username);
    pane.add(p2);
    JPanel p3 = new JPanel();
    p3.add(passwordLabel);
    p3.add(passwordField);
    pane.add(p3);
    JPanel p4 = new JPanel();
    p4.add(okButton);
    pane.add(p4);
    passwordDialog.pack();
```

Example 19-5. A GUI Authenticator (continued)

```
    ActionListener al = new HideDialog();
    okButton.addActionListener(al);
    usernameField.addActionListener(al);
    passwordField.addActionListener(al);

  }

  class HideDialog implements ActionListener {

    public void actionPerformed(ActionEvent e) {
      passwordDialog.hide();
    }

  }

  public PasswordAuthentication getPasswordAuthentication() {

    passwordDialog.show();

    // getPassword() returns an array of chars for security reasons.
    // We need to convert that to a String for
    // the PasswordAuthentication() constructor.
    String password = new String(passwordField.getPassword());
    String username = usernameField.getText();
    // Erase the password in case this is used again.
    // The provider should cache the password if necessary.
    passwordField.setText("");
    return new PasswordAuthentication(username, password);

  }
}
```

Most of this code is just for handling the GUI. Figure 19-4 shows the rather simple dialog box this produces.

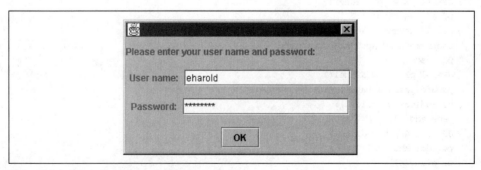

Figure 19-4. An authentication dialog

Interestingly, JPasswordField takes more pains to be secure than does PasswordAuthentication. JPasswordField stores passwords as an array of chars so that when you're done with the password, you can overwrite it with nulls. This means that the password exists in memory for less time and is less likely to be accidentally swapped out to disk and left there in a virtual memory system. However, PasswordAuthentication stores passwords as strings, which are immutable and therefore may be unintentionally stored on the disk.

Modifying the POP client to support this style of authentication is straightforward, as Example 19-6 demonstrates. We replace the hardcoded username and password with nulls and pass an instance of MailAuthenticator as the second argument to connect(). The only other change is that we call System.exit() at the end of the main() method, since the program will no longer exit when the main() method returns once the AWT thread has been started.

Example 19-6. A POP Client That Asks the User for the Password as Necessary

```
import javax.mail.*;
import javax.mail.internet.*;
import java.util.*;
import java.io.*;


public class SecurePOP3Client {

  public static void main(String[] args) {

    Properties props = new Properties();

    String host = "utopia.poly.edu";
    String provider = "pop3";

    try {

      // Connect to the POP3 server
      Session session = Session.getDefaultInstance(props,
       new MailAuthenticator());
      Store store = session.getStore(provider);
      store.connect(host, null, null);

      // Open the folder
      Folder inbox = store.getFolder("INBOX");
      if (inbox == null) {
        System.out.println("No INBOX");
        System.exit(1);
      }
      inbox.open(Folder.READ_ONLY);
```

Example 19-6. A POP Client That Asks the User for the Password as Necessary (continued)

```
      // Get the messages from the server
      Message[] messages = inbox.getMessages();
      for (int i = 0; i < messages.length; i++) {
        System.out.println("------------ Message " + (i+1)
          + " ------------");
        messages[i].writeTo(System.out);
      }

      // Close the connection
      // but don't remove the messages from the server
      inbox.close(false);
      store.close();

    }
    catch (Exception e) {
      e.printStackTrace();
    }

    // since we brought up a GUI returning from main() won't exit
    System.exit(0);

  }
}
```

Addresses

The `javax.mail.Address` class is very simple. It's an abstract class that exists mainly to be subclassed by other, protocol-specific address classes:

```
public abstract class Address extends Object
```

There are two of these subclasses in the standard JavaMail API: `InternetAddress` for SMTP email, and `NewsAddress` for Usenet newsgroups:

```
public class InternetAddress extends Address
public class NewsAddress extends Address
```

Providers of other mail protocols would also subclass `Address` with classes that represented their style of address.

The Address Class

The `Address` class itself is extremely simple. It has only three methods, all abstract and two of which are simple utility methods that override the corresponding methods in `java.lang.Object`:

```
public abstract String getType()
public abstract String toString()
public abstract boolean equals(Object o)
```

Since all three of these methods are abstract, there aren't any guarantees here about the methods' semantics, since all must be overridden in subclasses. However, this does require that subclasses provide their own implementations of `equals()` and `toString()` rather than relying on the rather generic implementations available from `java.lang.Object`. In general, the `getType()` method will return a string such as "rfc822" or "news" that indicates the kind of `Address` object this is.

The InternetAddress Class

An `InternetAddress` object represents an RFC 822–style email address. This is the standard Internet-style email address that is rapidly supplanting all other proprietary formats. It looks like *elharo@metalab.unc.edu* or *ask_tim@oreilly.com*. However, it can contain a name as well—for instance, *ask_tim@oreilly.com (Tim O'Reilly)*.

The state of an `InternetAddress` object is maintained by three protected fields:

```
protected String address
protected String personal
protected String encodedPersonal
```

The `address` field is the actual email address—for example, *ask_tim@oreilly.com*. The `personal` field is the name—for example, *Tim O'Reilly*. Although Java strings are pure Unicode that can express names like Erwin Schrödinger or ЕЛЬЦИН БОРИС НИКОЛАЕВИЧ, the strings used in mail headers must be pure ASCII in order to pass through most existing mail software. Consequently, Java's Unicode strings need to be converted to pure ASCII using a sort of hexadecimal escape. The details of this conversion are described in RFC 2047, *MIME (Multipurpose Internet Mail Extensions) Part Three: Message Header Extensions for Non-ASCII Text*. The encoded string is placed in the `encodedPersonal` field. All of these fields will be initially set in the constructor. There are four overloaded constructors for `InternetAddress` objects:

```
public InternetAddress()
public InternetAddress(String address) throws AddressException
public InternetAddress(String address, String personal)
  throws UnsupportedEncodingException
public InternetAddress(String address, String personal, String charset)
  throws UnsupportedEncodingException
```

They are used exactly as you'd expect. For example:

```
Address tim = new InternetAddress("ask_tim@oreilly.com", "Tim O'Reilly");
```

Although two of these methods are declared to throw `Unsupported-EncodingException`, this should happen only in the last method and then only if the name of the character set is not recognized by the VM. (For example, Java 1.1

does not recognize "ASCII", though in that case you don't really need to specify a character set.)

There are nine instance methods in this class—three setter methods, three getter methods, and three utility methods:

```
public void setAddress(String address)
public void setPersonal(String name, String charset)
  throws UnsupportedEncodingException
public void setPersonal(String name)
  throws UnsupportedEncodingException
public String getAddress()
public String getPersonal()
public String getType()
public String toString()
public boolean equals(Object o)
public int hashCode()
```

The setAddress() method sets the address field of the object to the specified value. The setPersonal() methods sets the personal and encodedPersonal fields to the specified value (after encoding it as necessary). The getAddress() and getPersonal() methods return the values of the address and personal or decoded encodedPersonal fields, respectively. Finally, the getType() method returns the string "rfc822".

The toString() method returns an email address suitable for use in a To: or From: field of an RFC 822 email message. The equals() and hashCode() methods have their usual semantics.

There are also five static utility methods, four of which convert addresses to and from strings:

```
public static String toString(Address[] addresses)
  throws ClassCastException
public static String toString(Address[] addresses, int used)
  throws ClassCastException
public static InternetAddress[] parse(String addressList)
  throws AddressException
public static InternetAddress[] parse(String s, boolean strict)
  throws AddressException
```

The InternetAddress.toString() methods convert an array of Address objects into a comma-separated list of addresses encoded in pure ASCII, possibly folded onto multiple lines. The optional used argument gives the number of characters that will precede this string in the header field, such as To: or Cc:, into which this string will be inserted. This lets toString() decide where it needs to break the lines. A ClassCastException is thrown if any of the Address objects in the array are not more specifically InternetAddress objects.

The two `parse()` methods perform this operation in reverse, converting a comma-separated `String` of addresses into an array of `InternetAddress` objects. Setting the optional `strict` argument to false changes the behavior so that strings that use whitespace instead of commas (or whitespace and commas) to separate email addresses are also understood. All four of these methods are useful for message header fields that contain multiple addresses; for example, a Cc: that's directed to six people.

Finally, the `getLocalAddress()` method checks several system properties (`mail.from`, `mail.user`, `mail.host`, and `user.name`) as well as `InetAddress.getLocalName()` to determine the email address of the current user:

```
public static InternetAddress getLocalAddress(Session session)
```

For example, this code fragment tries to use the user's own email address rather than one hardcoded into the program as a string:

```
msg.setFrom(InternetAddress.getLocalAddress());
```

However, there's no guarantee that any of these properties will necessarily give the user's true address.

The NewsAddress Class

Perhaps a little surprisingly, with an appropriate service provider, the JavaMail API can also access Usenet news. The API is mostly the same as for reading a POP or IMAP mailbox. However, instead of using an `InternetAddress`, you use a `NewsAddress`:

```
public class NewsAddress extends Address
```

A `NewsAddress` object represents a Usenet newsgroup name, such as *comp.lang.java.machine*. It may include the hostname for the news server as well. The state of a `NewsAddress` object is maintained by two protected fields:

```
protected String newsgroup
protected String host
```

The `newsgroup` field contains the name of the newsgroup—for example, *netscape.devs-java*. The `host` field is either null or contains the hostname of the news server—for example, *secnews.netscape.com*. Both of these fields are set in the constructor. There are three overloaded constructors for `NewsAddress` objects:

```
public NewsAddress()
public NewsAddress(String newsgroup)
public NewsAddress(String newsgroup, String host)
```

They are used exactly as you'd expect. For example:

```
Address netscape_java = new NewsAddress("netscape.devs-java.",
```

```
    "secnews.netscape.com");
```

There are eight instance methods in this class—three getter methods, two setter methods, and three utility methods:

```
    public String  getType()
    public String  getHost()
    public String  getNewsgroup()
    public void     setNewsgroup(String newsgroup)
    public void     setHost(String host)
    public String  toString()
    public boolean equals(Object o)
    public int      hashCode()
```

The setNewsgroup() and setHost() methods set the newsgroup and host fields of the object to the specified values. The getNewsgroup() and getHost() methods return the values of the newsgroup and host fields. Finally, the getType() method returns the string "news".

The toString() method returns the newsgroup name in a form suitable for the Newsgroups: header field of a Usenet posting. The equals() and hashCode() methods have their usual semantics.

There are also two static utility methods for converting addresses to and from strings:

```
    public static String toString(Address[] addresses)
      throws ClassCastException
    public static NewsAddress[] parse(String newsgroups)
      throws AddressException
```

The toString() method converts an array of Address objects into a comma-separated list of newsgroup names. A ClassCastException is thrown if any of the Address objects in the array are not more specifically NewsAddress objects. The parse() method reverses this operation, converting a comma-separated String of newsgroup names, such as "comp.lang.java.programmer,comp.lang.java. gui,comp.lang.java.help", into an array of NewsAddress objects. It throws an AddressException if the newsgroups argument is not a comma-separated list of newsgroup names.

Sun's implementation of the JavaMail API does not have a service provider for news, however; so although you can create news addresses, before you can actually read and post news, you'll need to install a service provider that does support it. Table 19-1 lists some possible sources of news providers. Once you've got one, reading news is as straightforward as talking to an IMAP server.

The URLName Class

`javax.mail.URLName` represents the name of a URL; that is, it treats a URL as a string, but does not attempt to connect to or resolve any of the parts of the string. URL names are mainly used as convenient ways to identify folders and stores with nonstandard URLs, such as *pop3://elharo:mypassword@mail.metalab.unc.edu:110/INBOX*, that don't have a matching protocol handler:

```
public class URLName Object
```

The methods of `URLName` are very similar to those of `java.net.URL` discussed in Chapter 7, except that all those involving actual connections have been deleted. What's left is a bunch of methods for breaking a URL string into its component parts or building a URL from pieces.

The Constructors

There are three overloaded `URLName` constructors. One takes the individual pieces of a URL as arguments; another takes a `java.net.URL` object; and a third takes a `String` containing a URL:

```
public URLName(String protocol, String host, int port, String file,
  String userName, String password)
public URLName(URL url)
public URLName(String url)
```

Constructing a `URLName` does not require that a protocol handler for the scheme be available. All the operations on the `URLName` take place with simple substring manipulation. This allows the `URLName` class to support very nonstandard URLs like *pop3://eharold:password@utopia.poly.edu/INBOX* or *imap://elharo@metalab.unc.edu/Speaking/SD99West*. These `URLName` objects can be used to refer to particular folders on the server.

Parsing Methods

These seven getter methods that return individual pieces of the URL are the main purpose for this class:

```
public int    getPort()
public String getProtocol()
public String getFile()
public String getRef()
public String getHost()
public String getUsername()
public String getPassword()
```

These can all be easily understood by analogy with the similarly named methods in `java.net.URL`. Except for `getPort()`, these all return null if the piece is missing. `getPort()` returns –1 if the port is not explicitly included in the URL.

There's also a `getURL()` method that converts a `URLName` to a `java.net.URL`. Since doing so requires that Java have a protocol handler for the URL's scheme, this method can throw a `MalformedURLException`:

```
public URL getURL() throws MalformedURLException
```

Finally, there are the usual three utility methods with the usual semantics:

```
public boolean equals(Object o)
public int     hashCode()
public String  toString()
```

The `toString()` method simply returns the string form of the URL.

We can use the `URLName` class to provide an interface for an email client that is completely protocol-independent. All information about protocol, host, and other details is provided by a URL read from the command line. Example 19-7 demonstrates.

Example 19-7. A Protocol-Independent Mail Client

```
import javax.mail.*;
import javax.mail.internet.*;
import java.util.*;
import java.io.*;


public class MailClient {

  public static void main(String[] args) {

    if (args.length == 0) {
      System.err.println(
      "Usage: java MailClient protocol://username:password@host/foldername");
      return;
    }

    URLName server = new URLName(args[0]);

    try {

      Session session = Session.getDefaultInstance(new Properties(),
       null);

      // Connect to the server and open the folder
      Folder folder = session.getFolder(server);
```

Example 19-7. A Protocol-Independent Mail Client (continued)

```
      if (folder == null) {
        System.out.println("Folder " + server.getFile() + " not found.");
        System.exit(1);
      }
      folder.open(Folder.READ_ONLY);

      // Get the messages from the server
      Message[] messages = folder.getMessages();
      for (int i = 0; i < messages.length; i++) {
        System.out.println("------------ Message " + (i+1)
         + " ------------");
        messages[i].writeTo(System.out);
      }

      // Close the connection
      // but don't remove the messages from the server
      folder.close(false);

    }
    catch (Exception e) {
      e.printStackTrace();
    }
  }
}
```

URLName does make the code a little more compact since it moves some information from the source code to the command line. Besides eliminating the obvious variables and string literals for username, host, and so forth, we've managed to eliminate any direct reference to the Store class. A typical run starts like this:

```
% java MailClient pop3://eharold:mypassword@utopia.poly.edu/INBOX
------------ Message 1 ------------
Received: (from eharold@localhost)
        by utopia.poly.edu (8.8.8/8.8.8) id QAA05728
        for eharold; Tue, 30 Nov 1999 16:14:29 -0500 (EST)
Date: Tue, 30 Nov 1999 16:14:29 -0500 (EST)
From: Elliotte Harold <eharold@utopia.poly.edu>
Message-Id: <199911302114.QAA05728@utopia.poly.edu>
To: eharold@utopia.poly.edu
Subject: test
Content-Type: text
X-UIDL: 87e3f1ba71738c8f772b15e3933241f0
Status: RO

hello you
```

For demonstration purposes, this program includes the password in the URL. In general, however, that's a huge security risk. It would be much better to use a runtime Authenticator as Example 19-6 did. Of course, ultimately it's very questionable whether this is really a superior interface to Example 19-6 and its ilk.

The Message Class

The `javax.mail.Message` class is the abstract superclass for all individual emails, news postings, and similar messages:

```
public abstract class Message extends Object implements Part
```

There's one concrete `Message` subclass in the standard JavaMail API, `javax.mail.internet.MimeMessage`. This is used for both email and Usenet news messages. Service providers are free to add classes for their own message formats. For instance, IBM might provide a `NotesMessage` class for Lotus Notes.

The `Message` class mainly declares abstract getter and setter methods that define the common properties of most messages. These properties include the addressees of the message, the recipients of the message, the subject and content of the message, and various other attributes. You can think of these as properties of the envelope that contains the message.

Furthermore, the `Message` class implements the `Part` interface. The `Part` interface mostly handles the body of an email message. It declares methods for getting and setting the content type of the message body, getting and setting the actual message body content, getting and setting arbitrary headers from the message, and getting input streams that are fed by the message body. The main body part of a message can contain other parts. This is used to handle attachments, message bodies that are available in multiple formats, and other multipart emails. Since the `Message` class is abstract and needs to be subclassed by concrete classes such as `MimeMessage`, most of these methods are not actually redeclared in `Message` but can be invoked by any actual instance of `Message`. We'll begin by discussing the methods actually declared in `Message`, then move on to those declared in `Part`.

Creating Messages

The `Message` class has three constructors:

```
protected Message()
protected Message(Folder folder, int messageNumber)
protected Message(Session session)
```

Since all the constructors are protected, these are primarily for the use of subclasses such as `MimeMessage`. If you're sending a message, you'll use one of the constructors in the subclass instead. If you're reading messages, then the `Folder` or `Session` you're reading from will create the `Message` objects and pass them to you.

Replying to messages

If you already have a **Message** object, one way to create a new **Message** object is to reply to the existing one using the **reply()** method:

```
public abstract Message reply(boolean replyToAll)
  throws MessagingException
```

This method creates a new **Message** object with the same subject prefixed with "Re: " and addressed to the sender of the original message. If **replyToAll** is true, then the message is addressed to all known recipients of the original message. The content of the message is empty. If you want to quote the original message, you'll have to do that yourself.

Getting messages from folders

You've already seen that when you're reading email, the JavaMail API creates **Message** objects to represent the messages it finds on the server. The primary means of doing this are the **getMessage()** and **getMessages()** methods in the **Folder** class:

```
public abstract Message getMessage(int messageNumber)
  throws MessagingException
public Message[] getMessages(int start, int end)
  throws MessagingException
public Message[] getMessages(int[] messageNumbers)
  throws MessagingException
public Message[] getMessages() throws MessagingException
```

The first three methods allow the caller to specify which messages it wants. The last simply returns all messages in the folder. What's actually returned are stubs holding the places of the actual messages. The text and headers of the message won't necessarily be retrieved until some method of the **Message** class is invoked that requires this information.

Basic Header Info

A typical RFC 822 message contains a header that looks something like this:

```
From levi@blazing.sunspot.noao.edu Fri Aug  5 10:57:08 1994
Date: Fri, 5 Aug 1994 10:57:04 +0700
From: levi@blazing.sunspot.noao.edu (Denise Levi)
To: volleyball@sunspot.noao.edu
Subject: Apologies
Content-Length: 517
Status: RO
X-Lines: 13
```

The exact fields can vary, but most messages contain at least a From: field, a To: field, a Date: field, and a Subject: field. Other common fields include Cc: (carbon copies) and Bcc: (blind carbon copies). In general, these will be accessible through getter and setter methods.

The From address

These four methods allow you to get and set the From: field of a message:

```
public abstract Address[] getFrom() throws MessagingException
public abstract void setFrom() throws MessagingException,
  IllegalWriteException, IllegalStateException
public abstract void setFrom(Address address)
  throws MessagingException, IllegalWriteException, IllegalStateException
public abstract void addFrom(Address[] addresses)
  throws MessagingException, IllegalWriteException, IllegalStateException
```

The getFrom() method returns an array of Address objects, one for each address listed in the From: header. (In practice, it's rare for a message to be *from* more than one address. It's quite common for a message to be addressed *to* more than one address.) It returns null if the From: header isn't present in the message. It throws a MessagingException if the From: header is malformed in some way.

The noargs setFrom() and addFrom() methods set and modify the From: headers of outgoing email messages. The noargs setFrom() method sets the header to the current value of the mail.user property or, as a fallback, the user.name property. The setFrom() method with arguments sets the value of the From: header to the listed addresses. The addFrom() method adds the listed addresses to any addresses that already exist in the header. All three of these methods can throw a MessagingException if one of the addresses they use isn't in the right format. They can also throw an IllegalWriteException if the From: field of the given Message object cannot be changed or an IllegalStateException if the entire Message object is read only.

The Reply-to address

Some messages contain a Reply-to: header indicating that any replies should be sent to a different address than the one that sent the message. There are two methods to set and get these addresses:

```
public Address[] getReplyTo() throws MessagingException
public void setReplyTo(Address[] addresses) throws MessagingException,
  MethodNotSupportedException, IllegalWriteException,
  IllegalStateException
```

The semantics of these methods are the same as for the equivalent getFrom() and setFrom() methods—in fact, the default implementation of getReplyTo()

simply returns `getFrom()`—with the single caveat that an implementation that doesn't support separate Reply-to: addresses may throw a `MethodNot-SupportedException` when `setReplyTo()` is invoked.

The recipient addresses

Whereas the sender of the message is generally found only in the From: header, the recipients of the message are often split across the To:, Cc:, and Bcc: fields. Rather than providing separate methods for each of these fields, the various `getRecipients()` and `setRecipients()` methods rely on a `Message.RecipientType` argument to determine which field's value is desired. `RecipientType` is a public inner class in `javax.mail.Message` whose private constructor limits it to exactly these three static objects:

```
Message.RecipientType.TO
Message.RecipientType.CC
Message.RecipientType.BCC
```

There are two methods to find the addressees of the `Message`:

```
public abstract Address[] getRecipients(Message.RecipientType type)
  throws MessagingException
public Address[] getAllRecipients() throws MessagingException
```

The `getRecipients()` method returns an array of `Address` objects, one for each address listed in the specified header. It returns null if the specified header isn't present in the message. It throws a `MessagingException` if the specified header is malformed in some way. The `getAllRecipients()` method does the same except that it combines the contents of the To:, Cc:, and Bcc: headers.

There are two methods to set the recipients of the message while replacing any previous recipients and two methods to add recipients to the message:

```
public abstract void setRecipients(Message.RecipientType type,
  Address[] addresses) throws MessagingException, IllegalWriteException,
  IllegalStateException
public void setRecipient(Message.RecipientType type, Address address)
  throws MessagingException, IllegalWriteException
public abstract void addRecipients(Message.RecipientType type,
  Address[] addresses) throws MessagingException,
  IllegalWriteException, IllegalStateException
public void addRecipient(Message.RecipientType type, Address address)
  throws MessagingException, IllegalWriteException
```

All four of these methods can throw a `MessagingException`, typically because one of the addresses used isn't in the right format. They can also throw an `IllegalWriteException` if the specified field of the given `Message` object cannot be changed or an `IllegalStateException` if the entire `Message` object is read-only.

The subject of the message

Since the subject is simply a single string of text, it's very easy to set and get with these two methods:

```
public abstract String getSubject() throws MessagingException
public abstract void    setSubject(String subject) throws
  MessagingException, IllegalWriteException, IllegalStateException
```

As with earlier setter methods, null is returned if the subject field isn't present in the message. An `IllegalWriteException` is thrown if the program isn't allowed to set the value of the Subject: field, and an `IllegalStateException` is thrown if the program isn't allowed to change the message at all.

The date of the message

Messages also have sent and received dates. Three methods allow programs to access these fields:

```
public abstract Date getSentDate() throws MessagingException
public abstract void setSentDate(Date date) throws MessagingException,
  IllegalWriteException, IllegalStateException
public abstract Date getReceivedDate() throws MessagingException
```

The underlying implementation is responsible for converting the textual date format found in a message header like "Fri, 5 Aug 2000 10:57:04 +0700" to a `java.util.Date` object. As usual, a `MessagingException` indicates some problem with the format of the underlying message; an `IllegalWriteException` indicates that the field cannot be changed; and an `IllegalStateException` indicates that the entire message cannot be changed.

Example 19-8 is a simple example program that follows the basic pattern of the last several mail-reading programs. However, this one no longer uses `writeTo()`. Instead, it uses the methods in this section to print just the headers. Furthermore, it prints them in a particular order regardless of their order in the actual message on the server. Finally, it ignores the less important headers such as X-UIDL: and Status:. The static `InternetAddress.toString()` method converts the arrays that most of these methods return into simple, comma-separated strings.

Example 19-8. A Program to Read Mail Headers

```
import javax.mail.*;
import javax.mail.internet.*;
import java.util.*;

public class HeaderClient {

  public static void main(String[] args) {
```

Example 19-8. A Program to Read Mail Headers (continued)

```
if (args.length == 0) {
  System.err.println(
   "Usage: java HeaderClient protocol://username@host/foldername");
  return;
}

URLName server = new URLName(args[0]);

try {

  Session session = Session.getDefaultInstance(new Properties(),
   new MailAuthenticator(server.getUsername()));

  // Connect to the server and open the folder
  Folder folder = session.getFolder(server);
  if (folder == null) {
    System.out.println("Folder " + server.getFile() + " not found.");
    System.exit(1);
  }
  folder.open(Folder.READ_ONLY);

  // Get the messages from the server
  Message[] messages = folder.getMessages();
  for (int i = 0; i < messages.length; i++) {
    System.out.println("------------ Message " + (i+1)
     + " ------------");
    // Here's the big change...
    String from = InternetAddress.toString(messages[i].getFrom());
    if (from != null) System.out.println("From: " + from);
    String replyTo = InternetAddress.toString(
     messages[i].getReplyTo());
    if (replyTo != null) System.out.println("Reply-to: "
     + replyTo);
    String to = InternetAddress.toString(
     messages[i].getRecipients(Message.RecipientType.TO));
    if (to != null) System.out.println("To: " + to);
    String cc = InternetAddress.toString(
    messages[i].getRecipients(Message.RecipientType.CC));
    if (cc != null) System.out.println("Cc: " + cc);
    String bcc = InternetAddress.toString(
     messages[i].getRecipients(Message.RecipientType.BCC));
    if (bcc != null) System.out.println("Bcc: " + to);
    String subject = messages[i].getSubject();
    if (subject != null) System.out.println("Subject: " + subject);
    Date sent = messages[i].getSentDate();
    if (sent != null) System.out.println("Sent: " + sent);
    Date received = messages[i].getReceivedDate();
    if (received != null) System.out.println("Received: " + received);
```

Example 19-8. A Program to Read Mail Headers (continued)

```
      System.out.println();
    }

    // Close the connection
    // but don't remove the messages from the server
    folder.close(false);

  }
  catch (Exception e) {
    e.printStackTrace();
  }

  // Since we may have brought up a GUI to authenticate,
  // we can't rely on returning from main() to exit
  System.exit(0);

  }
}
```

Here's some typical output. Several of the requested strings were null because the fields simply weren't present in the messages in the INBOX; for instance, Cc: and Bcc:. HeaderClient checks for that and simply omits the fields if they're not present.

```
% java HeaderClient pop3://eharold@utopia.poly.edu/INBOX
------------ Message 1 ------------
From: Elliotte Harold <eharold@utopia.poly.edu>
Reply-to: Elliotte Harold <eharold@utopia.poly.edu>
To: eharold@utopia.poly.edu
Subject: test
Sent: Tue Nov 30 13:14:29 PST 1999

------------ Message 2 ------------
From: Elliotte Rusty Harold <elharo@macfaq.com>
Reply-to: Elliotte Rusty Harold <elharo@macfaq.com>
To: eharold@utopia.poly.edu
Subject: New system
Sent: Wed Dec 01 10:55:40 PST 1999

------------ Message 3 ------------
From: Dr. Mickel <Greatsmiles@mail.com>
Reply-to: Dr. Mickel <Greatsmiles@mail.com>
To: eharold@utopia.poly.edu
Subject: Breath RX Products now available Online!
Sent: Thu Dec 02 03:45:52 PST 1999
```

Notice that none of these messages have received dates. That's because the receive time is not part of the message envelope itself. It has to be provided by the server, and POP servers don't provide it. An IMAP server would be much more likely to include a received date, as will be shown in Example 19-9.

Saving changes

When you invoke one of the previous set or add methods, some implementations will store the changes immediately. Others, however, may not. The saveChanges() method commits the changes made to a Message object:

```
public abstract void saveChanges() throws MessagingException,
  IllegalWriteException, IllegalStateException
```

This is not quite a flush. The actual changes may not be committed to disk until the folder containing the message is closed. However, this method does ensure that the changes are stored in the folder and that they will be saved when the folder is saved.

Flags

Mail programs can save extra information about the messages that are not part of the messages themselves. For instance, Pine lets me know whether I've replied to a message, whether I've read a message, and so on. As Figure 19-5 shows, these are indicated by symbols and letters in the lefthand column. D means a message has been deleted; A means it's been answered; N is a new message that hasn't been read yet; and so forth. In the JavaMail API, these are all represented as *flags*. A flag is an instance of the javax.mail.Flags class:

```
public class Flags extends Object implements Cloneable
```

Seven flags are predefined as instances of the public static inner class Flags.Flag. These are:

```
Flags.Flag.ANSWERED
Flags.Flag.DELETED
Flags.Flag.DRAFT
Flags.Flag.FLAGGED
Flags.Flag.RECENT
Flags.Flag.SEEN
Flags.Flag.USER
```

In addition, some implementations may allow arbitrary user-defined flags. If so, the USER flag will be set.

The getFlags() method returns the flags of a particular message:

```
public abstract Flags getFlags() throws MessagingException
```

Figure 19-5. Pine shows flags as letters in the lefthand column

The isSet() method tests whether a specified flag is set for the given message:

```
public boolean isSet(Flags.Flag flag) throws MessagingException
```

Finally, the setFlags() and setFlag() methods set or unset (depending on the second argument) the flag indicated by the first argument:

```
public abstract void setFlags(Flags flag, boolean set)
  throws MessagingException, IllegalWriteException,
  IllegalStateException
public void setFlag(Flags.Flag flag, boolean set) throws
  MessagingException, IllegalWriteException, IllegalStateException
```

You delete messages by setting their Flags.Flag.DELETED flag to true. For example, to delete message:

```
message.setFlag(Flags.Flag.DELETED, true);
```

This only marks the message as deleted. It does not actually expunge it from the file on the server. Until the message is expunged, it can still be undeleted by setting Flags.Flag.DELETED back to false.

Example 19-9 is a slight modification of Example 19-8, HeaderClient, that prints the flags as well. As a general rule, POP servers won't report flags. Only a protocol that stores messages and forwards them, such as IMAP or mbox, will report flags.

Example 19-9. A Program to Read Mailbox Flags

```
import javax.mail.*;
import javax.mail.internet.*;
import java.util.*;
```

Example 19-9. A Program to Read Mailbox Flags (continued)

```java
public class FlagsClient {

  public static void main(String[] args) {

    if (args.length == 0) {
      System.err.println(
        "Usage: java FlagsClient protocol://username@host/foldername");
      return;
    }

    URLName server = new URLName(args[0]);

    try {

      Session session = Session.getDefaultInstance(new Properties(),
       new MailAuthenticator(server.getUsername()));

      // Connect to the server and open the folder
      Folder folder = session.getFolder(server);
      if (folder == null) {
        System.out.println("Folder " + server.getFile() + " not found.");
        System.exit(1);
      }
      folder.open(Folder.READ_ONLY);

      // Get the messages from the server
      Message[] messages = folder.getMessages();
      for (int i = 0; i < messages.length; i++) {
        System.out.println("------------ Message " + (i+1)
         + " ------------");
        // Get the headers
        String from = InternetAddress.toString(messages[i].getFrom());
        if (from != null) System.out.println("From: " + from);
        String replyTo = InternetAddress.toString(
         messages[i].getReplyTo());
        if (replyTo != null) System.out.println("Reply-to: "
         + replyTo);
        String to = InternetAddress.toString(
         messages[i].getRecipients(Message.RecipientType.TO));
        if (to != null) System.out.println("To: " + to);
        String cc = InternetAddress.toString(
        messages[i].getRecipients(Message.RecipientType.CC));
        if (cc != null) System.out.println("Cc: " + cc);
        String bcc = InternetAddress.toString(
         messages[i].getRecipients(Message.RecipientType.BCC));
        if (bcc != null) System.out.println("Bcc: " + to);
        String subject = messages[i].getSubject();
        if (subject != null) System.out.println("Subject: " + subject);
```

Example 19-9. A Program to Read Mailbox Flags (continued)

```
      Date sent = messages[i].getSentDate();
      if (sent != null) System.out.println("Sent: " + sent);
      Date received = messages[i].getReceivedDate();
      if (received != null) System.out.println("Received: " + received);

      // Now test the flags:
      if (messages[i].isSet(Flags.Flag.DELETED)) {
        System.out.println("Deleted");
      }
      if (messages[i].isSet(Flags.Flag.ANSWERED)) {
        System.out.println("Answered");
      }
      if (messages[i].isSet(Flags.Flag.DRAFT)) {
        System.out.println("Draft");
      }
      if (messages[i].isSet(Flags.Flag.FLAGGED)) {
        System.out.println("Marked");
      }
      if (messages[i].isSet(Flags.Flag.RECENT)) {
        System.out.println("Recent");
      }
      if (messages[i].isSet(Flags.Flag.SEEN)) {
        System.out.println("Read");
      }
      if (messages[i].isSet(Flags.Flag.USER)) {
        // We don't know what the user flags might be in advance
        // so they're returned as an array of strings
        String[] userFlags = messages[i].getFlags().getUserFlags();
        for (int j = 0; j < userFlags.length; j++) {
          System.out.println("User flag: " + userFlags[j]);
        }
      }

    System.out.println();
  }

  // Close the connection
  // but don't remove the messages from the server
  folder.close(false);

}
catch (Exception e) {
  e.printStackTrace();
}

// Since we may have brought up a GUI to authenticate,
// we can't rely on returning from main() to exit
```

Example 19-9. A Program to Read Mailbox Flags (continued)

```
    System.exit(0);


  }
}
```

Here's a sample run. The first message has been read and deleted. The second message has no set flags. It hasn't been read, deleted, or answered. The third message has been read and answered but not deleted. Notice that I'm using an IMAP server instead of a POP server:

```
% java FlagsClient imap://elharo@mail.metalab.unc.edu/INBOX
------------ Message 1 ------------
From: Mike Hall <mikehall@spacestar.com>
Reply-to: Mike Hall <mikehall@spacestar.com>
To: mrj-dev@public.lists.apple.com
Subject: Re: dialog box, parents & X-platform
Sent: Mon Dec 13 05:24:38 PST 1999
Received: Mon Dec 13 06:33:00 PST 1999
Deleted
Read


------------ Message 2 ------------
From: Kapil Madan <kapil.madan@MIT-MISYS.COM>
Reply-to: XML-INTEREST@JAVA.SUN.COM
To: XML-INTEREST@JAVA.SUN.COM
Subject: Re: first mail to the list!
Sent: Mon Dec 13 06:19:46 PST 1999
Received: Mon Dec 13 06:40:00 PST 1999


------------ Message 3 ------------
From: Jim Jackl-Mochel <jmochel@foliage.com>
Reply-to: Jim Jackl-Mochel <jmochel@foliage.com>
To: elharo@metalab.unc.edu
Subject: CPreProcessorStream
Sent: Mon Dec 13 07:14:00 PST 1999
Received: Mon Dec 13 07:08:00 PST 1999
Answered
Read
```

Folders

Messages received from the network (as opposed to being sent to the network) will generally belong to some `Folder`. The `getFolder()` method returns a reference to the `Folder` object that contains this `Message`:

```
public Folder getFolder()
```

It returns null if the message isn't contained in a folder.

Within a folder, messages are organized from first (message 1) to last. The getMessageNumber() method returns the relative position of this Message in its Folder:

```
public int getMessageNumber()
```

Messages that aren't in any folder have number 0. Message numbers may change while a program is running if other messages are added to or deleted from a folder.

There's also a protected setMessageNumber() method, but it's only for service providers, not for user code:

```
protected void setMessageNumber(int number)
```

We'll talk more about folders and what they can do at the end of this chapter. One of the things you can do with a folder is expunge messages from it. This physically deletes the message if it's already been marked deleted. (A merely deleted message can be "undeleted", whereas an expunged message cannot be.) If a message is expunged, there may still be a Message object pointing to the message but almost all methods on the message will throw a MessagingException. Thus, it may be important to check whether a message has been expunged before working with it. The isExpunged() method does that:

```
public boolean isExpunged()
```

There's also a protected setExpunged() method, but it's only for service providers, not for user code:

```
protected void setExpunged(boolean expunged)
```

Searching

The final method left in the Message class is match(). The match() method is used to determine whether a Message satisfies particular search criteria. We'll discuss this more in a bit when we talk about searching folders:

```
public boolean match(SearchTerm term) throws MessagingException
```

The Part Interface

The Part interface is implemented by both Message and BodyPart. Every Message is a Part. However, some parts may contain other parts. The Part interface declares three kinds of methods:

- Methods for getting and setting the attributes of the part
- Methods for getting and setting the headers of the part
- Methods for getting and setting the contents of the part

The attributes of the part are things such as the size of the message or the date it was received. These aren't explicitly specified in the message's header. The headers, by contrast, are name-value pairs included at the front of the part. Finally, the content of the part is the actual data that the message is trying to transmit.

Attributes

The JavaMail API defines five attributes for parts. These are:

Size
> The approximate number of bytes in the part

Line count
> The number of lines in the part

Disposition
> Whether the part is an attachment or should be displayed inline

Description
> A brief text summary of the part

Filename
> The name of the file that the attachment came from

Not all parts have all attributes. For instance, a part that does not represent an attached file is unlikely to have a filename attribute. Each attribute is mapped to a getter method:

```
public int    getSize() throws MessagingException
public int    getLineCount() throws MessagingException
public String getDisposition() throws MessagingException
public String getDescription() throws MessagingException
public String getFileName() throws MessagingException, ParseException
```

Generally, the getter method returns null or −1 if a part doesn't possess the requested attribute. It throws a `MessagingException` if there's some problem retrieving the message; for instance, if the connection goes down while the message is being retrieved.

The `getSize()` method returns the approximate number of bytes in the part. Depending on the server and protocol, this may or may not account for changes in the size caused by operations such as Base64 encoding the data.

The `getLineCount()` method returns the approximate number of lines in the content of the part or −1 if the number of lines isn't known. Again, the number returned may or may not account for changes in the size of the part caused by the part's encoding.

The `getDisposition()` method returns a string indicating whether the content should be presented inline or as an attachment. The value returned should either be null (the disposition is not known) or one of the two named constants `Part.INLINE` or `Part.ATTACHMENT`:

```
public static final String ATTACHMENT = "attachment";
public static final String INLINE     = "inline";
```

If the disposition is `Part.ATTACHMENT`, then the `getFileName()` method should return the name of the file to save the attachment in. Otherwise, `getFileName()` will probably return null. However, some email clients, including Netscape 4.5 for Windows, do not properly set the Content-disposition header for attachments. Consequently, when receiving messages with attachments that were sent by Navigator, you'll often get a null disposition but a non-null filename. In practice, it seems more reliable to assume that any body part with a non-null filename is an attachment regardless of the Content-disposition header, and any body part with no filename and no Content-disposition header should be displayed inline if possible. If it's not possible—for instance, if you can't handle the MIME type—then you can either ask the user for a filename or pick some reasonable default, such as *attachment1.tif*.

Normally, the filename includes only the actual name of the file but not any of the directories that the file was in. It's up to the application receiving the message to decide where to put the incoming file. For instance, Eudora generally stores attachments in the Attachments folder inside the Eudora folder. However, the user has an option to pick a different location. Since it's not uncommon to receive multiple attachments with the same name over time (*vcard.vcf* is a particularly common attachment), always check to see whether a file with the attached file's name already exists before writing out the attachment. If a similarly named file does exist, you'll have to rename the attachment in some reasonable fashion; for instance, by appending a 1 or a 2 to it; e.g., *vcard1.vcf, vcard2.vcf*, and so on.

The description, disposition, and filename attributes also have setter methods. However, the size and line count attributes are determined by the content of the part rather than a setter method:

```
public void setDisposition(String disposition) throws
  MessagingException, IllegalWriteException, IllegalStateException
public void setFileName(String filename) throws MessagingException,
  IllegalWriteException, IllegalStateException
public void setDescription(String description) throws
  MessagingException, IllegalWriteException, IllegalStateException
```

The setter methods all throw a `MessagingException` if there's some problem while changing the message. They can also throw an `IllegalWriteException` if the relevant attribute of the part is not allowed to be modified or an `IllegalStateException` if the part belongs to a read-only folder.

The `setDisposition()` method determines whether the part is to be viewed inline or as an attachment. Although it's declared to take a `String` as an argument, this `String` should be one of the two named constants `Part.INLINE` or `Part.ATTACHMENT`. Parts that are attachments will generally have a filename included in their meta-information. This name can be set with the `setFileName()` method. Finally, the `setDescriptionMethod()` can take any `String` at all to add a description to the part.

Example 19-10 is a simple program that connects to a mail server and reads the attributes of the messages in the mailbox. Since each message is itself a part (even if it contains other parts), we can invoke these methods on the entire message.

Example 19-10. A Program to Read Mail Attributes

```java
import javax.mail.*;
import javax.mail.internet.*;
import java.util.*;

public class AttributeClient {

  public static void main(String[] args) {

    if (args.length == 0) {
      System.err.println(
       "Usage: java AttributeClient protocol://username@host/foldername");
      return;
    }

    URLName server = new URLName(args[0]);

    try {

      Session session = Session.getDefaultInstance(new Properties(),
       new MailAuthenticator(server.getUsername()));

      // Connect to the server and open the folder
      Folder folder = session.getFolder(server);
      if (folder == null) {
        System.out.println("Folder " + server.getFile() + " not found.");
        System.exit(1);
      }
```

Example 19-10. A Program to Read Mail Attributes (continued)

```
      folder.open(Folder.READ_ONLY);

      // Get the messages from the server
      Message[] messages = folder.getMessages();
      for (int i = 0; i < messages.length; i++) {
        System.out.println("------------ Message " + (i+1)
         + " ------------");
        String from = InternetAddress.toString(messages[i].getFrom());
        if (from != null) System.out.println("From: " + from);
        String to = InternetAddress.toString(
         messages[i].getRecipients(Message.RecipientType.TO));
        if (to != null) System.out.println("To: " + to);
        String subject = messages[i].getSubject();
        if (subject != null) System.out.println("Subject: " + subject);
        Date sent = messages[i].getSentDate();
        if (sent != null) System.out.println("Sent: " + sent);

        System.out.println();
        // Here's the attributes...
        System.out.println("This message is approximately "
         + messages[i].getSize() + " bytes long.");
        System.out.println("This message has approximately "
         + messages[i].getLineCount() + " lines.");
        String disposition = messages[i].getDisposition();
        if (disposition == null) ; // do nothing
        else if (disposition.equals(Part.INLINE)) {
          System.out.println("This part should be displayed inline");
        }
        else if (disposition.equals(Part.ATTACHMENT)) {
          System.out.println("This part is an attachment");
          String fileName = messages[i].getFileName();
          if (fileName != null) {
            System.out.println("The file name of this attachment is "
            + fileName);
          }
        }
        String description = messages[i].getDescription();
        if (description != null) {
          System.out.println("The description of this message is "
           + description);
        }

      }

      // Close the connection
      // but don't remove the messages from the server
      folder.close(false);
```

Example 19-10. A Program to Read Mail Attributes (continued)

```
    }
    catch (Exception e) {
      e.printStackTrace();
    }

    // Since we may have brought up a GUI to authenticate,
    // we can't rely on returning from main() to exit
    System.exit(0);


  }
}
```

Here's some typical output. I used an IMAP server because most of these methods don't work nearly as well with POP servers. IMAP servers can give you the attributes of a message without making you download the entire message, but POP servers aren't that sophisticated:

```
% java AttributeClient imap://elharo@mail.sunsite.unc.edu/INBOX
------------ Message 1 ------------
From: "Richman, Jeremy" <jrichman@hq.ileaf.com>
To: 'xsl-list' <XSL-List@mulberrytech.com>
Subject: Re: New twist: eliminating nodes with duplicate content
Sent: Mon Dec 06 08:37:51 PST 1999

This message is approximately 3391 bytes long.
This message has approximately 87 lines.
------------ Message 2 ------------
From: schererm@us.ibm.com
To: Unicode List <unicode@unicode.org>
Subject: Re: Number ordering
Sent: Mon Dec 06 11:00:28 PST 1999

This message is approximately 1554 bytes long.
This message has approximately 18 lines.
------------ Message 3 ------------
From: John Posner <jjp@connix.com>
To: 'Nakita Watson' <nakita@oreilly.com>
Subject: RE: Another conference Call
Sent: Mon Dec 06 11:16:38 PST 1999
This message is approximately 1398 bytes long.
This message has approximately 19 lines.
```

Headers

Classes that implement the `Part` interface—for example, `Message`—generally declare methods to return specific headers such as To: or From:. The `Part` interface, by contrast, declares methods to get and set arbitrary headers regardless of name.

The getHeader() method gets the values of all the headers with a name that matches the name argument. Some headers such as Received: can have multiple values and can be included in a message multiple times, so this method returns those values as an array of strings. It returns null if no header with that name is present in this Part:

```
public String[] getHeader(String name) throws MessagingException
```

The setHeader() method adds a new header to an outgoing message:

```
public void setHeader(String name, String value) throws
  MessagingException, IllegalWriteException, IllegalStateException
```

If there's already a header with this name, then that header is deleted and the new one inserted in its place—unless the folder in which the message resides is read only, in which case an IllegalStateException is thrown.

By contrast, the addHeader() method adds header with the specified name but does not replace any that exist:

```
public void addHeader(String name, String value) throws
  MessagingException, IllegalWriteException, IllegalStateException
```

The removeHeader() method deletes all instances of the named header from this Part:

```
public void removeHeader(String name) throws MessagingException,
  IllegalWriteException, IllegalStateException
```

The getAllHeaders() method returns a java.util.Enumeration object containing all the headers in this message:

```
public Enumeration getAllHeaders() throws MessagingException
```

The Enumeration contains one javax.mail.Header object for each header in the message.

```
public class Header extends Object
```

The Header class is very simple with just a constructor to set the name and value of the header, and getName() and getValue() methods to return them:

```
public Header(String name, String value)
public String getName()
public String getValue()
```

Finally, the getMatchingHeaders() method returns an Enumeration containing all the headers in this message whose name is one of the strings in the argument names array. The getNonMatchingHeaders() method returns an Enumeration containing all the headers in this message whose name is *not* one of the strings in the argument names array. Again, the Enumeration contains Header objects:

```
public Enumeration getMatchingHeaders(String[] names)
  throws MessagingException
public Enumeration getNonMatchingHeaders(String[] names)
  throws MessagingException
```

You may recall that Example 19-8, HeaderClient, printed only a few prespecified headers, such as To: and From:. With the methods of the Part interface (that Message implements), it's easy to expand this to cover all headers in the message, whether known in advance or not. Example 19-11 demonstrates. This is important because Internet email can contain arbitrary headers. It's not limited to just a few headers mentioned in the relevant RFCs. For instance, some graphical mail clients for X Windows use a completely nonstandard X-Face: header whose value is a 48-pixel × 48-pixel, black-and-white, uuencoded bitmap of the sender's countenance. Other clients use custom headers for purposes both more serious and more silly.

Example 19-11. A Program to Read Mail Headers

```
import javax.mail.*;
import javax.mail.internet.*;
import java.util.*;


public class AllHeaderClient {

  public static void main(String[] args) {

    if (args.length == 0) {
      System.err.println(
        "Usage: java AllHeaderClient protocol://username@host/foldername");
      return;
    }

    URLName server = new URLName(args[0]);

    try {

      Session session = Session.getDefaultInstance(new Properties(),
        new MailAuthenticator(server.getUsername()));

      // Connect to the server and open the folder
      Folder folder = session.getFolder(server);
      if (folder == null) {
        System.out.println("Folder " + server.getFile() + " not found.");
```

Example 19-11. A Program to Read Mail Headers (continued)

```
        System.exit(1);
      }
      folder.open(Folder.READ_ONLY);

      // Get the messages from the server
      Message[] messages = folder.getMessages();
      for (int i = 0; i < messages.length; i++) {
        System.out.println("------------ Message " + (i+1)
         + " ------------");
        // Here's the difference...
        Enumeration headers = messages[i].getAllHeaders();
        while (headers.hasMoreElements()) {
          Header h = (Header) headers.nextElement();
          System.out.println(h.getName() + ": " + h.getValue());
        }
        System.out.println();
      }

      // Close the connection
      // but don't remove the messages from the server
      folder.close(false);

    }
    catch (Exception e) {
      e.printStackTrace();
    }

    // Since we may have brought up a GUI to authenticate,
    // we can't rely on returning from main() to exit
    System.exit(0);

  }
}
```

Here's a typical run:

```
% java AllHeaderClient pop3://eharold@utopia.poly.edu/INBOX
------------ Message 1 ------------
Received: (from eharold@localhost)
        by utopia.poly.edu (8.8.8/8.8.8) id QAA05728
        for eharold; Tue, 30 Nov 1999 16:14:29 -0500 (EST)
Date: Tue, 30 Nov 1999 16:14:29 -0500 (EST)
From: Elliotte Harold <eharold@utopia.poly.edu>
Message-Id: <199911302114.QAA05728@utopia.poly.edu>
To: eharold@utopia.poly.edu
Subject: test
Content-Type: text
```

```
X-UIDL: 87e3f1ba71738c8f772b15e3933241f0
Status: RO


------------ Message 2 ------------
Received: from russian.cloud9.net (russian.cloud9.net [168.100.1.4])
        by utopia.poly.edu (8.8.8/8.8.8) with ESMTP id OAA28428
        for <eharold@utopia.poly.edu>; Wed, 1 Dec 1999 14:05:06 -0500 (EST)
Received: from [168.100.203.234] (macfaq.dialup.cloud9.net [168.100.203.234])
        by russian.cloud9.net (Postfix) with ESMTP id 24B93764F8
        for <eharold@utopia.poly.edu>; Wed,  1 Dec 1999 14:02:50 -0500 (EST)
Mime-Version: 1.0
X-Sender: macfaq@mail.cloud9.net
Message-Id: <v04210100b46b1f97969d@[168.100.203.234]>
Date: Wed, 1 Dec 1999 13:55:40 -0500
To: eharold@utopia.poly.edu
From: Elliotte Rusty Harold <elharo@macfaq.com>
Subject: New system
Content-Type: text/plain; charset="us-ascii" ; format="flowed"
X-UIDL: 01fd5cbcf1768fc6c28f9c8f934534b5
Status: RO


------------ Message 3 ------------
Received: from russian.cloud9.net (russian.cloud9.net [168.100.1.4])
        by utopia.poly.edu (8.8.8/8.8.8) with ESMTP id HAA17345
        for <eharold@utopia.poly.edu>; Thu, 2 Dec 1999 07:55:04 -0500 (EST)
Received: from [168.100.203.234] (macfaq.dialup.cloud9.net [168.100.203.234])
        by russian.cloud9.net (Postfix) with ESMTP id C036A7630E
        for <eharold@utopia.poly.edu>; Thu,  2 Dec 1999 07:54:58 -0500 (EST)
Mime-Version: 1.0
X-Sender: elharo@luna.oit.unc.edu
Message-Id: <v04210100b46c0c686ecc@[168.100.203.234]>
Date: Thu, 2 Dec 1999 06:45:52 -0500
To: eharold@utopia.poly.edu
From: "Dr. Mickel" <Greatsmiles@mail.com>(by way of Elliotte Rusty Harold)
Subject: Breath RX Products now available Online!
Sender: elharo@metalab.unc.edu
Content-Type: text/plain; charset="us-ascii" ; format="flowed"
X-UIDL: 40fa8af2aca1a8c11994f4c56b792720
Status: RO
```

Content

Every part has a certain content that can be represented as a sequence of bytes. For instance, in a part that's a simple email message, the content is the body of the message. However, in multipart messages, this content may itself contain other parts. The content of each of these parts can be represented as a sequence of bytes. Furthermore, this sequence of bytes may represent some more specific content type, such as a uuencoded GIF image or a Base64 encoded WAV audio clip.

Reading the contents of the part

The Part interface declares two methods for determining a part's MIME content type. The getContentType() method returns the MIME content type of this part as a string; for example, text/plain; charset="us-ascii"; format= "flowed". It returns null if the content type can't be determined:

```
public String getContentType() throws MessagingException
```

The isMimeType() method returns true if this part has the specified MIME type and subtype. Additional parameters, such as charset, are ignored:

```
public boolean isMimeType(String mimeType) throws MessagingException
```

The Part interface also declares several methods that return the content as a variety of different Java objects including InputStream, String, DataHandler, and more. The getInputStream() method returns an InputStream from which the part's content can be read:

```
public InputStream getInputStream() throws IOException,
  MessagingException
```

If the part's content has been encoded in some way—for example, by Base64 encoding it—then the InputStream reads the decoded content. The JavaMail API supports all the common encodings except the BinHex format used for Macintosh files. If it encounters a BinHex-encoded attachment, then it strips the MIME headers but otherwise leaves the BinHex data untouched. BinHex documents are tough to deal with on most platforms because of the unusual two-fork nature of a Mac file. Unless you're a real Mac expert, you're probably better off using a third-party utility such as StuffIt Expander (*http://www.aladdinsys.com/*) to decode the file.

Another possibility is to request a DataHandler for the content with the getDataHandler() method. The DataHandler class comes from the Java Activation Framework. It declares methods to help you decide what to do with the content; for instance, by finding the right Java bean or helper application to display the content:

```
public javax.activation.DataHandler getDataHandler()
  throws MessagingException
```

A third possibility is to request the content as an unspecified Java object using the getContent() method:

```
public Object getContent() throws IOException, MessagingException
```

This is reminiscent of the getContent() method of java.net.URL. However, rather than relying on the poorly designed content handler mechanism, this getContent() method uses the Java Activation Framework, so the behavior is a little more clearly specified. Most of the time, if the content type is text/plain, then a String will be returned. If the content type is multipart, then regardless of the subtype, a javax.mail.Multipart object is returned. If the content type is some other type that is recognized by the underlying DataHandler, then an appropriate Java object is returned. Finally, if the type is unrecognized, then an InputStream is returned.

You can change which objects are returned for which content types by providing your own DataHandler. This would be installed with the setDataHandler() method:

```
public void setDataHandler(javax.activation.DataHandler dh) throws
    MessagingException, IllegalWriteException, IllegalStateException
```

Although this method is declared to throw the usual group of exceptions, it's perhaps a little less likely to actually do so, since setting the DataHandler affects only the Message object rather than the actual message stored on the server.

Writing the contents of the part

When sending a message, you naturally must set the message's contents. Since email messages are text, the most straightforward way is just to provide the text of the part with setText():

```
public void setText(String text) throws MessagingException,
    IllegalWriteException, IllegalStateException
```

The setText() method sets the MIME type to text/plain. Other objects can be made into content as well, provided the part has a DataHandler that understands how to convert them to encoded text. This is done with the setContent() method:

```
public void setContent(Object o, String type) throws
    MessagingException, IllegalWriteException, IllegalStateException
```

Another way to write the contents of a part is by using an OutputStream. The writeTo() method writes the content of the Part onto an OutputStream. If necessary, it will encode the content using Base64, quoted-printable, or some other format as specified by the DataHandler:

```
public void writeTo(OutputStream out) throws IOException,
    MessagingException
```

In fact, this not only writes the content of this Part; it also writes the attributes and headers of the part. Example 19-4 used this to provide a simple way of getting an entire email message in one fell swoop. It's most convenient, though, when you want to send an entire message to an SMTP server in one method call.

Finally, multiple parts can be added to a part by wrapping them in a `Multipart` object and passing that to `setContent()`:

```
public void setContent(Multipart mp) throws MessagingException,
  IllegalWriteException, IllegalStateException
```

In this case, the entire message will typically have a content type such as multipart/ mixed, multipart/signed, or multipart/alternative. The individual parts of the message are all enclosed in one envelope, but each part of the message has its own content type, content encoding, and data. The multiple parts may be used to present different forms of the same document (e.g., HTML and plain-text mail), a document and meta-information about the document (e.g., a message and the MD5 digest of the message), or several different documents (e.g., a message and several attached files). The next section expands on this process.

Multipart Messages and File Attachments

The way all the different text and binary file types are encoded into raw text that can be passed through 7-bit email gateways is fairly ingenious and rather detailed. Fortunately, the JavaMail API shields you from those details, interesting as they are. To send a multipart message using the JavaMail API, all you have to do is add the parts to a `MimeMultipart` object, then pass that object to the `Message`'s `setContent()` method. To receive a multipart message, you simply process each of the parts individually.

Most of the methods you use to build and deconstruct multipart messages are in the abstract `javax.mail.Multipart` class:

```
public abstract class Multipart extends Object
```

However, since this class is abstract, you'll generally start with a `javax.mail. internet.MimeMultipart` object instead:

```
public class MimeMultipart extends Multipart
```

Each part you add to a `Multipart` is an instance of the abstract `javax.mail. BodyPart` class that implements the `Part` interface of the last section:

```
public abstract class BodyPart extends Object implements Part
```

In Internet email, the concrete subclass of `BodyPart` you'll use is `javax.mail. internet.MimeBodyPart`:

```
public class MimeBodyPart extends BodyPart implements MimePart
```

Most of the methods you need in the `MimeBodyPart` and `BodyPart` classes are the ones you're already familiar with from the `Part` interface, methods such as `setContent()` and `setDataHandler()`. There are also three methods to read the contents of a `Multipart` object:

```
public String    getContentType()
public int        getCount() throws MessagingException
public BodyPart getBodyPart(int index)
  throws IndexOutOfBoundsException, MessagingException
```

The `getContentType()` method returns the MIME type of the entire `Multipart`, which is typically something like multipart/mixed or multipart/alternative. This is not the same as the MIME types of the individual parts, which are something like text/plain or image/gif.

The `getCount()` method returns the number of parts in this `Multipart`. The `getBodyPart()` method returns a particular part. Parts are numbered starting at 0 like the components of an array. `Multiparts` are not hierarchical. A `Multipart` may not contain another `Multipart`. This makes writing programs to parse multipart messages fairly straightforward. Example 19-12 is very similar to Example 19-11, `AllHeaderClient`. However, this adds the necessary code to handle the body of the message. If the message is a single-part message, then it's simply printed on `System.out`. However, if the message has multiple parts, then each part is handled separately. If the part has no filename, does not have the disposition `Part.ATTACHMENT`, and has MIME type text/plain, then it's assumed to be an inline message and is printed on `System.out`. Otherwise, it's assumed to be an attachment and is saved into an appropriate file. If necessary, the static `File.createTempFile()` method introduced in Java 1.2 is used to generate a reasonable name for the file.

Example 19-12. A Mail Client that Handles Multipart Messages with Attached Files

```
import javax.mail.*;
import javax.mail.internet.*;
import java.util.*;
import java.io.*;


public class AllPartsClient {

  public static void main(String[] args) {

    if (args.length == 0) {
      System.err.println(
        "Usage: java AllPartsClient protocol://username@host:port/foldername");
      return;
    }
```

Example 19-12. A Mail Client that Handles Multipart Messages with Attached Files (continued)

```
    URLName server = new URLName(args[0]);

    try {

      Session session = Session.getDefaultInstance(new Properties(),
       new MailAuthenticator(server.getUsername()));

      // Connect to the server and open the folder
      Folder folder = session.getFolder(server);
      if (folder == null) {
        System.out.println("Folder " + server.getFile() + " not found.");
        System.exit(1);
      }
      folder.open(Folder.READ_ONLY);

      // Get the messages from the server
      Message[] messages = folder.getMessages();
      for (int i = 0; i < messages.length; i++) {
        System.out.println("------------ Message " + (i+1)
         + " ------------");

        // Print message headers
        Enumeration headers = messages[i].getAllHeaders();
        while (headers.hasMoreElements()) {
          Header h = (Header) headers.nextElement();
          System.out.println(h.getName() + ": " + h.getValue());
        }
        System.out.println();

        // Enumerate parts
        Object body = messages[i].getContent();
        if (body instanceof Multipart) {
          processMultipart((Multipart) body);
        }
        else { // ordinary message
          processPart(messages[i]);
        }

        System.out.println();

      }

      // Close the connection
      // but don't remove the messages from the server
      folder.close(false);

    }
    catch (Exception e) {
```

Example 19-12. A Mail Client that Handles Multipart Messages with Attached Files (continued)

```
      e.printStackTrace();
    }


    // Since we may have brought up a GUI to authenticate,
    // we can't rely on returning from main() to exit
    System.exit(0);


  }



  public static void processMultipart(Multipart mp)
   throws MessagingException {

    for (int i = 0; i < mp.getCount(); i++) {
      processPart(mp.getBodyPart(i));
    }


  }

  public static void processPart(Part p) {

    try {
      String fileName = p.getFileName();
      String disposition = p.getDisposition();
      String contentType = p.getContentType();
      if (fileName == null && (Part.ATTACHMENT.equals(disposition)
       || !contentType.equalsIgnoreCase("text/plain"))) {"X
        // pick a random file name. This requires Java 1.2 or later.
        fileName = File.createTempFile("attachment", ".txt").getName();
      }
      if (fileName == null) { // likely inline
        p.writeTo(System.out);
      }
      else {
        File f = new File(fileName);
        // find a version that does not yet exist
        for (int i = 1; f.exists(); i++) {
          String newName = fileName + " " + i;
          f = new File(newName);
        }
        FileOutputStream out = new FileOutputStream(f);

        // We can't just use p.writeTo() here because it doesn't
        // decode the attachment. Instead we copy the input stream
        // onto the output stream which does automatically decode
        // Base-64, quoted printable, and a variety of other formats.
        InputStream in = new BufferedInputStream(p.getInputStream());
        int b;
```

Example 19-12. A Mail Client that Handles Multipart Messages with Attached Files (continued)

```
          while ((b = in.read()) != -1) out.write(b);
          out.flush();
          out.close();
          in.close();
        }
      }
    catch (Exception e) {
      System.err.println(e);
      e.printStackTrace();
    }
  }
}
```

You can also get a part from a multipart message by passing an `OutputStream` to the part's `writeTo()` method:

```
public abstract void writeTo(OutputStream out)
  throws IOException, MessagingException
```

However, this differs from the approach taken in Example 19-12 in that it does not decode the part before writing it. It leaves whatever Base64 or BinHex or quoted-printable encoding that the sender applied to the attachment alone. Instead, it simply writes the raw data.

Attaching files (or other documents) to messages you send is more complicated. To attach a file to a message, you first have to wrap the data in a `BodyPart` object and add it to the `Multipart` using one of the two `addBodyPart()` methods:

```
public void addBodyPart(BodyPart part)
  throws IllegalWriteException, MessagingException
public void addBodyPart(BodyPart part, int index)
  throws IllegalWriteException, MessagingException
```

The first variant simply appends the part to the end of the message. The second variant adds the given part at the specified position. If the position is greater than the number of parts in the message, then it's simply added to the end. If it's added somewhere in the middle, this may cause the positions of other parts to change. If the message can't be changed, then an `IllegalWriteException` is thrown.

The tricky part is creating the `BodyPart` object. To do this, you'll first need to guess a reasonable MIME content type for the file (text/plain and application/octet-stream are the most common types). Next you'll need to read the file and convert it into some class of Java object. Then you'll install a `javax.activation.DataHandler` class that knows how to convert your data class according to your chosen MIME type. Once you've done all this, you can create a new `MimeBodyPart` object and use the various methods of the `Part` interface to set attributes such as the filename and the content disposition.

There are also two `removeBodyPart()` methods that delete a specified part from the message, though these aren't as commonly used:

```
public boolean removeBodyPart(BodyPart part)
  throws IllegalWriteException, MessagingException
public void removeBodyPart(int index)
  throws IndexOutOfBoundsException, MessagingException
```

If the message can't be changed, then an `IllegalWriteException` is thrown. If the specified index doesn't identify a part, then an `IndexOutOfBoundsException` is thrown. If the specified part isn't present in the message, then a `MessagingException` is thrown.

MIME Messages

MIME was designed mainly for Internet email, and it was specifically organized so that it would be backward compatible with existing protocols and software. Therefore, a typical Internet email message is in fact a MIME message. The only concrete subclass of `Message` in the JavaMail API is `javax.mail.internet.MimeMessage`:

```
public class MimeMessage extends Message implements MimePart
```

This class declares almost seventy public and protected methods. However, with the natural exception of the constructors, almost all of these either override methods from the `Message` superclass or implement methods declared by the `Part` interface. The only new methods are a baker's dozen declared in the `MimePart` interface, a subinterface of `Part`:

```
public interface MimePart extends Part
```

Most of these methods are very similar to either methods in `Part` or methods in `Message`. However, they have features that are unlikely to be found in non-MIME messages. For instance, a MIME part may have an MD5 digest, which would be encoded as an extra header inside the part. Thus, the `MimePart` interface declares and the `MimeMessage` class implements two methods to set and get this digest:

```
public String getContentMD5() throws MessagingException
public void   setContentMD5(String md5) throws MessagingException,
  IllegalWriteException, IllegalStateException
```

The `addHeaderLine()` method adds a string of text to the header of the message. It's up to you to make sure that this string will actually make sense in the header:

```
public void addHeaderLine(String line) throws
  MessagingException, IllegalWriteException, IllegalStateException
```

The getHeader() method returns the value of every header in the message with the given name. If there are multiple headers with this name, then the string separates the values of the different headers with the specified delimiter string:

```
public String getHeader(String name, String delimiter)
  throws MessagingException
```

The getAllHeaderLines() method returns a java.util.Enumeration containing every header in the message. The Enumeration contains String objects, one per header. Each String contains the full name and value; for example, "Subject: Re: Java 2 support". It is not divided into a separate name and value:

```
public Enumeration getAllHeaderLines() throws MessagingException
```

The getMatchingHeaderLines() method returns all header lines whose names are given in the names argument array. The getNonMatchingHeaderLines() method does the same thing except that it returns all those header lines with a name not mentioned in the names argument:

```
public Enumeration getMatchingHeaderLines(String[] names)
  throws MessagingException
public Enumeration getNonMatchingHeaderLines(String[] names)
  throws MessagingException
```

The getEncoding() method returns the encoding of this MIME part as a String as given by the Content-transfer-encoding: header. The typical encoding for a plain-text email is 7-bit or perhaps 8-bit or quoted-printable. The typical encoding for a file attachment is Base64:

```
public String getEncoding() throws MessagingException
```

The getContentID() method returns a string that uniquely identifies this part as given by the part's Content-ID: field. A typical ID looks like <Pine.LNX.4.10. 9912290930220.8058@akbar.nevex.com>. It returns null if the part doesn't have a content ID:

```
public String getContentID() throws MessagingException
  IllegalWriteException, IllegalStateException
```

The getContentLanguage() method returns the value of the Content-language: header. This is a comma-separated list of two (or more) letter abbreviations for languages as defined by RFC 1766. For example, English is "en" and French is "fr". It returns null if the part doesn't have a Content-language: header.

```
public String[] getContentLanguage() throws MessagingException
```

There's also a setContentLanguage() method that you might use when sending a message:

```
public void setContentLanguage(String[] languages) throws
  MessagingException, IllegalWriteException, IllegalStateException
```

Finally, the two `setText()` methods set the content of the part with the MIME type text/plain. The second `setText()` method also lets you specify the character set; for example, us-ascii or ISO 8859-1:

```
public void setText(String text) throws MessagingException
public void setText(String text, String charset)
  throws MessagingException
```

Folders

So far, we've worked mostly with the INBOX folder. This is the default folder where most mail resides until the user filters or saves it into some other folder. On some systems, it may actually reside in a file called INBOX. On other systems, it may be called something different. Nonetheless, you can always access it from the JavaMail API using the name INBOX.

Most mail programs do allow you to organize your messages into different folders. These folders are hierarchical; that is, one folder may contain another folder. In particular, in the IMAP protocol, servers store the messages in different folders, from which clients retrieve and manipulate the messages as necessary. POP servers, by contrast, generally send all the messages to the user when the user connects, then rely on the client to store and manage them. The primary advantage of the IMAP approach over POP is that it allows a user to easily access his entire email archive from multiple client machines.

The JavaMail API represents IMAP-like folders as instances of the abstract `Folder` class:

```
public abstract class Folder extends Object
```

This class declares methods for requesting named folders from servers, deleting messages from folders, searching for particular messages in folders, listing the messages in a folder, and so forth. Most of these methods are declared abstract. When you ask a session, a store, or a folder to give you one of the folders it contains, it will give you an instance of a concrete subclass appropriate for the protocol in use: IMAP, POP, mbox, or whatever. The reference implementation of the JavaMail API knows how to do these operations only for IMAP servers. However, some third-party implementations provide these operations in local mailbox folders stored on the client's filesystem as well.

Opening Folders

You cannot create folders directly. The only constructor is protected:

```
protected Folder(Store store)
```

Instead, you get a `Folder` from a `Session`, a `Store`, or another `Folder` like this:

```
Folder outbox = container.getFolder("sent-mail");
```

There are actually three `getFolder()` methods, one each in the `Session`, `Store`, and `Folder` classes. They all have the same signature and behave similarly:

```
public abstract Folder getFolder(String name) throws MessagingException
```

These methods share an annoying idiosyncrasy with the `File` class. Getting a `Folder` object doesn't imply that the named `Folder` actually exists on the server. To tell whether the folder is really present, you have to test for it with the `exists()` method:

```
public boolean exists() throws MessagingException
```

When you first get a folder, it's closed. Before you can read the messages it contains, you have to open the folder using the `open()` method:

```
public abstract void open(int mode)
  throws FolderNotFoundException, MessagingException
```

The `mode` argument should be one of the two named constants `Folder.READ_ONLY` or `Folder.READ_WRITE`. Some but not all implementations allow you to open multiple read-only connections to one real folder using multiple `Folder` objects. However, all implementations allow at most one `Folder` object to have write access to a folder at one time.

Some operations discussed in this section such as searching or retrieving messages from a folder can be performed only on an open folder. Others such as deleting or changing the name of a folder can be performed only on a closed folder. The `isOpen()` method returns true if the folder is open, false if it's closed:

```
public abstract boolean isOpen()
```

Generally, trying to do something with a closed folder that requires the folder to be open or vice versa will throw a `java.lang.IllegalStateException`. This is a runtime exception, so it doesn't need to be explicitly caught or declared.

When you're done with a folder, you should close it using the `close()` method:

```
public abstract void close(boolean expunge)
  throws FolderNotFoundException, MessagingException
```

If the `expunge` argument is true, then any deleted messages in the folder are deleted from the actual file on the server. Otherwise, they're simply marked as deleted, but the message can still be undeleted.

Basic Folder Info

The `Folder` class has eight methods that return basic information about a folder:

```
public abstract String getName()
public abstract String getFullName()
public URLName        getURLName() throws MessagingException
public abstract Folder getParent() throws MessagingException
public abstract int    getType() throws MessagingException
public int            getMode() throws IllegalStateException
public Store          getStore()
public abstract char   getSeparator()
  throws FolderNotFoundException, MessagingException
```

The `getName()` method returns the name of the folder, such as "Reader Mail", whereas the `getFullName()` method returns the complete hierarchical name from the root, such as "books/JNP2E/Reader Mail". The `getURLName()` method includes the server; for instance, "imap://elharo@mail.metalab.unc.edu/books/JNP2E/Reader Mail". In this example, the slash character is used as a separator between parts of the folder. The separator can vary from implementation to implementation, but the `getSeparator()` method always tells you what it is.

The `getParent()` method returns the name of the folder that contains this folder; e.g., "JNP2E" for the previous Reader Mail example.

The `getType()` method returns an `int` indicating whether the folder can contain messages and/or other folders. If it can contain messages but not folders, then `getType()` returns the named constant `Folder.HOLDS_MESSAGES`. If it can contain folders but not messages, then `getType()` returns the named constant `Folder.HOLDS_FOLDERS`. If it can contain both folders and messages, then `getType()` returns the bitwise union `Folder.HOLDS_FOLDERS` & `Folder.HOLDS_MESSAGES`.

The `getMode()` method tells you whether a folder allows writing. It returns one of the two named constants `Folder.READ_ONLY` or `Folder.READ_WRITE` or –1 if the mode is unknown. Finally, the `getStore()` method returns the `Store` object from which this folder was retrieved.

Managing Folders

The `create()` method creates a new folder in this folder's `Store`:

```
public abstract boolean create(int type) throws MessagingException
```

The type of the folder should be one of the named constants `Folder.HOLDS_MESSAGES` or `Folder.HOLDS_FOLDERS` depending on whether it will hold other folders or messages. It returns true if the creation succeeded, false if it didn't.

The delete() method deletes this folder. It can do that only if the folder is closed. Otherwise, an IllegalStateException is thrown.

```
public abstract boolean delete(boolean recurse) throws
    IllegalStateException, FolderNotFoundException, MessagingException
```

If there are messages in this folder, then they are deleted along with the folder. If the folder contains subfolders, then the subfolders are deleted if the recurse argument is true. If the recurse argument is not true, then the folder will only be deleted if it does not contain any subfolders. If it does contain subfolders, then the delete fails. If the folder does contain subfolders and also contains messages, then it's implementation-dependent whether or not the messages will be deleted even though the folder itself isn't. If the delete succeeded, then the method returns true; otherwise, it returns false.

The renameTo() method changes the name of this folder. A folder must be closed to be renamed. Otherwise, an IllegalStateException is thrown. This method returns true if the folder is successfully renamed, false if it isn't:

```
public abstract boolean renameTo(Folder f) throws
    IllegalStateException, FolderNotFoundException, MessagingException
```

Managing Messages in Folders

On occasion, you may find a need to put a message in a folder. There's only one method to do this, appendMessages():

```
public abstract void appendMessages(Message[] messages)
    throws FolderNotFoundException, MessagingException
```

As the name implies, the messages are placed at the end of this folder.

The copyMessages() method copies messages into this folder from a specified folder given as an argument:

```
public void copyMessages(Message[] messages, Folder destination) throws
    IllegalStateException, FolderNotFoundException, MessagingException
```

The copied messages are appended to the destination folder. They are not removed from the source folder. To move a message, you have to copy it from the source to the destination, then delete it from the source folder, then finally expunge the source folder.

To delete a message from a folder, you set its Flags.Flag.DELETED flag to true. To physically remove deleted messages from a folder, you have to expunge it using the expunge() method:

```
public abstract Message[] expunge() throws MessagingException,
    IllegalStateException, FolderNotFoundException
```

After a message has been expunged, there may still be `Message` objects that refer to it. In this case, almost any method call on such an object, except `isExpunged()` and `getMessageNumber()`, will throw an exception.

Subscriptions

Some implementations (though not the default IMAP implementation) allow you to subscribe to particular folders. This would be most appropriate for an NNTP provider, where a typical server offers thousands of newsgroups, but the typical user will want to retrieve messages from a few dozen of these at most. Each newsgroup would be represented as a `Folder` object. A subscription to the news-group's `Folder` indicates that the user wants to retrieve messages from that news-group:

```
public boolean isSubscribed()
public void    setSubscribed(boolean subscribe)
  throws FolderNotFoundException, MethodNotSupportedException,
  MessagingException
```

If a provider doesn't support subscription, then `setSubscribed()` throws a `MethodNotSupportedException` and `isSubscribed()` returns false.

Listing the Contents of a Folder

Folders are hierarchical. That is, a folder can contain other folders. There are four methods to list the folders that a folder contains. These are:

```
public Folder[] list()
  throws FolderNotFoundException, MessagingException
public Folder[] listSubscribed()
  throws FolderNotFoundException, MessagingException
public abstract Folder[] list(String pattern)
  throws FolderNotFoundException, MessagingException
public Folder[] listSubscribed(String pattern)
  throws FolderNotFoundException, MessagingException
```

The first method returns an array containing all the folders that this folder contains. The second method returns an array containing all the subscribed folders that this folder contains.

The third and fourth methods repeat these first two except that they allow you to specify a pattern. Only folders whose full names match the pattern will be in the returned array. The pattern is a string giving the name of the folders that match. However, the string can contain the % character, which is a wildcard that matches any sequence of characters not including the hierarchy separator, and *, which matches any sequence of characters including the hierarchy separator.

Checking for Mail

The getMessageCount() method returns the number of messages in this folder:

```
public abstract int getMessageCount()
 throws FolderNotFoundException, MessagingException
```

This method can be invoked on an open or closed folder. However, in the case of
a closed folder, this method may (or may not) return –1 to indicate that the exact
number of messages isn't easily available.

The hasNewMessages() method returns true if new messages have been added to
the folder since it was last opened (not since the last time you checked!):

```
public abstract boolean hasNewMessages()
 throws FolderNotFoundException, MessagingException
```

The getNewMessageCount() method uses a slightly different approach for determining how many new messages there are. It checks the number of messages in
the folder whose RECENT flag is set:

```
public int getNewMessageCount()
 throws FolderNotFoundException, MessagingException
```

Unlike hasNewMessages(), getNewMessageCount() can be invoked on either
an open or a closed folder. However, in the case of a closed folder,
getNewMessageCount() may return –1 to indicate that the real answer would be
too expensive to obtain.

The getUnreadMessageCount() method is similar but returns the number of
messages in the folder whose SEEN flag is not set:

```
public int getUnreadMessageCount()
 throws FolderNotFoundException, MessagingException
```

Like getNewMessageCount(), getUnreadMessageCount() can be invoked on
either an open or a closed folder. However, in the case of a closed folder, it may
return –1 to indicate that the real answer would be too expensive to obtain.

Getting Messages from Folders

The Folder class provides four methods for retrieving messages from open folders. These are:

```
public abstract Message getMessage(int messageNumber) throws
 IndexOutOfBoundsException, FolderNotFoundException,
 IllegalStateException, MessagingException
public Message[] getMessages() throws FolderNotFoundException,
 IllegalStateException, MessagingException
public Message[] getMessages(int start, int end) throws
 IndexOutOfBoundsException, FolderNotFoundException,
```

```
IllegalStateException, MessagingException
public Message[] getMessages(int[] messageNumbers) throws
IndexOutOfBoundsException, FolderNotFoundException,
IllegalStateException, MessagingException
```

The getMessage() method returns the nth message in the folder. The first message in the folder is number 1 (not 0). Message numbers may change when messages are expunged from the folder. An IndexOutOfBoundsException is thrown if you ask for message n and there are $n-1$ or fewer messages in the folder.

The first getMessages() method returns an array of Message objects representing all the messages in this folder. The second getMessages() method returns an array of Message objects from the folder beginning with start and finishing with end, inclusive. The third getMessages() method returns an array containing only those messages specifically identified by number in the messageNumbers array.

All four of these methods create only the Message objects and fill in the minimal number of fields in those objects. The actual text and other content of the message will be fetched from the server only when the Message's methods that use those things are invoked. This means, for example, that you can't get all the messages from the server, then hang up your PPP connection and work with them offline. There is, however, a fetch() method, which fills in certain parts of the Message objects with actual data from the server:

```
public void fetch(Message[] messages, FetchProfile fp)
   throws IllegalStateException, MessagingException
```

The messages argument is an array containing the Message objects to be prefetched. The FetchProfile argument specifies which headers in the messages to prefetch. However, this is still just a suggestion. Implementations are free to ignore this request and fetch the message content only when it's actually needed.

You can request prefetching of individual headers such as Subject: by name. You can also request prefetching of three predefined blocks of information: the envelope (essentially the subject and addressees of the message), the flags of the message, or the content info of the messages. The three groups you can ask for are given as constant FetchProfile.Item objects. They are FetchProfile.Item. ENVELOPE, FetchProfile.Item.FLAGS, and FetchProfile.Item.CONTENT_ INFO.

The FetchProfile class has a simple noargs constructor as well as methods for constructing a new profile, for adding particular items and headers to the profile, and for testing whether a particular item is part of a particular profile. These are:

```
public FetchProfile()
public void add(FetchProfile.Item item)
```

```
public void add(String headerName)
public boolean contains(FetchProfile.Item item)
public boolean contains(String headerName)
public FetchProfile.Item[] getItems()
public String[] getHeaderNames()
```

For example, suppose you wanted to download just the subjects, the To addresses, and the content information of a block of messages. Then you would fetch them like this:

```
Message[] messages = folder.getMessages();
FetchProfile fp = new FetchProfile();
fp.add(FetchProfile.Item.CONTENT_INFO);
fp.add("Subject");
fp.add("To");
```

Searching Folders

If the server supports searching (as many IMAP servers do and most POP servers don't), it's easy to search a folder for the messages meeting certain criteria. The criteria are encoded in SearchTerm objects:

```
public abstract class SearchTerm extends Object
```

The SearchTerm class is abstract, but the JavaMail API provides many subclasses for performing common searches:

```
public abstract class AddressTerm         extends SearchTerm
public abstract class FlagTerm            extends SearchTerm
public abstract class StringTerm          extends SearchTerm
public final class    FromTerm            extends AddressTerm
public final class    FromStringTerm      extends AddressStringTerm
public final class    ReceipientTerm      extends AddressTerm
public final class    AddressStringTerm   extends StringTerm
public final class    BodyTerm            extends StringTerm
public final class    HeaderTerm          extends StringTerm
public final class    MessageIDTerm       extends StringTerm
public final class    SubjectTerm         extends StringTerm
public abstract class DateTerm            extends ComparisonTerm
public final class    ReceivedDateTerm    extends DateTerm
public final class    SentDateTerm        extends DateTerm
```

It also provides several classes for combining searches:

```
public final class AndTerm               extends SearchTerm
public abstract class ComparisonTerm     extends SearchTerm
public final class NotTerm               extends SearchTerm
public final class OrTerm                extends SearchTerm
```

And of course you can write your own subclasses that implement your own search logic. To implement a search, you have to write a subclass and override the subclass's match() method to describe your search:

```
public abstract boolean match(Message message)
```

This method returns true if the **message** argument satisfies the search and false if it doesn't.

You set up a SearchTerm matching your desired parameters, then pass it to one of these two search() methods in the Folder class:

```
public Message[] search(SearchTerm term) throws SearchException,
  FolderNotFoundException, IllegalStateException, MessagingException
public Message[] search(SearchTerm term, Message[] messages)
  throws SearchException, FolderNotFoundException,
  IllegalStateException, MessagingException
```

A SearchException indicates that the search term is more complicated than the implementation can handle. For example, this search term seeks out all messages from *billg@microsoft.com*:

```
Address billg  = new InternetAddress("billg@microsoft.com");
SearchTerm term = new FromTerm(billg);
```

This search term looks for all messages from *billg@microsoft.com* after 1999:

```
Address billg      = new InternetAddress("billg@microsoft.com");
SearchTerm term1 = new FromTerm(billg);
Date millennium  = Calendar.getInstance().set(2000, 0, 1).getTime();
SearchTerm term2 = new SentDateTerm(ComparisonTerm.GE, millennium);
SearchTerm term  = new AndTerm(term1, term2);
```

Example 19-13 is a simple variation of the MailClient program of Example 19-7. It allows the user to list email addresses on the command line after the initial URL like this:

```
% java SearchClient imap://elharo@mail.metalab.unc.edu/INBOX
willis@nvx.com billg@microsoft.com
```

Only those messages from the specified users will be returned. However, if no email addresses are given, then all messages will be returned.

Example 19-13. A Mail Client That Searches by From: Address

```
import javax.mail.*;
import javax.mail.search.*;
import javax.mail.internet.*;
import java.util.*;
import java.io.*;

public class SearchClient {
```

Example 19-13. A Mail Client That Searches by From: Address (continued)

```
public static void main(String[] args) {

  if (args.length == 0) {
    System.err.println(
     "Usage: java SearchClient protocol://username@host/foldername");
    return;
  }

  URLName server = new URLName(args[0]);

  try {

    Session session = Session.getDefaultInstance(new Properties(),
     new MailAuthenticator(server.getUsername()));

    // Connect to the server and open the folder
    Folder folder = session.getFolder(server);
    if (folder == null) {
      System.out.println("Folder " + server.getFile() + " not found.");
      System.exit(1);
    }
    folder.open(Folder.READ_ONLY);

    SearchTerm term = null;
    if (args.length > 1) {
      SearchTerm[] terms = new SearchTerm[args.length-1];
      for (int i = 1; i < args.length; i++) {
        Address a = new InternetAddress(args[i]);
        terms[i-1] = new FromTerm(new InternetAddress(args[i]));
      }
      if (terms.length > 1) term = new OrTerm(terms);
      else term = terms[0];
    }

    // Get the messages from the server
    Message[] messages;
    if (term == null) {
      messages = folder.getMessages();
    }
    else {
      messages = folder.search(term);
    }
    for (int i = 0; i < messages.length; i++) {
      System.out.println("------------ Message " + (i+1)
        + " ------------");

      // Print message headers
      Enumeration headers = messages[i].getAllHeaders();
```

Example 19-13. A Mail Client That Searches by From: Address (continued)

```
      while (headers.hasMoreElements()) {
        Header h = (Header) headers.nextElement();
        System.out.println(h.getName() + ": " + h.getValue());
      }
      System.out.println();

      // Enumerate parts
      Object body = messages[i].getContent();
      if (body instanceof Multipart) {
        processMultipart((Multipart) body);
      }
      else { // ordinary message
        processPart(messages[i]);
      }

      System.out.println();

    }

    // Close the connection
    // but don't remove the messages from the server
    folder.close(false);

  }
  catch (Exception e) {
    e.printStackTrace();
  }

  // Since we may have brought up a GUI to authenticate,
  // we can't rely on returning from main() to exit
  System.exit(0);

}

public static void processMultipart(Multipart mp)
 throws MessagingException {

  for (int i = 0; i < mp.getCount(); i++) {
    processPart(mp.getBodyPart(i));
  }

}

public static void processPart(Part p) {

  try {
    // I'd prefer to test the Content-Disposition header here.
    // However, too many common email clients don't use it.
    String fileName = p.getFileName();
```

Example 19-13. A Mail Client That Searches by From: Address (continued)

```
      if (fileName == null) { // likely inline
        p.writeTo(System.out);
      }
      else if (fileName != null) {
        File f = new File(fileName);
        // find a version that does not yet exist
        for (int i = 1; f.exists(); i++) {
          String newName = fileName + " " + i;
          f = new File(newName);
        }
        FileOutputStream out = new FileOutputStream(f);

        // We can't just use p.writeTo() here because it doesn't
        // decode the attachment. Instead we copy the input stream
        // onto the output stream which does automatically decode
        // Base-64, quoted printable, and a variety of other formats.
        InputStream in = new BufferedInputStream(p.getInputStream());
        int b;
        while ((b = in.read()) != -1) out.write(b);
        out.flush();
        out.close();
        in.close();
      }
    }
    catch (Exception e) {
      System.err.println(e);
      e.printStackTrace();
    }
  }
}
```

Flags

It's sometimes useful to be able to change the flags for an entire group of messages at once. The Folder class has two methods for doing this:

```
public void setFlags(Message[] messages, Flags flag, boolean value)
  throws IllegalStateException, MessagingException
public void setFlags(int start, int end, Flags flag, boolean value)
  throws IllegalStateException, MessagingException
public void setFlags(int[] messageNumbers, Flags flag, boolean value)
  throws IndexOutOfBoundsException, IllegalStateException,
  MessagingException
```

Ultimately, these are just conveniences. There's nothing you can do with these that you can't do by setting the flags on each message individually with the setFlags() method of the Message class. In fact, the default implementation simply invokes that method on each message in the specified block of messages.

The `Folder` class also has a `getPermanentFlags()` method to return the flags that this folder will supply for all messages. This includes all the flags except the user-defined flags, which are applied only to particular messages that the user has flagged. For instance, not all folder implementations may track whether messages have been answered:

```
public abstract Flags getPermanentFlags()
```

Event Handling

Many email programs such as Eudora and Pine can be configured to periodically check for incoming email in the background. One way to structure an email program is as a series of responses to unpredictable events. This is much like programming for a graphical user interface, and indeed the JavaMail API uses the same basic patterns to handle mail events that the AWT and Swing use to handle GUI events.

The JavaMail API defines six different kinds of mail events, all in the `javax.mail.event` package. These are all subclasses of `MailEvent`:

```
public abstract class MailEvent extends EventObject
```

The six concrete kinds of mail events, the first four of which involve folders, are:

ConnectionEvent
> A `Folder` (or `Store` or `Transport`) has been opened, closed, or disconnected.

FolderEvent
> A `Folder` has been created, deleted, or renamed.

MessageChangedEvent
> The message's envelope or flags have changed.

MessageCountEvent
> A message was added to or deleted from a `Folder`.

StoreEvent
> A notification or alert from a `Store`.

TransportEvent
> A notification from a `Transport` that a message was delivered, partially delivered, or failed to be delivered.

There are listener interfaces for each of these six kinds of events:

```
public interface ConnectionListener       extends EventListener
public interface FolderListener           extends EventListener
public interface MessageChangedListener   extends EventListener
public interface MessageCountListener     extends EventListener
public interface StoreListener            extends EventListener
public interface TransportListener        extends EventListener
```

Each of these interfaces declares one or more methods that must be provided by implementing classes. For example, the `ConnectionListener` class declares these three methods:

```
public void opened(ConnectionEvent e)
public void disconnected(ConnectionEvent e)
public void closed(ConnectionEvent e)
```

The `FolderListener` interface declares these three methods:

```
public void folderCreated(FolderEvent e)
public void folderDeleted(FolderEvent e)
public void folderRenamed(FolderEvent e)
```

Four of these events can be fired by folders. Consequently, there are 14 `addXXXListener()`, `removeXXXListener()`, and `notifyXXXListener()` methods in the `Folder` class:

```
public    void addConnectionListener(ConnectionListener l)
public    void removeConnectionListener(ConnectionListener l)
protected void notifyConnectionListeners(int type)
public    void addFolderListener(FolderListener l)
public    void removeFolderListener(FolderListener l)
protected void notifyFolderListeners(int type)
protected void notifyFolderRenamedListeners(Folder folder)
public    void addMessageCountListener(MessageCountListener l)
public    void removeMessageCountListener(MessageCountListener l)
protected void notifyMessageAddedListeners(Message[] messages)
protected void notifyMessageRemovedListeners(boolean removed,
  Message[] messages)
public    void addMessageChangedListener(MessageChangedListener l)
public    void removeMessageChangedListener(MessageChangedListener l)
protected void notifyMessageChangedListeners(int type, Message message)
```

The `addXXXListener()` methods are invoked to add an implementation of the particular interface to the list of listeners. The `removeXXXListener()` methods are invoked to remove an implementation from that list. The `notify XXXListener()` methods are not used directly. Instead, they're used by instances of `Folder` and its subclasses to notify registered listeners of particular events. All of this works exactly as it does in the AWT and Swing, just with different events.

Utility Methods

Finally, for completeness' sake, I'll note that the `Folder` class overrides two methods from `java.lang.Object`, `finalize()` and `toString()`:

```
protected void finalize() throws Throwable
public String toString()
```

Neither of these is especially important to the client programmer.

Index

A

H

About the Author

Elliotte Rusty Harold is an internationally respected writer, programmer, and educator, both on the Internet and off. He got his start by writing FAQ lists for the Macintosh newsgroups on Usenet, and has since branched out into writing books. He lectures about Java and object-oriented programming at Polytechnic University in Brooklyn. His Cafe au Lait web site at *http://metalab.unc.edu/javafaq/* has become one of the most popular independent Java sites on the Internet.

Elliotte is originally from New Orleans, Louisiana, where he returns periodically in search of a decent bowl of gumbo. However, he currently resides in the Prospect Heights neighborhood of Brooklyn with his wife Beth and cats Charm (named after the quark) and Marjorie (named after his mother-in-law). When not writing books, he enjoys working on genealogy, mathematics, and quantum mechanics. His previous books include *The Java Developer's Resource, Java Secrets, JavaBeans, XML: Extensible Markup Language, The XML Bible,* and *Java I/O.*

Colophon

Our look is the result of reader comments, our own experimentation, and feedback from distribution channels. Distinctive covers complement our distinctive approach to technical topics, breathing personality and life into potentially dry subjects.

Beverly Goldfarb was the copyeditor for *Java™ Network Programming, Second Edition.* Deborah English was the proofreader. Jeffrey Holcomb, Sarah Jane Shangraw, and Claire Cloutier performed quality control reviews. Nancy Crumpton wrote the index. Interior composition was done by Claire Cloutier, Sarah Jane Shangraw, Molly Shangraw, and Joan McGaw.

The image on the cover of this book is a river otter. The cover was designed by Emma Colby using a series design by Edie Freeman. The cover image is a 19th-century engraving from the Dover Pictorial Archive. Emma Colby produced the cover layout with QuarkXPress 4.1 using Adobe's ITC Garamond font. Alicia Cech and David Futato designed the interior layout.

The text was produced in FrameMaker 5.5.6 using a template implemented by Mike Sierra. The heading font is Bodoni BT; the text font is New Baskerville. The illustrations that appear in the book were created in Macromedia Freehand 8 and Adobe Photoshop 5 by Robert Romano and Rhon Porter.

Whenever possible, our books use a durable and flexible lay-flat binding. If the page count exceeds the lay-flat binding limit, perfect binding is used.